D0852067

EDITORIAL
BOARD

EDITOR IN CHIEF

C. Neal Tate
Professor and Chair, Department of Political Science and Professor of Law, Vanderbilt University

C. Neal Tate is Chair of the Department of Political Science at Vanderbilt University. Previously, he was Dean of the Toulouse School of Graduate Studies and Regents Professor of Political Science at the University of North Texas. He has published widely on comparative judicial politics and international human rights. Professor Tate has been Director of the Law and Social Science Program of the U.S. National Science Foundation; President of the International Political Science Association's Research Committee on Comparative Judicial Studies; President of the Southwest Political Science Association; and is President-Elect of the Southern Political Science Association.

ASSOCIATE EDITORS

Martin Edelman
Professor Emeritus, Department of Political Science, University at Albany, State University of New York

Stacia L. Haynie
Professor and Chair, Department of Political Science, Louisiana State University

Donald W. Jackson
Professor, Department of Political Science, Texas Christian University

Mary L. Volcansek
Dean, AddRan College of Humanities and Social Sciences and Professor, Department of Political Science, Texas Christian University

Governments of the World

A Global Guide to Citizens' Rights and Responsibilities

VOLUME 2

DOMINICA *to* ITALY

C. Neal Tate, *Editor in Chief*

MACMILLAN REFERENCE USA
An imprint of Thomson Gale, a part of The Thomson Corporation

Detroit • New York • San Francisco • San Diego • New Haven, Conn. • Waterville, Maine • London • Munich

JA
61
G645
2006
v. 2

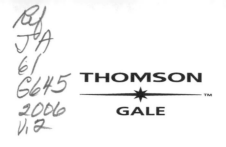

Governments of the World: A Global Guide to Citizens' Rights and Responsibilities

C. Neal Tate, Editor in Chief

© 2006 Thomson Gale,
a part of The Thomson Corporation.

Thomson, Star Logo and Macmillan Reference USA are trademarks and Gale is a registered trademark used herein under license.

For more information, contact
Macmillan Reference USA
An imprint of Thomson Gale
27500 Drake Rd.
Farmington, Hills, MI 48331-3535
Or you can visit our Internet site at
http://www.gale.com

ALL RIGHTS RESERVED

No part of this work covered by the copyright hereon may be reproduced or used in any form or by any means—graphic, electronic, or mechanical, including photocopying, recording, taping, Web distribution, or information storage retrieval systems—without the written permission of the publisher.

For permission to use material from this product, submit your request via Web at http://www.gale-edit.com/permissions, or you may download our Permissions Request form and submit your request by fax or mail to:

Permissions
Thomson Gale
27500 Drake Rd.
Farmington Hills, MI 48331-3535
Permissions Hotline:
248-699-8006 or 800-877-4253 ext. 8006
Fax: 248-699-8074 or 800-762-4058

Cover photograph: A European Community flag serves as the background of a ballot box (The Image Bank/Getty Images).

Since this page cannot legibly accommodate all copyright notices, the acknowledgments constitute an extension of the copyright notice.

While every effort has been made to ensure the reliability of the information presented in this publication, Thomson Gale does not guarantee the accuracy of the data contained herein. Thomson Gale accepts no payment for listing; and inclusion in the publication of any organization, agency, institution, publication, service, or individual does not imply endorsement of the editors or publisher. Errors brought to the attention of the publisher and verified to the satisfaction of the publisher will be corrected in future editions.

LIBRARY OF CONGRESS CATALOGING-IN-PUBLICATION DATA

Governments of the world: a global guide to citizens' rights and responsibilities / C. Neal Tate, editor-in-chief.
    v. cm.
    Includes bibliographical references and index.
    ISBN 0-02-865811-6 (set hardcover: alk. paper) — ISBN 0-02-865812-4 (vol 1) — ISBN 0-02-865813-2 (vol 2) — ISBN 0-02-865814-0 (vol 3) — ISBN 0-02-865815-9 (vol 4) — ISBN 0-02-866073-0 (e-book)
    1. Comparative government—Encyclopedias. I. Tate, C. Neal (Chester Neal), 1943-

    JA61.G645 2006
    320.3'03—dc22
    2005010436

This title is also available as an e-book.
ISBN 0-02-866073-0
Contact your Thomson Gale representative for ordering information.

Printed in the United States of America
10 9 8 7 6 5 4 3 2 1

EDITORIAL & PRODUCTION STAFF

Frank Menchaca, *Executive Vice President and Publisher*

Hélène Potter, *Director, New Product Development*

Jaime E. Noce, *Project Editor*

Jennifer Albers, Mark Drouillard, Jason Everett, Brad Morgan, *Contributing Editors*

Mark Springer, *Senior Editorial Systems Implementation Specialist*

Kari Bethel, Patti Brecht, Paul Greenland, Kathleen Roy, Drew Silver, *Copyeditors*

Christine Alexanian, Carol Brennan, Judy Clinebell, Eric Lowenkron,
    Eleanor Stanford, *Proofreaders*

Dawn DesJardins, Rebecca J. Frey, Lisa Frick, Jeremiah Garretson,
    Helene Kiser, Christine Tomassini, *Additional Editorial Support*

Linda Mamassian, *Indexer*

Pamela A.E. Galbreath, *Senior Art Director*

Dean Dauphinais, *Senior Editor, Image Research & Acquisitions*

Lezlie Light, *Coordinator, Imaging*

Michael Logusz, *Imaging Specialist*

Christine O'Bryan, *Graphics Specialist*

GGS Information Services, *Graphic Art Compilation*

Lisa Kincade, *Research Associate, Rights Acquisition & Management*

Jessica Schultz, *Fulfillment Associate, Rights Acquisition & Management*

Ron Montgomery, *Rights Acquisition Account Manager*

Evi Seoud, *Assistant Manager, Composition & Electronic Prepress*

Mary Beth Trimper, *Manager, Composition & Electronic Prepress*

Rhonda Dover, *Senior Buyer*

CONTENTS

Primary Source Documents

VOLUME 2

Primary Source Documents

Primary Source Documents

S

VOLUME 4

P

T

Q

R

Primary Source Documents

Keeping up with the ever-changing global political landscape can be daunting. *Governments of the World: A Global Guide to Citizens' Rights and Responsibilities* is designed to make the task easier. The volumes provide accessible, authoritative background information about governments, political issues, and citizen politics in 198 regions, including every independent nation of the world and several territories under the jurisdiction of sovereign countries. Because no nation operates in complete isolation, *Governments of the World* reaches beyond regional issues to explore the roles of international courts and supranational institutions such as the United Nations and the European Union.

The articles vary in length, ranging from 500 to 3,500 words. In general, we have provided shorter articles for countries that are comparatively small in geographic size or population or, in the judgment of the editors, of lesser economic or strategic significance. This does not mean countries represented by shorter articles are unimportant or uninteresting; many of them are fascinating, for any number of reasons. Common to all of the project's authors has been the diligent struggle to select only the most vital information for inclusion. Because the work we have prepared is an encyclopedia, not a library, authors were forced to select for readers only the essential facts key to the comprehension of the world's governments in the twenty-first century.

Understanding the structure of the world's governments, the interaction between governments and their citizens, and the intricacies of international relationships in a global environment entails much more than the study of isolated countries. To further the learning experience, a selection of articles present and explain in depth many of the institutions and concepts—including representation, dictatorship, and the role of political parties—crucial to the justification for and operations of governments and the roles played by citizens. Biographical sketches introducing readers to some of the most influential people in government and politics of the past century round out these 112 supporting articles.

Each of the 310 articles, arranged alphabetically over four volumes and thematically catalogued in the frontmatter, has been newly commissioned for this project. Entries represent the work of over 200 international contributors. Entry accessibility is enhanced by sidebars that explore key people, themes, and events. Numerous country maps, photos and illustrations help illuminate the text, while same-page definitions, entry-specific bibliographic citations, and cross-references help users delve more deeply into the topic. Ancillary materials—including a filmography, a glossary, and a cumulative index—provide additional tools for understanding the concepts presented in the set. A selection of primary documents, including international agreements and country-specific legislation, is reproduced in volume-specific appendices; these further explain the structure of governments and justifications and standards for promoting (or in some cases denying) citizen rights.

ACKNOWLEDGMENTS

Governments of the World has clearly been a group effort. The vision and contents of the work were shaped extensively by the members of the editorial board: Martin Edelman of the University at Albany, Stacia Haynie of Louisiana State University, and Donald Jackson and Mary Volcansek, both of Texas Christian University. The set's coverage and contents were initially developed in consultation with David O'Brien of the University of Virginia, Carl Baar of Brock and York Universities, and board members Edelman, Jackson, and Volcansek. When other commitments made it impossible for Professors O'Brien and Baar to continue their involvement, Professor Haynie and I came on board.

Governments of the World would have remained only a vision and a list of potential contents without the leadership and vital contributions of the staff at Thomson Gale. Hélène Potter, director of New Product Development, provided the stimulus and enthusiasm to get us going. Jaime Noce, our editor, was unfailingly supportive and resourceful; her gentle nudges kept us on schedule. Other members of the editorial and production staff worked behind the scenes to do everything necessary to turn rough drafts of individual articles into the polished and well-illustrated final product.

The excellent work of all these people would have been directed toward other projects but for the expertise and eloquence of the more than 200 authors of the individual articles. I learned from reading and editing their contributions more than I ever could have on my own. I frequently experienced a sense of real excitement and a desire to know more as I encountered new knowledge about the world's nations and their characteristics, the state of their citizens' rights and responsibilities, the dimensions of important concepts that help us understand the background and operations of those nations, and the lives and contributions of important individuals whose impacts on citizen rights and responsibilities, both positive and negative, have been substantial. All of us involved in bringing you *Governments of the World*—the associate editors, the editorial and production staff, the publishers, and, of course, the authors of the articles—hope you find it as informative and exciting as we have.

C. Neal Tate
Editor in Chief

Two of the more interesting items in my library are a world atlas published in the 1930s and the set of encyclopedias my parents bought for their growing family in the early 1950s. The former provides a picture of the world as it existed when my parents were in their adolescent years, before adulthood confronted my nineteen-year-old father in the form of a draft notice that sent him to World War II—ultimately, to a place he likely had never heard of before, the island of Guam. The latter depicts the world as it existed at the beginning of the Cold War between the United States and its allies and the Soviet Union and its communist allies in China and Eastern Europe. It captures the beginning of the end of European colonialism in Asia, but predates its wholesale demise in the 1960s that led to the creation of dozens of new nations in Africa and elsewhere.

THE INCREASING COMPLEXITY OF THE WORLD

In 1930, there were sixty-eight independent nation states in the world—twenty more than there were 100 years earlier. Certainly nations came and went during the late nineteenth and early twentieth centuries, but, on the average, people who wanted to keep up with the world across these ten decades had to learn about a new nation every five years. The pace of change in the map of the world was slow.

Despite the trauma and rapid change of World War II, territorially the map of the world looked only slightly different in 1950 than it had in 1930. The War brought small changes in some European borders, changes in colonial rulers for a small number of territories, and, soon, independence from colonial control for several significant Asian nations: India, Indonesia, Myanmar (Burma), Pakistan, the Philippines, and Sri Lanka. Politically, there were significant effects of the war, as the Soviet Union imposed communist regimes on territories that it had conquered from the Germans and Japanese: the eastern portion of Germany, the nations of Eastern Europe, and the northern half of Korea.

Twenty years later, in 1970, as my own family was growing, the map of the world's independent nations had changed more significantly than it had in the entire previous century, as the continent of Africa was transformed from colonial possessions to independent nations and numerous other dependencies became states. My young daughter—or anyone else who wanted to be informed about the world—lived in an era in which she had to keep up with 131 independent nations, fifty-two more than had existed two decades earlier.

The decade of the 1970s saw continued, though much slower, growth in the complexity of the world, as thirteen newly independent nations made their appearance on the world scene, and the decade of the 1980s saw very little change: the world gained only three newly independent nations from 1981 through 1990, reaching a total of 144. By 1993, however, shortly after my daughter reached adulthood, the world had once again changed rapidly. The number of independent states increased by seventeen, to a total of 161. More important, this sizable single decade increase was produced almost entirely by the breakup of the group of communist nations in Eastern Europe dominated by the Union of Soviet Socialist Republics (the Soviet Union) after World War II and during the Cold War, as well as the disintegration of the world's second super power, the Soviet Union itself.

Determining the number of independent nations in existence at any one time can be problematic. For example, the United States in 2005 recognized 192 independent states; some countries recognized Taiwan as the 193rd nation. Generally, data from the Polity IV project at the University of Maryland include nations that were independent members of the international system during a given year and that had a population of at least 500,000. According to the Polity IV criteria, there were 161 independent nations in 2003, but the United Nations had 191 independent member states, since it includes some very small nations, and the Vatican is not a member. For more information about sources of data on the world's nations, see the article on government data sets.

The consequence of all this change is that citizens of the world in the twenty-first century face a political reality that is by far the most complex in history. People whose formal education was completed some time ago find that much of what they had learned is now obsolete and that important world events often occur in places they never knew existed. People who are still completing their education, high school and college students, for example, face the same complex task of learning about a much more complicated world, albeit one in which they have grown up. Given that they have grown up in this more complicated world, people may lack understanding of the historical and political events and people responsible for making the world what it is. *Governments of the World: A Global Guide to Citizens' Rights and Responsibilities* has been created to provide the valuable reference information both groups need.

THE GROWTH OF THE DEMAND FOR HUMAN RIGHTS

Governments of the World is designed to do more than help its readers cope with a more complicated world of independent nation states. As its sub-title indicates, it also provides guidance to an array of citizen rights and responsibilities. This focus is the result of another major change that has affected the world and its governments in recent decades: a sharply increased emphasis on the importance of human rights and an insistence that the world's now large array of independent nation states respect and protect rights.

The acceptance of the proposition that human beings are entitled to exercise certain rights and liberties and to have them protected from abuse is not new. It has grown for centuries. The nineteenth century was important as the era in which almost all the world's nations came to reject the proposition that one human being should be able to own and control the destiny of another through the institution of slavery. It also saw

- the beginning of the acceptance of the previously radical proposition that government should be democratic, that the people—the mass of ordinary human beings, mostly men—should have the right to select and control their governments even if they were not wealthy, and
- the slow growth of acceptance by national governments of most of the basic rights and liberties expressed succinctly at the end of the eighteenth century in the Bill of Rights of the U.S. Constitution.

The twentieth century witnessed the continued expansion of national acceptance of the right of the people to select and control their governments. Where that right was accepted, the right to vote and participate in government was eventually extended to women on what was by mid-century a nearly universal basis. The rights and freedoms enumerated in the U.S. Bill of Rights also came into wider acceptance. Importantly, they were supplemented by a growing, though not universal, belief that citizens had a right to expect and governments a duty to provide fundamental social, educational, and economic services.

But the twentieth century was not a completely positive era for the expansion and protection of human rights. It also was the occasion for perhaps the most horrific and systematic attacks on human rights in history through the mechanisms of the brutal Nazi and Soviet dictatorships of Adolf Hitler and Joseph Stalin in the decades before and during World War II. Wholesale eradication and imprisonment of political opponents and class enemies under Stalin gave new and terrible meanings to the word "purge," while Hitler's ruthless extermination of population groups singled out as national or class enemies defined the term, "Holocaust."

Largely as a reaction to the atrocities accompanying World War II, much of the international community began efforts to reestablish democracy and to establish respect for human rights on a sounder and more universally accepted basis. Throughout the last half of the century and continuing with force into the twenty-first century, these and subsequent efforts have put citizen rights and responsibilities on the front burner for almost all of the world's governments. This does not mean, unfortunately, that citizen rights are secure everywhere—far from it, as many of the country descriptions in *Governments of the World* document. While worldwide democracy did indeed grow after the end of World War II, it did not continue to expand, but, rather, declined through the late 1980s, as the newly independent nations that came into being in that period had difficulty establishing and maintaining democratic governments and the communist regimes remained dictatorial. In fact, the human rights catastrophes of the first half of the twentieth century have not remained isolated instances, as recent accounts of genocide in such diverse locales as Bosnia, Rwanda, and Sudan and of assassination squads in various Latin American countries confirm.

Individual country articles in *Governments of the World* assess with impartiality the state of rights and responsibilities in ways that are appropriate for the countries being discussed. These volumes also contain numerous other articles that explain for readers the meaning and development of concepts that are crucial to understanding human rights and their condition around the world, descriptions of important organizations, and brief biographies of selected individuals who have had major impacts, either positive or negative, on the development of human rights.

ENVOI

This introduction has contended that we live in a world of possibly unprecedented political and governmental change. *Governments of the World: A Global Guide to Citizens' Rights and Responsibilities* has been created to help students and citizens understand and cope with that change. Its editors would be happy if it also assisted people in making important political choices related to their own ability to participate in civic life.

A resource like this can only be the beginning of the inquiry and reflection in which readers will engage as they pursue a civic-minded path. For one thing, given that we live in a period of very rapid change, it is impossible for any printed resource to anticipate and explain all the changes that are occurring constantly worldwide. Imagine, for example, the dismay that would have been felt by anyone completing a reference resource on the world in late 1988. Almost certainly, such an author or editor would not have anticipated the incredible change that was about to burst upon the world in the next three years as the communist governments disintegrated in Eastern Europe and the Soviet Union fell apart. If you encounter similarly unprecedented events as you seek further knowledge of our political world, remember that the only true constant is change.

C. Neal Tate, General Editor
Vanderbilt University

Biographies

Aquino, Corazon
Aung San Suu Kyi
Biko, Stephen
Dalai Lama
Gandhi, Mahatma
Gorbachev, Mikhail
Havel, Vaclav
Hitler, Adolf
Kelsen, Hans
King Jr., Martin Luther
Mandela, Nelson
Roosevelt, Eleanor
Stalin, Joseph
Yeltsin, Boris

Conventions and Documents

American Declaration of the Rights
    and Duties of Man and the
    American Convention on
    Human Rights
Bill of Rights
Convention Against Torture and other
    Cruel, Inhuman or Degrading
    Treatment or Punishment
Convention for the Elimination of All
    Forms of Discrimination against
    Women (CEDAW)

European Convention on Human
    Rights and Fundamental
    Freedoms
International Covenant on Civil
    and Political Rights
International Covenant on
    Economic, Social, and
    Cultural Rights
Magna Carta
Universal Declaration of
    Human Rights

Country and Region Profiles

Afghanistan
Albania
Algeria
Angola
Antigua and Barbuda
Argentina
Armenia
Australia
Austria
Azerbaijan
Bahamas
Bahrain
Bangladesh
Barbados
Belarus
Belgium

This outline provides a general overview of the conceptual structure of *Governments of the World*. The outline is organized under eight categories, with entries listed alphabetically within each category. Because the section headings are not mutually exclusive, certain entries are listed in more than one section.

Belize
Benin
Bhutan
Bolivia
Bosnia and Herzegovina
Botswana
Brazil
British Virgin Islands
Brunei
Bulgaria
Burkina Faso
Burundi
Cambodia
Cameroon
Canada
Cape Verde
Caribbean Region
Central African Republic
Chad
Chile
China (PRC)
Colombia
Comoros
Congo, Democratic Republic of
  (Zaire)
Congo, Republic of the
Costa Rica
Côte d'Ivoire
Croatia
Cuba
Cyprus
Czech Republic
Denmark
Djibouti
Dominica
Dominican Republic
East Timor
Ecuador
Egypt
El Salvador
Equatorial Guinea
Eritrea
Estonia
Ethiopia
European Microstates
Fiji
Finland
France
Gabon
Gambia, The
Gaza Strip
Georgia
Germany

Ghana
Greece
Grenada
Guatemala
Guinea
Guinea-Bissau
Guyana
Haiti
Honduras
Hong Kong and Macau
Hungary
Iceland
India
Indonesia
Iran
Iraq
Ireland
Israel
Italy
Jamaica
Japan
Jordan
Kazakhstan
Kenya
Kiribati
Korea, North
Korea, South
Kosovo
Kuwait
Kyrgyzstan (Kyrgyz Republic)
Laos
Latvia
Lebanon
Lesotho
Liberia
Libya
Lithuania
Luxembourg
Macedonia
Madagascar
Malawi
Malaysia
Maldives
Mali
Malta
Marshall Islands
Mauritania
Mauritius
Mexico
Micronesia, Federated States of
Moldova
Mongolia
Morocco

Mozambique
Myanmar (Burma)
Namibia
Nauru
Nepal
Netherlands, The
Netherlands Antilles and Aruba
New Zealand
Nicaragua
Niger
Nigeria
Northern Ireland
Norway
Oman
Pakistan
Palestine
Panama
Papua New Guinea
Paraguay
Peru
Philippines
Poland
Portugal
Qatar
Romania
Russia
Rwanda
Saint Kitts and Nevis
Saint Lucia
Saint Vincent and
  the Grenadines
Samoa
São Tomé and Príncipe
Saudi Arabia
Senegal
Serbia and Montenegro
Seychelles
Sierra Leone
Singapore
Slovakia
Slovenia
Solomon Islands
Somalia
South Africa
Spain
Sri Lanka
Sudan
Suriname
Swaziland
Sweden
Switzerland
Syria
Taiwan

Tajikistan
Tanzania
Thailand
Togo
Tonga
Trinidad and Tobago
Tunisia
Turkey
Turkmenistan
Tuvalu
Uganda
Ukraine
United Arab Emirates
United Kingdom
United States
Uruguay
Uzbekistan
Vanuatu
Vatican
Venezuela
Vietnam
West Bank
Yemen
Zambia
Zimbabwe

Forms of Government

Apartheid
Bicameral Parliamentary Systems
Colonies and Colonialism
Confederations
Constitutional Monarchy
Constitutions and
    Constitutionalism
Democracy
Dictatorship
Elections
Federalism
Liberal Democracy
Majoritarian Party Systems
Nationalist Movements
Oligarchy
Parliamentary Systems
Political Parties
Political Party Systems
Popular Sovereignty
Presidential Systems
Primaries
Representation
Republic

Totalitarianism
Transitional Political Systems

History

American Civil Liberties
    Union
Campaign Finance
Censorship
Ethnic Cleansing
Gender Discrimination
Genocide
Government Data Sets
Immigration and Immigrants
Political Corruption
Racism
Refugees
Stateless People

International and Supranational Entities

American Declaration of
    the Rights and Duties
    of Man and the American
    Convention on Human
    Rights
Amnesty International
Convention Against Torture and
    other Cruel, Inhuman or
    Degrading Treatment or
    Punishment
Convention for the
    Elimination of All Forms
    of Discrimination against
    Women (CEDAW)
European Convention on Human
    Rights and Fundamental
    Freedoms
European Court of Human
    Rights
European Court of Justice
European Parliament
European Union
Inter-American Commission and
    Court of Human Rights
International Court of Justice
International Covenant on Civil
    and Political Rights

International Covenant on
    Economic, Social, and
    Cultural Rights
International Criminal Court
Non-governmental Organizations
Peacekeeping Forces
United Nations
United Nations Commission on
    Human Rights

Law and the Courts

Civil Law
Common Law
Constitutional Courts
Crimes Against Humanity
Due Process of Law
Equal Protection of the Law
Equality Before the Law
European Court of Human Rights
European Court of Justice
Halakhah
Inter-American Commission
    and Court of Human Rights
International Court of Justice
International Criminal Court
International Human Rights Law
International Humanitarian Law
Judicial Independence
Judicial Review
Judicial Selection
Shari'a
Universal Criminal Jurisdiction
War Crimes

Rights, Responsibilities, and Freedoms

American Civil Liberties Union
Bill of Rights
Children's Rights
Citizenship
Civil Liberties in Emergencies
Civil Rights Movement in the
    United States
Economic, Social, and Cultural
    Rights

Freedom of Assembly and
   Association
Freedom of Expression
Freedom of Information
Freedom of the Press
Freedom of Religion and the State
Freedom of Religion, Foundations
Human Rights

Indigenous Peoples' Rights
Interest Groups
Juries
Magna Carta
Naturalization
Ombudsmen
Political Protest
Referendums and Plebiscites

Reproductive Rights
Right to Privacy
Student Rights
Suffrage
Universal Declaration
   of Human Rights
Voting Rights
Women's Rights

Mounah Abdel Samad
*Ph.D. Candidate, Public
Administration
University at Albany, State
University of New York*

Jordan
Lebanon
Oman
United Arab Emirates
Yemen

Janet Adamski
*Visiting Assistant Professor,
Political Science
Southwestern University*

Economic, Social, and Cultural Rights
European Union
Parliamentary Systems

Felix Ronkes Agerbeek
*Référendaire, Cabinet of
Advocate General Poiares
Maduro, Court of Justice of the
European Communities
Luxembourg*

European Court of Justice

Felipe Agüero
*Associate Professor,
International Studies
University of Miami*

Chile

Klint Alexander
*Adjunct Professor, Political
Science*

Vanderbilt University

Common Law
Constitutions and Constitutionalism

Klaus Armingeon
*Professor, Political Science
University of Berne*

Switzerland

Victor Asal
*Assistant Professor, Political
Science
University at Albany, State
University of New York*

Ethnic Cleansing

Florence Attiogbe
*Independent Scholar
Detroit, MI*

Togo

Godfrey Baldacchino
*Associate Professor, Sociology
and Anthropology
University of Prince Edward
Island*

Malta

Asoka Bandarage
*Professor, Government
Georgetown University*

Sri Lanka

Sherrie L. Baver
*Associate Professor, Political
Science*

Sherrie L. Baver *(continued)*
City College and The Graduate Center, the City University of New York

Dominican Republic

Al Bavon
Associate Professor, Public Administration
University of North Texas

Ghana

Joan E. Bertin
Executive Director, National Coalition Against Censorship
New York, NY

Censorship

Morris Bidjerano
Lecturer, Rockefeller College of Public Affairs and Policy
University at Albany, State University of New York

Poland

George E. Bisharat
Professor, Law
University of California Hastings College of the Law

Gaza Strip
Palestine
West Bank

John C. Blakeman
Associate Professor, Political Science
University of Wisconsin–Stevens Point

Constitutional Courts
Constitutional Monarchy
Judicial Review
United Kingdom

J. Blondel
Professor Emeritus, Political and Social Sciences
European University Institute

Majoritarian Party Systems
Political Party Systems

Isa Blumi
Visiting Lecturer, History
Trinity College

Kosovo

Joseph B. Board
Professor Emeritus, Government
Union College

Sweden

Jeanette Bolenga
Fellow, Pacific Institute of Advanced Studies in Development and Governance
University of the South Pacific

Vanuatu

John J. Brandon
Director, International Relations, The Asia Foundation
Washington, DC

Myanmar (Burma)

Peter Breiner
Associate Professor, Political Science
University at Albany, State University of New York

Democracy
Oligarchy
Republic

Bryan Brophy-Baermann
Associate Professor, Political Science
University of Wisconsin–Stevens Point

Campaign Finance
Elections

Julia Brotea
Graduate Student, Political Science
University of Calgary

Political Protest

Julie M. Bunck
Associate Professor, Political Science
University of Louisville

Cuba

Isa Camyar
Ph.D. Candidate, Political Science
Louisiana State University

Maldives

Henry F. Carey
Associate Professor, Political Science

Georgia State University

Haiti

Maya Chadda
Professor, Political Science
William Paterson University

Nepal

Cheng Chen
Assistant Professor, Political Science
University at Albany, State University of New York

China (PRC)
Nationalist Movements

Ann Marie Clark
Associate Professor, Political Science
Purdue University

Amnesty International

Andrew Coleman
Lecturer, Business Law and Taxation
Monash University

International Court of Justice

Melissa Comenduley
Research Assistant, Sociology
University of Washington

Estonia
Latvia
Lithuania

Linda Cornett
Assistant Professor, Political Science
University of North Carolina at Asheville

Refugees

Jennifer Corrin Care
Executive Director, Comparative Law, Centre for Public International and Comparative Law
University of Queensland TC Beirne School of Law

Fiji
Solomon Islands

Emily Corwin
Ph.D. Candidate, Political Science
Louisiana State University

Interest Groups

Andrew Costello
Independent Scholar
Hicksville, NY

Apartheid
Biko, Stephen
Mandela, Nelson
Racism
South Africa

Eric W. Cox
Assistant Director, Leadership
Center
Texas Christian University

International Human Rights Law
International Humanitarian Law
United Nations Commission on
    Human Rights
Universal Declaration of Human
    Rights

Jefferson Cumberbatch
Senior Lecturer, Faculty
of Law
University of the West
Indies–Cave Hill

Antigua and Barbuda

Lucy Dadayan
Ph.D. Candidate, Rockefeller
College of Public Affairs
and Policy
University at Albany, State
University of New York

Armenia
Azerbaijan
Georgia
Hungary

John Daniel
Research Director, Human
Sciences Research Council
Durban, South Africa

Swaziland

Maria Elisabetta de Franciscis
Professor, Political Science
Università degli Studi di Napoli
Federico II

Vatican

Hassan S Dibadj
Ph.D. Candidate, Rockefeller
College of Public Affairs and
Policy
University at Albany, State
University of New York

Afghanistan
Iran
Iraq

Susan Dicklitch
Associate Professor, Government
Franklin and Marshall College

Uganda

Scott A. Dittloff
Assistant Professor, Political
Science
University of the Incarnate
Word

Saint Vincent and the Grenadines

Michael Dodson
Professor, Political Science
Texas Christian University

El Salvador
Guatemala
Honduras
Nicaragua

Ernest A. Dover Jr.
Chair, Political Science
Midwestern State University

Mozambique
Tunisia
Zambia

Mark A. Drumbl
Associate Professor, Law
Washington and Lee University

Rwanda

Graciela Ducatenzeiler
Professor, Political Science
Université de Montréal

Argentina

John C. Dugas
Assistant Professor, Political
Science
Kalamazoo College

Colombia

Martin Edelman
Professor Emeritus, Political
Science
University at Albany, State
University of New York

Bill of Rights
Citizenship
Halakhah
Israel
Naturalization

Emily Edmonds-Poli
Assistant Professor, Political
Science
University of San Diego

Mexico

Eric S. Einhorn
Professor, Political Science
University of Massachusetts,
Amherst

Denmark

Kisangani N. F. Emizet
Associate Professor, Political
Science
Kansas State University

Congo, Democratic Republic
    of (Zaire)

Shawn Flanigan
Ph.D. Candidate, Public
Administration and Policy
University at Albany, State
University of New York

Albania
Macedonia

Ronald Flowers
Professor Emeritus, Religion
Texas Christian University

Freedom of Religion and the State

Jon Fraenkel
Senior Research Fellow,
Pacific Institute of Advanced
Studies in Development &
Governance
University of the South Pacific

Marshall Islands

Vanuatu

Gerrit Franssen
Professor, Centre for Sociology
of Law
University of Antwerp

Belgium

Bogdan Alex Fratiloiu
Independent Scholar
Bucharest, Romania

Czech Republic
Romania
Slovakia

Barbara A. Frey
Director, Human Rights
Program

Barbara A. Frey *(continued)*
University of Minnesota
Stateless People

Douglas Friedman
Associate Professor, Political Science
College of Charleston
Brazil

Brian Galligan
Chair, Political Science
University of Melbourne
Australia

Andrew Geddis
Senior Lecturer, Faculty of Law
University of Otago
New Zealand

Yana N. Georgieva
Ph.D. Candidate, Political Science
Southern Illinois University, Carbondale
Bulgaria

Hamid Ghany
Dean, Faculty of Social Sciences
University of the West Indies–St. Augustine
Trinidad and Tabago

Steven Gibens
Professor, Centre for Sociology of Law
University of Antwerp
Belgium

Mark Gibney
Professor, Political Science
University of North Carolina at Asheville
Immigration and Immigrants
Refugees

Tom Ginsburg
Professor, Law
University of Illinois
Mongolia

Rachel M. Gisselquist
Ph.D. Candidate, Political Science
Massachusetts Institute of Technology
Peacekeeping Forces

James J. Gobert
Professor, Law
University of Essex
Juries

Kenneth Good
Professor, Political Science
University of Botswana
Botswana

Timothy Gordinier
Policy Director, Institute for Humanist Studies
Albany, NY
Freedom of Religion,
Foundations

Dennis R. Gordon
Professor, Political Science
Santa Clara University
Caribbean Region

Ross Grainger
Lecturer, Faculty of Law
University of Wollongong
Hong Kong and Macau

Cecilia A. Green
Assistant Professor, Sociology
University of Pittsburgh
Dominica

Gregory Green
Curator, Southeast Asia Collection
Northern Illinois University Libraries
Laos

Joanne Connor Green
Associate Professor, Political Science
Texas Christian University
Reproductive Rights
Roosevelt, Eleanor

Ivelaw Lloyd Griffith
Dean, Honors College
Florida International University
Colonies and Colonialism
Guyana

Leny E. de Groot-van Leeuwen
Associate Professor, Faculty of Law

University of Nijmegen
Netherlands, The

Helgi Gunnlaugsson
Professor, Sociology
University of Iceland
Iceland

Sten Hagberg
Associate Professor, Cultural Anthropology and Ethnology
Uppsala University
Burkina Faso

Johann J. Hagen
Professor, Basic Sciences
Universität Salzburg
Austria

Kare Hagen
Associate Professor, Public Governance
Norwegian School of Management
Norway

Linn A. Hammergren
Senior Public Sector Management Specialist,
The World Bank
Washington, DC
Peru

M. Donald Hancock
Professor, Political Science
Vanderbilt University
Germany
Hitler, Adolf

Robert Harmsen
Senior Lecturer, European Studies
Queen's University, Belfast
European Convention on Human
Rights and Fundamental
Freedoms
European Court of Human Rights

Dirk Haubrich
Research Officer, Politics and International Relations
University of Oxford
Civil Liberties in Emergencies

Eric Heinze
Reader in Legal Theory, Faculty of Laws

University of London, Queen Mary

Children's Rights

Metin Heper
Dean, School of Economics, Administrative, and Social Sciences
Bilkent University

Turkey

Andrew Herod
Professor, Geography
University of Georgia

Tonga

Gerti Hesseling
Director, African Studies Centre
Leiden, The Netherlands

Senegal

Larry B. Hill
Professor, Political Science
University of Oklahoma

Ombudsmen

Abdourahmane Idrissa
Ph.D. Candidate, Center for African Studies
University of Florida

Niger

Guy-Erik Isaksson
Associate Professor, Political Science
Åbo Akademi University

Bicameral Parliamentary Systems

Deborah Isser
Rule of Law Program, United States Institute of Peace
Washington, DC

Bosnia and Herzegovina

Donald W. Jackson
Professor, Political Science
Texas Christian University

Bahamas
Barbados
Convention Against Torture and other Cruel, Inhuman or Degrading Treatment or Punishment
Convention for the Elimination of All Forms of Discrimination Against Women (CEDAW)

Crimes Against Humanity
Equal Protection of the Law
Equality Before the Law
International Covenant on Civil and Political Rights
International Covenant on Economic, Social and Cultural Rights
Right to Privacy
Student Rights
Universal Criminal Jurisdiction

Sarita D. Jackson
Ph.D. Candidate, Political Science
Brown University

Panama

Rounaq Jahan
Senior Research Scholar, Southern Asian Institute
Columbia University

Bangladesh

Richard Janikowski
Associate Professor, Criminology and Criminal Justice
University of Memphis

Genocide

Gregory Johnston
Ph.D. Candidate, Political Science
Louisiana State University

Angola
Comoros
Madagascar

Lisa A. Joyner
Contract Management Specialist
Albany, NY

Thailand

Jimmy D. Kandeh
Associate Professor, Political Science
University of Richmond

Sierra Leone

David L. Kenley
Associate Professor, History
Marshall University

Taiwan

Michael Keren
Professor, Political Science
University of Calgary

Political Protest

Amal I. Khoury
Ph.D. Candidate, School of International Service
American University

Bahrain
Brunei
Kuwait
Qatar
Saudi Arabia

George Klay Kieh Jr.
Associate Professor and Chair, Political Science
Morehouse College

Liberia

John Kincaid
Director, Meyner Center for the Study of State and Local Government
Lafayette College

Confederations
Federalism

Kris Kobach
Professor, School of Law
University of Missouri–Kansas City

Referendums and Plebiscites

Paul J. Kubicek
Associate Professor, Political Science
Oakland University

Finland

Azzedine Layachi
Associate Professor, Government and Politics
St. John's University

Algeria

Stephen Levine
Professor, Political Science
Victoria University of Wellington

Tuvalu

David Lewis
Reader in Social Policy
London School of Economics and Political Science

Non-governmental Organizations

Timothy C. Lim
Assistant Professor, Political Science

Timothy C. Lim *(continued)*
California State University,
Los Angeles

Korea, North
Korea, South

Robert B. Lloyd
Professor, International Relations
Pepperdine University

Zimbabwe

Richard A. Lobban Jr.
Professor, Anthropology
Rhode Island College

Sudan

Michelle S. Lyon
Adjunct Professor, Law
Washington & Lee University

Rwanda

Pedro Magalhães
Investigator, Instituto de
Ciências Sociais
Universidade de Lisboa

Portugal

Alvin Magid
Professor Emeritus, Political
Science
University at Albany, State
University of New York
Dictatorship
Popular Sovereignty

Kate Malleson
Senior Lecturer in Law
London School of Economics
and Political Science

Judicial Selection

Rodelio Cruz Manacsa
Ph.D. Candidate, Political
Science
Vanderbilt University

Aquino, Corazon
Philippines

Christopher P. Manfredi
Professor and Chair, Political
Science
McGill University

Canada

Marianne Marty
Ph.D. Candidate, Centre
d'Etude d'Afrique Noire

Bordeaux, France

Mauritania

Diane K. Mauzy
Professor, Political Science
University of British Columbia

Malaysia
Singapore

Shelley A. McConnell
Senior Associate Director,
Americas Program
The Carter Center,
Washington, DC

Ecuador

Kathryne McDorman
Associate Professor, History
Texas Christian University

Magna Carta

Brian W. Meeks
Professor, Government
University of the West
Indies–Mona

Jamaica

Albert P. Melone
Professor, Political Science
Southern Illinois University,
Carbondale

Bulgaria

Agustín José Menéndez
Professor, Basic Public Rights
University of Leon, Spain

Spain

Peter J. Messitte
U.S. District Court Judge for
Maryland
Baltimore, MD

Civil Law

Arnauld Miguet
Lecturer in European Politics
London School of Economics
and Political Science

France

Mark C. Miller
Professor and Chair,
Government and International
Relations
Clark University

Luxembourg

Ted H. Miller
Assistant Professor, Political
Science
University of Alabama

Representation

H. Mbella Mokeba
Instructor, Political Science
Louisiana State University

Cameroon
Central African Republic
Chad
Congo, Republic of the
Equatorial Guinea

Carlo Mongardini
Professor, Political Science
University La Sapienza, Rome

Italy

Gabriella R. Montinola
Associate Professor, Political
Science
University of California, Davis

Political Corruption

Derwin Munroe
Lecturer, Political Science
University of Michigan–Flint

British Virgin Islands
Saint Kitts and Nevis

Stephen N. Ndegwa
Associate Professor, Program of
African Studies
Northwestern University

Kenya

Léonce Ndikumana
Associate Professor, Economics
University of Massachusetts,
Amherst

Burundi

Brian Nelson
Associate Professor, Political
Science
Florida International
University

Totalitarianism

David M. O'Brien
Professor, Government and
Foreign Affairs
University of Virginia

Judicial Independence

Rory O'Connell
*Lecturer, Human Rights
Centre
Queen's University of Belfast
School of Law*

Northern Ireland

Ayo Ogundele
*Assistant Professor, Political
Science
Texas A&M
University–Commerce*

Benin
Gambia, The
Nigeria

Henry Okole
*Lecturer, Political Science
University of Papua New
Guinea*

Papua New Guinea

John V. Orth
*Professor, School of Law
University of North Carolina*

Due Process of Law

Sunita A. Parikh
*Associate Professor, Political
Science
Washington University in
St. Louis*

Pakistan

Gianfranco Pasquino
*Professor, Political Science
University of Bologna*

Transitional Political Systems

Pamela Paxton
*Associate Professor, Sociology
The Ohio State University*

Suffrage

Tony Pederson
*Chair, Journalism
Southern Methodist University*

Freedom of Information

Glenn Petersen
*Professor, Anthropology and
International Affairs
Bernard Baruch College,
City University of
New York*

Micronesia, Federated States of

Miguel Poiares Maduro
*Advocate General, Court of
Justice of the European
Communities
Luxembourg*

European Court of Justice

Ralph R. Premdas
*Professor, Behavioural
Sciences
University of the West Indies–St.
Augustine*

Saint Lucia

Elisabeth Prügl
*Associate Professor,
International Relations
Florida International University*

Gender Discrimination
Women's Rights

Marc-Georges Pufong
*Associate Professor, Political
Science
Valdosta State University*

Samoa
Seychelles

Nicol Rae
*Professor and Chair, Political
Science
Florida International
University*

Primaries

Tapio Raunio
*Professor, Political Science
University of Tampere*

European Parliament

Alison Dundes Renteln
*Professor, Political Science and
Anthropology
University of Southern
California*

Human Rights

Cara Richards
*Graduate Student
University at Albany, State
University of New York*

Kazakhstan
Kyrgyzstan (Kyrgyz Republic)
Tajikistan
Turkmenistan
Uzbekistan

Dylan Scott Rickards
*Ph.D. Candidate, Political
Science
Louisiana State University*

Voting Rights

James W. Riddlesperger Jr.
*Professor and Chair, Political
Science
Texas Christian University*

Civil Rights Movement in the United
States
King Jr., Martin Luther
United States

Ann E. Robertson
*National Council for Eurasian
and East European Research
Washington, DC*

Gorbachev, Mikhail
Russia
Stalin, Joseph
Yeltsin, Boris

Robert S. Robins
*Professor Emeritus, Political
Science
Tulane University*

Gandhi, Mahatma
India

Siniša Rodin
*Professor, Faculty of Law
University of Zagreb*

Croatia
Serbia and Montenegro
Slovenia

Andrea Rogers
*Independent Scholar
Clifton Park, NY*

Belarus
Moldova
Ukraine

Wannes Rombouts
*Associate Professor, Faculty
of Law
University of Nijmegen*

Netherlands, The

Jonathan Rosenberg
*Associate Professor, Political
Science
University of Alaska–Fairbanks*

Grenada

Susan Dente Ross
Associate Professor, Journalism
Washington State University

Freedom of Assembly and
Association

Emile Sahliyeh
Associate Professor, Political
Science
University of North Texas

Shari'a
Egypt

Paul Khalil Saucier
Ph.D. Candidate, Sociology and
Anthropology
Northeastern University

Cape Verde
Guinea-Bissau

Christopher Saunders
Professor, Historical Studies
University of Cape Town

Namibia

Michael P. Scharf
Professor and Director,
Frederick K. Cox International
Law Center
Case Western Reserve University
School of Law

International Criminal Court

Birgit Schmook
ECOSUR
Chetumal, Mexico

Belize

Gerhard Seibert
Researcher, Centro de Estudos
Africanos e Asiáticos
(CEAA)
Instituto de Investigação
Científica Tropical

São Tomé and Príncipe

Dinah Shelton
Professor, Law
George Washington University
Law School

American Declaration of the Rights
and Duties of Man and the
American Convention on Human
Rights
Inter-American Commission and
Court of Human Rights

Gerry Simpson
Reader in Law
London School of Economics
and Political Science

War Crimes

Holly Sims
Associate Professor, Public
Administration and Policy
University at Albany, State
University of New York

Aung San Suu Kyi
Dalai Lama

Anthony L. Smith
Senior Research Fellow, Asia-
Pacific Center for Security
Studies
Honolulu, HI

East Timor

Zeric Kay Smith
Management Systems
International
Washington, DC

Mali

Dimitri A. Sotiropoulos
Assistant Professor, Political
Science
University of Athens

Greece

Roger Southall
Distinguished Research Fellow,
Human Sciences Research
Council
Pretoria, South Africa

Lesotho

Henry F. Srebrnik
Professor, Political Studies
University of Prince Edward
Island

Mauritius

Ronald Bruce St John
Independent Scholar
Dunlap, IL

Libya
Syria
Vietnam

Paige Johnson Tan
Assistant Professor, Political
Science

University of North Carolina
Wilmington

Indonesia

C. Neal Tate
Professor and Chair, Political
Science
Vanderbilt University

Bhutan
Government Data Sets
Guinea
Kiribati
Nauru
Netherlands Antilles and Aruba
Somalia
Suriname
Tanzania

Moses Kangmieve Tesi
Professor, Political Science
Middle Tennessee State
University

Côte d'Ivoire

Andreas Theophanous
Director General, Research
and Development
Center
Intercollege

Cyprus

Erica E. Townsend-Bell
Ph.D. Candidate, Political
Science
Washington University in
St. Louis

Uruguay

Brian Turner
Associate Professor and Chair,
Political Science
Randolph-Macon College

Paraguay

Kheang Un
Visiting Assistant Professor,
Political Science
Northern Illinois University

Cambodia

Mark Ungar
Associate Professor, Political
Science
Brooklyn College, City
University of New York

Venezuela

Koen Van Aeken
*Director, Centre for Sociology
of Law
University of Antwerp*
Belgium

Ingrid van Biezen
*Senior Lecturer, Political
Science and International
Studies
University of Birmingham*
Political Parties

Donna Lee Van Cott
*Assistant Professor, Political
Science
Tulane University*
Bolivia

Mary L. Volcansek
*Dean, AddRan College of
Humanities and Social
Sciences
Texas Christian University*
European Microstates
Havel, Vaclav
Kelsen, Hans
Presidential Systems

Peter VonDoepp
*Assistant Professor, Political
Science
University of Vermont*
Malawi

Samuel Walker
*Professor, Criminal Justice
University of Nebraska at
Omaha*
American Civil Liberties Union

Jerold Waltman
*Professor, Political Science
Baylor University*
Freedom of Expression
Freedom of the Press

Bradley C. S. Watson
*Chair, American and Western
Political Thought
Saint Vincent College*
Liberal Democracy

Liam Weeks
*Ph.D. Candidate, Political Science
Trinity College, University of
Dublin*
Ireland

Helena Whall
*Project Officer, Indigenous
Rights in the Commonwealth
Project
Commonwealth Policy Studies
Unit*
Indigenous Peoples' Rights

Nigel D. White
*Professor, International
Organisations*

*University of Nottingham School
of Law*
United Nations

Michael J. Willis
*Fellow, Middle East Studies
St. Antony's College, Oxford
University*
Morocco

Bruce M. Wilson
*Associate Professor, Political
Science
University of Central Florida*
Costa Rica

Matthew J. Wilson
*Associate Dean and Director,
School of Law
Temple University Japan*
Japan

Mulatu Wubneh
*Professor and Chair, Planning
East Carolina University*
Djibouti
Eritrea
Ethiopia

Ralph A. Young
*Senior Lecturer, Government
and International Politics
University of Manchester*
Gabon

Dominica

Dominica is a mountainous island of volcanic origin in the Lesser Antilles in the Caribbean, located midway between Puerto Rico to the north and Trinidad to the south. It is 754 square kilometers (291 square miles) in area and in 2004 had a population of approximately 69,400. The majority of its inhabitants are of African descent, with about 77 percent adhering to the beliefs of the Roman Catholic Church and 15 percent to those of Protestant denominations.

After Christopher Columbus (1451–1506) landed on the island in 1493, its inhabitants, the Carib, managed to fend off rival colonial claims from the French and British but were eventually defeated and nearly decimated. France formally **ceded** Dominica to Great Britain in 1763. Despite several French attempts to reclaim the territory, it remained a British colony for another two centuries, with a limited representative government similar to those of older West Indian colonies.

cede: to relinquish political control of lands to another country; surrender

In 1831, with the passage of the Brown Privilege Bill, free nonwhites were granted full political and civil rights. After the final abolition of slavery in 1838, Dominica immediately elected a nonwhite majority, a situation that lasted until 1898 when Crown Colony Rule was adopted under intense colonial pressure. In 1903 a reserve was officially established for the surviving Caribs. Continued agitation for representative government led to constitutional reforms in 1924 and 1936, which introduced through the electoral process a minority component into the legislature.

In 1951 a new constitution granted universal adult **suffrage**. In 1956 a ministerial system was introduced, giving unofficial members seats on the Executive Council and responsibility for government departments. In 1957 the first election involving a political party representing the masses took place. Franklin Andrew Merrifield Baron (b. 1923), who led a post-election majority **coalition** in the Council, became the island's first chief minister in 1960 when further constitutional changes went into effect. In 1967 Dominica was transformed into a fully self-governing state in association with Great Britain, which retained

suffrage: to vote, or, the right to vote

coalition: an alliance, partnership, or union of disparate peoples or individuals

responsibility for external defense. In the 1970 general elections the number of constituencies increased from eleven to twenty-one. On July 12, 1978, the Dominica Assembly passed a resolution seeking to terminate its association with Britain. Later that month Dominica was granted independence. Like Trinidad and Tobago and Guyana, two other former colonies, Dominica elected to become a **republic**, with a president as head of state and prime minister as head of government. The official name, the Commonwealth of Dominica, was chosen to distinguish the state from the larger Spanish-speaking country to the north, the Dominican Republic.

POST–1945 MAJOR POLITICAL EVENTS

Edward Oliver (E. O.) Leblanc (1923–2004) led the Dominica Labour Party (DLP), the country's first major party, to several victories after the 1957 election in which it won four seats in the House of Assembly. The DLP subsequently swept the 1958 federal elections that were held under the aegis of the short-lived West Indies Federation (1958–1962). Leblanc led popularly elected governments in 1961, 1966, and 1970 before resigning as prime minister in 1974 over mass protests against a proposed censorship law. The DLP won sixteen out of twenty-one seats in the 1975 elections under the leadership of Patrick Roland John (b. 1938), who took over from Leblanc and eventually led the island to independence.

John had already proved to be a controversial figure when he sponsored and oversaw passage of the draconian Dread Act of 1974, which drew widespread international condemnation. The act was directed against a loose association of **dissident** youth, mostly males, known as "dreads," due to their signature dreadlocks hairstyle. Persons whose mere appearance indicated membership in prohibited societies were subject to arrest without warrant and imprisonment without bail. The act exempted from civil or criminal liability any civilian injuring or killing a "dread" found inside a dwelling house and assumed to be trespassing. John ran into more serious trouble in 1979 after he was implicated in a series of shady behind-the-scenes deals. Opposition mounted to legislation he had proposed, and thousands of protestors swarmed the government headquarters on May 29. The island's Defence Force opened fire on the crowd, killing one man and critically injuring several others. A major political and constitutional crisis was thus provoked, with John rejecting calls to resign from a broad coalition, the Committee for National Salvation. When a number of cabinet members defected and the president fled the country, a new acting president was sworn in and an **interim** prime minister installed on June 21, thereby revoking John's appointment as prime minister. The government of Prime Minister Oliver Seraphin (b. 1946), an ex-cabinet member in the discredited John **regime**, lasted about a year, during which the country faced the devastation of a natural catastrophe, Hurricane David. On July 20, 1980, new elections occurred, bringing into power the twice-defeated conservative Dominica Freedom Party (DFP), with Mary Eugenia Charles (b. 1919) at its helm.

Charles, an attorney by training, became the Caribbean's first woman prime minister. She went on to win two more elections, finally retiring after her third term in office ended in June 1995. The DFP was replaced in power by a new party with broad social-democratic leanings, the United Workers' Party (UWP), under the leadership of Edison James (b. 1943). In 2000, the UWP was narrowly defeated by a reinvigorated DLP under the charismatic leadership of Roosevelt Bernard Douglas (1942–2002). The DLP formed an alliance with the greatly diminished DFP that had won two seats in the House

republic: a form of democratic government in which decisions are made by elected representatives of the people

dissident: one who disagrees with the actions or political philosophy of his or her government or religion

interim: for a limited time, during a period of transition

regime: a type of government, or, the government in power in a region

of Assembly, to the DLP's ten and UWP's nine. Douglas died of a sudden heart attack after only eight months in office. He was succeeded by Pierre Charles (1954–2004), who suffered the same fate after serving for a little over three years as prime minister. On January 8, 2004, Charles was succeeded by Roosevelt Skerrit (b. 1972), who at thirty-two was the youngest-ever Caribbean prime minister.

NATURE OF GOVERNMENT

Dominica has a **Westminster**-style parliamentary government, and there are three political parties: the DLP (the majority party), the UWP, and the DFP. A president and prime minister make up the executive branch; however, the role of the president is largely ceremonial. Nominated by the prime minister in consultation with the leader of the opposition party, the president is elected for a five-year term by the parliament. The president appoints as prime minister the leader of the majority party in the parliament and also appoints, on the prime minister's recommendation, members of the parliament from the ruling party as cabinet ministers. The prime minister and cabinet are responsible to the parliament and can be removed on the basis of a no-confidence vote.

The unicameral parliament, called the House of Assembly, is composed of twenty-one regional representatives and nine senators, with the speaker and one ex-officio member bringing the total to thirty-two. Regional representatives are elected by universal suffrage and, in turn, decide whether senators are to be elected or appointed. If appointed, the president chooses five of them on the advice of the prime minister and four on the advice of the opposition leader. If elected, senators are selected through the vote of regional representatives. Dominica's laws require that elections for representatives and senators occur at least every five years, although the prime minister can call for elections at any time.

Dominica's legal system is based on English common law, and the country enjoys an independent judiciary. There is a multilevel judicial system, including Lower or Magistrate's Courts and a High Court, with appeals made to the Eastern Caribbean Supreme Court and, ultimately, the Judicial Committee of the Privy Council in London, which in 2005 was scheduled to be replaced by a regional Caribbean Court of Justice. The Dominica Police is the only security force, the Defence Force having been abolished by the Charles regime. It remains answerable to the democratically elected government, which alone determines its powers.

POLITICAL LIFE AND HUMAN RIGHTS

The turbulent period of the 1970s and early 1980s, which included two foiled coup attempts, was an unusual one for Dominica. Its governments since the late twentieth century have, in general, respected the rights of their citizens. Serious political intimidation remained rare, and elections continued to be free and fair. All individuals—except those suffering from

Westminster: a democratic model of government comprising operational procedures for a legislative body, based on the system used in the United Kingdom

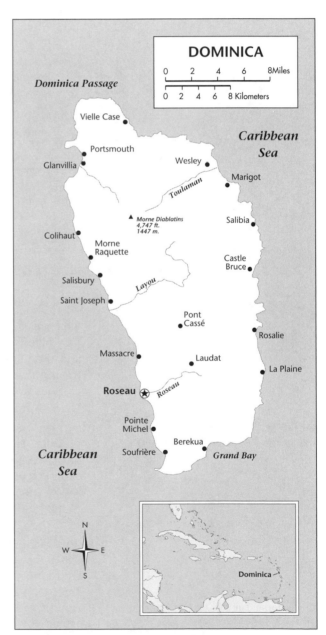

(MAP BY MARYLAND CARTOGRAPHICS/THE GALE GROUP)

indigene: a person who has his origin in a specific region

mental incompetence or having a criminal record—who are citizens of Dominica, are over eighteen years of age, and have resided in Dominica for at least twelve months prior to the voter registration deadline are qualified to vote. However, human rights abuses do exist in several areas: the use of excessive force by police, poor prison conditions, societal violence against women and children, discrimination against **indigenous** Caribs, and discrimination against female Caribs in mixed marriages.

See also: Caribbean Region.

BIBLIOGRAPHY

Andre, Irving W. and Gabriel J. Christian. *In Search of Eden: The Travails of a Caribbean Mini State*. Upper Marlboro, MD: Pond Casse Press, 1992.

Baker, Patrick L. *Centring the Periphery: Chaos, Order and the Ethnohistory of Dominica*. Jamaica: The Press—University of the West Indies, 1994.

Government of Dominica. *Aspects of Dominican History*. Roseau, Dominica: Government Printery, 1972.

Honychurch, Lennox. *The Dominica Story*. London: Macmillan Education, 1995.

Trouillot, Michel-Rolph. *Peasants and Capital: Dominica in the World Economy*. Baltimore, MD: The Johns Hopkins University Press, 1988.

Cecilia A. Green

Dominican Republic

The Dominican Republic is located in the central Caribbean and covers 48,322 square kilometers (18,657 square miles) of the island of Hispaniola, which it shares with Haiti. In 2003 the republic's population was roughly 8.7 million. The country is bounded by the Atlantic Ocean on its north coast and the Caribbean Sea on its south coast. Mountain chains, or *cordilleras,* frame the fertile Cibao valley; the country also has humid lowlands and several rivers. The Dominican capital of Santo Domingo was the first city in the Western Hemisphere.

per capita: for each person, especially for each person living in an area or country

The Dominican Republic's relatively high 2002 **per capita** gross domestic product ($6,300) masks the country's marked income inequality. After spectacular economic growth in the late 1990s and early 2000s, the Dominican economy experienced a major bank collapse in mid–2003. This resulted in a severe economic downturn accompanied by inflation and a sharp devaluation of the peso.

authoritarianism: the domination of the state or its leader over individuals

Although the Dominican Republic was a Spanish colony for three hundred years, the country gained its independence from Haiti in 1844. Until 1961, the republic experienced periods of instability and brutal dictatorships, most notably that of Rafael Leonidas Trujillo Mólina (1891–1961) from 1930 to 1961. After a brief democratic respite in 1962, a U.S. military intervention in 1965, and an **authoritarian** regime for the next twelve years under Trujillo loyalist Joaquin Balaguer (1907–2002), democracy began to take root in 1978.

This democratic shift occurred with the election of Dominican Revolutionary Party (PRD) candidates Antonio Guzman (1911–1982), who served from 1978 to 1982, and Salvador Jorge Blanco (b. 1926), who served from 1982 to 1986. In a series of increasingly fraudulent elections, the Social Christian Reformist Party's (PRSC) Joaquin Balaguer served as president again between 1986 and 1996. Signaling the emergence of a younger generation of political actors, the Dominican Liberation Party's (PLD) Leonel Fernández (b. 1953) served as president from 1996 to 2000 and was reelected for the 2004–2008 term. The PRD's Hipolito Mejia (b. 1941) was president from 2000 to 2004.

The Dominican Republic is a representative democracy, based on a 1966 constitution that was adopted after the U.S. military intervention of 1965. The government has executive, legislative, and judicial branches. In reality, in this presidential system the executive has overwhelming power, so much that the practice of government has been labeled "neosultanistic" (Hartlyn 1998, p. 17). For the most part, the Dominican bureaucracy remains **centralized** and politicized.

Historically, the **bicameral** legislature has been a rubber stamp for the president, although since the democratic transition in 1978 the Congress has had some autonomy. A Supreme Court exercises judicial power at the national level and over lower courts created by Congress. Although judicial reform began in the late 1990s, the courts remain characterized by a high degree of politicization, corruption, and a lack of citizen access. The Dominican Republic's legal system is based on the French model.

With the democratic transition in 1978 came more respect for democratic freedom and rights, a greater role for political parties and interest groups, and progress toward fair and free elections. Three political parties—the Dominican Revolutionary Party (PRD), Dominican Liberation Party (PLD), and Social Christian Reformist Party (PRSC)—dominated the political scene during

centralize: to move control or power to a single point of authority

bicameral: comprised of two chambers, usually a legislative body

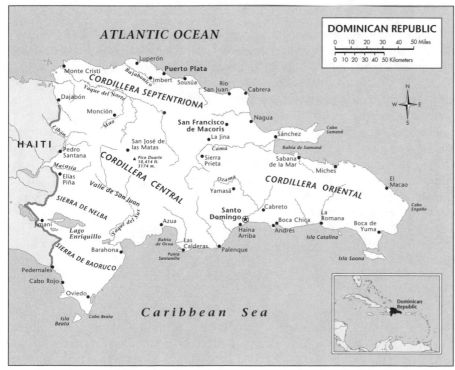

(MAP BY MARYLAND CARTOGRAPHICS/THE GALE GROUP)

the 1990s and early 2000s. However, these parties remained personalist (i.e., focused on certain individuals) and did little between elections. The main broadly based pressure group was the Collective of Popular Organizations (COP).

Elections in the Dominican Republic have been considered fair since 1996, with the electoral board playing its mandated role of creating accurate voter lists. Most notable is the growth of civic associations since the 1990s. Organizations such as *Participacion Ciudadana* are promoting political participation not only through voting, but also by educating Dominicans that government institutions should be held accountable. The media generally are free of censorship.

In terms of personal security and justice, rights are respected more for the wealthier and lighter-skinned Dominican citizens. Human rights groups have cited the Dominican government for abuses against Haitian workers or darker-skinned Dominicans who may "look Haitian."

See also: Caribbean Region.

BIBLIOGRAPHY

Hartlyn, Jonathan. *The Struggle for Democratic Politics in the Dominican Republic*. Chapel Hill: University of North Carolina Press, 1998.

Moya Pons, Frank. *The Dominican Republic: A National History*. New Rochelle, NY: Hispaniola Books, 1995.

Sherrie L. Baver

Due Process of Law

Due process of law describes proper legal procedures but also has additional meanings in American constitutional law. The essential guarantee of due process is fairness, although its implementation in practice depends on the particular institutions of a given legal system; trial by jury, adversary proceedings, and certain rules of evidence, for instance, are specific to the common law system and not necessarily universal requirements. In general, procedural propriety means that disputes are resolved according to law; that is, courts are open and available to litigants, decisions are rendered by learned and impartial judges, and judgments are promptly and effectively enforced. All U.S. state constitutions expressly guarantee due process of law, using either those words or the synonymous phrase "by the law of the land." The U.S. Constitution, in keeping with the **federal** form of American government, contains two guarantees: The Fifth Amendment in the Bill of Rights (1791) prohibits the federal government from depriving any person of "life, liberty, or property, without due process of law," and the Fourteenth Amendment, adopted in 1868 to constitutionalize the results of the U.S. Civil War (1861–1865), extends the same prohibition to the states.

As developed by American courts, both state and federal, due process has a substantive as well as a procedural component. Procedural due process summarizes proper procedure generally and authorizes judges to fill gaps left by express procedural guarantees. Substantive due process, like its procedural counterpart, authorizes the judicial protection of rights not expressly **enumerated** elsewhere

federalism: a system of political organization, in which separate states or groups are ruled by a dominant central authority on some matters, but are otherwise permitted to govern themselves independently

enumerate: to expressly name, as in a list

in the constitutional texts. Substantive due process may be further divided into economic substantive due process, concerned with economic freedom, especially freedom of contract, and noneconomic (or social) substantive due process, concerned with the right to privacy. Although one may find correlations in many of the world's legal systems, the rights protected by substantive due process in the United States are not elsewhere subsumed under the general phrase "due process," but are given more specific labels. Even in American jurisprudence, due process is often interchangeable with other juristic concepts, such as equal protection or the separation of powers.

jurisprudence: the body of precedents already decided in a legal system

HISTORICAL BACKGROUND

The pedigree of the phrase "due process of law" may be traced back to the Magna Carta (1215), in which the embattled English King John was forced by his rebellious barons to swear that he would take no action against any free person *nisi per legem terrae* (except by the law of the land). Hundreds of years later the influential English jurist Sir Edward Coke associated the Latin phrase *per legem terrae* with a French phrase (French being the language of English law in the centuries after the Norman Conquest), *en due process a la commune lei*; he translated it as "by due process according to the common law." In time the phrase was honed to "due process of law." Although in England, the land of its birth, due process as a phrase gradually went out of fashion, the concept survived in a similar expression, "rule of law." Before that happened, however, American constitution-makers, conscious of the role due process had played in English constitutional history, enshrined it in America's founding documents. Heirs of the English common law tradition—American judges—using their power to review statutes for compliance with the constitutions, proceeded to develop the demands of due process over the years in an accumulating series of precedents.

jurist: a person learned in legal matters; most often, a judge

statute: a law created by a legislature that is inferior to constitutional law

precedent: an established ruling, understanding, or practice of the law

PROCEDURAL DUE PROCESS

In the United States, state and federal constitutions contain a host of procedural guarantees, many of them quite specific and historically conditioned, such as indictment by grand jury and limitations on the review of facts found by a trial jury. When gaps have been discovered, the general guarantee of due process has been invoked. In *Tumey v. Ohio* (1928), for example, the U.S. Supreme Court reviewed a state statute that gave a magistrate a share of the fines imposed in case of conviction and held that for a judge to have a financial interest in the outcome of a case "deprives a defendant in a criminal case of due process of law." In state constitutions that expressly prohibit the practice, such as the constitution of North Carolina, the problem would be addressed as a violation of the more specific provision.

magistrate: an official with authority over a government, usually a judicial official with limited jurisdiction over criminal cases

In civil cases, too, express guarantees have been supplemented by recourse to the general requirements of due process. In *Goldberg v. Kelly* (1970) the Supreme Court ruled that before a state could terminate welfare benefits due process required a fair hearing, and provided a comprehensive summary of precisely what that meant:

recourse: a resource for assistance

1. adequate notice,
2. an opportunity to be heard,
3. the right to present evidence,
4. confrontation of opposing witnesses,
5. the right to cross-examine those witnesses,

6. disclosure of all adverse evidence,
7. the right to an attorney if desired,
8. a decision based solely on the evidence produced at the hearing,
9. a statement of reasons for the decision,
10. an impartial decision maker.

In code-based legal systems these rights would more likely be expressly guaranteed, rather than derived by judicial development from the general concept of due process.

Because the U.S. Bill of Rights applies only to action by the federal government and specifies a number of rights not included in the text of the Fourteenth Amendment, which applies only to state action, the due process clause of the Fourteenth Amendment has become the vehicle through which most of the Bill of Rights has been applied to the states. The Fourteenth Amendment is said to "incorporate" the Bill of Rights, a doctrine that may be seen as a judicial response to criticism that the bare phrase "due process " is too open to interpretation: Reference to the rights enumerated in the Bill of Rights guides judicial discretion. When the only role of the due process clause of the Fourteenth Amendment is to incorporate parts of the Bill of Rights, due process is not itself the source of the constitutional limitations but only the vehicle through which those limitations are applied to the states.

Before the acceptance of the incorporation doctrine, the U.S. Supreme Court addressed claims of violations of due process by the states by asking general questions, such as whether a challenged practice violates "fundamental principles of liberty and justice" or whether it "shocks the conscience." Before incorporation, for example, it held in *Rochin v. California* (1952) that state law enforcement officers' use of incriminating evidence obtained by pumping the stomach of an unwilling suspect violated due process in general. Although this approach was finally abandoned in favor of incorporating the more specific provisions of the Bill of Rights, such as the privilege against self-incrimination in the Fifth Amendment, it suggests an approach to be used in searching for counterparts to the American law of due process in other legal systems; that is, whatever means those systems use to safeguard "fundamental principles" or to avoid abusive government practices may be analogs to due process as understood in the American constitutional system. The European Convention on Human Rights and Fundamental Freedoms, for example, provides expressly that "everyone is entitled to a fair and public hearing within a reasonable time by an independent and impartial **tribunal** established by law." In the United States the guarantee of due process has been held to mean just that and more.

tribunal: a type of court of law, usually military in nature

SUBSTANTIVE DUE PROCESS

Substantive due process is far less intuitive than its procedural counterpart. To some extent, it can be explained by reference to the relative generality of the rights expressly protected by due process: life, liberty, and property. But it also reflects the American judiciary's strong commitment to the notion of limited government. Just as with procedural due process, substantive due process has been used to fill gaps left by more specific guarantees. Because the U.S. Constitution nowhere speaks about freedom of contract or the right to privacy, the courts located such rights in the concepts of liberty and property. Economic substantive due process is best exemplified by the Supreme Court's decision in *Lochner v. New York* (1905) holding unconstitutional a state statute that limited the working hours of bakers. Due process was violated because the statute was determined to be "an unreasonable, unnecessary and **arbitrary** interference with the right of the individual" to contract with respect to hours of labor. The decision meant that much regulatory legislation, including much early labor law, was subject to searching judicial inquiry and possible veto. For example, both state and federal statutes that prohibited employers from requiring as a condition of employment that workers agree not to join a labor organization were held to violate due process. Although much social legislation survived judicial scrutiny, the risk of **litigation** and judicial invalidation delayed the emergence of modern welfare systems in American states.

The constitutional guarantee of freedom of contract, recognized in the heyday of laissez faire, was not finally abandoned until 1937, when the Court acknowledged in *West Coast Hotel Co. v. Parrish* (1937) that, in fact, "the Constitution does not speak of freedom of contract." The next year in *United States v. Carolene Products Co.* (1938) the Court announced that it would from that point forward presume the constitutionality of "regulatory legislation

arbitrary: capricious, random, or changing without notice

litigate: to bring a disagreement or violation of the law before a judge for a legal decision

NEW YORK STATE SUPREME COURT JUSTICE CHARLES TEJADA LISTENS TO COURT PROCEEDINGS IN DECEMBER 2002. In the United States, every state constitution guarantees its citizens due process, according to state and federal laws. The form of due process may vary state to state or even case by case, but the legality of the proceedings is expected to remain. (SOURCE: AP/WIDE WORLD PHOTOS)

affecting ordinary commercial transactions," but at the same time warned that it would not extend the presumption to restrictions on civil rights, implicitly splitting the judicial concept of liberty into economic and noneconomic components. Thereafter economic rights were accorded less generous protection by the courts than noneconomic or social rights. Although freedom of contract is no longer recognized as a constitutional right, the takings clause of the Fifth Amendment, prohibiting the government from seizing private property for public purposes without just compensation, has been invoked in challenges to state regulations that would once have been scrutinized for deprivations of property without due process.

Non-economic substantive due process is associated with the right to privacy, eventually located, although not without some difficulty, in the requirement of due process. Reaction to the freedom-of-contract cases made the Court wary at first of adopting an expansive reading of the due process clause, so when the Court in *Griswold v. Connecticut* (1965) invalidated state statutes outlawing the distribution of birth control materials to married persons, it rationalized its holding by a complicated theory of privacy protected by the "penumbras," or shadows, cast by a variety of rights enumerated in the Bill of Rights—notably not including the due process guaranteed by the Fifth Amendment. When a few years after *Griswold* its holding was extended to unmarried persons in *Eisenstadt v. Baird* (1972), the result was technically justified by the guarantee of "the equal protection of the laws" contained in the Fourteenth Amendment. The same law, it was held, must be applied to married and unmarried couples alike, but as the Court explained its decision, it implicated issues far beyond equality of treatment: "If the right of privacy means anything, it is the right of the individual, married or single, to be free from unwarranted governmental intrusion into matters so fundamentally affecting a person as the decision whether to bear or beget a child."

Roe v. Wade (1973), finding a state ban on virtually all abortions "violative of the Due Process Clause of the Fourteenth Amendment," followed almost inevitably. Retrospectively, the cases that had invalidated restraints on the distribution of birth control materials were reconceptualized as due process cases. A comprehensive statement of the law was attempted two decades later in *Planned Parenthood of Southeastern Pennsylvania v. Casey* (1992), largely reaffirming *Roe* and explaining that the liberty protected by due process included "personal decisions relating to marriage, procreation, contraception, family relationships, child rearing, and education." To intrude into such personal decisions, the state needed a compelling reason.

After initial rejection, due process was found to protect private consensual sexual activity more generally; *Lawrence v. Texas* (2003) held state sodomy laws to be unconstitutional. The guarantee of due process is not found only in the federal constitution nor is the development of substantive due process a monopoly of federal courts. In *Goodridge v. Department of Public Health* (2003) the Massachusetts Supreme Judicial Court, extending the reasoning in *Lawrence,* held that the state's refusal to recognize the marriage of same-sex couples was a violation of the due process protected by the state constitution's law-of-the-land clause. It may be that the emptying of due process by the incorporation doctrine of much of what once was considered its content and leaving it as a residual category, invoked in only the most controversial cases, explains many of the difficulties surrounding its current use in the United States.

Once again the incorporation of the Bill of Rights in the due process clause of the Fourteenth Amendment has added specificity to the general concept. But again the earlier inquiry provides a guide to what sorts of counterparts to the American law of due process exist in other legal systems. The Supreme Court of Canada in *R. v. Morgentaler* held that a restrictive abortion law **infringed** on the constitutional "right to life, liberty and security of the person and the right not to be deprived thereof except in accordance with the principles of fundamental justice," while in South Africa it was held in *National Coalition for Gay and Lesbian Equality v. Minister of Justice* that the common law crime of sodomy infringes on the "right to dignity" protected by the South African constitution. In the United States the demands of due process continue to be developed incrementally by judicial decision and encompass both procedural and substantive rights, while in other systems similar problems are addressed more self-consciously under various, usually more specific, provisions of law.

infringe: to exceed the limits of; to violate

See also: Bill of Rights; European Convention on Human Rights and Fundamental Freedoms; Magna Carta; Right to Privacy.

BIBLIOGRAPHY

Brandeis, Louis D., and Samuel D. Warren. "The Right to Privacy." *Harvard Law Review* 4 (1890):193–220.

Gilman, Howard. *The Constitution Besieged: The Rise and Demise of Lochner Era Police Powers Jurisprudence.* Durham, NC: Duke University Press, 1993.

Kens, Paul. *Judicial Power and Reform Politics: The Anatomy of* Lochner v. New York. Lawrence: University Press of Kansas, 1990.

Nowak, John E., et al. *Constitutional Law.* St. Paul, MN: West, 1983.

Orth, John V. *Due Process of Law: A Brief History.* Lawrence: University Press of Kansas, 2003.

Phillips, Michael J. *The Lochner Court, Myth and Reality: Substantive Due Process from the 1890s to the 1930s.* Westport, CT: Praeger, 2001.

Pound, Roscoe. "Liberty of Contract." *Yale Law Journal* 18 (1909):454–487.

Siegel, Stephen A. "Lochner Era Jurisprudence and the American Constitutional Tradition." *North Carolina Law Review* 70 (1991):1–111.

Stoner, James, Jr. *Common Law and Liberal Theory: Coke, Hobbes, and the Origins of American Constitutionalism.* Lawrence: University Press of Kansas, 1992.

Strong, Frank R. *Substantive Due Process of Law: A Dichotomy of Sense and Nonsense.* Durham, NC: Carolina Academic Press, 1986.

Tribe, Laurence H. *American Constitutional Law.* Mineola, NY: Foundation Press, 1978.

Court Cases

Goldberg v. Kelly, 397 U.S. 254 (1970).

Goodridge v. Department of Public Health, 798 NE2d 941 (Massachusetts 2003).

Lawrence v. Texas, 123 S.Ct. 2472 (2003).

Lochner v. New York, 198 U.S. 45 (1905).

National Coalition for Gay and Lesbian Equality v. Minister of Justice, (1) SALR 6 (CC) (1999).

Planned Parenthood of Southeastern Pennsylvania v, Casey, 505 U.S. 833 (1992).

R. v. Morgentaler, 1 S.Ct. 30 (1988).

Rochin v. California, 342 U.S. 165 (1952).

Roe v. Wade, 410 U.S. 113 (1973).

Tumey v. Ohio, 273 U.S. 510 (1928).

United States v. Carolene Products Co., 304 U.S. 144 (1938).

West Coast Hotel Co., v. Parrish, 300 U.S. 379 (1937).

John V. Orth

East Timor

East Timor is Southeast Asia's newest independent country of approximately 925,000 inhabitants. Situated on the eastern half of the Timor Island, and also including a small enclave on the western side, it consists of flat coastal areas separated by a rugged mountain range and features distinct tropical dry and rainy seasons. The population of East Timor is made up of a dozen separate indigenous groups that share a common experience of colonialism under Portugal and Indonesia. As a result, Tetum (the language spoken in the capital, Díli), Portuguese, and Indonesian vie for prominence as the language of school and government—the first two are official languages.

East Timor's most valuable and only exportable crop lies in the extensive plantations of Arabica coffee in the mountainous interior. Oil and gas reserves, in abundance in the Timor Sea, are still untapped pending negotiations with neighboring Australia and individual oil companies. East Timor remains extremely poor. Per capita income is around $520, according to the World Bank's 2002 estimate, and the majority of the population is engaged in **subsistence farming**.

subsistence farming: farming which does not turn a profit, providing only enough food for the farmers themselves

Portugal refused to give independence to its colonies after World War II (1939–1945) but abruptly changed course in 1974. In East Timor two parties emerged to promote independence: Fretilin and the Timorese Democratic Union. After a brief civil war between the two in 1975, the more left-wing Fretilin emerged as the winner and established the government through a **unilateral** declaration of independence. Few countries had recognized this government when Indonesian troops invaded the territory on December 7, 1975, and **annexed** the territory.

unilateral: independent of any other person or entity

annex: to incorporate; to take control of politically and/or physically

Indonesian atrocities in East Timor, costing more than one hundred thousand lives over more than two decades, brought the country's plight to the attention of the international community. East Timor's circumstances changed in 1999, however, when Indonesia allowed the East Timorese to hold a **referendum**, in which 78.5 percent of the population opted for independence. Pro-Indonesia militia destroyed East Timor when this result became known, prompting an international peacekeeping force to assume control of the territory.

referendum: a popular vote on legislation, brought before the people by their elected leaders or public initiative

super-majority: a legislative majority so large that the party can pass whatever legislation it wishes

sovereignty: autonomy; or, rule over a political entity

unicameral: comprised of one chamber, usually a legislative body

East Timor held elections for an assembly to draft a constitution on August 30, 2001. The constitutional assembly then stayed on to serve as a parliament. Fretilin reemerged as a political power in a multiparty environment, winning fifty-five of the eighty-eight seats. The party made subsequent political deals to give it a **super-majority** in parliament. Fretilin also appointed the prime minister, Marí Alkatiri (b. 1949), and the house speaker, Francisco "Lú-Olo" Guterres (b. 1954). On April 14, 2002, Xanana Gusmão (b. 1946), the former head of Falintil, the armed resistance movement during Indonesian occupation, was overwhelmingly elected president with 82.7 percent of the vote. Gusmão is regarded by East Timorese as the father of their independence, and his influence on government far outweighs the formal powers granted to him in the constitution. On May 20, 2002, the United Nations officially handed over **sovereignty** to East Timor.

East Timor's constitution, largely based on the examples of Mozambique and Portugal, provides for a semi-presidential system. The president is head of state with the resulting ceremonial duties but also has the power of veto over parliamentary legislation and supply. Parliament is **unicameral** and sits for a five-year term. Seventy-five of the eighty-eight seats are determined by proportionality, and the remaining thirteen are reserved for each district. There is adherence to civil rights for citizens, parties, and the media.

The Supreme Court of Justice is the highest judicial authority, and its independence is guaranteed under East Timorese law. The constitution is secular but makes reference to the historic role of the Catholic Church.

Under international tutelage and aid, East Timor's democracy has remained stable, although its political and developmental challenges are formidable.

See also: Indonesia; International Court of Justice; Peacekeeping Forces.

BIBLIOGRAPHY

Dunn, James. *East Timor: A Rough Passage to Independence*, 3rd ed. Double Bay, New South Wales, Australia: Longueville Books, 2003.

East Timor Action Network, ed. *Constitution of the Democratic Republic of East Timor*. <http://www.etan.org/etanpdf/pdf2/constfnen.pdf>.

Fox, James J., and Dionisio Babo Soares, eds. *Out of the Ashes: Destruction and Reconstruction of East Timor*, 2d ed. Canberra: Australian University Press, 2003.

Hill, Hal, and João M. Saldanha, eds. *East Timor: Development Challenges for the World's Newest Nation*. Singapore: Institute of Southeast Asian Studies, 2001.

Smith, Anthony L. "East Timor: Elections in the World's Newest Nation." *Journal of Democracy* 15, no. 2 (2004):145–159.

Anthony L. Smith

EAST TIMOR

0   25   500 Miles

0   25   500 Kilometers

Makassar Strait

Ujungpandang

Banda Sea

Kepulauan Kai

Bali Sea   *Flores Sea*   Dili

Bali   Sumbawa   Flores

Sumba   West Timor   East Timor

Waingapu   Timor   Kupang

Kepulauan Tanimbar

Timor Sea

LESSER SUNDA ISLANDS

INDIAN OCEAN

East Timor

AUSTRALIA

(MAP BY MARYLAND CARTOGRAPHICS/THE GALE GROUP)

Economic, Social, and Cultural Rights

Citizens of modern states enjoy a number of rights. Civil and political rights shape individuals' interactions with states' legal and political systems. Economic, social, and cultural rights, on the other hand, address freedoms often exercised in private life. Examples include access to sufficient food, education, health care, and employment. Although economic, social, and cultural rights offer different guarantees than do civil and political rights, the international community treats them as indivisible. Because they reinforce each other, together they help to ensure social justice. For example, without the political right of free association, the economic right to form unions would be meaningless. Equally, the social and cultural right to an education would be worthless to those imprisoned because they do not enjoy the civil right to be free from **arbitrary** detention.

arbitrary: capricious, random, or changing without notice

ORIGINS

Widespread human suffering during World War I (1914–1918) and World War II (1939–1945) gave great traction to the idea of internationalizing human rights. Many leaders agreed that only universal recognition and protection of rights would be sufficient to prevent another such tragedy. Although World War II's devastation was the immediate catalyst, drafters of human rights documents built on multiple foundations. In **delineating** these rights, authors drew from many sources, including religious and philosophic traditions.

delineate: to depict, portray, or outline with detail

Many religious traditions believe that humans embody certain rights because of the way that a Supreme Being structured the universe. Further, these advocates argue that such "natural" rights are beyond human transformation or negotiation. They believe that human reason allows the discovery of God's plan, and people must govern themselves based on these discovered laws. Additionally, as **natural rights** predate the creation of governments and exist independently of human created law, these believers maintain that these fundamental rights are superior to human decisions.

natural right: a basic privilege intrinsic to all people that cannot be denied by the government

Many of the world's religions recognize not only human rights but also human responsibilities to protect the rights of others. Religious teachings range from Judeo-Christian lessons such as "love thy neighbor as thyself" (Leviticus 19:18) to Islamic instruction about tolerance and respect for "People of the Book" to a Buddhist focus on the interconnectedness of all beings. These conceptions of a community's responsibility to all its members have particularly helped to shape economic, social, and cultural rights, going beyond civil and political rights to so-called "second-generation" rights.

Various philosophic schools also contributed to rights development. The idea of individual civil and political rights drew from such Enlightenment thinkers as John Locke, (1632–1704) an English liberal philosopher who wrote of the inalienable rights of all people. Although **legal positivists** such as British Utilitarian philosopher Jeremy Bentham (1748–1832) indicated a different source for the legitimacy of human rights—the sovereignty of law creators— they acknowledged both human rights and duties. From these differences come some of the variations in the concept of rights as either universal or culturally bound. Those who see rights as attaching to the people envision the same rights for all. Those who rest authority in the rights' creator, on the other hand, could expect different rights from dissimilar sovereigns. Later philosophers, including the German founder of socialism, Karl Marx (1818–1883), contributed ideas that supported second-generation rights, including those related to a minimum required standard of living and other material provisions.

legal positivism: a philosophy that laws have no moral standing, being merely man-made

Although rights originally attached to the individual, many rights now are seen as belonging to groups as well. **Intergovernmental** institutions, such as the Organization of African Unity, and private organizations, such as Human Rights Watch, have pushed to expand human rights definitions to include members of

intergovernmental: between or involving multiple governments, with each government retaining full decision-making power

collectives. Advocates often reason that certain groups such as children or minority populations are vulnerable and therefore need clear protections, especially for rights that are particular to them. Examples include the right to an education, to practice a minority religion, or to communicate in a minority language. Otherwise, groups' lack of a dominant political voice can leave them at the mercy of unsympathetic majorities. Collective rights also may require new rights, such as access to public education in minority languages.

Additionally, the gross atrocities committed in World War II, especially the Holocaust, following closely on the brutalities of World War I, forced states to face their need for a means to guarantee human rights. In response, they created the United Nations (UN). The UN charter's first article addresses "respect for human rights and for fundamental freedoms for all without distinction as to race, sex, language or religion" (United Nations, 1945). However, while establishing that all UN members had an obligation to protect rights, the charter did not lay out these rights and freedoms with any specificity. The UN's General Assembly began to address this with passage of the Universal Declaration of Human Rights in December 1948.

DEVELOPMENT

Recognition and protection of economic, social, and cultural rights developed along two tracks. International institutions, especially the UN, serve as one forum for their development. Simultaneously, many states, through organizations linked to a particular geographic region, pursue additional human rights regimes.

The Universal Declaration of Human Rights passed in the UN General Assembly without a dissenting vote. It outlined thirty principles basic to human development and dignity, including not only economic, social, and cultural rights, but also civil and political rights. Following passage, the body asked the Commission on Human Rights to put the general language of the Universal Declaration into a form legally binding on states with a treaty outlining specific rights and their implementation. This eventually led to two treaties: the International Covenant on Cultural and Political Rights (ICCPR) and the International Covenant on Economic, Social, and Cultural Rights (ICESCR). Signaling the political disputes involved, neither covenant passed the General Assembly until 1966. Each required an additional ten years, until 1976, before receiving the thirty-five votes required for **ratification**.

ratify: to make official or to officially sanction

In part, countries debated whether economic, social, and cultural rights require different implementation than do civil and political rights. Either legislative or administrative actions, or a combination of both, usually suffice to ensure civil and political rights. Economic, social, and cultural rights, however, demand a positive action by government. Thus, rather than states agreeing not to do something (negative right), states or some other entity must agree to take action or to provide something (positive right).

self-determination: the ability of a people to determine their own destiny or political system

The ICESCR addresses a number of specific issues, including the right to an adequate standard of living, to an education, to **self-determination**, and to participation in cultural life. Further, it specifies equal rights for men and women, the right to work, to form and join trade unions, and to have just and favorable conditions for work, as well as the right to the best standards of physical and mental health, to social security and to social insurance, and to enjoy the benefits of scientific progress. These positive rights mean that employers, for instance, rather than governments, should enact the right to "enjoy just and favorable conditions of work . . . [including] fair wages and equal remuneration for work of equal value" (Article 7, ICESCR). Obviously, implementation is complex, as states often do not provide these rights directly but take responsibility for outcomes dependent on their provision. For example, although private clinics might deliver medical care, the state guarantees its citizens the right to good health.

CHILDREN WORKING AT A BUILDING SITE IN 1996 IN YANGON, MYANMAR. In 1990 the UN Convention on the Rights of the Child came into force by recognizing the basic rights of children. Although Myanmar (Burma) acceded to the convention in 1991, a report by the UN Commission on Human Rights found that children continued to suffer from a lack of education, child labor, and malnourishment. (SOURCE: AP/WIDE WORLD PHOTOS)

signatory: one who signs an agreement with other parties and is then bound to that agreement

Additionally, states' varied levels of economic development and wealth made the ICESCR's drafters cautious about stipulating a specific time frame for implementation. Instead, the covenant anticipated "achieving progressively the full realization of the rights" covered (Article 2, ICESCR). This differed from the ICCPR, which required immediate implementation of its rights.

The ICESCR called for supervision by the UN's Economic and Social Council. In 1985, the Economic and Social Council replaced the monitoring Committee of Experts with the Committee for Economic, Social, and Cultural Rights (CESCR), which enjoys greater power. The CESCR reviews **signatories'** progress using several sources of information. First, each state must report on its advancement and plans for the future at intervals specified by the committee, as well as explain any retreat from its provision of treaty rights. Next, specialized UN agencies, including the International Labour Organization, the World Health Organization, and the Food and Agriculture Organization, provide the committee with information about states' progress. Domestic and international non-governmental organizations also may report to the CESCR. As well, the CESCR is considering an Optional Protocol to the ICESCR that would allow individuals to lodge a complaint.

Additional UN treaties, more limited in scope than the ICESCR, also address some or all of the various economic, social and cultural rights. These include the Convention on the Prevention and Punishment of the Crime of Genocide (1948), the Declaration on the Granting of Independence to Colonial Countries and Peoples (1960), and the Convention Against Torture and other Cruel, Inhuman or Degrading Treatment or Punishment (1984). Additionally, specific groups gained protections under the Convention on the Status of Refugees (1951), the International Convention on Elimination of All Forms of Racial Discrimination (1965), the Convention on the Elimination of All Forms of Discrimination Against Women (1979), and the Convention on the Rights of the Child (1989).

Regional organizations also produced agreements that obligate signatory states to provision and protection of economic, social, and cultural rights. In some instances, these rights regimes are different from those created within the UN, and they rely on a variety of means to enforce and protect these rights.

The African Charter on Human and Peoples' Rights, passed by the Organization of African Unity in 1981, differs from the ICESCR, as it includes collective rights and protections of groups as well as the rights of individuals. Further, the charter protects the family unit, recognizing it as the "natural unit and basis of society" (Article 18) and the keeper of traditional values and morals. The charter allows governments to suspend or limit certain rights for such reasons as national security. The charter also instituted the African Commission on Human and Peoples' Rights, which studies African rights issues, gathers information, publicizes the charter and the rights it protects, and suggests to signatories ways to improve their rights regimes and resolve outstanding problems.

Africa is not alone in this endeavor. The Organization of American States (OAS) passed the American Declaration on the Rights and Duties of Man in 1948 and the American Convention on Human Rights in 1969. These resolutions address civil and political, as well as economic, social, and cultural rights. The OAS added an Additional Protocol in the Area of Economic, Social, and Cultural Rights (1988). This addendum includes rights related to work, unions, health, food, education, and protection of such groups as the handicapped, children, the elderly, and families. The Inter-American Commission on Human Rights, created in 1959, and the Inter-American Court of Human Rights, created in 1969, resolve complaints and aid in the implementation and protection of rights. Signatories agreed to implement these rights on a progressive basis.

The Council of the League of Arab States created a Permanent Arab Commission on Human Rights (1968) and passed the Arab Charter on Human Rights (1994). The charter calls for reports by signatories and created a Committee of Experts to monitor state actions. Some Arab countries took part in the 1990 meeting of the Organization of the Islamic Conference. The subsequent Cairo Declaration on Human Rights in Islam states that Allah defines all rights and that they are subject to protection under Islamic Shari'a law. This interpretation of human rights, particularly in terms of the rights of men and women, often differs from the UN's human rights regime.

The European Council (EC) enacted the European Convention on Human Rights and Fundamental Freedoms (1953), which has since been amended by several additional protocols. The EC agreed to the European Social Charter in 1961, which included supplementary economic and social rights. Council members revised the charter in 1996, adding additional rights and protections. Those who believe they have suffered violation of their rights can complain to the European Commission on Human Rights. The European Court of Justice may **adjudicate** cases the commission cannot resolve. In 1999 the council created an Office of the Commissioner of Human Rights. The charter and its revision include core obligations that immediately bind signatories, while allowing progressive implementation of the remainder. The depth and breadth of its protection of human rights makes Europe an enviable model for rights activists.

Asia remains the only continent without regional protection of the rights of their citizens. Some leaders from the region argue that human rights historically have been defined and implemented in culturally biased ways. Thus, they believe the current protections reflect the **hegemony** of Western ideas rather than universal norms applicable to all states and people.

ISSUES OF IMPLEMENTATION

The UN has been a leader in the development and implementation of international human rights agreements. Non-governmental organizations—sometimes in cooperation and sometimes in conflict with governments—have helped the UN by providing information to states and to their citizens, and by publicizing states' failures to meet their obligations.

Although the old East–West tensions of the Cold War have faded, they colored the development of the rights regimes. Soviet-bloc states emphasized economic and social rights, arguing that economically disenfranchised citizens would be unlikely to participate fully in a political life. Further, socialist governments refused to give up state power, which guarantees of civil and political rights require. Western states, led by the United States, gave primacy to civil and political rights. Coming from a liberal tradition, with limited governments and a focus on individual freedoms, these states were not well structured to provide economic, social, and cultural rights. Further, they argued that free individuals could best guarantee their own economic, social, and cultural development. Each side used the issue of rights to criticize the systems developed by the other.

Differences in economic resources and focus now separate many developed countries, (often labeled the "North") from less developed states (often called the "South" or "Global South"). Although developed states criticized the Soviet **bloc**'s weak civil and political rights, these same states supported repressive regimes in the South if they were anticommunist. Thus, some in the South regard the rights regimes encouraged by Northern states with skepticism.

adjudicate: to settle a case by judicial procedure

hegemony: the complete dominance of one group or nation over another

bloc: a group of countries or individuals working toward a common goal, usually within a convention or other political body

■ ■ ■
WEB-BASED RESOURCES

The following is a list of Web-based resources for issues concerning economic, social, and cultural rights.

African Union. <http://www.africa-union.org/>.

Council of Europe. <http://www.coe.int>.

European Court for Human Rights. <http://www.echr.coe.int/>.

The European Union's Human Rights and Democratisation Policy: Overview. <http://europa.eu.int/comm/external_relations/human_rights/intro/>.

Human Rights Watch. <http://www.hrw.org>.

Organization of American States. <http://www.OAS.org>.

Organization of the Islamic Conference. <http://www.oic-oci.org/>.

Office of the United Nations High Commissioner for Human Rights. <http://www.ohchr.org/english/>.

University of Minnesota Human Rights Library. <http://www1.umn.edu/humanrts/>.

United Scholar Workstation at Yale University. <http://www.library.yale.edu/un/>.

Further, Southern states believe rights related to economic development are just as critical as the civil and political rights that are championed by Northern states. The Southern states argue that free elections are meaningless to people without shelter or sufficient food. Additionally, many in the South focus on provision of such collective rights as self-determination and racial equality, whereas Northern leaders often look to individual freedoms as the best way to achieve all human rights.

Some states have sharpened the argument by insisting that, rather than being universal, rights regimes reflect Western values. This push for culturally relevant rights often is associated with Asia and the Middle East. Additionally, some Asian states note that their cultures' traditional focus on families and groups, rather than individuals, may make individual rights inappropriate. Further, the tenet of equality between men and women, they say, ignores fundamental differences. Finally, some characterize universal rights as a **neo-imperialist** tool for interference in national sovereignty.

Attendees of the World Conference on Human Rights (1993), however, affirmed the universality of human rights in their final report. They noted, "All human rights are universal, indivisible and interdependent and interrelated" (UN, 1993, No. 5). Despite the conference's broad participation, these disputes remain topical with continuing claims that the rights embedded in liberal democracies are not universal, and that equality between the sexes and protection of children—especially female children—from traditional practices **infringe** unacceptably on their religious, ethnic, and cultural practices.

See also: American Declaration of the Rights and Duties of Man and the American Convention on Human Rights; Convention Against Torture and Other Cruel, Inhuman or Degrading Treatment or Punishment; Convention for the Elimination of All Forms of Discrimination Against Women; European Convention on Human Rights and Fundamental Freedoms; European Court of Human Rights; Human Rights; International Human Rights Law; United Nations; Universal Declaration of Human Rights.

neo-imperialism: the belief in the building of political or cultural empires in the contemporary world

infringe: to exceed the limits of; to violate

BIBLIOGRAPHY

African Commission on Human and Peoples' Rights. *African Charter on Human and Peoples' Rights*, 1979. <http://www.achpr.org/english/_info/charter_en.html>.

Brown, Seyom. *Human Rights in World Politics*. New York: Longman, 2000.

Donnelly, Jack. *International Human Rights*, 2d ed. Boulder, CO: Westview Press, 1997.

Donnelly, Jack. *Universal Human Rights in Theory and Practice*, 2d ed. Ithaca, NY: Cornell University Press, 2002.

Falk, Richard. *Human Rights Horizons: The Pursuit of Justice in a Globalizing World*. New York: Routledge, 2000.

Ishay, Micheline R., ed. *The Human Rights Reader: Major Political Essays, Speeches, and Documents from the Bible to the Present*. New York: Routledge, 1997.

Meijer, Martha. *Dealing with Human Rights: Asian and Western Views on the Value of Human Rights*. Bloomfield, CT: Kumarian Press, 2001.

Office of the High Commissioner for Human Rights. *International Covenant on Economic, Social and Cultural Rights*. <http://www.unhchr.ch/html/menu3/b/a_cescr.htm>.

Steiner, Henry, and Philip Alston. *International Human Rights in Context, Law Politics and Morals*, 2d ed. London: Oxford University Press, 1995.

United Nations. *Charter of the United Nations*, 1945. <http://www.un.org/aboutun/charter/>.

United Nations. *Vienna Declaration and Programme of Action*, 1993. <http://www.unhchr.ch/huridocda/huridoca.nsf/(Symbol)/A.CONF.157.23.En?OpenDocument>.

Janet Adamski

Ecuador

Ecuador is a South American country situated on the equator at the western edge of the continent. Its 283,561 square kilometers (109,483 square miles) includes the Gálapagos Islands. Roughly one-third of its 13.7 million citizens are under fifteen years of age. *Blanco-mestizos* of mixed Caucasian and Amerindian ethnicity dominate the population (65%). One-quarter of Ecuadorians are Amerindian, and there are small Spanish (7%) and black (3%) populations. Spanish is the official language, but Quechua and other Amerindian languages are widely used. The population is 95 percent Roman Catholic.

The Andean highlands of central Ecuador are dotted with active volcanoes, including one overshadowing the capital city of Quito. To the west lies the Pacific coastal plain where the country's largest city and business center, Guayaquil, is located. To the east is sparsely populated jungle. In 1942 Ecuador **ceded** 200,000 square kilometers (124,280 square miles) of disputed territory to Peru. Sporadic border clashes culminated in renewed hostilities until a peace agreement stabilized territorial boundaries in 1998.

cede: to relinquish political control of lands to another country; surrender

Ruled by the Incas from 1450 to 1526, Ecuador became a Spanish colony in 1543. It won independence in 1822 after Antonio Josáe de Sucre (1795–1830) defeated Spanish royalists and joined with Colombia, Venezuela, and modern-day Panama to form Gran Colombia. When the federation collapsed in 1830, Ecuador became a **constitutional republic** governed by conservative and liberal *caudillos*, or local strongmen, well into the twentieth century. The military was active in politics, and throughout the 1970s Ecuador endured military **authoritarian** rule. Democracy was restored in 1979, but enthusiasm for it faded. In 2004 the Latinobarometer poll indicated that just 46 percent of Ecuadorians preferred democracy, and 30 percent said an authoritarian government might be preferable. Government remained highly **centralized**.

constitutional republic: a system of government marked by both a supreme written constitution and elected officials who administer the powers of government

authoritarianism: the domination of the state or its leader over individuals

centralize: to move control or power to a single point of authority

Instability and corruption have plagued Ecuador's presidency. In 1997 the country's Congress removed President Abdala Bucaram (b. 1952) after a year in office, judging him mentally unfit to serve following widespread protest against his policies and personal corruption. His successor, Fabian Alarcon Rivera (b. 1947) also was accused of corruption and briefly jailed. President Jamil Mahuad (b. 1949) was ousted in January 2000 by **indigenous** protesters and their military allies, making Ecuador the first South American country to undergo a **coup** d'etat in nearly a quarter century. Constitutional succession was preserved when his vice president, Gustavo Noboa (b. 1937), filled out the term. However, he too was eventually charged with malfeasance and fled into exile. In response to this pattern, the Civic Commission for Control of Corruption was founded and granted state authority by the 1998 constitution.

indigene: a person who has his origin in a specific region

coup: a quick seizure of power or a sudden attack

Pardoned coup-leader Lucio Edwin Gutierrez (b. 1957) went on to win the presidency in 2002, with 54.3 percent of the vote in a second-round run-off direct election. Relatively equal population distribution between the rival highland and coastal regions virtually assures close presidential races. The executive branch also features an elected vice president and appointed cabinet.

unicameral: comprised of one chamber, usually a legislative body

The one hundred deputies in Ecuador's **unicameral** National Congress are popularly elected from the twenty-two provinces to four-year terms. The Congress is typically fragmented among a multitude of small parties. Because defections are commonplace, the distribution of seats fluctuates. Starting in the late 1990s, Amerindians became increasingly politically active—winning mayoral races, voicing demands in Congress through the *Pachakutik* Movement, and joining protest marches organized by the Confederation of Indigenous Nationalities of Ecuador (CONAIE) and other groups.

rule of law: the principle that the law is a final grounds of decision-making and applies equally to all people; law and order

The **rule of law** remains weak in Ecuador. Although citizens enjoy civil liberties such as freedom of expression and labor rights, and their human rights are largely respected, informal discrimination against Amerindians persists. The judicial branch, headed by a supreme court, became politicized in the 1980s by party control of lower-level judicial appointments. A Byzantine legal framework is further complicated by corruption, making contracts difficult to enforce and taxes difficult to collect, and crowding jails with defendants awaiting trial. In 2004, political maneuvering of dubious constitutionality by the Congress in cooperation with the executive branch influenced selection not only of the Supreme Court of Justice, but also of members of the Constitutional Court and the highest electoral authority, illustrating that separation of powers is ineffective.

Ecuador exports oil, bananas, and shrimp, and the nation has enjoyed a booming tourist economy. Nevertheless, as a result of low oil prices, weather-related damage caused by El Niño, a banking crisis, and mismanagement, in 1999 Ecuador became the first country to default on its Brady bonds. (Former U.S. Secretary of the Treasury Nicholas Brady first conceived of these government-issued bonds, which are underwritten by the U.S. Treasury, in 1982 as a way to help Latin America retire its debt.) In 2000 inflation reached 96 percent; to control it, Ecuador made the U.S. dollar its currency. The strategy worked to lower inflation in the short term, and the economy recovered when oil prices shot up to a historic high. In 2005, however, two-thirds of Ecuadorians continued to live in poverty. Although 92 percent of Ecuadorians are at least minimally literate, only two-thirds finish six years of schooling. Ecuador ranked ninety-seventh among the 175 countries assessed via the 2002 United Nations Human Development Index. Privatization of state industries has faltered, and many Ecuadorians reject neo-liberal policies that cut subsidies and shrink state employment. Completion of a second oil pipeline now under contract, however, could improve the economy by increasing the quantity and price of future oil exports.

See also: Constitutions and Constitutionalism; Democracy; Freedom of Expression; Human Rights.

(MAP BY MARYLAND CARTOGRAPHICS/THE GALE GROUP)

BIBLIOGRAPHY

"Ecuador." In *CIA World Factbook*. Washington, DC: Central Intelligence Agency, 2005. <http://www.cia.gov/cia/publications/factbook/geos/ec.html>.

Gerlach, Allen. *Indians, Oil, and Politics: A Recent History of Ecuador*. Wilmington, DE: Scholarly Resources, 2003.

McConnell, Shelley A. "Ecuador's Centrifugal Politics." *Current History* 100, no. 643 (2001): 73–79.

"South America, Central America and the Caribbean." In *Regional Surveys of the World*, 11th ed. New York: Europa Publications, 2003.

"Informe–Resumen Latinobarómetro 2004: Una decada de mediciones." Corporación Latinobarómetro. December 2004. <http://www.latinobarometro.org>.

U.S. Department of State, Bureau of Public Affairs. *Background Note: Ecuador.* Washington, DC: U.S. Department of State, 2005.

ViewsWire Ecuador Economist Intelligence Unit. December 2003. <http://www.viewswire.com>.

Shelley A. McConnell

Egypt

Egypt is located at the northeastern tip of Africa and is surrounded by Libya to the west, Israel and Palestine to the east, Sudan to the south and the Mediterranean Sea to the north. Egypt's population in 2004 was estimated at 76 million people, 90 percent of whom are Sunni Muslims and 10 percent Coptic Orthodox Christians. Most of the country is desert, and virtually the entire population lives in the valley of the Nile River, which has been the central feature of Egyptian geography and civilization for many centuries.

Egypt gained its independence from Britain in 1922 and for the next thirty years functioned as a constitutional monarchy. In July 1952 a group of Egyptian army officers led by Gamal Abdel Nasser (1918–1970) and Anwar el-Sadat (1918–1981) overthrew the monarchy, and in 1953 they made Egypt a **republic**. Nasser ruled Egypt until his death in 1970. In September 1970, Sadat assumed power until his assassination in October 1981. Since 1981 Egypt has been ruled by President Mohammed Hosni Mubarak (b. 1928).

republic: a form of democratic government in which decisions are made by elected representatives of the people

THE STRUCTURE OF THE EGYPTIAN GOVERNMENT

The 1971 Egyptian constitution divides the government into three branches: executive, legislative, and judicial. The executive power rests with the president, who is elected once every six years. Article 77 of the constitution allows the president to be reelected for successive terms, and Article 76 specifies the procedures of electing the president. It states that the lower house of the Egyptian parliament (the People's Assembly) nominates the presidential candidate by a two-thirds majority vote. The candidate is then confirmed through a popular **referendum**. Although the constitution empowers the president to designate one or more vice presidents, Mubarak has not chosen a vice president since he assumed power in 1981.

referendum: a popular vote on legislation, brought before the people by their elected leaders or public initiative

According to the constitution, the president has the power to appoint and dismiss the prime minister and the cabinet and to appoint the governors of Egypt's twenty-six **governorates**. Article 136 gives the president the power to dissolve the parliament, provided that new parliamentary elections are held within sixty days. The constitution also designates the president as the supreme commander of the armed forces and the head of the police.

governorate: a political subdivision, often associated with Middle Eastern states

The Egyptian parliament consists of two houses. Articles 86 through 125 of the constitution define the powers and the procedures governing Egypt's *Majlis Al-Sha'ab* (People's Assembly). The *Majlis* has 454 members: 444 are elected every five years in three rounds of elections, and the remaining 10 are appointed by the president. The *Majlis* does not play any significant role in economic and social policymaking, and Article 115 of the constitution does not allow it to modify the budget without governmental approval.

Article 195 of the constitution defines the powers of Egypt's second house, the *Majlis El-Shura* (Consultative Assembly). The article stipulates that the *Majlis El-Shura* functions solely as an advisory body in amending the constitution, passing legislation dealing with social and economic development, **ratifying** treaties with foreign powers, and passing presidential draft laws. It consists of 264 members: 176 members are elected by popular vote, and the remaining 88 are appointed by the president. There are no constitutional limits on the terms that legislators can serve.

Chapter 4 of the constitution defines the powers of the judicial branch. Articles 165 and 166 guarantee the independence of the judiciary, stating that the judges are independent and subject only to the authority of the law. Article 175 creates the Supreme Constitutional Court as the highest judicial authority in the country, allowing it to review the constitutionality of governmental laws and regulations and settle conflicting rulings of lower courts. In addition, Article 173 creates the Supreme Judicial Council to supervise the judicial branch, ensure its independence, and recommend to the president a list of candidates to fill judicial vacancies. Article 172 also establishes the Council of State as an independent judicial organization to review cases involving governmental officials, civil servants, and disciplinary cases within the judiciary.

In addition, the Egyptian parliament created four levels of courts of criminal and civil **jurisdiction**. The district tribunal court has one judge and has jurisdiction over minor criminal and civil cases. The tribunal of first instance court has a three-judge panel and exercises jurisdiction over major criminal and civil cases involving long-term imprisonment or the death penalty. The next level of courts is the five courts of appeals. Each of these courts has a three-judge panel and hears appeals from lower courts in its region. The court of cassation has five judges and has final jurisdiction over criminal and civil appeals in Egypt. Egypt's judicial system does not employ juries and is based on Napoleonic codes, English common law, and Islamic Shari'a.

THE STATUS OF POLITICAL FREEDOMS AND CIVIL LIBERTIES

Since its independence, Egypt has been struggling with the challenge of **democratization**, economic development, and the governmental respect of human rights. The 1971 constitution guarantees universal **suffrage** for men and women who have reached the age of eighteen. Article 40 bans discrimination on the basis of language, race, ethnic origin or religion, and Articles 46 through 48 guarantee freedom of religious belief and worship as well as freedoms of expression, speech, and the press. Articles 41, 42, and 44 extend some rights of personal integrity and privacy to citizens. They protect detainees against police torture and require police officers to obtain search and arrest warrants from a judge or the prosecutor before arresting citizens, searching their homes, monitoring their movements and correspondence, or wiretapping their phones.

Despite these constitutional guarantees, the government has placed serious limitations on its citizens' rights and civil liberties. The Egyptian constitution grants Egyptian men and women the right to vote; voting is **compulsory** and those citizens who abstain from voting have to provide an explanation for their failure to vote. In its 1997 human rights report, the U.S. Department of State observed that the freedom of press in Egypt is restricted by the 1993 Press Law

ratify: to make official or to officially sanction

jurisdiction: the territory or area within which authority may be exercised

democratization: a process by which the powers of government are moved to the people of a region or to their elected representatives

suffrage: to vote, or, the right to vote

compulsory: mandatory, required, or unable to be avoided

and the penal codes that make it illegal for journalists to print certain information that is deemed to be disrespectful or endangering to the public order or national economy. The Department of State report further added that journalists who criticize the government may be subject to five years' imprisonment.

The passage of the antiterrorism law in 1992 gave the government additional powers to restrict political activities and civil and political rights. In 1993 Egypt's supreme constitutional court ruled that the president may use the emergency law, which has been in effect since June 1967, to refer criminal cases to military courts. The rulings of these courts cannot be appealed. In 2000 and again in 2003, the Egyptian government secured the approval of the parliament to extend the state of emergency for additional three years. The leaders of the opposition protested the extension, claiming that the emergency law denies them the right of political participation. It permits the government to detain prisoners indefinitely without trial, to try citizens in military courts, and to rule the country by presidential decrees.

Several Egyptian and international human rights organizations besides the U.S. Department of State have also documented repeated abuse and torture of detainees by the state security forces. The 1997 U.S. Department of State's human rights report asserted that the law allowed the police to use wiretaps, intercept mail, search persons and places without court order, and arrest citizens on the ground that the detained individuals pose a danger to security and public order. In its *World Report 2003*, Human Rights Watch also observed that the Egyptian government has not relaxed its restrictions on civil liberties. It concluded that the government has continued to crack down on Islamic and leftist opposition, limit

(MAP BY MARYLAND CARTOGRAPHICS/THE GALE GROUP)

the activities of civil society institutions, detain thousands of citizens without trial, and try detainees before state security courts without right of appeal.

Although Articles 54, 55, and 56 give the people the right to form political associations, unions, and societies, these rights have been severely restricted. A 1923 law mandates that Egyptians must secure the advanced approval from the Ministry of Interior before holding public meetings, rallies, or protest marches. Likewise, in 1999 the Egyptian parliament passed a law regulating the activities of civil society institutions and non-governmental organizations (NGOs). The law prohibits NGOs from engaging in political activities that are considered the domain of political parties, trade unions and professional associations. It also requires NGOs to register with the government, which has the power to deny licenses to such organizations if their work is deemed a threat to public order, morality, or national unity. The law requires civil society institutions to obtain advanced governmental approval before receiving foreign financial aid. As a result of this law, several human rights organizations have been denied the right to operate or have been forced to turn down outside funding.

With regard to the formation of political parties, the parliamentary Political Parties Committee, which is controlled by the pro-government National Democratic Party (NDP), licenses the creation of new political parties. The government has also used the state-of-emergency laws to curtail the activities of Islamist and leftist political groups and ban them from contesting parliamentary elections.

In the 2000 parliamentary elections, the NDP captured 388 seats out of the 444 elected seats, candidates affiliated with the Islamic movement won 19 seats, the Wafd Party gained 7 seats, the Progressive National Unionist Rally won 6 seats, and the remaining 24 seats went to independent candidates and smaller leftist parties. The NDP advocates social welfare programs such as public housing, construction of new urban centers, improvement of education and health services, enforcement of religious values and traditions, and the spreading democracy. By contrast, the outlawed Muslim Brotherhood opposes **secularism** and Western influence in Egypt and calls for the application of Islamic Shari'a. The Wafd party advocates multiparty democracy, governmental respect for human rights and public freedom, and the Progressive National Unionist Rally highlights the importance of national independence, emphasizes the Arab character of Egypt, supports the Palestinian people, and fights against exploitation.

secularism: a refutation of, apathy toward, or exclusion of all religion

SOCIAL WELFARE

Despite the harsh restrictions on political rights and civil liberties, the government's social welfare record has been impressive. Several articles of the Egyptian constitution obligate the government to provide social welfare services to the citizens. For instance, Articles 20 and 21 commit the government to provide free education and Article 18 makes education obligatory through the elementary level. Likewise, Article 13 considers work as a right for the citizens, and Article 14 guarantees job security for public sector workers. Article 17 obligates the state to provide social and health insurance to the citizens and pensions to senior citizens, the unemployed, and the disabled.

As a result of these constitutional rights, the government has allocated a significant amount of its budget to the well-being of the Egyptian people, including the Social Insurance Program, which provides social security and retirement benefits for all government employees. Administered by the Ministry of Social

Insurance, the program also provides for the elderly, the disabled, and the poor. The Ministry of Health provides medical benefits for the sick, as well as for pregnant women and workers and their dependents. In addition, the government has gradually been extending the social insurance program to students, although it continues to exclude from coverage agricultural workers, domestic servants and the self-employed.

Egypt's social welfare programs, however, have been hampered by the poor performance of the public sector and the population surge. A number of international organizations, such as the World Bank and multiple NGOs, have offered financial and technical assistance to the Egyptian government to control population growth. The program promotes the use of contraceptives and the education of both men and women in family planning. The World Bank also extended loans to Egypt to create the Social Fund Project, which aims at decreasing poverty. The Community Development Program, a segment of the Social Fund Project, attends to the needs of women, the poor, and the unemployed, whereas the Enterprise Development Program enables banks to provide credit and loans and technical assistance to entrepreneurs.

In addition to the social welfare services, the Egyptian government reformed its family law in 2000. The new law extends equal divorce rights to women and enables them to **unilaterally** divorce their husbands. The law stipulates that a divorce becomes final after a three-month period of court-supervised reconciliation efforts. It also secures for women a part of their husband's wages and enables them to draw wages from a special state bank in case the husband disappears or is unable to pay. The law, however, stipulates that women who initiate divorce against the objections of their husband should return the dowry, including any money or property paid to her at the time of the marriage.

unilateral: independent of any other person or entity

EGYPT'S ECONOMY

Until the 1960s, Egypt's economy was primarily **agrarian**. However, the oil boom of the 1970s, remittances from Egyptian workers working in the Persian Gulf, financial aid from the oil-rich Gulf countries, American foreign assistance, and revenue from the Suez Canal and tourism enabled the government to grow. It initiated numerous industrial projects, subsidized goods at prices below production cost, and expanded employment in the public sector. This latter action was grounded in the constitution's designation of Egypt as a **socialist** republic. Articles 24, 30, and 33 highlight the pivotal role of the public sector, Article 31 subordinates the private sector to the public sector interests, and Article 24 refers to the people as the owners of the means of production.

agrarian: having to do with farming or farming communities and their interests; one involved in such a movement

socialism: any of various economic and political theories advocating collective or governmental ownership and administration of the means of production and distribution of goods

By the 1980s and the 1990s the public sector and state-owned industries were facing many problems. The oil boom was accompanied by a large-scale migration from the rural areas to the urban centers and to the Persian Gulf countries. The migration resulted in the shrinkage of the agricultural sector and the rapid growth of the informal labor market. The significant decline in agricultural output forced the government in the 1990s to import 70 percent of its foodstuffs and to subsidize their cost.

In addition, public corporations turned out to be too expensive to maintain, and the government had to borrow heavily to subsidize these corporations. The state-owned industry **monopoly** of the domestic market and the lack of competition resulted in poor quality public-sector goods. The price of these goods was high, which made them uncompetitive in the international market. Furthermore, the continued **subsidies** of consumer goods and public corporations as well as

monopoly: the domination of a market by one firm or company

subsidy: a government grant used to encourage some action

EGYPTIAN PRIME MINISTER GAMAL ABDEL NASSER ATTENDS A RALLY IN CAIRO ON JUNE 19, 1956 TO ANNOUNCE THE COUNTRY'S COMPLETE INDEPENDENCE FROM THE BRITISH MONARCH. Nasser served as prime minister (1954–1956) until being elected president in 1956; he retained the post until his death in 1970. Although Nasser was viewed as an influential modern-day leader, he ruled as an authoritarian who disallowed political parties and advocated censorship. (SOURCE: AP/WIDE WORLD PHOTOS)

maintaining redundant labor became very costly. This situation became even more critical in the wake of the high interest payments on foreign debt, the plummeting in the price of oil during the mid-1980s, the decline in workers' remittances, and the drop in the revenue from tourism.

As a result of these problems, the government reluctantly attempted to privatize the public sector, reduce the number of imports, promote Egypt's exports, cancel or postpone many public works projects, and limit food subsidies to only those citizens in real need. The World Bank and the International Monetary Fund also pressured the Egyptian government to introduce economic and political reforms. However, the government's occasional efforts to reduce food subsidies and limit the size of the public sector resulted in periodic massive popular uprisings and opposition by the labor unions and the managers of public corporations. The economic hardships also increased the popularity of the Islamist groups.

Political **liberalization** and economic reforms are the two most serious challenges that continue to face Egypt. Although long-term economic liberalization would help solve the country's economic problems, the

liberalization: the process of lowering trade barriers and tariffs and reducing government economic regulations

dilemma is that it would also, for the short term, increase poverty, raise unemployment, and generate discontent among the workers in the public sector. In addition to inadequately addressing the immediate needs of the Egyptian people for food and housing, market reforms would likely to lead to widespread poverty and increase the popularity of the Islamic opposition. Such economic hardships in the absence of genuine democratic reforms, the restrictions of civil liberties, and the manipulation of the electoral system could further undermine governmental political legitimacy, detach it even more from the people, and unite the various Islamic and leftist groups against the government.

See also: Shari'a.

BIBLIOGRAPHY

Abdalla, Ahmed. "Egypt's Islamists and the State: From Complicity to Confrontation." *Middle East Report* 183 (1993):28–31.

Brownlee, Jason. "The Decline of Pluralism in Mubarak's Egypt." *Journal of Democracy* 13, no. 4 (2002):6–14.

"Egypt." In *CIA World Factbook*. Washington, DC: Central Intelligence Agency, 2005. <http://www.cia.gov/cia/publications/factbook/geos/eg.html>.

Egypt Constitution. Egypt Government Service Portal. <http://www.egypt.gov.eg/english/laws/constitution/index.asp>.

Egyptian State Information Service. "Current Political Parties in Egypt." <http:// www.sis.gov.eg/egyptinf/politics/parties/html/parts.htm>.

Egyptian State Information Service. "Know Egypt: Politics." <http://www.sis.gov.eg/eginfnew/politics/pres/html/pres01.htm>.

"Egypt's Parliamentary Elections: An Assessment of the Results." *The Estimate: Political & Security Intelligence Analysis of the Islamic World and Its Neighbors* 12, no. 23 (2000). <http://www.theestimate.com/public/111700.html>.

Human Rights Watch. "Egypt." *World Report 2003*. <http://www.hrw.org/wr2k3/mideast2.html>.

Richards, Alan, and John Waterbury. *A Political Economy of the Middle East*, 2nd ed. Boulder, CO: Westview Press, 1998.

Schneider, Howard. "Women in Egypt Gain Broader Divorce Rights." *Washington Post* (April 14, 2000): A16. <http://www.library.cornell.edu/colldev/mideast/divrua.htm>.

Social Security Administration. "Egypt." *Social Security Programs Throughout the World, 2003*. <http://www.ssa.gov/policy/docs/progdesc/ssptw/2002-2003/africa/egypt.html>.

Emile Sahliyeh

El Salvador

With only 21,476 square kilometers (8,260 square miles) of territory, El Salvador is Central America's smallest state, but its 6.3 million inhabitants make it the region's most densely populated nation. Traditionally, Salvadorans have professed Roman Catholicism, but evangelical Protestants constitute a growing minority. **Indigenous** groups gave up their Native American dress and customs following the 1932 peasant uprisings that the government brutally suppressed, but in 2004 more than 90 percent of Salvadorans were considered mestizos (persons of mixed European and Indian heritage). The national

indigene: a person who has his origin in a specific region

literacy rate of 80 percent is relatively high for Central America, although the rate is lower in rural areas.

El Salvador's traditional agro-export economy, which was heavily dependent on coffee, has diversified to the extent that commerce (27.2%), services (18.7%), and manufacturing (17.6%) employed nearly two-thirds of the workforce in the early twenty-first century. The country has positioned itself to be a leader in *maquila* manufacturing (the assembly of finished goods from parts manufactured elsewhere), and its political leadership has sought strong ties with the United States as well as membership in the Central American Free Trade Agreement. El Salvador was the first Central American country to "dollarize" its economy, introducing the dollar as legal tender on January 1, 2001.

El Salvador is a unitary **republic**. The president is popularly elected to a five-year term, whereas representatives in the **unicameral** National Assembly are elected to three-year terms: Sixty-four are elected in multiseat constituencies and twenty by **proportional representation**. An independent Electoral Commission runs national elections, which, since the signing of the Chapultepec Peace Accords in 1992, have been contested by political parties from across the political spectrum. Since the accords, the government has made sustained efforts to strengthen judicial independence and create a more professional judiciary consistent with republican principles.

For much of its modern history, a landowning **oligarchy** dominated Salvadoran politics. Because this elite ruling class depended on a system of forced labor to harvest major export **commodities** such as coffee, the Salvadoran regime came to rely heavily on internal security forces and the armed forces to assure stability. This authoritarian and repressive political system has been described as "reactionary despotism" because of the way it militarized political life and violently resisted social change. From the late 1970s to the early 1990s the country was wracked by a devastating internal war, which killed 75,000 citizens. The crucial turning point toward a more democratic system occurred when the government and the armed opposition,

republic: a form of democratic government in which decisions are made by elected representatives of the people

unicameral: comprised of one chamber, usually a legislative body

proportional system: a political system in which legislative seats or offices are awarded based on the proportional number of votes received by a party in an election

oligarchy: government by a few or an elite ruling class, whose policies are often not in the public interest

commodity: an article of trade or commerce that can be transported, especially an agricultural or mining product

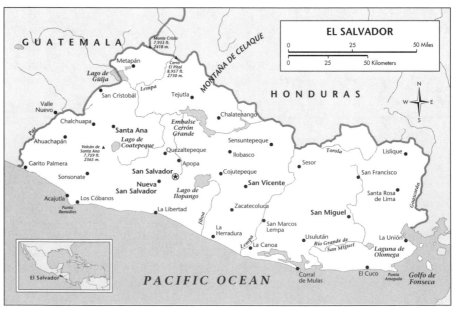

(MAP BY MARYLAND CARTOGRAPHICS/THE GALE GROUP)

the Farabundo Martí National Liberation Front (FMLN), signed the 1992 Peace Accords, which called for extensive political reforms and demilitarization. Critical reforms included disbanding the internal security forces, which had committed terrible human-rights abuses during and before the war, purging the military leadership and depoliticizing the army, creating a national human rights **ombudsman**, and forming a new national civilian police force.

Since 1992 El Salvador has held open elections, but with steadily declining voter participation. Power has been transferred peacefully from one administration to the next. Executive power has resided with the right-wing National Republican Alliance (ARENA) party throughout the period of democratic transition, while seats in the National Assembly have been nearly evenly divided between the left-wing FMLN (now a legal political party) and the right-wing ARENA. For example, the FMLN won a **plurality** of thirty-one seats in the 2003 elections, whereas ARENA garnered twenty-seven seats. Parties of the center had lost appeal in the early 2000s and held few seats in the assembly; the Christian Democratic Party, for example, won only five seats in 2003. ARENA policy makers have promised to promote free trade and **macroeconomic** growth, reduce crime, and increase employment. The enormous social and economic losses caused by three major earthquakes in January and February 2001 greatly complicated the government's efforts to fulfill these policy goals. Nevertheless, in the March 2004 elections ARENA captured the presidency for the fourth consecutive time.

See also: Ombudsmen.

ombudsman: a government official that researches the validity of complaints and reports his findings to an authority

plurality: more votes than any other candidate, but less than half of the total number of votes

macroeconomics: a study of economics in terms of whole systems, especially with reference to general levels of output and income and to the interrelations among sectors of the economy

BIBLIOGRAPHY

Baloyra, Enrique. *El Salvador in Transition*. Chapel Hill: University of North Carolina Press, 1982.

Byrne, Hugh. *El Salvador's Civil War: A Study of Revolution*. Boulder, CO: Lynne Rienner, 1996.

Danner, Mark. *The Massacre at El Mozote*. New York: Vantage Books, 1994.

Popkin, Margaret. *Peace Without Justice: Obstacles to Building the Rule of Law in El Salvador*. University Park: Pennsylvania State University Press, 2000.

Michael Dodson

Elections

Whether the subject is political transition in the former Soviet Union, South Africa, Romania, or Iraq, the movement toward democracy has been, and continues to be, symbolized by elections. If "the people" do not have a say in determining who governs, through free and fair elections, one does not recognize that country as a democracy. Elections are so central to this basic idea of democracy that once elections have been adopted, **suffrage** is generally universal for citizens eighteen and older. This generality holds for countries thought to be more restrictive of civil liberties and civil rights: Iran (a **theocracy**)—which even drops the age to fifteen—and China (still communist). A few exceptions exist: Felons lose their suffrage in the United States while in prison or on parole, and lose it completely in fourteen states upon conviction. In Guatemala active members of the military are not allowed to vote and must remain inside their barracks on election day. In Kuwait women cannot vote; in Saudi Arabia no one can vote. The larger concern

suffrage: to vote, or, the right to vote

theocracy: a state governed by its religious leaders

about free and fair elections in many parts of the world derives from unwritten rules or illegal actions that hamper turnout or render electoral results suspicious. These violations include intimidating voting environments, insecure ballot boxes (ballot stuffing), nonsecret voting, threats of retaliation, a lack of independent supervision of polling centers, and government monopoly of the media.

This is not to say that one only encounters elections in democratic systems. Elections have been used by many types of **authoritarian** or **totalitarian** regimes to legitimize leaders and systems. In such regimes, this is the only role of elections. Although elections also legitimize nonauthoritarian regimes, they do much more than confer the right to govern. Elections provide the official, universal connection between citizens and their government. They allow citizens the opportunity to provide input into the governing process (a prospective force), and they allow citizens to hold a government accountable for its policies (a retrospective force). Perhaps most important, elections provide for the peaceful, legitimate transfer of power between groups, without which political, social, and economic stability could be threatened. How do elections accomplish these goals in practice?

authoritarianism: the domination of the state or its leader over individuals

totalitarianism: a form of absolute government that demands complete subjugation by its citizens

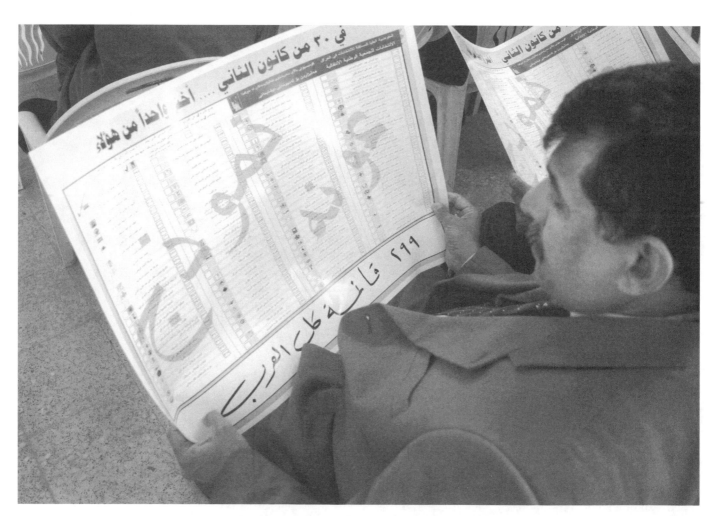

AT AN ELECTION MEETING IN KIRKUK, IRAQ IN 2005, AN IRAQI MAN REVIEWS A BALLOT PAPER. Despite overwhelming fears of violence, nearly 60 percent of Iraqi citizens exercised their right to vote for the first time in a free election on January 30, 2005. The 275-member Iraqi National Assembly, the country's transitional legislative body, was chosen. (SOURCE: MARWAN IBRAHIM/AFP/GETTY IMAGES.)

TYPES OF ELECTIONS

Although a number of variations exist throughout the world on these basic themes, most electoral systems in democratic countries follow the general rules outlined by two approaches: single-member district (SMD) representation or **proportional representation** (PR). A third approach (e.g., the system in Germany and New Zealand) combines the two (SMD-PR). SMD representation works as follows. A given territory is divided into political pieces, and the number of those pieces is equal to the total number of representatives called for in one of the houses of the legislature. SMD is often used in "lower" houses and other selection measures are often used in "upper" houses (state or regional representation, appointment). In the United States, a **bicameral** system, the number of political pieces created equals the number of representatives in the House of Representatives. Senate membership is based on geography, with two representatives per state. Elections are held within each piece and one winner is chosen. The winner in SMD systems is often the candidate who receives the most votes (a **plurality**, not necessarily the majority). For the U.S. House, the representative body is composed of 435 individual winners.

Proportional representation systems differ from SMD systems in two main ways: geographic area of representation and vote choice. Take the same political territory and erase all the dividing lines for the pieces discussed above. One now has a single large area without small subsections; however, more than one representative is wanted. The Israeli parliament, the Knesset, is a good example in this regard because the **nation-state** of Israel is a single electoral district (with 120 members). When elections are held, the voters choose a preferred party, not a preferred candidate. All the votes are counted (in most PR systems a minimum threshold exists for any party to overcome before it may be counted at all) and the parties are ranked by the percentage of the total vote received. Each party is allowed to translate that percentage of vote received into a percentage of all possible seats in the house/parliament in question. In the Israeli example, a party receiving 20 percent of the vote would send twenty-four representatives to the Knesset. This vote-to-representative translation process continues until 100 percent of the seats are filled. Thus, 120 winners result instead of just one, but these winners did not all win individual contests; each party won something and the individuals sent to the legislature represent that win. Mixed systems (sometimes called personalized proportional systems) combine these two strategies to take advantage of the benefits of both. In the lower house of the German parliament, the *Bundestag*, about half its members are chosen by SMD and about half by PR.

The advantages of SMD and PR can be summarized as follows. SMD systems connect the voters to representatives who are local, who have traits voters like to evaluate in elections, and who can be held directly responsible for their actions in the legislature. PR systems provide for a wider variety of interests to be represented because there is more than one winner per election; they focus voters' attention on ideas and policies rather than the traits of specific individuals; and they are a more realistic reflection of the distribution of political preferences in a population.

SMD and PR electoral systems do more than give voters different kinds of choices in the voting booth. They also shape the party structure that is likely to emerge once a system is put into place. Two major parties usually dominate SMD systems. When there is only one winner and that winner must win the most votes, few incentives exist for any party representing a small segment of the population to expend the time, energy, and resources to contest an election. If that party is never likely to receive the most votes, it will never claim any share of the representative body. This leads to the formation of two general, or catch-all,

proportional system: a political system in which legislative seats or offices are awarded based on the proportional number of votes received by a party in an election

bicameral: comprised of two chambers, usually a legislative body

plurality: more votes than any other candidate, but less than half of the total number of votes

nation-state: a relatively homogeneous state with only one or few nationalities within its political borders

parties, both capable of generating support from a broad segment of the population, both capable of winning any given election with the help of a few undecided or independent voters. PR systems have the exact opposite effect on the number of parties participating in elections. With multiple winners, and when winning means getting some percentage of the total popular vote greater than a minimal threshold, parties of all kinds have an incentive to contest elections. Some larger, more general parties form, but many parties stay focused on specific constituencies (like farmers or workers) or issues (like the environment). These are called particularistic parties. The overall result is this: SMD systems lead to middle-of-the-road, or centrist, political parties and political cultures and PR systems tend to lead to a more diversified, or wider, variety of parties and political cultures.

Given these basics, how do these electoral systems affect leadership? Leaders in PR systems are forced to compromise with competing political forces because they often have to govern with a **coalition**; that is, two or three parties must band together to gain a functional majority in the legislature, and in parliamentary systems, to select a prime minister. Given the need to satisfy these coalitions, PR leaders are more likely to have a diverse executive branch (or "government") by including members of several parties in the cabinet of ministers. These leaders, then, cannot focus simply on what they want to do; they must balance their **constituents**' desires with those of their coalition partners' constituents. This can slow down the legislative process, but the resulting legislation is often more widely accepted among all constituencies. SMD systems promote the opposite: less need to compromise, a more single-minded executive, and more **polarized** legislation.

PR systems focus elections on ideas, so leadership is more often affected by how citizens assess the successes and failures of the parties in power. A focus on the effectiveness of the coalition encourages voters to think along the lines of maintaining the status quo of the government as a whole or replacing it. SMD systems focus on individuals, so leadership is more often affected by how citizens assess the competence and integrity of their specific representative (that one representative of 435). This parochial perspective downplays the importance of thinking about maintaining or changing the government as a whole. Overall, one finds more frequent change in the leadership structures of PR systems than SMD systems. Stability is the rule of the day, however. The differences in leadership changes between PR and SMD become muted when the fact that most parties in governing coalitions stay in governing coalitions over time is considered. More often a change occurs in the rank order of the top two or three parties rather than the wholesale replacement of all the top parties with a set of all new parties.

Although there are many exceptions to the rule, these different approaches appear to affect voter turnout: It is generally lower in SMD systems than PR systems. Setting aside complicated models, giving people a wider choice of viable parties, connecting a wider variety of voters to their leadership by including more groups in governance, and allowing for the greater possibility of dramatic change in those controlling the levers of government (or promoting the appearance of a greater ability to hold leaders accountable)—these are all factors that seem to strengthen the connection between citizens and leaders. This does not mean political cultures could be changed easily by electoral rules, or that PR is necessarily more democratic or better than SMD, but it should provide some insight into why citizens of some countries interact with their leaders in very different ways than citizens of other countries.

See also: Political Parties; Suffrage.

coalition: an alliance, partnership, or union of disparate peoples or individuals

constituency: the people who either elect or are represented by an elected official

polarize: to separate individuals into adversarial groups

BIBLIOGRAPHY

Almond, Gabriel A., G. Bingham Powell, Jr., and Kaare Strøm, et al. *Comparative Politics Today: A World View,* 7th ed. New York: Longman, 2003.

Foreign Government Resources on the Web. University of Michigan Documents Center. <http://www.lib.umich.edu/govdocs/foreign.html>.

Sodaro, Michael J. *Comparative Politics: A Global Introduction.* Boston: McGraw Hill, 2001.

U.S. Central Intelligence Agency. *The World Factbook.* Washington, DC: U.S. Central Intelligence Agency, 2005. <http://www.odci.gov/cia/publications/factbook/index.html>.

Bryan Brophy-Baermann

Equal Protection of the Law

It should be noted at the outset that the provision for the equal protection of the law in the United States, set forth in the Fourteenth Amendment of the U.S. Constitution, applies only to discrimination that results from the actions or policies of governments. Purely private discrimination cannot be prosecuted under the Fourteenth Amendment (although it may be reached in limited circumstances by other means). The Equal Protection Clause of the Fourteenth Amendment (ratified in 1868 as a consequence of the Civil War, which ended in 1865) seemed to offer the prospect of protecting former slaves against discriminatory state laws. In fact, with only a few exceptions, it provided little effective protection against racial discrimination until the period following World War II (1939–1945). The principal obstacle was the Supreme Court's decision in *Plessy v. Ferguson* (1896), which established the "separate but equal" doctrine, a concept that effectively condoned racial segregation in public schools and supported an environment in which racial segregation could flourish. Under the separate but equal doctrine, the Supreme Court held in 1899 that the County Board of Education of Richmond County, Georgia, could, within its discretion, allocate its resources to provide several alternatives for high school education for white students, while providing only primary education for black students. The proper conclusion at the time was that equal protection of the law had become an empty promise.

REVIVING THE EQUAL PROTECTION CLAUSE

Indeed, it was not the Supreme Court that spontaneously revived the Equal Protection Clause, but rather a series of cases brought by the National Association for the Advancement of Colored People (NAACP). This group's primary strategy was to show how the "equal" requirement of *Plessy* had been entirely ignored by bringing lawsuits demanding equal allocations of resources.

The rejection of racial segregation in public education in *Brown v. Board of Education* in 1954 flowed directly from decisions handed down about segregated graduate and profession education in the 1940s and early 1950s. These decisions were especially important when viewed in combination with the language of the Supreme Court decision in *Korematsu v. United States* in 1944. Although that decision eventually became notorious for its support of wartime exclusion and internment orders against Japanese Americans during

World War II, it did contain the important prescription that laws "which curtail the civil rights of a single racial group are immediately suspect," and federal courts "must subject them to rigid scrutiny."

LEVELS OF SCRUTINY

Probably the key to understanding the Supreme Court's twenty-first-century approach to equal protection is to review the three levels of equal protection scrutiny that the justices have developed over time. The first and highest level of scrutiny applies to all instances of racial or ethnic discrimination, as declared in *Korematsu*. The result is that the use of any racial or ethnic category in public policy is inherently suspect; indeed, it is presumptively invalid. This has been the case since *Brown* and its progeny were decided in the 1950s and 1960s. Strict scrutiny has the consequence of shifting the burden of justification to the government that has used a racial category by forcing it to demonstrate that there is a compelling public necessity for the policy, and that no other available means would achieve its purpose. As shall be seen below, this raises questions about the constitutionality of affirmative action programs. These policies are designed to remediate the consequences of years of public discrimination by taking race into account to favor those minorities who formerly were the subjects of discrimination.

The second level of equal protection of scrutiny was developed in cases involving gender discrimination. Specifically, in *Craig v. Boren* (1976), the Supreme Court through Associate Justice William Brennan restated the "heightened scrutiny" standard. Thus, when a government applies a policy involving a gender distinction, it is required to show that the use of gender involves an important governmental objective and that gender distinction is substantially related to the achievement of that objective. Gender is subjected to heightened scrutiny, rather than strict scrutiny, because the Court recognizes that there are instances in which gender distinctions may be appropriate, as, for example, in policies that protect pregnant workers in employment. However, except for the occasions in which race-based affirmative action programs have been approved by the Court, the use of racial distinctions cannot be justified under the strict scrutiny standard.

The third level of scrutiny is the one under which governments most often prevail. When a categorical distinction that has not been included under strict or heightened scrutiny is contained in a public policy and challenged in court, those who challenge the policy have the burden of demonstrating that the policy has no rational basis. In effect, the plaintiff must prove that the policy is **arbitrary**, capricious, and unreasonable. That is a difficult standard for a plaintiff to meet. A hypothetical example would be the use of standardized tests, such as the SAT, for college admissions decisions. Sorting applicants by test scores creates categories of those who are admitted and those who are rejected. A lawsuit challenging the use of such test scores as discriminatory would have to demonstrate that the tests provide no rational basis for admissions decisions. At best, that is a difficult and expensive burden to meet. Most plaintiffs will fail. Therefore, in equal protection cases the key decision is which of the three standards shall be applied.

THE KEY DECISION: BROWN V. BOARD OF EDUCATION

Brown v. Board of Education of Topeka, Kansas (1954) is by far the most famous equal protection case the Supreme Court has yet decided. The holding that racially segregated public schools were inherently unequal and could not

arbitrary: capricious, random, or changing without notice

be made equal was a clarion call for the use of the equal protection clause by advocates of racial justice. The follow-up enforcement decision in 1955, however, revealed a faint-hearted court that allowed federal district judges to enforce *Brown* with "all deliberate speed." In most instances the word "speed" in *Brown* became much like the word "equal" in *Plessy*, and it was not until Congress passed major civil rights legislation in 1964 and 1965 that much serious enforcement resulted.

One of the key problems in enforcing school desegregation lay in the distinction between de jure (required by law) and de facto (existing in fact) racial segregation. When segregated public education was required or permitted by law, it was relatively simple to strike down the offending legislation, but that did not necessarily mean that integrated schools would follow. Neighborhood residential patterns often reflected the fact of de jure segregation, but eliminating only the formal laws usually would not change the reality of (de facto) segregated neighborhoods. To be sure, some public schools could be integrated within adjacent neighborhoods, but as distances between homes and schools increased, other methods became necessary to achieve any real integration.

INTEGRATING PUBLIC EDUCATION

One answer came in the case of *Swann v. Charlotte–Mecklenburg* (1971). The public schools in Mecklenburg County, North Carolina, had been consolidated in 1960 into one countywide system. The unintended result was that the

ON MAY 17, 1954, THURGOOD MARSHALL (CENTER) IS VICTORIOUS AS THE CHIEF LAWYER IN THE BATTLE AGAINST SEGREGATION IN THE *BROWN V. BOARD OF EDUCATION* CASE. In 1896 the U.S. Supreme Court legalized racial segregation with their decision in *Plessy v. Ferguson* by invoking the principle of "separate but equal." In 1954 Chief Justice Earl Warren led the court's unanimous decision to abolish the practice, citing its violation of the Fourteenth Amendment's civil rights guarantee. (SOURCE: © BETTMANN/CORBIS)

consolidation made possible a metropolitan plan for integrating schools when a suit was brought challenging the segregated county system. It was through the *Swann* opinion that a majority of the Supreme Court embraced an understanding of equality that measured the achievement of an integrated school system by examining the degree to which racial proportions in individual schools matched those of the school district as a whole.

DIFFERENT MEANINGS OF EQUALITY

In his 1981 book *Equalities*, Douglas Rae formulated an important structural grammar of equality. Usually, most people argue that equality means that everyone ought to be treated alike. Rae calls this "individual-regarding equality," with its broadest application as an inclusionary standard that describes an egalitarian society as one in which everyone is treated alike without regard to race, creed, color, age, gender, sexual orientation, and so on. Individualism is an important cultural principle in the United States—a principle that most Americans recognize and support without much reflection—but it is important to recognize that individual-regarding equality is only one version of equality. It is a particularly American version.

Another version, often favored in other cultures, can be found in "group-regarding equality." Recognizing that in real societies there are all sorts of social categories and divisions, equality can also be achieved when one group, taken as a whole, does as well as another comparable group. With respect to racial and gender equality, for example, an equal society would be achieved when blacks as a group do as well as whites as a group, or when women do as well as men. The approved policy in *Swann* was much like this. It measured success by comparing the outcomes for each racial group taken as a whole. A strong argument for this solution lies in the fact that racial discrimination is in fact directed at a group's characteristics (e.g., African Americans), not at the characteristics of individuals. Since discrimination has been group-directed, the remedy should also be. Most group-directed programs are **remedial**. Thus, they are enforced only until the vestiges of prior group discrimination have been removed. The arguments in favor of remedial affirmative action programs are consistent with group-regarding equality, whereas arguments against affirmative action are consistent with individual-regarding equality. Each view has its advocates, which is why affirmative action programs have been so controversial.

remedial: intended as a solution

■ ■ ■
U.S. SUPREME COURT CASES ADDRESSING EQUALITY

Brown v. Board of Education, 347 U.S. 483 (1954), 349 U.S. 294 (1955)

Craig v. Boren, 429 U.S. 190 (1976)

Cummings v. County Board of Education of Richmond County, Georgia, 175 U.S. 628 (1899)

Korematsu v. U.S., 323 U.S. 214 (1944)

Lawrence v. Texas, 539 U.S. 558 (2003)

Milliken v. Bradley, 418 U.S. 717 (1974)

Missouri ex rel Gaines v. Canada, 305 U.S. 337 (1938)

Plessy v. Ferguson, 163 U.S. 537 (1896)

Romer v. Evans, 615 U.S. 620 (1996)

Sipuel v. Board of Regents of the University of Oklahoma, 332 U.S. 631 (1948)

Swann v. Charlotte–Mecklenburg Board of Education, 402 U.S. 1 (1971)

Sweatt v. Painter, 339 U.S. 629 (1950)

For all the promise that *Swann* seemed to offer, it rested on the voluntary 1960 consolidation of many school districts into a single countywide metropolitan district. That singularity became evident in the 1974 decision *Milliken v. Bradley*. In this case, a federal judge ordered fifty-three adjacent school districts in metropolitan Detroit to be combined into a single district for which a comprehensive plan of desegregation would be devised. However, this time there was no voluntary consolidation; instead, there was steadfast resistance. To support the consolidation, Chief Justice Warren Burger's opinion in *Milliken* required a finding of fact that each district which had been brought into the metropolitan Detroit system had contributed to the de jure segregation that the federal courts sought to **redress**. This, of course, was not practicable. The consequence has been that most metropolitan areas with multiple school districts cannot be effectively integrated.

redress: to make right, or, compensation

Since the 1954 decision in *Brown v. Board of Education*, equal protection cases have fallen into two broad groups. The first group includes all the cases involving affirmative action programs. Some of these are pure equal protection cases, but a greater number rely on federal **statutes**, such as Title VII (discrimination in employment) of the Civil Rights Act of 1964. The second group includes all the cases that "discover" new forms of categorical discrimination and seek to bring them within a new understanding of equal protection of the law.

statute: a law created by a legislature that is inferior to constitutional law

AFFIRMATIVE ACTION

Affirmative action cases are too numerous and too complex to cover in much detail here. In general terms, affirmative action programs in employment cases (mostly statutory cases involving hiring, retention, and promotion) have been upheld in the federal courts when it has been shown that an institution or employer has discriminated in the past and that an affirmative action program, which addresses a category such as race or gender, is designed as a form of compensatory relief to repair the damage of historic discrimination. When racial or gender **parity** is achieved in a particular employment sector, the relevant affirmative action program would no longer be required.

parity: a state of equality, or being identical

Affirmative action in public higher education admissions cases has most often been upheld when states have included among their admissions objectives the achievement of a racially or ethnically diverse student body, provided that race or ethnicity is only one factor taken into account (not the single or dominant factor) and also that racial or ethnic quotas are not employed in the admissions process.

THE EVOLUTION OF CATEGORICAL DISCRIMINATION

As to the evolution of categorical discrimination, in the 1971 case of *Reed v. Reed*, the Supreme Court found discrimination based on gender to be covered by the equal protection clause, and in 1976 it established the heightened scrutiny standard that would be applied to gender discrimination. Since then, most public policies that have rested on sexual stereotypes, rather than physiological differences between men and women, have been set aside. Other discrimination cases have considered illegitimacy, poverty, age, alien status, state residency requirements, mental retardation, and other forms of disability as possible objects of prohibited categorical discrimination, but with mixed results. Race remains the best example of a classification viewed suspiciously by the Supreme Court, and gender has been its only consistent rival in the enforcement of equal protection.

The most interesting aspect of equal protection law in the late twentieth and early twenty-first century has been the open-ended character of its application. This is best illustrated by cases involving sexual orientation. Thus, in 1996 in *Romer v. Evans*, the Supreme Court struck down Colorado's constitutional amendment that prohibited state and local governments from enforcing policies that would afford legal protection to gays and lesbians. In 2003 in *Lawrence v. Texas*, the Court overturned a Texas law criminalizing sodomy between consenting adults that, in fact, had only been enforced against homosexual couples. At the time of its decision in *Lawrence*, only thirteen states still had laws against sodomy, and the laws of only four of those applied solely to homosexual conduct. Those states that still had general laws against sodomy normally enforced them only against homosexuals. *Lawrence* can be read chiefly as a privacy case that allows homosexual adults the right to engage in sexual conduct in the privacy of their homes, but the opinion of Associate Justice Anthony Kennedy goes beyond that, recognizing their dignity as free persons and holding that no legitimate state interest can justify intrusion into their personal and private lives.

In November 2003 the Massachusetts Supreme Judicial Court held that its state laws limiting marriage to heterosexuals represented a violation of the Massachusetts Constitution that requires "equality before the law." The Supreme Court has yet to go this far, but the issue is at the cutting edge of the law. It seems possible that sexual orientation will eventually be accorded at least the same heightened scrutiny that has been applied in cases involving gender discrimination. But that will take time and will likely also involve intense **litigation**.

See also: Civil Rights Movement in the United States; Equality Before the Law; Gender Discrimination; Racism.

litigate: to bring a disagreement or violation of the law before a judge for a legal decision

BIBLIOGRAPHY

Baer, Judith. *Equality under the Constitution: Reclaiming the Fourteenth Amendment.* Ithaca, NY: Cornell University Press, 1983.

Jackson, Donald W. *Even the Children of Strangers: Equality under the U.S. Constitution.* Lawrence: University Press of Kansas, 1992.

Kluger, Richard. *Simple Justice.* New York: Vintage Books, 1975.

Rae, Douglas. *Equalities.* Cambridge, MA: Harvard University Press, 1981.

Woodward, C. Vann. *The Strange Career of Jim Crow.* New York: Oxford University Press, 1968.

Donald W. Jackson

Equality Before the Law

Equality provisions appear in international conventions and in the human rights documents of many countries. For example, Article 7 of the Universal Declaration of Human Rights holds that "all [people] are equal before the law and are entitled without any discrimination to the equal protection of the law." Article 3 of the International Covenant on Civil and Political Rights (ICCPR) provides that states must "undertake to ensure the equal right of men and women to the enjoyment of all civil and political rights" contained in the Covenant, whereas Article 2 of the International Covenant on Economic, Social and Cultural Rights (ICESCR) requires its **signatories** to guarantee that the rights **enumerated** in this Covenant "will be exercised without discrimination of any kind as to race, colour, sex, language, religion, political or other opinion, national or social origin, property, birth or other status." Article 14 of the European Convention on Human Rights contains language almost identical to that of the ICESCR.

Perhaps the most interesting equality provision is that contained in the Canadian Charter of Rights and Freedoms (1982), which in Section 15(1) provides for equality "before and under the law" as well as the right to "the equal protection and equal benefit of the law" without discrimination based on "race, national or ethnic origin, colour, religion, sex, age or mental or physical disability."

Several of the provisions mentioned here are significantly different from the Equal Protection Clause of the Fourteenth Amendment of the U.S. Constitution, which lists in detail prohibited forms of discrimination. These variations represent two interesting legal developments. First, the articles themselves establish the categories of discrimination and are not subject to judicial interpretation of broad language, as is the case with the equal protection clause, from which U.S. Supreme Court justices have had to develop a list of categories. Second, the clear specification of categories may make it more difficult for future courts to include previously unforeseen forms of discrimination. Is it better for certain kinds of discrimination to be identified and included in laws by elected representatives or judges? The answer seems to be contingent on one's national or political perspective.

The other interesting feature of the Canadian Charter is its Section 15(2), which makes clear that the earlier section guaranteeing equality before the law and equal protection, Section 15(2), "does not preclude any law, program or activity that has as its object the amelioration of conditions of disadvantaged individuals or groups including those that are disadvantaged because of race, national or ethnic origin, colour, religion, sex, age or mental or physical disability." As a result of this specific provision in the Charter, Canada was able to **mandate** affirmative action programs, policies that have been a source of considerable legal controversy in the United States since their inception in the 1960s.

Other countries have followed a similar course. For example, Articles 15(4) and 16(4) of the Indian Constitution provide for affirmative action programs for the disadvantaged in public educational institutions and in government employment.

The strong preference of most U.S. judges to focus on the principle of individual equality (whereby every person ought to be treated alike) is not always shared by judges in other countries. Both the Canadian and Indian legal systems are more concerned with group equality, whereby outcomes are often assessed in terms of the relative treatment of groups rather than individuals. In India, for example, *dalits* (untouchables) have been the chief beneficiaries of affirmative action given their continuing negative treatment as a result of the traditional Hindu caste system. A number of affirmative action provisions based on group equality date back to the founding of the Indian nation in 1949, but subsequent decisions of the Indian Supreme Court go even further. For example, its decision in 1976 to support other forms of affirmative action stated that: "Equality means **parity** of treatment under parity of condition. Equality does not connote **absolute** equality." The opinion of Justice K.K. Mathew of the Indian Supreme Court in *State of Kerala v. Thomas* makes the case for looking beyond simple individual equality:

> If we are to be treated in the same manner, that must carry with it the important requirement that none of us should be better or worse in upbringing or education than anyone else which is an unattainable ideal for human beings of anything like the sort we now see. (1976, pp. 513–4)

signatory: one who signs an agreement with other parties and is then bound to that agreement

enumerate: to expressly name, as in a list

mandate: to command, order, or require; or, a command, order, or requirement

parity: a state of equality, or being identical

absolute: complete, pure, free from restriction or limitation

Such analysis leads one to conclude that the legal principles of equality require governments to eliminate all sources of inequality and "to provide for opportunities for the exercise of human rights and claims." (1976, p. 516) This particular view, however, is unpopular in certain quarters, especially among many U.S. citizens.

AT THE 2004 WORLD SOCIAL FORUM (WSF) IN BOMBAY, INDIA, AN INDIAN *DALIT* PROTESTS AGAINST THE INEQUITIES OF THE COUNTRY'S CASTE SYSTEM. Since 2001 the World Social Forum (WSF) has assembled annually for those seeking alternatives to globalization efforts. The fourth conference in January 2004 in Mumbai, India, with about 75,000 participants, focused on cultural diversity and addressed the sufferings of the *Dalit*. (SOURCE: INDRANIL MUKHERJEE/AFP/GETTY IMAGES)

See also: Equal Protection of the Law.

BIBLIOGRAPHY

Galanter, Marc. *Competing Equalities: Law and the Backward Classes in India*. Berkeley: University of California Press, 1984.

Jackson, Donald W. *Even the Children of Strangers: Equality Under the U.S. Constitution*. Lawrence: University Press of Kansas, 1992.

Loenen, Titia, and Peter R. Rodrigues. *Non-Discrimination Law: Comparative Perspectives*. The Hague, The Netherlands: Kluwer Law International, 1999.

Donald W. Jackson

Equatorial Guinea

As late as the early 1990s, Equatorial Guinea was often presented as a backward and unappealing country. The country was not only bankrupt but also suffering from moral decay. By the early 2000s, stories on Equatorial Guinea made international headlines and Malabo (its capital) had become more appealing, awash with cash from major oil companies. Although these developments offered some promise for the future of this country, there has been little change in the bleak living conditions of most of the population.

Equatorial Guinea is located on the western coast of Africa, between Cameroon and Gabon. The total land area is about 28,051 square kilometers (10,828 square miles), and its total population is about 510,000. The country consists of a mainland area (Rio Muni Province) and five islands, the largest of which is Bioko. Several languages are spoken, including Fang, but Spanish is the official language. Equatorial Guinea is surrounded mostly by French-speaking countries, however; consequently, it belongs to the International Organization of Francophonie (French-speaking countries).

In 1778 Spain claimed Equatorial Guinea as its only colony in Africa. The country gained local autonomy in 1963 and independence in 1968. Since then it has been governed by two leaders, Francisco Macias Nguema (1924–1979) and his nephew Teodoro Obiang Nguema Mbasogo (b. 1942), who seized power in a 1979 palace **coup**. Spain has had troubled relations with Equatorial Guinea because of corruption and misrule. Most of the democratic opposition leaders live in exile in Spain. Under Macias Nguema, about one-third of the population was killed or fled into exile.

coup: a quick seizure of power or a sudden attack

Despite the democratic wave of the 1990s, Equatorial Guinea is far from being democratic. A multiparty system is in place, but there is constant military intimidation of the political opposition, including arrest and torture. The presidential elections of 2002 led to the victory of President Obiang for another seven-year term. Most foreign observers described the election as neither free nor fair.

The political system is strictly presidential. In his last cabinet reshuffle, President Obiang described the team as a "transitional government," but not much transition has taken place. Instead, the president lives under tight security and constantly confronts rumors and threats of a coup. A plot in March 2004 had a peculiar international flavor; Zimbabwe arrested scores of foreigners, including Europeans and Africans, who were planning to fly to Malabo to overthrow the government. Arrests were also made within the country itself, and hundreds of foreigners were expelled.

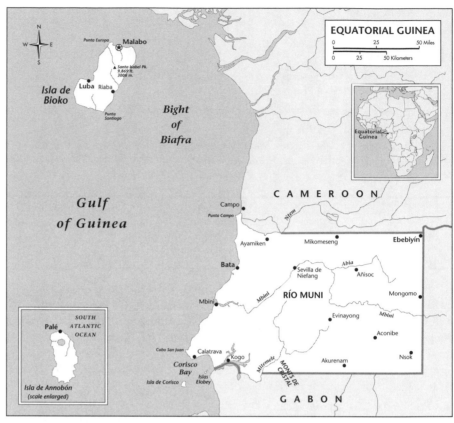

EQUATORIAL GUINEA

(MAP BY MARYLAND CARTOGRAPHICS/THE GALE GROUP)

unicameral: comprised of one chamber, usually a legislative body

The legislative branch of government is the **unicameral** House of People's Representatives. In 2004 membership was increased from eighty to one hundred lawmakers. The president's party, the Democratic Party of Equatorial Guinea, held a near monopoly.

The president appoints the prime minister and other government officials, and he can also dismiss them at will. The judiciary is partly based on Spanish civil law and is also influenced by tribal customs. There is a Supreme Tribunal, where the wishes of the president prevail, especially regarding summary executions.

Increasingly, President Obiang's son, who spends most of his time living abroad, has made key decisions. He also manages the family's huge assets deposited in foreign banks. Corruption is widespread in the country, and the oil wealth has only made things worse. The heavy reliance on oil means that the country still has to import food from neighboring countries to deal with rising malnutrition.

This country has great economic prospects. However, the political climate will ultimately determine just how much Equatorial Guinea's people benefit from its oil wealth.

See also: Presidential Systems.

BIBLIOGRAPHY

"Equatorial Guinea." In *CIA World Factbook*. Washington, DC: Central Intelligence Agency, 2005. <http://www.cia.gov/cia/publications/factbook/geos/ek.html>.

Klitgaard, Robert. *Tropical Gangsters*. New York: Basic Books, 1990.

Mars, Laura, director. *Nations of the World: A Political, Economic and Business Handbook*. Millerton, NY: Grey House Publishing, 2003.

Ramsay, F. Jeffress, ed. *Global Studies: Africa*. 10th ed. Guilford, CT: McGraw Hill/Dushkin, 2004.

H. Mbella Mokeba

Eritrea

With an area of 121,300 square kilometers (46,800 square miles) and an estimated population of 4.5 million, Eritrea is a relatively small state located on the Red Sea. It is bounded on the north and west by Sudan, on the south by Ethiopia, and on the east by the Red Sea and Djibouti. Eritrea has close to 1,100 kilometers (670 miles) of coastline and it is located along one of the busiest oil transit sea routes in the world. Asmara, the capital city, is estimated to have a population of 500,000.

Eritrea was an Italian colony from 1885 to 1941, when Italy was forced to relinquish its East African colonies to Allied powers after World War II (1939–1945). Between 1941 and 1952 the British administered Eritrea as a United Nations (UN) Trust Territory, and in 1952 the UN federated Eritrea with Ethiopia. Ethiopia incorporated Eritrea in 1962.

Resistance to the union with Ethiopia started in the early 1960s. The Eritrean Liberation Front and, subsequently, the Eritrean People's Liberation Front (EPLF) conducted an armed struggle against the Ethiopian government that lasted thirty years.

In 1991, the Ethiopian People's Democratic Front ousted the repressive government of **communist** leader Mengistu Haile Mariam (b. 1937) and took control of the Ethiopian government. The EPLF soon captured Asmara and set up a transitional government. In a **referendum** on the independence of Eritrea held in 1993, over 98 percent of the Eritrean people supported independence.

Following this vote, a transitional government began to chart the course for establishing a constitutional government and a pluralistic political system. The EPLF leader Isaias Afewerki (b. 1946) was elected as the head of state. In 1994 the EPLF adopted the new name—the People's Front for Democracy and Justice—and transformed itself into the only political party in Eritrea. It set up an eighteen-member executive committee and a seventy-five-member central committee, with Afewerki as the president. In 1997 a Constituent Assembly adopted a constitution authorizing political pluralism and a presidential system that allows the president to serve a maximum of two five-year terms. The president was to appoint the prime minister and judges of the Supreme Court, subject to approval by the National Assembly.

The first post-independence election was scheduled for 1999, but it was later postponed following outbreak of hostilities between Ethiopia and Eritrea. Elections were once again postponed in December 2001. As of 2005, the constitution had not been implemented and the likelihood of pluralistic elections remains slim. President Afewerki, who is the chief of state, head of the government, and head of the State Council and the National Assembly, has assumed an increasingly **authoritarian** position, dismissing cabinet ministers and the chief justice of the Supreme Court and dissolving the electoral commission. In May 2001 a group of influential Eritreans, including some government officials, wrote a letter to President Afewerki accusing him of operating illegally. By late 2001, eleven

communism: an economic and social system characterized by the absence of class structure and by common ownership of the means of production and subsistence

referendum: a popular vote on legislation, brought before the people by their elected leaders or public initiative

authoritarianism: the domination of the state or its leader over individuals

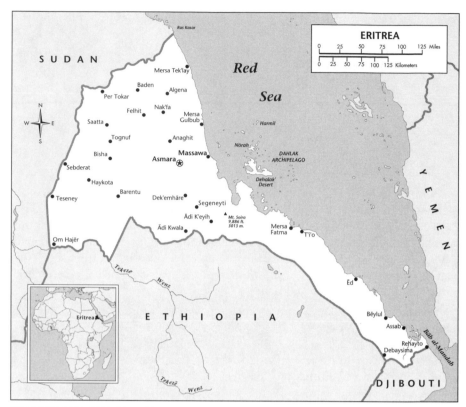

(MAP BY MARYLAND CARTOGRAPHICS/THE GALE GROUP)

of the fifteen government officials who signed the letter had been arrested, and the independent press was suspended.

Hostilities between Ethiopia and Eritrea started soon after independence because of conflicting border claims. A war that broke out in 2000 claimed the lives of eighty thousand people and displaced thousands more. The conflict subsided after Ethiopia and Eritrea agreed to settle their border conflict based on the decisions of an independent boundary commission to be set up by the UN. The commission gave its rulings in 2002, but the border demarcation and peace process that were to follow the commission report had still not been implemented as of early 2005. Eritrea's citizens continued to live in a repressive state.

See also: Ethiopia.

BIBLIOGRAPHY

Clapham, Christopher. *Transformation and Continuity in Revolutionary Ethiopia*. Cambridge, UK: Cambridge University Press, 1988.

"Eritrea." In *CIA World Factbook*. Washington, DC: Central Intelligence Agency, 2005. <http://www.cia.gov/cia/publications/factbook/geos/er.html>.

Gebre-Medhin, Jordan. *Peasants and Nationalism in Eritrea*. Trenton, NJ: Red Sea Press, 1988.

Markakis, John. "The Nationalist Revolution in Eritrea." *Journal of Modern African Studies* 26, no. 1 (1988):51–70.

Negash, Tekeste. *Eritrea and Ethiopia: The Federal Experience*. New Brunswick, NJ: Transaction, 1997.

Negash, Tekeste, and Kjelil Tronvoll. *Brothers at War: Making Sense of the Eritrean and Ethiopian War*. Oxford, UK: James Currey, 2000.

U.S. Department of State, Bureau of Democracy, Human Rights, and Labor. "Eritrea." *Country Reports on Human Rights Practices 2003*. Washington, DC: U.S. Department of State, Bureau of Democracy, Human Rights, and Labor, 2004. <http://www.state.gov/g/drl/rls/hrrpt/2003/27726.htm>.

Yohannes, Okbazghi. *Eritrea: A Pawn in World Politics*. Gainesville: University of Florida Press, 1991.

Mulatu Wubneh

Estonia

The Republic of Estonia, with a population of 1.4 million people, lies on the eastern shore of the Baltic Sea and shares its borders with Latvia and Russia. Russia continues to dispute border agreements reached in 1994. Estonia's proximity to Scandinavia and Russia contributed to the use of its land for territorial wars. These wars led to centuries of foreign rule by Germans, Swedes, Poles, and Russians.

At the beginning of the 1800s, Estonians revived a sense of national identity after serfdom was abolished by the Russian Empire. This development led to increased cultural expression through literature, education, and music. Growing **nationalism**, coupled with the collapse of the Russian Empire after World War I (1914–1918), led to the declaration of Estonia as an independent state on February 24, 1918. The first constitution of the Republic of Estonia was enacted in 1920, and the country adopted a parliamentary government. The effective independence of Estonia ended in 1940, when it was conquered and absorbed into the Union of Soviet Socialist Republics (USSR). On August 20, 1991, Estonia declared and established independence for a second time as the USSR disintegrated.

Estonian voters approved a new draft constitution on June 28, 1992. The constitution established a parliamentary government with a president as head of state and prime minister as head of government. The *Riigikogu,* or parliament, is comprised of 101 members who are selected through open, direct, uniform elections by secret vote based on a **proportional system**. The *Riigikogu* elects a president through direct, secret ballot. The president's duties include representing Estonia in international matters as well as appointing office holders to the judicial and executive branches of government, including the prime minister. After the *Riigikogu* authorizes that appointment, the prime minister selects a Cabinet of Ministers to assist in the day-to-day operations of the government.

In January 1995 the *Riigikogu* reinstated a 1938 citizenship law that guaranteed **cultural autonomy** to minority groups. Minorities comprise at least three thousand people in Estonia, including Jews and resident aliens. The religious majority consists of Evangelical Lutherans, Baptists, and members of the Orthodox Church of Estonia. This law gives minorities an active voice in society and local government, although only Estonian citizens are allowed to vote in state elections and serve as members of political parties.

The constitution of Estonia provides equality before the law for all residents. The constitution also grants free education, freedom of speech and thought, protection of health through social services, as well as the duty to uphold the Estonian constitution and laws. Anyone who is the object of discrimination, torture, or degradation may seek **redress** through the court system.

Estonia's transition into the European Union (EU) modernized the judicial branch, creating a system to address issues of constitutionality. This increases the system of checks and balances on the government. The handling of human

nationalism: the belief that one's nation or culture is superior to all others

proportional system: a political system in which legislative seats or offices are awarded based on the proportional number of votes received by a party in an election

cultural autonomy: the state in which a group's beliefs and behavior patterns do not incorporate influences from other groups

redress: to make right, or, compensation

ESTONIA

FINLAND

(MAP BY MARYLAND CARTOGRAPHICS/THE GALE GROUP)

rights issues continues to improve, but still falls short of the EU minimum standard. The most frequently reported human rights violations involve police brutality, excessive force, and verbal abuse. The trafficking of humans and the illegal drug trade are also obstacles to freedom that Estonia must address.

See also: European Union; Latvia; Parliamentary Systems; Russia.

BIBLIOGRAPHY

"Estonia." In *CIA World Factbook.* Washington, DC: Central Intelligence Agency, 2005. <http://www.cia.gov>.

Laar, Mart. *Estonia: Little Country That Could.* London: Centre for Research and Post-Communist Economies, 2002.

Raun, Toivo U. *Estonia and the Estonians.* Stanford, CA: Hoover Institution Press, 2001.

Smith, David J. *Estonia: Independence and European Immigration.* New York: Routledge, 2001.

United Nations Online Network in Public Administration and Finance. <http:// www.unpan.org>.

University of Washington, Baltic States Studies. *Encyclopedia of Baltic History.* <http://depts.washington.edu/baltic/encyclopedia.html>

U.S. Department of State, Bureau of European and Eurasian Affairs. *Background Note: Latvia.* <http://www.state.gov>.

Melissa Comenduley

Ethiopia

Ethiopia, with an area of 1.13 million square kilometers (437,600 square miles), is located in northeastern Africa, also known as the Horn of Africa. The country has a wide range of agro-ecological zones, ranging from 120 meters (394 feet) below sea level in the *Dalol* (northeast) to 4,620 meters (15,158 feet) high in the *Ras Dashen* (northwest). The Ethiopian landscape is dominated by a massive highland of mountains and plateaus. The Great Rift Valley, running in a northwest-southeast direction, bisects the highland area.

Although Ethiopia is in the tropics, a large part of the country enjoys a temperate climate. Most places enjoy two rainy seasons: *Meher* (the main rainy season), lasting from June to September, and *Belg* (a shorter season with lighter rain), lasting from February to April, with a long dry season from April to June.

With a population of 67 million, as estimated in 2004, Ethiopia is the most populated country in sub-Saharan Africa, second only to Nigeria. Most of the population is concentrated in the Ethiopian highland. Over 80 percent of the population lives in rural areas; however, urbanization is growing at a steady rate.

Ethiopia is an ancient country with a history extending over three thousand years. It is the oldest independent country in Africa, with the exception of its five-year occupation by fascist Italy from 1936 to 1941. Ethiopia's best-known twentieth-century ruler was Emperor Haile Selassie (1892–1975), who reigned from 1930 to 1974. He was an **absolute** monarch who enjoyed supreme authority. Although the 1955 constitution called for the establishment of a Chamber of

absolute: complete, pure, free from restriction or limitation

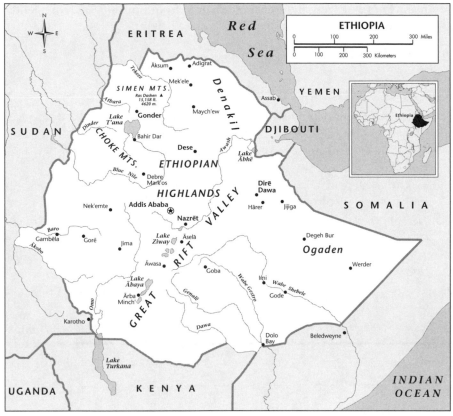

(MAP BY MARYLAND CARTOGRAPHICS/THE GALE GROUP)

Deputies and a Senate to serve as parliament, the emperor controlled the members of both bodies.

In 1974 Selassie was overthrown by a military body known as the Derg (Committee). Mengistu Haile Mariam (b. 1937) emerged as the leader of the **coup**, and the country soon plunged into a Marxist-socialist political and economic system. Mengistu's rule was characterized by repression, civil war, and the suppression of opposition groups. Thousands perished under Mengistu's **regime** when they opposed the brutality of the military government.

In 1991 the Ethiopian People's Revolutionary Democratic Front (EPRDF), a **coalition** of rebel groups led by the Tigrayan People's Liberation Front (TPLF), forced Mengistu to flee the country. Melese Zenawi (b. 1955), the leader of the group, assumed power the same year.

The EPRDF developed a new constitution, which was approved in 1994, and the country was transformed into a federal republic with nine ethnic-based regions. The new constitution also called for the establishment of a **bicameral** parliament: the People's Representatives with 548 seats and the House of Federation with 108 seats.

In 1995 Negasso Gidada (b. 1943) became the president and Zenawi became the head of government (prime minister). Elections were held in May 2000, and despite complaints of election irregularities and violence, the EPRDF remained in power. Zenawi continued as prime minister, and in October 2001 Girma Woldegiorgis (b. 1924) replaced Gidada as the country's president.

Members of the Federal Supreme Court and other federal judges are named by the prime minister and subject to approval by the House of the People's Representatives. Political parties are allowed to exist, but there have been

coup: a quick seizure of power or a sudden attack

regime: a type of government, or, the government in power in a region

coalition: an alliance, partnership, or union of disparate peoples or individuals

bicameral: comprised of two chambers, usually a legislative body

complaints of the government restricting them from operating independently and preventing the press from freely exercising its rights.

See also: Eritrea; Federalism.

BIBLIOGRAPHY

Clapham, C. *Transformation and Continuity in Revolutionary Ethiopia.* Cambridge, UK: Cambridge University Press, 1988.

Markakis, John. *Ethiopia: Anatomy of a Traditional Polity.* New York: Oxford University Press, 1974.

Ofcansky, Thomas, and La Verle Berry, eds. *Ethiopia: A Country Study*, 4th ed. Washington, DC: Federal Research Division, Library of Congress, 1992.

Ullundorff, E. *The Ethiopians: An Introduction to the Country and the People*, 3rd ed. London: Oxford University Press, 1973.

Wubneh, Mulatu, and Yohannis Abate. *Ethiopia: Transition and Development in the Horn of Africa.* Boulder, CO: Westview Press, 1988.

Zewde, Bahru. *A History of Modern Ethiopia, 1855–1991*, 2d ed. Oxford, UK: James Currey, 2001.

Mulatu Wubneh

Ethnic Cleansing

Ethnic cleansing is a relatively new term for the ancient practice of expelling a people, using a variety of means, from a geographic area to secure it for another people's exclusive use. The term began to be used extensively in an international context during the early 1990s in relation to the wars surrounding the collapse of Yugoslavia. It was a translation of a Serbo-Croatian phrase for the practice of using forced deportation, random attacks, and systematic rape to encourage people of a specific ethnic origin to leave a region. Ethnic cleansing was practiced to varying degrees by several sides in the conflict as a strategic goal to help establish ethnically **homogeneous** areas that could then be incorporated into a larger **nation-state**.

Since its use to describe events in Yugoslavia, the term has been widely utilized by reporters, international governmental organizations such as the United Nations (UN), and social scientists to characterize other ethnic conflicts, both current and historic. Distinguishing ethnic cleansing from related phenomena such as genocide and ethnically targeted governmental repression is not easy, and any effort to do so must examine the goals of the perpetrators. Ethnic cleansing is best understood as a conscious policy of population removal by a variety of means to achieve firm political control of a region by establishing "facts on the ground"; that is, establishing a strong position by removing people from an unwanted ethnic group.

Ethnic cleansing has not always been portrayed in a negative light. Certainly, many extreme nationalists throughout history have extolled the value of creating, by force if necessary, ethnically homogeneous areas that will help to build and defend a nation. More interestingly, some political scientists have suggested that the resulting separation of communities created by ethnic cleansing or population transfers may help to reduce ethnic conflict and promote peace. The majority opinion, however, both in the social sciences and among human rights

homogeneous: simple; consisting of components that are identical or similar

nation-state: a relatively homogeneous state with only one or few nationalities within its political borders

organizations, is that ethnic cleansing is clearly a violation of human rights, and that international efforts must try to end or prevent ethnic cleansing from occurring and correcting the damage caused by it.

ETHNIC CLEANSING OVER THE CENTURIES

The transfer of population as a policy of war is almost as old as the recorded history of war. Assyria, one of the first historic empires (existing from around 2400 to 612 B.C.E. in the region of today's Turkey, Syria, and Iraq), practiced transfer of population as a regular policy of state to secure its hold on newly conquered areas. When Assyria conquered the Israelites in 722 B.C.E., the victorious Assyrians expelled a majority of the population, replacing the Hebrews with settlers from more politically sympathetic peoples. This policy of population transfer as a tool of empire building was practiced by other **imperial** powers that followed. In Europe during the Middle Ages and early modern era, the practice of ethnic cleansing frequently took on a religious cast, and the targets were most often Jews, who were expelled from England, France, Hungary, Austria, Portugal, and Spain (in this instance, along with the Muslim population).

The expulsion of Jews and Muslims from Spain was an important turning point, because scholars have identified this ethnic cleansing as central to Spain's formation as a state. Indeed, several scholars have argued that efforts to homogenize a population through ethnic cleansing or genocide have been essential to the formation of many states. Scholars who make this argument point not only to Spain but also to the persecution of the Huguenots in France, the forced relocation and killing of Native Americans in the United States from the 1830s to 1880s, and the English expulsion of Irish Catholics from the Ulster area of Northern Ireland during the 1700s.

The Spanish repression of Protestants in the Low Countries illustrates that it can sometimes be difficult for historians to differentiate ethnic repression

imperialism: extension of the control of one nation over another, especially through territorial, economic, and political expansion

"The transfer of population as a policy of war is almost as old as the recorded history of war."

■ ■ ■

TREATY OF LAUSANNE

The expulsion of Greeks from Turkish lands and corresponding expulsion of Turks from Greek territory in the period between the two world wars is an example of ethnic cleansing as an attempt to stabilize international relations. The redrawing of European national boundaries at the end of World War I (1918) created several nation-states that contained large ethnic minorities. Mass transfer of these minority groups was proposed as a way to prevent ethnic separatist movements within the newly defined countries. The Treaty of Lausanne, which was signed on July 24, 1923, defined the political boundaries of Turkey and Greece, and required a population exchange between the two countries.

The population transfer involved 1.2 million Greeks and 400,000 Turks. Although the exchange was supposedly peaceful and humane, it was in reality a harsh and brutal process. Many people died during their journeys, and Greece in particular was overwhelmed by a large number of diseased and starving people. The 1923 treaty had specified monetary compensation for people uprooted from their homes but these debts were never paid. Instead of easing relations between Greece and Turkey, the forced transfer of populations led to decades of bitterness and anger between the two countries.

from ethnic cleansing. More than a hundred thousand Protestants fled that area in the sixteenth century, but many other Protestants remained in the region. Although Spain did engage in religious and ethnic repression, it is not clear whether this particular policy qualifies as ethnic cleansing.

During the twentieth century, ethnic cleansing reached new heights; the old tools of expulsion, massacres, and deportations were superseded by the planned extermination of entire ethnic groups. One of the first groups to suffer this fate were the Armenians during World War I (1914–1918). The Armenians had previously endured an attempt at ethnic cleansing toward the end of the nineteenth century at the hands of the Ottoman Empire (1899–1922). During World War I Turkey renewed this effort to annihilate the remaining Armenians with particular vigor, representing one of the first genocides of the twentieth century. The war's end also witnessed other episodes of mass ethnic cleansing: Turkey's attempts to eliminate Greeks, Greece's attempts to obliterate Turks, and Bulgaria's attempts to kill off both groups.

The Nazi campaign of ethnic cleansing against the Jews began with their expulsion from Germany and the occupied lands, but it escalated quickly to an attempt to exterminate them as a people. The same could be said of Nazi policies toward the Roma (or gypsies). Nazi policy toward the Poles, however, more closely corresponded to the classic model of ethnic cleansing; the Third Reich expelled over a million Poles from areas that German dictator Adolf Hitler (1889–1945) wanted to incorporate into Germany.

Aside from the Nazis, several other major examples of ethnic cleansing are associated with World War II (1939–1945) and its aftermath. The former Soviet Union ordered the deportation of Volga Germans, Crimean Tartars, and Chechens to Central Asia in 1944. At the war's end, Russian forces also expelled ethnic Germans from Eastern Prussia. In addition, Poland, Czechoslovakia, Hungary, Yugoslavia, and Romania expelled many ethnic Germans.

■ ■ ■

THE INDIAN WARS

Relocation and killing of Native Americans as official policies of the U. S. federal government occurred between 1830 and 1890. Before 1830 Indian tribes living east of the Mississippi interacted with the governments of individual states. During the presidential campaign of 1828, however, victorious candidate Andrew Jackson promised to achieve Indian removal: the relocation of Eastern tribes to lands west of the Mississippi. Congress passed the Indian Removal Act in 1830, which ordered the relocation of the Chickasaw, Choctaw, Creek, Seminole, and Cherokee nations to Oklahoma and Kansas. The Seminoles resisted removal, however, resulting in the Second Seminole War (1835–1842).

After the Civil War ended in 1865, the U. S. Army was involved in a series of conflicts with the Native American tribes in the Great Plains and the Southwest. The so-called Indian Wars resulted from the country's rapid westward expansion and the closing of the frontier, in which the U.S. government gave away the Native Americans' land to homesteading pioneers traveling west from the former British colonies and Europe. Not only did this practice deprive the western tribes of their ancestral lands, it also drastically reduced available land upon which the relocated eastern Indians could be resettled. In addition, the farming practices of the pioneers threatened the buffalo with extinction, eliminating a major source of food and shelter for the Plains tribes. Many tribes chose to fight rather than give up their ancestral lands. The Indian Wars ended in defeat for the tribes and their relocation to reservations throughout the American West.

Native Americans regained political power in the 1970s, following several years of protests and court cases. As of the early 2000s, federal law regards Native American tribes as political communities with powers of self-government greater than those given to the U.S. states. The tribes are not, however, considered independent nations.

ETHNIC CLEANSING AFTER WORLD WAR II

Despite the growth of human rights norms and the UN Declaration of Human Rights, ethnic cleansing remains a significant problem on an international scale. Europe continues to see cases of ethnic cleansing, such as the expulsion of ethnic Greeks from Turkish-occupied Cyprus and ethnic Turks from the rest of Cyprus after Turkey's invasion of the island in 1975. Toward the end of the 1990s, Yugoslavia engaged in policies of ethnic cleansing in Kosovo toward ethnic Albanians. After the **North Atlantic Treaty Organization** (NATO) intervened on the side of the ethnic Albanians, reverse efforts to ethnically cleanse Kosovo of all Serbs occurred. In Bulgaria during the late 1980s the government engaged in the expulsion and repression of those ethnic Turks who had remained after the forced removals of the interwar period.

Ethnic cleansing is not just a European phenomenon, however. Ethnic cleansing took place during the creation of India and Pakistan in 1947, with countless Muslims forced to flee to the north, and Sikhs and Hindus to the south. During the 1990s Armenia expelled all Azeris from the region of

North Atlantic Treaty Organization: a military alliance chiefly involving the United States and Western Europe that stated that, in the event of an attack, the member countries would have a mutual defense

A FRENCH SOLDIER USES A BULLDOZER TO PLACE VICTIMS OF THE RWANDA GENOCIDE INTO A MASS GRAVE IN 1994. After Rwanda's president Juvenal Habyarimana was assassinated in April 1994, ethnic hostilities escalated resulting in the Hutu-led genocide of about 800,000 Tutsis and moderate Hutus. The massacre ended when Tutsi rebels claimed the capital, Kigali, and approximately two million Hutus fled to Zaire (now the Democratic Republic of Congo). (SOURCE: AP/WIDE WORLD PHOTOS)

Nagorno-Karabakh, laying claim to the entire region. Others have characterized the continuing ethnic repression in Sudan and the 1994 genocide in Rwanda as examples of ethnic cleansing.

INTERNATIONAL RESPONSE

Throughout most of history there was no immediate international response to episodes of ethnic cleansing, and international law remained silent on the issue. Starting with the development of rules of war and human rights law, however, this situation began to change. The practice is clearly illegal under the 1949 Geneva Conventions and qualifies as a crime against humanity as defined by the 1945 charter that established the International Military Tribunal (IMT) at Nuremberg, Germany. Even as international law was being developed after World War II, however, the 1945 Potsdam Conference, at which the United States, Union of Soviet Socialist Republics, and United Kingdom were key participants, authorized the expulsion of ethnic Germans from wide areas of Eastern Europe.

Indeed, for most of the second half of the twentieth century the international community's response to ethnic cleansing has been ineffective and mute. In a European context at least, this began to change with the end of the Cold War and NATO's involvement in the Bosnian conflict, which pushed all sides to come to peace terms and resulted in the **repatriation** of expelled peoples to their former homes. In the case of Kosovo and the former Yugoslavia, international involvement led to NATO forces remaining in both areas, policing the regions to maintain tenuous levels of ethnic peace, protecting ethnic minorities from ethnic majorities, and in some cases preventing the reverse situation. These conflicts in the Balkans, in fact, led to the establishment of the International Criminal Tribunal for the Former Yugoslavia (ICTY), which continues to prosecute those individuals involved in ethnic cleansing during the war.

See also: Crimes Against Humanity; Dictatorship; Genocide.

repatriate: to return to the country of one's birth or citizenship

BIBLIOGRAPHY

Bell-Fialkoff, Andrew. "A Brief History of Ethnic Cleansing." *Foreign Affairs* 72, no. 3 (1993):110–122.

Kaufman, Chaim D. "When All Else Fails. Ethnic Population Transfers and Partitions in the Twentieth Century." *International Security* 23, no. 2 (1998).

Petrovic, Drazen. "Ethnic Cleansing: An Attempt at Methodology." *European Journal of International Law* 5, no. 3 (1994).

Preece, Jennifer. "Ethnic Cleansing as an Instrument of Nation-State Creation: Changing State Practices and Evolving Legal Norms." *Human Rights Quarterly* 20, no. 4 (1998).

Rae, Heather. *State Identities and the Homogenization of Peoples.* New York: Cambridge University Press, 2002.

Walling, Carrie Booth. "The History and Politics of Ethnic Cleansing." *International Journal of Human Rights* 4, no. 3 and 4 (Autumn–Winter 2000).

Victor Asal

European Coal and Steel Community

See European Union.

European Community

See European Union.

European Convention on Human Rights and Fundamental Freedoms

The Convention for the Protection of Human Rights and Fundamental Freedoms, commonly known as the European Convention on Human Rights (ECHR), lies at the heart of a highly sophisticated regional legal order developed under the authority of the Council of Europe based in Strasbourg, France. The Convention initially provided for a two-tier system of supervisory institutions, consisting of the European Commission of Human Rights and the European Court of Human Rights. In 1998, these two part-time institutions were replaced by a single-tier, full-time European Court of Human Rights. By 2004, the Court's **jurisdiction** extended to all of the Council of Europe's forty-six member states.

The origins of the ECHR may be traced back to the Western European federalist movements that gained a degree of prominence in the years immediately after the end of the Second World War in 1945. The initial proposal for the creation of a European human rights jurisdiction was made at the famous Congress of The Hague in May 1948. European governments, however, appeared singularly reserved about the possible development of this incursion into their traditional sphere of **sovereignty**. Indeed, the Committee of Ministers of the newly established Council of Europe initially refused to place the question of human rights on the agenda of the inaugural session of the organization's Consultative Assembly in August 1949. Nevertheless, faced with the assembly's strong insistence on the question, the Committee of Ministers recanted its initial position.

Given the opportunity to deal with the issue, the assembly proceeded to produce a draft convention of human rights based on the "Teitgen Report", so named for its principal drafter, Pierre-Henri Teitgen (1908–1997)—which it submitted to the Committee of Ministers in September 1949. A series of expert meetings and **intergovernmental** negotiations were then held over the course of the following year, producing the definitive text of the ECHR. The treaty was opened for signature in Rome on November 4, 1950. The ECHR entered into force, for an initial group of ten **ratifying** states, on September 3, 1953.

The document, as agreed in 1950, encompassed only a comparatively limited range of rights; its scope is notably narrower than that of the United Nation's 1948 Universal Declaration of Human Rights. The ECHR is focused on a core of political and **procedural rights**, to the exclusion of the broader social and economic rights proclaimed in the Universal Declaration. For the proponents of the European system, there was a necessary trade-off between the creation of an effective international mechanism for human rights protection and the range of rights that it might, at least initially, encompass.

jurisdiction: the territory or area within which authority may be exercised

sovereignty: autonomy; or, rule over a political entity

intergovernmental: between or involving multiple governments, with each government retaining full decision-making power

ratify: to make official or to officially sanction

procedural right: a right to due process of the law when defending other liberties

Reflecting an interesting blend of English common law and continental European civil law drafting techniques, the ECHR encompassed the following rights: the right to life (Article 2); the prohibition of torture (Article 3); the prohibition of slavery and forced labor (Article 4); rights to liberty and security, significantly concerned with the conditions of detention (Article 5); the right to a fair trial (Article 6); the right for punishment to be inflicted only in terms established by law (Article 7); the right to respect for private and family life (Article 8); the right to freedom of thought, conscience, and religion (Article 9); freedom of expression (Article 10); freedom of assembly and association (Article 11); the right to marry (Article 12); the right to an effective remedy (Article 13); and a prohibition of discrimination as regards the exercise of any of the aforementioned rights (Article 14).

Further substantive rights have been incorporated into the Convention by way of six additional protocols, which bind only those states that choose to ratify them. Protocol No. 1—arguably the most important of these additional protocols—was opened for signature in March 1952 and entered into force in May 1954. This protocol essentially allowed for the optional inclusion of three provisions that had proved too controversial to be included in the initial text of the ECHR: a right to property, a right to education, and an obligation on the states' parties to hold free and fair elections at regular intervals.

Both Protocol No. 4 (opened for signature in 1963 and entered into force in 1968) and Protocol No. 7 (opened for signature in 1984 and entered into force in 1988) contain somewhat diverse packages of provisions that further develop and extend the core political and procedural rights of the initial ECHR text, in line with the recommendations of the expert committees established by the Council of Europe. An evolving European consensus on the abolition of the death penalty has also found expression in the addition of two protocols to the Convention. Protocol No. 6 (opened for signature in 1983 and entered into force in 1985) provides for the peacetime abolition of capital punishment; the more recent Protocol No. 13 (opened for signature in 2002 and entered into force in 2003) takes this one step further and prohibits the imposition of the

■ ■ ■

THE TEITGEN REPORT

The Teitgen Report of September 8, 1949, is the most important document that preceded the drafting of the European Convention of Human Rights (ECHR) in 1950. The report, which was given to the Consultative Assembly of the Council of Europe, represented the conclusions of the Assembly's Committee on Legal and Administrative Questions. Pierre-Henri Teitgen (1908–1997), a French law professor and cabinet minister, was the chief author of the report.

The committee had been asked to study proposals for a European organization that would provide a collective guarantee of human rights. The Teitgen Report listed ten rights from the Universal Declaration of Human Rights that should be guaranteed. It also recommended the establishment of a European Court of Justice and a European Commission of Human Rights. The provisions of the Teitgen Report were stronger in two

important respects than those of the later ECHR—the Report gave individual citizens full access to the Court and the Commission, and it did not make the Committee of Ministers the final judge of cases not referred to the Court.

Teitgen himself had suffered at the hands of the Gestapo during the German occupation of France (1940–1944); his father and brother had died in concentration camps. When some delegates to the 1949 Consultative Assembly expressed concerns about the loss of national sovereignty, Teitgen replied that "the only sovereignty worth dying for . . . the sovereignty of justice and the law" (Council of Europe, p. 50).

Source: Council of Europe. *Collected edition of the "travaux préparatoires" of the European Convention on Human Rights*, volume 1. The Hague: Council of Europe, 1975.

death penalty in any circumstances. Finally, Protocol No. 12 (opened for signature in 2000 and entered into force in 2005) invests the European Court of Human Rights with a broader, freestanding antidiscrimination jurisdiction.

While not discounting the importance of the specific measures adopted, the development of the ECHR by the addition of further substantive rights has, overall, remained relatively limited. Most notably, more ambitious proposals to effect a qualitative expansion of the system's jurisdiction to encompass social and economic rights or minority rights have failed to win the necessary support of the contracting states. In each case, distinctive instruments have been developed within the wider Council of Europe system, such as the European Social Charter (operational since 1965 in its initial form) and the Framework Convention for the Protection of National Minorities (operational since 1998), which do not provide for a form of judicial **recourse** on the ECHR model.

recourse: a resource for assistance

JURISPRUDENTIAL DEVELOPMENT

The ECHR has been the subject of an expansive **jurisprudential** development by the European Court of Human Rights and (prior to 1998) by the European Commission on Human Rights. Already in the 1961 case of *Austria v. Italy*, the Human Rights Commission clearly set apart the interpretive principles that were to govern the development of the Convention from more traditional understandings of international law. The case concerned a complaint brought by the Austrian government related to the trial of six youths who had been convicted for the murder of an Italian customs officer in the border province of Alto Adige. The Italian government, interpreting the Convention as creating **reciprocal** obligations between the contracting states, argued that Austria lacked standing to bring the case as it had not been a party to the ECHR when the events took place. The Commission rejected the Italian position, stressing that the ECHR was to be interpreted as an instrument establishing a common public order for all democracies within Europe. As such, conditions of reciprocity were not applicable. The ECHR created objective rights for all those who found themselves in the jurisdiction of any one of the contracting states.

jurisprudence: the body of precedents already decided in a legal system

reciprocity: mutual action or help that benefits both parties

This expansive understanding of the ECHR has been further developed by the Strasbourg institutions through the use of object and purpose interpretive techniques. In the 1968 case of *Wemhoff v. Germany*, the Court of Human Rights pointedly rejected the view that the ECHR, as an international treaty, should be interpreted in the manner most restrictive of states' obligations. Rather, the Court argued that the Convention must be interpreted in light of its overall object and purpose, which is that of the creation of an effective system of human rights protection, in accord with the shared values and political goals of the community of contracting states.

The practical implications of this interpretive technique may be illustrated with reference to the 1975 case of *Golder v. United Kingdom*. This case concerned a complaint brought by a prisoner who had been prohibited from communicating with a solicitor in respect of a civil suit that he wished to bring against the prison authorities. The core issue was whether Article 6 of the ECHR, establishing the right to a fair trial, could be construed to encompass an implicit right of access to a court, in the absence of any explicit reference to this effect. The majority opinion of the Court, citing the overall object and purpose of the Convention, held that such a prior right of access does, in fact, exist, thus siding with the plaintiff.

The Strasbourg institutions have further ensured that the Convention remains a living instrument, reflective of changing social attitudes and legal practice in the community of contracting states. A technique of dynamic or evolutive

AUTHOR OF THE HUMAN RIGHTS DRAFT THE "TEITGEN REPORT," FRENCH POLITICIAN PIERRE-HENRI TEITGEN (CENTER) IN SEPTEMBER 1947 AT THE SIGNING OF THE ECONOMIC CONFERENCE REPORT. The formation of the European Convention on Human Rights (ECHR) in 1950 was based upon French politician and lawyer Pierre-Henri Teitgen's draft dubbed the "Teitgen Report." Implemented in 1953 by the Council of Europe, the ECHR was designed to ensure human rights and protect freedom for its member states. (SOURCE: YALE JOEL/TIME LIFE PICTURES/GETTY IMAGES)

interpretation has thus been used. In keeping with this doctrine, the Court of Human Rights found the practice of judicial corporal punishment (birching) on the Isle of Man to constitute degrading punishment in the 1978 case of *Tyrer v. United Kingdom*. Although the Isle of Man authorities could point to overwhelming popular and parliamentary support for the practice, the Court held that it was unacceptable in light of the generally accepted standards of the Council of Europe member states. The Court has similarly pointed to an evolving consensus of member-state practice in a series of decisions, beginning with *Dudgeon v. United Kingdom* in 1981, which found breaches of the Convention regarding national legislation that treated homosexual acts between consenting adults as a criminal offense.

Although the jurisprudence of the European Court of Human Rights has generally been marked by a vigorous affirmation of European human rights standards, it has also displayed an awareness of the inherent limits of the Convention system. As the Court has itself repeatedly affirmed, the ECHR can provide only a **subsidiary** guarantee of human rights protection; national authorities must necessarily continue to hold the principal responsibility for the maintenance and development of human rights, with the European system acting only to secure a baseline minimum standard.

subsidiary: a small component of a larger entity

In keeping with this division of responsibilities, the Court has had frequent recourse to a "margin of appreciation" doctrine in its interpretation of the Convention. The margin of appreciation refers to the area of discretion enjoyed by the contracting parties as regards the discharge of their obligations under the ECHR. This doctrine recognizes that democratic societies may legitimately make different policy choices in light of differing national cultures and circumstances. The precise balance struck between state interference and individual freedom will thus not be the same across all contracting parties. Nevertheless, insofar as a common minimum standard of human rights protection is maintained, the doctrine holds that it is not properly the place of an international court to question these choices.

The margin of appreciation is differentially applied. Notably, no margin is accorded to states as regards Articles 2 through 4 of the Convention, whereas it comes most prominently into play regarding Articles 8 through 11. The application of the doctrine—and the problems that attach to it—may be illustrated with reference to the Article 10 guarantee of freedom of expression. In this area, the Court has allowed states a relatively broad margin of appreciation as regards questions of public morals (*Handyside v. United Kingdom*, 1976) or sensitivity toward local religious sensibilities (*Otto-Preminger Institute v. Austria*, 1995).

Conversely, the margin has been markedly more circumscribed in relation to questions of disclosure in the public interest (*The Sunday Times v. United Kingdom*, 1979), political commentary (*Lingens v. Austria*, 1986), or journalistic freedom of expression (*Jersild v. Denmark*, 1994).

For proponents of the margin of appreciation, this pattern of decisions is reflective of the necessary—if necessarily difficult—balance that the Court must strike between the acceptance of legitimate national differences and the affirmation of European standards. Yet, critics of the doctrine would argue that the use of a discretionary construct of this type leads to significant inconsistencies in the Court's case law, running the risk of producing a longer term loss of legitimacy for the European human rights system as a whole.

NEW CHALLENGES

The Convention system has faced major new challenges from the 1990s onward. In the mid-1990s, the Court of Human Rights was confronted with a series of cases alleging the severe and systematic abuse of human rights by Turkish authorities in their treatment of the country's Kurdish minority. Violations of the Convention were found to have taken place in relation to allegations of torture (*Aksoy v. Turkey*, 1996), rape (*Aydin v. Turkey*, 1997), and the destruction of private homes (*Akdivar v. Turkey*, 1996). The case of *Loizidou v. Turkey* (1998), concerned with the exercise of property rights in northern Cyprus, marked the first instance in the Convention's history of a state directly refusing to comply with a judgment of the Court. The Turkish government executed the Court's judgment in the *Loizidou* case only in 2003 after protracted negotiations and the sustained application of international pressure.

The problems raised by the Turkish cases must not, however, be seen in isolation. The progressive enlargement of the Council of Europe since the end of the Cold War to encompass the vast majority of post-communist successor states in Central and Eastern Europe has markedly changed the character of the Convention community. The Court of Human Rights must now deal with a much wider diversity of both states and issues than had previously been the case in the context of an exclusively Western European system.

In particular, although many of the new contracting states have rapidly and successfully completed processes of democratic transition, other recent adherents nonetheless continue to exhibit significant structural failings regarding their ability to comply with Convention obligations. Thus, for example, in the case of *Kalashnikov v. Russia* (2002), the Court of Human Rights found typical Russian prison conditions to constitute a form of inhuman treatment in violation of the ECHR.

At the same time, the growing prominence of the European Union (EU) as a human rights actor is also posing new challenges for the Convention system. The adoption by the EU of its own declaratory Charter of Fundamental Rights in 2000, which may acquire binding force as part of a new constitutional treaty, has posed the question of the relationship between the EU and the ECHR. At the limit, one could imagine that the Luxembourg-based Court of Justice of the European Communities might, on the basis of the Charter, pursue a human rights jurisprudence that diverged significantly from that of the Strasbourg-based European Court of Human Rights. This risk should not, however, be overemphasized. Although there have been occasional divergences between the two courts in the past, the Luxembourg Court has nonetheless shown a growing awareness of Strasbourg jurisprudence. Rather, the issue at stake is more that of ensuring an overall, coherent system of European human rights protection.

At present, although the implementation of EU law by national governments may give rise to a case against the government concerned under the ECHR system (for example, *Matthews v. United Kingdom*, 1999), there is no means by which EU acts may directly be brought before the Court of Human Rights. This would be possible only if the EU itself were to become a party to the ECHR. A broad consensus now appears to exist in principle supporting this accession, but it remains for the necessary measures to be taken.

The ECHR has thus reached a historical turning point. The highly sophisticated system of regional human rights protection that emerged in Western Europe over the course of the post-World War II period must now, in the post-Cold War era, secure its position as a pan-European institution. As it strives to meet this

■ ■ ■

CONGRESS OF THE HAGUE, 1948

The Congress of the Hague, which was held between May 7 and May 11, 1948, was one of the most important events in the process leading to the formation of the European Union. The Congress was preceded by two meetings in July and November 1947, in which four different groups advocating closer relationships among European governments first merged and then renamed themselves the Joint International Committee for European Unity.

The Committee organized the 1948 Congress at the Hague and invited eight hundred delegates from twenty European countries as well as observers from Canada and the United States. There were three major committees at the Congress, which discussed cultural, economic and social, and political issues, respectively. The committees then drafted

resolutions calling for such measures as a common European currency and economic union as well as the formation of an international court and a charter of human rights. These resolutions were submitted to the delegates in three plenary sessions and formally adopted by the Congress. Five months later, the Joint International Committee for European Unity officially changed its name to the European Movement.

The delegates to the 1948 Congress included notable figures in the arts and literature as well as politicians. In addition to well-known political leaders such as Winston Churchill, Harold Macmillan, Konrad Adenauer, François Mitterrand, and Paul-Henri Spaak, the Congress was attended by philosophers (Raymond Aron and Bertrand Russell), novelists (Ignazio Silone), and poets (Willem Asselbergs).

challenge, the ECHR system will continue to be of central interest to students of both international human rights and European integration.

See also: European Court of Human Rights; European Union; Human Rights; International Human Rights Law.

BIBLIOGRAPHY

Blackburn, Robert, and Jörg Polakiewicz, eds. *Fundamental Rights in Europe: The ECHR and Its Member States, 1950–2000*. Oxford, UK: Oxford University Press, 2001.

Council of Europe. <http://www.coe.int/DefaultEN.asp>.

European Court of Human Rights. <http://www.echr.coe.int/>.

Harris, David J., Michael O' Boyle, and Colin Warbrick. *Law of the European Convention on Human Rights*. London: Butterworths, 1995.

Jackson, Donald W. *The United Kingdom Confronts the European Convention on Human Rights*. Gainesville: The University Press of Florida, 1997.

Janis, Mark, Richard Kay, and Anthony Bradley. *European Human Rights Law: Text and Materials*. 2nd ed. Oxford, UK: Oxford University Press, 2000.

Merrills, John G., and Arthur H. Robertson. *Human Rights in Europe: A Study of the European Convention on Human Rights*. Manchester, UK: Manchester University Press, 2001.

Mowbray, Alastair. *Cases and Materials on the European Convention on Human Rights*. London: Butterworths, 2001.

Ovey, Claire, and Robin C.A. White. *European Convention on Human Rights*, 3rd ed. Oxford, UK: Oxford University Press, 2002.

Robert Harmsen

European Court of Human Rights

The European Court of Human Rights is an institution of the Council of Europe (CoE), based in Strasbourg, France. The Court is the supervisory institution established by the 1950 European Convention on Human Rights (ECHR). Initially, the Court, together with the European Commission of Human Rights, formed part of a two-tier institutional system. These two part-time institutions were replaced by a single-tier, full-time European Court of Human Rights in 1998. The Court is composed of one judge elected in right of each of the CoE's forty-six member states.

Reflecting the reservations of national governments, the Convention originally provided for only a comparatively limited **compulsory** system of supervision. States, in **ratifying** the ECHR, had only to accept a right of interstate complaint. Under the terms of this mechanism, any state party to the Convention could bring a case before the European Commission of Human Rights against any other state party. The Commission, after taking evidence, would then transmit its opinion to the CoE's Committee of Ministers for a decision (the finding of a violation requiring a two-thirds majority among the members of the Committee).

The Convention, however, also provided for the possibility of states accepting a more robust system of control. Article 25 of the ECHR set out an optional provision, whereby states could accept the right of individual **petition**. Following a state's acceptance of this mechanism, any person, non-governmental organization (NGO), or group of individuals who deemed themselves to have been the victim(s) of a violation of the rights guaranteed by the Convention could lodge a petition with the

compulsory: mandatory, required, or unable to be avoided

ratify: to make official or to officially sanction

petition: a written appeal for a desired action, or, to request an action, especially of government

TABLE 1

Member States of the Council of Europe

Date of membership in parentheses.

Albania (July 13, 1995)
Andorra (November 10, 1994)
Armenia (January 25, 2001)
Austria (April 16, 1956)
Azerbaijan (January 25, 2001)
Belgium (May 5, 1949)
Bosnia and Herzegovina (April 24, 2002)
Bulgaria (July 5,1992)
Croatia (November 6, 1996)
Cyprus (May 24, 1961)
Czech Republic (June 30, 1993)
Denmark (May 5, 1949)
Estonia (May 14, 1993)
Finland (May 5, 1989)
France (May 5, 1949)
Georgia (April 27, 1999)
Germany (July 13, 1950)
Greece (August 9, 1949)
Hungary (November 6, 1990)
Iceland (March 7, 1950)
Ireland (May 5, 1949)
Italy (May 5, 1949)
Latvia (February 10, 1995)
Liechtenstein (November 23, 1978)
Lithuania (May 14, 1993)
Luxembourg (May 5, 1949)
Malta (April 29, 1965)
Moldova (July 13, 1995)
Monaco (October 5, 2004)
Netherlands (May 5, 1949)
Norway (May 5, 1949)
Poland (November 26, 1991)
Portugal (September 22, 1976)
Romania (October 7, 1993)
Russian Federation (February 28, 1996)
San Marino (November 16, 1988)
Serbia and Montenegro (April 3, 2003)
Slovakia (June 30, 1993)
Slovenia (May 14, 1993)
Spain (November 24, 1977)
Sweden (May 5, 1949)
Switzerland (May 6, 1963)
Former Yugoslav Republic of Macedonia
    (November 9, 1995)
Turkey (August 9, 1949)
Ukraine (November 9, 1995)
United Kingdom (May 5, 1949)

SOURCE: Adapted from *The Council of Europe's Member States*. Council of Europe. <http://www.coe.int/DefaultEN.asp>.

---

polarize: to separate individuals into adversarial groups

docket: a list or schedule of cases to be heard by a court

Commission. The admissibility of such petitions was made subject to a number of conditions, including the exhaustion of domestic remedies. Article 46 of the ECHR provided for the optional acceptance by state parties of the jurisdiction of the European Court of Human Rights. This provision allowed, after the delivery of the Commission's opinion, for the referral of a case to the Court rather than to the Committee of Ministers. The referral could be made either by the Commission itself or a state party concerned. The initial acceptance of the optional provisions was something of a patchwork, with member states variously accepting one or both of the articles. Nevertheless, in the long term, there was a clear trend toward generalized acceptance of the full system of control. From 1989 on the ratification of the ECHR, together with the immediate acceptance of both Articles 25 and 46, became a condition of admission to the CoE for new member states.

Nevertheless, the very success of the ECHR system in establishing itself engendered new problems. Already in the early 1980s, the growing caseload of the Commission and (to a lesser extent) the Court led to extensive discussions concerning the possible reform of the system. The reform discussions centered around two competing institutional projects. On the one hand, the initial phase of discussions was dominated by a Swiss-inspired proposal for the merger of the two supervisory institutions, creating a single-tier, full-time Court. On the other hand, the Dutch and Swedish governments advanced a counterproposal that sought to preserve the existing two-tier system, while upgrading the status of the Commission so as to become a fully judicial institution in its own right (empowered to render final decisions, rather than only advisory opinions). After a period of increasingly **polarized** negotiations, a compromise was finally reached between proponents of the two plans at a meeting in Stockholm in May 1993. The Stockholm Compromise, which formed the basis for the Eleventh Protocol to the ECHR, mandated the creation of a single-tier Court structure, but provided for the rehearing of cases within that unitary structure.

Protocol No. 11 to the ECHR was opened for signature in 1994 and entered into force in 1998. While leaving the rights guaranteed by the ECHR untouched, it effected a major reform of the Convention's structures. A single, full-time Court was established, while the right of individual petition was made an integral part of the Convention. Under the new procedures, individual petitions are first reviewed by a committee of three judges, who may unanimously declare an application inadmissible. Cases passing this initial hurdle will then normally be heard by a seven-member chamber of the Court. However, a provision also exists for a seventeen-member grand chamber of the Court to hear cases of exceptional importance—either when a chamber has relinquished jurisdiction or, on a discretionary basis, after a chamber judgment. The Committee of Ministers no longer plays any role in the decision-making process, although it remains responsible for supervising the execution of judgments. Relative to the previous system, Protocol No. 11 may thus be seen to have created a more streamlined process, as well as fully securing the judicial character of the system. The rather awkward provisions that govern the rehearing of cases within a single court (where the national judge and the chamber president will sit at both stages of the case) have, however, been the subject of strong criticism.

Although the new system has resulted in a substantial increase in the number of cases dealt with every year, it has not been able to keep pace with the demands placed on the Convention system. The steady increase in the number of petitions from longstanding member states, coupled with the expanding volume of cases from post-Communist states that have joined the CoE since the end of the Cold War, has produced an almost exponential growth in the Court's **docket**. Almost 41,000 applications were lodged with the Court in 2004. By way

PRESIDENT-ELECT LUZIUS WILDHABER OF SWITZERLAND (RIGHT) AT THE INAUGURATION OF THE REVAMPED EUROPEAN COURT OF HUMAN RIGHTS (ECHR) ON NOVEMBER 3, 1998. The ECHR hears violations from citizens of its 46 member states and is comprised of a matching number of judges. Consolidated by an amendment in 1997 to a single unit, the court is divided into four sections that are headed by section presidents while the entire body is overseen by a president. (SOURCE: AP/WIDE WORLD PHOTOS)

of comparison, the Strasbourg institutions, in the entire period from 1955 to 1988, had addressed approximately 44,000 such petitions.

Faced with this increasingly unmanageable volume of business, discussions concerning further reform of the Court started very shortly after the entry into force of Protocol No. 11. Following a series of evaluation reports and expert recommendations, Protocol No. 14 to the ECHR was opened for signature in May 2004. If the protocol is ratified by all state parties, admissibility decisions may be made by a single judge, while repetitive cases (those that concern recurring patterns of violations, where the points of law are already clearly established) may be dealt with by a three-member committee of judges. New possibilities also will be created for the Committee of Ministers to bring matters directly before the Court, in the interest of a better enforcement of decisions. Most controversially, Protocol No. 14 would additionally establish a new admissibility criterion, whereby the Court may choose not to hear a case when it is deemed that the petitioner has not suffered a "significant disadvantage" that no general issue under the ECHR is raised by the case; and that the case has received due consideration by a domestic tribunal.

The new admissibility criterion potentially introduced by Protocol No. 14 acutely raised the more general question of the future direction of the Strasbourg

redress: to make right, or, compensation

Court. Prominent voices within the Court have argued that it must strategically limit its docket, redefining itself as a constitutional court concerned primarily with establishing general principles of human rights law. Equally prominent voices have, however, conversely argued that the very essence of the system lies in its ability to provide effective **redress** in all meritorious cases. The Court must thus confront the dilemma of balancing the expectations of individual petitioners against the broader demands of its institutional role. The future of the European Court of Human Rights will largely be shaped by where, and how successfully, this balance is struck.

See also: European Convention on Human Rights and Fundamental Freedoms; Human Rights.

BIBLIOGRAPHY

Blackburn, Robert, and Jörg Polakiewicz, eds. *Fundamental Rights in Europe: The ECHR and Its Member States, 1950–2000.* Oxford, UK: Oxford University Press, 2001.

The Council of Europe's Member States. Council of Europe. <http://www.coe.int/DefaultEN.asp>.

European Court of Human Rights. <http://www.echr.coe.int/>.

Harris, David J., Michael O' Boyle, and Colin Warbrick. *Law of the European Convention on Human Rights.* London: Butterworths, 1995.

Janis, Mark, Richard Kay, and Anthony Bradley. *European Human Rights Law: Text and Materials,* 2nd ed. Oxford, UK: Oxford University Press, 2000.

Merrills, John G., and Arthur H. Robertson. *Human Rights in Europe: A Study of the European Convention on Human Rights.* Manchester, UK: Manchester University Press, 2001.

Mowbray, Alastair. *Cases and Materials on the European Convention on Human Rights.* London: Butterworths, 2001.

Ovey, Claire, and Robin C. A. White. *The European Convention on Human Rights,* 3rd ed. Oxford, UK: Oxford University Press, 2002.

Robert Harmsen

European Court of Justice

federalism: a system of political organization, in which separate states or groups are ruled by a dominant central authority on some matters, but are otherwise permitted to govern themselves independently

The European Court of Justice (ECJ), which is seated in Luxembourg, is the highest court of the legal order of the European Union (EU). It has developed a **federal** constitutional architecture for the EU. This architecture includes the principles of supremacy and direct effect for European Community rules on national legal orders, the protection of fundamental rights, the expansion of Community competences, and the understanding of the European Community as a "community of law." The ECJ does not interpret the European Community treaties simply as an agreement between states but as having been created for the "peoples of Europe." In landmark decisions such as Van Gend & Loos (1963) and Francovich (1991) the ECJ contributed to the process of European integration while at the same time protecting the legal positions of individual citizens vis-à-vis the member states. For some, this has made the ECJ the hero of European integration, and for others, the villain.

The creation of a European legal order was only possible through the cooperation of different national actors, in particular the national courts. This cooperation was fundamental in both promoting the developments of the

European legal order and securing its legitimacy. The ECJ is open to questions posed by national courts and often relies on national legal traditions when interpreting Community rules. The national courts in requesting and applying rulings from the ECJ provide ECJ decisions with the same authority as national judicial decisions. In this light, the judicial system of the EU should, in effect, be described as composed of both the European courts, which consist of the ECJ and a **Court of First Instance** (CFI), and the national courts responsible for the application of EU law in national proceedings.

court of first instance: the first or lowest court in which a case or suit can be decided

COMPOSITION OF THE COURT OF JUSTICE

The ECJ and the CFI each consist of one judge per member state, which means that there are twenty-five judges on each court. The ECJ is also composed of eight advocates general who are members of the court with the same status as judges. Therefore, in total, the ECJ is composed of thirty-three members. Every three years, in the ECJ as well as in the CFI, the judges elect the president of their court from among their numbers for a renewable term of three years.

Cases coming to the ECJ are distributed to different chambers, usually composed of three or five judges. A case will be decided by the grand chamber—consisting of thirteen judges with a quorum of nine—when the ECJ considers this appropriate or when this is requested by a Member State or a European institution that is party to the proceedings. Only in extraordinary cases will the ECJ sit as a full court. The quorum for the full court is fifteen.

The members of the ECJ (judges and advocates general) are appointed for a term of six years by common accord of the member states. Often they previously held high political or administrative offices or were senior members of the national judiciary, academics, or practicing lawyers. Court rules provide that their independence "shall be beyond doubt." Observers of the court conclude that this rule is obeyed and that, rather than being representatives of their national governments, the judges are remarkably "European-minded."

To protect the perceived independence of the judges, judgments are delivered as collegiate decisions without separate concurring or dissenting opinions.

THE ROLE OF THE ADVOCATE GENERAL

The ECJ is assisted in its work by eight advocates general. Each case that is filed in the ECJ is assigned to one of the advocates general. After the parties have made their submissions to the Court, the advocate general publicly delivers an impartial and independent opinion on how, in the advocate general's view, the case at hand should be resolved. The opinion does not bind the Court, and the advocate general does not take part in the subsequent deliberations. However, the advocates general have an important influence on the development of Community law and their opinions form an integral part of the Court's **jurisprudence**. Only when the Court considers that a case raises no new point of law, it may decide, at the end of the written part of the proceedings, to determine the case without the advocate general's opinion.

jurisprudence: the body of precedents already decided in a legal system

JURISDICTION OF THE COURT OF JUSTICE

The **jurisdiction** of the ECJ mainly follows from provisions of the EU Treaty and the European Community Treaty. It is the European Community Treaty that established the ECJ. The ECJ can review the legality of decisions of the

jurisdiction: the territory or area within which authority may be exercised

European Community institutions and may annul them or declare them invalid if they are not in conformity with higher rules of Community law. In addition, the Court has an important role in enforcing EU law in the member states and may even impose liability for violations of EU law and penalty payments if member states do not remedy their **infringements**. Perhaps most important, the Court assists national judicial bodies in interpreting Community law.

Because the EU Treaty borrows the institutions from the European Community, the ECJ is part of the single institutional framework of the EU. However, in the policy areas covered by the EU Treaty—notably the common foreign and security policy and police and judicial cooperation in criminal matters—the role of the ECJ is limited.

ACTIONS BEFORE THE COURT OF JUSTICE

The ECJ is authorized by the European Community Treaty to hear preliminary references and direct actions. Preliminary references are sent to the Court by national judicial bodies who, in proceedings before them, encounter a problem of

infringe: to exceed the limits of; to violate

THE EUROPEAN COURT OF JUSTICE, LOCATED IN THE KIRCHBERG, LUXEMBOURG. Acting as the judicial branch for the European Union (EU) since 1957, the European Court of Justice (ECJ) is assembled from one judge from each member state, selected for a six-year term, and eight advocates general. (SOURCE: AP/WIDE WORLD PHOTOS)

interpretation or application of Community law. Direct actions are brought before the Court by a member state, an institution, or a private individual. The direct actions are the infringement procedure, the action for annulment, the action for failure to act and the action for damages.

Under the infringement procedure member states can be forced to comply with Community law. The defendant in this procedure is always a member state. The action can be brought by one member state against another, but normally it is brought by the Commission. The infringement procedure is an important way for the Commission, the institution that is at the centre of the management of the EU system, to perform its role as "guardian of the Treaties." A significant proportion of the infringement procedure cases regards the timely and proper implementation of directives. The outcome of a successful Court action is a declaratory judgment that a state has committed an infringement. If a member state fails to remedy the infringement, the Commission, in a subsequent procedure, may ask the Court to impose a monetary penalty. Some have voiced skepticism about the cumbersome procedure that eventually leads to the imposition of a penalty and about the scenario that would unwind if a member state refuses to pay. In practice, however, most disputes are settled during the procedure the Commission is obliged to follow before it may refer the matter to the Court.

Reviews of the legality of Community acts and omissions occur through the action for annulment and the action for failure to act. Article 230 of the European Community Treaty offers the possibility of an action for annulment to challenge the legality of any Community act (other than an act of the ECJ itself) that has binding force. If the action is well-founded, the Court can declare the act void in whole or in part. As a general rule the act is then considered never to have existed.

Parallel to the action for annulment is the action for failure to act. The applicant must demonstrate that there was an obligation to act and that, even after having been called on, the institution concerned failed to do so. If the action is successful, the Court will pronounce a declaratory judgment to the effect that the defendant institution must take measures.

Member states, institutions, and private applicants may in principle all bring an action for annulment, but different conditions for standing to do so apply depending on the identity of the applicant. There are three categories of applicants: privileged, semi-privileged and nonprivileged. The Council, the institution in which government ministers meet to reconcile national interests and enact EU legislation, is a privileged applicant. So are the European parliament, the Commission, and the member states. They have standing to challenge any act regardless whether they can demonstrate an interest in bringing the action. The Court of Auditors and the European Central Bank are semi-privileged applicants. They have standing whenever their prerogatives are in issue.

All other applicants, including regional or local governments, fall within the category of nonprivileged applicants. Their actions for annulment are only admissible if the act challenged directly affects their interests. Consequently, it is extraordinarily difficult for a private applicant to challenge more general legislative measures through the action for annulment. The Court has often been urged to alter its stance on the strict requirement of individual concern but thus far to no avail.

Liability of the Community: The Action for Damages. Article 288 of the European Community Treaty governs claims for compensation for damage against the Community. In cases arising from contractual liability the court applies the law that is applicable to the contract according to the rules of private international law. In noncontractual liability cases—in which the Court has exclusive jurisdiction—the Court applies rules that it has developed from national legal traditions.

The rules on admissibility are considerably more lenient for the action for damages than they are for the action for annulment. An action for damages may be brought up until five years after the damage occurred, and the identity of the appellant sets no limits on admissibility. However, the substantive criteria for establishing Community liability can be very strict.

THE PRELIMINARY REFERENCE PROCEDURE

Under Article 234 of the European Community Treaty a national court may refer a question to the ECJ on the interpretation of a Community rule whenever it considers it necessary to give a judgment in a case pending before it. Courts against whose decisions there are no appeals are obliged to stay the case and refer the question to the ECJ. Because of its increased workload, however, the ECJ has put forward a set of criteria that may excuse national courts from the obligation to refer a case to the ECJ when the question to be raised has been effectively answered in a previous decision of the ECJ. When the national proceedings require the national court to determine the validity of a Community act, those national courts are obliged to refer the question to the ECJ. Only this court can decide on the validity of the Community act.

The preliminary reference procedure performs a pivotal function in the European Community legal system. It forges a direct relationship between the ECJ and the national courts, who may have to set aside national law when Community law is relied on by parties before them.

THE ECJ AND FUNDAMENTAL RIGHTS

Although the ECJ is often labelled the "constitutional court" of the EU, its role in respect to the protection of fundamental human rights is not equivalent to that of federal constitutional courts of, for example, Germany or the United States because the "basic constitutional charter" (the European Community Treaty), although imparting rules and competences that ultimately could affect fundamental rights, has a limited scope and purpose. As a result, the ECJ can only undertake human rights review in cases that fall within the scope of Community law—and even that definition of the Court's role was established by case law, in recognition of the tenet that the application of those treaties would have to occur in conformity with fundamental human rights. This case-law was codified as follows in Article 6 of the EU Treaty in 1992:

> The Union shall respect fundamental rights, as guaranteed by the European Convention for the Protection of Human Rights and Fundamental Freedoms signed in Rome on 4 November 1950 and as they result from the constitutional traditions common to the Member States, as general principles of Community law.

In 2000 a Charter of Fundamental Rights was adopted but without legally binding effect. Still, the Charter may have a guiding value in determining the fundamental rights that correspond to the common constitutional traditions of the member states.

Fundamental Rights and the Member States. The reasons why the role of the ECJ regarding fundamental rights is the topic of continuing political and academic debate are numerous and closely related. The issue is important and sensitive when actions or legislation of a member state are at stake. It raises the following question: To what extent do fundamental rights, as general principles of Community law, impose limits and obligations on member states? The case *Grogan* (1991) may serve as illustration.

In *Grogan* the ECJ was confronted with an Irish prohibition to assist pregnant women in Ireland to obtain abortions by informing them of the location of abortion clinics abroad. When various student associations distributed information about the availability of legal abortion in the United Kingdom, an anti-abortion organization instituted legal proceedings against them and requested an injunction restraining the distribution. In their defense, the student associations argued that a ban would contravene their right to freedom of expression and that it would impair the freedom to provide and receive services (in breach of Article 43 European Community). The High Court of Ireland referred the matter to the ECJ for a preliminary ruling. Before the ECJ could examine the argument relating to freedom of expression, it had to determine whether the case raised an issue of Community law. According to the ECJ, it did not. This, in turn, meant that the Court could not examine the argument relating to freedom of expression. Some have criticized the judgment in *Grogan*, claiming that the ECJ adopted a narrow view of the scope of Article 43 European Community to avoid difficult questions on abortion and the freedom of expression.

Fundamental Rights and the European Institutions. The main focus of the human rights debate is not on the member states, but on the European institutions themselves. Here the wider context of the EU's perceived lack of democratic legitimacy is apparent. While often contested in democratic terms, the EU has the power to adopt legislation that supersedes national laws and constitutions. There consequently needed to be a guarantee that the EU would not threaten the fundamental rights usually protected at the level of the member states. Even though the original treaties made no reference to fundamental rights, the ECJ held in *Stauder* (1969) and subsequent cases that it would protect those rights. This currently has a firm basis in Article 6 EU. Nevertheless, Article 6 EU hardly settles the debate on human rights in the EU. The member states appear to be in consensus that the Charter of Fundamental Rights should be incorporated in binding EU law and that the EU itself should become party to the European Convention of Human Rights (ECHR) which could make its actions subject to scrutiny by the European Court of Human Rights.

DIVISION OF TASKS BETWEEN THE ECJ AND THE CFI

Although the Court of Justice of the European Communities is one institution, it in fact consists of two Courts: the ECJ and the CFI. The CFI was created in 1989 to help relieve the ECJ of its case load and originally served as a court of first instance for direct actions brought by natural or legal persons against the Community institutions. The division of competences has become considerably more complex.

Nevertheless, with some exceptions, the general rule still applies that the CFI is competent for actions brought by natural and legal persons (e.g., an action for damages against the Community), whereas the ECJ has jurisdiction in preliminary rulings and actions brought by the member states, institutions, or the European Central Bank. The ECJ functions as a court of appeal against decisions of the CFI.

CASE LOAD AND LENGTH OF PROCEEDINGS

According to legend, on the day that the first preliminary reference made by a national judicial body was received—in 1961, almost four years after the Court was established—there was abundant popping of champagne corks in the **deliberation** room. In the early twenty-first century the Court receives well over 200 references per year—a number that is expected to increase significantly as a result of the enlargement of the EU from fifteen to twenty-five member states. The average length of the preliminary ruling procedure is approximately two years—a disquieting statistic as the procedure is an incident staying the national main proceedings. Preliminary references account for about half of the case load of the ECJ. Direct actions and appeals account for the other half. In total, more than 500 proceedings were brought before the ECJ in 2004, while at the end of that year nearly 900 cases were still pending. In addition, well over 500 direct actions were initiated before CFI, and 1,000 cases were pending at the end of 2004.

See also: European Court of Human Rights; European Union.

BIBLIOGRAPHY

Alter, Karen J. "The European Court's Political Power." *West-European-Politics* 19 (1996): 458–487.

Dehousse, Renaud. *The European Court of Justice: The Politics of Judicial Integration*. New York: St. Martin's Press, 1998.

Gibson, James L., and Gregory Caldeira. "Changes in the Legitimacy of the European Court of Justice: A Post-Maastricht Analysis." *British Journal of Political Science* 28 (1998):63–91.

Hartley, Trevor C. *The Foundations of European Community Law*, 5th ed. Oxford, UK: Oxford University Press, 2003.

Kenney, Sally J. "Beyond Principals and Agents: Seeing Courts as Organizations by Comparing Referendaires at the European Court of Justice and Law Clerks at the U.S. Supreme Court." *Comparative Political Studies* 33 (2000):593–625.

Mancini, G. F. *Democracy and Constitutionalism in the European Union*. Oxford, UK: Hart, 2000.

Mattli, W., and A. Slaughter. "Revisiting The European Court of Justice." *International Organization*. 52 (1998):177–210.

Poiares Maduro, Miguel. "Contrapunctual Law: Europe's Constitutional Pluralism in Action." In *Sovereignty in Transition*, ed. Neil Walker. Oxford, UK: Hart, 2003.

Schermers, H.G. and Waelbroeck, D.F. *Judicial Protection in the European Union*. New York: Kluwer Law International, 2001.

Stone Sweet, Alec, and T. Brunell. "The European Court and the National Courts: A Statistical Analysis of Preliminary References, 1961–65." *Journal of European Public Policy* 5 (1998):66–97.

Tridimas, P. "The Role of the Advocate General in the Development of Community Law: Some Reflections." *Common Market Law Review* 34 (1997):1349–1378.

Volcansek, Mary L. "The European Court of Justice: Supranational Policy Making." *West European Politics* 15 (1992):109–21.

Miguel Poiares Maduro

---

deliberate: to present contradicting arguments and choose a common course of action based upon them, or, characterized by such careful discussion

European Economic Community

See European Union.

European Microstates

Andorra, Liechtenstein, Monaco, and San Marino qualify as microstates, and each is nestled in a different part of Europe. The total population of the four slightly exceeds 150,000, and Andorra accounts for almost 69,000. Their geographic sizes are also small: Andorra occupies 464 square kilometers (179 square miles); Liechtenstein, 160 square kilometers (62 square miles); San Marino, 61 square kilometers (24 square miles); and Monaco, only 1.95 square kilometers (0.75 square miles). What is remarkable about the four is that each has managed to retain its sovereignty and its national character, despite being squeezed by larger neighbors. Andorra is a wedge of land between Spain and France, San Marino is surrounded by Italy, Monaco is located near the southeastern part of France, and Liechtenstein sits between Switzerland and Austria.

Monaco is the smallest of the four, but is larger than the Vatican. Now a constitutional monarchy, it has been in the control of the Grimaldi family since the thirteenth century. Up until 2002, the throne was inherited through the male line; since Prince Rainer III's (1923–2005) son, Albert, had no male heir, he adjusted the constitution to allow his daughters to inherit the throne. San Marino claims to be the world's oldest republic, tracing its founding to the third century and its republican form of government to the thirteenth century. Liechtenstein was recognized as a principality in 1719 but was absorbed and later separated from other entities until 1866, when it achieved its full national sovereignty. It is a constitutional hereditary monarchy and has been, since 1921, a parliamentary democracy. Andorra has existed continually since 1288 and was governed by the founding feudal judgments until 1993, when a democratic constitution was written.

All four microstates are strongly influenced by the nations that surround them. For example, Italian is spoken in San Marino, French in Monaco, German in Liechtenstein, and Catalan—the language of a neighboring region of Spain—in Andorra. In all three nations, however, a multiplicity of languages are commonly spoken, which demonstrates the porous nature of their boundaries and cultures.

Both Liechtenstein and Andorra have carved out an economic niche in the fields of banking and finance. San Marino relies more heavily on tourism and the sale of commemorative stamps and coins of interest to collectors. Monaco depends entirely upon income from tourism, real estate, financial services, and small, non-polluting industry. All four have entered

(MAP BY MARYLAND CARTOGRAPHICS/THE GALE GROUP)

(MAP BY MARYLAND CARTOGRAPHICS/THE GALE GROUP)

(MAP BY MARYLAND CARTOGRAPHICS/THE GALE GROUP)

(MAP BY MARYLAND CARTOGRAPHICS/THE GALE GROUP)

into a number of international treaty obligations, and although all have some associated relationship with the European Union, none is a full member. All four are sovereign nations, although San Marino has relinquished some rights to Italy, for which the Italian government pays an annual subsidy.

All four of these mini-states have undergone some significant political or constitutional changes in the last decades of the twentieth century. For example, Andorra adopted a new constitution in 1993 that for the first time legalized political parties and trade unions and harmonized legislation with international treaties. It retained a head of state arrangement that includes co-princes, the president of the Republic of France, and the Catalan bishop of the Roman Catholic Church, but real power is exercised by the head of government who is elected by the Andorran parliament. The new constitution also provided for a constitutional court that can review legislation for constitutionality.

HUMAN RIGHTS

San Marino, Liechtenstein, Monaco, and Andorra are all signatories to the European Convention on Human Rights and Fundamental Freedoms and members of the Council of Europe. They have all, with some reservations, accepted the jurisdiction of the European Court of Human Rights. Andorra is continuing, as part of its democratization process, to move closer to complying with international norms on human rights. Freedom House, an independent advocacy foundation, gives Andorra, Liechenstein, and San Marino its highest ratings as completely free nations; Monaco is also rated as free, with perfect civil liberties and nearly perfect political rights.

See also: European Convention on Human Rights and Fundamental Freedoms; Malta; Vatican.

BIBLIOGRAPHY

Duursma, Jorri. *Fragmentation and the International Relations of Micro-States: Self-Determination and Statehood.* New York: Cambridge University Press, 1996.

Hemmerle, Norbert. *Liechtenstein—Principality in the Heart of Europe.* Vaduz, Liechtenstein: Press and Information Office, 2000.

Freedom House. "Table of Independent Countries." *Freedom in the World 2005.* New York: Freedom House, 2005. <http://www.freedom house.org/research/freeworld/2005/countryratings/ table2005.pdf>.

Kritzer, Herbert M. "San Marino." *Legal Systems of the World,* ed. Herbert M. Kritzer. Santa Barbara, CA: ABC-CLIO, 2002.

"Monaco." *Worldmark Encyclopedia of the Nations,* 11th edition. Detroit, MI: Gale, 2004. *Student Resource Center.* <http://galenet. galegroup.com/servlet/SRC>.

Poblet, Marta. "Andorra." *Legal Systems of the World,* ed. Herbert M. Kritzer. Santa Barbara, CA: ABC-CLIO, 2002.

"Prince Rainier III, Chief of State of Monaco." *Worldmark Encyclopedia of the Nations: World Leaders.* Detroit, MI: Gale, 2003. *Student Resource Center.* <http://galenet.galegroup.com/servlet/SRC>.

Walch, Ernst J. "Liechtenstein." *Legal Systems of the World*, ed. Herbert M. Kritzer. Santa Barbara, CA: ABC-CLIO, 2002.

Mary L. Volcansek

European Parliament

Parliaments are the central institutions in European systems of representative democracy. Traditionally, the idea that parliament is at the core of democracy has been intertwined with the existence of the independent **nation-state**. Although international organizations often also have assemblies of national representatives, these are not directly elected and they mainly function as consultative bodies without any legislative powers.

Reflecting the mix of **intergovernmental** and **supranational** modes of governance in the European Union (EU), the European Parliament (EP) is directly elected and has considerable influence over policy making, but is deprived of many of the powers that have traditionally been the prerogative of the parliaments at the national level. The EP lacks the right of legislative initiative, it largely holds no formal powers in those policy areas that within the EU are still based on intergovernmental bargaining (such as foreign policy), and it has no influence in policy areas that fall outside of the competence of the EU altogether (such as taxation or the core policies of the **welfare state**).

However, the Parliament nonetheless possesses significant powers in the EU's political system. The Parliament has enjoyed the right to dismiss the entire commission since its inception in the 1950s, provided that an **absolute** majority of members and two-thirds of the votes cast support a no-confidence motion. The Maastricht Treaty (signed in 1992) also gave the Parliament the right to approve the entire commission with a simple majority of votes cast. Testing its new powers after the 1994 elections, the chamber first held a vote on Jacques Santer, the European Council's candidate for commission president, who only narrowly escaped defeat. The Parliament then subjected the prospective commissioners to detailed hearings in its committees. Finally, the Parliament gave its approval to the commission. In this way, the Parliament itself established the practice formally introduced by the Amsterdam Treaty (signed in 1997), according to which a commission president must receive the support of the EP before assembling his or her team of commissioners. The Parliament is also consulted on the appointment of members to the Court of Auditors, and the president and board of the European Central Bank.

The legislative influence of the Parliament varies considerably between policy areas. The consultation procedure is the oldest legislative process. Under this procedure, the role of the EP is advisory, that is, it must be heard but its opinions are not binding on the commission or the Council. The Single European Act (SEA, signed in 1986) introduced the cooperation procedure. From 1987 to 1999 it covered a broad set of policy areas, including much of the internal market legislation. The procedure provided the EP with a limited ability to amend or veto commission proposals. SEA also introduced the assent procedure that applies only to a small but important number of issues, such as the incorporation of new member

nation-state: a relatively homogeneous state with only one or few nationalities within its political borders

intergovernmental: between or involving multiple governments, with each government retaining full decision-making power

supranational: between or involving multiple governments, with all governments sharing control, usually through independent representatives and majority rule

welfare state: a political state that assumes liability for the wellbeing of its people through government-run social programs

absolute: complete, pure, free from restriction or limitation

states into the EU and certain international agreements. Under this procedure, the EP cannot change the proposal, but its support is required for the proposal to be adopted. The Maastricht Treaty introduced the codecision procedure. The procedure involves two readings, and if the Council and EP fail to reach an agreement, the matter is referred to a conciliation committee composed of an equal number of Council and EP representatives. The codecision procedure currently applies to most of the issues previously decided by the cooperation procedure. Hence, the extended application of the codecision procedure means that the EU is gradually moving toward a **bicameral** system, in which the Council represents the states and the EP the peoples of Europe.

In terms of its economic power, the Parliament can amend and veto the annual EU budget. However, its budgetary rights are restricted to the so-called noncompulsory expenditure, which covers approximately half of the EU's budget. Moreover, the Parliament must respect the multiannual financial frameworks (budget ceilings) decided by the national governments. Nevertheless, the Parliament has within these limits forced the Council to accept increases in several policy areas, including education, job training, culture, and social and employment policies.

INTERNAL ORGANIZATION AND ELECTIONS

In the last few decades of the twentieth century and the early years of the twentieth-first century, committees have become increasingly powerful within European national legislatures, both in terms of legislative work and control of the executive. This development is primarily explained by the need to acquire policy expertise through **sectoral specialization**. The same applies to the Parliament. Committees process all legislative initiatives considered by the EP, and this consideration is based on the work of a **rapporteur** whose task is to produce a draft report on the proposal.

The EP party system is primarily based on the left–right dimension. The main groups are officially the parliamentary groups of their Euro-parties: social democrats (Party of European Socialists, PES), conservatives/Christian democrats (European People's Party, PP), liberals (European Liberal, Democrat and Reform Party), and the greens (European Green Party). PES and EPP have been the two dominant groups, controlling more than half of the seats after each election. A notable discontinuity exists among the smaller groups, which have tended to be rather loose **coalitions**. The composition of the smaller groups often undergoes significant changes during a five-year electoral term.

The position of the Parliament can be undermined by its failure to connect with European peoples. Direct elections to the Parliament are almost exclusively heralded as a disappointment by both the media and political scientists. Before the first elections held in 1979, a wide range of Members of the European Parliament (MEPs) and federalists entertained high hopes for the forthcoming unique experiment in supranational democracy. However, their optimistic expectations have largely failed to materialize. Turnout in Euro-elections has steadily fallen since the first elections, and various public opinion surveys suggest that only a small minority of EU citizens possesses even an elementary understanding of the powers and work of the Parliament. In the fifth round of elections in June 1999 only 49.8 percent of 289 million eligible voters bothered to cast their votes. Turnout tends to be high only in those member states with **compulsory** voting or when elections are held concurrently with elections to the national parliament. Although the initial

bicameral: comprised of two chambers, usually a legislative body

sectoral specialization: the ability of a country to organize its economy in such a way that it dominates or performs better in a specific sector

rapporteur: one that reports on a committee's work

coalition: an alliance, partnership, or union of disparate peoples or individuals

compulsory: mandatory, required, or unable to be avoided

STRASBOURG, FRANCE'S LOUISE WEISS BUILDING OF THE EUROPEAN PARLIAMENT. In 1999 the newly-constructed Louise Weiss Building replaced the Palace of Europe as the European Parliament's home in Strasbourg, France for its monthly one-week plenary meetings. (SOURCE: © ARCHITECTURE STUDIO/VINCENT KESSLER/REUTERS/CORBIS)

expectations regarding turnout were probably unrealistic, the main concern for the EP is the fact that turnout has declined at the same time as the legislative powers of the Parliament have considerably increased.

See also: European Union; Parliamentary Systems; Political Parties.

BIBLIOGRAPHY

Corbett, Richard, Francis Jacobs, and Michael Shackleton. *The European Parliament,* 5th ed. London: J. Harper, 2003.

Hix, Simon, and Roger Scully, eds. "The European Parliament at Fifty." *Special Issue of the Journal of Common Market Studies* 41 (2003):2.

Judge, David, and David Earnshaw. *The European Parliament.* London: Palgrave, 2003.

Kreppel, Amie. *The European Parliament and the Supranational Party System: A Study of Institutional Development.* Cambridge, UK: Cambridge University Press, 2002.

Tapio Raunio

European Union

The European Union (EU) is a grouping of states from Western, Eastern, and Central Europe. Those interested in politics view the EU with great interest because it is unique among regional and international power arrangements. Even non–political scientists study the entity; following its 2004 enlargement, it represented approximately 450 million people and 25 percent of the world's economic production, making it a significant international actor.

States created the EU and states make up its members. Unlike most other international organizations, however, the EU holds a measure of power over members' policies, especially in the realm of economics. This difference has led to debate about whether the EU has an intergovernmental (states alone hold power) or supranational (states and EU institutions together hold power) character. The answer depends on where one looks—which institutions and policy areas—as evidence for both characterizations exists. In the early twenty-first century students of the EU have turned to explanations provided by "multilevel governance" and "two-tiered bargaining." For many, these theoretical models better capture the reality of Europe's multiple arenas of bargaining, and the varied interests, actors, and influences that collaborate to create policy in the EU.

This sometimes untidy, always complex entity results from a long historical process. During its evolution, citizens of member states witnessed the completion of a single market encompassing all their economies, the removal of most barriers to intra-EU movement, as well as the adoption of a single currency (euro) and monetary policy by most member governments. Further, the November 1993 Maastricht Treaty on European Union (TEU) committed members to "deepening" integration. They agreed to coordinate a common foreign and security policy and justice and home affairs (police and legal functions). In addition, the EU continues to widen its membership, admitting ten states from Central and Eastern Europe (Cyprus, the Czech Republic, Estonia, Hungary, Latvia, Lithuania, Malta, Poland, Slovenia, and Slovakia) in 2004. Romania and Bulgaria are scheduled to join the EU in 2007 and Turkey in 2010. The EU is a fascinating experiment in new ways of organizing power, **sovereignty**, and citizenship.

sovereignty: autonomy; or, rule over a political entity

HISTORY OF EUROPEAN INTEGRATION

Following World War II (1939–1945), France and other states sought to "cage" Germany so that it could never again threaten its neighbors. This effort led first to the Brussels Treaty Organization (BTO) in 1948; its member states were Belgium, the Netherlands, and Luxembourg (Benelux), as well as France and the United Kingdom. The BTO evolved into the Western European Union (WEU) with the addition of West Germany (formed in 1949 from the British, French, and U.S.–occupied sectors of defeated Germany) and Italy in 1955. In 1950, BTO's members plus Canada, Denmark, Iceland, Italy, Norway, Portugal, and the United States became the North Atlantic Treaty Organization (NATO), formed to protect against military threats from the Soviet-led East **bloc**.

bloc: a group of countries or individuals working toward a common goal, usually within a convention or other political body

The Allies focused on rebuilding Europe to insulate it from perceived threats by the Communist Union of Soviet Socialist Republics (USSR). To stretch scarce European resources, the United States conditioned Marshall Plan aid (initiated in 1947) on recipients preparing integrated recovery plans. This requirement helped countries develop cooperative habits that served the community's later integrative efforts.

THE EUROPEAN UNION (EU) CONVENES IN BRUSSELS, BELGIUM IN 2002. Comprised of 25 member states, the EU expanded by 10 countries in May 2004 and expected two more to join in 2007. The focus of the EU has included economic unity, creation of a single monetary unit, and the enactment of a European Constitution. (SOURCE: AP/WIDE WORLD PHOTOS)

Integration took place in stages: first, the European Coal and Steel Community (ECSC); next, the European Economic Community (EEC); then the European Community (EC); and finally the EU. From a limited agenda and membership, European unity now encompasses vast new policy areas and reflects a much wider association.

France's Jean Monnet, regarded as the Father of Europe, and West Germany's Chancellor Konrad Adenauer notably provided the political finesse and inspiration for the ECSC. It came into existence after the Benelux states, France, Italy, and Germany signed the Treaty of Paris in 1951. Although the "Six" invited the United Kingdom to participate, domestic politics prevented British membership. The ECSC assumed regulatory authority over the production and sale of coal and steel. In focusing on these important products—essential to war and industry— the ECSC helped appease members' fears regarding their neighbors' ability to wage war during post-World War II reconstruction.

The ECSC was composed of a supranational High Authority, an intergovernmental Council of Ministers, an independent Court of Justice, and an advisory Assembly. The High Authority served as the executive. To ensure its supranationality, members pledged to take no instruction from their home governments. The authority had significant autonomy, including the power to fine firms, raise and invest money, arrange loans for members, and finance the retraining and resettlement of workers. In addition, it regulated the common market for coal and steel.

The Council of Ministers and Court of Justice both limited the authority. The council's members came from the Six's national cabinets, usually in the person of the minister of economics or industry. It could set the authority's agenda and block its initiatives. The council also exercised budgetary control. The Court of Justice also could check the authority through **judicial review**. Council members could ask the Court to examine whether the authority had overstepped its **mandate** or acted contrary to ECSC law.

On the other hand, the Assembly, made up of representatives from members' national legislatures, had little influence; it could not directly stop authority initiatives. The assembly could only censure the authority as a whole, forcing its resignation. Also, the assembly held limited proposal power regarding the budget.

This system of checks and balances created several important legacies. The High Authority showed great reluctance—and perhaps great wisdom—in refusing to exercise its powers contrary to explicit member preferences. Clearly, states' wishes restrained the authority's supranationality. This delicate balance continues in the EU. In addition, the court's capacity to evaluate and overturn the authority's decisions legitimized the use of judicial review, which later courts have employed to enhance European supranationality. Finally, the assembly, with its limited powers and non-elected members, does not always represent popular opinion, a serious deficiency for an organization of democratic states. The EU continues to struggle with this "democratic deficit," seeking to remedy this problem through bestowing greater power on the European Parliament (EP).

The ECSC's successes inspired its members to integrate additional policy areas. When an attempt to incorporate defense and security through the European Defense Community failed in 1954, ECSC members contemplated other possibilities. In 1957 they signed the Treaties of Rome that created the European Atomic Energy Community (Euratom) for peaceful atomic development and the EEC for construction of a common market in a wider array of goods in addition to ECSC products. Again, the British were invited to participate; again, they declined.

In the 1960s the EEC removed barriers to trade and freed the movement of labor within the Community, two prerequisites to a common market. Additionally, members negotiated the politically sensitive Common Agricultural Program (CAP), which provided Community support for farming (this **subsidy** remains a significant budget item). Moreover, in 1965, the states signed a Merger Treaty—fusing the ECSC, Euratom, and EEC into the EC—and created common institutions.

This same year witnessed the Empty Chair Crisis, in which France refused to move from unanimous to majority voting (on some issues) in the Council of Ministers as envisioned by the Treaties of Rome. Majority voting would have forced states that were opposed to an action to accept it if enough other states agreed. This reflected the ongoing debate over the nature of the Community's character. French President Charles de Gaulle (b. 1948) refused to **cede** any national prerogatives and withdrew France's representative. The 1966 Luxembourg Compromise filled France's "empty chair," allowing unanimity on any issue deemed very important by a member. This agreement gave each state a veto, preserving intergovernmentalism. Although this slowed the momentum of the EC, even the most intergovernmental states began to feel more secure.

judicial review: the ability of the judicial branch to review and invalidate a law that contradicts the constitution

mandate: to command, order, or require; or, a command, order, or requirement

subsidy: a government grant used to encourage some action

cede: to relinquish political control of lands to another country; surrender

By 1968 the Europeans completed the Common Market and again began to consider expansion. After two attempts to join, which were vetoed by de Gaulle (who considered Great Britain a rival), the United Kingdom entered the EC in 1973, along with the Republic of Ireland and Denmark. (Norway's citizens rejected EC membership by **referendum**.)

This period reflected great economic uncertainty. In 1971 the United States delinked the dollar—the peg of the international currency system—from a fixed relationship with gold. The Community responded, in 1972, with the Snake in the Tunnel policy (the "snake" represented tightly joined European currencies, while the "tunnel" symbolized their more flexible relationship to the U.S. dollar). That same year, the Organization of Petroleum Exporting Countries (OPEC) drastically increased the price of oil, which led to wide swings in EC currency values. The Europeans decided to create a better system and, in 1979, launched the European Monetary System (EMS). Another reform in 1979 was direct elections of Members of the European Parliament (MEPs), an important step toward democracy.

The 1980s witnessed significant activity, from widening membership to deepening integration. Beginning with Greece (1981), followed by Spain and Portugal (1986), the Community grew. In addition, the Council of Ministers named Jacques Delors as Commission president in 1985. Under his energetic leadership, the Community made great progress, including passage of the 1986 Single European Act outlining the steps remaining for, and committing members to, the completion of a Single Market. The 1989 Delors Report by central bankers detailed the steps toward a Economic and Monetary Union (EMU). Finally, the Council of Ministers dropped the requirement for unanimity on many issues, eroding the Luxembourg Compromise and easing EC operations.

The enthusiasm and optimism of the 1980s swept the EC forward with ambitious plans. In 1990 most members signed the Schengen Treaty that eliminated internal borders. Given its problems with domestic terrorism, the United Kingdom declined to sign the treaty (with Ireland abstaining), as did Norway, which sought to preserve travel agreements with non–EC Nordic states. Member states—including a newly unified Germany—signed the TEU in 1992, greatly expanding Community competencies. **Ratification** meant coordination of common foreign and security policies, as well as policing, immigration, political asylum, and legal procedures under the rubric "justice and home affairs." Members' initial steps toward the EMU included making central banks autonomous, coordinating monetary policies, and irrevocably linking participating states' currencies. In 1995 Sweden, Finland, and Austria joined the EU. Additionally, the group considered numerous new candidates for membership, mostly from the former Soviet bloc.

Economic difficulties, citizen revolt, and Commission scandal undermined these positive steps, however. In 1992 and 1993 the EMS underwent speculative attacks that led to its virtual collapse. In addition, states seeking to join the EMU often had to cut social spending, raise taxes, and even practice creative accounting to meet stringent entrance criteria. Such actions, especially in high unemployment areas, led many of them to question the desirability of membership. Political repercussions included Danish rejection of the TEU (later reversed) and France's ratification of the treaty by less than a 1 percent margin. The entire Commission, led by Jacques Santer, resigned in 1999 following reports of fraud, **nepotism**, and mismanagement of resources.

The early twenty-first century saw the EU focus on the ambitious agenda of the TEU, enlargement, and institutional reform. On January 1, 2002, citizens of

referendum: a popular vote on legislation, brought before the people by their elected leaders or public initiative

ratify: to make official or to officially sanction

nepotism: favoritism for one's own family in the appointment to positions or granting of other benefits

■■■
THE EUROPEAN COAL AND STEEL COMMUNITY

The European Coal and Steel Community (ECSC) was the first organization established by treaty that led to the eventual formation of the European Union. The ECSC is sometimes called the Schuman Plan, after the French foreign minister who proposed it in 1950. It was originally intended to pool French and German coal and steel production. By the time the Treaty of Paris was signed on April 18, 1951, however, the ECSC involved six countries (Italy, Belgium, Luxembourg, and the Netherlands in addition to France and Germany). The treaty went into effect on July 24, 1952 and was scheduled to expire fifty years later on July 23, 2002.

The six members agreed to create a common market for coal and steel, to lift restrictions on imports and exports, and to set up a unified labor pool. The structure of the ECSC included a nine-member High Authority, a Council of Ministers, an Assembly, and a Court of Justice. This organizational structure served as the model for the later European Union. The ECSC was an economic success in its early years; it raised iron and steel production in the member nations by 75 percent between 1952 and 1960, and general industrial production by 58 percent.

The ECSC's assets were turned over to the European Community when it went out of existence in July 2002.

■■■
---

lobby: to advocate for a specific political decision by attempting to persuade decision makers

bureaucracy: a system of administrating government involving professional labor; the mass of individuals administering government

the twelve "euroland" states began using paper euros. The EU also began developing an autonomous military "rapid reaction force," for use in a variety of situations. Further, members are coordinating asylum and immigration policies and other justice and policing activities.

The EU's enlargement by ten new members, in 2004, highlighted the need for institutional reform. The Treaty of Nice, signed in 2000, furthered reforms mandated by the 1996 Treaty of Amsterdam. Both agreements left many issues unsettled, however, in anticipation of a future constitutional conference. Reallocation of power and budget responsibilities particularly troubled members that wanted no reduction in the first or increase in the second, but such disagreements were overcome and leaders agreed to the EU Constitutional Treaty in the summer of 2004. Although many countries support the new constitution, France and the Netherlands do not. When put to a vote, both the French and the Dutch people rejected it. Unless the treaty receives a unanimous vote, the new constitution cannot be ratified.

INSTITUTIONS OF THE EU

The institutions governing the EU distribute power and responsibility uniquely. Functions overlap, creating unfamiliar authorities and responsibilities compared to national governments. This, in large measure, reflects the starting point provided by the ECSC and the evolutionary nature of the institutions' development.

European Council. This intergovernmental body should not be confused with the Council of Europe. The head of the country holding the presidency of the Council of Ministers convenes at least two meetings of this council during his or her six-month term. Here, national leaders set the EU's extraordinary agenda for the near future and approve previous efforts, usually in the form of treaties (e.g., the Single European Act). Originally an informal forum of heads of member states, the Community in 1974 accorded this meeting legal status. This move shifted the supranational/intergovernmental balance, returning power to the states. At the same time, it allowed bold expansion into new areas, for example, security and defense, that less senior diplomats could not propose, given political ramifications.

Commission. The supranational Commission, heir to the High Authority, serves both legislative and executive functions. Currently each member appoints one Commissioner, although that may change with future enlargements. After gaining approval from the Council of Ministers' (based on qualified majority voting) and European Parliament, commissioners serve five-year renewable terms. While many have served prominently in national governments, commissioners swear to forsake allegiance to any national agenda and agree to put EU interests first. The Commission president assigns commissioners to the twenty-three functionally distinct directorates-general and various services. The EP may censure and remove the commission en masse for failure to fulfill its commitments.

As a legislative body, the Commission proposes bills in consultation with the EP, states, and **lobbyists**, with direction from the European Council. Its submissions make up much of the Council of Ministers' agenda. As an executive body, the commission supervises implementation of legislation at the EU level through oversight of a **bureaucracy** of "Eurocrats," as well as at the state level by monitoring members' implementation of regulations and directives. (Regulations are immediately applicable and binding on member states, whereas directives outline objectives that states must achieve through means determined in national legislation.) In this executive capacity, the commission often writes guidelines for the implementation of legislation, giving it significant interpretative powers.

The Council of the European Union. This body, formerly, the Council of Ministers, representing states' national interests, counterbalances the commission's supranational bias. Several different councils do, in fact, exist, as membership varies based on the issue. In all cases, national ministers compose the council. The six-month council presidency rotates among members. The state holding this office also presides over the European Council. Ministers' dual role—both national and EU responsibilities—dictates additional support. Thus, the Council of Permanent Representatives (COREPER), a permanent bureaucracy of national civil servants, and a General Secretariat aid ministers.

The Council of Ministers performs a legislative function. Although formerly one could summarize operations as "the Commission proposes, the Council disposes," given increasing parliamentary responsibility, this no longer holds true in most instances. While the council still approves, amends, or rejects commission proposals, now, after it acts, proposals often move to the EP for approval (co-decision). In other situations, however, the Council still need only consult the EP or gain its assent.

Council ministers enjoy a different number of votes, weighted according to their states' sizes. Thus, the five largest members represent about 60 percent of total votes. After the Luxembourg Compromise, the council often required unanimity, but in treaties beginning with the TEU, it has added a growing number of issues to those decided by qualified majority voting (QMV). To ensure the protection of states' interests, QMV voting requires more than a simple majority. According to the Treaty of Nice, passage by "qualified majority" requires assent by a majority of member states, holding at least 72.3 percent of total Council votes and representing at least a majority of member states and at least 62 percent of the EU's population. The Constitutional Treaty further addresses this system.

European Parliament (EP). Since 1979 Europeans have elected MEPs directly, to five-year terms, with each **delegation**'s size based on its state's population. After the 2004 enlargement, the EP's size grew, but it should return to 535 in 2009. In the EP, MEPs sit in **transnational** party groupings. In addition, the EP has structured parliamentary activity and funding to enhance these cross-border political identities. Still, EP elections more often serve as referendums on national governments rather than reflecting voter opinions on European issues.

Parliament's authority varies depending on the issue, because European treaties have awarded it different roles. From humble "consultation" under the Treaties of Rome, the EP won the powers of cooperation and co-decision in the Single European Act and Maastricht Treaty, respectively. Honoring the EP's consultation role, the council must listen to its views, but it is not obliged to act on them. When operating under the cooperation procedure, the EP can amend or reject council proposals, although the ministers, acting unanimously, may overturn the EP's decision. Finally, co-decision gives the EP veto power over legislation approved by both commissioners and ministers. Such increases in EP power are one way to address the previously mentioned democratic deficit.

European Court of Justice. The EU's legal system encompasses several specialized bodies, for example, the Court of Auditors and two general courts: the Court of First Instance and the European Court of Justice (ECJ). The Community created the Court of Auditors, in 1977, to ensure that the budget is

delegate: to assign power to another, or, one who represents another

transnational: extending beyond the jurisdiction of one single nation

spent correctly and the Court of First Instance, in 1988, to relieve the ECJ's heavy caseload. Members each appoint one judge to the ECJ. With the 2004 enlargement, the number of judges increased to twenty-five, each serving a six-year term. These judges rarely sit en masse, meeting instead in smaller panels to hear cases. Judges consider suits involving EU institutions, firms, individuals, and member states. The court system has increased Europe's supranational character in two important ways. As discussed earlier, ECSC members accepted judicial review of the High Authority. The later ECJ also reviews actions by member states, in some cases ruling against national legislation. This derives from the ECJ judgment that European legislation is supreme over conflicting national legislation. Thus, ECJ rulings have driven forward the EU's agenda, in some cases against members' legislated preferences.

CONCLUSION

As the EU looks forward, it faces new and continuing challenges. The 2004 enlargement highlighted the need for additional reform of its institutions and budget. In addition, worries by many about the fairness of representation (the democratic deficit) persist, despite a strengthened EP. The nature of the EU and whether true authority lies with the states alone, or with the institutions of the EU, remains contentious. Further, such debate spotlights the difficulty of agreement in new areas of involvement: foreign policy, security, justice, and domestic affairs. The EU's recent and planned expansions also bring it into increasingly close contact with developing areas of the world (e.g., the Balkans, the former Soviet republics, and Turkey) with special needs. The EU remains an important international actor as it addresses these internal and external challenges.

See also: European Court of Justice; European Parliament.

BIBLIOGRAPHY

Archive of European Integration. <http://aei.pitt.edu/>.

De Giustino, David. *A Reader in European Integration.* London: Longman, 1996.

Eur-Lex. *Portal to European Law.* <http://europa.eu.int/eur-lex/en/index.html>.

European Research Paper Archive. <http://www.wu-wien.ac.at/erpa/>.

European Union. <http://www.eurunion.org>.

Gilbert, Mark. *Surpassing Realism.* Lanham, MD: Rowman & Littlefield, 2003.

McCormick, John. *Understanding the European Union: A Concise Introduction,* 2d ed. New York: Palgrave Macmillan, 2002.

Urwin, Derek W. *The Community of Europe*, 2d ed. London: Longman, 1995.

Wood, David, and Birol Yesilada. *The Emerging European Union*, 2d ed. New York: Longman, 2002.

Janet Adamski

Federalism

Federalism and its related terms (e.g., federal and federation) refer to a type of government that is established voluntarily to achieve unity while preserving diversity by constitutionally uniting separate political communities into a single limited, but encompassing, political community, such as a nation-state like the United States of America. Power is divided and shared in a federal system between (1) a general (or national) government that has certain areawide (or nationwide) responsibilities, such as national defense and monetary policy, and (2) constituent territorial governments (e.g., states, provinces, or cantons) that have broad local responsibilities such as highways, health care, and policing.

A key feature of a federal **polity** is that both the national (or federal) government and the constituent governments act directly on the people by enacting laws (e.g., criminal laws, tax laws) that directly affect the individuals within their **jurisdiction**. Furthermore, each order (or level) of government is supreme within its constitutional sphere of authority. Thus, in the United States the U.S. Constitution is supreme with respect to all matters within its jurisdiction, whereas within each of the fifty constituent states the state constitution, when not in conflict with the federal Constitution, is supreme with respect to all matters within its jurisdiction.

Approximately twenty-five countries can be termed *federal* to a greater or lesser degree: Argentina, Australia, Austria, Belgium, Bosnia and Herzegovina, Brazil, Canada, Comoros, Ethiopia, Germany, India, Malaysia, Mexico, Micronesia, Nigeria, Pakistan, Russia, Saint Kitts and Nevis, Serbia and Montenegro, South Africa, Spain, Switzerland, the United Arab Emirates, the United States, and Venezuela. These federal countries account for 39 percent of the world's population.

Scholars disagree on a precise definition of federalism and on which countries can properly be called *federal* because no two federal systems are identical. In practice, federal ideas are applied in various ways, thus making it impossible for one definition to fit all cases exactly.

polity: a form of government held by a specific country or group

jurisdiction: the territory or area within which authority may be exercised

FIRST U.S. SECRETARY OF THE TREASURY ALEXANDER HAMILTON. A dedicated proponent of a centralized federal government, Alexander Hamilton was author and editor of the 85 essays of *The Federalist,* published in 1788, that aided in the passing of the U.S. Constitution and has been utilized by the Supreme Court.

■-■-■

secularism: a refutation of, apathy toward, or exclusion of all religion

devolve: to move power or property from one individual or institution to another, especially from a central authority

apartheid: an official policy of racial segregation in the Republic of South Africa with a goal of promoting and maintaining white domination

ORIGINS AND DEVELOPMENT

The word *federal* comes from the Latin *foedus*, meaning *covenant*. A covenant signifies a partnership in which individuals or groups voluntarily consent to unite for common purposes without giving up their fundamental rights or identities. The covenant idea originated in the Hebrew Bible, which emphasizes the idea that all relationships—between God and humans and among humans themselves—should be established by mutual and voluntary consent and signified by a covenant or compact of mutual promise and obligation.

The covenant idea was universalized in Western civilization when Christianity adopted the Hebrew Bible as its Old Testament; however, theological and political concepts of covenant did not become prominent until the outbreak of the Protestant Reformation in 1517. With the breakdown of medieval forms of religious and political governance, Reformed Protestants developed a political theology of covenant, which held that the only legitimate way to form church congregations and larger church structures is through the consent of individual members and congregations. Similarly, in their revolts against Catholic princes, reformers combined the covenant idea with popular sovereignty in order to develop theories of revolution, equality, freedom, and the right of people to organize their own governments through mutual consent.

The first systematic political ideas articulated in North America were those of the Puritans' federal or covenant theology. The first political covenant was the Mayflower Compact of 1620. For the Puritans and other Reformed Protestants, individuals covenanted together in marriage to form families, families covenanted to form congregations and towns, and local congregations and towns covenanted to form larger structures of government.

Nonreligious reformers later **secularized** the covenant idea. The first full-fledged political theory of federalism is attributed to Johannes Althusius (1557–1638), who wrote *Politicia Methodice Digesta* (1614). The covenant idea is central to Thomas Hobbes's (1588–1679) *Leviathan* (1651) as well as to John Locke's (1632–1704) *Two Treatises of Government* (1690), in which Locke used the word *compact* to signify a political covenant. The notion of covenant also appears in the works of other English and Scottish political philosophers of the seventeenth century. The covenant idea also was widely applied to international relations by such thinkers as Hugo Grotius (1583–1645).

The framers of the U.S. Constitution, who invented the modern concept of federalism in 1787–1788, were strongly influenced intellectually by these secular philosophers as well as by the predominance of covenant-based religions in North America (e.g., Baptists, Calvinists, Congregationalists, Huguenots, Jews, Quakers, and Presbyterians).

REASONS TO FORM A FEDERAL POLITY

Essentially, a federal polity can be established in one of two ways. First, different states and political communities can come together to form a federal nation-state, as in the cases of Australia in 1901, Switzerland in 1848, and the United States in 1787–1788. Second, a unitary national government can **devolve** powers to regional and local governments, as occurred, for example, in Germany (after the Nazi era) in 1949, South Africa (after the **apartheid** era) between 1994 and 1996, and Spain (after the Franco era) in 1978. In Spain, such groups as the Basques, Catalans, and Galicians insisted on constitutional rights of autonomous self-government for themselves.

The most common historical reason to form a federal system is to establish peace and security. By uniting, small states and political communities can establish a more effective defense against foreign aggression. They also can establish domestic peace and security by creating rules and procedures that prevent war among themselves. These were important motivations for the founders of the Canadian and U.S. federal systems.

Another common reason for the formation of federal systems is economic, namely, to establish a large common market or zone for **free trade** that fosters economic development and prosperity by eliminating trade and tax barriers among the states that make up the federal union. This was another important motivation for the framers of the U.S. Constitution.

A common contemporary reason to form a federal polity is to unite diverse, territorially based national, racial, ethnic, religious, and/or linguistic communities into one nation-state. In these federations each constituent government (e.g., state, canton, or province) usually is dominated by a particular group. Switzerland, with its Protestant and Roman Catholic and French-, German-, and Romansch-speaking cantons, is a leading example. Other examples are Canada, India, Nigeria, and Russia.

Another major reason is to establish or preserve liberty and rights for individuals and communities. A federal system, argued James Madison (1751–1836) in *The Federalist 51* (1787–1788/1961), provides "a double security" for the rights of individuals because power "is first divided between two distinct governments" (federal and state) and then, within each, subdivided among branches of government (i.e., the separation of powers) (Hamilton, Madison, and Jay, 1787–1988/1961, p. 351). A federal system also protects rights and liberties for constituent communities by guaranteeing them autonomous powers to govern themselves on many matters. As such, a key principle of federalism is to prevent a tyranny of the majority by which one group of people or **coalition** of groups can constitute a majority and trample on the rights of minorities by outvoting those minorities on all matters. For example, the French-speaking minority in Canada values the self-governing autonomy of Quebec within Canada's federation as a protection against unfriendly policies that otherwise could be imposed on them by the English-speaking majority.

There can, however, be conflicts between individual and communitarian liberty. In the antebellum (pre–Civil War) United States, for example, the liberty of states to govern themselves allowed southern states to maintain slavery in gross violation of the liberty and rights of African Americans. In turn, national guarantees of individual rights can reduce communitarian liberty by prohibiting states from legislating in many areas that might reflect local values. For instance, no U.S. state can outlaw abortion even if the majority of the population desires it.

PRINCIPAL CHARACTERISTICS

Modern federalism is an invention of the framers of the U.S. Constitution of 1787–1788, who transformed the confederation established by the Articles of Confederation (1781) into a federation. Before 1787 the word *federal* referred to what is now called *confederal* .

Federal Authority to Legislate for Individuals.
In *The Federalist* Alexander Hamilton (1755?–1804) argued that the singular innovation of the U.S. Constitution was the granting of authority to the federal government to legislate

---

"The most common historical reason to form a federal system is to establish peace and security."

---

free trade: exchange of goods without tariffs charged on importing or exporting

coalition: an alliance, partnership, or union of disparate peoples or individuals

■-■-■

conscript: to draft an individual into the armed services against his will

for individuals. That is, under the Articles of Confederation the confederal government could not tax, arrest, or **conscript** individuals into the military, nor could it regulate commerce. It could act only through the states (much as the United Nations cannot tax, arrest, or conscript individuals or regulate commerce). Under the U.S. Constitution, however, the federal government can tax, arrest, and conscript individuals and regulate commerce, among other things.

This highlights another distinction between a federation and a confederation that was created by the founders of the United States. A federal union is intended to establish a nation-state rather than a mere alliance or league. A federation thus has a national government that possesses significant independent powers.

Written Constitution. A federal form of government is almost always established by, and based on, a written constitution that is intended to serve as a perpetual covenant. The constitution can be amended to adapt to changing times, but amendments usually require extraordinary procedures, as well as the concurrent consent of the national and constituent governments. The constitution sets forth the reasons for union, the terms of union, the rights of individuals (and sometimes constituent political communities as well), the structures of government, rules governing relationships among the orders (or levels) of government, and, most important, the allocation of powers among the orders of government. Most federal constitutions recognize only two orders of government: national (or federal) and state (or provincial or cantonal). A few federal constitutions (e.g., India and Nigeria) recognize local (usually municipal) government as a third order.

Allocation of Powers. The constitution usually allocates certain powers exclusively to various governments. In the United States, for example, the power to declare war rests exclusively with the U.S. Congress. The constitution also may prohibit certain powers to certain governments. For instance, no U.S. state can enter into any treaty, alliance, or confederation without the consent of Congress. A few federal constitutions, such as that of India, also list concurrent powers; these powers can be exercised by the federal or state governments. Although the U.S. Constitution does not list concurrent powers, there are in practice many areas of concurrent federal and state action, such as taxation, criminal justice, environmental protection, and consumer protection.

Symmetry. The powers of the constituent governments (e.g., states or provinces) can by symmetrical or asymmetrical. Their powers are said to be symmetrical when all the constituent governments are on an equal footing and have the same constitutional powers of self-government and same rights vis-à-vis the federal government. This is true of all fifty states in the United States. Powers are asymmetrical when different constituent governments possess different degrees of constitutional powers of self-government and different rights vis-à-vis the federal government. This is the case in Russia and Spain, for example.

Implied Powers. Some constitutions recognize implied powers, that is, the authority of a government to exercise powers that are not expressly listed in the constitution but are deemed "necessary and proper" (U.S. Constitution, Art. I, Sec. 8: 18) to carry out a government's **enumerated** powers.

enumerate: to expressly name, as in a list

Reserved or Residual Powers. Most federal constitutions stipulate the location of residual powers, that is, all possible remaining powers that are not enumerated in the constitution. Through the U.S. Constitution, for example, the people of the states delegated certain limited powers to the U.S. government. The federal government can exercise only those powers enumerated in the U.S. Constitution and no others. Hence, as the Tenth Amendment to the U.S. Constitution states, all other powers not delegated to the U.S. government or prohibited by the Constitution to the states are reserved to the states or to the people. By contrast, in Canada, the residual powers rest with the federal government, not the provinces.

Multiple Governments. A federal system therefore has multiple, semi-independent governments, each of which possesses autonomous and independent constitutional authority to legislate for individuals. In the United States, for example, the federal government levies an income tax independently of the states. In turn, forty-three states levy their own separate income taxes independently of the federal government and each other.

Forum Shopping. Multiple governments also foster forum shopping, by which individuals who do not get satisfaction from one government **petition** another government. Unable to end racial segregation through state governments, for example, black Americans appealed to the federal government for relief in the 1950s and 1960s.

petition: a written appeal for a desired action, or, to request an action, especially of government

Policy Diversity. Multiple governments give rise to policy diversity. In the United States thirty-eight states permit capital punishment whereas twelve states prohibit it. Hence, another common feature of a federal system is an agreement to disagree. When agreement cannot be reached on a particular national policy, constituent states can enact different policies that reflect their citizens' preferences. Federalism also permits policy experimentation. As U.S. Supreme Court Justice Louis Brandeis (1856–1941) argued in *New State Ice Co. v. Liebmann* (1932), "It is one of the happy accidents of the federal system that a single courageous state may, if its citizens choose, serve as a laboratory, and try novel social and economic experiments without risk to the rest of the country." A more contemporary example is Oregon—the only U.S. state that permits physician-assisted suicide.

Fiscal Federalism. A common feature of federal systems is transfers of money between governments, most commonly grants-in-aid given by the

■ ■ ■
FORUM SHOPPING

"Forum shopping" is an informal term that refers to a plaintiff's attempts to have his case heard in the court most likely to give him a favorable decision. The plaintiff may be able to choose between a local and a federal court or between two different local courts. Since the 1990s, most well-known instances of forum shopping have concerned patents and inventions, child custody, antitrust cases, or trials of alleged terrorists.

In the 1950s and 1960s, however, black Americans used forum shopping as a way to advance the cause of civil rights. Blocked by state courts and legislatures, such organizations as the National Association for the Advancement of Colored People (NAACP) began to look to federal courts to overturn previous decisions at the state level that upheld segregation.

The landmark case was *Brown v. Board of Education*, decided by the Supreme Court in 1954. *Brown* was actually a combination of four separate cases from different states (Kansas, South Carolina, Virginia, and Delaware). Although *Brown* did not order the desegregation of restaurants and other public facilities owned by private persons, it paved the way for such provisions in the Civil Rights Act of 1964.

Boynton v. Virginia (1960) is another example of forum shopping. The case concerned a law student arrested for trespassing by entering a whites-only restaurant in a bus terminal. The U. S. Supreme Court ruled that segregation in public transportation was illegal because it violated the Interstate Commerce Act (1887).

federal government to state and local governments and given by states to local governments. In the United States about 23 percent of state and local budgets consists of grant-in-aid money from the federal government. For example, the federal government provides about 90 percent of the money for interstate highway construction; states provide the other approximately 10 percent. Most federal countries, although not the United States, have a fiscal equalization policy by which the federal government gives money to poor states or provinces to enable them to provide a national-average level of public services to their citizens.

intergovernmental: between or involving multiple governments, with each government retaining full decision-making power

Intergovernmental Relations. A key political and administrative feature of federal systems is relations among governments: **intergovernmental** relations between different orders of government (sometimes referred to as vertical federalism) and interjurisdictional relations among multiple governments of the same order, such as interstate and interlocal relations (sometimes called horizontal federalism). Although it is important for governments in a federal system to cooperate in order to serve citizens effectively, conflict among governments is common as well. Competition among governments also is important to serve citizens more efficiently and to reduce the possibility of one order of government gaining too much power and thus dominating the federal system. Collusion among governments also can occur when government officials in different orders of government work together to increase their budgets or power at the expense of taxpayers. In turn, one criticism of intergovernmental relations is that it is often difficult for citizens to hold public officials accountable because citizens cannot determine easily who is responsible for particular policies, especially policies that fail.

EVALUATION

Some federal countries, such as Australia, Canada, Switzerland, and the United States, are among the world's oldest, most successful, most prosperous, and most democratic countries. India, a federation since 1950, is the world's largest democracy in terms of population. Furthermore, seven of the world's eight territorially largest countries are federal: Argentina, Australia, Brazil, Canada, India, Russia, and the United States. (Only China is not federal or democratic.) At the same time, federal countries such as Ethiopia, Nigeria, Pakistan, and Russia demonstrate that federalism is not always a highly successful government in terms of human rights, economic prosperity, and vibrant democracy. In some countries it is very difficult to achieve constitutional and political covenants that promote unity without local resistance, general violence, or **centralized** authoritarianism.

centralize: to move control or power to a single point of authority

See also: Confederations; Democracy; Republic.

BIBLIOGRAPHY

Elazar, Daniel J. *American Federalism: A View from the States*, 3rd ed. New York: Harper & Row, 1984.

Elazar, Daniel J. *Exploring Federalism*. Tuscaloosa: University of Alabama Press, 1987.

Elazar, Daniel J., and John Kincaid, eds. *The Covenant Connection: From Federal Theology to Modern Federalism*. Lanham, MD: Lexington Books, 2000.

Griffiths, Ann L. ed. *Handbook of Federal Countries, 2002*. Montreal, Canada: McGill Queen's University Press, 2002.

Hamilton, Alexander, James Madison, and John Jay. *The Federalist* (1787–1788), ed. Jacob E. Cooke. Middletown, CT: Wesleyan University Press, 1961.

Kenyon, Daphne A., and John Kincaid, eds. *Competition among States and Local Governments: Efficiency and Equity in American Federalism*. Washington, DC: Urban Institute Press, 1991.

Kincaid, John. "Values and Value Tradeoffs in Federalism." *Publius: The Journal of Federalism* 25, no. 2 (1995):29–44.

Kincaid, John, and G. Alan Tarr, eds. *Constitutional Origins, Structure, and Change in Federal Countries*. Montreal, Canada: McGill-Queen's University Press, 2005.

New State Ice Co. v. Liebmann, 285 U.S. 262, 1932.

Riker, William H. *Federalism: Origin, Operation, Significance*. Boston: Little, Brown, 1964.

Sutton, Robert P. *Federalism*. Westport, CT: Greenwood Press, 2002.

Watts, Ronald L. *Comparing Federal Systems*. 2nd ed. Kingston, Canada: Institute of Intergovernmental Relations, Queen's University, 1999.

John Kincaid

Fiji

The Republic of Fiji Islands (or Fiji) lies in the South Pacific Ocean. It is made up of 332 islands, with a total landmass of 18,270 square kilometers (7,000 square miles). The land is mostly mountainous forest of volcanic origin. Fiji claims natural resources of timber, fish, gold, and copper. It has a population of about 833,000, made up of Fijians (51%), Fijian Indians (43%), and Europeans, other Pacific Islanders, Chinese, and mixed races (6%). Sugar exports and the tourist industry are the major sources of foreign exchange.

In 1865 Fiji's first constitution was drawn up and signed by seven paramount chiefs. The arrangement collapsed in 1867, and Fiji was **ceded** to Great Britain as a colony in 1874. It finally became independent in 1970. Two military **coups** occurred in 1987, and in 1990 a new constitution, which weighted government representation in favor of Fijians, came into effect. In 1997 the Constitution of the Sovereign Democratic Republic of Fiji, designed to balance the demands of the two major ethnic groups, replaced that document.

In May 2000 the Indo-Fijian prime minister and members of parliament were taken hostage in a civilian-led coup. An **interim** military government formed in July of that year; it negotiated the release of the hostages and established an interim civilian government. The Court of Appeal upheld a challenge to the validity of the civilian government and ruled that the 1997 constitution remained the supreme law of Fiji. The interim civilian government refused to step down and was validated by the 2001 national election results.

Fiji is a republic and a member of the Commonwealth. The constitution established a **Westminster**-style system of parliamentary democracy. The national legislature is **bicameral**. There are seventy members in the House of Representatives. Thirty-seven seats are reserved for Fijians, twenty-seven for Indians, one for a Rotuman, and five for other ethnic groups. Elections are based on the preferential system of voting. The Senate consists of thirty-two members appointed by the president on the advice of the *Bose Levu Vakaturaga* (Great Council of Chiefs) (which recommends fourteen

cede: to relinquish political control of lands to another country; surrender

coup: a quick seizure of power or a sudden attack

interim: for a limited time, during a period of transition

Westminster: a democratic model of government comprising operational procedures for a legislative body, based on the system used in the United Kingdom

bicameral: comprised of two chambers, usually a legislative body

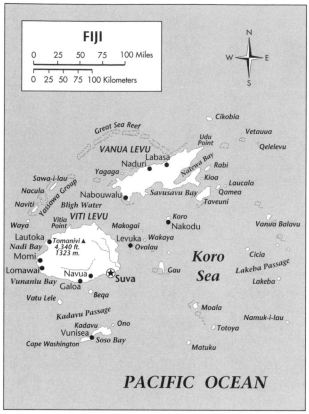

FIJI

0   25   50   75   100 Miles

0   25 50 75 100 Kilometers

Great Sea Reef

Cikobia

Vetauua

VANUA LEVU

Udu
Point

Qelelevu

Labasa

Naduri

Natewa Bay

Rabi

Yagaga

Kioa

Sawa-i-lau

Laucala

Nacula

Savusavu Bay

Qamea

Nabouwalu

Taveuni

Naviti

Bligh Water

Yasawa Group

VITI LEVU

Koro

Waya

Vitia
Point

Makogai

Nakodu

Vanua Balavu

Lautoka

Tomanivi ▲
4,340 ft.
1323 m.

Levuka

Wakaya

Nadi Bay

Ovalau

Cicia

Momi

Koro
Sea

Lakeba Passage

Lomawai

Navua

Gau

Lakeba

Vunaniu Bay

Suva

Galoa

Beqa

Vatu Lele

Moala

Kadavu Passage

Namuk-i-lau

Kadavu

Ono

Totoya

Vunisea

Cape Washington

Soso Bay

Matuku

PACIFIC OCEAN

(MAP BY MARYLAND CARTOGRAPHICS/THE GALE GROUP)

members), the prime minister (nine members), the leader of the opposition (eight members), and the Council of Rotuma (one member). Bills originate in the House of Representatives and normally must pass both houses and secure the president's consent. The functions of the *Bose Levu Vakaturaga* include advising the president, making recommendations for the benefit of the Fijian people, and considering draft legislation related to Fijians.

The executive authority of the state is vested in the president, who is appointed by the *Bose Levu Vakaturaga,* after consultation with the prime minister, for a term of five years. The president appoints the prime minister on the basis of majority support in the House of Representatives. The prime minister is under duty to establish a multiparty cabinet. In 2002 the Court of Appeal declared the prime minister, Laisenia Qarase (b. 1941), to be in contravention of this provision. That decision was upheld by the Supreme Court in 2003.

Judicial power in the state lies with the High Court, the Court of Appeal, the Supreme Court, and any other courts created by law. The constitution contains a "Bill of Rights" establishing a Human Rights Commission. The constitution also contains a compact that governs interpretation of the constitution and laws formulated according to it.

See also: Constitutional Monarchy.

BIBLIOGRAPHY

Corrin Care, Jennifer. "Unfinished Constitutional Business: Human Rights in Fiji Islands." *Alternative Law Journal* 25, no. 4 (2000):223–226.

Corrin Care, Jennifer, Teresa Newton, and Donald Paterson. *Introduction to South Pacific Law.* London: Cavendish, 1999.

Lal, Brij V., and Tomasi R. Vakatora. *Fiji in Transition.* Suva, Fiji Islands: School of Social and Economic Developmment, University of the South Pacific, 1997.

Ministry of Information. *Fiji Government Online.* <http://fiji.gov.fj/>.

Paterson, Donald, and Stephen Zorn. "Fiji." In *South Pacific Island Legal Systems*, ed. Michael Ntumy. Honolulu: University of Hawaii Press, 1993.

University of the South Pacific, School of Law. *2000–2001 Crisis in Fiji Islands.* <http://www.vanuatu.usp.ac.fj/journal_splaw/Special_Interest/Fiji_2000/Fiji_Main.html>.

Jennifer Corrin Care

Finland

Finland is a highly developed democratic country situated in northeastern Europe. It borders Russia to the east, Sweden to the west, Norway to the north, and the Baltic Sea to the south. Since gaining independence from Russia in 1917, Finland has had a democratic form of government. From 1945 to 1991, Finland, although a democratic state with historical ties to Western Europe, pursued an official policy of **neutrality** and maintained close ties with the Soviet Union. With the Cold War's end came a tilt to the West in Finnish foreign policy, and Finland joined the European Union (EU) in 1995. Finns enjoy an advanced and productive economy, extensive social welfare programs, and one of the highest standards of living in the world.

BASIC FACTS

Finland is a presidential/parliamentary **republic** that is 337,115 square kilometers (130,160 square miles) in area, approximately the size of Montana, with its capital in Helsinki. The population is estimated at 5.2 million; the ethnic breakdown is as follows: Finns (93%), Swedes (6%), and small numbers of Saami (Lapps), Romani (gypsies), and Tatars. The overwhelming majority of Finland's citizens are Lutheran (89%). The gross national product (GNP) **per capita** is 26,800 euros. Both Finnish and Swedish are the official languages of the nation.

HISTORICAL DEVELOPMENT

The origins of the Finnish people remain relatively obscure, but most agree that they arrived in Finland thousands of years ago from Siberia. Finns speak an Finno-Ugric language that is distantly related to Turkish and Mongolian and far removed from West European languages. The first written accounts of Finnish history recount a Swedish "crusade" in the 1150s to spread Christianity to the Finns and incorporate Finnish lands into the Swedish Crown. For over 600 years Finland was an integral part of the Swedish kingdom. Finns played a prominent role in many aspects of the state, particularly the military, but the land-owning elites on the territory of today's Finland were Swedish-speaking. Meanwhile, the peasants engaged in small-scale farming—the majority of the population—and retained Finnish as their native tongue. This heritage is important, as there was still a sizable Swedish-speaking minority in Finland in the early twenty-first century and Swedish has been recognized as one of the official languages of the state.

As Russia began to emerge as a great power in the 1700s, Finland and adjoining lands on the Baltic coast became targets of Russian expansionism. At the same time the Swedish state was becoming militarily weaker, and Sweden and Russia fought several wars for control of the Baltic region. In 1809 Finland was conquered by the armies of Czar Alexander I of Russia and incorporated into the Russian Empire as a semiautonomous **grand duchy**. With this status Finland enjoyed a high degree of self-rule, including for a time its own diet or parliament. Ironically, it was under Russian rule that Finland began to experience a **nationalist** renaissance, led by intellectuals and an emerging middle class. The publication in 1835 of *The Kalevala*, an epic of Finnish myths and legends, would rank as one of the most important events in the Finnish national movement. Although Finland enjoyed the political **liberalization** pursued by Czar Alexander II (1855–1881) (a statue of whom may be found in Helsinki today), by the 1890s "Russification" and a curtailment of Finnish rights began to provoke more resistance, culminating in the assassination of the Russian **governor-general** in 1904. The 1905 revolution in Russia brought another round of liberalization to Finland, including the first freely elected parliament in 1906.

On December 6, 1917, shortly after the Bolsheviks seized power in Russia, Finland declared its independence from Russia. This was recognized by the Soviet leader Vladimir Lenin (1870–1924). In 1918 a civil war broke out in Finland between Reds (communists) and Whites (noncommunists), with the latter prevailing. In 1919 Finland adopted a democratic constitution, and Finnish

neutrality: the quality of not taking sides, as in a conflict

republic: a form of democratic government in which decisions are made by elected representatives of the people

per capita: for each person, especially for each person living in an area or country

grand duchy: a territory ruled by a grand duke or duchess

nationalism: the belief that one's nation or culture is superior to all others

liberalization: the process of lowering trade barriers and tariffs and reducing government economic regulations

governor-general: a governor who rules over a large territory and employs deputy governors to oversee subdivided regions

democracy would survive throughout the interwar period despite marked tensions between the extreme right and extreme left. In November 1939 the Soviet Union invaded Finland, and even though the Finns fought ferociously, they agreed to a peace accord in March 1940. From 1941 to 1994 Finland, as an ally of Nazi Germany, would fight the Soviets, with an end to the conflict declared after Finland made territorial concessions and promised to expel the Nazis, which occurred in 1945.

MAJOR DEVELOPMENTS SINCE 1945

Finland's most immediate task after World War II was to repair relations with the Soviet Union. Finland and the Soviets signed a peace treaty at Paris in February 1947 limiting the size of Finland's military forces and providing for the cession, to the Soviet Union, of the Petsamo area on the Arctic coast, the Karelian Isthmus in southeastern Finland, and other territory along the former eastern border. In 1948 Finland and the Soviet Union concluded the Treaty of Friendship, Cooperation and Mutual Assistance, which pledged, among other items, that neither side would enter into an alliance against the other. This essentially guaranteed Finnish neutrality during the Cold War, and some referred to Finnish deference to the Soviets on foreign policy questions as "Finlandization." Finland joined the United Nations (UN) in 1955 and was active in UN peacekeeping operations. Finland did not, however, join the **North Atlantic Treaty Organization** (NATO) or the European Economic Community.

Postwar Finnish politics was dominated by three political figures: President Juho Paasikivi (1870–1956) was elected in 1946 and served until 1956; Urho Kekkonen (1900–1986), was president from 1956 until 1981; and President Mauno Koivisto (b. 1923) held power from 1982 until 1994. Paasikivi and Kekkonen were credited with securing Finnish independence and managing periodic crises with the Soviet Union during which the Soviets attempted to meddle in Finnish domestic politics. Under Kekkonen a politics of social consensus between right and left and between business and labor developed and contributed to Finnish development. Koivisto was the first postwar president from the Social Democratic Party and, as the Cold War ended, reoriented Finnish foreign policy toward the West. Finland **unilaterally abrogated** restrictions imposed by the 1947 and 1948 treaties and gave unofficial encouragement to independence movements in Estonia, Lithuania, and Latvia. In 1995 Finland, together with Sweden, joined the European Union (EU), and in 1999 Finland gave up its currency and joined eleven other countries in creating the euro, the currency for the EU. Finland also joined NATO's Partnership for Peace program.

SOCIOECONOMIC CONDITIONS

Finland is one of the most developed countries in the world. On a variety of measures, such as literacy (100%), infant mortality (3.8 in 1,000), low poverty rates, and life expectancy (for males 74, for females 81), Finland ranks among the best in the world. According to the 2003 United Nations Human Development Report, which takes into account life expectancy, literacy, educational enrollment, and GDP per capita, Finland ranked fourteenth among all the countries in the world. By 2002 the country was 67 percent urban, with the main population centers in the south of the country.

For much of its history the Finnish economy was dominated by agriculture even though **arable land** is in short supply and is concentrated in the south. In the nineteenth century the timber industry began to develop, and after World War II

North Atlantic Treaty Organization: a military alliance chiefly involving the United States and Western Europe that stated that, in the event of an attack, the member countries would have a mutual defense

unilateral: independent of any other person or entity

abrogate: to abolish or undo, usually a law

arable land: land suitable for the growing of crops

metalworking and shipbuilding assumed a prominent role in the economy. By the end of the twentieth century electronics had become Finland's main export, as the country was a world leader in such sectors as cellular phones and environmental equipment. However, services (e.g., finance, insurance, public services) employed more workers (45%) than did industry (21%). Unemployment in 2002 stood at 9.1 percent.

Aside from timber, Finland has few natural resources and imports much of its energy and many of its consumer goods, such as textiles and cars. For much of the postwar period the Soviet Union was Finland's largest trading partner, but by 2002 Germany topped the list for both exports and imports. Over half of Finland's trade is with other EU countries. It joined the euro effort in 1999, and in the first years of the new currency Finland's economy outperformed euro-area partners in terms of economic growth and public finance.

STRUCTURE OF GOVERNMENT

Finland adopted a new constitution in 1999, which went into effect in 2000. Finland is a presidential/parliamentary republic, similar to France. This means that there are two executives. One is a president, who is directly elected by voters for a six-year term (with a two-term maximum limit). Any party that has a representative in the *Eduskunta* (parliament) can nominate a candidate, and if no candidate receives a majority of the vote, there is a run-off election between the top two vote-getters. The president is the official head of the Finnish state and traditionally has overseen foreign policy and defense (the president is commander in chief of the armed forces), oversees numerous appointments in the government, can veto legislation, and has the right to initiate legislation. Whereas in the past the president was the dominant figure in Finland, the president's powers have been reduced by the new constitution (e.g., the *Eduskunta* now elects the prime minister and the president can dismiss the *Eduskunta* only on the recommendation of the prime minister).

In Finland the prime minister is the head of government and traditionally, as in France, has been responsible for the day-to-day running of the government, leaving the most important issues for the president to decide. Whereas in the past the prime minister was appointed by the president, now the prime minister is elected by the *Eduskunta*, typically by a **coalition** of parties that agree to form a government. The prime minister, together with the president, then appoints a Council of State (a cabinet) of up to seventeen ministers to oversee various government departments. As was noted, the power of the prime minister has grown in recent years, and with Finnish ascension to the EU and less distinction between domestic and foreign affairs, the prime minister has become nearly equal to the president in power, having formal responsibility for relations with the EU.

This system, as in France, functions rather smoothly when the president and prime minister are from the same party. However, conflict may arise if the two come from different parties, resulting in what is called cohabitation between the two executives.

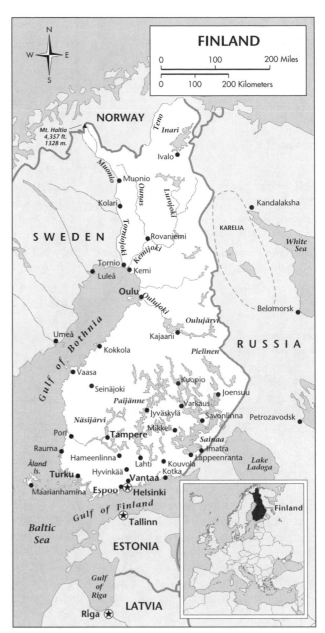

FINLAND

(MAP BY MARYLAND CARTOGRAPHICS/THE GALE GROUP)

coalition: an alliance, partnership, or union of disparate peoples or individuals

proportional system: a political system in which legislative seats or offices are awarded based on the proportional number of votes received by a party in an election

judicial review: the ability of the judicial branch to review and invalidate a law that contradicts the constitution

jurisdiction: the territory or area within which authority may be exercised

litigate: to bring a disagreement or violation of the law before a judge for a legal decision

appellate: a court having jurisdiction to review the findings of lower courts

communal: something owned or used by the entire community

■ ■ ■

WOMEN AND POLITICS IN FINLAND

Finland has one of the best records in the world regarding female participation in politics. In 1906 Finland became the second country in the world (after New Zealand) to give women the right to vote at the national level. In the postwar period the number of female members of parliament steadily increased, rising from 8.5 percent of the total in 1945 to 37.5 percent of the total in 2003, placing Finland among the top three countries in the world (together with Norway and Sweden) in terms of female composition of the legislature. Generous social benefits such as maternity leave and day care also have contributed to a growing role for Finnish women in the work force. In 2000 Tarja Halonen (b. 1943) of the Social Democratic Party became the first female president, and in 2003 the leader of the Center Party, Anneli Jaatteenmaki (b. 1955), became Finland's first female prime minister.

The *Eduskunta* is a single body of 200 elected representatives. Representatives are elected through a system of **proportional representation** in multimember districts, thereby allowing several parties to gain seats in the *Eduskunta*. Elections are held every four years unless the *Eduskunta* is dismissed by the president. The *Eduskunta* is the supreme governing body in the country. It makes the laws and can override presidential vetoes, and its decisions are not subject to **judicial review**. It elects the prime minister and can remove the prime minister with a no-confidence vote, meaning that a majority of the members vote for his or her removal.

The judicial system is divided between courts with regular civil and criminal **jurisdiction** and special courts with responsibility for **litigation** between the public and the administrative organs of the state. Finnish law is codified, and much of it dates back to the years of Swedish rule. The Finnish court system consists of local courts, regional **appellate** courts, and a supreme court of twenty-one judges. Judges are appointed for life, and the president appoints judges to the supreme court.

For administrative purposes the country is divided into six provinces, with the Aland Islands (populated by Swedish speakers) enjoying a degree of special autonomy. Below the provincial level the country is divided into cities, townships, and communes administered by municipal and **communal** councils elected by proportional representation once every four years. At the provincial level the five mainland provinces are administered by provincial boards composed of civil servants, each headed by a governor. The boards are responsible to the Ministry of the Interior and play a supervisory and coordinating role within the provinces.

PARTIES, INTEREST GROUPS, AND POLITICAL PARTICIPATION

Finland's proportional representation system fosters the creation of a multiparty system. In the 2003 parliamentary elections, for example, eight parties gained parliamentary seats. Traditionally, Finnish politics has been dominated by two parties: the Social Democratic Party (SDP) and the Center (formerly Agrarian) Party. The primary constituency of the SDP is urban professionals and workers, whereas the Center Party has catered more to rural interests. Since World War II one of these parties, if not both in a coalition, has served in every Finnish government. Finland also formerly had a sizable Communist Party (which in the 1950s received as much as 20 percent of the vote), but this group suffered from internal dissension in the 1970s and after the end of the Cold War lost much of its appeal, although it still exists as the Leftist Alliance. The National Coalition Party has been the leading party on the right but rarely has joined a coalition government. Since the 1980s the greens have become a sizable party on the left, and there is also a Swedish Peoples' Party whose primary constituency is the Swedish-speaking population.

Finland experienced a great deal of political instability from 1919 through the 1960s as coalition governments would fall over such issues as labor unrest and relations with the Soviet Union. In the 1960s, however, Finland, like other Scandinavian countries, developed a "social consensus" model of government that featured grand coalition governments between the left and right, strong support for social welfare programs, and a prominent role for trade unions in economic policy making. Unionization rates (80% in 2001) remain high in Finland, and organized labor remains by far the most important interest group in the country.

Finns enjoy a wide range of political and economic rights, and Finland ranks as one of the freest countries in the world in terms of civil liberties and political rights. All Finns over eighteen have the right to vote, and voter turnout has generally been high, reaching 85 percent in 1962, although it has declined (70% in 2003). There is universal male **conscription**, in which all men serve in the military from six to twelve months. As of 1995 women were permitted to serve as volunteers.

See also: European Union; France; Political Party Systems; Russia; Sweden.

BIBLIOGRAPHY

Allison, Roy. *Finland's Relations with the Soviet Union.* New York: St. Martin's, 1985.

Arter, David. *Politics and Policy-Making in Finland.* New York: St. Martin's, 1987.

Constitution of Finland. <http://www.om.fi/constitution/3340.htm>.

Kirby, D. G. *Finland in the Twentieth Century.* Minneapolis: University of Minnesota Press, 1979.

Raunio, Tapro, and Teija Tiilikainen. *Finland in the European Union.* London: Frank Cass, 2003.

Solsten, Eric, and Sandra Meditz, eds. *Finland: A Country Study.* Washington, DC: Library of Congress, 1990.

Vehvilainen, Olli. *Finland in the Second World War: Between Germany and Russia.* New York: Palgrave, 2002.

Virtual Finland. <http://www.virtual.finland.fi>.

Paul J. Kubicek

conscript: to draft an individual into the armed services against his will

France

Situated on the western fringes of continental Europe, France has three coast-lines—on the English Channel and North Sea, on the Atlantic, and on the Mediterranean—and has continental borders, stretching from north to south, with Belgium, Luxembourg, Germany, Switzerland, and Italy. France also has borders with Spain and the Principality of Andorra in the southwest and is linked to the United Kingdom by the Channel Tunnel in the northeast. With a total surface area of 549,000 square kilometers (211,914 square miles), metropolitan France is the largest country in the European Union (EU). In addition, France has a number of overseas departments and territories—**vestiges** of the former French colonial empire created after the discovery of the Americas.

vestige: a remnant of a lost or vanished entity, as in a nation or an institution

In 2005 France had 60.7 million inhabitants, which represents an increase of 44 percent since 1940. The origins of the French population are very diverse. The strong influence of the Gallo-Romans and Francs has been accompanied by that of the Bretons in the west, Germanics in the east, and Catalans, Basques, and Provencals in the south. In addition, during the nineteenth and twentieth centuries France witnessed the arrival of Italian and Polish immigrants and political refugees from central Europe and, more recently, influxes of migrants from former French colonies in North Africa and those from other EU member states.

BRIEF HISTORY

France is one of the oldest **nation-states**. The state is older than the nation, the nation having been affirmed by the French Revolution of 1789. A distinction often is drawn between the period before the Revolution,

nation-state: a relatively homogeneous state with only one or few nationalities within its political borders regime: a type of government, or, the government in power in a region

absolute: complete, pure, free from restriction or limitation

republic: a form of democratic government in which decisions are made by elected representatives of the people

coup: a quick seizure of power or a sudden attack

known as the *Ancien Régime*, and modern France. The latter has had a troubled political history, with a succession of unstable political **regimes**. It can be said definitively that over a period of two centuries France has tried every possible form of government. These forms include **absolute** monarchies, constitutional monarchies under the Empires (of which there were two), and as many as five **republics**, both parliamentary and presidential, all this without taking into account the Vichy Régime and the provisionary regimes that were established in anticipation or in the absence of a constitution. Wars, **coups** d'etat, and revolutions can be identified as the direct causes of this instability, with each new constitution establishing the opposite kind of regime to its predecessor. The French have had no fewer than sixteen constitutions since the adoption of their first constitution on June, 20, 1789. However, it was not until 1877 that republicanism was established as the undisputed constitutional basis of government in France.

MAJOR POLITICAL LEADERS SINCE 1945

Since 1945 the French political landscape has been dominated by the figure of General Charles de Gaulle (1890–1970), and today politicians from all parties lay claim to his legacy. As the hero and leader of France during World War II (1939–1945), de Gaulle returned to power in 1958 at the height of the Franco–Algerian War when he founded and became the first president of the Fifth Republic.

Pierre Mendès-France (1907–1982), who acted as a guardian of republican values under the Fourth Republic and brought an end to the war in Indochina, has also had a considerable influence on the French political life.

The Nobel Prize winner and former French foreign minister under the Fourth Republic, Robert Schuman (1886–1963), was, along with the economist Jean Monnet (1888–1969), one of the founding fathers of the EU and a strong advocate of European integration.

François Mitterrand (1916–1996), despite having been an ardent critic of the Fifth Republic Constitution and General de Gaulle during the establishment and consolidation of the regime in the late 1950s and early 1960s, adapted well to the office of president of the Republic after his election in 1981 and re-election in 1988. He is recognized as France's longest-serving head of state since 1789.

As successor to General de Gaulle in 1969, Georges Pompidou (1911–1974) presided over the rejuvenation and modernization of postwar France. Valéry Giscard d'Estaing (b. 1926) was the first of France's presidents to espouse a more liberal economic outlook and, along with Mitterrand, was instrumental in strengthening Franco–German relations, which in turn were to act as a powerful motor toward further European integration.

SOCIOECONOMIC CONDITIONS

The French economy is the second largest in Western Europe and the fourth largest in the world after the United States, Japan, and Germany. Agricultural and farm products, together with the services industry and French culture, make up the bulk of French exports. A considerable part of France's economic clout is derived from French-based multinationals that make up some of the world's largest commercial companies: L'Oréal, Airbus, France Télécom, Carrefour, Danone, Total Fina Elf, and Matra are among the best known examples. France's gross domestic product (GDP) reached 1,463.7 billion euros in

TABLE 1

Political Leaders under V Republic, 1959–2007

President	Tenure
Charles de Gaulle	1959–1969
Georges Pompidou	1969–1974
Valéry Giscard d'Estaing	1974–1981
François Mitterrand	1981–1995
Jacques Chirac	1995–2007

Prime ministers	Date of appointment
Michel Debré	January 8, 1959
Georges Pompidou	April 14, 1962
Maurice Couve de Murville	July 10, 1968
Jacques Chaban-Delmas	June 20, 1969
Pierre Messmer	July 5, 1972
Jacques Chirac	May 27, 1974
Raymond Barre	August 25, 1976
Pierre Mauroy	May 21, 1981
Laurent Fabius	July 17, 1984
Jacques Chirac	March 20, 1986
Michel Rocard	May 10, 1988
Édith Cresson	May 15, 1991
Pierre Bérégovoy	April 26, 1992
Édouard Balladur	March 29, 1993
Alain Juppé	May 17, 1995
Lionel Jospin	June 2, 1997
Jean-Pierre Raffarin	May 6, 2002

SOURCE: Courtesy of author.

(MAP BY MARYLAND CARTOGRAPHICS/THE GALE GROUP)

2001, and with a GDP **per capita** of 24,220 euros, France is one of the richest countries in the world.

In 2001, France's budget amounted to 266 billion euros, with a public deficit of 3 percent of the GDP. In spite of policies aimed at curbing inflation, unemployment in France stood at 9.4 percent of the workforce in 2004, and France devoted a quarter of its GDP to social security payments.

The economic strength of France cannot be detached from the country's membership in the EU, especially given that the single market has facilitated the development of French agriculture and **free trade**.

NATURE OF THE GOVERNMENT

The political regime in France is the Fifth Republic, which was approved in a **referendum** by a large majority of the population and promulgated on October 4, 1958. The Fifth Republic is relatively young in constitutional terms compared to the American presidential regime or the British parliamentary model. Yet given France's chaotic institutional history, the Fifth Republic has been something of a haven of stability.

The Fifth Republic was born out of the exceptional circumstances of the Algerian War and an exceptional man, General de Gaulle. It was the successor to the Fourth Republic, which, although having made a significant contribution to

per capita: for each person, especially for each person living in an area or country

free trade: exchange of goods without tariffs charged on importing or exporting

referendum: a popular vote on legislation, brought before the people by their elected leaders or public initiative

postwar reconstruction in France and to the inception of the European project from 1950 onward, remains one of the least-loved French regimes because of the political and governmental instability it engendered and the wars of decolonization that dominated its short tenancy. The Fourth Republic was a parliamentary regime but, given the dominance of the legislature over the executive, commonly is referred to as the Assembly Regime and was even dubbed the "Parties' Regime" by General de Gaulle. The Fifth Republic hence was the inverse of the Fourth: It strengthened executive power at the expense of the legislature.

Basis for the Government. The Fifth Republic Constitution consists of a preamble and eighty-nine articles. The regime is democratic, based on popular sovereignty and the principle of representation. The Preamble reaffirms the nation's attachment to the Declaration of the Rights of Man of 1789 as confirmed and complemented by the economic and social rights of the Preamble of the Fourth Republic Constitution of 1946. This is complemented by the various articles relating to political freedom, freedom of conscience, and the freedom of individuals. Furthermore, these freedoms are guaranteed by a new judicial institution, the Constitutional Council, which rules on the constitutionality of laws.

The organization of powers under the Fifth Republic is dominated by the principle of separation. This is seen in the separation of legislative and executive powers, the incompatibility of concurrent governmental and parliamentary office, and the distinction between specific areas of legislation passed by parliament and all other lawmaking, which is left to the discretion of the government.

The French executive is **bicephalic**, with a president elected by direct universal **suffrage** for five years and a prime minister appointed by the president but responsible to the National Assembly. The National Assembly is the lower house of the **bicameral** French parliament, in which representatives are elected by direct universal suffrage; the president of the Republic has the power to dissolve the parliament. The upper house of the parliament, the Senate, is elected by indirect universal suffrage.

The Constitution of the Fifth Republic is short in length but ambiguous in character. The crucial ambiguity contained within the Constitution concerns the leadership of the executive. The text includes elements that are typical of both presidential and parliamentary regimes. In practice, if not in theory, the regime leans more toward presidentialism. The Constitution was drafted to put an end to the perceived excesses of parliamentarism of previous regimes, and the legislative procedures laid out in the text enable the government to remain master of the legislative game. The Fifth Republic often is referred to as a "mixed" or "hybrid" regime and, more formally, as a semipresidential, presidentialist, or rationalized parliamentary regime.

Government in Legal Principle. The Fifth Republic does not correspond to the norms of classical constitutional law. On reading the constitution, it is possible to distinguish certain similarities with the British parliamentary system as well as with the American presidential system.

The prime minister and government are responsible before parliament, and the executive has the power to dissolve the National Assembly. However, the dual nature of the executive means that although the prime minister directs the operation of the government, which determines and conducts national policy, it is the president—who is not responsible before parliament—who has the power to dissolve the National Assembly.

The regime also displays characteristics in common with presidential systems: The president is elected by direct universal suffrage and is invested with

bicephalic: possessing two heads, as in government with two heads of state

suffrage: to vote, or, the right to vote

bicameral: comprised of two chambers, usually a legislative body

FIGURE 1

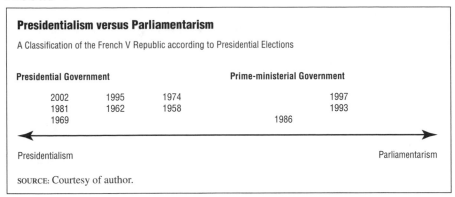

Presidentialism versus Parliamentarism

A Classification of the French V Republic according to Presidential Elections

Presidential Government			Prime-ministerial Government
2002	1995	1974	1997
1981	1962	1958	1993
1969			

1986

←————————————————————————————————→

Presidentialism   Parliamentarism

SOURCE: Courtesy of author.

significant presidential prerogatives, such as the power to submit any government bill to referendum, and emergency powers under Article 16 of the Constitution. The president thus can be considered a "republican monarch," and the presidency, the cornerstone of the Fifth Republic institutions.

Government in Practice. In areas that fall under what is commonly termed the "reserved domain," namely, defense and foreign affairs, the president is able to make policy decisions even if these policy-making powers are not expressly stated in the text of the constitution. The 1962 constitutional reform, which provided for the direct election of the president by all French citizens, provided for the president a democratic legitimacy that exceeded that of all other political mandates in France. Thus the president has considerable influence over the political system. Only in periods when the parliamentary majority is politically opposed to the president's political base is the government's dependence on the head of state called into question. During such times, commonly referred to as "cohabitation," the prime minister, with a **mandate** derived from and supported by a parliamentary majority, implements the government's political program and the president is relegated to a principally ceremonial role, more akin to that of the queen of England than that of the president of the United States. Yet during such periods the president continues to have considerable influence. In 2000 a constitutional amendment sought to put an end to the difficulties experienced during the three periods of opposition parliamentary control by reducing the presidential mandate from seven years to five and consequently making it coincide with the legislative term of the National Assembly.

Thus it is possible to put forward contradictory interpretations of the Fifth Republic regime depending on whether it is the text of the constitution or the actual practice of the constitution that is being examined. In short, France under the Fifth Republic has two constitutions in one.

mandate: to command, order, or require; or, a command, order, or requirement

DIVISION OF POWERS: THE ROLE OF LEGISLATOR

In France, as in many other countries, the role of the parliament has been weakened, and the 577 deputies and 322 senators have seen many of their powers and prerogatives reduced. Europeanization, **globalization**, **decentralization**, the increased powers of the judiciary and the media, and the power of the executive are among the principal causes of the legislature's diminished power and influence. Nonetheless, parliament remains a critical forum for democratic debate and the legitimization of power in France.

globalization: the process of expanding regional concerns to a worldwide viewpoint, especially politics, economics, or culture

decentralize: to move power from a central authority to multiple periphery government branches or agencies

The French parliament has three functions: to represent the democratically expressed wishes of the electorate, to make decisions, and to act as a check on the executive. Under the Fifth Republic the parliament's activities in relation to all three functions have been controlled strictly. The government has at its disposal a whole range of measures that enable it to restrain the parliament.

The power to legislate is divided between the legislature and the executive. Parliament can legislate only in the specific areas defined in Article 34 of the Constitution because Article 37 states that all other areas are considered to fall within the government's prerogative. Yet arguably the most powerful weapon in the government's armory is the its ability to make parliament vote on a bill that has not been subjected to any debate in either the National Assembly or the Senate. According to Article 49.3 of the Constitution, unless a motion of censure is carried by the National Assembly, thus precipitating the resignation of the government, the bill is considered to have been adopted.

ROLE OF THE JUDICIARY AND OTHER INSTITUTIONS

The constitutional tradition in France has been to have judicial authorities rather than a judicial power, and the constitution does not deviate from this rule. The history of the French judicial system is one of frequent conflict—first between monarchs and parliaments composed of judges and then between revolutionaries and Napoleon Bonaparte (1769–1821). The **authoritarian** nature of Napoleon I's conception of power meant that he also wanted to avoid being controlled by ordinary judges. Hence, he established an administrative justice system that was designed to pass judgment on conflicts arising from the relationship between the public and the state.

There is a single judicial system, although it enjoys multiple jurisdictions and essentially is made up of two branches: a civil and criminal branch with the *Cour de cassation* as the highest **ordinary court** and an administrative branch with the Council of State as the highest administrative court. One major innovation of the Fifth Republic was the creation of the Constitutional Council, which fulfils the essential role of ruling on the constitutionality of legislation. The French judicial system professes to be independent, although its independence is guaranteed by the *Conseil supérieure de la magistrature*, which in turn is presided over by the president of the republic.

POLITICAL PARTIES AND INTEREST GROUPS

French political parties generally align themselves on a left–right dimension. Although the origins of the left–right divide in France can be traced back to the revolution, political parties in France emerged later than in many other democracies, and contemporary parties are comparatively recent political groupings. The first modern political parties were founded on the left, including the Radical Party in 1901, the Socialist Party in 1905, and the Communist Party in 1920. It was only after the liberation of France from Germany's occupation in 1944 that the right began to organize itself along the lines of structured political parties.

Officially recognized by the constitution and an essential element of democratic life, French political parties are great in number, are generally top-down in their organizational structure, and have a tendency to change their names frequently. Parties in contemporary France tend to have relatively few members and are more accurately described as white-collar rather than mass parties. From 2002 through 2004 the center-right Union for a Popular Movement was in

authoritarianism: the domination of the state or its leader over individuals

ordinary court: a court that hears civil cases, especially in the United Kingdom

government and the center-left Socialist Party was the largest opposition party. Aside from the Union for a Popular Movement and the Socialist Party, French political life is animated by a multitude of parties ranging from the National Front on the extreme right to the Communist Revolutionary League and Workers' Struggle on the extreme left. A number of parties that started life as single-issue groupings, such as the conservative Hunting, Fishing, Nature Traditions and the progressive Green Party, have secured political representation in France at a local, national, and European level.

The electoral system together with the presidentialization of the Fifth Republic helped engender a two-bloc presidential party system, which pits

ILLUSTRATED POSTER IN SUPPORT OF THE FRENCH REVOLUTION OF 1789: "UNITY, INDIVISIBILITY OF THE REPUBLIC, LIBERTY, EQUALITY, FRATERNITY, OR DEATH." The French bourgeoisie class toiled in the late 18th century at the hands of the privileged nobility and clergy. An economic recession burdened workers with exorbitant taxes to fund the recovery. The French Revolution (1789–1799) provided an overhaul of the country's political and social composition with the eradication of its feudal system. (SOURCE: © TIME LIFE PICTURES/GETTY IMAGES)

coalition: an alliance, partnership, or union
of disparate peoples or individuals

a **coalition** of the left, principally the Socialist and Communist Parties, against a coalition of the Gaullist right with other center-right parties for power. However, the French party system fragmented somewhat in the 1980s after the formation of new political parties, such as the National Front and the Greens, and the decline of the Communist Party. The 2002 presidential and parliamentary election results demonstrated the extent to which the so-called "parties of government" have lost favor with the electorate while smaller opposition or extremist parties have become more appealing.

As with political parties, French trade unions are officially recognized by the state and are weak and multiple in number. Decline in the trade union movement has been as pronounced in France as elsewhere in Western Europe. Although 25 percent of workers were unionized in the 1950s, in the early 2000s less than 8 percent of French workers belonged to a union, and the union movement as a whole has been highly divided. Yet although the representativeness of trade unions is clearly open to question, they have retained considerable influence over French public life.

ELECTIONS, VOTING, AND CITIZEN PARTICIPATION

There are no fewer than six different kinds of direct elections in France. Two national elections (the presidential and legislative) are held every five years (except when the National Assembly has been dissolved or the presidency has been unexpectedly vacated), using a two-round **majoritarian** electoral system. Other direct elections are held on regional, departmental, municipal (since 1986), and European (since 1979) levels. In European elections voters elect French representatives to the European Parliament, using a system of **proportional representation**.

majoritarianism: the practice of rule by a
majority vote

proportional system: a political system in
which legislative seats or offices are awarded
based on the proportional number of votes
received by a party in an election

In addition, French voters are called on to vote in referendums, a key element of French political life. Since 1958 there have been eight referendums on issues ranging from the adoption of the Fifth Republic Constitution in October 1958 to the reduction of the presidential mandate from seven to five years in September 2000.

Active citizen participation in political life has not been limited to elections and referendums; the French also frequently resort to more spontaneous and less organized forms of public expression such as marching and demonstrating.

At the beginning of the twenty-first century it was possible to distinguish a shift in the relationship between the French public and the political elite. The increasing volatility of the electorate and the considerable rise in the rate of abstention are symptoms of the French public's dissatisfaction with and disinterest in the political class.

See also: European Parliament; European Union; Political Parties; Presidential Systems.

BIBLIOGRAPHY

Bell, John. *French Constitutional Law*. New York: Oxford University Press, 1992.

Carcassonne, Guy. *La Constitution*. Paris: Editions du Seuil, 2002.

Charlot, Jean. *La Politique en France*. Paris: Livre de Poche, 1994.

Cole, Alistair. *French Politics and Society*. New York: Prentice Hall, 1998.

Duhamel, Olivier. *Le pouvoir politique en France, vertus et limites*. Paris: Seuil, 1993.

Elgie, Robert. *Political Institutions in Contemporary France*. Oxford, UK: Oxford University Press, 2003.

International Labour Office Bureau of Statistics. *LABORSTA: Labour Statistics Database*. <http://laborsta.ilo.org>.

Knapp, Andrew, and Vincent Wright. *The Government and Politics of France*. London: Routledge, 2001.

McMillan, James. *Modern France: 1880–2002*. Oxford, UK: Oxford University Press, 2003.

Mény, Yves. *The French Political System*. Paris: Documentation française, 1998.

Ministry for Employment, Labour and Social Cohesion. *Research and Statistics*. <http://www.travail.gouv.fr/etudes/etudes_f.html>.

National Institute of Statistics and Economic Studies. *France in Facts and Figures*. <http://www.insee.fr/en/ffc/accueil_ffc.asp>.

Safran, William. *The French Polity*. New York: Longman, 2003.

Stevens, Anne. *Government and Politics of France*. New York: Palgrave Macmillan, 2003.

United Nations, Population Division. *World Population Prospects*. <http://esa.un.org/unpp/>.

Arnauld Miguet

Freedom of Assembly and Association

As with many aspects of U.S. law, the freedoms of assembly and association in the United States draw heavily on English origins. The 1670 arrest of the founder of the Pennsylvania colony, William Penn (1644–1718), in London helped shape the first official right of association recognized within a state declaration of rights. Penn had been locked out of the Grace Church Street Friends Meetinghouse in London and forbidden to preach in any building in the city. Therefore, he preached in the street outside the hall to an orderly group of several hundred Quakers. He then was charged with unlawful assembly, disturbing the peace, and inciting a riot. Penn vigorously fought the charges against him as a thinly veiled attempt to silence his nonconformist religious views. Despite fines and imprisonment, the jury refused to find him guilty, and Penn took that experience with him to the newly formed state of Pennsylvania when he helped craft its declaration of rights in 1701.

In his 1776 work *Fragments on Government* Jeremy Bentham (1748–1832) described freedom of association as "the security with which malcontents may communicate their sentiments, concert their plans, and practice every mode of opposition short of actual revolt, before the executive power can be legally justified in disturbing them" (Levy 1985, p. 167). In 1791, the year in which the U.S. Bill of Rights was adopted, Thomas Paine (1737–1809) published *The Rights of Man*. He wrote that "the end of all political associations is the preservation of the rights of man, which rights are liberty, property, and security" (Paine 1791). This premise, Paine asserted, became evident after the French and American revolutions renovated "the natural order of things [and discovered] a system of principles as universal as truth and the existence of man, and combining moral with political happiness and national prosperity" (Paine 1791).

"The distinctive conceptual feature of freedom of association is its hybrid character as both an individual and a collective right," according to the scholar Stephen Neff (Neff 1995, p. 1). In this view the right incorporates the individual right to associate casually with one individual and others, but it also provides the right to associate more permanently as a **collectivity** that has its own right to

collectivity: the state of being whole or complete, as a group

function effectively without undue government restraint. Such a right would encompass the right of an organization to raise funds and affiliate with other organizations to generate change.

APPLICATION IN THE UNITED STATES

Although the "right of the people peaceably to assemble" was incorporated into the U.S. Bill of Rights, the U.S. Constitution offers no explicit protection for a right of association. Instead, beginning in the twentieth century, U.S. courts led by the U.S. Supreme Court interpreted the First Amendment's guarantees of freedom of speech, assembly, and **petition** to include the affiliate right of free association. In 1958, for example, Justice John Marshall Harlan wrote, "It is beyond debate that freedom to engage in association for the advancement of beliefs and ideas is an inseparable aspect of 'liberty' . . . which embraces freedom of speech" (*NAACP v. Alabama*, at 460). In 1980 then Chief Justice Warren Burger noted that the right of association was among the "unarticulated rights . . . implicit in enumerated guarantees" of the Constitution (*Richmond Newspapers v. Virginia*, at 579).

The fundamental logic involved in providing constitutional protection to free association is that people must form relationships and affiliations to engage in free speech, express their ideas, advance shared interests, and participate effectively in political debate, oversight of government, and broad self-governance. Thus, the freedom to associate is a **natural right** that is both an extension and a foundation of free speech and the cornerstone of democratic participation. As the Supreme Court upheld in 1876, "The very idea of a government, republican in form, implies a right on the part of its citizens to meet peaceably for consultation in respect to public affairs" (*United States v. Cruikshank*, at 552). And in 1960 Justice Potter Stewart wrote, "Like freedom of speech and a free press, the right of peaceable assembly was considered by the Framers of our Constitution to lie at the foundation of a government based upon the consent of an informed citizenry" (*Bates v. Little Rock*, at 523).

Despite the vital role of association and assembly in a democracy, these rights are not **absolute** in the United States. In fact, the Supreme Court has stated consistently that when speech is intermingled with conduct, as when people gather to demonstrate, march, or picket on public roads or sidewalks, the conduct may be subject to reasonable regulations (usually as to time, place, and manner) designed to advance important government interests. The Court has determined that the right of individuals to assemble to share and express ideas must be balanced, for example, against countervailing government interests in community safety and the safe and efficient passage of cars and pedestrians. In addition, the personal right to privacy and freedom from harassment in the sanctity of one's own home or inside a health-care facility limits how and when people may assemble on adjoining public property. Because the courts' weighting of the competing interests is subject to political, economic, and social influences, the right to assemble in the United States is variable.

Like other First Amendment rights, the right to assemble is likely to contract during times of conflict and strife in the nation. However, the Supreme Court's assembly and association decisions often have protected unpopular groups as a source of alternative ideas and divergent voices. Also, the Court has held repeatedly "that publicly owned streets, sidewalks, and parks are so historically associated with the exercise of First Amendment rights that access to them for purposes of exercising such rights cannot be denied absolutely" (*Lloyd Corp. v. Tanner* 1972, at 559).

petition: a written appeal for a desired action, or, to request an action, especially of government

natural right: a basic privilege intrinsic to all people that cannot be denied by the government

absolute: complete, pure, free from restriction or limitation

CONGRESS OF INDUSTRIAL ORGANIZATIONS (CIO) LABOR UNION AUTO WORKERS PICKET AT THE DETROIT GENERAL MOTORS BUILDING. From 1935 through 1955, the CIO operated in conjunction with the United Auto Workers (UAW) to promote unions, a right protected by the European Convention on the Protection of Human Rights and Fundamental Freedoms. (SOURCE: © AP/WIDE WORLD PHOTOS)

Beginning in the 1930s and continuing through the Cold War the Supreme Court's decisions related to the American Communist Party established the parameters of the right of individuals to associate with organizations the government deems subversive. In an early decision the Court struck down the conviction of an organizer and speaker at a Communist Party meeting in support of a **maritime** workers strike. The Court ruled in 1937 that the right of association provides an individual with the right to conduct meetings "for peaceable political action" and to belong to an organization that may advocate violence or illegal activity (*DeJonge v. Oregon* 1937, at 365). In subsequent cases the Supreme Court generally rejected the notion of guilt by association, holding that individuals may be punished only when they specifically intend to advance illegal goals through the organization.

This has not always assured that government would not punish individuals for mere membership in disfavored organizations. The Supreme Court, in fact,

maritime: relating to the sea or the coast

turned a blind eye to the pernicious reasons for state laws requiring both the Ku Klux Klan and the National Association for the Advancement of Colored People (NAACP) to disclose their lists of members. Without requiring evidence that the groups were engaged in illegal acts, the Court determined that the government could force disclosure of the names and addresses of group members to control the illegal activities of both groups.

Nevertheless, the Supreme Court twice refused to allow states to demand the names of NAACP members. The Court reasoned that disclosure constituted a type of official harassment and intimidation of the NAACP, then the leading black equal rights organization in the nation. Compelled membership disclosure, the Court said, violated the First Amendment rights of the members of this "wholly legitimate organization" (*Gibson v. Florida Legislative Investigative Committee* 1963, at 555) to freely and privately associate and chilled the likelihood that other groups would form to advance "**dissident** beliefs" (*NAACP v. Alabama* 1958, at 462). In 1982 the Court used similar reasoning to strike down a state law requiring the Socialist Workers Party to disclose the names of its donors. Many believe that the right of association in the United States protects the privacy of such lists, although the full impact of the USA Patriot Act (passed soon after the September 11, 2001, terrorist attacks) on this protection is unknown.

Supreme Court decisions on the rights of association and assembly may have been critical to the vitality and effectiveness of the civil rights movement and other groups advocating social change in the United States. In 1940, for example, the Court struck down a state ban on labor picketing. The decision in *Thornhill v. Alabama* acknowledged that picketing was an important means for labor to mobilize, counterbalance the power of business owners, and affect public attitudes and policy by publicizing the facts of a labor dispute. In the years since that time the Court has held that states have the authority to regulate the number of picketers, the volume of their chanting, the disruption caused by mass protests, and the economic harm of targeted pickets. However, the Court has determined that the Constitution prohibits an outright ban on demonstrations and protests because they are "indispensable to the effective and intelligent use of the processes of popular government" (quoting *Thornhill v. Alabama* 1940, at 103).

During the 1960s several Supreme Court rulings protected organizations and activities designed to advance racial equality and end **de facto** segregation in the South. In 1963, in *NAACP v. Button,* the Court said that states could not punish the NAACP for helping individuals find and pay for lawyers to fight racial discrimination. Virginia courts had ruled that this NAACP practice violated a state ban on legal solicitation. However, the Court asserted that the First Amendment protected the right of the NAACP and its members to express grievances and seek **redress** through orchestrated lawsuits. Indeed, the Court proffered such **litigation** as an essential and constitutionally protected means of expressing dissident political views.

The Supreme Court also relied on First Amendment protection for assembly and association to rule that states could not impose criminal **sanctions** for disturbing the peace against nonviolent, lawful civil rights assemblies. In 1961, for example, the Court in *Garner v. Louisiana* struck down the state breach-of-the-peace convictions of five blacks who had engaged in a peaceful sit-in at a whites-only lunch counter in Baton Rouge. In 1963 the Court overturned criminal sanctions imposed on black students who had marched peacefully on the statehouse carrying signs proclaiming, "Down with Segregation." In that case, *Edwards v. South Carolina,* the Court determined

dissident: one who disagrees with the actions or political philosophy of his or her government or religion

de facto: (Latin) actual; in effect but not officially declared

redress: to make right, or, compensation

litigate: to bring a disagreement or violation of the law before a judge for a legal decision

sanction: economic, political, or military reprisals, or, to ratify

that the U.S. Constitution clearly and unequivocally protected "the peaceful expression of unpopular views."

At times, however, U.S. courts have allowed the government to punish disfavored groups and associations of minorities, aliens, and dissidents. Protection for associations ends when gatherings, parades, demonstrations, or pickets trespass on private property, destroy or vandalize property, or threaten the health and safety of individuals or communities. Critics assert that the right of association in the United States discriminates against the poor and the disenfranchised in favor of property owners. Such individuals cite the Supreme Court's 1988 decision holding that the government may ban picketing that targets individuals in their own homes. In 1988 in *Frisby v. Schultz* the Court determined that a city could ban picketing of residences that prohibited marching outside the home of an abortion provider. The Court stated that the privacy rights of "captive" homeowners who do not wish to hear the message of protesters outweigh the rights of "focused" picketers.

In the 1990s, amid bombings of abortion clinics and murders of abortion providers, the High Court ruled that laws establishing no-protest buffer zones around abortion facilities could limit the assembly and association rights of would-be protesters to protect the health and privacy of health-care clients. City and state governments also have imposed similar no-protest zones around political conventions, schools, courthouses, polling places, and meetings of the World Trade Organization, for example, as essential to protect the safety of congregating participants, prevent the destruction of property, and preserve peace and order. The Supreme Court has determined that such laws do not violate the Constitution because they regulate the location of speech and association and do not target or silence a specific group or idea.

In the United States the right to associate sometimes—but only sometimes—encompasses the right not to associate. Freedom of association logically requires the right to determine with whom to join. Thus, the government generally cannot require individuals to associate with particular groups or **ideologies** without violating this freedom. This means that small private organizations that assume no public or quasi-public role have the right to exclude individuals who violate core tenets of the organization. The Court has ruled that the right to be free from undesired associations enables private

ideology: a system of beliefs composed of ideas or values, from which political, social, or economic programs are often derived

NAACP V. ALABAMA

NAACP v. Alabama (357 U.S. 449, 1958) was a landmark civil rights case as well as an important decision regarding the freedoms of assembly and association. In 1956 the attorney general of Alabama sued the National Association for the Advancement of Colored People (NAACP), claiming that the organization had violated a state law requiring "foreign" corporations to qualify before doing business in Alabama. The NAACP believed that the 'state's suit violated its rights to freedom of assembly and freedom of speech. The state of Alabama also issued a subpoena for the 'NAACP's records, including the organization's bank statements and leases as well as a list of its Alabama members.

The NAACP appealed repeatedly to the United States Supreme Court until the justices finally agreed to consider the case. The court decided unanimously in favor of the NAACP on June 30, 1958. The opinion, delivered by Justice John Harlan II, held that forced disclosure of membership lists would violate the 'petitioners' rights to free association. Harlan went on to say that the freedom of people to associate with groups devoted to the "advancement of beliefs and ideas" is covered by the due process clause of the Fourteenth Amendment.

owners of a shopping mall to prevent war protesters from distributing handbills in the mall. It allowed the Boy Scouts of America, a group that proclaims its foundation on religious principles, to expel an openly gay leader, and it held that the private organizers of the huge, annual, city-licensed St. Patrick's Day Parade in Boston could refuse to allow a gay-lesbian-bisexual association to participate. However, the Supreme Court also has ruled that the U.S. Jaycees (Junior Chamber of Commerce), a politically influential, historically male national organization whose members include many government officials and business owners, may not discriminate on the basis of gender. In a legal context the size and power of the association, as well as the nature of the discrimination, determine when an association may exclude certain individuals.

APPLICATION AROUND THE WORLD

All the primary international treaties on human rights guarantee the right of freedom to associate. The first of these international covenants was enacted in 1953. Article 11 of the European Convention on the Protection of Human Rights and Fundamental Freedoms, which has been adopted by more than forty members of the Council of Europe (CoE), states that:

1. Everyone has the right to freedom of peaceful assembly and to freedom of association with others, including the right to form and to join trade unions for the protection of his interest.
2. No restrictions shall be placed on the exercise of these rights other than such as are prescribed by law and are necessary in a democratic society in the interests of national security or public safety, for the prevention of disorder or crime, for the protection of health or morals or for the protection of the rights and freedoms of others.

Similar regional conventions have been adopted in American states and African nations. The most recent international commitment to freedom of association, the UN Declaration on Human Rights Defenders adopted in 1999, establishes that "everyone has the right, individually and in association with others, at the national and international levels, to meet or assemble peacefully; to form, join and participate in non-governmental organizations, associations or

∎ ∎ ∎

RICHMOND NEWSPAPERS V. VIRGINIA

Richmond Newspapers v. Virginia (448 U.S. 555, 1980) was a case that involved public access to criminal trials. A trial judge in Virginia had closed a murder trial to reporters and the general public after three mistrials. The defense had asked for closure and the prosecution did not object. Two reporters on the staff of Richmond Newspapers then challenged the judge's action. The case came before the United States Supreme Court in February 1980. At issue was whether the closure of the trial was a violation of the First Amendment (freedom of speech) or the Sixth Amendment (right to a public trial in criminal cases).

The Court's 7-to-1 decision, handed down on July 2, 1980, was a landmark ruling because it extended the First Amendment's guarantee of freedom of speech to include the right of public and media access to government information, including access to the courtroom. The Supreme Court also noted that the First Amendment applied to the right to assembly in such public places as courtrooms. The majority opinion stated that "certain unarticulated rights" were implicitly contained in the guarantees listed in the Bill of Rights.

groups; and to communicate with non-governmental or **intergovernmental** organizations." However, many believe that Article 22 of the International Covenant on Civil and Political Rights (ICCPR) is the "most important international human rights treaty dealing with freedom of association and assembly" (Irish and Simon 2001, p. 37). The ICCPR basically adopts the relevant language from the European Convention on the Protection of Human Rights and Fundamental Freedoms. The UN's International Labour Organization conventions also has made significant contributions to **delineating** these rights.

International laws define the freedom of association broadly as the right of individuals to join together in groups to pursue common goals. The Human Rights Committee, established under the ICCPR, interprets that international law in accordance with the Siracusa Principles adopted in 1984 by a panel of thirty-one international experts. The ICCPR allows restrictions on the freedom of association for certain narrow and clearly specified reasons. Freedom of association may be restricted only when its exercise poses a real, clear, immediate, and serious threat of harm to the nation, its territory, or its independence and when the restrictions are essential to ensuring the peaceful functioning of society.

Governments must justify any limits imposed on the freedom of association and may not use vague, **arbitrary**, or sweeping limits as a means to repress or suppress opposition. Limits should advance, not undermine, the basic democratic tenets of pluralism and tolerance, respond to a pressing public need, and be carefully tailored to impose only the restrictions necessary to address the specific cause of the limit. Accordingly, governments may abolish or ban a specific group or type of association only in the most extreme case and only after all less restrictive alternatives have been examined carefully and found to be inadequate.

Article 8 of the International Covenant on Economic, Social, and Cultural Rights goes a bit further. It recognizes that the simple right to form and join an association, specifically a trade union, is not sufficient without the right for that organization to "function freely." If governments must confer official "non-government organization" status on an association before it may enjoy certain legal benefits, for example, governments might use this power coercively. Thus, human rights groups suggest that registration requirements should be minimal and the registration process quick, simple, and reviewable.

Despite some concern in the early twenty-first century that governments were developing increasingly subtle and sophisticated methods to limit the freedom of association, an international group of experts that produces an annual study of the state of freedom in the world determined that the last three decades of the twentieth century witnessed "dramatic progress in the [worldwide] expansion of freedom and democratic governance" and growth in the number of nations that enjoy "a climate of respect for civil liberties [and] significant independent civic life" (Karatnycky 2003).

See also: Freedom of Expression.

intergovernmental: between or involving multiple governments, with each government retaining full decision-making power

delineate: to depict, portray, or outline with detail

arbitrary: capricious, random, or changing without notice

BIBLIOGRAPHY

Bentham, Jeremy. *Fragments of Government* (1776). London: University of London Athlone Press, 1977.

Brant, Irving. *The Bill of Rights: Its Origin and Meaning.* Indianapolis, IN: Bobbs-Merrill, 1965.

European Convention on the Protection of Human Rights and Fundamental Freedoms. <http://conventions.coe.int>.

Irish, Leon E., and Karla W. Simon. "Recent Developments Regarding the 'Neglected Right.' " *American Society of International Law Human Rights Interest Group Newsletter* 9, no. 1/2 (2001):37.

Joseph, Sarah, Jenny Schultz, and Melissa Castan. *The International Covenant on Civil and Political Rights: Cases, Materials and Commentary,* 2nd ed. Oxford, UK: Oxford University Press, 2004.

Karatnycky, Adrian. *Freedom in the World 2003: Liberty's Expansion in a Turbulent World: Thirty Years of the Survey of Freedom*, 2003. <http://www.freedomhouse.org/research/freeworld/2002/webessay2003.pdf>.

Lawyers Committee for Human Rights. *The Neglected Right: Freedom of Association in International Human Rights Law,* 1997. <http://www.lchr.org/pubs/neglrt.htm>.

Levy, Leonard. *Emergence of a Free Press.* Oxford, UK: Oxford University Press, 1985.

Neff, Stephen. "Report of Mission to Egypt." *Human Rights First* 1 (November 1995):1–2.

Nowak, Manfred. *UN Covenant on Civil and Political Rights: CCPR Commentary.* Arlington, VA: N.P. Engel, 1993.

Paine, Thomas. *The Rights of Man* (1791). <http://www.infidels.org/library/historical/thomas_paine/rights_of_man/index.shtml>.

"Symposium: The Siracusa Principles on the Limitation and Derogation Provisions in the International Covenant on Civil and Political Rights." *Human Rights Quarterly* 7, no. 1 (Special Issue, February 1985):1–157.

UN General Assembly. *Declaration on the Right and Responsibility of Individuals, Groups and Organs of Society to Promote and Protect Universally Recognized Human Rights and Fundamental Freedoms.* <http://www.unhchr.ch/huridocda/huridoca.nsf/(Symbol)/A.RES.53.144.En?OpenDocument>.

Court Cases

Amalgamated Food Employees Union v. Logan Valley Plaza, 391 U.S. 308 (1968).

Bates v. Little Rock, 361 U.S. 516 (1960).

DeJonge v. Oregon, 299 U.S. 353 (1937).

Edwards v. South Carolina, 372 U.S. 229 (1963).

Frisby v. Schultz, 484 U.S. 1003 (1988).

Gibson v. Florida Legislative Investigative Committee, 372 U.S. 539 (1963).

Lloyd Corp. v. Tanner, 405 U.S. 1015 (1972).

NAACP v. Alabama, 357 U.S. 449 (1958).

Richmond Newspapers v. Virginia, 448 U.S. 555 (1980).

Thornhill v. Alabama, 310 U.S. 88 (1940).

United States v. Cruikshank, 92 U.S. 542 (1876).

Susan Dente Ross

Freedom of Expression

Freedom to express one's views is both a basic human right and a bedrock principle of democracy. If people are denied the right to speak their minds, something essential to their sense of autonomy is removed. Democracy cannot function without opponents being able to criticize the actions of those in power. Elections are meaningless charades if those challenging the government are muzzled.

Freedom of expression took a long time to develop. Governments everywhere and at all times usually prefer to hear praise rather than criticism. In the past, most governments were unable or unwilling to separate disagreement with their policies from outright disloyalty. While critics were sometimes tolerated, governments were loathe to recognize freedom of expression as a right. In Western civilization, seventeenth-century England primarily was where the idea of a "loyal opposition" first began to take hold.

Though the concept is now widespread, the right to freedom of expression is by no means universally practiced. Throughout the world, people are imprisoned, or worse, for merely expressing opposition to their government's policies. Countries such as China, Cuba, and Saudi Arabia are decidedly not free. At the other end of the spectrum are a number of countries where freedom of expression is given constitutional status and usually respected. In between, there are other countries that can be labeled "partly free."

THE UNITED STATES

As the first country to enshrine freedom of expression in its constitution, the United States still gives this right broader protection than most other nations. The Constitution's First Amendment, adopted soon after the original document's **ratification**, says: "Congress shall make no law . . . abridging the freedom of speech." The "due process" clause of the Fourteenth Amendment, ratified in 1868, has been interpreted in such a way that this prohibition applies to the states as well.

ratify: to make official or to officially sanction

Read carefully, the First Amendment seems to be **absolute**. However, only very rarely can a legal command be absolute in actual practice. Consequently, individual Supreme Court justices have developed three approaches to interpreting these words: near absolute protection, a preferred position, and balancing of interests. The first position, held by a few individual justices but never by a majority, contends that the phrase "no law" should be read as literally as possible. If government wants to regulate any kind of speech, it has to show that there is a "compelling governmental interest" at stake and that the regulation in question is "narrowly tailored." It is very unlikely that government will be able to meet this test. The preferred position doctrine does not go quite so far. It asserts that freedom of speech is the most basic of rights. If it comes into conflict with some other provision of the Constitution, it maintains a preferred but not absolute position that can be overcome when other compelling values are demonstrated. The third approach argues that the First Amendment must simply be read in light of the entire document, and that freedom of speech should be balanced against other important interests.

absolute: complete, pure, free from restriction or limitation

There are at least seven problem areas regarding freedom of expression. The first involves war and national security. Revealing military secrets or troop movements during wartime obviously can have serious consequences, and in general the court has upheld the government's right to prosecute those who communicate such things. Another issue involves whether sharp criticism of the government's war policies is considered protected speech. A landmark case arose during World War I (1914–1918) when German sympathizers urged young men not to report for the draft. The Court laid out the "clear and present danger" rule, stating that, considering the place and circumstances, if speech was seen as being likely to lead to a serious evil that the government had the duty to resist, then it could be regulated. Over the years, the Court has retreated from this rule, affording greater protection to political speech even in dangerous times.

Save Freedom of Speech, Buy War Bonds (Norman Rockwell, 1943). In 1941 President Franklin D. Roosevelt encouraged U.S. citizens to purchase war bonds as a patriotic act that not only funded the American military fighting in World War II but also served as a personal financial investment. (SOURCE: © SWIM INK 2, LLC/CORBIS. PRINTED BY PERMISSION OF THE NORMAN ROCKWELL FAMILY AGENCY. COPYRIGHT © 1943 THE NORMAN ROCKWELL FAMILY ENTITIES. SECONDARY SOURCE: 506059, NORMAN ROCKWELL FAMILY AGENCY.)

The second problem area is symbolic "speech." Although the Constitution refers to "speech," we often communicate through the use of symbols, and the Supreme Court has extended the meaning of "speech" to include such symbols. For example, wearing a black arm band to school (to protest the Vietnam War between 1964 and 1975) and burning an American flag have both been protected from government attempts to punish the perpetrators.

A third and more vexing problem involves hate speech. Should people be free to hurl potentially harmful invective statements at others, or does the need for public civility and the decent treatment of all citizens trump one's right of expression? This is a classic case of two desirable goods coming into conflict. A particularly cogent example of this dilemma occurred in 1978, when a handful of American Nazi Party members wanted to march in Skokie, Illinois, home to many Holocaust survivors. The march and rally had no purpose other than to provoke the residents by dragging up hateful memories. Nevertheless, the Supreme Court upheld the rights of the marchers rather than the watchers. By and large, in the United States the courts have come down on the side of allowing the maximum amount of speech, no matter how vile its content. The fear has been that if one person's speech is made dependent on someone else's reaction to it, there is a danger that groups will press government to silence their political opponents.

The fourth problem area involves sexually oriented communication, especially the extreme sexually oriented material called pornography. Pornographic communication, by definition, contributes nothing to the public good and is not subject to protection under the First Amendment. However, if government is allowed to freely regulate sexually oriented communication, there is always the danger it will use that power to stifle artistic creativity, and perhaps even political expression, rather than only genuine pornography. The Court has repeatedly held that pornography is not protected by the First Amendment, but it has been unable to define what is genuinely pornographic. As a result, governmental attempts to regulate pornography have often been struck down on vagueness grounds. The Internet has made this issue even more difficult, but the Court has tended to strike down regulations. This is because of the difficulty of distinguishing protected, if sexually explicit, speech from pornography.

A fifth problem area relates to communication in political campaigning. Modern campaigns for public office have become very expensive. Therefore, candidates must either be wealthy or able to raise large amounts of money from contributors. Does this fact give those with the most resources to contribute to campaigns an undue influence over politicians or political contributors who are not wealthy, thereby harming the equality of political participation that is essential to electoral democracy? Government is allowed to regulate campaign finance in the interest of promoting transparency and responsibility and avoiding corruption. However, can government—even in the interest of fair elections—regulate the amount individuals can give to candidates, or does such regulation **infringe** on a candidate's or contributor's freedom of speech? In 2003 the Supreme Court upheld some modest limitations Congress had put on campaign contributions, diminishing its previously near **absolutist** position.

infringe: to exceed the limits of; to violate

absolutism: a way of governing, usually monarchic, that reflects complete control and an unwillingness to compromise or deviate from dogma or principles

The sixth problem area involves libel. The law of libel, holding people accountable for damage that flows from their speech, is very old. It is based on a simple principle: if someone stands outside a butcher shop and falsely and knowingly claims that the owner puts poison in his meat, the butcher can recover damages for lost business. Freedom of speech provides the speaker no protection. On the other hand, if someone satirizes or even makes false statements about the president or a member of Congress, they would be protected by the First Amendment. Because the behavior of public officials must be subject to unfettered criticism in a democracy, the U.S. Supreme Court considers them fair game and does not find utterances about them to be libelous—even though they might clearly be so if directed at a private individual. The Supreme Court generally has held that utterances about celebrities and other "public figures" usually are also protected by the First Amendment. They cannot sue successfully for libel unless they can show that the comments about them were deliberate falsehoods or were made with reckless disregard for the truth.

The final problem that arises in connection with freedom of expression is the matter of commercial speech. Most of the speech covered above has direct or indirect political implications that make it worthy of basic protection under the First Amendment. On the other hand, pure commercial advertising does not. In the past, governments and quasi-governmental bodies like professional associations sometimes regulated commercial advertising for a variety of purposes that they regarded as in the public interest. For example, states attempted to regulate the advertising of prices for special **commodities** such as prescription drugs. However, the Supreme Court has thwarted many such regulations, ruling that commercial speech, though not absolute, enjoys some First Amendment protection.

There is an inherent tension between **majoritarian** democracy and the First Amendment. Any policy enacted by an elected legislature likely enjoys the support of the people. When a court voids an attempt by the federal or state governments to regulate speech, it is acting against the presumed will of the people. However, the whole purpose of the First Amendment is to take certain issues off the political agenda. Freedom of speech is not open to a show of hands. The issue for the Court is deciding whether or not the type of speech at issue falls under the First Amendment's protection. If so, then the regulation must fall.

OTHER FREE SOCIETIES

The American approach is unique in the extensive protection it gives to freedom of speech. A large number of other countries have similarly worded guarantees written into their constitutions, but their courts are much more deferential toward governmental regulations, particularly in such sensitive areas as hate speech. Canada and Germany offer useful comparisons.

The Canadian Charter of Rights and Freedoms provides that "Everyone has the following fundamental freedoms: . . . (b)freedom of thought, belief, opinion and expression. . ." (section 2). However, the document contains two important qualifications. The first is that the Charter "guarantees the rights and freedoms set out in it subject only to such reasonable limits as can be demonstrably justified in a free and democratic society." (section 1). This suggests that the preferred position or balancing approaches are the only ones open to the Canadian courts. The second qualification is that either the federal parliament or a provincial legislature may insert a clause into a **statute** that immunizes it from judicial invalidation for five years (at which point it can be renewed). This ultimately puts freedom of speech in the hands of the legislature. Although this second provision is seldom used, it always lies at the ready.

Given its Nazi past, Germany has faced several special problems in building a democracy. For example, while political parties are free to organize, the constitution stipulates that "Parties which, by reason of their aims or the behavior of their adherents, seek to impair or abolish the free democratic basic order" may be banned by the courts (Article 21). Both the Nazi and Communist Parties were outlawed under this provision at one time or another. Furthermore, racially tinged speech prompts a special sensitivity. The constitution guarantees freedom of expression in these words: "Everyone shall have the right freely to express and disseminate his opinion." However, the right is "limited by the provisions of the general laws, the provisions of law for the protection of youth, and by the right to inviolability of personal honor." (Article 5). In 2000 the

commodity: an article of trade or commerce that can be transported, especially an agricultural or mining product

majoritarianism: the practice of rule by a majority vote

statute: a law created by a legislature that is inferior to constitutional law

German constitutional court upheld a law that made denial of the Holocaust an offense, and applied it to postings on the Internet. An Australian citizen who had placed such material on the Internet was sentenced to seven months in prison when he traveled to Germany.

PARTLY FREE NATIONS

Russia provides an instructive example of a partly free society. For years, the communist government (and the tsarist government before that) rigidly controlled expressions of every type. This history creates immense problems for the development of freedom of expression. No one serving in government is conditioned to live with the day-to-day criticism that leaders of long-standing democracies usually face. This makes it very difficult for them to distinguish between legitimate criticism and that which might pose a real danger to the state's security. The long war in Chechnya (1994–) has added additional stress on this front. Opposition candidates are regularly harassed by government agents at election time, and news reporters can face serious penalties for running afoul of the government.

Thus, the old organizations of repression often veer toward their previous habits. It is often noted that Russian President Vladimir Putin (b. 1952) worked in the internal security police for years. Freedom of expression faces an uncertain future in Russia.

INTERNATIONAL EFFORTS

There have been three major international efforts to effect freedom of expression: the European Convention on Human Rights (1950), the United Nations Universal Declaration of Human Rights (1948), and the International Covenant on Civil and Political Rights (1976).

The European Convention was a treaty aimed at forestalling any renewal of **totalitarian** government. It provides that "Everyone has the right to freedom of expression. This right shall include freedom to hold opinions and to receive and impart information and ideas without interference by public authority and regardless of frontiers." (Article 10). A special court of human rights was established to hear cases brought by individuals against governments who signed the treaty and made it applicable internally (as most Western European nations have). Through the years, it has grappled with several serious issues similar to those brought to the United States Supreme Court, and has struck down the policies of several governments.

totalitarianism: a form of absolute government that demands complete subjugation by its citizens

The United Nations (U.N.) Declaration was passed by the General Assembly in 1948. It contains the following provision: "Everyone has the right to freedom of opinion and expression; this right includes the freedom to hold opinions without interference and to seek, receive and impart information and ideas through any media and regardless of frontiers." (Article 19). Implementing the declaration falls to the U.N. Human Rights Commission, made up of fifty-three nations selected by the Economic and Social Council, another U.N. body.

Membership on the Human Rights Commission has proved controversial, as some of the world's worst human rights violators, including Sudan and Libya, have been given seats. Thus, its legitimacy is often suspect. Furthermore, the only power the commission has is to listen to complaints and make recommendations. Seldom is there any follow-through by the governments involved.

The International Covenant on Civil and Political Rights was adopted by the General Assembly of the United Nations in 1966. It entered into force in 1976. The covenant created a Human Rights Committee that is charged with monitoring compliance.

ENFORCEMENT

The example of the U.N. Commission on Human Rights underscores the importance of enforcement in the freedom of expression arena. Since it is a government that is denying someone freedom of expression, who is going to stop them? With only a handful of exceptions, the countries with the best records in protecting freedom of expression possess strong and independent courts. No country lacking freedom of expression has independent courts, and "partly free" countries tend to be weak and often swayed by corruption. Thus, an independent court system is a major ingredient in maintaining freedom of expression.

The next question is why do governments in the free countries obey court orders? After all, courts have no police forces under their command. It is here that we realize that a political culture that prizes freedom of expression is an essential part of the equation. A few countries have such a strong commitment to freedom of expression that they can function with relatively weak courts. This formerly was the situation in Britain in the past, for example. Even there, however, there has been a renewed emphasis on using courts to help secure freedom of expression. Thus, a combination of a citizenry that prizes liberty and an independent court system is the best formula to protect freedom of expression.

See also: Constitutions and Constitutionalism; Freedom of Assembly and Association; Freedom of the Press; Freedom of Religion.

BIBLIOGRAPHY

Canadian Charter of Rights and Freedoms, 1982. <http://laws.justice.gc.ca/en/charter/>.

Curtis, Michael Kent. *Free Speech, "The People's Darling Privilege": Struggles for Freedom of Expression in American History*. Durham, NC: Duke University Press, 2000.

European Convention on Human Rights and Fundamental Freedoms, 1950. <http://conventions.coe.int/Treaty/EN/CadreLiskTraites.htm>.

Fiss, Owen M. *Liberalism Divided: Freedom of Speech and the Many Uses of State Power*. Boulder, CO: Westview Press, 1996.

Freedom in the World. Freedom House. <http://www.freedomhouse.org>.

German Basic Law, 1949.

Glendon, Mary Ann. *A World Made New: Eleanor Roosevelt and the Universal Declaration of Human Rights*. New York: Random House, 2001.

Passavant, Paul A. *No Escape: Freedom of Speech and the Paradox of Rights*. New York: New York University Press, 2002.

Smolla, Rodney A. *Free Speech in an Open Society*. New York: Knopf, 1992.

Steele, Richard W. *Free Speech in the Good War*. New York: St. Martins, 1999.

Sunstein, Cass. *Democracy and the Problems of Free Speech*. New York: Free Press, 1995.

United Nations Universal Declaration of Human Rights, 1948. <http://www.un.org/Overview/rights.html>.

Jerold Waltman

Freedom of Information

Freedom of information generally means access to information about any governmental entity involved in the operation of government. This includes access to reports, budgets, correspondence, and other documents related to the operational aspects of a governmental body, whether it is legislative or executive.

In the early twenty-first century the concepts of freedom of information and access to information are closely aligned with democracy. Throughout history democracy and freedom of information have been limited. Public discourse and exchange of information and ideas about government were common in the development of Greek democracies beginning in the fifth century B.C.E. Greek citizens were welcome to attend open forums, debate issues, make proposals, and hear about matters of public debate. Around the same time the Roman Senate was a public body. Originally it was composed of the 100 leading citizens of Rome who advised the executive authority. Neither the Greeks nor the Romans practiced democracy in the modern sense, and neither society recognized equality among its citizens. Nonetheless, each saw the need for public participation in government and, in order for that government to prove effective, for citizens to be aware of the issues of the day and understand the workings of government.

During the Middle Ages in Europe the concept of the divine right of kings developed. This right held that because kings answered only to God, they were exempt from criticism from the public. With kings enjoying such an exalted position and insulation, public participation in government was limited. Because kings did not answer to the public, there was little necessity for them to communicate information to the public or respond to public requests. Laws prohibiting criticism of the government or government officials, known as insult laws, still exist in many countries around the world. Although these laws are not always enforced, their existence, which limits speech and information, is considered a major hindrance to freedom of expression and freedom of information.

Ideas related to freedom of information are freedom of the press and freedom of expression. Shortly after Johannes Gutenberg (1390–1468) invented printing in the mid-fifteenth century, the Catholic Church imposed censorship on any books not approved by the Church. In England, beginning with King Henry VIII (1491–1547) in the 1530s, censorship and the repression of ideas and information were common.

English poet John Milton (1608–1674) in his famous essay *Areopagitica*, written in 1644, argued passionately for freedom of ideas and information and against the licensing and printing **monopoly** common in England at that time. In some of the most famous lines in Western literature Milton wrote: "And though all the winds of doctrine were let loose to play upon the earth, so Truth be in the field, we do injuriously by licensing and prohibiting to misdoubt her strength. Let her and Falsehood grapple; who ever knew truth put to the worse, in a free and open encounter?" (Rhys, 1946, p. 36). The concept of the marketplace of ideas was thus born, one in which people would have access to all information and individuals would be free to publish their own ideas and opinions without fear of retribution. The fundamental belief behind the marketplace of ideas is that the people, not government, the church, or any other group, should decide what is the truth.

The founders of the U.S. Constitution were inspired by the marketplace of ideas in the eighteenth century and sought to include it in the formation of a representative democracy and guarantee the free flow of information. James

monopoly: the domination of a market by one firm or company

Madison (1751–1836) was the primary author of the Bill of Rights. In an frequently quoted letter to W. T. Barry (1785–1835) written in 1822, Madison said: "A popular Government, without popular information, or the means of acquiring it, is but a prologue to a farce or a tragedy; or, perhaps, both. Knowledge will forever govern ignorance; and a people who mean to be their own governors must arm themselves with the power which knowledge gives" (Hunt, 1910, vol. 9, p. 103).

Although general openness and access to information were traditions early on in the United States, laws in the twentieth century made the process more formal and outlined specific procedures for securing information. The Federal Freedom of Information Act was passed in 1966 and signed by President Lyndon B. Johnson (1908–1973). During that time period many individual states enacted open records and open meetings acts, part of a so-called sunshine law movement. "Government in the sunshine" became an expression of openness and accessibility to government just as the United States was making major reforms in civil rights and improving opportunities for women.

The access to information law in Sweden is the oldest in the world, dating from 1766. Freedom of the press and freedom of information received a major push from various international organizations during the mid-twentieth century. Article 19 of the United Nations Universal Declaration on Human Rights, adopted in 1948, states: "Everyone has the right to freedom of opinion and expression; this right includes freedom to hold opinions without interference and to seek, receive, and impart information and ideas through any media and regardless of frontiers."

As of 2004 more than fifty countries around the world had laws specifying access to information. That number continues to increase, as there is an active movement to enact such laws. Among those countries enacting access laws in the early twenty-first century is India, the world's second most populous country. Access to information laws are common in Europe, and about half the countries in Latin America have some type of law regarding citizens' right to information. Mexican President Vicente Fox (b. 1942) signed such a bill into law in 2002. In the first year of its existence the law in Mexico was used by thousands of citizens and journalists seeking specific types of information from the government.

■ ■ ■

THE FEDERAL FREEDOM OF INFORMATION ACT

The federal Freedom of Information Act (FOIA) and its 1996 amendments define and protect the public's right to obtain information from government agencies. The FOIA itself was signed into law by President Lyndon B. Johnson on July 4, 1966, with amendments covering electronic media signed on October 2, 1996 by President Bill Clinton. The FOIA is supplemented by the Privacy Act of 1974, which allows citizens to see government records about themselves, correct these records when needed, and sue the government for violations of the Act.

Most of the controversies over the FOIA and the Privacy Act concern the exemptions to these acts. There are nine exemptions to the FOIA that allow the government to withhold information in the interest of national security, defense, or foreign policy. Similarly, there are ten exemptions to the Privacy Act. Whether the government has abused these exemptions since 1966 is a subject of vigorous debate among private citizens as well as government officials.

The Department of Justice (DOJ) has set up a FOIA Home Page at <http://www.usdoj.gov/04foia> with links to the full texts of the FOIA and the Privacy Act as well as links to the *DOJ Freedom of Information Act Guide* and the *DOJ Privacy Act Overview*. In addition, a number of individual states have enacted similar legislation applying to state and municipal governments.

SUPREME COURT RELEASES PENTAGON PAPERS. The *Washington Post*'s chief of presses, William Frazee, celebrated the Supreme Court's decision in June 1971 that permitted newspapers to publish the Pentagon Papers, a highly-classified report by the U.S. government detailing its troubled involvement in the Vietnam War. (SOURCE: © BETTMANN/CORBIS)

The laws on access to information vary from country to country, but standard components exist in most cases. It is common for the laws to outline a specific procedure for securing information, usually in writing to the specific authority or agency holding the documents sought. The government is given a specific time limit, usually a number of days, in which to respond. There is typically an appeals process if the authority holding the documents believes it should not release them.

Access laws include exceptions to disclosure, meaning the government is not obligated to release every document it holds. In the United States, for example, some law enforcement records, especially those related to ongoing investigations, are exempted. Also exempted are certain personnel documents that contain sensitive information, such as medical records, trade secret information, records dealing with national security and intelligence activities, and information on financial institutions that are regulated by the government.

Part of the response to terrorism in light of the attacks on September 11, 2001, has been to restrict information that once was available to the public. In the United States government directives and the USA Patriot Act of 2001 have limited access to information. For example, the availability of detailed maps of energy transmission lines and energy facilities is much more restricted. Access to information about the designs of nuclear power plants, shipping ports, and major public structures that might be targets for terrorism also is more limited.

Limits also have been placed on some legal proceedings, such as those for persons being held on suspicion of terrorism and immigration hearings for detainees the U.S. government suspects might have ties with terrorist groups.

Freedom of information advocates have complained about these restrictive policies, claiming that governments are acting arbitrarily, even overreacting, and that terrorists have seldom if ever used public information to plan attacks. The appropriate response to terrorism will be one of the ongoing issues of debate as freedom of information advocates seek to regain access to information that the government has made inaccessible.

The right to attend legislative and judicial proceedings has come to be a major component of the right to freedom of information. In the United States judicial proceedings have remained open through tradition and the constitutional guarantee of a public trial. Acts mandating open meetings became common in the 1960s to guarantee public participation in governmental and legislative deliberations. Even with the open meetings acts, exceptions exist. Closed or "executive" sessions are permitted for a range of exceptions, including deliberations on personnel issues, **litigation** consultations, and consideration of real estate transactions.

Judicial documents may or may not be covered by general freedom of information laws. Depending on the legal system, judicial documents have varying degrees of accessibility by the public. Access to judicial proceedings was part of the early tradition in the United States, based on the tradition of English law. There are a few exceptions to this general rule, however, such as the closing of legal proceedings involving under-age minors. The general trend is toward opening more judicial proceedings as governments adopt democratic principles and seek to make the judiciary accountable.

The trend toward democracy worldwide is expected to continue the movement favoring laws for access to information. A number of advocacy groups and international agencies continue to encourage the adoption of such laws. The weakening of **communism** late in the twentieth century and the push for freedom of the press have accelerated the movement. In addition, technological advances such as the Internet have created more readily available tools for access as well as making it more difficult for the government to control information.

See also: Censorship; Freedom of Expression; Freedom of the Press.

litigate: to bring a disagreement or violation of the law before a judge for a legal decision

communism: an economic and social system characterized by the absence of class structure and by common ownership of the means of production and subsistence

BIBLIOGRAPHY

Banisar, David. *The Freedominfo.org Global Survey.* <http://www.freedominfo.org>.

Dahl, Robert A. *Democracy and Its Critics.* New Haven, CT: Yale University Press, 1989.

Freedom of Information Center, University of Missouri. <http://foi.missouri.edu/international.html>.

Hunt, Gaillard, ed. *The Writings of James Madison.* New York: G.P. Putnam's Sons, 1910.

James Madison Center, James Madison University. <http://www.jmu.edu/madison/center/home.htm>.

Rhys, Ernest, ed. *Areopagitica and Other Prose Works by John Milton.* New York: E.P. Dutton & Co., 1946.

Walden, Ruth. *Insult Laws: An Insult to Press Freedom.* Reston, VA: World Press Freedom Committee, 2000.

Tony Pederson

Freedom of the Press

Freedom of the press is a type of freedom of expression. Two factors make it different from freedom of speech. First, since it involves publication, there ordinarily is an interval of time between composition and public dissemination. If governmental authorities learn of the impending publication of material they wish to keep from the public, they have a period of time in which to act. Even in the broadcast area of the media, there usually is a script or even a tape of the story made before it is put on the air. Second, while speech is often done by a lone individual, the press is mostly made up of organizations—newspapers, magazines, radio stations, and television stations.

JUSTIFICATIONS FOR PRESS FREEDOM

Every citizen, including those who write for and edit publications, enjoys a fundamental human right to impart and receive information. In addition, a free press is an important check on government. Governments usually want their citizens to believe that those in power are wise and trustworthy, and that their policies are working flawlessly. Thus, they customarily expend a good bit of energy trying to let the public know how well things are going. However, a free press will find its own sources of information and report what is actually happening. By exposing misguided policies, incompetence, dishonesty, and corruption, a free press helps to hold government accountable.

This possibility is, in fact, what makes governments so sensitive about press freedom. Every government wants the press to portray it in a positive light, and the only way they can guarantee that is by regulation or outright control.

THREE IMPORTANT DISTINCTIONS

There is an important difference between the print side of the press and the broadcast side. Newspapers and magazines can be produced without limit, and often at a fairly low cost. Radio and television outlets, however, rely on the allocation of broadcast frequencies, which almost have to be regulated by government to prevent chaos. Through its involvement in assigning frequencies, the government automatically has more control over radio and television than over the print media.

Second, there is a difference between the freedom to express opinions and the freedom to publish facts. Those who defend freedom of the press agree that opinions should be printed without hindrance. However, facts are another matter. Sometimes there are facts that could damage national security if made public (disclosure of "cutting edge" military technology, for example). Outside the area of national security, in most modern societies governments control many facts that may be needed for the public to make informed judgments about candidates for office, or whether certain policies are having their intended impact. Examples include the health effects of certain prescription drugs, the effects of pesticides, the treatment of prisoners, and automobile safety tests. The degree to which the press should be able to demand access to such information is a matter of debate.

Finally, although a connection exists between democracy (governments chosen by open and fair elections) and freedom of the press, no universal correlation exists between democracy and press freedom. Some non-elected governments allow freedom of the press, and there have been times when democratically elected governments have moved to silence the press.

RUSSIAN NEWSPAPERS ON DISPLAY AT A NEWSSTAND AT ST. PETERSBURG STATE UNIVERSITY IN 1992. Despite the fall of communism in 1991, the level of freedom of the press has steadily declined in Russia, particularly during the authoritarian rule of President Vladimir Putin. As of 2004 all independent television networks had been shut down and, in July 2004, Putin created laws to prohibit journalists from scrutinizing political candidates. In October 2004 the constitutional court rejected these laws. (SOURCE: © STEVE RAYMER/CORBIS. REPRODUCED BY PERMISSION.)

PRIOR RESTRAINT

Even in countries with the strongest protections for freedom of the press, newspapers and other media outlets are not immune from prosecution for what they publish. If they cause harm to someone—such as the loss of a job—and if what they published was false, the press can be held financially responsible for committing libel. Furthermore, every country has laws prohibiting the sharing of legitimate military and security secrets. If material of this type came into the possession of a newspaper and they chose to publish it, they might well find themselves facing criminal charges.

The more important question is whether the government can engage in prior restraint and prohibit the publication of such information beforehand. The United States provides a good example of the issues involved in prior restraint. The Constitution's First Amendment provides that: "Congress shall make no law . . . abridging the freedom . . . of the press." During the Vietnam War (1964–1975), a stolen copy of a government report on the war (the so-called "Pentagon Papers") was given to the *New York Times*. The president's advisers learned of the newspaper's possession of the document. Alleging that it contained sensitive national security information, they asked the federal courts to issue an order forbidding its publication. The Supreme Court refused to issue the order, saying that any request for prior restraint would have to prove beyond any doubt that irreparable harm would follow publication. Thus, in the United States it is exceedingly difficult for the government to obtain prior restraint.

However, there is one important exception. Under some circumstance, a trial judge may issue a "gag order" to the press. Securing a fair trial is such an important value that it may trump the right of the press to publish information about the trial, even if that information might be of interest to the public.

The attempt by Third World governments to establish a New World Information and Communication Order (NWICO) in the 1970s was an important threat to freedom of the press. Some of this program's backers, although not all, had benign motives, which illustrates that purity of motive does not always guarantee purity of outcome.

In support of NWICO, many less developed countries argued that the dominance of world media by Western communications organizations produced a one-way flow of messages from developed to developing nations that tended to paint a distorted picture of them. When less developed nations were not ignored, which was most of the time, their failures were emphasized while their accomplishments were downplayed. The former Soviet Union and its satellites joined in this critique.

While the accusing governments were trying to challenge the dominance of the Western press in the international realm, they were arguing for what they called "development journalism" in their own nations. According to this argument, the overriding goal of Third World governments was to secure economic development. Accordingly, all national resources, including the mass media, should be marshaled toward that end. In short, government must control the press for the greater good until a certain level of economic development was reached, at which time the "luxury" of a free press could be granted.

At the 1976 meeting of the United Nations Educational, Scientific, and Cultural Organization (UNESCO), a group of these nations proposed making all governments "responsible for the activities in the international sphere of all mass media under their jurisdiction." (Sussman 2003, 15). Then, they sought to establish a legal "right to reply" to any objectionable coverage. Such an approach would have had serious repercussions for freedom of the press. After a number of acrimonious meetings over several years that led the United States and the United Kingdom to temporarily withdraw from UNESCO, the proposal was finally put to rest. The issues behind the dispute remain, however, and there are periodic calls in international forums for a resurrected NWICO.

jurisdiction: the territory or area within which authority may be exercised

TECHNIQUES OF CONTROL

The most severe restrictions on freedom of the press occur in those countries that have laws that explicitly forbid freedom of the press and provide severe punishment for anyone breaking them. This usually is combined with outright government ownership of all media. Examples include Iraq under Saddam Hussein (b. 1937), and sometimes communist China.

Short of such draconian measures, governments have utilized a variety of laws to keep the press docile and cooperative. For example, some countries have "security laws." These measures make it a crime to publish anything damaging to national security. National security is then defined so broadly that almost anything (news about a rise in prices, a housing shortage, and so forth) can be construed as falling under its rubric. Another approach is the enactment

communism: an economic and social system characterized by the absence of class structure and by common ownership of the means of production and subsistence

of "insult laws" that forbid the insulting of a public official. Under these acts, even the slightest criticism can be deemed an insult. Finally, some countries have passed laws requiring "responsible journalism." While it is true that the press can be irresponsible, when government officials are able to decide what is sober, reflective journalism and what is unmerited ranting, the formula for intimidation is firmly in place.

Some nations also have experimented with laws that require journalists to procure a license from the government. This scenario does not necessarily allow only pro-government journalists to work. For example, Costa Rica—a relatively free society—once had a journalists' license law. However, such a law can easily be manipulated to accomplish that end.

Even without legal **sanctions**, there are other ways to create a more pliable press. Sadly, a common one is to have police or unofficial militias detain, abuse, or threaten journalists who probe into sensitive areas. A softer approach is to use economic pressure, such as the placing of government ads in friendly papers but not elsewhere.

sanction: economic, political, or military reprisals, or, to ratify

INTERNATIONAL STATEMENTS

Freedom of the press has been written into a variety of international agreements. The most widely applicable one is the United Nations Universal Declaration of Human Rights, which was adopted in 1948. It provides that "Everyone has the right to freedom of opinion and expression; this right includes freedom to . . . receive and impart information and ideas through any media and regardless of frontiers." (Article 19). The European Convention on Human Rights, adopted in 1950, holds that "Everyone has the right to freedom of expression. This right shall include freedom to hold opinions and to receive and impart information and ideas without interference by public authority and regardless of frontiers." However, it adds that "This article shall not prevent

NEW WORLD INFORMATION AND COMMUNICATION ORDER (NWICO)

The New World Information and Communication Order (NWICO) is a phrase that was popularized by a 1980 United Nations Educational, Scientific, and Cultural Organization (UNESCO) report called "Many Voices, One World." Although NWICO was never precisely defined, the term reflected the belief that transnational corporations' domination of mass media threatened national identity and self-respect in developing countries. The "Many Voices" report was issued by the MacBride Commission, chaired by the Irish politician Seán MacBride. The report was highly controversial in its recommendations that developing countries should have the right to control the content of news reports about themselves; that journalists should be licensed and asked to subscribe to a code of conduct; and that communications resources should be redistributed.

Most Western journalists were opposed to NWICO on the grounds that it represented a threat to freedom of the press, particularly the freedom to report unfavorable news about developing countries. Other experts pointed out that better distribution of media technology would not automatically fix the economic and political problems of the poorer nations. The United States, the United Kingdom, and Singapore withdrew from UNESCO in response to the MacBride report—although the United Kingdom eventually rejoined in 1997, followed by the United States in 2003.

The rise of the Internet has reopened the 1980s debates about NWICO. The February 2005 UNESCO conference on "Freedom of Expression in Cyberspace" renewed journalists' concerns that the United Nations wants to control the Internet in order to impose global censorship rules.

States from requiring the licensing of broadcasting, television or cinema enterprises." (Article 10). In 1978 most Western Hemisphere nations signed the American Convention on Human Rights. One of its provisions stated: "Everyone has the right to freedom of thought and expression. This includes freedom to seek, receive, and impart information and ideas of all kinds, regardless of frontiers, either orally, in writing, in print, in the form of art, or through any other medium of one's choice." (Article 13)

The methods used to enforce these documents vary. The United Nations relies on a largely ineffective body of fifty-three nations called the United Nations Commission on Human Rights to study complaints and issue reports. The European Convention created a multinational court to which individuals in the affected countries may bring actions. Most of the **signatory** countries have incorporated the convention into their domestic law, giving the court's decisions legal status inside a country. Therefore, in many cases the actions of governments have been overturned and implementation has followed. The American Convention is enforced by a hybrid. There is an Inter-American Commission that investigates complaints and makes recommendations. If satisfaction is not obtained, there is the Inter-American Court on Human Rights. Although it has had some successes to its credit, the American Convention is not incorporated into the domestic law of the signatories. Therefore, national governments are free to ignore it if they so choose.

signatory: one who signs an agreement with other parties and is then bound to that agreement

GOVERNMENT VERSUS PRIVATE ACTION

In addition to the actions of governments, private actions also are used to silence the press. In some instances, militant religious or **ideological** groups threaten or even kill journalists. In others, economic pressure is brought to bear. Depending on the circumstances, these factors can be very effective. Governments sometimes move to protect the press. However, at other times private groups may be acting with the acquiescence or even the support of the government.

ideology: a system of beliefs composed of ideas or values, from which political, social, or economic programs are often derived

LONG-TERM TRENDS

Despite numerous instances where freedom of the press has been denied in the contemporary world, long-run trends have been favorable. At the beginning of the twentieth century, colonial powers controlled much of Africa and Asia, and granted little freedom of any kind. Throughout Eastern Europe and the Middle East, old-fashioned autocracies of one sort or another ruled and freedom of the press was unheard of. The press situation in most of Latin America also was quite precarious. Only in a handful of Western nations was there anything approaching a free press, and it often was rather restricted by contemporary standards.

The 1930s to the 1980s witnessed the rise of ruthless **totalitarian** states such as Nazi Germany, Joseph Stalin's (1879–1953) Soviet Union, Mao Tse-tung's (1893–1976) China, and a variety of imitators. As previously noted, many of the Third World's newly independent states practiced "development journalism" after World War II (post-1945).

totalitarianism: a form of absolute government that demands complete subjugation by its citizens

By the 1990s, freedom of the press was making inroads almost everywhere. The collapse of communism opened the doors to press freedom in many places formerly under Soviet rule. While some of the successor states (Turkmenistan in particular) have developed into dictatorships and some (such as Ukraine and Russia) have since moved to restrict freedom of the press, the situation is still

pluralism: a system of government in which all groups participate in the decision-making process

statute: a law created by a legislature that is inferior to constitutional law

more fluid than in the past. Russian President Vladimir Putin (b. 1952) closed the last independent television station in early 2003, and print journalists have been intimidated on a number of occasions. However, even Putin felt obliged to meet with leaders of the European Union (EU) in 2001 and agreed that "Freedom of speech and **pluralism** in the media are essential democratic principles and core values for a genuine EU-Russia partnership" (freedomforum.org, 2001).

There also has been a decided change in thinking about economic development, with the new orthodoxy being that a free press is a necessary ingredient for, and not a barrier to, economic growth. Nobel Prize-winning economist Amartya Seen (b. 1933), stated that freedom of the press is "an integral component of development." (Sussman 2003, 27). The World Bank also has taken the position that a press free of government ownership will aid economic development.

At the same time there has been growth in Freedom of Information laws, or **statutes** that allow journalists to obtain information more readily from government agencies. Great Britain, which long resisted such a law, has now enacted one. Mexico also adopted such a measure in 2000.

During the early twenty-first century, there still were places around the world where the press was not free, where citizens could not impart or receive information freely, and where there virtually were no checks on government. In addition, the impact of terrorist attacks on established democracies was a potential threat to press freedom. Even so, the long-run trend seems to favor the expansion of press freedom.

See also: Censorship; Freedom of Expression; Freedom of Information; International Covenant on Civil and Political Rights; Universal Declaration of Human Rights.

BIBLIOGRAPHY

American Convention on Human Rights, 1978.

De Volpi, A., et al. *Born Secret: The H-Bomb, The Progressive Case and National Security*. New York: Pergamon Press, 1981.

European Convention on Human Rights, 1950.

Karlekar, Karin Deutsch, ed. *Freedom of the Press 2003: A Global Survey of Media Independence*. Lanham, MD: Rowman & Littlefield Publishers Inc., 2003.

Levy, Leonard W. *Emergence of a Free Press*. New York: Oxford University Press, 1985.

Powe, Lucas A. Jr. *The Fourth Estate and the Constitution: Freedom of the Press in America*. Berkeley: University of California Press, 1991.

Reporters without Borders. <http://www.rsf.org/>.

"Russian President Putin Pledges Free Speech and a Free Press." *Freedomforum.org*, May 18, 2001. <http://www.freedomforum.org/templates/document.asp?documentID=13957>.

Siebert, Fredrick Seaton. *Freedom of the Press in England, 1476–1776: The Rise and Decline of Government Controls*. Urbana: University of Illinois Press, 1965.

Sussman, Leonard R. "Press Freedom, the Past Quarter Century: The Vile and the Valiant." In *Freedom of the Press 2003*. Edited by Karin D. Karlekar. Lanham, MD: Rowman & Littlefield, 2003.

United Nations Commissioner for Human Rights. <http://www.ohchr.org/english/>.

United Nations Universal Declaration of Human Rights, 1978. <http://www.un.org/Overview/rights.html>.

Jerold Waltman

Freedom of Religion and the State

Simply defined, freedom of religion is the ability of persons to be religious or not, the ability to believe (respond to what one perceives as the divine), the ability to worship alone or collectively, and the ability to change religion, all without interference by the state or government. Religious freedom is determined largely by a government's attitude toward religion. The shorthand term for this is "church–state relations." There are four basic historic categories of church–state relations:

- *Hostility.* Here government opposes religion because religious belief is perceived to compete with the government for the loyalty of the people. The government tries to suppress religion or tightly control it so that it might serve the state. Religious freedom does not exist.
- *Establishment.* Establishment is an official relationship between religion and civil authority. Government approves of, supports, and promotes a religion. The state benefits because it relies on religion to teach people to be moral and to obey civil law. Religion benefits because it utilizes the state's police power to compel people to believe and worship correctly. Religious freedom prevails for those practicing the favored religion; it is restricted for those adhering to disfavored religions.
- *Toleration.* This may be called "establishment light." Among the religions in the country, the government favors one. It allows others to exist; it tolerates them. The favored religion receives political and financial benefits, but the others do not. Tolerated religions exist at the pleasure of the government, which may repress or destroy them at any time. Religious freedom is rather complete for adherents of the favored religion. It is available to tolerated religions too, but the government may withdraw toleration, causing religious freedom to disappear.
- *Disestablishment/religious freedom.* Here there is no official relationship between religion and government. Religion exists without support or opposition from the government. Religious diversity thrives. Freedom of belief is **absolute**; one can believe in any religion or none. Religious action is prevented only when it is contrary to public welfare.

absolute: complete, pure, free from restriction or limitation

EXAMPLES

Hostility. **Communist** China usually has been hostile to religion and often represses religious freedom. Communism asserts that religious faith diverts people from the effort to create a **socialist** society. Thus, it advocates state **atheism**. China maintains this attitude. China is a huge country and issues of religious freedom are not addressed uniformly, but generalizations can be made. The government recognizes Buddhism, Islam, Taoism, and Christianity (Catholicism and Protestantism). These individual **sects** must register with the government so that officials can keep them under control. The government's goal is for religion to serve the state until it disappears from Chinese society.

Registered religions are treated rather well so long as they publicly support government policies and/or denounce unacceptable religions. Unacceptable religions are unregistered religions. Some religions refuse to register to avoid government control. Other religions are not allowed to register. In either case they pay a price, for they are illegal. Their clergy often are harassed with jail time or forced "reeducation" in labor camps. The government frequently destroys the property of unregistered groups. Consequently, unregistered Protestants,

communism: an economic and social system characterized by the absence of class structure and by common ownership of the means of production and subsistence

socialism: any of various economic and political theories advocating collective or governmental ownership and administration of the means of production and distribution of goods

atheism: the belief that God does not exist

sect: a group of people with a common distinctive view of religion or doctrine

persecute: to belittle, harass, injure, or otherwise intimidate, especially those of a different background or group

Catholics, and Muslims have formed what are known as house churches, underground groups, to try to avoid **persecution**. The strategy has not worked; the government consistently harasses house churches.

The Chinese government teaches atheism in schools. Neither military personnel nor public officers are allowed to be religious. Foreigners cannot perform missionary activity. The government has banned so-called cults, the principal one of which is Falun Gong. The government has arrested the leaders and followers of Falun Gong, subjecting them to reeducation, imprisonment, torture, and sometimes death.

North Korea is also hostile to religion. Similarly dedicated to state atheism, North Korea aggressively oppresses religion. Although it is a closed society and verifiable information is hard to obtain, refugees tell of widespread persecution. Registered religious groups (Buddhists, Catholics, and Protestants) remain under tight control. The government presumes that "all religions are opium," and so those believing in God or the gods are insane. They must be repressed to protect society. The civil religion is Juche, a combination of the state **ideology** of self-reliance and **veneration** of the former leader Kim Il Sung and current ruler Kim Jong Il. Reverence of government leaders is the spiritual foundation for the nation; a refusal to venerate them is considered opposition to the national interest.

ideology: a system of beliefs composed of ideas or values, from which political, social, or economic programs are often derived

venerate: to hold something or someone in extremely high regard

Establishment. In Saudi Arabia, Islam is the official religion and the law requires all citizens to be Muslims. The Qur'an (the Scriptures of Islam) and the Sunna of Muhammad (tradition, or what the Prophet said, did, or permitted) make up the constitution of the country. Its legal system is based on Shari'a, Islamic law. The government prohibits the public practice of non-Muslim religions, although such believers are allowed to worship in private. This usually means in secret because even privately worshipping non-Muslims have been arrested and sentenced to hard labor, beatings, or deportation.

However, the official religion is not any form of Islam but only what is called Wahhabi, a conservative interpretation of Islam. Therefore, Shiite Muslims or even moderate Sunni Muslims are harassed in Saudi Arabia. The government prohibits the teaching of any Muslim perspective other than Wahhabi. Shiite

JAMES MADISON ON RELIGIOUS FREEDOM

The following is an excerpt from James Madison's "A Memorial and Remonstrance Against Religious Assessments." It was written in 1785 to arouse popular opposition to a bill in the Virginia legislature that would have authorized government support for teaching religion.

[W]e hold it for an fundamental and undeniable truth, "that Religion or the duty which we owe to our Creator and the manner of discharging it, can be directed only by reason and conviction, not by force or violence." The Religion then of every man must be left to the conviction and conscience of every man; and it is the right of every man to

exercise it as these may dictate. This right is in its nature an unalienable right.

[I]t is proper to take alarm at the first experiment on our liberties . . . . Who does not see that the same authority which can establish Christianity, in exclusion of all other Religions, may establish with the same ease any particular sect of Christians, in exclusion of all other Sects? That the same authority which can force a citizen to contribute three pence only of his property for the support of any one establishment, may force him to conform to any other establishment in all cases whatsoever?

Muslims are severely restricted in practicing their understanding of Islam. They are discriminated against in government employment and in admission to higher education. Wahhabi religious education is mandatory in the nation's public schools.

Non-Muslim clergy who want to lead worship are banned from the country. Non-Muslim missionary activity is prohibited. Any Muslim who converts to another religion risks the death penalty. The Hindu community in Saudi Arabia is continually on guard, for Hinduism is regarded as polytheistic, and unacceptable to the regime.

The Saudi government enforces these regulations through its religious police, who, in tandem with the civil police, may arrest those who break religious law. This applies to restrictions on women's dress and any other matters of religious decorum. There is little religious freedom in Saudi Arabia.

Toleration. Denmark is a good example of toleration. The Evangelical Lutheran Church (ELC) is the state church and the only religion subsidized by the government. The ELC alone receives funds through the tax system. The government pays the pastors of the ELC but not those of other groups, of which there are many.

The Danish government does not compel other religious groups to register with the government, but nonregistered groups do not qualify for income tax exemption. Also, the religious ceremonies of nonregistered groups, especially weddings, must have the government's permission to be recognized as valid. The government has given such permission to some nonregistered groups but not all. Such matters are administered by the Ministry of Ecclesiastical Affairs. To receive permission, unregistered groups must submit to the ministry detailed documentation of their theology and rituals, organization, and leadership that can be held accountable to the government. There is considerable government monitoring of religious groups.

Missionary activity is permitted. The Evangelical Lutheran faith is taught in public schools, but students with their parents' consent are excused from the classes. Denmark has a long history of welcoming religious minorities and in recent times has been hospitable to a large number of Muslim immigrants. Religious freedom exists, but not equality. The government could diminish the freedoms of groups other than the ELC, but Danish history suggests that such a course of action is not likely.

The United Kingdom also has state churches: the Church of England (Anglican) and the Church of Scotland (Presbyterian). No religious group is required to register with the government, and none, not even the state churches, receive government funds. Religious groups do enjoy exemption from most taxes if they use their income for religious and/or charitable purposes. Religion is taught in public schools. Curricula must reflect the prominent place of Christianity in society, but teaching may be tailored to reflect the dominant religions in different regions of the country.

Toleration is so broad that about the only advantage the state churches have is political. The monarch is the supreme governor of the Church of England and must always be a member in good standing. He or she appoints Church of England officials, particularly the Archbishop of Canterbury, the leader of the church, on advice from the prime minister. (The Church of Scotland appoints its own leaders.) In addition, the Archbishops of Canterbury and York, with twenty-four other bishops, receive automatic membership in the House of Lords, the upper house of Parliament. Important clergy of other denominations or religions do not have this privilege.

MEMBERS OF THE FALUN GONG CARRY BANNERS FOR A PROTEST IN HONG KONG IN 2003.
Banned by the Chinese government after being labeled a "cult" in 1999, members of the Falun Gong spiritual movement do not purport to practice politics. Rather, its followers are said to believe in good health, meditation, and exercise as taught by founder Li Hongzhi. (SOURCE: © AP/WIDE WORLD PHOTOS)

Disestablishment/religious freedom. The United States originated this style of church–state relations. It was the first nation to write disestablishment and governmentally guaranteed religious freedom into its basic law. The First Amendment of the Constitution states: "Congress shall make no law respecting an establishment of religion, or prohibiting the free exercise thereof." This created a **secular** state—however, a state not hostile to religion but supportive of religious belief and behavior.

secularism: a refutation of, apathy toward, or exclusion of all religion

In the American system freedom of religious belief is absolute; one can be religious or not and, if religious, can hold any belief without government interference. Freedom of belief would be meaningless if one could not act out one's beliefs. Thus, the free exercise of religion also is guaranteed. Such religious behavior may not be contrary to individual or public welfare nevertheless.

Missionary activity is permitted; one can convert from one religion to another. Holding public office is not conditional on religious belief. The government does not finance religious groups or, until recently, religious schools. The income of religious organizations is tax-exempt, however. Because of the separation of church and state and its corollary, religious freedom, religion has flourished in America.

INTERNATIONAL STANDARDS

Countries have expressed the goal of religious freedom as the norm for behavior within nations and for relations between nations. Several documents and treaties attest to this ambition; the concept has become part of international law. The most celebrated document is Article 18 of the Universal Declaration of Human Rights, adopted by the United Nations (UN) in 1948. It asserts:

> Everyone has the right to freedom of thought, conscience and religion; this right includes freedom to change his religion or belief, and freedom, either alone or in community with others and public or private, to manifest his religion or belief in teaching, practice, worship and observance.

Article 9 of the European Convention on Human Rights and Fundamental Freedoms (adopted in 1950) reproduces the language of Article 18 language and adds:

> Freedom to manifest one's religion or beliefs shall be subject only to such limitations as are prescribed by law and are necessary in a democratic society in the interests of public safety, for the protection of public order, health or morals, or the protection of the rights and freedoms of others.

Article 18 of the International Covenant on Civil and Political Rights (formulated in 1966) contains similar language.

Thirty-five nations signed the Helsinki Accords in 1975. Section 1(a)VII states:

> The participating States will respect human rights and fundamental freedoms, including the freedom of thought, conscience, religion or belief, for all without distinction as to race, sex, language, or religion. . . . Within this framework the participating States will recognize and respect the freedom of the individual to profess and practice, alone or in community with others, religion or belief acting in accordance with the dictates of his own conscience.

In 1981 the UN in General Assembly Resolution 36/55 passed the Declaration on the Elimination of All Forms of Intolerance and of Discrimination Based on Religion or Belief. This document describes the rights of religious freedom in elaborate detail. At the same time, the UN created the office of Special **Rapporteur** on Religious Intolerance. This individual investigates abuses of religious freedom and reports them directly to the UN.

rapporteur: one that reports on a committee's work

Principle 16 of the Concluding Document of the Vienna Conference on Security and Cooperation in Europe, adopted in 1989 by thirty-five nations, addresses the need to enforce religious liberty. This lengthy passage asserts the rights of religious liberty in intricate detail.

WATCHDOGS

Because international law reinforces the concept of religious freedom, some organizations monitor alleged abuses of it and progress toward religious freedom in the world. Their purpose is to observe and publicize government violations of religious freedom. Believing that the first step in preventing or correcting abuses is to report such instances, these organizations attempt to alert the world community with the hope that informed citizens will pressure offending countries to change their ways.

Some of these watchdogs are informal sources—privately, rather than governmentally, operated. One is Forum 18 News, based in Oslo, Norway. It is named for Article 18 of the Universal Declaration of Human Rights. Dedicated to universal religious freedom, it is a worldwide news service that reports threats and actions against religious freedom as quickly and accurately as possible.

The Ontario (Canada) Consultants on Religious Tolerance is both an advocacy organization and an information source. Its purpose is best summed up in its **mandate** ("To promote religious tolerance and freedom. To describe religious faiths in all their diversity. To describe controversial topics from all points of view.") and motto ("No peace among the nations without peace among the religions. No peace among religions without dialogue between the religions. No dialogue between the religions without investigation of the foundations of the religions.").

In the United States, Freedom House has promoted global freedom and democracy since 1941. In 1986 the organization created a subdivision, the Center for Religious Freedom, that reports on religious persecution around the world. It urges the U.S. government to advocate, through diplomacy, for religious freedom. It publishes timely news reports and annually ranks each country on its commitment to religious freedom.

In 1998 the United States Congress passed the International Religious Freedom Act to promote religious freedom as a U.S. policy goal and to combat

mandate: to command, order, or require; or, a command, order, or requirement

---

FALUN GONG

Falun Gong is the name commonly used in the West for a Chinese spiritual movement known as Falun Dafa. Its founder, Li Hongzhi, left China for Brooklyn, New York in 1996. Li maintains that Falun Gong was handed down as a secret tradition for generations before he made it public in 1992. By 2005 the movement claimed to have 70 million followers in China and 30 million elsewhere; however, the Chinese government disputes these figures, as do others familiar with China. The government estimates that there are about ten million.

China officially outlawed Falun Gong on July 22, 1999, claiming it is a superstition that deceives people and causes social unrest. Although the government regards Falun Gong as a type of cult, its members deny that it is a religion in the usual sense of the term. It is best described as a spiritual movement that combines elements of Buddhism and Taoism. Falun Gong has no paid clergy, no formal worship, and no dues; its central practice is a set of five exercises said to purify the mind and body. It teaches three basic moral principles: truthfulness, compassion, and forbearance. Falun Gong also claims not to be a political movement, although it has conducted public protests in China.

Government hostility to Falun Gong has several causes:

- Government unease with religion (predating Communist rule) as an alternative or rival source of social authority.
- Political infighting among various government officials.
- The potential of Falun Gong to become a focus of political opposition.

religious persecution in other countries. To that end it formed a Commission on International Religious Freedom to monitor religious freedom globally and advise the president, secretary of state, and Congress on how best to promote it. It also created an Office of International Religious Freedom in the State Department and an Ambassador-at-Large for International Religious Freedom. Both the Commission and the State Department publish annual reports on the status of religious freedom in the world.

RELIGIOUS FREEDOM IN THE UNITED STATES

Despite America's constitutional guarantees and history of (imperfectly) implemented religious freedom, the Supreme Court in the last decade of the twentieth century upheld the principle but seriously compromised its application. The law provides that government may prohibit religious behavior that is harmful. In the case of *Sherbert v. Verner* (374 U.S. 398 [1963]) the Court ruled that the government had to demonstrate a "compelling interest" before it could interfere with religious action. Religious freedom was broad; the possibility of government interference was narrow. The Court changed this standard with its decision in *Employment Division of Oregon v. Smith* (494 U.S. 872 [1990]). The new standard is that a general law that does not target religious behavior prevails over religious freedom. After *Smith* the possibility of government interference with the free exercise of religion became much greater.

See also: Freedom of Assembly and Association; Freedom of Expression; Freedom of Religion, Foundations; Halakhah; Shari'a.

BIBLIOGRAPHY

Boyle, Kevin, and Juliet Sheen, eds. *Freedom of Religion and Belief: A World Report.* London: Routledge, 1997.

Forum 18 News. <http://www.forum18.org/index.php>.

Freedom House Center for Religious Freedom. <http://www.freedomhouse.org/religion/>.

Gaustad, Edwin S. *Proclaim Liberty Throughout All the Land: A History of Church and State in America.* New York: Oxford University Press, 1999.

Keston Institute. <http://www.starlightsite.co.uk/keston/>.

Madison, James. "A Memorial and Remonstrance Against Religious Assessments." 1785. <http://religiousfreedom.lib.virginia.edu/sacred/madison_m&r_1785.html>.

Marshall, Paul, ed. *Religious Freedom in the World: A Global Report on Freedom and Persecution.* Nashville, TN: Broadman and Holman, 2000.

Ontario Consultants on Religious Tolerance. <http://www.religioustolerance.org/welcome.htm>.

United States Commission on International Religious Freedom. <http://www.uscirf.gov/index.php3?scale=1152>.

United States Department of State. Office of International Religious Freedom. <http://www.state.gov/g/drl/irf/>.

Van der Vyver, Johan D., and John Witte, Jr., eds. *Religious Human Rights in Global Perspective: Legal Perspectives.* The Hague, Netherlands: Martinus Nijhoff, 1996.

Witte, John, Jr., and Johan D. van der Vyver, eds. *Religious Human Rights in Global Perspective: Religious Perspectives.* The Hague: Martinus Nijhoff, 1996.

Ronald Flowers

Freedom of Religion, Foundations

Freedom of religion is recognized as a fundamental right in both the United States Constitution and international law. Those who oppose religious freedom usually do so because they believe that obedience to religious authority is more important than freedom of conscience or that religious thought is a superstitious belief system that impedes progress and rational thinking. However, by most modern standards fostering a regime of religious freedom generally is deemed to be a desirable aim of government because it provides individuals with the ability to structure their existence around a set of core beliefs that give their lives meaning.

Evaluating what is meant conceptually by religious freedom, or even what constitutes a religion, is a difficult undertaking, however, and raises many serious concerns. Should government have the authority to treat spiritual beliefs in a legal manner, whether favorable or not, that is different from the way it treats other belief systems that are based on philosophical, political, aesthetic, moral, or cultural principles? Does **atheism**, or disbelief in the supernatural, qualify as falling under the protection of religious freedom? What about Scientology or Falun Gong? Can a state that financially and/or symbolically promotes a specific religious viewpoint, or promotes religion generally, still be said to be religiously free if it otherwise allows individuals to worship as they please?

These thorny questions indicate some of the initial difficulties one encounters when attempting to define what constitutes religious freedom, much less agree on legal standards for its propagation, and this is a difficulty faced even by modern, **secular** nations. Such a situation is complicated further by the wide disparity that sometimes exists between declarations made by countries that claim to safeguard religious liberty and empirical studies that indicate that the same governments often use a variety of official and unofficial methods to persecute disfavored religious **sects**.

Article 18 of the *Universal Declaration of Human Rights*, a document that nearly every nation has signed, asserts that all individuals are entitled to the right to freedom of thought, conscience, and religion and that this condition is required if the dignity and **self-determination** of each individual are to be preserved and enhanced. It is important to note that this international definition of freedom goes beyond religious thought and embraces nonbelief. Most nations also make some provision in their laws and constitutions to guarantee religious freedom, although, again, such assertions are no guarantee that this freedom will be protected in reality, no matter how generously the right is defined.

HISTORY

In the West some of the first major steps forward for religious freedom and tolerance came during the Renaissance, Reformation, and Enlightenment periods. Although Protestant groups that broke away from the Roman Catholic Church often did not extend tolerance to other groups, the view that individuals were responsible for their own salvation, or could interpret the Bible on their own without clerical mediation, was a major departure from the Catholic notion of the church strictly regulating matters of faith.

English philosopher John Locke (1634–1704), in his "A Letter Concerning Toleration" (1689), urged tolerance for all faiths except Catholicism and atheism. He did not attack Catholicism on theological grounds but rather on the basis that a Catholic subject's true political allegiance would be given to a foreign prince (the pope), a concern that resonated centuries later with the

atheism: the belief that God does not exist

secularism: a refutation of, apathy toward, or exclusion of all religion

sect: a group of people with a common distinctive view of religion or doctrine

self-determination: the ability of a people to determine their own destiny or political system

candidacy of John F. Kennedy (1917–1963) in the 1960 U.S. presidential election. Atheists also were excluded from similar consideration because it was thought that nonbelievers could not be trusted to be truthful or principled in their words or actions. Beyond these two exceptions Locke felt that a leader should not be concerned, on religious grounds, with belief or the conduct that emanated from it. A leader simply should remain blind to theological matters and regulate religion indirectly only when it violated the peace and good order of the community. Thomas Jefferson and James Madison followed and expanded on these views by indicating that they would extend toleration to Catholics, nonbelievers, skeptics, and other free thinkers, as did Roger Williams (c. 1603–1683) before them, when he established the colony of Rhode Island on the basis of religious tolerance. It should be noted, however, that for Williams tolerance did not mean what it does today—respect for other religions—but simply meant legal forbearance. Williams, a Puritan minister, looked on other religions as **heretical** but outside his power to regulate.

heresy: an opinion about religion that contradicts that of an organized church

BELIEF AND PRACTICE

Even with the best intentions to see it flourish, the concept of religious freedom becomes problematic when it moves beyond the realm of belief and applies to practices and customs that spring from religious thought—especially when such conduct is not necessarily required by the tenets of a religion. Because any behavior potentially can pose a threat to its practitioner or others, governments traditionally have had a free hand in regulating conduct, whether religious or not, with the consequence that religious practices often are burdened. In the United States, for example, there is an long-running debate about whether religious freedom should only protect religious conduct from government attempts to discriminate based on hostility to a group's theological or doctrinal tenets—or whether that freedom should extend to protecting religious groups from the incidental burdens placed on religion by otherwise valid, secular laws.

In the former instance the scope of the freedom would only prohibit efforts by government to regulate the conduct of belief systems because of a theologically based view that a group is heretical or is worshipping incorrectly. (This also would prohibit atheistic government officials from attempting to base legislation on hostility to religion generally and forbid a requirement in religiously diverse states that nonreligious people had to embrace some faith to avoid prejudicial treatment.) At most this interpretation would legally safeguard the practice of innocuous conduct such as religious services, rituals, gestures, or the wearing of distinctive religious apparel. At the very least it would forbid attempts to apply discriminatory classifications against a religious group by forbidding its members from engaging (or requiring them to engage) in certain behavior that other individuals were free (or were not required) to engage in. Otherwise, as long as government could demonstrate a genuine secular purpose for prohibiting or requiring certain behavior, it would not be required to accommodate the burdened religious group by granting it an exemption from compliance with the law. This interpretation of religious freedom would provide complete protection for belief and the communication of belief but would draw the line at conduct that the state would be free to regulate.

In the latter, broader interpretation of religious freedom a religious group would not have to demonstrate that a government action is based on a hostile intent in order to receive relief from the burden placed on its religious conduct. Accommodation also would extend to instances in which a generally applicable, religiously neutral law inadvertently burdened a religious group. On such occasions government would be constitutionally required to exempt religious groups from otherwise valid laws that encumber them even while all others would continue to comply with those laws, with the caveat that truly objectionable behavior such as human sacrifices would not be accommodated.

In its first controversy touching on this matter, *U.S. v. Reynolds* (1879), a case involving **polygamous** marriages, the U.S. Supreme Court upheld a federal law outlawing the practice. Interpreting the Free Exercise Clause of the First

polygamy: the practice of having more then one mate or spouse at one time

Freedom of Worship (Norman Rockwell, 1943). During the height of World War II, an address by President Franklin D. Roosevelt to the U.S. Congress discussed post-war life and featured the "four freedoms": freedom of religious worship, freedom of speech, freedom from want, and freedom from fear. In 1943 artist Norman Rockwell completed four posters highlighting these principles. (SOURCE: © CORBIS. PRINTED BY PERMISSION OF THE NORMAN ROCKWELL FAMILY AGENCY. COPYRIGHT © 1943 THE NORMAN ROCKWELL FAMILY ENTITIES. SECONDARY SOURCE: 506059, NORMAN ROCKWELL FAMILY AGENCY.)

Amendment narrowly, the Court held that religious freedom did not mean that individuals could become "a law onto themselves" if their religious beliefs and practices happened to conflict with positive law. In *Sherbert v. Verner* (1964) and a line of similar cases dealing with government entitlements the Court seemed to move toward a more robust interpretation of religious freedom by requiring that government provide unemployment benefits to Sabbatarians whose religious beliefs forbade them from working on Saturday. This broader interpretation found its fullest articulation in *Wisconsin v. Yoder* (1973), a case that mandated the excusing of Amish children from otherwise required attendance at school, although the Court as a general rule never has directly advanced the principle that religious people, as a constitutional norm, automatically receive an exemption from obeying the same laws obeyed by the rest of society.

Interestingly, the opposing viewpoint that religious persons should never receive voluntary exemptions at the discretion of legislative or executive bodies because such exemptions would constitute improper favoritism over secular belief systems has never been considered seriously. Accommodation of religion in the United States, although not constitutionally required by the Free Exercise Clause, is not forbidden by the Establishment Clause. In 1990 the *Reynolds'* view was reiterated with more force in *Employment Division v. Smith*, a case that examined whether the Free Exercise Clause required the state of Oregon to exempt Native Americans from its general laws prohibiting all use of the hallucinogenic substance peyote. The Supreme Court ultimately held that the state was under no obligation to exempt the drug for ceremonial use in Indian rituals and that the clause had been intended only to prevent government from singling out religious groups for special disability. However, because of some ambiguities in the majority opinion, there is still the possibility that a broader interpretation of free exercise may prevail in future cases, such as claims for unemployment benefits made by religious persons.

As a matter of principle, the Smith/Reynolds approach still could be questioned on the basis of need and not evenhandedness. The fact that government treats everyone alike does not mean that government is treating all people the way they ought to be treated. Many believe that religious people should receive special consideration above others seeking accommodation in secular circumstances because, it is claimed, the Establishment Clause places special impediments on the dissemination of religious thought in the public sphere.

Another difficulty in distinguishing between these two approaches to religious freedom is that both U.S. laws and other nations' laws ultimately are based on the dominant religious tradition(s) of a nation, even when a secular rationale can be offered to justify a law. Again, to use *Reynolds* as an example, the question of whether a polygamist Mormon was being discriminated against because of hostility to his religion is debatable. One might see laws restricting marriage to monogamous relationships as ultimately driven by a religious (mainstream Christian) justification even though a secular argument could be made that monogamy is a more manageable system of marital relations in a well-ordered society.

Even if agreement existed that religious freedom ends with direct attempts by government to curtail practices because of hostility to the underlying theological tenets of a religion, it still is difficult sometimes to determine whether government actions are genuinely guided by legitimate secular motives. Though the incidence of concealed government hostility toward religion is probably not substantial in contemporary America, this is certainly not true in assessing the status and well-being of religious freedom on a global scale.

mandate: to command, order, or require; or, a command, order, or requirement

ideology: a system of beliefs composed of ideas or values, from which political, social, or economic programs are often derived

communism: an economic and social system characterized by the absence of class structure and by common ownership of the means of production and subsistence

fundamentalism: a philosophy marked by an extreme and literal interpretation of religious texts and an inability to compromise on doctrine or policy

inculcate: to teach through repetition

theocracy: a state governed by its religious leaders

INTERNATIONAL RELIGIOUS FREEDOM

Globally, the incidence of religious freedom runs the gamut from theocratic states that allow very little—who ruthlessly use government institutions and other social instruments to **mandate** that religious beliefs, speech, and conduct conform to a particular orthodoxy—to the promotion of extensive liberty by some nations, which frequently make vigorous, proactive legal efforts to accommodate religious minorities whenever an otherwise valid law interferes with the practice(s) of a faith.

As far as human rights are concerned, the worst type of religious oppression is an inquisitional approach that attempts to probe people's minds to ensure that their thoughts are in line with a dominant **ideology**, with harsh punishments meted out to those who do not embrace certain articles of faith or dogma. This kind of oppression can be found in rigid **communist** nations such as North Korea and theocratically inclined states such as Iran and Saudi Arabia. Although persecution by religious **fundamentalists** is most prevalent today in Islamic nations, the same oppression prevailed and still exists to some degree in predominantly Christian and other non-Islamic nations.

Some states go to great lengths to promote a particular religious worldview even if they are not directly engaged in the persecution of disfavored sects. Some Latin American and European nations that are mainly Roman Catholic in character often attempt to blend religious institutions with the structure of the government, and this leads to laws that reflect theological positions, such as codes that prohibit practices like divorce, homosexuality, and abortion.

Occasionally an attempt to accommodate several religions as corporate entities within the structure of the state has the paradoxical effect of impinging on the religious freedom of the individuals who belong to those faiths. For example, in Israel this may occur because the legal system gives the orthodox clergy of various religious communities quasi-governmental authority to regulate social functions such as performing marriages and granting divorces.

In addition, atheistic communistic or postcommunistic regimes often go to great lengths to persecute particular religious/cultural groups, such as China's persecution of Tibetan Buddhism. China, North Korea, and Vietnam are cited frequently for human rights violations because they oppress religion and religious practices generally, especially proselytizing efforts led by foreign missionaries, even though these regimes often claim to respect the right of conscience.

Nor is religious oppression limited to atheistic or theocratic states. In many modern secular democracies, such as France and Turkey, there is a sustained effort by government to **inculcate** the populace with secular principles, and this sometimes extends to banning the wearing of religious icons or apparel in schools and other public spaces. Rather than functioning as a **theocracy** or officially sponsoring atheism, some governments attempt to discourage religion in public and to relegate it to the private sphere.

Although the U.S. judicial system probably would view such aggressive attempts at secularization as a violation of freedom of belief, many of these nations justify such actions as necessary because they claim to be struggling against fanatical religious minorities who are using extra-legal means to impose their beliefs and conduct socially on their own people (such as forcing women to wear scarves or veils), which runs counter to general legal norms protecting individual choice.

Somewhere closer to the middle of the spectrum are nations such as Norway that give financial and symbolic support to an established church but otherwise make no effort to impede others from worshipping or not worshipping as they please. England goes a step further by making heresy or ridicule of the Anglican Church an actionable offense, and this seems not to comport with liberal principles of free speech that allow such criticism.

Many nations, such as Belgium, Germany, and Holland, have even devised a system of largesse by which government funds go to religious groups—including systems predicated on disbelief such as **humanism**—and calculate such subsidization proportionally on the basis of the number of adherents of these groups. This attempt to be evenhanded would be considered unacceptable by men like Jefferson or Madison, who believed that even taxation to support one's own mode of worship violated the principles of religious liberty. This line separating acceptable accommodation of religion from what might be deemed its improper promotion has remained a contested point, resulting in many different standards for assessing government neutrality.

humanist: one who places a great deal of importance on humankind and its experiences

In many ways the U.S. government's relationship with religion is unique. This was the first government to formulate a constitutional principle prohibiting establishment of religion and one promoting its free exercise. The irony here is that although the United States is officially a nation without an establishment, it has a higher level of religious fervor than does "post-Christian" Europe, often leading to undue religious influences on legal and governmental practices. For example, some might consider the motto "In God We Trust" on the nation's currency or the inclusion of "under God" in the Pledge of Allegiance to be violations of the nonestablishment rule, whereas others would view these words as harmless ceremonial deism.

CONCLUSIONS

In the early twenty-first century the debate continues as to what constitutes religious freedom, although for most secular democratic states a large degree of acceptance on broad principles exists. Although the United Nations continues to push for some of the most inclusive and expansive views of freedom of conscience, there are still many areas of the world where harsh religious persecution persists. In many states secularist doctrines such as separation of religion and government do not constitute the governing norms of those in authority, and it appears that such liberal principles will have difficulty taking root in these territories in the foreseeable future.

See also: Freedom of Assembly and Association; Freedom of Expression; Freedom of Religion and the State.

BIBLIOGRAPHY

Drinan, Robert A. *Can God and Caesar Coexist? Balancing Religious Freedom and International Law.* New Haven, CT: Yale University Press, 2004.

Employment Division v. Smith, 494 U.S. 872 (1990).

First Amendment Center. *Religious Liberty in Public Life.* <http://www.firstamendment-center.org/rel_liberty/free_exercise/index.aspx>.

"Free Exercise of Religion." University of Missouri–Kansas City. <http://www.law.umkc.edu/faculty/projects/ftrials/conlaw/freeexercise.htm>.

Locke, John. *Two Treatises of Government and a Letter Concerning Toleration*, ed. by Ian Shapiro. New Haven, CT: Yale University Press, 2003.

Madison, James. "Memorial and Remonstrance Against Religious Assessment." In *Basic Documents Relating to the Religious Clauses of the First Amendment*. Washington, DC: Americans United for the Separation of Church and State, 1965.

Peters, Shawn Francis. *The Yoder Case: Religious Freedom, Education, and Parental Rights*. Lawrence: University Press of Kansas, 2003.

Sanna, Ellyn, Sheila Nelson, and Jack N. Rakove. *The Northern Colonies: The Quest for Religious Freedom, 1600–1700*. Broomal, PA: Mason Crest, 2005.

Sherbert v. Verner, 374 U.S. 398 (1963).

United Nations Universal Declaration of Human Rights. <http://www.un.org/Overview/rights.html.>.

United States v. Reynolds, 345 U.S. 1 (1953).

U.S. State Department, Office of International Religious Freedom. <http://www.state.gov/g/drl/irf/>.

Wisconsin v. Yoder, 406 U.S. 205 (1972).

Timothy Gordinier

Gabon

Formerly part of French Equatorial Africa, the Republic of Gabon gained independence in August 1960. Gabon has an area of 267,669 square kilometers (103,347 square miles), and in 2003 its population was estimated at 1.32 million, which is divided into various small to medium-size ethnic groupings. The three largest constitute only 55 percent of the total. Gabon's **export economy** initially was based on tropical wood, manganese, and uranium, but oil has provided its linchpin since the early 1970s, and Gabon remains a leading African oil producer.

Leon M'Ba (1902–1967) served as Gabon's first president from 1961 until his death in 1967. His successor, Albert-Bernard (later Omar) Bongo Ondimba (b. 1935), is Africa's second longest-serving head of state. Gabon became a one-party state soon after independence in 1960. After surviving a **coup** attempt in 1964, the **regime** enjoyed both political stability and rapid economic growth until the late 1980s, when economic difficulties sparked pressures for political reform that produced a restoration of multiparty politics in 1990.

Gabon's constitutional framework reflects the influence of the French Fifth Republic, with a president joined by a prime minister and council of ministers. The National Assembly has 120 deputies, and the Senate consists of ninety-one members who are elected indirectly. The reintroduction of competitive politics also saw the creation of a separate Constitutional Court alongside the Supreme Court and a National Communications Council to regulate the newly emergent privately owned media; an independent electoral commission was introduced in 1996.

The greater institutional dispersion of authority that followed the democratic opening of 1990 coincided with a continuing **centralization** of power in the presidency—a tendency accentuated by President Bongo Ondimba's undoubted leadership skills, a fragmented political opposition, and the cohesion of the ruling *Parti démocratique gabonais,* the only effective national party. In the seven legislative or presidential elections since 1990 the party's power has never been challenged seriously, enabling Bongo Ondimba frequently to

export economy: an economy dominated by selling products internationally as opposed to domestically

coup: a quick seizure of power or a sudden attack

regime: a type of government, or, the government in power in a region

centralize: to move control or power to a single point of authority

include opposition figures in his cabinet. The nearly thirty opposition parties are tied to individual leaders or anchored to narrow ethnic interests. Few have significant representation in the National Assembly.

Gabon's democratic foundations thus appear shallow. Certainly, electoral management has improved greatly since the early l990s; opposition parties campaign largely without hindrance, and the Constitutional Court has shown independence in **adjudicating** disputed electoral outcomes. However, question remains over the integrity of the electoral rolls and, more recently, the use of the National Communications Council to harass independent newspapers. Despite high levels of urbanization, civil society remains weakly organized. Voting turnout declined steadily from the early 1990s and stood at only 44 percent in the 2001 National Assembly elections (under 20 percent in the capital of Libreville).

Since the late 1990s oil production has been in decline, and uranium exports ceased in 1999. Gabon still has one of the highest national incomes per capita in Africa, but underlying tensions arising from the marked regional and socioeconomic inequalities have considerable disruptive potential. Bongo Ondimba's skills in balancing competing ethnic and regional interests are likely to be tested increasingly, although as of 2004 the *Parti démocratique gabonais* regime's dominance appeared secure for the immediate future.

adjudicate: to settle a case by judicial procedure

(MAP BY MARYLAND CARTOGRAPHICS/THE GALE GROUP)

BIBLIOGRAPHY

Decalo, Samuel. *The Stable Minority: Civilian Rule in Africa, 1960–1990*. Gainesville: Florida Academic Press, 1998.

Englebert, Pierre, with Ralph A. Young. "Gabon: Recent History." In *Africa South of the Sahara 2004*, ed. Katy Murison. London: Europa, 2004.

Gardinier, David. *Gabon*. Oxford, UK: Clio Press, 1992.

Yates, Douglas A. *The Rentier State in Africa: Oil Rent Dependency and Neocolonialism in Gabon*. Trenton, NJ: Africa World Press 1996.

Ralph A. Young

Gambia, The

With a total area of 11,295 square kilometers (4,000 square miles), the Republic of The Gambia is the smallest country on the continent of Africa. It is bordered by Senegal on all sides except on the Atlantic coast, and for this reason the two countries have many ethnic and cultural ties. The Gambia's population, estimated at 1,501,050 in 2003, consists primarily of Muslim ethnic groups, but 10 percent of the population is Christian. English is the official language, although a number of African dialects are spoken widely. The capital of the country is Banjul (called Bathurst until 1973).

The Gambia came under total British control in 1902 and was a British colony until 1965. A system of local rule was established until World War II

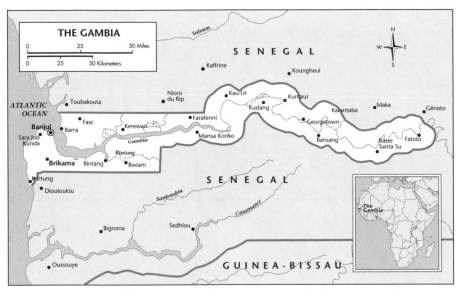

(MAP BY MARYLAND CARTOGRAPHICS/THE GALE GROUP)

(1939–1945), when Britain began to prepare the country for independence. The Gambia achieved self-governance in 1963 and independence on February 1965. After a referendum in 1970 the country became a republic.

The Gambia is a multiparty democracy with a presidential–parliamentary system of government. The government is headed by a president who is popularly elected for a five-year term. The unicameral legislature, the House of Representatives, consists of forty-nine members; forty-five members are elected, and five are appointed by the president. The Alliance for Patriotic Reorientation and Construction, headed by President Yahya Jammeh (b. 1965), was the ruling party as of 2005. The opposition parties have remained weak and divided.

The constitution provides for an independent judiciary, headed by a Supreme Court. Although the lower courts sometimes are subject to corruption and executive branch influence, the judiciary in general has shown its independence on many occasions. The Gambia's legal system is based on English common law, Qur'anic law, and customary law. Administratively, The Gambia consists of five divisions and one city, the capital.

The Gambia's system of government is the culmination of a chain of events that began in 1981 with an unsuccessful coup attempt (suppressed with the intervention of Senegalese troops) by a group of junior-ranking officers. Until that time the country had been one of the democratic oases on the continent of Africa, defying the conventional view that Islam and democracy are incompatible. Within the next ten years the country formed and dissolved a confederation with Senegal, experienced coups and countercoups and elections in between, and finally reverted to democratic rule in 2001.

Once among the best in Africa, The Gambia's human rights record was poor during the military takeover that lasted from 1994 until 2001. Since that time the situation has improved considerably, but the combination of repressive measures and political intimidation during elections earned The Gambia a rating of "partially free" in Freedom House's rankings in 2003.

See also: Parliamentary Systems; Presidential Systems; Republic.

referendum: a popular vote on legislation, brought before the people by their elected leaders or public initiative

unicameral: comprised of one chamber, usually a legislative body

customary law: a law created by the traditions of a community but never officially declared in force

coup: a quick seizure of power or a sudden attack

BIBLIOGRAPHY

Freedom House. "The Gambia." *Freedom in the World 2004*. New York: Freedom House, 2004. <http://www.freedomhouse.org/research/freeworld/2004/countryratings/gambia.htm>.

"Gambia, The." In *CIA World Factbook*. Washington, DC: Central Intelligence Agency, 2005. <http://www.cia.gov/cia/publications/factbook/geos/ga.html>.

U.S. Department of State, Bureau of Democracy, Human Rights, and Labor. "The Gambia." *Country Reports on Human Rights Practices*. Washington, DC: U.S. Department of State, Bureau of Democracy, Human Rights, and Labor, 2005. <http://www.state.gov/g/drl/rls/hrrpt/2004/41605.htm>.

Ayo Ogundele

Gandhi, Mahatma

INDIAN RELIGIOUS LEADER
1869–1948

Mohandas Karamchand Gandhi, the world-renowned leader of India's struggle for independence from Great Britain, is best remembered for his doctrine of peaceful resistance. Gandhi's traditional title, *Mahatma* (Great soul), refers to this philosophy.

Gandhi was born into a middle-caste political family. His grandfather and father were prime ministers of Porbandar, a minor princely state. After studying law in Britain, Gandhi returned to India but was unable to establish a successful legal practice. In 1893 he **emigrated** to the wealthy British colony of Natal, South Africa. There, as a prosperous lawyer, Gandhi became a leading figure in the Indian community's pursuit of equal rights. In 1914 Gandhi returned to India, where he soon assumed a leadership role in the Indian National Congress (INC), an organization advocating self-rule.

Gandhi's **pacifist** philosophy was grounded in the Hindu principle of nonviolence. It also was inspired by the New Testament, Buddhist writings, and the work of the English essayist John Ruskin (1819–1900). The essence of Gandhi's philosophy is that God is universally present and is identical to love. This inner love exists in everyone, even the worst oppressors. Gandhi argued that one must appeal to the oppressor through a combination of persuasion and noncooperation (*satyagraha*). Justice and peace then can be achieved by nonviolent means (*ahimsa*). Although India has never been a particularly nonviolent society, Gandhi succeeded in reducing dramatically the level of bloodshed required to win India's independence. When bloody riots broke out at independence in 1947, fueled by long-standing antagonism between Hindus and Sikhs on the one hand and Muslims on the other, his influence was a key factor in preventing hostilities from spreading to Bengal.

Gandhi's influence, first in India and later worldwide, has promoted the peaceful settlement of otherwise bloody conflicts. He has served as the model for other activist groups, most notably the American civil rights movement led by Dr. Martin Luther King, Jr. (1929–1968). In practice Gandhi's philosophy is restricted to societies, for example, the United States and Great Britain, where the "oppressor" has a strong tradition of peaceful conflict resolution and is open to moral suasion. The limitation of Gandhi's doctrine was illustrated in 1938 when he counseled German Jews to "offer

emigration: the migration of individuals out of a geographic area or country

pacifism: the belief that war and violence are inferior methods of conflict resolution, to be avoided

"... Gandhi succeeded in reducing dramatically the level of bloodshed required to win India's independence."

satyagraha" to Nazi leader Adolf Hitler, which he predicted would convert the Nazis "to an appreciation of human dignity" (Chadha 1997, p. 367).

Although traditionally portrayed as an idealist, Gandhi was a skillful politician who accepted the necessity of military conflict. He supported the British in the Boer War (1899–1902), recruited British Indian forces during World War I (1914–1918), and, after independence, supported India's use of force against Pakistan. Gandhi was, however, a consistent opponent of all forms of violence and discrimination against innocent civilians. It was his pleas on behalf of India's Muslims, Christians, and lower castes that provoked a Hindu extremist to assassinate him on January 30, 1948.

■ ■ ■

GANDHI'S LIFE: A TIMELINE

October 2, 1869: Born in minor princely state of Porbandar, India.

September 1888: Departs to Great Britain for legal education.

July 1891: Returns to India from England.

August 1893: Departs for South Africa.

July 1914: Returns to India from South Africa.

February 1919: Opposes British rule and soon becomes leader of Nationalist movement.

Summer 1942: Demands immediate British withdrawal from India and is imprisoned.

May 1944: Released near end of World War II.

August 1947: India is partitioned between independent India and Pakistan; widespread violence breaks out.

January 30, 1948: Assassinated by Hindu extremist in Delhi, India.

MAHATMA GHANDI (LEFT) DURING THE HISTORIC SALT MARCH IN 1930 WITH INDIAN POET AND POLITICIAN SAROJINI NAIDU. Powerful for its message of Indian independence to the British government, Mahatma Gandhi's "Salt March" in 1930 symbolized the peaceful resistance movement of the Indian leader. (SOURCE: HULTON ARCHIVE/GETTY IMAGES)

See also: India; King Jr., Martin Luther.

BIBLIOGRAPHY

Chadha, Yogesh. *Gandhi.* New York: John Wiley and Sons, 1997.

Duvall, Jack, and Peter Ackerman. *A Force More Powerful. A Century of Non-Violent Conflict.* New York: St Martin's Press, 2001.

Gandhi, Mohandas Karamchad. *An Autobiography, the Story of My Experiments with Truth*, trans. Mahadev Desai. Boston: Beacon, 1957.

Holmes, Robert L. *Nonviolence in Theory and Practice.* Long Grove, IL: Waveland Press, 2001.

Robert S. Robins

Gaza Strip

The Gaza Strip is part of Palestine, a term that refers to the entity which has governed the Palestinian Arabs of the West Bank and the Gaza Strip since 1994. As of 2005 Palestine had not yet become an independent **sovereign** state, but it was widely seen as a state-in-the-making for the Palestinian people.

The Gaza Strip is an area of 360 square kilometers (139 square miles) along the Mediterranean coast between Egypt's Sinai Peninsula and Israel. Mostly composed of sandy plains and low, rolling hills, with 1.3 million inhabitants, the region is one of the most densely populated in the world. The population is overwhelmingly Palestinian Arab and Muslim (98.7%). However, a Christian Palestinian minority of about 1 percent does exist. Approximately 75 percent of the residents of Gaza are refugees from Palestine. Until 2005 there was also a post-1967 Jewish population of settlers which numbered about 7,000.

The Gaza Strip economy is primarily based on agriculture. **Remittances** from migrant laborers—the vast majority of whom work in adjacent Israel—and from the Palestinian diaspora provide vital sources of income. Since the 1990s employment within the emergent Palestinian bureaucracy, with its southern administrative center in Gaza City, has also sustained many Palestinian families.

The Gaza Strip was formerly part of the Palestine Mandate, administered by Great Britain from 1923 to 1948. During the war that followed Israel's declaration of independence in 1948, the Gaza Strip fell under Egyptian rule and was administered by an Egyptian military governor. Although Egypt maintained political control, the Gaza Strip was never **annexed**. Instead, it was held "in trust" for the Palestinian people, and its laws, court system, and bureaucracy were kept relatively unchanged.

Israel conquered the Gaza Strip during the Arab-Israeli War in June 1967. It did not annex the Gaza Strip, but through a military government controlled almost every aspect of Palestinian life. Israel has also sponsored the settlement of Palestinian lands by Israeli settlers, an action the United Nations (UN) has rejected as illegal.

The Gaza Strip fell under a so-called Palestinian Authority (PA) that was created in the Oslo Accords, a series of agreements concluded between Israel and the Palestine Liberation Organization (PLO) in 1993. In 1996 PLO leader Yasser Arafat (1929–2004) was elected president of the PA; eighty-eight members of the Palestine Legislative Council were also elected. The Gaza Strip has been a stronghold of

sovereignty: autonomy; or, rule over a political entity

remittance: a shifting of funds from one entity to another

annex: to incorporate; to take control of politically and/or physically

GRAFFITI FROM SUPPORTERS OF THE PALESTINE LIBERATION ORGANIZATION (PLO) COVERS A LOCAL POST OFFICE AFTER THE PEACE SETTLE-MENT BETWEEN THE PLO AND ISRAEL IN SEPTEMBER 1993. Following the 1993 peace agreement between Palestine and Israel, large portions of the Gaza Strip were allocated to the Palestinian Authority (PA), as established by the accord, while some sections remain under Israeli control. (SOURCE: © PETER TURNLEY/CORBIS)

Islamist opponents of peace negotiations with Israel, who have boycotted the PA elections and advocated violence to end Israeli military occupation.

According to the terms of the Oslo Accords, the PA is not a sovereign state; it lacks full functional and territorial control over the region. Arafat's **authoritarian** tendencies and charges of both corruption and incompetence within the PA led to reforms in 2002 and 2003. In 2004 Israel mounted a series of raids into the Gaza Strip, ostensibly to stem weapons-smuggling from across the border in Egypt, but also crippling much of the PA **infrastructure** and demolishing scores of Palestinian homes in the process. After Arafat's death in November 2004, West Bank and Gazan Palestinians elected Mahmoud Abbas as president of the Palestinian Authority. Abbas, a principal architect of the Oslo Accords, declared an end to the armed *intifada* (uprising) against Israel and promoted negotiations toward a final peace. In 2005, the Israeli government forced all Israeli settlers to leave Gaza, withdrawing its troops and leaving the Gaza Strip to the PA.

See also: Gaza Strip; Israel; Palestine.

authoritarianism: the domination of the state or its leader over individuals

infrastructure: the base on which a system or organization is built

BIBLIOGRAPHY

Brown, Nathan. *Palestinian Politics After the Oslo Accords: Resuming Arab Palestine*. Berkeley: University of California Press, 2003.

Robinson, Glenn. *Building a Palestinian State: The Incomplete Revolution*. Bloomington: University of Indiana Press, 1997.

George Bisharat

Gender Discrimination

Gender discrimination is unfair or unequal treatment directed at a person because of his or her sex or gender. It results most typically from the stereotypical association of certain character traits with women and men, the identification of feminine character traits as less desirable, and the disadvantages that result from this for women. Although gender discrimination also can, at least in principle, be directed at men, its victims are overwhelmingly women.

Cross-culturally and throughout history societies have imputed social significance to gender, assigned different roles to women and men, and used gender-biased language and symbols to suggest a categorical difference between women and men. Categorical distinctions become unfair discrimination when women are identified persistently as subordinate and weaker. All over the world governments, organizations, firms, and households have used gender distinction to allocate burdens and rewards to women and men differentially. Frequently societies have considered gender inequalities part of a natural or divine order and justified discrimination by referring to religion and biology.

THE FEMINIST MOVEMENT

Since the mid-nineteenth century feminists have attacked gender discrimination. They have argued that gender differences are not natural but instead are products of society. They have contended that people are made feminine or masculine through socialization and social institutions and practices and that the world is conceived of as masculine and feminine as a result of the symbols and language that are employed.

Feminist movements have challenged legislation that discriminates against women in politics, economics, and the private sphere. They have gained equal voting rights for women almost universally. They have challenged the exclusion of women from certain jobs, discriminatory pay, and unequal treatment in the workplace. In many places they still are fighting the restriction of women's property rights and rights to contract, their unequal access to education, their unequal rights in families, and their lack of rights to inherit or serve as guardians for their children. The United Nations' Convention on the Elimination of All Forms of Discrimination Against Women is the most authoritative international document condemning gender discrimination at the international level.

DE FACTO DISCRIMINATION

Although women's equal rights have become an international norm and governments have adjusted their laws, in practice gender discrimination is widespread in all parts of the world. Women are severely underrepresented in the political arena. For example, women made up an average of only 15.2 percent of the members of parliaments worldwide in 2003, and of the 192 countries in

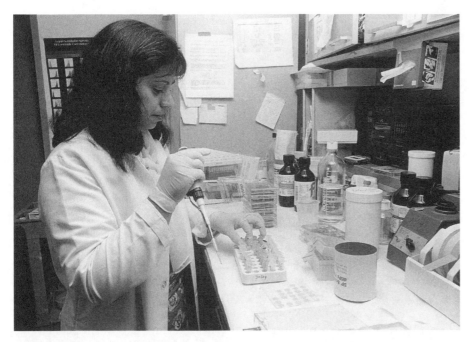

USING MICROPIPETTING TECHNIQUES, A GENETIC ENGINEERING RESEARCH SCIENTIST WORKS IN HER LAB. The potential for DNA manipulation for gender selection of an embryo has given rise to a bioethical debate over the possible discriminatory implications. (SOURCE: MARTHA TABOR/WORKING IMAGES PHOTOGRAPHS. REPRODUCED BY PERMISSION.)

the world only 12 had a female head of state. Women are still much less likely than men to be active in the paid labor market (63 women for every 100 men). However, they work more hours per day than men do. Almost half of women's workday involves nonmarket activities compared to 20 to 30 percent for men.

Women make up 70 percent of the world's 1.3 billion poor (i.e., those living on the equivalent of less than one dollar a day). Women around the world still earn less than men for the same work, their skills tend to be undervalued, and they tend to be concentrated in low-paying and insecure jobs in the informal sector. In Europe the farther women move up the career ladder, the larger the wage differential becomes, with those in the top 10 percent of the salary scale earning on average 35 percent less than do their male counterparts. Clearly, aggregate statistics speak of pervasive discrimination.

CAUSES AND ISSUES

Why is there such a discrepancy between international commitments to nondiscrimination and political and economic realities? Feminist theorists have provided different answers to this question. Some have argued that correcting discrimination against women is a matter or time, of educating biased people, and of strengthening and enforcing laws of nondiscrimination. Others have insisted that a purely legal strategy is insufficient. Because ideas about gender difference are deeply embedded in societies, it is necessary to change informal rules and practices in all spheres of society. This entails a vast change of culture, the language and symbols that suggest women's inferiority, and the practices of public and private organizations, governments, and firms. A commitment to nondiscrimination, in this perspective, needs to be incorporated into all aspects of policy planning and implementation in all issues areas.

Other feminists take a sharply different perspective. They argue that the problem lies with a society that has built its economic and political structures on the presumption that all individuals are the same. This presumption suppresses difference and persuades people to approximate the masculine standard of autonomous, rational individuals. The liberal economic idea that people are competing freely in the labor market implicitly suggests that people have no attachments to families and no care obligations. The liberal idea of citizenship also ignores the differential rights and duties assigned to women and men in the family to create a fiction of a public sphere in which all voices are equal. Equality in these constructions becomes sameness, and gender, racial, ethnic, age, and other differences are denied.

Gender equality tends to be associated with a country's wealth. Typically the countries ranked highest in the United Nations's Development Program's (UNDP) gender-related development index (which measures gender differences in life expectancy, literacy, school enrollment, and earned income) are industrialized countries. However, the UNDP's gender empowerment measure (which weighs women's participation in politics, their proportion among professional and technical workers, and the wage gap) places relatively poorer countries, such as the Bahamas, Costa Rica, and Barbados, in the ranks of the top twenty whereas Japan moves down to forty-fourth place. Wealth thus is an important but not a sufficient predictor of discrimination. Norway, Iceland, and Sweden, the top three countries on both UNDP measures, like the Bahamas, Costa Rica, and Barbados, have strong **welfare states** and a strong presence of women in legislatures. Social policy and government intervention clearly matter.

In addition, culture has a significant impact. In countries where women's and men's roles are considered to be fundamentally different and complementary, women's status tends to be lower. This is the case in conservative and often strongly religious countries such as Saudi Arabia, Yemen, Ecuador, and Ireland, all of which show extreme income differentials between women and men. Furthermore, since the 1980s neo-liberal economic policies have had a definite, if highly complex, impact on women's status. Women have entered low-wage labor markets, increasing their representation in the global labor force, but doing so disproportionately in insecure jobs.

In sum, gender discrimination persists because of a combination of cultural commitments and policy preferences. The neo-liberal perspective that sees the welfare state as an obstacle to economic growth has been problematic for the fight against gender discrimination.

See also: Convention for the Elimination of All Forms of Discrimination Against Women; United Nations; Women's Rights.

welfare state: a political state that assumes liability for the wellbeing of its people through government-run social programs

BIBLIOGRAPHY

Benería, Lourdes. *Gender, Development, and Globalization: Economics as If All People Mattered*. New York: Routledge, 2003.

International Confederation of Free Trade Unions. "Equality through Pay Equity." *Trade Union World Briefing* 2 (March 2003). <http://www.icftu.org/www/pdf/PayequityE.pdf>.

International Labour Organization. *Global Employment Trends for Women 2004*. Geneva: International Labour Organization, 2004. <http://kilm.ilo.org/GET2004/DOWNLOAD/trendsw.pdf>.

Inter-Parliamentary Union. *Women Elected in 2003: The Year in Perspective*. Geneva: Inter-Parliamentary Union, 2004. <http://www.ipu.org/wmn-e/March04.pdf>.

Tong, Rosemarie Putnam. *Feminist Thought: A More Comprehensive Introduction*. Boulder, CO: Westview Press, 1998.

United Nations Development Programme. *Human Development Report*. New York: Oxford University Press, 2003. <http://hdr.undp.org/reports/global/2003/>.

United Nations Women's Fund. *Progress of the World's Women: Vol. 2. Gender Equality and the Millennium Development Goals*. New York: United Nations Women's Fund, 2002. <http://www.unifem.org/index.php?f_page_pid=10>.

Elisabeth Prügl

Geneva Conventions

See International Humanitarian Law.

Genocide

Throughout history there have been attempts to destroy groups of human beings because of their race, religion, or nationality. However, until the twentieth century, no international body or document had adopted a formal legal definition of such concerted action. Attempts to develop humanitarian laws, including various treaties and the Geneva Conventions, focused on war crimes and crimes against humanity committed during times of war. Genocide as a legal concept has its origins in the Nazi barbarism of World War II (1939–1945). The Nazis' extermination of 6 million Jews during the Holocaust, recognized by Sir Winston Churchill (1874–1965), prime Minister of Great Britain, as the "crime that has no name," caused the international community to recognize genocide as an international crime.

THE HOLOCAUST

The ascension of Adolf Hitler (1889–1945) to power in 1933 as the head of the National Socialist Party in Germany laid the foundation for the Holocaust and the death of over 11 million people. Nazi **ideology**, based on a belief in racial purity, declared the Aryan race to be the supreme race in the world. Skillfully using propaganda to demonize Jews as the cause of Germany's post-World War I (1914–1918) social and economic ills, the Nazis imposed laws and policies discriminating against Jews and, with adoption of the Nuremberg Laws in 1935, Jews were denied all rights of citizenship.

ideology: a system of beliefs composed of ideas or values, from which political, social, or economic programs are often derived

Initially the Nazis attempted to drive the Jewish population from Germany through **pogroms**, the destruction of Jewish communities, forced relocation to ghettos and labor camps, and forced **emigration**. Subsequently, Nazi leadership devised a "Final Solution" for the Jewish question, the use of liquidation squads and concentration camps as centers for mass murder. By World War II's end the Nazi **regime** had murdered over 6 million Jews.

pogrom: a planned annihilation of a specific people, especially the Jews

emigration: the migration of individuals out of a geographic area or country

regime: a type of government, or, the government in power in a region

In addition, the Nazis targeted other ethnic groups, nationalities, and persons considered social deviants: homosexuals, the mentally ill, and the physically disabled. Some sources have estimated that overall 3 million non-Jewish Poles, 500,000 Romani (gypsies), and thousands of those regarded as socially undesirable were killed in concentration camps. Poles not killed in the camps became forced laborers; many were sent to work in factories in Germany under conditions of extreme starvation and deprivation.

DEFINING GENOCIDE

seminal: original; at the basis of

The term "genocide" was first used by Raphael Lemkin, an international law scholar, who had fled the Nazi occupation of Poland in 1939. Searching for a word to describe the organized destruction of racial, religious, or social groups, Lemkin coined the word genocide by combining the Greek *genos* (race or tribe) with the Latin-*cide* (killer or act of killing). Writing in 1944 during the height of the Holocaust, Lemkin in his **seminal** work *Axis Rule in Occupied Europe* identified genocide as any synchronized plan intended to eliminate a group of people by destroying the "essential foundations" of the life of that group.

Genocide was first officially recognized as a legal concept in the indictment of Nazi war criminals before the International Military Tribunal (IMT) at Nuremberg in 1945. Count III of the war crimes indictment specifically addressed "deliberate and systematic genocide; viz., the extermination of racial and national groups, against the civilian population of certain occupied territories in order to destroy particular races and classes of people, and national, racial, or religious groups, particularly Jews, Poles, and Gypsies" (Article 6).

ratify: to make official or to officially sanction

The legal concept of genocide was affirmed by the United Nations (UN) General Assembly in 1946 when it adopted Resolution 96(I) that described genocide as follows: "a denial of the right of existence of entire human groups, as homicide is the denial of the right to live of individual human beings; such denial of the right of existence . . . is contrary to moral law and to the spirits and aims of the United Nations." In 1948 the General Assembly unanimously adopted the Convention on the Prevention and Punishment of the Crime of Genocide, which came into force in 1951 and has been **ratified** by 133 countries.

Article I of the Genocide Convention recognizes genocide, whether committed during times of war or peace, as a crime under international law. In Article II the Convention defines genocide as:

[A]ny of the following acts committed with intent to destroy, in whole or in part, a national, ethnical, racial or religious group as such:

(a) Killing members of the group;

(b) Causing serious bodily or mental harm to members of the group;

(c) Deliberately inflicting on the group conditions of life calculated to bring about its physical destruction in whole or in part;

(d) Imposing measures intended to prevent births within the group. . . . .

enumerate: to expressly name, as in a list

As such, the Convention created a category of international crime requiring three elements: (1) the commission of one of the four **enumerated** acts, (2) its direction against one of the specified groups; and (3) its specific intent to destroy that group in whole or in part.

Scholars, particularly social scientists, finding the legal definition too narrow, have also attempted to define genocide to assist in understanding how governments become involved in mass murder. Some well-known and frequently utilized examples of these definitions include the following:

Genocide is the successful attempt by a dominant group, vested with formal authority and/or with preponderant access to the overall resources of power, to reduce by coercion or lethal violence the number of a minority group whose ultimate extermination is held desirable . . . and whose respective vulnerability is a major factor. (Dadrian 1975, p. 201–202)

perpetrate: to commit a crime or injustice

collectivity: the state of being whole or complete, as a group

Genocide is a sustained purposeful action by a **perpetrator** to physically destroy a **collectivity** directly or indirectly, through interdiction of the biological and social reproduction of group members, sustained regardless of the surrender or lack of threat offered by the victim. (Fein 1993, p.24)

YOUNG VICTIMS OF GENOCIDE IN TURKEY. In 1915 the Turkish government initiated the genocide of 600,000 Armenians after incarcerating about 200 Armenian community leaders. The systematic annihilation of Armenians lasted three years. (SOURCE: HULTON ARCHIVE/GETTY IMAGES)

Genocide is a form of one-sided mass killing in which a state or other authority intends to destroy a group, as that group and membership in it are defined by the perpetrator. (Jonassohn 1992, p. 19)

Unfortunately, even with an internationally recognized prohibition against genocide and increased attention by scholars to understanding the causes and dynamics of genocide as a prelude to preventing, or at a minimum reducing, its incidence, genocidal events still arose in the later part of the twentieth century and continue in the twenty-first.

OTHER TWENTIETH-CENTURY EXAMPLES OF GENOCIDE

In 1990 simmering political tensions in Rwanda erupted into civil war. A former Belgian colony, Rwandan society was divided into two primary social groups: the Hutu making up approximately 85 percent of the population and the Tutsi representing the other 15 percent. Historically the Tutsi had been politically privileged through a Tutsi monarchy and system of highly personal patron-client relationships known as *ubuhake*. The resulting social divisions were based more on the Tutsis' societal roles and occupational characteristics rather than their ethnic classification. However, Belgian colonial rule, in asserting a belief in the racial superiority of the Tutsi and instituting

■ ■ ■

CAMBODIAN GENOCIDE

Cambodia was the site of a tragic genocide between 1975 and 1979. Led by the despot Pol Pot (1925–1998), the Khmer Rouge (or Red Cambodians) came to power by overthrowing the weak and unpopular government of Gen. Lon Nol (1913–1985), which had with the help of the United States overthrown the neutralist government of Prince Sihanouk (b. 1922). The Khmer Rouge tried to turn Cambodia into a self-contained Communist agrarian society. The country, which was renamed the Democratic Republic of Kampuchea, is thought to have lost between one and two million people—perhaps as much as a quarter of its total population—during the purges, mass executions, and starvation that marked the four years of Pol Pot's rule.

Imitating Mao Tse-tung's policies of population relocation, Pol Pot forcibly emptied the major cities of Cambodia. The inhabitants were moved into rural areas at gunpoint and put to work in slave labor camps that came to be known as "killing fields." Many died there of disease, overwork, and malnutrition.

The country was also "purified" of Western influences. All foreigners were expelled; the use of foreign languages was forbidden; and newspapers, radio, and television stations were closed. Banks were closed, and money was abolished. Social groups that represented the "old" Cambodia, including anyone with higher education as well as Buddhist clergy and former government officials, were relentlessly purged. In addition, ethnic minorities, such as the Vietnamese and Chinese, were scheduled for elimination. It is estimated that half the ethnic Chinese living in Cambodia in 1975 died under the Khmer Rouge regime.

The genocide ended after the Vietnamese, in response to several years of Khmer Rouge provocation, as well as thousands of refugees coming over the border, invaded Cambodia in late 1978 and overthrew the Khmer Rouge regime. Pol Pot fled Cambodia in January 1979. He died in exile in Thailand in April 1998.

administrative policies that legitimized Tutsi rule, created an environment whereby social divisions began to be viewed along ethnic lines.

Hutu uprisings between 1959 and 1961 resulted in large-scale ethnic violence leading to the murder of 10,000 Tutsi and the flight of another 336,000 into exile. By 1990 it was estimated that between 600,000 and 700,000 Tutsi were in exile. Within Rwanda, a new Hutu elite institutionalized discrimination against the remaining Tutsi. In neighboring countries, Tutsi exile groups increased in militancy, became more organized, and in 1990 launched an invasion of Rwanda under the banner of the Rwandan Patriotic Front (RPF). During the next three years of civil war, the Rwandan government sponsored a series of massacres of Tutsi within the country. In 1993 the government and RPF signed a peace accord; almost immediately, however, the government began to train and arm radical Hutu **militia**. Simultaneously ethnic tensions between Tutsi and Hutu in neighboring Burundi erupted into fighting that led to ethnic massacres responsible for some 50,000 deaths. When a plane carrying the presidents of both Rwanda and Burundi was shot down in 1994, Rwandan military forces and radical Hutu militias began a murderous campaign, executing Tutsi and moderate Hutu throughout the country. Between 500,000 and a million people were killed during a four-month period (April through July of 1994).

During this same time period, the republic of Bosnia-Herzegovina, formerly part of Yugoslavia, became the site of another genocide. Yugoslavia, created in World War I's aftermath, had within its borders numerous religious and ethnic groups driven by historical rivalries: In particular, enmity had long existed between Serbs (Orthodox Christians), Croats (Catholics), and ethnic Albanians (Muslims). Following the death of its **communist** leader, Josip Broz Tito (1892–1980), the country quickly became mired in political and economic chaos. By 1991 Yugoslavia had fragmented, with a number of republics

militia: a group of citizens prepared for military service in emergency situations

communism: an economic and social system characterized by the absence of class structure and by common ownership of the means of production and subsistence

announcing their independence. In response, the Yugoslav military dominated by Serbs under the control of Slodoban Milosevic (b. 1941), a **nationalist** who had gained power by inflaming religious hatred, invaded Croatia. During this invasion Serbs massacred hundreds of Croat men and buried them in mass graves. Although a cease-fire had been brokered by the end of 1991, a new crisis emerged when the United States and the European community formally recognized the independence of Bosnia. The capital of Bosnia, Sarajevo, soon came under attack by Serb forces. Moving through the country, in what came to be known as a campaign of "**ethnic cleansing**," Serb forces rounded up local Muslims and perpetrated mass executions, rape, the forced depopulation of towns and villages, and imprisonment of men and boys in concentration camps. It is estimated that by the time a peace accord was reached in 1995, 200,000 Muslim Bosnians had been killed, more than 20,000 were missing, and over 2,000,000 persons had become refugees.

See also: Armenia; Bosnia and Herzegovina; Crimes Against Humanity; Ethnic Cleansing; Hitler, Adolf; International Criminal Court; Rwanda; War Crimes.

nationalism: the belief that one's nation or culture is superior to all others

ethnic cleansing: the systematic murder of an entire ethnic group

BIBLIOGRAPHY

Charny, Israel W. *The Widening Circle of Genocide.* New Brunswick, NJ: Transaction Publishers, 1994.

Dadrian, Vahakn N. "A Typology of Genocide." *International Review of Modern Sociology* 5 (Fall 1975):201–212.

Fein, Helen. *Genocide: A Sociological Perspective.* Newbury Park, CA: Sage, 1993.

Horowitz, Irving L. *Taking Lives: Genocide and State Power,* 4th ed. New Brunswick, NJ: Transaction Publishers, 1997.

Indictment: Count Three. The Avalon Project. <http://www.yale.edu/lawweb/avalon/imt/proc/count3.htm>.

Jonassohn, Kurt. "What is Genocide?" In *Genocide Watch,* ed. Helen Fein. New Haven, CT: Yale University Press, 1992.

Lemkin, Raphael. *Axis Rule in Occupied Europe: Laws of Occupation, Analysis of Government, Proposals for Redress.* Clark, NJ: Lawbook Exchange, 2005.

Nuremberg Trial Proceedings, Volume 1, Article 6,

Prunier, Gerard. *The Rwanda Crisis: History of a Genocide.* New York: Columbia University Press, 1995.

Rummel, R. J. *Death by Government: Genocide and Mass Murder Since 1900.* New Brunswick, NJ: Transaction Publishers, 1994.

Richard Janikowski

Georgia

Georgia, bordered by Russia on the north, Azerbaijan and Armenia on the southeast, Turkey on the southwest, and the Black Sea on the west, is situated on the dividing line between Europe and Asia. The total territory of Georgia is 69,700 square kilometers (43,312 square miles).

The total population of Georgia was estimated at 4.7 million in 2004. Approximately 70 percent of the people are Georgians. The rest are Armenian

(8.1%), Russian (6.3%), Azeri (5.7%), Ossetian (3%), Abkhaz (1.8%), and other (5%). About 65 percent of the total population is Georgian Orthodox, 11 percent Muslim, 10 percent Russian Orthodox, 8 percent Armenian Apostolic, and 6 percent unknown. Tbilisi is the capital city.

After decades of domination by czarist Russia, Georgia became an independent country in May 1918. However, in 1921 Georgia was absorbed into the Union of Soviet Socialist Republics (USSR). A native son of Georgia, Joseph Stalin (1879–1953), was the Soviet Union's most brutal dictator from the 1920s until his death in 1953. After seventy years of the Soviet **communist** regime, Georgia declared its independence in 1991, when the USSR disintegrated.

Zviad Gamsakhurdia (1939–1993) was elected president in 1991 but was unseated in 1992 by a **coup** that installed Eduard Shevardnadze (b. 1928) as head of state. Shevardnadze subsequently won the presidential elections: first in 1995 and again in 2000. In 1995 and 1998 two assassination attempts were made against Shevardnadze. The irregularities of the 2003 parliamentary elections forced Shevardnadze to resign. Mikhail Saakashvili (b. 1967) resigned as Minister of Justice in 2001 and founded the United National Movement (later the National Movement), a political party under whose banner he won the 2004 presidential elections, garnering more than 96 percent of the vote.

In February 2004 the parliament amended the 1995 constitution to establish a French-style presidential-parliamentary system that passed power from the legislative to the executive. The president appoints a prime minister after consulting with the leaders of parliament. The prime minister then names ministers with the approval of the president. The president alone appoints the ministers of security, defense, and interior. The parliament can consider motions of confidence in the government and dismiss them with a majority vote. The president has the right to dismiss the parliament if the parliament fails to approve the government three times in a row or approve the nation's budget.

The president is elected by direct **suffrage** with a term of five years for a maximum of two consecutive terms. Georgia's **unicameral** parliament is the

communism: an economic and social system characterized by the absence of class structure and by common ownership of the means of production and subsistence

coup: a quick seizure of power or a sudden attack

suffrage: to vote, or, the right to vote

unicameral: comprised of one chamber, usually a legislative body

(MAP BY MARYLAND CARTOGRAPHICS/THE GALE GROUP)

supreme representative body of the country and exercises legislative power and general control over the Cabinet of Ministers. The parliament consists of 150 deputies elected by a **proportional system** and 85 deputies elected by a **majoritarian** system, all for a period of four years.

The judicial system is headed by the Supreme Court and the Constitutional Court. The Constitutional Court has nine members; three are appointed by the president, another three are elected by parliament, and the remaining three are appointed by the Supreme Court. The chief justice and judges of the Supreme Court are nominated by the president and elected by the parliament for a period of not less than ten years.

Most political parties are weak and unstable. Nevertheless, President Saakashvili's party won almost two-thirds of the seats in the March 2004 parliamentary elections.

Georgia is considered to have a democratic government. However, it has embarked on an uncertain path of democratic transition in the wake of the dissolution of the communist regime. Freedom House rates it as only partly free and gives it a middle rating of 4 on both its political rights and civil rights and liberties scales.

See also: Gorbachev, Mikhail; Russia; Stalin, Joseph.

proportional system: a political system in which legislative seats or offices are awarded based on the proportional number of votes received by a party in an election

majoritarianism: the practice of rule by a majority vote

BIBLIOGRAPHY

The Constitution of Georgia. <http://www.parliament.ge/LEGAL_ACTS/CONSTITU-TION/consten.html>.

"Georgia." In *CIA World Factbook.* Washington, DC: Central Intelligence Agency, 2005. <http://www.cia.gov/cia/publications/factbook/geos/gg.html>.

International Institute for Democracy and Electoral Assistance. *Georgia and the South Caucasus: Challenges to Sustainable Democracy.* Stockholm: International Institute for Democracy and Electoral Assistance, 2001.

Karatnycky, Adrian, et al., eds. *Nations in Transit 2003: Democratization in East Central Europe and Eurasia.* Baltimore, MD: Rowman & Littlefield, 2003.

Phillips, David L. *Stability, Security, and Sovereignty in the Republic of Georgia.* New York: Center for Preventive Action, 2004. <http://www.cfr.org/pdf/Georgia.pdf/>.

Lucy Dadayan

Germany

Germany is Western Europe's most populous nation, with 82.5 million inhabitants (compared to approximately 58.7 million in both France and the United Kingdom and 57.4 million in Italy), and claims the third largest economy in the world after those of the United States and Japan. Germany is strategically situated at the geopolitical and economic crossroads of Europe, bordering nine countries. Its neighbors are France, Luxembourg, Belgium, and the Netherlands to the west; Denmark to the north; Poland to the east; the Czech Republic and Austria to the southeast; and Switzerland to the south. Germany is a prominent member of the North Atlantic Treaty Organization (NATO) and a founding member of the European Union.

Germany's geographical features include rolling countryside dotted with farms and forests throughout much of the country, sandy beaches on the shores

decentralize: to move power from a central authority to multiple periphery government branches or agencies

totalitarianism: a form of absolute government that demands complete subjugation by its citizens

socioeconomic: relating to the traits of income, class, and education

communism: an economic and social system characterized by the absence of class structure and by common ownership of the means of production and subsistence

liberalization: the process of lowering trade barriers and tariffs and reducing government economic regulations

bloc: a group of countries or individuals working toward a common goal, usually within a convention or other political body

dissident: one who disagrees with the actions or political philosophy of his or her government or religion

of the Baltic and North seas, mountains in the south—including a slice of the Alps on the border with Austria—and the Black Forest in the southwest. The most important rivers are the Rhine in the west and the Elbe in the east.

Urban and industrial centers are more **decentralized** in Germany than in many European countries (notably France and Britain). The three largest cities are Berlin (the country's capital) near the Polish border in the east, Hamburg on the North Sea, and Munich (the capital of the state of Bavaria) in the south. Other cities of note include Cologne and Frankfurt in the western part of the country and Leipzig, Dresden, and Magdeburg in the east.

FROM DIVISION TO UNIFICATION

One of the most dramatic events of late-twentieth-century European politics was the unification of Germany in 1990. This proved a momentous capstone to a long and tortuous pattern of political development rooted in historical traditions of territorial fragmentation, political instability, and military aggression. Germany achieved artificial unity with the creation of the Imperial Reich in 1871, helped provoke World War I (1914–1918), and experienced revolutionary and counterrevolutionary upheavals during the formation of the ill-fated Weimar Republic (1918–1919). Adolf Hitler (1889–1945) and his National Socialist (Nazi) henchmen abolished democracy with the ruthless imposition of the **totalitarian** Third Reich in 1933 and immediately proceeded with plans to launch another Europe-wide war. They also instigated the arrest and execution of millions of Jews and other regime "outsiders." At the end of World War II (1939–1945) the wartime Allies—the United States, Britain, France, and the Soviet Union—divided Germany into four occupation zones, which were consolidated in 1949 into two antagonistic political and **socioeconomic** systems: the capitalist democratic Federal Republic of Germany in the West (also known as West Germany) and the **communist** German Democratic Republic (GDR) in the East (also known as East Germany).

The Federal Republic quickly developed a successful and stable economic and political system. Unprecedented material growth and prosperity contributed to the emergence of a cohesive democratic political culture and the legitimation of the West German political system. In contrast, communist leaders in the East created a dictatorial political and economic system modeled after that of the Soviet Union. Political, economic, and institutional power was centralized in the hands of the monopolistic Marxist–Leninist Socialist Unity Party (SED).

The GDR was never able to attain the levels of prosperity and political legitimacy achieved in the Federal Republic. As a result millions of East German citizens fled to the west. The continuing loss of skilled labor forced the SED to close the border between East and West Berlin by erecting the Berlin Wall in August 1961. The communists maintained themselves and the political system in power through a policy of constant vigilance and repression, enforced by a well-organized and efficient secret police.

Mikhail Gorbachev's (b. 1931) rise to power in the Soviet Union in 1985 unleashed a process of **liberalization** throughout the communist **bloc**. By 1989 tens of thousands of mainly younger East Germans had left the GDR via Hungary (which opened its borders to neighboring Austria) and Czechoslovakia. **Dissidents** who chose to stay at home began taking to the streets in massive demonstrations, demanding freedom, democracy, and (increasingly) unification with the Federal Republic. Hard-line Stalinist rulers were forced to resign in October 1989. Their successors reluctantly agreed with opposition leaders in January 1990 to schedule East Germany's first free elections. The elections were held in March 1990 and resulted in a resounding victory by pro-democratic parties.

A **coalition** East German government then negotiated unification treaties with West Germany, providing for economic, monetary, and social union and establishing the constitutional basis for political unification. West Germany and East Germany constitutionally merged in October 1990 to form an expanded Federal Republic, and all-German elections were held on December 2. The victors were the center-right Christian Democrats and the liberal Free Democrats, which formed the first postwar all-German government. Thus, Germany became territorially, institutionally, and politically unified for the second time in its history.

coalition: an alliance, partnership, or union of disparate peoples or individuals

CONSTITUTIONAL PRINCIPLES

The united Federal Republic embodies traditional features of German governance and a number of important postwar innovations. Historical elements include a written constitution (the first national constitution was adopted when Imperial Germany was established in 1871) and a federal system of government. Federalism is a logical and necessary development from Germany's historical legacy of territorial fragmentation among numerous independent kingdoms,

(MAP BY MARYLAND CARTOGRAPHICS/THE GALE GROUP)

city-state: a system of government common in ancient Greece, marked by a city with authority over surrounding territory

jurisdiction: the territory or area within which authority may be exercised

judicial review: the ability of the judicial branch to review and invalidate a law that contradicts the constitution

incumbent: one who currently holds a political office, or, holding a political office

principalities, and **city-states** before the country's initial unification. Both Imperial Germany and the Weimar Republic were federal systems, with political power divided between a national government and regional states (*Länder*). Hitler abolished federalism with the creation of a unitary state under totalitarian Nazi control, but the Western Allies reconstituted federalism in their zones of occupation after 1945. West German federalism was anchored in the Basic Law, which was adopted in 1949 as the constitutional basis for the Federal Republic. Federal principles were extended to former East Germany in 1990.

Similar to the American constitution, the Basic Law provides for a system of national, concurrent, and state **jurisdiction**. The federal government in Berlin exercises exclusive authority over foreign policy, citizenship, the defense of democracy and the constitution, the criminal police, and other all-German policies. It shares concurrent legislation with the country's sixteen states (ten in western Germany, five in eastern Germany, and Berlin) in such areas as civil and criminal law, public welfare, economic policy, and refugee matters. The states exercise primary jurisdiction over public education, the public media, cultural institutions, and policies of strictly regional concern.

German constitutional provisions include the legal protection of individual freedoms similar to those contained in the U.S. Bill of Rights—such as freedom of assembly, opinion, and religion—as well as a number of positive freedoms characteristic of more modern constitutions in Europe and elsewhere. The latter provisions include the protection of human dignity, the sanctity of marriage and families, the protection of illegitimate children, the right of citizens to join unions and professional groups and pursue an occupation of their choice, and safeguards governing private ownership of property and inheritance. Capital punishment is prohibited under the Basic Law.

An important postwar constitutional innovation was the creation of a Federal Constitutional Court, modeled after the U.S. Supreme Court, with powers of **judicial review** over national and state legislation. The Federal Constitutional Court also is empowered to rule on the constitutionality of political parties. The court twice has banned parties because of their antidemocratic principles.

INSTITUTIONAL ACTORS

Principles of federalism and democracy are institutionalized on both the federal and state levels of government. Germany's head of state is an indirectly elected federal president who is chosen for a five-year term by a special electoral college made up of an equal number of national and state legislators. The president represents Germany to the international community, receives foreign dignitaries, and conducts goodwill visits abroad. Otherwise the president exercises few substantive powers. Depending on the personality and political convictions of the **incumbent**, the most important role of the federal president is to serve as Germany's moral conscience, for example, exhorting citizens to be exemplary democrats. Up to the year 2005 nine men had served as president since 1949. Horst Koehler (b. 1943), a Christian Democrat, was narrowly elected over a Social Democratic candidate in May 2004.

The most important executive power is vested in a federal chancellor (the equivalent of a prime minister) who is constitutionally empowered to determine general policy guidelines and goals. The chancellor is elected by a majority of the members of the lower house of parliament and can be ousted from office only through a vote of no confidence in which a majority of deputies simultaneously elect a successor. This provision has been evoked twice: unsuccessfully in

1972 and successfully in 1982. Once elected, the federal chancellor nominates members of the cabinet to the federal president for formal appointment to office. The powers of the federal chancellor broadly resemble those of the British prime minister, especially with respect to setting the national political agenda and determining policy priorities.

Legislative power on the national level is divided between a directly elected lower house, the *Bundestag*, and an appointive upper house, the *Bundesrat*. Both bodies constitute modified institutional reincarnations of legislative assemblies from Germany's past—especially those in the Weimar Republic. *Bundestag* deputies are elected for four-year terms (unless a special election intervenes, as occurred in 1982) on the basis of a dual ballot that combines direct **constituency** elections and **proportional representation**. A key postwar constitutional innovation is the requirement that parties must receive either 5 percent of the popular vote or three direct mandates to be represented in parliament. Members of the *Bundesrat* are appointed by the sixteen state governments, which in turn are formed on the basis of staggered elections to *Länder* assemblies.

The number of representatives from each state varies from three to six, depending on the size of a state's population. *Bundesrat* deputies do not vote as

constituency: the people who either elect or are represented by an elected official

proportional system: a political system in which legislative seats or offices are awarded based on the proportional number of votes received by a party in an election

A SESSION OF THE BUNDESTAG IN BERLIN, GERMANY IN 2005. After the decline of communism and the reunification of East Germany with West Germany in 1990, Germans voted in 1991 throughout the new republic for its inaugural bicameral legislature including the lower house *Bundestag* and upper house *Bundesrat*. (SOURCE: MARCUS BRANDT/AFP/GETTY IMAGES)

a matter of personal conscience but instead vote as a bloc on instructions from their state governments. The *Bundestag* is politically the more powerful of the two houses in that it elects the federal chancellor and provides the institutional basis for most legislative initiatives. At the same time the *Bundesrat* shares legislative jurisdiction with the lower house in most matters and may exercise an **absolute** veto over constitutional amendments and changes in *Länder* boundaries.

PARTIES, ELECTIONS, AND LEADERS

One of Germany's historical legacies was a complex, highly fragmented party system dating from preunification times and continuing through the Imperial times and Weimar regimes. Most parties were doggedly **ideological**, often unable to compromise **partisan** differences. Their failure to seek a common policy response to the crisis of the Great Depression (1929–1933) was an indirect cause of Hitler's rise to power in 1933. Postwar parties have evolved in a significantly different manner.

The wartime Allies authorized the creation of a multiparty system in their four zones of occupation during the spring and summer of 1945. The parties included the center-right Christian Democratic Union (CDU) and a Bavarian sister party, the Christian Social Union (CSU); a liberal Free Democrats (FDP); the Social Democrats (SPD); and the Communist Party (KPD). In the Soviet zone of occupation the KPD and SPD were merged forcibly to form the communist Socialist Unity Party (SED) in 1946, and the remaining satellite parties were reduced to a subordinate political status. In West Germany, in contrast, a vibrant competitive party system emerged that was dominated by the CDU/CSU, the FDP, and the SPD. The KPD became increasingly **marginalized** during the formative years of the Federal Republic, first because it failed to surmount the 5 percent electoral threshold by the mid-1950s and later because the Federal Constitutional Court banned it as antidemocratic.

During Germany's political division from 1949 until the move toward unity in 1990, the SED monopolized political power in East Germany, while West Germany's democratic parties—the CDU/CSU, the FDP, and the SPD—alternated in power in various coalitions. The CDU/CSU and the FDP emerged as early advocates of a social **market economy** policy that combined government support for capitalism and extensive welfare provisions, German participation in European integration, and membership in NATO.

Although all three of West Germany's mainstream political parties resolutely affirmed democratic principles and institutions, SPD leaders initially were skeptical of policy measures that in their view would deepen the country's political division. A crucial consequence of these differences was that the CDU/CSU and the FDP handily won national elections—and therefore formed federal governments—from 1949 well into the 1960s. The SPD abandoned ideological rigidity in 1959 with the adoption of a moderate party program that affirmed German membership in NATO and the European Economic Community (now the European Union). Largely because of the party's shift to the center, the SPD joined the CDU/CSU as junior partners in a grand coalition government in 1966. They subsequently governed in coalition with the FDP from 1969 to 1982 and formed a coalition government with the Greens in 1998 (which was renewed in 2002).

The Greens emerged as a national political force in the early 1980s as part of a Europe-wide phenomenon of citizen protest against environmental pollution and nuclear armament. Their success in surmounting the 5 percent electoral barrier in 1983 transformed the West German system from a two-and-a-half-party system dominated by the CDU/CSU, SPD, and FDP into a multiparty system.

absolute: complete, pure, free from restriction or limitation

ideology: a system of beliefs composed of ideas or values, from which political, social, or economic programs are often derived

partisan: an ideologue, or a strong member of a cause, party, or movement

marginalize: to move to the outer borders, or to move one to a lower position

market economy: an economy with little government ownership and relatively free markets

German unification in 1990 resulted in the transformation of the former SED into a postcommunist democratic party that was named the Party of Democratic Socialism (PDS). The PDS entered parliament as a fifth national party in 1990. In elections since 1990 the PDS polled an average of 4 percent of the popular vote compared to 7 percent for the Greens, 37 percent for the SPD, and 38 percent for the CDU/CSU.

National leaders who have played key roles in shaping postwar German political development and a domestic democratic consensus include politicians from all the major parties. Among them are Theodor Heuss (1884–1963), a member of the FDP who served as the first federal president (1949–1959); Konrad Adenauer (1876–1967), a founding member of the CDU who served as the first federal chancellor (1949–1963); Willy Brandt (1913–1992), a member of the SPD who **emigrated** to Scandinavia after the rise of national socialism to power in 1933 and returned to Germany at the end of the war to become an internationally respected mayor of West Berlin and later federal chancellor (1969–1974); Helmut Kohl (b. 1930), a CDU chancellor who presided over German unification in 1990; and Gerhard Schroeder (b. 1944), a member of the SPD who presided over a coalition SPD-Green government formed after national elections in 1998 and 2002.

emigration: the migration of individuals out of a geographic area or country

ACHIEVEMENTS AND ISSUES

A historic achievement of postwar German politics has been the firm anchorage of the Federal Republic in the North Atlantic community. Previous regimes, from Imperial Germany through the Third Reich, had pursued a "special path" (*sonderweg*) of domestic development and foreign policy—with disastrous consequences for Germany and the world. Postwar anchorage in a larger community of nations has taken multiple forms, including the Federal Republic's eagerness to help launch the European integration movement in the early 1950s and its membership by the mid-1950s in NATO. Germany subsequently became a major player in both the European Union and North Atlantic security affairs. In addition, Germany's status as Europe's principal "economic locomotive" has contributed to the European Union's emergence as an important global economic actor.

A number of problems confronted contemporary Germany at the start of the twenty-first century. Although Germany is once again unified, East and West Germans have not been fully integrated in a single society. Unemployment is significantly higher and wages are lower in the eastern states than in the "old" Federal Republic. Many East Germans feel their Western "cousins" treat them as second-class citizens, and many West Germans resent the unexpectedly high cost of unification (much of it paid through tax surcharges). In the late 1990s and early 2000s Germany's economic performance faltered somewhat; its annual growth rate slowed, and unemployment increased in the country as a whole.

See also: European Union.

BIBLIOGRAPHY

Adenauer, Konrad. *Memoirs 1945–53*. Chicago: Regnery, 1955.

Basic Law for the Federal Republic of Germany. <http://www.psr.keele.ac.uk/docs/german.htm>.

Bracher, Karl Dietrich. *The German Dictatorship*. New York: Praeger, 1970.

Brandt, Willy. *In Exile. Essays, Reflections and Letters 1933–1947.* Philadelphia: University of Pennsylvania Press, 1971.

Braunthal, Gerard. *Parties and Politics in Modern Germany.* Boulder, CO: Westview Press, 1996.

Bullock, Alan. *Hitler: A Study in Tyranny*, rev. ed. New York: Harper & Row, 1963.

Conradt, David P. "Changing German Political Culture." In *The Civic Culture Revisited*, ed. Gabriel A. Almond and Sidney Verba. Boston: Little, Brown, 1980.

Conradt, David P., ed. *Germany's New Politics: Parties and Issues in the 1990s.* Providence, RI: Berghahn Books, 1995.

Dalton, Russell. *Citizen Politics: Public Opinion and Political Parties in Advanced Industrial Democracies*, 3rd ed. New York: Chatham House Publishers/Seven Bridges Press, 2002.

Hancock, M. Donald, and Helga Welsh, eds. *German Unification: Process and Outcomes.* Boulder, CO: Westview Press, 1994.

Merkl, Peter, ed. *The Federal Republic at Forty-Five: Union Without Unity.* New York: New York University Press, 1995.

Merkl, Peter, ed. *The Federal Republic of Germany at Fifty: The End of a Century of Turmoil.* New York: New York University Press, 1999.

Padgett, Stephen, William E. Paterson, and Gordon Smith, eds. *Developments in German Politics.* Basingstoke, UK: Palgrave Macmillan, 2003.

Pond, Elizabeth. *Friendly Fire: The Near-Death of the Transatlantic Alliance.* Pittsburgh, PA: European Union Studies Association, 2004.

M. Donald Hancock

Ghana

Located on the coast of West Africa, Ghana occupies a total land area of 228,000 square kilometers (88,000 square miles). The population, estimated in 2004 to be approximately 20.3 million, is comprised of several tribal groups, including the Akan, Moshi-Dagomba, Ewe, and Ga. According the World Bank, the gross national income per capita in 2002 was $270. The climate is tropical; the weather is warm and comparatively dry along the southeast coast, hot and humid in the southwest, and hot and dry in the north. The terrain consists mostly of low plains, with a dissected plateau in the south-central area. Ghana is home to Volta Lake, the world's largest artificial lake.

A former British colony, Ghana became the first country in sub-Saharan Africa to gain its independence in 1957 under the leadership of Kwame Nkrumah (1909–1972). Beginning in 1964, a series of coups resulted in the suspension of three constitutions until a fourth was approved in 1992, which has since remained the basis for government. Becoming effective on January 7, 1993, the 1992 Constitution of the Republic of Ghana incorporates provisions and institutions drawn from British and U.S. constitutional models. Like the American system, it provides for the sharing of powers among a president, a legislature, and an independent judiciary through a system of checks and balances designed to limit the power of any one branch of government.

The president has executive authority as head of state, head of government, and commander in chief of the armed

"Ghana became the first country in sub-Saharan Africa to gain its independence . . ."

forces. As in the United States, the president is limited to two four-year terms. Jerry Rawlings (b. 1947) won presidential elections in 1992 and 1996 and was succeeded by John Kufuor (b. 1938) in a free and fair election in 2000. The National Parliament, a **unicameral** body of two hundred members, performs legislative functions. Members of parliament are popularly elected by universal adult **suffrage** to four-year terms. Unlike the American system, members of parliament can also hold dual positions as ministers appointed by the president. The president, who has a qualified veto over all bills (except those to which a vote of urgency is attached), must consent to any legislation before it becomes law. The structure and the power of the judiciary are independent of all other branches of government. The Supreme Court has broad powers of **judicial review**, and it has the authority to rule on the constitutionality of any legislative or executive action at the request of any aggrieved citizen.

A salient feature of the 1992 constitution is the inclusion of fundamental human rights and freedoms enforceable by the courts. In a further effort to guarantee these basic human rights and freedoms, the constitution provides for an autonomous Commission on Human Rights and Administrative Justice,

unicameral: comprised of one chamber, usually a legislative body

suffrage: to vote, or, the right to vote

judicial review: the ability of the judicial branch to review and invalidate a law that contradicts the constitution

(MAP BY MARYLAND CARTOGRAPHICS/THE GALE GROUP)

which is empowered to investigate alleged human-rights violations, injustice, corruption, abuse of power, and unfair treatment of any person by a public officer. This commission can also take action to remedy proven abuses. The constitution guarantees the freedom and independence of the media and makes any form of censorship unconstitutional. Although there have been a few challenges to the implementation of these constitutional provisions, experts believe the foundation has been laid for improvement in democratic governance, an independent press, and the active participation of civic society in Ghana. Freedom House, therefore, rated Ghana as a "free" country in 2003.

See also: Constitutions and Constitutionalism; Dictatorship.

BIBLIOGRAPHY

Aryee, Joseph R. "Ghana." In *Public Administration in Africa: Main Issues and Selected County Studies*, ed. Ladipo Adamolekun. Boulder, CO: Westview Press, 1999.

Freedom House. "Ghana." *Freedom in the World 2004.* New York: Freedom House, 2004. <http://www.freedomhouse.org/research/freeworld/2004/countryratings/ghana.htm>.

"Ghana." In *CIA World Factbook.* Washington, DC: Central Intelligence Agency, 2005. <http://www.cia.gov/cia/publications/factbook/geos/gh.html>.

World Bank. *African Development Indicators.* Washington, DC: The World Bank, 2004.

Al Bavon

Gold Coast

See Ghana.

Gorbachev, Mikhail

FORMER PRESIDENT OF THE UNION OF SOVIET SOCIALIST REPUBLICS 1931–

Mikhail Sergeyevich Gorbachev was born on March 2, 1931, to a peasant family in the Stavropol region of Russia. He excelled in both the classroom and the local collective farm, winning admission to Moscow State University. While attending the university, Gorbachev joined the **Communist** Party of the Soviet Union (CPSU) and earned a law degree.

Gorbachev pursued his early career in Stavropol. Unlike other CPSU general secretaries, he never worked outside Russia, making it difficult for him to comprehend the ethnic problems that his reforms would unleash. He began his efforts in the local Communist Youth League and was eventually promoted to first secretary of the Stavropol region. Gorbachev transferred to Moscow in 1978 when he was named a secretary of the Central Committee. Two years later he became the youngest member of the Politburo. His youth proved to be an asset. Following the rapid deaths of three elderly CPSU general secretaries between November 1982 and March 1985, the Central Committee, perhaps hoping for stability, elected Gorbachev as its general secretary in March 1985.

communism: an economic and social system characterized by the absence of class structure and by common ownership of the means of production and subsistence

"[Gorbachev] never worked outside Russia, making it difficult for him to comprehend the ethnic problems that his reforms would unleash."

Gorbachev sought to improve, not revolutionize, the Union of Soviet Socialist Republics (USSR). He introduced three key domestic policy initiatives: *glasnost, perestroika,* and **democratization**, all of which quickly outpaced his original intent. He had tremendous success in foreign policy, but he was much more popular abroad than at home. Gorbachev and U.S. President Ronald Reagan (1911–2004) built a solid working relationship that led to numerous summit meetings and ostensibly ended the Cold War. Gorbachev withdrew Soviet troops from Afghanistan and refused to prop up other communist leaders in Eastern Europe. For these efforts, he was awarded the Nobel Peace Prize in 1990.

Glasnost (openness) encouraged broad discussion of the problems facing the USSR. Strict censorship and official secrecy eased, while newspapers and magazines began filling in the blank spots of history. But as secrets were revealed, the foundation of communist rule began to crumble.

Perestroika (restructuring) relaxed central controls on the economy to improve efficiency and encourage initiative. Gorbachev removed the "command"

democratization: a process by which the powers of government are moved to the people of a region or to their elected representatives

SOVIET PRESIDENT MIKHAIL GORBACHEV AND U.S. PRESIDENT RONALD REAGAN SIGN AN ARMS TREATY IN 1987. As Mikhail Gorbachev entered office in 1985, his policies focused on rebuilding the USSR's economic and social structures along with creating an open environment in the media and political system. (SOURCE: AP/WIDE WORLD PHOTOS)

in the Soviet economy, but without mandated production levels, output dropped. Severe shortages and hoarding resulted.

With democratization, Gorbachev sought to shift political control away from the CPSU. This brought him tremendous criticism; hardliners claimed he was going too fast, while reformists complained he was not doing enough. In 1988 he introduced a new parliament, the Congress of People's Deputies. Elections for the new Congress were held in 1989, and although multiple parties were not permitted, multiple candidates and non-Party members were. In 1990 Gorbachev ended the CPSU's monopoly on power, but he still sought to control the reform process. He gave parliament, not the people, authority to select the new president of the USSR. Gorbachev assumed the post himself.

Elections for seats in the newly established, republic-level Congress of People's Deputies in early 1990 resulted in a legislature that called for **self-determination** and even independence. Gorbachev ordered the drafting of a new Union Treaty to reconfigure center-periphery relations, a process that considered extensive changes. When he submitted a document that effectively gave six republics their independence, Party hardliners seized control. The August 1991 **coup** attempt quickly collapsed, but momentum had shifted from Gorbachev to Boris Yeltsin (b. 1931).

Gorbachev spent the remainder of 1991 trying to cobble together a new Soviet state. With all of the republics proclaiming independence, however, Gorbachev resigned on December 25, 1991. In his retirement he established a think tank, wrote his memoirs, and became president of the Green Cross International, an environmental organization working for sustainable development.

See also: Russia.

BIBLIOGRAPHY

Brown, Archie. *The Gorbachev Factor* . New York: Oxford University Press, 1996.

Gorbachev, Mikhail. *Memoirs* . New York: Doubleday, 1996.

Ann E. Robertson

self-determination: the ability of a people to determine their own destiny or political system

coup: a quick seizure of power or a sudden attack

Government Data Sets

Here are some questions that many of us are likely to ask or to be asked at some time:

- What is the largest nation in the world in area? In population?
- Are the people of the United States free? Healthy? Long-lived? Rich?
- Is the government of the United States a democratic nation?
- Is the government of the United States upright, rather than corrupt?

Although we may or may not know the answers, questions such as "What is the largest nation in the world in area?" appear to be simple. We could certainly figure out the answer to this question ourselves: We would simply use modern tools and techniques to measure the number of square miles (or hectares) occupied by all the territory within the boundaries of each nation in the world and then search our findings to see which resulting number is largest. Of course a few technical decisions would be required. In the case of one of the inevitable disputes about just where a certain national boundary lies, whose answer should we accept? In calculating the size of a nation's territory, should we count bodies of water such as lakes, rivers, or open ocean that may lie between island territories or off a nation's coast? And just when are we going to have the time and where are we going to find the money we would need to do all the measuring that would be required?

Naturally we all understand that we don't really have to do all the measuring and make all these technical decisions to find out which is the world's largest nation in area. All we really have to do is look up the answer in an *authoritative source*, one whose creators have already made the technical decisions necessary to provide us with the answer we seek. For example, if we looked up any given nation's area in the U.S. Central Intelligence Agency's (CIA) *World Factbook 2005*, we could access a table of territories rank ordered by area (http://www.cia.gov/cia/publications/factbook/rankorder/2147rank.html). That table would tell us that the largest nation in the world is Russia (at just over 17 million square kilometers; 6.6 million square miles) followed by Canada (10 million square kilometers; 3.85 million square miles), the United States (just over 9.6 million square kilometers; 3.72 million square miles), China (just under 9.6 million square kilometers; 3.7 million square miles), and Brazil (8.5 million square kilometers; 3.29 million square miles). While we were at it, we could use the same source to discover that the largest nation in the world in population was China (1.3 billion people), followed by India (1.1 billion), the United States (296 million), Indonesia (242 million), and Brazil (186 million).

Answering even transparently simple questions is not as simple as it appears, and we rely on authoritative sources of data to give us answers. And yet questions about national area and population are simple and uncontroversial compared to many other questions that may interest us vitally. For example, many of us might answer in the affirmative to questions about whether the people of the United States are in general free, healthy, long-lived, and rich. We would be pretty sure that the United States was indeed democratic and relatively upright. But suppose we wanted to know whether the people of the United States were the freest, healthiest, or most long-lived in the world, or whether the United States was the most democratic or the least corrupt? Unless we were convinced that we already knew the answers and did not wish to be confused by any "facts," we would once again want to turn to authoritative sources to help find the information we needed to find the answers. To use these authoritative sources, we would again have to accept the definitions and technical decisions their creators had had to make to come up with the information we need to get our answers. This is always a characteristic and, perhaps, a limitation we must accept if we are to use such authoritative sources.

The rest of this article reviews several categories of the most useful authoritative sources of data about the nations and government of the world and the rights and duties of their citizens. But before we do so, perhaps we should answer the remaining questions with which we began. Are the people of the United States the world's freest? According to the rankings in *Freedom in the World 2005*, the United States falls in the category of the world's freest nations (along with forty-five others), so, according to one source we can use to answer this question, the answer is certainly "yes," or at least "they are as free as any other people in the world." Are the people of the United States the world's healthiest? On most such reasonable measures of a people's health the United States is a healthy nation, but not the healthiest in the world: The infant mortality rate of the United States, for example, is higher than that of forty-six other nations or territories that are rank ordered in the CIA's *World Factbook 2005*. Is the United States an upright or a corrupt nation? According to corruption perception surveys and indices compiled annually by researchers working with Transparency International, the United States was in 2004 tied for seventeenth among the 146 nations for which this source gives data. So most observers would agree that, on the basis of these data, the United States is (perceived to be) one of the world's "not corrupt" nations, but not the least corrupt in the world.

A GENERAL DATA SOURCE ON GOVERNMENT, POLITICS, SOCIETY, AND ECONOMY

Far too many authoritative sources of data exist about the government, politics, societies and economies of the world's nations to cite or include each in the bibliography of this article. A good starting point, however—and one of the most useful general sources on many of these characteristics of the nations of the world—is the *World Factbook*, produced by the CIA. It is an outgrowth of the U.S. government's civilian intelligence operations that began in 1947. The *World Factbook* itself has been published since 1962 but was a classified (secret) document until 1971. Since then the CIA's *World Factbook* has been published each year as a unclassified printed volume intended for use by U.S. government officials but available for general purchase from the U.S. Government Printing Office. For several years, the current edition of the *World Factbook* has also been available via the World Wide Web as an online resource, which has greatly enhanced its usability and also has allowed the CIA to update it dynamically. The breadth of the information contained in the *World Factbook*'s profiles is indicated by the major topics it treats. Following a brief background paragraph, the *Factbook* has sections presenting extensive facts about geography, people, government, economy, communications, transportation, military, and **transnational** issues. It provides a map of the country and regional maps that put its location into context. The biggest limitation the *World Factbook* is that it presents its information in a relatively formal and nonjudgmental fashion. Users may come away from the *Factbook* knowing a lot more basic information about a nation, its government, and society but still feeling that they do not understand the nature of its government—the state of the rights and liberties of its citizens experience, for example.

CITIZEN RIGHTS, DEMOCRACY, AND FREEDOM

Another annual U.S. Government publication, the U.S. State Department's annual *Country Reports on Human Rights Practices*, usually called the *Human Rights Reports* differs distinctly from the *World Factbook* because it has the specific purpose of presenting comprehensive evaluative information about the state of citizen rights. The *Human Rights Reports* are explicitly judgmental with respect to their subject, that is, the human rights practices of the world's independent nations. The U.S. State Department's Bureau of Democracy, Human Rights, and Labor has issued the *Human Rights Reports* annually under a directive from the U.S. Congress since the early 1970s. They are available as printed volumes from the U.S. Government Printing Office, but reports since 1993 are also easily accessed online. Each country report begins with a summary of current political conditions affecting human rights. This introduction is followed by more detailed sections dealing (in the 2004 report, for example) with respect for the right to personal integrity, respect for civil liberties, respect for political rights, the right of citizens to change their government, governmental attitude regarding international and non-governmental investigation of alleged violations of human rights, discrimination, societal abuses, and trafficking in persons, and worker rights. In the past, the *Human Rights Reports* were criticized for alleged bias—they were

transnational: extending beyond the jurisdiction of one single nation

accused of overlooking or minimizing human rights violations committed by allies of the United States. In the last fifteen years, however, accusations of such bias have diminished or disappeared.

Reports on the state of human rights in the world's nations are also produced by several important non-governmental organizations, notably Amnesty International and Human Rights Watch, among others. Although they are usually shorter, Amnesty International's annual reports mirror those of the U.S. State Department in that they are very comprehensive in their coverage—in recent years their reports contain a specific report on the vast majority, if not all, of the world nations—and are available both in print and online. Amnesty's reports also are available since 1975, although the reports for earlier years are much less comprehensive in coverage than recent reports. The annual and other reports of Human Rights Watch can be accessed online as well. Because neither Amnesty International nor Human Rights Watch is government supported, one can assume that their reports are not likely to be shaped by possible policy biases that might affect government-sponsored reports, although this does not rule out the possibility that their reports might reflect other biases held by the organizations' staff or financial supporters.

Another important source of information on citizen rights and responsibilities is Freedom House's *Freedom in the World* reports, published annually since 1978 and available online since 2001. Freedom House focuses broadly on democratic rights. The annual volumes of *Freedom in the World* provide essays assessing the state of democratic rights in all the nations of the world, and their coverage is very comprehensive. In addition, Freedom House has provided since 1973 an annual ordinal rating on a 1 ("least free") to 7 ("most free") scale of the state of freedom for each country for its political rights and civil liberties, and, from a combination of these two ratings, a classification of each country as "free," "partly free," or "not free." These useful ratings make it possible to compare the state of citizen political rights and civil liberties for individual countries at any point in time since 1973 or to examine how the state of citizen rights has changed within a country over time.

The Freedom House ratings, especially the political rights scale, have frequently been used as measures of the level of democracy present in the countries Freedom House rates. Although this is a very appropriate use of the Freedom House data, the political rights scale is not the only widely used measure of democracy. Also very widely used are the "**polity**" indexes and their supporting data initially created by the political scientist Ted Robert Gurr and annually updated and maintained as of this writing by Monte Marshall and Keith Jaggers in the *Polity IV Project*. Like the Freedom House scales, the *Polity IV Project* data provide ordinal ratings, in this case for the world's 161 largest countries. Unlike the Freedom House scales, the *Polity IV* indexes are not published in print format.

The *Polity IV* indexes rate countries from zero to ten on two related but not simply inverse measures: levels of democracy and of **authoritarianism**. The *Polity IV* indexes are, in turn, the sum of a country's scores on several partial assessments of the nature of its government and politics. These assessments can themselves also be used to compare countries. Finally, for the 161 nations it assesses, the *Polity IV* data are very long term: They cover the period from 1800 through the latest possible year (2003 as of this writing). Although they are very useful measures of democracy and authoritarianism, the *Polity IV* data's are archived and presented in a format that is intended mostly for use by those with some professional training in the social sciences or related disciplines and who understand statistical analysis.

FAST FACTS

Freedom House was founded in 1943 by a group of Americans, including Eleanor Roosevelt and Wendell Willkie.

polity: a form of government held by a specific country or group

authoritarianism: the domination of the state or its leader over individuals

A different approach to rating the world's nations on the freedoms they extend to their citizens focuses on the extent to which they regulate or interfere in their economies. The *Index of Economic Freedom* has been generated and distributed in various print and electronic formats by the conservative Heritage Foundation each year since 1995. The 2005 version of the index covers 161 countries. The index itself is the average of a series of freedom ratings from 1 ("most free") to 5 ("least free") given each country on ten aspects of its economy (trade, fiscal burden, government intervention, monetary policy, foreign investment, banking, wages and prices, property rights, regulation, and informal market). An electronic version of the *2005 Index of Economic Freedom* —the book commenting on issues of economic freedom, documenting the 2005 index and summarizing the performance of each country—and a spreadsheet containing all the economic freedom index scores from 1995 to date were available for download from the Heritage Foundation.

ECONOMIC AND SOCIAL DATA

More purely economic data and much social and demographic data can be secured from many sources. Two of the most useful are the *Human Development Report* by the United Nations Development Program and the World Bank's *World Development Report*. Both are published annually in print and electronic formats. The *Human Development Report* was created to provide a richer, more flexible, and more accurate assessment of the actual quality of life for the citizens of the world's nations than could be achieved by looking only at traditional economic data such as gross national product **per capita**. The human development index rates national quality of life by combining measures of raw wealth economic with other factors relevant to a good quality of life. The *World Development Report* concentrates on more traditional indicators of wealth and economic activity, although it, too, has become more creative in its approach to measuring world development.

Those who do not wish to purchase the printed *Human Development Report* can freely download the full text of the report for recent years, including its extremely valuable data tables. Selected data from the *World Development Report* can be accessed and downloaded online for no charge, but the World Bank sells the full database in various formats.

See also: Amnesty International.

per capita: for each person, especially for each person living in an area or country

BIBLIOGRAPHY

Amnesty International. *Amnesty International Report 2004*. London: Amnesty International, 2005. <http://web.amnesty.org/report2004/index-eng>.

Derksen, Wilfried. *Elections Around the World*, 2005. <http://www.electionworld.org>.

Federal Research Division of the Library of Congress. *Country Studies*, 1986–1998. <http://www.countrystudies.us/>.

Freedom House. *Freedom in the World 2004*. New York: Freedom House, 2005. <http://www.freedomhouse.org/research>.

Heritage Foundation. *Index of Economic Freedom*. Washington, DC: Heritage Foundation, 2005. <http://www.heritage.org/research/features/index/index.cfm>.

Heston, Alan, Robert Summers, and Bettina Aten. *Penn World Table Version 6.1* Philadelphia: Center for International Comparisons at the University of Pennsylvania, 2002. <http://pwt.econ.upenn.edu/php_site/pwt_index.php>.

Human Rights Watch. *Documents by Country*. New York: Human Rights Watch, 2005. <http://www.hrw.org/countries.html>.

Inter-Parliamentary Union. *Your Site on Parliamentary Democracy*. Geneva, Switzerland: Inter-Parliamentary Union, 2005. <http://www.ipu.org/english/home.htm>.

Marshall, Monty G., and Keith Jaggers, principal investigators. *Polity IV Project*. College Park: Center for International Development and Conflict Management, University of Maryland, 2005. <http://www.cidcm.umd.edu/inscr/polity/>.

Organisation for Economic Co-operation and Development. <http://www.oecd.org>.

Schemmel, B. *Rulers*. <http://www.rulers.org>.

Transparency International. *Corruption Perceptions Index 2004*. New York: Transparency International, 2005. <http://www.transparency.org/cpi/2004/cpi2004.en.html#cpi2004>.

United Nations Development Programme. *Human Development Report 2004: Cultural Liberty in Today's Diverse World*. New York: Oxford University Press, 2004. <http://hdr.undp.org/reports/global/2004>.

United Nations Statistics Division, 2005. <http://unstats.un.org/unsd/default.htm>.

U.S. Central Intelligence Agency. *2005 World Factbook*. Washington, DC: Central Intelligence Agency, 2005. <http://www.cia.gov/cia/publications/factbook>.

U.S. Central Intelligence Agency. *Chiefs of State and Cabinet Members of Foreign Governments*. Washington, DC: Central Intelligence Agency, 2005. <http://www.odci.gov/cia/publications/chiefs/index.html>.

U.S. Department of State, Bureau of Democracy, Human Rights, and Labor. *Country Reports on Human Rights*. Washington, DC: U.S. Department of State, Bureau of Democracy, Human Rights, and Labor, 2005. <http://www.state.gov/g/drl/hr/c1470.htm>.

World Bank. *World Development Report 2004: Making Services Work for Poor People*. Washington, DC: The World Bank, 2003. <http://econ.worldbank.org/wdr/wdr2004/text-30023>.

World Bank. *World Development Indicators 2004 CD-ROM*. Washington, DC: The World Bank, 2004.

World Bank. *World Development Report 1978–2004 with Selected World Development Indicators 2003: Indexed Omnibus CD-ROM Edition*. Washington, DC: The World Bank, 2004.

Zárate, Roberto Ortiz de. *Zárate's Political Collections: Dates and Figures of the Worldwide Leadership Since 1945*. <http://www.terra.es/personal2/monolith/home.htm>.

C. Neal Tate

Greece

Situated at the crossroads between the West and the East, Greece has been subjected to multiple and contradictory political, economic, and cultural influences since it became an independent state in 1830. Although for most of the nineteenth and twentieth centuries the Greek economy was predominantly agricultural and Greek society bore traditional characteristics, the country modernized rapidly during the second half of the twentieth century. Since the 1950s Greece has grown economically, and in 1974 a successful transition to democracy opened the way for the firm placement of the country among the core Western democracies. Greece was admitted to the European Community

(MAP BY MARYLAND CARTOGRAPHICS/THE GALE GROUP)

(now the European Union) in 1981, became a member of the euro zone (by which the euro became the legal currency) in 2001, and hosted the Olympic Games in August 2004.

BASIC COUNTRY CHARACTERISTICS

Greece is a relatively small country situated in southeastern Europe. Its land area is only 4.1 percent of the total area of the European Union (i.e., the fifteen original member states). Greece is known for its naval tradition, including naval commerce, and has benefited significantly from tourism directed toward its coasts and islands. To the north of the country lies the mainland of the Balkan peninsula; to the south, the Mediterranean Sea; to the west, the Ionian Sea; and to the east, the Aegean Sea. These seas have hundreds of large and small islands, of which about fifty have adequate modern infrastructure and are inhabited.

The mainland of the country is mountainous. In the few plains of the central and northern regions cotton, olives, wine, vegetables and fruits are produced. However, 40 percent of the population is concentrated around the capital city of Athens (and its port, Piraeus) and a few other urban centers.

According to the last census (taken in 2001), the population of Greece totals 10,960,020. The country is also home to a large undeclared labor force of immigrants, mostly from Albania, Bulgaria, Poland, and the Philippines. In the past there were large, successive migratory movements of Greeks who **emigrated** from Greece to go to the United States, Western Europe, and Australia; they formed a Greek diaspora of about 4 million people.

In terms of economic prosperity, Greece ranks forty-fifth among the 208 countries of the world. In 2003, according the World Bank, the **per capita** national income for Greece was $13,720. According to the United Nation Development Program's Human Development Index, which takes into account life expectancy at birth, adult literacy rate, and enrollment ratio for schools, Greece ranks twenty-fourth among 177 countries.

BRIEF HISTORY

Less than two centuries ago Greece was an economically underdeveloped and politically marginal area in the Ottoman Empire, (1299–1922). As a result of the War of Independence (1821–1827), Greece became an independent **nation-state**. In the 1830s the regime of Greece was an **absolute** monarchy under German-born King Otto I (1815–1867). An uprising in 1843 led to a short period of constitutional monarchy from 1843 to 1864, until Otto was overthrown and replaced by a prince of Danish descent, George I (1890–1947). George ruled within the legal framework of the Constitution of 1864, which signaled the beginning of a long period of crowned democracy.

At that time political parties were no more than groups of notables rallying around a few leaders who fought for power in general elections. Since 1864 the majority of male adults have been eligible to vote, although women did not get the right to vote until 1952. Political participation meant the forging of patronage ties between the masses and political elites. However, compared to other Western nation-states, universal male **suffrage** and parliamentary life were achieved quite early in Greece.

During the nineteenth century and the first quarter of the twentieth century Greek politicians were consumed by the idea of pushing the frontiers of Greece to the north and the east, where Greek-speaking and other populations still lived under Ottoman rule. **Nationalism**, the hallmark of politics in nineteenth-century Europe, permeated Greece's foreign policy. However, the domestic political scene was characterized by **polarization** between modernizing and traditional politicians.

Tensions became more acute in 1911, when the Greek premier Eleutherios Venizelos (1864–1936) passed a liberal constitution that met with resistance from the pro-German King Constantine I (1868–1923), who also objected to his attempt to align Greece with Western powers during World War I (1914–1918). A national **schism** followed, but finally Greece sided with the Allied forces. In 1922 Greece's attempt to invade lands of the former Byzantine Empire, which still had a thriving Greek population, was defeated by Turkey, bringing to an end the idea of further enlargement of Greece. In the interwar period parliamentary life was interrupted by a military **coups** d'etat. Democracy broke down in 1936 with the rise to power of the authoritarian leader Ioannis (also known as John) Metaxas (1871–1941).

Although the Greek army was able to repel an Italian invasion during World War II (1939–1945), Germany occupied the country in 1941. Resistance against the Germans flourished, and the occupation ended in 1944. However, a civil war ensued between 1946 and 1949, bitterly fought between the left-wing army, which had contributed to the resistance against the Germans, and the governmental army, which safeguarded the traditional political elites and the throne. The government army won, and a parliamentary regime—albeit heavily monitored by the

emigration: the migration of individuals out of a geographic area or country

per capita: for each person, especially for each person living in an area or country

nation-state: a relatively homogeneous state with only one or few nationalities within its political borders

absolute: complete, pure, free from restriction or limitation

suffrage: to vote, or, the right to vote

nationalism: the belief that one's nation or culture is superior to all others

polarize: to separate individuals into adversarial groups

schism: a separation between two factions or entities, especially relating to religious bodies

coup: a quick seizure of power or a sudden attack

king, the army, the police, and the U.S. embassy—was installed. The postwar Greek regime was still a crowned democracy, but some freedoms were curtailed and **communists** and sympathizers of the left were prosecuted. Thus democracy was monitored to some extent by nonelected, nonaccountable powers.

In the postwar period between 1949 and 1967 conservatives won most of the general elections. The most prominent leaders of that time were the conservative Constantine Karamanlis (1907–1998) and his major opponent, the **centralist** George Papandreou (1888–1968). Elected governments ruled within the limits allowed by the extra-institutional powers previously mentioned. In July 1965 a confrontation over who would hold the post of the minister of defense arose between Prime Minister Papandreou and King Constantine II (b. 1940). When the king insisted on imposing his preference, the prime minister resigned. The king, instead of dissolving the parliament to hold new elections, nominated successive prime ministers, who were not able to obtain the parliament's vote of confidence. A period of political instability ensued, and in April 1967 the democratic regime was brought down by a military coup d'etat staged by colonels from the Greek army.

The colonels built an authoritarian regime that lasted for seven years (1967–1974) but collapsed under the weight of events in Cyprus. In July 1974 a military coup d'etat, masterminded by the Greek military regime and staffed by nationalist Greek Cypriots, brought down the legitimate government of Cyprus. Turkey claimed that Turkish Cypriots were in danger, invaded Cyprus, and occupied the northern part of the island.

Faced with the Turkish invasion, the colonels were unable to control the crisis and **ceded** power to politicians of the preauthoritarian period. Karamanlis formed a government of national unity and carefully executed the transition to democracy. Free general elections were held in November 1974, and a **referendum** on the nature of the government—especially the fate of the monarchy—was held in December 1974. Karamanlis and his conservative party won the elections, and 69 percent of the electorate voted in favor of a **republic** and against a crowned democracy.

From 1974 to 1981 the conservative party New Democracy (ND) was in power but was constantly challenged by a new party, the Panhellenic Socialist Movement (PASOK). The emergence of the PASOK signaled the emergence of mass political parties in Greece, and its rise to power in 1981 signaled the consolidation of Greek democracy.

THE BASES OF THE GOVERNMENT

The Constitution of 1975 reflected the developments and conflicts of recent events. Upon the **promulgation** of that constitution, Greek politics stabilized. The political regime became a multiparty parliamentary democracy, functioning in a unitary (i.e., nonfederal) state. The central government is organized into nineteen ministries and numerous public agencies and corporations. Despite some privatizations that took place after 1996, the public **bureaucracy**, which employs approximately 12 percent of the labor force, is still sprawling, top-heavy, and quite politicized.

The country is divided into thirteen regions. Each region is divided into smaller units, the prefectures. Each prefecture encompasses different **munici-palities**. Even though the governors of prefectures (the prefects) and the mayors are elected every four years, the country is not nearly as **decentralized** as most of the other member-states of the European Union. Local government

communism: an economic and social system characterized by the absence of class structure and by common ownership of the means of production and subsistence

centralize: to move control or power to a single point of authority

cede: to relinquish political control of lands to another country; surrender

referendum: a popular vote on legislation, brought before the people by their elected leaders or public initiative

republic: a form of democratic government in which decisions are made by elected representatives of the people

promulgation: an official declaration, especially that a law can start being enforced

bureaucracy: a system of administrating government involving professional labor; the mass of individuals administering government

municipality: local governmental units, usually cities or towns

decentralize: to move power from a central authority to multiple periphery government branches or agencies

in Greece still lacks financial independence and substantive administrative autonomy from the central government.

General elections are held every four years. All adults, male and female, over eighteen years old are eligible to vote. According to the law, they are obliged to register to vote and voting is **compulsory**. Parties fight to win the majority of the 300 parliamentary seats. After the election the president of the republic assigns to the leader of the party that holds the largest number of seats the responsibility of forming a cabinet and obtaining a vote of confidence from the parliament. As soon as this is achieved, the prime minister rules virtually unchallenged until the next general election.

In the elections of March 2004 the conservative ND party obtained 165 of the 300 parliamentary seats and formed a single-party government. The socialist party, PASOK, obtained 117 seats and fell from power after controlling the government from 1981 to 2004, during which time it had ruled virtually unchallenged (the conservative party was in power only between 1990 and

compulsory: mandatory, required, or unable to be avoided

THE PARLIAMENT BUILDING IN SYNTAGMA SQUARE IN ATHENS, GREECE. Built in 1836 as King Otto's (1815–1867) residence, the Old Palace Mansion became the Hellenic Parliament's home in Athens, Greece in 1930. The 300-member unicameral parliament shares the structure with other government officials such as the president and prime minister. (SOURCE: © DAVID BALL/CORBIS)

1993). The remainder of parliamentary seats were allocated to the communist party and a smaller pro-European party of the left.

DIVISION OF POWERS

In legal principle power rests with the executive branch of the government, which in Greece means with the cabinet and particularly with the prime minister. In postauthoritarian Greece **coalition** governments have been rare. Parliamentary life has been dominated by the party in power, which can count on a solid parliamentary majority. Members of parliament of the governing party consistently support the government's policies. This means that the parliament is subject to the effective control of either conservative or socialist single-party **majoritarian** governments. The emergence of strong parliamentary majorities has been facilitated by the control of party leaders over electoral tickets and by electoral systems (variations of **proportional representation**) that are meant to promote the formation of strong cabinets, uninhibited by parliamentary opposition.

Following the general civil law model, the Greek judiciary has two branches, a "civil" **jurisdiction** that includes both civil and criminal courts and is headed by the Civil Supreme Court and an "administrative" jurisdiction that is headed by an Administrative Supreme Court. There is also a third "supreme" court, the Court of Auditors, which specializes in controlling the expenditures of government. There is no specialized Constitutional Court, as there is in many other European democracies. All courts are bound to refuse to apply unconstitutional laws. Conflicts among the various supreme courts are resolved by a Special Supreme Court. Only that court has the power to annul an act of the parliament on grounds of unconstitutionality. The justice system is independent but may to some extent be influenced by the party in power because in Greece the government decides on the selection of higher judges who fill the top-ranking posts of the supreme civil and administrative courts.

CITIZEN PARTICIPATION, RIGHTS, AND LIBERTIES

Between 1974 and 2004 two political parties contested power and systematically won the largest share of the votes. The conservative ND party, founded by Constantine Karamanlis, was led as of fall 2004 by his nephew, Costas Karamanlis (b. 1956), who won the elections of March 2004. The socialist party, PASOK—founded by Andreas Papandreou (1919–1996), the son of George Papandreou, in 1974 just after the fall of the colonels' regime—was led in 2004 by Andreas Papandreou's son, George A. Papandreou (b. 1952). Although this may create the impression that the country is run by two families alternating in power, the political reality is more complex. Although the two major political parties are the strongest players in the political system, other players are actively involved in the political process.

First, strong associations of business leaders and ship owners exist within the country, and liberal professionals are well represented in parliament as most members of parliament are lawyers, doctors, engineers, and economists. Other strong interest groups are labor unions in the service sectors, particularly those of public corporations and banks. The influence of such groups is shown in matters such as social security policy and taxation, where each group attempts to safeguard previously obtained privileges.

Second, although the two smaller parties of the left, which at times have been able to obtain approximately one-tenth of the votes cast in general

coalition: an alliance, partnership, or union of disparate peoples or individuals

majoritarianism: the practice of rule by a majority vote

proportional system: a political system in which legislative seats or offices are awarded based on the proportional number of votes received by a party in an election

jurisdiction: the territory or area within which authority may be exercised

elections, have little influence in parliament, they are influential within certain labor unions, and their capacity to mobilize workers and employees can be high.

Third, since the mid-1980s the role of the mass media in politics has increased. Mass media owners and journalists can dictate the political agenda and have partly assumed the function of political representation fulfilled by political parties, interest groups, and members of parliament—as has been the tendency in all contemporary Western democracies, where the political marketing of individual party leaders has taken precedence over political debate. At the same time, electoral campaigns have become very expensive, and political parties cannot afford to run elections unless they have accumulated large sums of money.

Moreover, in Greece as in other Western democracies, large business enterprises have increased their involvement in multiple sectors of the economy, including the politically sensitive sectors of mass media, opinion polling, armaments production, and public works. Decision makers in the corresponding public policy fields are caught in a web of business and political ties, and this has made democratic politics less transparent and less attractive.

Fourth, there has been a gradual increase of political apathy. Between 1974 and 1985 Greeks participated in politics by joining political parties and turning out to vote in large numbers. However, since the mid-1980s the combination of rising living standards and new consumption habits, fatigue with self-reproducing political elites, and the worldwide sway of the neo-liberal idea that **interventionist** politics may hamper the functioning of the market system have contributed to political apathy. Politics is assigned a diminishing role in economic development and in society. Political programs on Greek television have become much less popular than they used to be, the circulation of the largest Greek newspapers has dwindled since the early 1990s, labor unions have seen their membership decrease dramatically, and political parties have realized that their internal party life has become a formality.

interventionism: the policy of involving oneself in another's affairs, especially one nation to another

These tendencies are in sharp contrast with the usual polarized nature of Greek politics in the past. However, the new trends indicate that Greece gradually has converged with the rest of Western democracies, where contentious elections, military coups, and **ideological** polarization are things of the past.

ideology: a system of beliefs composed of ideas or values, from which political, social, or economic programs are often derived

PERSONAL SECURITY

Greek democracy was consolidated after the fall of the colonels' regime and is stronger than in any other period of modern Greek political history. Civil liberties are protected both by constitutional guarantees and by the everyday practice of the authorities. Individual and social rights are protected by law. There is freedom from torture, imprisonment, disappearance, and death. The press is free, and there is a large number of national and local private media, which are not subjected to control or manipulation by any governmental authority. In 2001 another constitutional revision expanded the scope of rights, including the protection of genetic identity and personal data. In all these respects Greek citizens feel secure.

There are exceptions, of course, which concern the treatment of minorities, including the Albanians who temporarily work in Greece, the Roma (ethnic minority), and the Jehovah's Witnesses (religious minority). Non-governmental organizations such as Amnesty International have protested against the treatment of members of those minorities by the justice system and the sporadic **infringement** of their rights by the police or local authorities.

infringe: to exceed the limits of; to violate

See also: European Union; Parliamentary Systems; Political Parties; Turkey.

BIBLIOGRAPHY

Allison, Graham T., and Kalypso Nicolaidis, eds. *The Greek Paradox*. Cambridge, MA: MIT Press, 1997.

Charalambis, Dimitris, Laura Maratou-Alipranti, and Andromachi Hadjiyani, eds. *Recent Social Trends in Greece, 1960–2000*. Montreal, Canada: McGill-Queen's University Press, 2002.

Clogg, Richard. *A Short History of Modern Greece*, 2nd ed. Cambridge, UK: Cambridge University Press, 1992.

Close, David H. *Greece Since 1945*. London: Pearson Education, 2002.

Gallant, Thomas W. *Modern Greece*. London: Arnold, 2001.

Hellenic Parliament. <http://www.parliament.gr/english/default.asp>.

Koliopoulos, John S., and Thanos Veremis. *Greece. The Modern Sequel: From 1831 to the Present*. London: Hurst, 2002.

McNeill, William H. *The Metamorphosis of Greece Since World War II*. Chicago: University of Chicago Press, 1978.

National Statistical Service of Greece [English version]. <http://www.statistics.gr/Main_eng.asp>.

Office of the Prime Minister of the Hellenic Republic [English version]. <http://www.primeminister.gr/gr/lang/en/primeminister.asp>.

United Nations Development Programme. *Human Development Report 2004*. New York: United Nations Development Programme, 2004. <http://hdr.undp.org/reports/global/2004/pdf/hdr04_complete.pdf>.

Dimitri A. Sotiropoulos

Grenada

Grenada is a country of approximately 89,500 inhabitants situated in the Windward Islands of the Eastern Caribbean. The land is of volcanic origin, with good harbors, a heavily forested and mountainous interior, and rich but limited arable areas. The population is principally of African origin, the result of slavery under French and British colonial rule.

Sugar and cocoa dominated the economy until the 1930s, when nutmeg, mace, and bananas became leading export crops. Grenada is the world's second largest exporter of nutmeg; however, light industry, tourism, and construction are the most important sources of export earnings and employment. By global standards Grenada is a lower-middle-income country with a well-educated population. In 1991, the **per capita** gross domestic product (GDP) was $3,965 and adult literacy 98 percent. Public education is **compulsory** and free, but students pay for books, supplies, and uniforms. Grenada belongs to the Organization of Eastern Caribbean States and uses its common currency, the Eastern Caribbean dollar.

Christopher Columbus sighted Grenada in 1498, but resistance by Caribs, the local Indians, delayed European colonization for a century. The French defeated the Caribs in 1651 and **ceded** control to Great Britain in 1763 at the end of the Seven Year's War between those two nations.

Grenada developed a parliamentary democracy under British rule. In the early twentieth century pressure from activists such as journalist T. A. Marryshow and labor leader "Buzz" Butler resulted in limited self-rule. The 1925 constitution established a legislative council and gave the vote to male property owners. In the early

per capita: for each person, especially for each person living in an area or country

compulsory: mandatory, required, or unable to be avoided

cede: to relinquish political control of lands to another country; surrender

1950s the charismatic labor leader Sir Eric Matthew Gairy (1922–1997) organized the country's first mass-based political party. In 1967 Grenada was granted associate statehood and control over its internal affairs. During this period a group of young, progressive intellectuals organized the New Jewel Movement (NJM) to oppose Prime Minister Gairy. Gairy violently suppressed the NJM and held on to power when Grenada gained its independence on February 7, 1974. In 1979, responding to economic decline and increasing repression, Maurice Bishop (1944–1983) and the NJM overthrew Gairy in a bloodless coup. With support from Cuba, the NJM government instituted popular programs of **agrarian** reform, public works, and social services. On October 19, 1983, a radical Marxist movement within the NJM deposed Bishop, who was executed by the military under the direction of Bernard Coard, leader of that NJM faction. Six days later, citing national security and the safety of U.S. medical students attending St. George's University as his justification, President Ronald Reagan (1911–2004) ordered an invasion by U.S. Marines. The revolutionaries were overthrown.

During a brief U.S. occupation political stability was restored. The army of the People's Revolutionary Government was defeated. Bernard Coard and his closest associates (the so-called Grenada 17) were tried and imprisoned. Some of the social and economic programs of the revolutionary period were halted or reversed, but multiparty elections resumed, leading to regular, peaceful transfers of power and political stability. Queen Elizabeth II (b. 1926) is the official head of state; she is represented by a **governor-general**. The government consists of a prime minister and cabinet selected by a parliamentary majority. The parliament is bicameral, with a fifteen-member House of Representatives elected to five-year terms from single-member districts and a thirteen-member Senate appointed by the governor-general in consultation with the prime minister and the leader of the opposition. The 1974 constitution guarantees basic civil and political liberties and the right to work. Rights generally are respected by the government, but evidence of de facto gender discrimination in employment does exist. All citizens over the age of eighteen may vote. The press is free and **partisan** and criticizes the government without fear of reprisal. The Eastern Caribbean Supreme Court acts as the ultimate court of appeals in Grenadian legal matters but does not review acts of parliament for constitutionality.

Grenada continues to struggle with problems of economic underdevelopment. Environmental problems such as coastal zone erosion and habitat loss are gaining worldwide attention.

See also: Caribbean Region.

agrarian: having to do with farming or farming communities and their interests; one involved in such a movement

governor-general: a governor who rules over a large territory and employs deputy governors to oversee subdivided regions

partisan: an ideologue, or a strong member of a cause, party, or movement

BIBLIOGRAPHY

Brizan, George. *Grenada: Island of Conflict*. London: Macmillan, 1998.

Ferguson, James. *Grenada: Revolution in Reverse*. London: Latin American Bureau, 1990.

"Grenada." In *CIA World Factbook*. Washington, DC: Central Intelligence Agency, 2005. <http://www.cia.gov/cia/publications/factbook/geos/gj.html>.

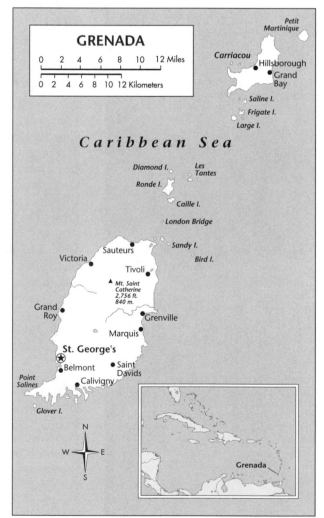

(MAP BY MARYLAND CARTOGRAPHICS/THE GALE GROUP)

Payne, Anthony, Paul Sutton, and Tony Thorndike. *Grenada: Revolution and Invasion.* New York: St. Martin's Press, 1984.

United Nations Development Programme. *2003 Human Development Report, Millennium Development Goals: A Compact Among Nations to End Human Poverty.* New York: Oxford University Press, 2003.

Jonathan Rosenberg

Guatemala

Guatemala is Central America's most populous nation, with one 2002 study having estimated 12 million inhabitants in a territory of 108,890 square kilometers (42,000 square miles). Nearly 2.5 million people live in the capital, Guatemala City, but Guatemala also has a large rural population spread throughout the western highlands and along the coastal plains. The vast mineral-rich province known as El Petén in the north of the country is very lightly populated. The northernmost country in Central America, Guatemala is very mountainous, and the climate ranges from hot in coastal areas, to temperate in mountain valleys, to chilly at higher elevations. Guatemala exhibits the most complex racial and ethnic mix of any country in Central America. Nearly 60 percent of the population is descended from **indigenous** Mayan peoples, and this sector of the population speaks some two dozen indigenous languages. Roman Catholicism is the predominant religion, but Protestant evangelicalism has made rapid advances, and among the Maya a **syncretism** of Catholicism and traditional Mayan religion is common.

Traditionally, Guatemala has had an agro-export economy in which coffee, sugar, cotton, and bananas have figured prominently. Agricultural products have accounted for about 75 percent of exports. In the last two decades of the twentieth century Guatemala became a petroleum exporter and positioned itself to compete in textile manufacturing through the establishment of *maquila* industries, assembling finished goods from parts manufactured in other countries in order to take advantage of low-cost labor. In 2001 agriculture accounted for 22.3 percent of the gross domestic product (GDP), industry 19.2 percent, and services 58.4 percent. Approximately 50 percent of the workforce is engaged in agriculture, much of it at the level of **subsistence farming**. Guatemala has exhibited extreme land concentration, which remains a contributing factor to national poverty rates. In 2000, 56 percent of the population, or 6.4 million Guatemalans, lived in poverty, about 16 percent of them in extreme poverty. At the same time 81 percent of the poor live in rural areas. Poverty affects 68 percent of children under the age of six. Finally, poverty is most concentrated in the highland regions populated by the Maya. The literacy rate of 55.6 percent is low, as might be expected in a poor country where wealth distribution is extremely unequal, and social unrest and **guerrilla insurgency** long convulsed the countryside. In 2003 Guatemala ranked 119 on the United Nations (UN) Human Development Index, just above Nicaragua, which was the lowest-ranked Central American country.

Before the Spanish conquest Guatemala was a center of Mayan civilization. During Spanish colonial rule it was the seat of colonial administration for Central America and was known as the Kingdom of Guatemala. After achieving independence in 1821, Guatemala briefly belonged to Mexico and later the federation known as the United Provinces of Central America, before becoming fully independent in 1830, when the federation collapsed.

indigene: a person who has his origin in a specific region

syncretism: an attempt to meld disparate or opposing schools of thought

subsistence farming: farming which does not turn a profit, providing only enough food for the farmers themselves

guerrilla: a soldier engaged in non-traditional methods of warfare, often separate from any structured military group

insurgency: a rebellion against an existing authority

Strong Liberal Party leaders shaped Guatemalan society and politics in the second half of the nineteenth century and early twentieth century. They established so-called republican dictatorships that rigged elections and **centralized** political power, and their ascendancy led to a severe decline in the power of Conservatives. Liberals forged close ties with foreign economic interests and promoted modernization through export agriculture. The most important of those leaders was Justo Rufino Bários (1835–1885), whose policies encouraged foreign immigration and investment, strengthened state services in support of the export sector, and opened Indian communal lands to commercial exploitation. Those policies directly benefited the landed elite and the ladino middle class. They also encouraged the creation of a forced labor system that **subjugated** the labor of the Maya to the economic demands of the **agrarian** elite. This model of development was maintained by dictatorial rule until the mid-1940s. It made control over land the overriding issue in politics, pitted the interests of landowners against those of Mayan peasants, and concentrated wealth to an extreme degree.

centralize: to move control or power to a single point of authority

subjugate: to force into submission

agrarian: having to do with farming or farming communities and their interests; one involved in such a movement

THE GOVERNMENTAL SYSTEM

Guatemala experienced little constitutional government throughout most of its history. Except for a brief interlude between 1944 and 1954, twentieth-century Guatemala was governed directly by the military or a civilian elite backed by the army. That **authoritarian** form of rule persisted until 1985. A representative

authoritarianism: the domination of the state or its leader over individuals

(MAP BY MARYLAND CARTOGRAPHICS/THE GALE GROUP)

legislature sometimes existed on paper, but in practice the executive dominated policy making to an extreme degree, and the judiciary lacked independence. However, since a democratic transition commenced in 1985 (the current constitution went into effect in January 1986), the basic elements of a formal constitutional government have been put into place. The constitution was reformed in 1993 with an eye to strengthening the separation of powers and curbing the dangers of executive dominance in the political system.

Guatemala is a **republic** whose president is elected by popular vote to a single four-year term. Re-election is prohibited. The president has veto power, although not the line-item type of veto (by which the executive can reject specific provisions of a bill without rejecting the entire piece of legislation), but Congress can override a presidential veto with a two-thirds majority. The vice president may run for the presidency, but only after being out of office for one term. The legislature is a **unicameral** body whose members are elected concurrently with the president, also to four-year terms. Guatemala has a civil law system. Legislation is the only formal source of law, and there is **judicial review** of legislative acts. The Supreme Court of Justice stands at the head of the judicial system, and Congress elects the Court's thirteen justices to five-year terms. The chief justice is elected to a one-year term by a two-thirds vote of the sitting justices. A separate Constitutional Court reviews the constitutionality of actions involving the government. The office of the Human Rights Ombudsman was created after the adoption of the 1985 constitution. The Ombudsman is appointed by Congress to a five-year term and is responsible for hearing citizen complaints of human rights violations, investigating those complaints, and, when necessary, censuring public officials who abuse their authority. A Supreme Electoral Tribunal, whose members are elected to six-year terms by Congress, supervises national elections and serves as the nation's highest court to settle election disputes.

Numerous political parties exist in Guatemala, but few parties have a long history because of the country's authoritarian past. Furthermore, most political parties do not have a large mass membership but instead tend to be formed as vehicles to advance the presidential ambitions of a caudillistic, or dictatorial, figure. In this sense Guatemala has a weak party system, which raises questions about the effectiveness of representation and the accountability of elected candidates to the public.

POLITICAL HISTORY

In 1944 middle-class reformers pressured Jorge Ubico (1878–1946), who had governed Guatemala as a dictator for thirteen years, to resign the presidency in the October Revolution. Juan José Arévalo (1904–1990) won the ensuing national election and instituted important social reforms aimed at improving the conditions of the working classes. Although President Arévalo promoted union and peasant organizing, he did not address the issue of the extreme maldistribution of land. That reform fell to his successor, Jacobo Arbenz Guzmán (1913–1971), who backed the 1952 Agrarian Reform Law, which sought to redistribute land to 100,000 peasants. When the Arbenz government **nationalized** lands belonging to the United Fruit Company, which had close ties to the U.S. government, and legalized the Communist Party (called the Guatemalan Labor Party), the United States attempted to destabilize and overthrow the Arbenz regime. A CIA-backed **coup** in June 1954, led by Colonel Carlos Castillo Armas (1914–1957), achieved that goal and initiated three decades of military rule.

The reform-minded leaders of the October Revolution had attempted to implement a more balanced model of capitalist development. They promoted

republic: a form of democratic government in which decisions are made by elected representatives of the people

unicameral: comprised of one chamber, usually a legislative body

judicial review: the ability of the judicial branch to review and invalidate a law that contradicts the constitution

nationalization: the process of giving control or ownership of an entity to the government

coup: a quick seizure of power or a sudden attack

public education and the rights of workers to organize into unions, and they pushed for agrarian reform. However, when succeeding military governments reversed those reforms and repressed dissent, armed opposition to the government evolved.

In the early 1960s armed insurgent groups began to emerge in Guatemala in response to authoritarian rule. Although the insurgents initially came from the ranks of disaffected army officers, the resulting guerrilla organizations eventually adopted a Marxist **ideology** and the tactics of rural guerrilla warfare. In response the government greatly expanded its counterinsurgency operations, and the influence of the armed forces over government policy deepened. In the 1970s two Indian-based guerrilla organizations, the Guerrilla Army of the Poor and the Organization of the People in Arms, joined the rural insurgency against military rule. Meanwhile, peasant organizing through the Peasant Unity Committee added another political dimension to the growing resistance to the military governments. Those conflicts culminated in the tragic "scorched earth" policies of the late 1970s and early 1980s, which claimed the lives of tens of thousands of Maya, razed hundreds of highland villages, and created hundreds of thousands of refugees. The intense repression carried out in the countryside was accompanied by plans for a transition to civilian rule under military auspices. In 1985 Christian Democrat Vinicio Cerezo (b. 1942) was elected president, and civilian government was restored.

ideology: a system of beliefs composed of ideas or values, from which political, social, or economic programs are often derived

Guatemala's transition toward democracy began while armed insurgency continued. President Cerezo supported the Esquipulas peace process, which helped end wars throughout Central America, but was unsuccessful in forging a peace agreement with the Guatemalan insurgents. Cerezo transferred power peacefully to Jorge Serrano Elías (b. 1945) in 1991, completing the nation's first smooth transition from one elected civilian government to another. The Serrano administration successfully pressured the powerful armed forces to begin serious peace negotiations with the National Revolutionary Unity (URNG), but then, in a setback for democracy, it attempted to dissolve Congress (known as a "self-coup"). Resistance in civil society to the self-coup led to Serrano's resignation and his replacement by the nation's Human Rights Ombudsman, Ramiro de León Carpio (1942–2002). This was a turning point because President Carpio, despite having no political party base, enjoyed wide popularity. He used that popularity to push the armed forces and guerrillas, under UN auspices, into completing the bargaining process. This led to the historic signing of the Comprehensive Peace Accords in 1996, thereby enhancing Guatemala's chances for a successful democratic transition.

There have been three presidential elections, unmarred by military intervention, since the **interim** presidency of Carpio. Álvaro Arzú (b. 1946) of the conservative National Advancement Party (PAN) served as president until 1999. The historic Guatemalan Peace Accords were signed during his administration. Arzú was succeeded by Alfonso Portillo (b. 1951) of the Republican Front Party (FRG), a right-wing **populist** party whose leader, Efraín Ríos Montt (b. 1926), was ineligible to run because of his participation in a 1980s military coup. As a leader Portillo was so unpopular (widespread allegations of corruption plagued his administration, and he fled the country after leaving office) that his party fared poorly in the 2003 elections. Oscar Berger (b. 1946) of the Grand National Alliance (GANA) won the presidential election and assumed office in January 2004, promising to end corruption and vigorously implement the Peace Accords.

interim: for a limited time, during a period of transition

populist: someone who advocates policies for the advancement of the common man

CONTEMPORARY POLITICAL LIFE

Despite strong early resistance from the armed forces to a negotiated settlement with the URNG, after the attempted self-coup by President Serrano a broad range of civil society organizations mobilized for peace. The peace process moved toward resolution when both sides agreed to allow the UN to become moderator of peace talks, and an agenda-setting framework accord was signed in January 1994. A distinctive feature of the Guatemalan peace process was the formation of a Civil Society Assembly that brought together diverse sectors to provide **grassroots** input to the talks between the government and guerrillas. Because various groups in civil society had long been excluded from political participation, this aspect of the peace process marked a milestone in the transition to democracy. The government and the URNG signed a breakthrough Comprehensive Agreement on Human Rights (which became one of several separate agreements contained in the Comprehensive Peace Accords) in March 1994, which allowed the UN to establish a verification mission, the United Nations Mission in Guatemala (MINUGUA). MINUGUA took up its monitoring responsibilities before any of the remaining agreements were signed and helped provide an international presence that encouraged both parties to negotiate in good faith. MINUGUA's carefully researched reports also helped quell the political violence that might have overwhelmed the peace process. In that context the parties reached agreement on a broad range of reforms affecting nearly every aspect of Guatemalan life.

By way of example, the 1996 Peace Accords called for the establishment of the Historical Clarification Commission, commonly known as the truth commission, to investigate the nature and extent of human rights violations committed during the war, obligated the government to resettle the tens of thousands persons displaced by the war, outlined steps to subordinate the armed forces to civilian political authority, and called for reforms to strengthen democratic institutions. The Accords also allowed the URNG to enter the political process as a legal party. With the agreement on democratic institutions, the government committed to undertake judicial and police reform and to invest in strengthening all institutions associated with the **rule of law**. Negotiating those wide-ranging agreements was a delicate and difficult process. Implementation has perhaps been even more challenging, as one or two important examples may illustrate.

Demilitarizing political life was a major aim of the Peace Accords. To that end the Accords mandated a reduction in troop levels and a revised mission focused on external defense. Meanwhile, a National Civilian Police (PNC) force was set up to take over internal security. However, efforts to establish an effective democratic police force were slow to gain traction. Crime rates rose dramatically in the postwar milieu, fostering a widespread sense of personal insecurity among Guatemalans. Two responses had troubling implications for demilitarization and democratic policing. One was the rise of vigilante justice. Human rights monitors have recorded rising numbers of **extrajudicial** executions, assassinations, and lynchings of suspected criminals by citizens impatient with a weak police presence. The second, and related, response has been the call for the armed forces to assist the police, which opened the door to a remilitarization of public security in Guatemala. Such a development would be contradictory to the aims of the Peace Accords.

A second example concerns human rights and the rule of law, which stood at the heart of the Peace Accords. "Truth telling" was a major goal of the Accords. Guatemala followed the example of other Latin American nations that had endured repressive dictatorships, such as Chile, Argentina, and El Salvador, when it committed to confronting and acknowledging the past.

grassroots: at the lowest level, often referring to support from members of the public rather than from political elites

rule of law: the principle that the law is a final grounds of decision-making and applies equally to all people; law and order

extrajudicial: outside the legal system; lacking the legitimating authority of the government

GUATEMALAN PEASANTS AND INDIGENOUS PEOPLES CALL FOR CULTURAL RIGHTS AND LAND REFORMS IN GUATEMALA CITY IN 2004. Although in 1996 the Agreement on Socio-Economic Issues and Agrarian Situation was designed to balance unfair land distribution and the resulting poverty of Guatemala's rural population, it had yet to be implemented in 2005. Government officials estimated that one-half million peasant families live in extreme poverty due to their inability to grow crops while six million farmers await the activation of the agrarian policy. AP/WIDE WORLD PHOTOS

Two separate entities undertook investigations into human rights violations committed under military rule: the Catholic Church and the Historical Clarification Commission established by the Accords. The Catholic Church issued its report, *Nunca Más* (Never again), in April 1998. Based on the testimony of 6,000 persons, the report documented massive rights violations, 85 percent of which were committed by the army and **paramilitary** forces linked to it. Two days after the report was presented, the man most visibly responsible for it, Bishop Juan José Gerardi Conedera (1922–1998), was assassinated. The government's investigation was so slow and inept as to suggest a lack of political will to solve the crime. When a case finally was brought against several military officers, the initial prosecutor and presiding judge received death threats and fled the country.

The Gerardi case, involving a very high-profile figure and attracting intense international media attention, illustrated the critical problem of **impunity** in Guatemala's democratic transition. To strengthen the rule of law, Guatemala's judicial institutions must overcome a long history of intimidation and politicization and demonstrate that no one is above the law. As of 2004 the reform

paramilitary: modeled after a military, especially as a possible supplement to the military

impunity: an exemption from punishment

and strengthening of those institutions were slow and incomplete. Polls at that time suggest that Guatemalans are deeply skeptical that judicial reform has enabled the state to hold powerful individuals accountable when they commit crimes or authorize others to do so. Indeed, opinion surveys showed that Guatemalan citizens have little faith in any of their major political institutions.

Despite such pessimistic findings, it must be noted that international observers declared the 2003 elections to be free and fair, and voter participation, at 60 percent, was up from previous elections. An equally positive sign for the sustainability of democracy was the signing by all registered parties, including the current governing party, of the Shared National Agenda, a program to restore implementation of the Peace Accords to the national agenda.

See also: Belize; Elections; Indigenous Peoples' Rights; Ombudsmen.

BIBLIOGRAPHY

Dunkerly, James. *The Pacification of Central America.* London: Verso, 1994.

Falla, Ricardo. *Massacres of the Jungle.* Boulder, CO: Westview Press, 1994.

Jonas, Suzanne. *Of Centaurs and Doves: Guatemala's Peace Process.* Boulder, CO: Westview Press, 2000.

McCreary, Rachel M. "Guatemala's Postwar Prospects." *Journal of Democracy* 8, no. 2 (1997):129–143.

Perera, Victor. *Unfinished Conquest: The Guatemalan Tragedy.* Berkeley: University of California Press, 1993.

Sanford, Victoria. *Buried Secrets: Truth and Human Rights in Guatemala.* New York: Palgrave Macmillan, 2003.

Sieder, Rachel, ed. *Guatemala After the Peace Accords.* London: Institute of Latin American Studies, 1998.

Smith, Carol A. *Guatemalan Indians and the State, 1540–1988.* Austin: University of Texas Press, 1990.

Stoll, David. *Between Two Armies in the Ixil Towns of Guatemala.* New York: Columbia University Press, 1993.

Michael Dodson

Guinea

Guinea is located on the west coast of Africa, bordering the Atlantic Ocean. It has turbulent neighbors: Guinea-Bissau, Senegal, Mali, Côte d'Ivoire, Liberia, and Sierra Leone. Guinea occupies 245,857 square kilometers (94,900 square miles), slightly smaller than the U.S. state of Oregon. Its population was estimated to be 9,246,462 in July 2004, and its **per capita** income at $2,100 in 2003, about the same as Ghana, Nicaragua, and Pakistan.

Guinea is ethnically diverse. The Peuhl people constitute 40 percent of its population; the Malinke, 30 percent; the Soussou, 20 percent; and smaller ethnic groups, 10 percent. Religiously, Guinea's is not diverse: 85 percent of its population is Muslim, with Christians accounting for 8 percent and followers of **indigenous** beliefs, 7 percent. With a life expectancy of less than 49 years and an adult literacy rate estimated at between 36 and 41 percent (and a literacy rate for women of 22 percent), the United Nations *Human Development Report 2004* ranked Guinea 160 out of 177 nations for whom it calculated its Human Development Index.

per capita: for each person, especially for each person living in an area or country

indigene: a person who has his origin in a specific region

(MAP BY MARYLAND CARTOGRAPHICS/THE GALE GROUP)

In ancient times, the territory that became Guinea was a part of the great West African empires of Ghana, Songhai, and Mali. It became a French colony in the nineteenth century and remained one until 1958, when its citizens voted to end its association with France, the first of France's numerous African colonies to do so. It began its existence as an independent **republic** under the **authoritarian** leadership of its pro-independence leader, Sekou Touré (1922–1984), a strong nationalist and Pan-African proponent. Touré's rule was tumultuous.

When Touré died in 1984, the army staged a military **coup** that installed Lansana Conté (b. 1934) as chief executive. Conté ruled from his position at the head of the military **junta** until December 1993, when he was elected president as a civilian. He was nearly ousted in 1996 in a military revolt, but loyal forces finally helped him overcome the threat. After surviving this challenge, he was reelected in 1998 in "an election that was marred by violence and civil unrest, widespread irregularities, and the arrest and detention of major opposition candidates during vote counting" (U.S. Department of State 2003). Conté was elected to a third 5-year term in 2003 with more than 95 percent of the vote.

Guinea is officially a constitutional republic with a very strong president who is popularly elected. The 114 members of its unicameral National Assembly are elected for 5-year terms. Elections for president and for the National Assembly have not generally been regarded as free or fair. President Conté and his political party, the Party for Unity and Progress, have dominated the elections on the basis of appeals to the Sousou ethnic group.

The U.S. Department of State's 2003 country report on the human right situation in Guinea noted that the judiciary, which includes **courts of first instance**, two Courts of Appeal, and the Supreme Court, has not demonstrated

republic: a form of democratic government in which decisions are made by elected representatives of the people

authoritarianism: the domination of the state or its leader over individuals

coup: a quick seizure of power or a sudden attack

junta: a group of individuals holding power, especially after seizing control as a result of a coup

court of first instance: the first or lowest court in which a case or suit can be decided

the independence that Guinea's constitution guarantees it. Instead, "judicial authorities routinely deferred to executive authorities in politically sensitive cases . . . [and] influential members of the Government often were . . . above the law" (U.S. Department of State 2003).

In sum, the state of citizen rights in Guinea is nearly as poor as the economy. Freedom House rated it in 2003 as "Not Free."

See also: Presidential Systems.

BIBLIOGRAPHY

Amnesty International. "Guinea." *Amnesty International Report 2004.* New York: Amnesty International, 2004. <http://web.amnesty.org/report2004/gin-summary-eng>.

Freedom House. "Guinea." *Freedom in the World 2003: The Annual Survey of Political Rights and Civil Liberties.* New York: Freedom House, 2004. <http://www.freedomhouse.org/research/freeworld/2003/countryratings/Guinea.htm>.

"Guinea." In *CIA World Factbook* . Washington, DC: Central Intelligence Agency, 2005. <http://www.cia.gov/cia/publications/factbook/geos/gv.html>.

Turner, Barry. "Guinea." *SYBworld: The Essential Global Reference.* <http://www.sybworld.com>.

United Nations Development Programme. *Human Development Report 2004.* New York: United Nations Development Programme, 2004. <http://hdr.undp.org/reports/global/2004/pdf/hdr04_HDI.pdf>.

U.S. Department of State. "Guinea." *Country Reports on Human Rights Practices—2003.* Washington DC: Department of State Bureau of Democracy, Human Rights, and Labor, 2003. <http://www.state.gov/g/drl/rls/hrrpt/2003/27731.htm>.

C. Neal Tate

Guinea-Bissau

Occupying 36,120 square kilometers (13,950 square miles), about three times the size of the U.S. state of Connecticut, the Republic of Guinea-Bissau is bounded on the south by the Republic of Guinea and on the north by Senegal. Its population was estimated in July 2004 at 1,388,363.

Historically known for its powerful kingdoms and as a major entry point of explorers, missionaries, and traders, Guinea-Bissau was colonized by the Portuguese in 1879. The campaign for independence began in the 1950s under the leadership of Amilcar Cabral (1924–1973) and the African Party of Independence of Guinea and Cape Verde. After more than a decade of armed struggle this small West African country gained its independence on September 10, 1974. For the first six years of independence Guinea-Bissau was led by Amilcar Cabral's half-brother, Luis de Almeida Cabral (b. 1931). In 1980 then-vice president Joao "Nino" Vieira (b. 1939) led a successful **coup** against Cabral, thus terminating any plans for political unity between Cape Verde and Guinea-Bissau. Despite several coup attempts against his regime, Vieira remained in power from 1980 to 1999.

Under Vieira's tenure as president and at times prime minister and commander in chief of the armed forces, Guinea-Bissau moved from a single-party state to a multiparty democracy in 1994. In the country's first multiparty elections, Vieira was reelected president by defeating opposition candidate Kumba Yalla of the Party for Social Renovation. Unfortunately, the advent of

coup: a quick seizure of power or a sudden attack

multipartyism meant at best a minor step toward democracy, for in 1998 an army uprising triggered a bloody civil war, and in 1999 a military **junta**, led by Kumba Yalla, ousted Vieira from power. In 2000, after transparent elections, Yalla took office and dissolved the People's National Assembly (ANP), only to be over-thrown in a bloodless coup three years later. Under the leadership of interim president Henrique Rosa in 2004 Guinea-Bissau was considered to be both polit-ically and economically unstable, ranking among the poorest countries in the world, with an estimated per capita income of $800 in 2003.

Legislative power has been vested in the ANP since independence. The ANP passes laws, **ratifies** decrees, and can revise the state constitution at any time, thus making it officially the highest political body in Guinea-Bissau. For instance, a new constitution was approved by the ANP in 1984, which was subsequently amended in 1991, 1993, and 1996. Further, constitutional amendments as approved by the ANP in 1991 provided for the operation of a multiparty political system. New polit-ical parties seeking registration must obtain 1,000 signatures, with at least 50 from each of the nine administrative regions. As a result, more than fifteen political parties were introduced after the legislation.

The ANP consists of 100 members, all whom are elected by universal adult **suffrage** to serve a four-year term. Similarly, the president is elected to a five-year term by universal adult suffrage, and in turn appoints a prime minister. Both the president, who is also head of government, and the prime minister are part of the Council of State and the Council of Ministers. Further, the judicial branch in Guinea-Bissau consists of a Supreme Court, nine regional courts, and twenty-four sectional courts. Under the provisions of the 1984 Constitution the president appoints nine Supreme Court jus-tices. The Supreme Court is the final court of appeals in all civil and criminal cases. The regional courts are the first courts of appeal and hear all felony and civil cases. The sectional courts, where the judges are not necessarily lawyers, hear all civil cases under $1,000.

Despite economic and electoral chaos the government of Guinea-Bissau has maintained numerous international rela-tions, including relationships with the African Union, the Economic Community of West African States, United Nation's Group of Seventy-Seven (G-77), the International Monetary Fund, the United Nations, the United Nations Educational, Scientific, and Cultural Organization (UNESCO) and the World Health Organization.

See also: Cape Verde.

BIBLIOGRAPHY

Forest, Joshua. *Guinea-Bissau: Power, Conflict, and Renewal in a West African Nation.* Boulder, CO: Westview, 1992.

"Guinea-Bissau." In *CIA World Factbook.* Washington, DC: Central Intelligence Agency, 2005. <http://www.cia.gov/cia/publications/factbook/geos/ek.html>.

Lobban, Richard, and Peter K. Mendy. *Historical Dictionary of the Republic of Guinea-Bissau.* Lanham, MD: Scarecrow Press, 1997.

Paul Khalil Saucier

multipartyism: the state of having multiple parties in a party system

junta: a group of individuals holding power, especially after seizing control as a result of a coup

ratify: to make official or to officially sanction

suffrage: to vote, or, the right to vote

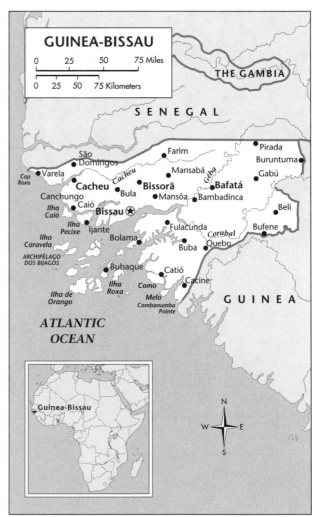

(MAP BY MARYLAND CARTOGRAPHICS/THE GALE GROUP)

Guyana

constitutional republic: a system of government marked by both a supreme written constitution and elected officials who administer the powers of government

authoritarianism: the domination of the state or its leader over individuals

Guyana is a **constitutional republic** in northern South America. It has an area of 214,970 square kilometers (83,000 square miles) and an estimated population of 702,100. Once a Dutch colony, Guyana was ruled by Great Britain from the early nineteenth century until 1966, when it gained its independence. Since that time the country has experienced both political stability and instability, the latter influenced by racially driven politics and episodes of **authoritarian** rule, which dominated most of the almost two decades of rule by Forbes Burnham (1923–1985). Burnham was a charismatic leader, as was his nemesis, Cheddi Jagan (1918–1997), who won the presidency in 1992 in what is considered the country's first free and fair election after independence. Upon Jagan's death in 1997, he was succeeded by his wife Janet Jagan (b. 1920), who resigned in 1999 because of poor health. Her successor, Bharrat Jagdeo (b. 1964), was reelected in 2001. As of 2005 he headed the executive branch, and his People's Progressive Party-Civic (PPP-Civic) party commanded the majority of seats in the sixty-eight-member unicameral National Assembly.

Although only five parties are represented in parliament, several other political parties exist, including the Alliance for Guyana; the Guyana Labor Party; the Working People's Alliance; the Guyana Action Party; the People's National Congress/Reform; Rise, Organize, and Rebuild; the United Force; and the ruling PPP-Civic. The judiciary, at the top of which sits the Supreme Court, is independent-minded and forms the third branch of government. Civil and political rights are constitutionally guaranteed but often violated by the police and other authorities. The legal system is based on English common law with certain features of Roman-Dutch law. The governmental bureaucracy revolves around ministries led by government ministers on the political side and permanent secretaries as heads of the professional civil service. There also are numerous government corporations, boards, and commissions.

Political mismanagement, ideologically driven destabilization by foreign powers, corruption, and inefficiency have combined to produce a situation in which Guyana, although it possesses considerable natural resources—including gold, bauxite, diamonds, and rich agricultural lands—is the third poorest nation in the Western Hemisphere, behind Haiti and Nicaragua. According to 2003 statistics, the gross domestic product (GDP) per capita was a mere $920, and GDP growth from 2000 has averaged 1.4 percent. The nation faces massive foreign debt, $1.2 billion at the end of 2003, despite debt relief from the United States, Canada, Britain, and some multilateral lending institutions. Almost one-third of the population lives in poverty. Hence, remittances from nationals living abroad, especially those in the United States, Canada, and Britain, are critical for both the survival of thousands of citizens and the buoyancy of the national economy, given the boost in foreign exchange that occurs with remittances.

A crisis in public security developed in the early twenty-first century. Murders and other violent crimes rose, and kidnappings

(MAP BY MARYLAND CARTOGRAPHICS/THE GALE GROUP)

for ransom continue to be a burgeoning criminal enterprise. Despite the combined use of the army and the police in anticrime efforts, the lack of manpower, equipment, training, and intelligence that security forces face has prevented them from adequately addressing the situation. In 2003 the resulting climate of fear had begun to affect foreign investment. It also led to an increase in the number of private security agencies, which created a balloon effect, shifting some of the crime from various parts of the nation to other areas.

See also: Caribbean Region; Colonies and Colonialism.

BIBLIOGRAPHY

Burnett, Graham D. *Masters of All They Surveyed: Exploration, Geography, and a British El Dorado.* Chicago: University of Chicago Press, 2000.

Griffith, Ivelaw L. "Political Change, Democracy, and Human Rights in Guyana." *Third World Quarterly* 18, no. 2 (1997):267–285.

Guyana News and Information. <http://www.guyana.org/>.

Mars, Joan. R. *2002. Deadly Force, Race, Colonialism, and the Rile of Law: Police Violence in Guyana.* Westport, CT: Greenwood Press, 2001.

Seecoomar, Judaman. *Contributions Towards the Resolution of Conflict in Guyana.* Leeds, UK: Peepal Tree, 2002.

Ivelaw L. Griffith

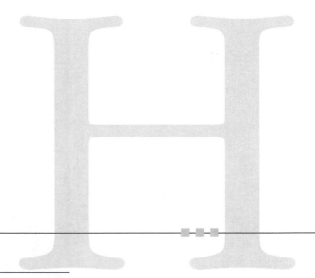

Haiti

The Republic of Haiti is a small, mountainous country on the western one-third of the island of Hispaniola in the Caribbean Sea. Haiti was originally the Arawak name for the island, meaning "mountainous land," Haiti's area is 27,560 square kilometers (10,641 square miles) Its population, estimated at 7,656,166 in July 2004, is the poorest in the Western Hemisphere and resides mostly in crowded rural villages and urban slums. Life expectancy is 49.7 years for men and 56.1 years for women, compared to the Latin American average of 69. The racial distribution is 94 percent black, 4 percent mulatto, and 1 percent each Middle Eastern and white. The official languages are Kreyol (Creole) and French, but only Kreyol is widely spoken.

Haiti is the poorest country in the Americas, and one of the few countries to have become poorer in the last decades of the twentieth century. The United Nations (UN) Conference on Trade and Development has labeled it an "economy in regress" to draw attention to the collapse in living conditions. Between 1980 and 1994 the gross domestic product fell some 45 percent, while the average of all less-developed countries rose by 4 percent. In 2002 Haiti ranked 146th out of 173 countries in the UN Development Programme's Human Development Index, and most of the lower-ranking countries were in postwar situations. Three-fourths of the population live in conditions of abject poverty. In the cities, unemployment rates are well over 50 percent.

BRIEF HISTORY

Haiti celebrated its bicentennial on January 1, 2004, as the second independent state in the new world and the first where everyone was a citizen. Haiti's independence attained additional significance because it was the result of the only successful slave revolt in history, led to initial success by the brilliant ex-slave Touissant L'Ouverture (1743?–1803). Subsequently, when Napoleon Bonaparte (1769–1821) reneged on an independence agreement and L'Ouverture was captured by the French, transported to France, and allowed to die of neglect in

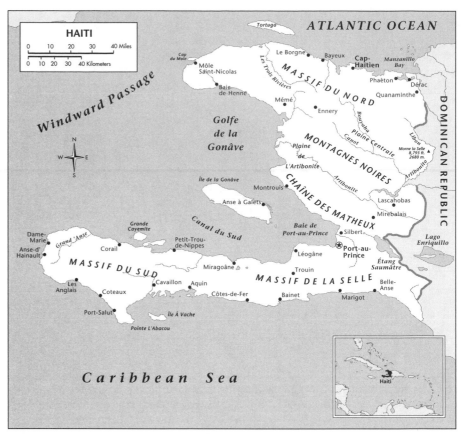

(MAP BY MARYLAND CARTOGRAPHICS/THE GALE GROUP)

factionalism: a separation of people into competing, adversarial, and self-serving groups, usually in government

a remote prison, Haiti's revolt was reinitiated and brought to a successful conclusion by one of his former lieutenants, Jean-Jacques Dessaline (1758–1806), who proclaimed himself emperor of Haiti. Dessaline ruled brutally and corruptly, but briefly—he was assassinated in 1806 in a plot organized by leaders of the light-skinned (mulatto) elite who were disenchanted with his rule. Conflict between mulatto (northern) and the dark-skinned (black and southern) political **factions** continued to characterize Haiti's politics into the twenty-first century.

Since independence, Haiti has experienced political instability, secessionist efforts, and dictatorships of varying durations, as well as a U.S. Marine occupation from 1915 to 1934, which was effectively another period of dictatorship.

The background events that have led to the political conditions of contemporary Haiti begin with the ascension to power of François (Papa Doc) Duvalier (1907–1971), who was elected president in 1957 in a military-guided election. Duvalier was a black medical doctor who attracted parts of the overwhelming black majority by appealing to traditional Haitian culture and the Voodou religion and advocating against the dominant mulatto elite.

insurgency: a rebellion against an existing authority

militia: a group of citizens prepared for military service in emergency situations

Duvalier crushed the vestiges of a mulatto resistance to his election. He declared himself president for life in 1964 and successfully resisted five invasions by Haitian **insurgents**, terrorizing the public after each. He counterbalanced the power of the armed forces by unleashing a civil **militia** based around gangs of youths from the slums known as the Volunteers for National Security, colloquially known as the *Tonton Macoutes* ("bogeyman" in Kreyol).

Duvalier died of natural causes in 1971 and was succeeded by his son, Jean Claude (Baby Doc) Duvalier (b. 1951), who also declared himself president for life. Duvalier increasingly fell under the influence of the mulattos, alienating his father's poor, black power base. His repression of political opponents became increasingly severe as his popularity evaporated. After ruling for somewhat longer than his father, Baby Doc was overthrown and fled the country after a popular uprising in early 1986.

A civil–military transitional **junta** ruled until 1987 when General Henri Namphy (b. 1932) was declared president following elections marred by the unleashing, once more, of the *Tonton Macoutes*. The army decided to rid the country of their own man barely a year into Namphy's presidency and installed General Prosper Avril (b. 1937) to power following a **coup**. Avril fled the country in 1990 under international pressure, and fresh elections were organized.

Last-minute candidate Jean-Bertrand Aristide (b. 1953), a former Roman Catholic priest and popular anti-Duvalier activist, became president following the first democratic transfer of power in Haitian history. Aristide's rhetoric of class warfare—his slogan was *lavalas* (flood)—and his personality cult quickly offended the traditionally powerful elements of Haitian society, and he was overthrown by a bloody military coup in September 1991, which installed a civilian government with military backing.

With the help of foreign embassies, Aristide escaped to the United States. The international community refused to recognize the government put in place by General Raoul Céval (b. 1949), and Aristide was finally restored to power when UN forces, led by U.S. troops, landed in September 1994.

President Aristide served the remaining fifteen months of his term in office until the 1995 elections. Aristide's protégé, René Préval (b. 1943), won the presidency in the name of the Lavalas party. However, he was later seen as having come under the influence of the old institutions of Haitian power—the mulattos, the military, and the *Tonton Macoutes*—and Aristide broke with Préval to found his own party, *La Fanmi Lavalas*.

Haiti was effectively without a functioning government from 1997, when controversial legislative elections led to the resignation of the prime minister, until Aristide was reelected president in the flawed November 2000 elections. During this period President Préval's nominees for prime minister were rejected by parliament, which was in turn disbanded by Préval in January 1999. Fresh parliamentary elections were initially announced for December of that year but did not take place until May 2000. They were mired in controversy and described by the international community, including the United States, the European Union, and Organization of American States (OAS), as deeply flawed.

Opposition parties continued their protest, boycotting the presidential elections in November 2000, allowing Aristide to return to power. The opposition rejected proposals mediated by the OAS and the Caribbean Community and Common Market (CARICOM) to end the stand-off and refused to recognize Aristide as president. Continuing negotiations were disrupted in July 2001 by a series of attacks on police targets by armed men in military uniform that left five officers dead and led to a spate of recriminations that rapidly undid the progress made earlier in the year. Violent protest continued and, by early 2004, armed opposition rebels had taken control of several towns around the country.

The United States and France induced President Aristide's resignation on February 29, 2004. Following an overnight UN Security Council resolution, the United States led an international force of more than 3,600 soldiers into Haiti to support a provisional government which, as of early 2005, continued to be opposed by Aristide's *Lavalas* party.

junta: a group of individuals holding power, especially after seizing control as a result of a coup

coup: a quick seizure of power or a sudden attack

■ ■ ■

TOUSSAINT L'OUVERTURE (1743–1803)

Born into slavery, Toussaint L'Ouverture became a military mastermind who defeated the French, Spanish, and British who occupied the West Indian island of Santo Domingo (earlier known as Hispaniola). The island is now split between Haiti and the Dominican Republic.

L'Ouverture was born (as Toussaint Breda, with the surname of his owner) on a plantation near what is now Cap-Haïtien, Haiti. His master recognized his intelligence and took a liking to him, offering him less taxing jobs like driver, waiter, and steward. This allowed L'Ouverture to learn some French, which the slaves were not taught. He also had access to the plantation's library and purportedly liked to read about historic military campaigns.

The black slaves of the French-controlled western part of the island, known as Saint-Domingue, revolted in 1791. The French Declaration of the Rights of Man of 1789 had raised their hopes, but its application to Saint-Domingue was suppressed by the white planters. Following the uprising L'Ouverture saved his former master (he had been freed in 1776), then joined the black forces. Soon, he recruited his own soldiers and trained them in guerrilla warfare. He took L'Ouverture as his surname in 1793. When the French government offered emancipation to slaves who would fight the counterrevolutionary planters on the island, L'Ouverture allied with the French. L'Ouverture was short and small-framed but transmitted enormous energy and authority on the battlefield. At one point L'Ouverture had control of the entire island. Forces of the Napoleonic government, seeking to regain control of Saint-Domingue, eventually arrested him during a pretended negotiation and sent him to the prison fortress at Joux in eastern France, where he died.

Aristide's February 2004 departure on a U.S. plane into exile in Africa was not without controversy. Aristide himself contended that he did not leave voluntarily, that he was in effect "kidnapped." The United States, France, and the commander of Aristide's own private security force denied his claim, insisting that he left voluntarily when confronted with the possibly disastrous consequences of an attempt to retain power. Regardless of the accuracy of Aristide's claim, the controversy over his 2004 departure from power did little for the ability to govern by the **interim** regime of Prime Minister Gerard Latortue (b. 1934) that replaced him.

interim: for a limited time, during a period of transition

A second UN peacekeeping phase of the mission in Haiti began in June 2004 with a handover from the United States to a team of UN peacekeepers from nine nations. Despite the presence of the UN peacekeepers, as of early 2005 political, economic, and social conditions in Haiti appeared to have improved little, if at all, and its citizens continued to have little freedom or personal security.

POLITICAL LIFE UNDER THE REGIME

federalism: a system of political organization, in which separate states or groups are ruled by a dominant central authority on some matters, but are otherwise permitted to govern themselves independently

bicameral: comprised of two chambers, usually a legislative body

Haiti's generally ignored 1987 constitution provides for a **federal** republic with a **bicameral** legislature, a directly elected president, and a parliamentary government, similar to the French Fifth Republic. This semipresidential system in Haiti divides authority between a president and a prime minister, mandating just the kind of cooperation that Haiti's political elites lack. Instead, politicians have pursued relative gains in power to control the state for personal gain.

Haiti's ineffective institutions do not protect Haitian citizens. Aristide was the first president to aspire credibly to reform the justice and military agencies, as well as the incentives that corrupt them. Unfortunately, Aristide refused to give up personal political control and the extralegal use of force. The attempt to develop the rule of law has been undermined most by illegal security forces linked to newly elected officials.

Judges in Haiti are underpaid and often corrupt and incompetent. Intimidation of judges in politically sensitive court cases is common. The police conduct searches without judge-issued warrants and detain those arrested without legal recourse. Defendants are often not informed of their rights. Most Haitians cannot afford a lawyer, and the state is not required to provide one. Thus, denial of due process is the norm. There is no protection for property rights and the enforcement of contracts, as well as the functioning of the judiciary is generally lacking.

Ostensibly the criminal code prohibits all forms of corruption, but Haiti has never had the political will to stop it. Indeed, politicians have sought political power to obtain and illicitly use public funds. Aristide declared repeatedly that he would wage war on corruption, and one of his greatest achievements was the abolition of the army and its rural section chiefs, which curtailed the prevalent practice of armed extortion of peasants. However, in terms of use of public funds and allocation of public businesses and licenses—primarily for imports— to cronies, the Aristide presidency was as corrupt as its predecessors. In 2004 Transparency International ranked Haiti as tied (with Bangladesh) for most corrupt of the 146 countries in its complete Corruption Perceptions Index.

Drug trafficking is another large source of corruption in Haiti. The police, if not high government officials as well, are widely believed to be corrupted by the drug trafficking trade. It is likely that some money laundering takes place through Haiti's poorly regulated banks and currency exchanges as well. The impact of reform efforts in these regards has been limited.

A major scandal in 2001 and 2002, which was publicized because of its extensive effects on the general population, involved the bankruptcies of cooperatives in which President Aristide had encouraged people to make deposits. After Rosemond Jean, the coordinator of the National Society of Victims of Failed Cooperatives, called on the Haitian state for full reimbursement for victims, he was imprisoned for six months on nebulous charges of drug trafficking. Complaints from human rights groups led to his release in early 2003.

CITIZEN PARTICIPATION, RIGHTS, AND LIBERTIES

Haiti's civil and criminal codes have nominally protected civil rights for much of the past two centuries, but they have been consistently ignored in practice. Political and civil rights gained greater de jure protection with the 1987 constitution, which included prohibitions of unnecessary force and arbitrary arrest and detention and mandated free assembly, but all rights are routinely denied in practice. In late 1988 Haiti signed and ratified the International Covenant on Civil and Political Rights, but little enabling legislation has been enacted or institutional reform carried out since then.

Haiti has practically no checks to ensure that the police force respect citizens' physical and psychological integrity, nor does it have any system of **redress** for rights violations. The forty-eight- to seventy-two-hour limit on detention without charge is often violated, with months or years passing before prisoners obtain judicial orders for release. Effective petition and redress by state authorities generally do not occur, except under intense international pressure or in a few landmark cases.

Haiti's constitution does not specifically prohibit discrimination on the grounds of race, sex, disability, language, or social status, although the ratified International Covenant mandates such protections. The constitution does require equal working conditions without discrimination based on gender,

■ ■ ■

THE SLAVE REVOLT OF 1791

During the eighteenth century, the Caribbean island colony of Saint-Domingue (now Haiti) was home to thriving plantations run by white Frenchman that relied on black slave labor. The French Revolution (1789–1799) touched off a fierce revolt of landowning blacks and mixed-race mulattoes. They expected to be granted more autonomy in accordance with the French declaration of the *Rights of Man*, but the white colonists of Saint-Domingue ignored this provision, leading to a mulatto uprising in 1790 that was easily quashed.

Black slaves, however, were inspired by the events to rebel against French rule and the slaveholding system. By August 1791 an uprising was underway that evolved into the Haitian revolution. As slaves escaped, they banded together in ragtag armies and wreaked havoc by slaughtering whites and torching their property.

Former slave Toussaint L'Ouverture (1743–1803) is often credited with masterminding the revolt, but scholars say that claim cannot be substantiated. Whether or not the rebellion was his idea, however, he eventually joined the fray and led his troops to victory against the Spanish, British, and French armies on the island. In November 1803 Haiti became an independent republic.

■ ■ ■

redress: to make right, or, compensation

beliefs, or marital status, but women continue to hold the lowest paying jobs in the economy. There is, however, a ministry for women and various state programs that have had important symbolic impacts for women.

The constitution protects religious freedom, which the government largely respects. However, significant conflict has grown among Protestants and Catholics and also between voodoo practitioners and their rivals both inside and outside the voodoo religion. In addition, Catholics loyal to the hierarchy, which has supported the opposition to Aristide, have clashed with those loyal to the populist church leaders, which include Aristide himself.

Freedom of association and collective organizing and bargaining are legally protected. In practice, however, armed intimidation and selective arrests of political leaders and non-governmental organization protesters restrict these rights.

POLITICAL PARTIES AND INTEREST GROUPS

Violent factionalism both between and within the country's political parties has continued to poison the democratic process. The *Lavalas* movement includes violent gangs who intimidate opposition sympathizers. Former army soldiers and officers, as well as disgruntled members of the national police force, which came into existence in 1995, are also prone to intervene in the political crisis.

Immediately following the December 2001 coup attempt—which the Aristide government alleged was led by disgruntled former police and army officers, not the opposition—*Lavalas* shock troops, called *chiméres*, attacked and demolished opposition party headquarters, opposition leaders' homes, Radio Metropole, an independent radio station, and a French cultural center. These militia groups are not necessarily **ideological**; their services can be bought with money or alcohol, as they have been since at least the 1950s.

See also: Caribbean Region.

ideology: a system of beliefs composed of ideas or values, from which political, social, or economic programs are often derived

BIBLIOGRAPHY

Dupuy, Alex. *Haiti in the World Economy: Class, Race and Underdevelopment since 1700*. Boulder, CO: Westview Press, 1988.

Farmer, Paul. *The Uses of Haiti: Updated Edition*. Monroe, ME: Common Courage Press, 2003.

Fatton, Robert. *Haiti's Predatory Republic: The Unending Transition to Democracy*. Boulder, CO: Lynne Rienner, 2002.

Freedom House. "Haiti." *Freedom in the World 2004*. New York: Freedom House, 2004. <http://www.freedomhouse.org/research/freeworld/2004/countryratings/haiti.htm>.

"Haiti." In *CIA World Factbook*. Washington, DC: U.S. Central Intelligence Agency, 2005. <http://www.cia.gov/cia/publications/factbook/geos/ha.html>.

Nicholls, David. *From Dessaline to Duvalier: Race, Colour and National Independence in Haiti*. New Brunswick, NJ: Rutgers University Press, 1995.

O'Neill, William. *Judicial Reform in Haiti*. New York: National Coalition for Haitian Rights, 1995. <http://www.nchr.org/hrp/jud_reform_eng.htm>.

Schmidt, Hans. *The U.S. Occupation of Haiti, 1915–1934*. New Brunswick, NJ: Rutgers University Press, 1995.

Transparency International. *Transparency International Corruption Perceptions Index 2004*. Berlin: Transparency International, 2004. <http://www.transparency.org/cpi/2004/cpi2004.en.html#cpi2004>.

United Nations Development Programme. *Human Development Report 2002*. New York: Oxford University Press, 2002. <http://www.undp.org/hdr2002/complete.pdf>.

U.S. Department of State, Bureau of Democracy, Human Rights, and Labor. "Haiti." *Country Reports on Human Rights Practices*. Washington, DC: U.S. Department of State, Bureau of Democracy, Human Rights, and Labor, 2005. <http://www.state.gov/g/drl/rls/hrrpt/2004/41764.htm>.

Henry F. Carey

Halakhah

Jewish law (*Halakhah*) is rooted in the three-thousand-year history of the Jews. Jewish law contains elements that are central to both the religious and national development of the Jews. Until the end of the eighteenth century, Jewish law regulated every aspect of Jewish life, private and public. Individuals or groups who did not recognize the authority of *Halakhah* were excluded from the Jewish community. Since then, only that segment of the Jewish people known as Orthodox still feels bound by *Halakhah*; other Jews observe *Halakhah* to a lesser degree or not at all.

When the Jews came into existence as a distinct people—according to tradition, with the exodus from Egypt and the divine revelation at Mount Sinai—all nations had their own gods specifying the particular norms that were to govern every aspect of their lives. That is what it meant to be a distinct, separate nation. Thus, not only did the divine commands embedded in Jewish law specify the relationship of Jews to God, but by specifying the relationships among members of the community, *Halakhah* defined the distinct practices of the Jewish people.

Halakhah has always been a case-oriented legal system designed to resolve specific issues. Because Jewish law was traditionally believed to have its origins in divine commands—the Ten Commandments and the remainder of the Torah (the Five Books of Moses)—its interpretation and application have remained in the hands of religious leadership. At first this was the function of the prophets and the hereditary priestly class. When the Romans destroyed the Second Temple (in C.E. 70), the rabbis—men who were learned in the law—became the unchallenged expositors of the norms governing the behavior of Jews within their own communities. Their rulings were collected in the Mishnah and the Babylonian and Palestinian Talmuds, compiled between 100 B.C.E. and C.E. 500. The rabbinic **sages** who lived after the **codification** of the Talmuds continued their interpretation and development as the authoritative basis of Jewish law.

Halakhic norms covered every aspect of Jewish life. Jews were seen as a distinct people and continued to live in separate communities even when they were dispersed around the world. Jewish courts were central elements of that **communal** autonomy. Jewish law, therefore, was applied not only to all aspects of religious observance, but also to all aspects of private civil law—property, contracts, family law, and the like—as well as to many aspects of public law.

In the late eighteenth century, Jews came to be recognized as individual members of the **nation-states** where they resided. Jewish courts lost the authority to decide matters within the community; those functions were handled by state courts. Moreover, with the spread of rationalistic, scientific modes of thought, most Jews began to treat even the remaining Halakhic norms—those relating to religious practices—primarily as part of the historic

sage: a wise person

codification: the making of official law

communal: something owned or used by the entire community

nation-state: a relatively homogeneous state with only one or few nationalities within its political borders

JEWS GATHER IN A TUNISIAN SYNAGOGUE FOR THE SIMCHAT TORAH. Simchat Torah is the last day of the autumnal Sukkot festival that marks the end of the harvest. Such Jewish celebrations are essential components of *Halakhah,* or Jewish Law, which provides a guide to daily living through rules and practices. However, not all those in the Jewish community follow *Halakhah,* as some believe it should evolve from generation to generation. (SOURCE: HULTON ARCHIVE/GETTY IMAGES)

secularism: a refutation of, apathy toward, or exclusion of all religion

Judaic tradition. Only Orthodox Jews continue to feel obligated to follow Halakhic norms in all aspects of their lives.

The establishment of Israel in 1948 raised the question of the role of Jewish law in the self-proclaimed Jewish state. The majority believed that Israel, as a **secular** state, should be governed by the democratically enacted laws of its parliament. Orthodox Jewish Israelis, however, believed that, as the Jewish state, Israel ought to be governed by divinely inspired *Halakhah* as interpreted and applied by rabbinic authorities. In the early twenty-first century this conflict was an important feature of Israeli public life.

See also: Israel; Shari'a.

BIBLIOGRAPHY

Dorf, Elliot N., and Arthur Rosett. *A Living Tree: The Roots and Growth of Jewish Law*. Albany: State University of New York Press, 1988.

Edelman, Martin. *Courts, Politics, and Culture in Israel*. Charlottesville: University Press of Virginia, 1994.

Elon, Menachem. *Jewish Law: History, Sources, Principles*. Philadelphia: Jewish Publication Society, 1994.

Gordis, Robert. *The Dynamics of Judaism: A Study of Jewish Law*. Bloomington: Indiana University Press, 1990.

Martin Edelman

Havel, Vaclav

FORMER PRESIDENT OF CZECHOSLOVAKIA
1936–

Vaclav Havel is a Czech intellectual, writer, dramatist, and **dissident** who became the first president of Czechoslovakia after the yoke of the communist dictatorship was discarded as a consequence of the "Velvet Revolution" in 1989. He was viewed by many in Czechoslovakia and in the larger West as one of the founding fathers of democracy in post-Cold War Europe.

Vaclav Havel was born in 1936 to bourgeois parents who would lose much after the communist takeover of Czechoslovakia after World War II (1939–1945). He was apparently a precocious child, and by the time he was fifteen, he was writing poetry, had founded a literary group among his high school friends that organized symposia, and even published a typewritten magazine. Despite his interests in the arts, he was not admitted to the Academy of Performing Arts and, instead, entered the Czechoslovak University of Technology to study economics. After only one year of study, he was conscripted into the military.

Writing was Havel's vocation, and he has written numerous plays, essays and poetry. His work often has a political theme, such as his April 1968 essay, "On the Theme of Opposition," published in *Literarni listy*, which argued for political **pluralism**. Publication of that essay coincided with the move toward democratization in Czechoslovakia that Alexander Dubcek (1921–1992), first secretary of the Communist Party, began discussing in 1968. The Soviet Union blunted that initiative, and Soviet tanks invaded and occupied the country beginning in August 1968. Dubcek was removed from office the following April and replaced with hardliner, Gustav Husak (1913–1991). In April 1975, Havel wrote a letter to Husak pleading for an end to the "drastic suppression of history." Husak never responded, but the letter was widely circulated and had an impact on the rise of dissidents in Czechoslovakia.

Havel was a founder of the opposition group Charter 77. Tried in 1977 for allegedly smuggling a colleague's manuscript out of the country, he was convicted and sentenced to fourteen months in prison. He was later arrested in 1989 for allegedly inciting a demonstration, convicted, and imprisoned for another nine months. His release coincided with the beginnings of the Velvet Revolution, which would eventually lead to the retreat of the Soviets from Czechoslovakia and the introduction of democratic institutions. Havel was named by the Czechoslovakian parliament to be the nation's first president before the end of the year.

dissident: one who disagrees with the actions or political philosophy of his or her government or religion

"[Havel] was viewed by many in Czechoslovakia and in the larger West as one of the founding fathers of democracy in post-Cold War Europe."

pluralism: a system of government in which all groups participate in the decision-making process

VACLAV HAVEL, IN OTTAWA, CANADA IN 1999. Vaclav Havel was a playwright whose Civic Forum group rallied against communism and the USSR. Upon its dissolution in 1989, he became president of Czechoslovakia, leaving office in 1992 only to be elected president of the newly-formed Czech Republic in 1993. (SOURCE: AP/WIDE WORLD PHOTOS)

secede: to break away from, especially politically

Havel and his advisors were suspicious of a parliament that included a large contingent of communists; more important, they were writers and intellectuals who understood little about constitutions, legalities, and government. As a result, Havel was often seen as not respecting the role of parliament.

Havel presided over the **secession** of Slovakia from the nation in 1992 and then resigned as president. The so-called "velvet divorce" of the two nations was official on New Year's Eve 1992. Havel was elected president of the Czech Republic in January 1993. He attempted to move the Czech Republic into the larger, Western world and began negotiations for the Czech Republic to enter the European Union (which occurred in 2005), the North Atlantic Treaty Organization, and the Organization for Economic Cooperation and Development. He retired from the presidency in 2003. Notably, he is the author of seven books, two written while he was president, and twelve plays.

See also: Czech Republic.

BIBLIOGRAPHY

Havel, Vaclav. *Disturbing the Peace: A Conversation with Karel Hvizdala*, trans. Paul Wilson. New York: Alfred A. Knopf, 1990.

Havel, Vaclav. *Open Letters: Selected Writings 1965–1990*. New York: Alfred A. Knopf, 1991.

Keane, John. *Vaclav Havel: A Political Tragedy in Six Acts*. New York: Basic Books, 2000.

Kriseova, Eda. *Vaclav Havel: The Authorized Biography*. New York: St. Martin's Press, 1993.

Mary L. Volcansek

Hitler, Adolf

GERMAN DICTATOR

1889–1945

Adolf Hitler (1889–1945) was national **socialist** dictator of Germany's **totalitarian** Third Reich from January 1933 until his suicide in the closing days of World War II (1939–1945). He ranks alongside the Soviet Union's Joseph Stalin (1879–1853) and China's Mao Tse-tung (1893–1976) as one of the modern world's most ruthless and maniacal political figures.

Hitler was born on April 20, 1889, in eastern Austria. He enjoyed a pampered childhood and adolescence, was an indifferent student, and failed to graduate from secondary school. In 1907 Hitler moved to Vienna, where he developed basic convictions that formed the subsequent basis of his political ideology. These included a commitment to pan-German **nationalism** coupled with a radical racial anti-semitism; an appreciation of the power of mass mobilization in politics; and his rejection of liberalism, socialism, Marxism, and democracy. While debating politics on a daily basis, Hitler also developed exceptional skills as an impassioned orator.

In 1913 Hitler left for Munich, the capital of Bavaria, and enthusiastically joined a Bavarian regiment at the onset of World War I. The war—including Germany's defeat in 1918—was a pivotal experience for Hitler, who became obsessed with perpetuating war. "That is how he looked at politics as a career— as a means for gaining power which would make possible a new war, this one, however, fought according to his ideas until final victory was won" (Bracher 1970, pp. 66–67).

Hitler resigned from the military to join the German Workers Party, a radical right group formed in Munich to oppose postwar Germany's fledgling democratic **regime** (the Weimar Republic). He quickly became party leader (*führer*), changed the party's name to the German National Socialist Workers Party (NSDAP), and initiated a *Putsch* (attempted seizure of power) against the Bavarian government in November 1923. Hitler was arrested, tried for treason, and sentenced to five years in prison, during which time he wrote *Mein Kampf*, an inflammatory autobiography. The book later inspired millions of Germans and other Europeans to accept Hitler's claim to leadership and the Nazi agenda.

After his early release from prison in December 1924, Hitler devoted his energies to the reorganization of the NSDAP and extending its political appeal. He obtained the support of sympathetic voters and the German military in a calculated strategy to achieve a legal rise to political power. Hitler's targets included Jews, socialists, liberals, and **pacifists**. These groups had allegedly conspired to bring about Germany's defeat in 1918 and the Treaty of Versailles, which had imposed territorial, financial, and political costs on the Weimar Republic.

Initially, the NSDAP's prospects seemed dismal; it received only 2.6 percent of the national vote in 1928. However, support for the party surged to 18.3 percent in 1930 and 37.3 percent in July 1932. Key factors in Hitler's growing popularity included the onset of the Great Depression and resulting mass unemployment, the persuasiveness of his ideological oratory, and a parallel increase in support for the **Communist** Party that frightened many middle-class voters. Another factor was the failure of democratic leaders to devise credible measures to combat the effects of the Depression, or to unite in defense of the republic against its radical opponents on both the right and

socialism: any of various economic and political theories advocating collective or governmental ownership and administration of the means of production and distribution of goods

totalitarianism: a form of absolute government that demands complete subjugation by its citizens

nationalism: the belief that one's nation or culture is superior to all others

regime: a type of government, or, the government in power in a region

pacifism: the belief that war and violence are inferior methods of conflict resolution, to be avoided

communism: an economic and social system characterized by the absence of class structure and by common ownership of the means of production and subsistence

coalition: an alliance, partnership, or union of disparate peoples or individuals

absolute: complete, pure, free from restriction or limitation

left. Although the NSDAP's strength sagged marginally in the November 1932 election (to 33.1 percent), conservative politicians persuaded Weimar President Paul von Hindenburg (1847–1934) to appoint Hitler as chancellor of a **coalition** NSDAP-conservative government on January 30, 1933.

Once in office, Hitler proceeded swiftly to consolidate power. In 1933 he coerced the parliament into granting his cabinet dictatorial powers to deal with the "national crisis." The Nazis quickly outlawed other political parties and mass organizations, subordinated the economy and all social and educational institutions to party control, imposed censorship on all media, rejected the Versailles treaty, and began a systematic program of rearmament in preparation for the resumption of war. Upon Hindenburg's death in 1934, Hitler combined the offices of chancellor and president into his personal role as **absolute** *führer*. Following the views expounded in *Mein Kampf*, the Nazis launched a coordinated program of overt discrimination, subsequent imprisonment, and later the mass extermination of millions of Jews and other regime "outsiders." In foreign policy, Hitler engineered—with British and

ADOLF HITLER IN 1933. Hilter's appointment as chancellor of a coalition German National Socialist Workers Party (NSDAP)-conservative government on January 30, 1933 set Germany on the path toward a consolidation of government and Hitler's dictatorship. (SOURCE: HULTON ARCHIVE/GETTY IMAGES)

French acquiescence—the annexation of Austria and most of Czechoslovakia in 1938. When the Western powers subsequently balked at his demands to seize Polish territory on Germany's eastern border, Hitler launched World War II on September 1, 1939.

Hitler's demise—and that of the Third Reich—came as a result of a military alliance between the United States, Britain, and the Soviet Union in 1941, after Germany's invasion of the Soviet Union and Japan's attack on Pearl Harbor. The advance of the Red Army through eastern Germany into Berlin and a relentless drive by Anglo-American forces through Germany in the West convinced Hitler that he had no **recourse** but to take his life and entrust what remained of the Third Reich and its armed forces to others. He shot himself in an underground bunker in Berlin on April 30, 1945. A week later, German military officers surrendered unconditionally to the wartime allies. Most of the bunker remains (unmarked), but Hitler's body was taken by the Red Army and was never officially interred.

recourse: a resource for assistance

See also: Crimes Against Humanity; Dictatorship; Ethnic Cleansing; Genocide; Germany; Totalitarianism; War Crimes.

BIBLIOGRAPHY

Bracher, Karl Dietrich. *The German Dictatorship: The Origins, Structure, and Effects of National Socialism,* trans. Jean Steinberg. New York: Praeger Publishers, 1970.

Bullock, Alan. *Hitler, a Study in Tyranny.* Completely revised ed. New York: Harper & Row, 1962.

Speer, Albert. *Inside the Third Reich. Memoirs,* trans. Richard and Clara Winston. New York: Macmillan, 1970.

M. Donald Hancock

Honduras

The Republic of Honduras is located on the Atlantic coast of Central America; it is the region's second largest country. Honduras's 6.5 million people are 90 percent mestizo and largely Roman Catholic, and they inhabit a mountainous nation that has relied heavily on export agriculture. Principal exports are coffee, bananas, and beef. Although agriculture employs one-third of the work force, it accounts for only 12 percent of the gross domestic product (GDP); nearly 50 percent of the populace works in the service sector. The official literacy rate of 78.5 percent is comparable to that of neighboring Nicaragua and El Salvador. The effects of 28 percent unemployment are compounded by high rates of underemployment, which has left about half the population living below the poverty line. On the United Nations Human Development Index in 2004, Honduras ranked 115, near the bottom of the "medium development" category.

A pattern of traditional **authoritarian** rule in Honduras during the first half of the twentieth century gave way to more reform-minded military rule after 1954. Military governments of the 1960s and 1970s promoted land reform, permitted labor organizing, and presided over rapid economic growth and the development of the country's infrastructure. Honduras has been undergoing a transition to a civilian, democratic government since the 1981 elections and its

authoritarianism: the domination of the state or its leader over individuals

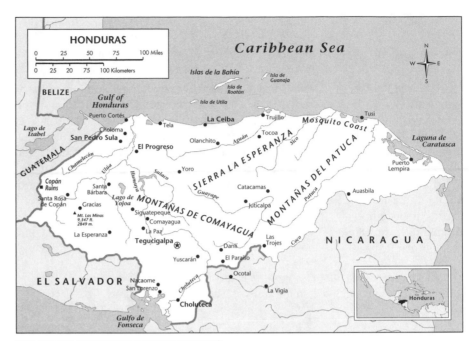

HONDURAS

Caribbean Sea

(MAP BY MARYLAND CARTOGRAPHICS/THE GALE GROUP)

unicameral: comprised of one chamber, usually a legislative body

proportional system: a political system in which legislative seats or offices are awarded based on the proportional number of votes received by a party in an election

rule of law: the principle that the law is a final grounds of decision-making and applies equally to all people; law and order

adoption of a new constitution in 1982. The end of military rule reflected the influence of the United States, which encouraged the transition to electoral democracy while building up its own military presence in Honduras as part of the Contra war against Nicaragua.

Since 1982 the country has experienced regular elections in which the Liberal and National Parties have vied for control of the presidency and congress. The president is head of state and is elected for a single four-year term. Honduras has a **unicameral** legislature composed of 128 deputies who are elected through a system of **proportional representation**. A National Elections Tribunal administers the elections, but it has been criticized for lacking independence because its office holders come from the country's political parties. The judiciary is technically independent, but has historically been controlled by the executive through appointments and patronage, and due to the short tenure of office. Substantial reform of the judicial system commenced toward the end of the 1990s.

Because Honduras's transition to democracy in the early 1980s took place within the context of the United States's "low-intensity war" with Nicaragua, efforts to establish democracy were attenuated by the country's national security situation. The armed forces functioned autonomously with regard to security matters. In that sense, security forces operated outside the control of law, and grave human rights abuses, including forced disappearances and assassinations, were committed against the civilian population. With the signing of the Esquipulas Peace Accords in 1987, Honduras was able to begin a process of demilitarization, which has allowed broader institutional reforms to go forward aimed at strengthening the **rule of law**. Honduras created a position in the government for a commissioner for human rights, which has investigated human rights violations committed during the war, promoted efforts to strengthen the rule of law, and publicized government corruption.

Although civil society is still relatively weak in Honduras, the mobilization that occurred in the aftermath of Hurricane Mitch has strengthened this spirit of democracy. The hurricane, which struck Central America in November 1998, killed 17,000 Hondurans, caused over $3 billion in damage, and left hundreds of thousands homeless. Driven by necessity, human rights organizations, women's organizations, worker and peasant organizations, and other such activist groups exerted mounting pressure on the government for reform. The emergence of such **factions** reflects a growing popular participation in political life, which could deepen Honduran democracy in the future.

See also: Belize; Caribbean Region; Inter-American Commission and Court of Human Rights.

BIBLIOGRAPHY

Barry, Tom, and Kent Norsworthy. *Honduras: The Essential Guide to Its Politics, Economy, Society and Environment.* Albuquerque, NM: Resource Center Press, 1994.

Merrill, Tim L. *Honduras: A Country Guide.* Washington, DC: U.S. Government Printing Office, 1995.

Schulz, Donald E. *The United States, Honduras, and the Crisis in Central America.* Boulder, CO: Westview Press, 1994.

Michael Dodson

Hong Kong and Macau

Hong Kong comprises an extension of China's Guangdong province and some 235 islands including Hong Kong Island. It has a land area of 1,100 square kilometers (425,000 square miles) and had an estimated population of 6,855,125 in 2004. Level land is at a premium as most of Hong Kong consists of rugged hills and mountains. A large percentage of Hong Kong's people live and work in high density areas on the northern side of Hong Kong Island and across the water at Kowloon. Since the early 1950s an increasing number of refugees from China forced the government to build large housing estates in selected areas throughout the southern part of an area north of Kowloon known as the New Territories. Dotted throughout the New Territories and most of the smaller islands are numerous traditional villages where life has remained relatively unchanged over the past 100 years.

BRITISH COLONY TO CHINESE SPECIAL ADMINISTRATIVE REGION

Hong Kong was made a Special Administrative Region within the People's Republic of China (PRC) on July 1, 1997, after being a British Crown Colony for some 156 years. Prior to British settlement Hong Kong Island was a haven for smugglers, fishermen, and those fleeing from or plotting against **imperial** rule. While British colonial rule gradually ameliorated the worst excesses of the local Chinese population, it did not temper their sense of adventure and desire for both wealth and freedom. In the early days of colonial rule, Hong Kong developed a reputation as a dynamic but unsavory place where the opium trade, organized crime, and unscrupulous entrepreneurs who paid little heed to ethics, law, and protocol thrived.

Throughout the twentieth century Hong Kong gradually established itself as a major port and a center for business and trade. From the 1970s, Hong Kong entered a period of record economic growth which, along with the other East

factionalism: a separation of people into competing, adversarial, and self-serving groups, usually in government

imperialism: extension of the control of one nation over another, especially through territorial, economic, and political expansion

HONG KONG

CHINA

South China Sea

Hong Kong

(MAP BY XNR PRODUCTIONS, INC./THE GALE GROUP)

sovereignty: autonomy; or, rule over a political entity

motherland: one's country or region of origin

political autonomy: the state of a country or region within a country that holds sovereignty over its own affairs

democratization: a process by which the powers of government are moved to the people of a region or to their elected representatives

Asian "dragon" economies of Singapore, Taiwan, and South Korea, created the phenomena now known as the East Asian Economic Miracle.

Until the 1990s the people of Hong Kong were recognized only for their energy and financial acumen and were thought to be disinterested in politics. As recently as the transfer of Hong Kong to Chinese **sovereignty** in 1997, most commentators were still describing the people of Hong Kong as politically apathetic.

Britain gained increasing control over Hong Kong in three successive stages over a sixty-year period. It began with the raising of the British flag on Hong Kong Island on January 20, 1841. After a number of territorial disputes between Britain and China, the British managed to establish full sovereignty over Hong Kong Island and a perpetual lease over the Kowloon peninsula in 1860. Toward the end of the nineteenth century a number of European powers as well as Japan and Russia began to seize Chinese territory. The British feared Hong Kong would be attacked and sought a 99-year lease from China over the New Territories to establish a defensible border at the Shenzen River.

During the later colonial period the political expression of the people of Hong Kong became increasingly focused on establishing rights and freedoms within the British system. There was no serious effort on the part of any group of Hong Kong residents either to reunite with China or to gain independence. Hong Kong, therefore, is one of the few European colonies where there was no independence movement of any significance and where there were only a handful of people who thought unification with the **motherland** would be desirable.

When it became obvious in the early 1980s that the Chinese would not renew the New Territories lease the British realized that Hong Kong would no longer be a viable entity with only the Hong Kong Island and Kowloon. In the following negotiations, China made it obvious that while it would accept nothing less than full sovereignty, it did concede it would have to allow Hong Kong a high degree of **political autonomy** to preserve stability and prosperity. At the same time, many prominent political figures in Hong Kong were beginning to realize that only by democratizing the structures of government and allowing only local candidates to stand for election could they limit the power of the central government in Beijing.

In 1984 Britain and China signed the Sino-British Joint Declaration (SBJD), which allowed the orderly transfer of Hong Kong to Chinese sovereignty in 1997. The SBJD guaranteed that the common-law legal system would continue for the next fifty years. The SBJD also stated that the political structure would be subject to a number of stages that would ultimately lead to the full **democratization** of the Legislative Council and left the possibility open that the chief executive officer's (CEO) post could be subject to a similar process after 2007. Until that time, the CEO would be selected by an 800-person election committee appointed by the central Chinese government.

Up until 1984, Hong Kong had been administered by a governor and the legislative and executive councils. The roles of both councils had been largely advisory. The British now proposed that an increasing number of seats in the Legislative Council would be subject to election and that both the legislature and the executive should play a greater role in decision-making. In both the 1984 and the 1988 Legislative Council elections, twelve members were elected through functional constituencies such as law, social services, and education, and another twelve were elected via an electoral college.

BASIC LAW

The people of Hong Kong were far from satisfied with what they saw as a token attempt at democracy. They became even more concerned when China presented its mini-constitution for Hong Kong, known as the Basic Law.

Following China's suppression of pro-democracy activists in Beijing's Tiananmen Square in June 1989, over a million Hong Kong residents took part in a demonstration against China's brutal treatment of its own people. David Wilson (b. 1935), Hong Kong's governor from 1987 to 1992, responded by allowing the creation of political parties and making eighteen indirectly elected seats open to direct election through the geographic **constituency** model for the 1991 Legislative Council elections. The British government responded to what it saw as merely incremental changes and the shabby treatment of its prime minister, John Major (b. 1943), on a recent trip to Beijing by dismissing Wilson and appointing a career politician, Chris Patten (b. 1944), as its governor.

Although Patten realized his proposals for political change would have to comply with the Basic Law, they were still a marked improvement in terms of democracy and political participation. The net effect of the Patten reforms was to extend the electoral **franchise** to 2.7 million voters and make every one of the sixty seats in the Legislative Council subject to either direct or indirect election.

The Basic Law thus provides that Hong Kong's chief of government is the CEO, elected by an 800-member electoral committee that reflects the preferences of Beijing. There is also a sixty-seat Legislative Council: half elected by popular vote and half elected by functional constituencies. The judiciary is headed by Court of Final Appeal for the Hong Kong region. Although the Basic Law does allow democratization to proceed in a number of stages, the main focus is on methods to ensure law and order and to ensure that the CEO has similar powers to a British colonial governor until at least 2007.

In the Legislative Council elections held in September 1995 the pro-democracy candidates won nineteen of the twenty-five directly elected seats and fell only a few seats short of achieving a majority. Hong Kong's **retrocession** to Chinese sovereignty in 1997 has not changed the voting pattern. Rather, voting turnout numbers have increased along with support for pro-democracy parties and candidates.

BEIJING'S INFLUENCE

The first CEO selected by the China-appointed election committee, Tung Chee-hwa (b. 1937), installed on July 1, 1997, was seen by critics as weak, indecisive, and willing to go along with Chinese demands without consulting the people of Hong Kong. They argue that he failed to carry through with the democratic reforms outlined in both the Basic Law and the SBJD and also to introduce measures that would stimulate Hong Kong's flagging economy.

Under Tung's tutelage the Chinese exerted increasing control over business, the legal process, local politics, and security, and the civil liberties enshrined in both the SBJD and the Basic Law have been steadily eroded. In 1999 he allowed the powers inscribed in the Basic Law for the Court of Final Appeal to be, essentially, transferred to the National People's Congress in Beijing. A year later Pacific Century Cyberwork acquired one of Hong Kong's

constituency: the people who either elect or are represented by an elected official

franchise: a right provided by statutory or constitutional law; to give such a right

retrocession: the act of returning, as in territory

largest companies, Cable & Wireless HKT, making it obvious that China was backing one of its "patriotic" protégés, media mogul Richard Li, and that this practice was now becoming commonplace.

In July 2003, Tung was forced by the weight of public opinion to withdraw a bill that would have allowed the same draconian laws in operation in China, regarding free speech, civil liberties, and media censorship, to apply to Hong Kong. The passing of the bill would have outlawed large public demonstrations and groups such as Falun Gong in Hong Kong. The large protest rallies held over a number of days against the bill led to its withdrawal and the resignation of two of Tung's most prominent cabinet ministers.

By the middle of 2004 the people of Hong Kong had become increasingly concerned regarding Beijing's attempt to influence the outcome of the Legislative Council elections and threatening those prominent in the democracy movement. A number of leaders from the usually pro-China business community claimed that the democratic movement was now so large and broadly based that China's attempts to muzzle it were proving counterproductive and that the destabilizing effects of China's constant intervention in Hong Kong's affairs was posing a threat to Hong Kong's economic future.

At the same time, leading figures in the pro-democracy movement—including founding chairman of Hong Kong's Democratic Party, Martin Lee (b. 1938); professor and former chairman of the Democratic Party, Yeung Sum (b. 1947); and legislator Audrey Eu (b. 1953)—realized that, although most Hong Kongers desired democracy, they also wanted political stability and did not wish to see confrontation with Beijing continue. For the first time since 1997, a spirit of compromise took hold in which all parties, including the Chinese, began trying to find a way to solve the ongoing problems of political stability, autonomy, and civil rights, as well as discussing ways to improve Hong Kong's business environment.

Tung Chee-hwa resigned in 2005, two years before his term was ended. While he claimed to have left due to ill health, there is belief that Beijing may have played a role in his resignation.

MACAU

Macau lies some 50 miles west of Hong Kong and sits at the mouth of the Pearl River Delta. Macau comprises the geographic extension of China's Guangzhou province and the islands of Taipa and Coldane. Macau is considerably smaller than Hong Kong as it is only 18 square kilometers (7 square miles) and is home to approximately 450,000 residents. With the advent of large ocean growing vessels Macau lost its role as a trading port some time ago and for the past 150 years has mainly survived on gambling, tourism, and activities generally associated with organized crime.

Like Hong Kong, Macau was declared a Special Administrative Region of China in 1999 after being a Portuguese possession since 1557. Throughout Macau's long colonial history China has played a far greater role in its affairs than it has in Hong Kong. China did not recognize Portuguese sovereignty until 1862. Since the communist-inspired riots of 1966 and 1967 Portuguese authority has been in decline while Chinese influence has steadily increased.

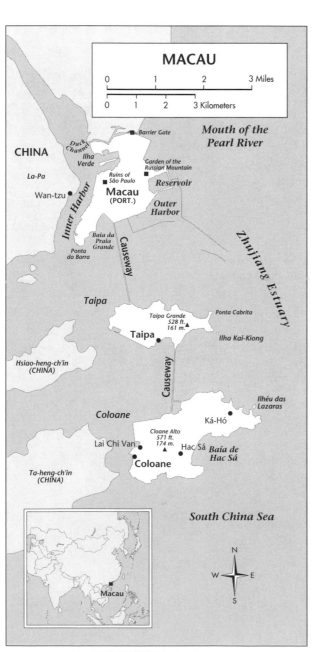

(MAP BY MARYLAND CARTOGRAPHICS/THE GALE GROUP)

On April 25, 1974, Portugal experienced a **coup** d'etat and the new government informed China that it wished to hand control of Macau back to China. Fearing that Chinese control would lead to the destabilization of Hong Kong, the Chinese government refused to discuss the issue. However, in 1979 Portugal and China came to a secret agreement that stated Macau was Chinese territory under temporary Portuguese administration. In 1987 China and Portugal signed an agreement in which sovereignty was officially transferred to China on December 20, 1999, and that Macau would become a Special Administrative Region with its own mini-constitution.

There are, however, some significant differences between the arrangements made for postcolonial Hong Kong and postcolonial Macau. Those who held Portuguese passports in 1999 were able to transfer Portuguese citizenship to their children and grandchildren while remaining residents of Macau. This was not the case in Hong Kong, where some people were left stateless in 1997. Although the desire for democratic governance is not as strong in Macau as it is in Hong Kong, China has allowed for partial democratization to occur in a number of stages.

coup: a quick seizure of power or a sudden attack

CAUSEWAY BAY ON HONG KONG ISLAND. In 1842 the British took control of Hong Kong from China as a result of the First Opium War. An agreement between the two countries in 1984, the Sino-British Joint Declaration (SBJD), returned Hong Kong to China but made it a Special Administrative Region (SAR) in 1997 that operates with economic independence until at least 2047. (SOURCE: RICHARD A. BROOKS/AFP/GETTY IMAGES)

In 2001 the number of democratically elected seats to Macau's *Assemblia Legislativa* (Legislative Assembly) rose from eight to ten out of twenty-seven members. In 2004 the number of democratically elected seats rose to twelve out of twenty-nine members. Macau's mini-constitution, also called the Basic Law, allows for the full democratization of the *Assemblia Legislativa* but does not stipulate a date. Like Hong Kong, Macau is, essentially, governed by a China-appointed CEO who selects seven of the members to the *Assemblia Legislativa*. The remaining members are appointed by local civic associations comprised of Macau's financial elite. In practice, the CEO, business groups, and Chinese officials get together and appoint all members that are not elected.

The low support for pro-democracy candidates suggests that the Macanese readily accept what is, in effect, indirect rule from Beijing and that this is unlikely to change in the near future. Edmund Ho (b. 1955), appointed Macau's CEO in 1999, has claimed that the main challenge facing Macau is the reduction of the strong influence exercised by organized crime on most aspects of public life. However, as the profits of gambling provide half the government's revenue and the role of the sex trade has only increased along with tourism since 1999, there is little likelihood that issues relating to human and civil rights will be given any prominence as organized crime and China's political interests seems destined to maintain a stranglehold.

See also: China (PRC).

BIBLIOGRAPHY

Callick, Rowan. *Comrades & Capitalists: Hong Kong Since the Handover*. Sydney, Australia: University of New South Wales University Press, 1998.

Cheng, J. Y. S. "Sino-British Negotiations and Problems of the British Administration." In *From Colony to SAR: Hong Kong's Challenge's Ahead*, ed. J. Y. S. Cheng and S. S. H. Lo. Hong Kong: The Chinese University of Hong Kong, 1995.

Ching, Frank. "Cleared for Action." *Far Eastern Economic Review* 155, no. 42 (October 22, 1992):20–21.

Dimbleby, Jonathan. *The Last Governor: Chris Patten and the Handover of Hong Kong*. London: Little, Brown, 1997.

Edmonds, R. "Macau and Greater China." In *Greater China: The Next Superpower?*, ed. David Shambaugh. Oxford, UK: Oxford University Press, 1995.

Guilen-Nunez, Cesar. *Macau*. New York, Oxford University Press, 1984.

Hopkins, Keith. "Public and Private Housing in Hong Kong." In *The City as a Centre of Change in Asia* (pp. 200–215), ed. D. J. Dwyer. Hong Kong: Hong Kong University Press, 1972.

Largue, David. "Democracy: The Heat is On." *Far Eastern Economic Review* 166, no. 29 (July 24, 2003):28–31.

Largue, David. "In the Eye of the Storm." *Far Eastern Economic Review* 166, no. 30 (July 31, 2003):24–25.

Roberti, Mark. *The Fall of Hong Kong: China's Triumph and Britain's Betrayal*. New York: Wiley, 1994.

Tsai, Jung-Fang. *Hong Kong in Chinese History: Community and Social Unrest in the British Colony*. New York: Columbia University Press, 1993.

Vatikiotis, Michael. "Talk of Compromise." *Far Eastern Economic Review* 167, no. 26 (July 1, 2004):28–29.

Ross Grainger

Human Rights

In the twentieth century the international community embraced human rights as a way to promote justice for individuals in communities around the world. As the standards were **promulgated**, scholars raised questions about the origins of the idea, the conceptual boundaries of such rights, methods of enforcement, and the potential impact of human rights in the future. Although international human rights norms are widely accepted, their interpretation and enforcement remain controversial. Sometimes governmental officials have manipulated the standards to avoid being held accountable, claiming that human rights are incompatible with their own political traditions. The fundamental dilemma for human rights is that states play a dual role: They are expected to uphold human rights standards, but at the same time they are usually the perpetrators of gross violations of human rights.

Although the idea of human rights usually is traced to the European Enlightenment (1600–1790), some analysts contend that historical antecedents exist. They frequently make mention of the Greek playwright Sophocles' (c. 496 B.C.E. –406 B.C.E.) *Antigone*, the play in which the heroine is in a predicament: Antigone is caught between the positive law—the king's decree forbidding the burial of traitors, including her brother who fought against the city—and the higher law requiring that one always give relatives a decent burial. Most often commentators in the Western tradition derive human rights norms from antiquity, the Bible, and the Enlightenment.

Jurists point to other bodies of public international law to show that precursors of human rights exist. Other branches of international law generated humanitarian principles that are considered historical antecedents to twentieth-century human rights standards. For instance, the notion that torturing prisoners of war is strictly prohibited is one such norm. Other ancient ideas that are part of the **customary law** of war support the general idea that individuals, even if they are enemies, should be treated with dignity.

International humanitarian law is not the only field containing norms that are related to modern human rights norms. The duty of states to safeguard the rights of aliens is another; states must ensure that no harm comes to aliens while they reside within a state's borders, that no unjustified **expropriation** of property occurs, and the like. It often also is claimed that the standards set by the International Labor Organization should be considered the first human rights instruments.

SOURCES OF HUMAN RIGHTS

As jurists have dominated the field of human rights, they have tended to define human rights by referring to written instruments. The International Bill of Rights consists of the Universal Declaration of Human Rights, the International Covenant on Civil and Political Rights, and the International Covenant on Civil and Political Rights. In addition to treaties, the other major source of human rights norms is customary international law, whose existence is demonstrated by state practice and *opinio juris*. State practice means that the behavior of states supports the norm, and *opinio juris* means that there is a sense of legal obligation on the part of the state not to **infringe** on the human right. Whereas treaties are binding only on states that choose to **ratify** them,

promulgation: an official declaration, especially that a law can start being enforced

"The fundamental dilemma for human rights is that states play a dual role: They are expected to uphold human rights standards, but at the same time they are usually the perpetrators of gross violations of human rights."

jurist: a person learned in legal matters; most often, a judge

customary law: a law created by the traditions of a community but never officially declared in force

expropriate: to take property from its owner and give it to another, especially oneself; usually accomplished through government decree or legal procedures

infringe: to exceed the limits of; to violate

ratify: to make official or to officially sanction

customary law is, by definition, binding on all states. Many of the most significant human rights conventions, such as the Convention Against Genocide, the Convention Against Torture, and the Convention on the Rights of the Child represent the **codification** of customary law. Hence, some human rights are said to be both conventional and customary.

Some human rights norms are deemed so important that they are *ius cogens*, or peremptory norms. This status usually is construed to mean that they are "non-derogable," that is, can never be suspended. Such norms include the rights against genocide, piracy, slavery, and torture. These most basic rights are conceived as "super norms," which are not subject to negotiation. As a *ius cogens* norm is **absolute** in character, it can be superseded only by another *ius cogens* norm (though no example of one that would trump another appears in the scholarship on this subject). No matter what sort of crisis a government might face, officials may not **derogate** from the obligation to respect human rights that have the status of being *ius cogens*.

THE QUESTION OF THE UNIVERSALITY OF HUMAN RIGHTS

Human rights scholars have grappled with the question of whether the legal standards promulgated by the United Nations (UN) reflect universal or Western (or Eurocentric) values. This debate is partly motivated by a desire to respond to the theory of cultural **relativism**, which holds that different societies have divergent value systems. The question is whether the existence of multiple moral codes poses a threat to the universality of international human rights standards. Ignoring the reality of diverse traditions, the vast majority of analysts have simply presumed the validity of universal human rights standards.

Some have taken a different approach. One scholar, Jack Donnelly (1982), conceded that human rights norms are derived from the European Enlightenment and contended that the concept of human rights simply is not found in Asian and African traditions. His response to the challenge of cultural relativism was to argue that the Western method of guaranteeing human dignity is the best, compared with approaches taken in other societies, and therefore should be adopted or imposed in other countries.

In contrast to Eurocentric interpretations of human rights, some scholars have advocated taking a comparative approach. One notable example is Raimundo Panikkar (1982), whose expertise in comparative religious ethics led him to use an innovative methodology. Rather than looking for the precise Western formulation of human rights in the English language, Panikkar searched for the homeomorphic equivalent to human rights in ethical systems across the globe to identify shared universal principles. Others scholars also have argued for conducting cross-cultural empirical research to find consensus that would support particular human rights standards. Although a comparative analysis of human rights might offer a way of identifying cross-cultural universals, little serious scholarship of this sort has been undertaken.

The debate about the universality of human rights has continued in other contexts. The question whether "Asian values" or Islamic law is incompatible with human rights represents a variation on this theme. Some scholars who come from non-Western countries contend that the human rights discourse should be challenged because of its colonial legacy or maintain that human rights advocates are missionaries attempting to impose their worldviews on others. Even if these scholars are correct in their supposition that human rights standards are associated with European political traditions, the discourse of human rights may prove to be useful to advocates around the world.

codification: the making of official law

absolute: complete, pure, free from restriction or limitation

derogate: to remove or deny, as a right; to disparage or belittle

relativism: a belief that ethical values are dependent on individuals or groups and are not common to all humanity

Scholarship on the role of human rights non-governmental organizations in **transnational** networks reveals that the international instruments empower local campaigns for human rights. Regardless of their origins, activists have found international human rights to be useful. Ultimately, the experience of activities attests to the capacity of human rights norms to empower **marginalized** groups despite their European origins.

NEW HUMAN RIGHTS

There is no question that new substantive human rights norms have appeared on the global horizon. After first-generation human rights (i.e., civil and political rights) were established, the debate over second-generation rights (i.e., economic, social, and cultural rights) began. Although there is said to be no implicit **hierarchy** among the two sets of human rights **enumerated**, many have inferred that first generation rights are more well accepted. Some Anglo-American scholars go so far as to deny that economic rights count as human rights mainly because it is unrealistic to expect states to provide for rights they cannot afford, and the assumption, perhaps unjustified, is that economic rights such as the right to shelter and the right to food are more costly than the right to freedom of speech or religion (negative rights).

Some have argued that the classifications are arbitrary because the determination of whether a right is political may hinge on whether it is found in a constitution. Furthermore, some rights, such as the right to form a trade union and the right of **self-determination**, are found on both lists.

Controversy also raged over whether third-generation rights, which include collective or group rights, are genuine human rights. The concern about such rights is that guaranteeing group rights may lead states to trample on individual rights. Another worry has been to avoid construing the right of self-determination in a way that supports a right of **secession** because international law has been understood as almost entirely opposed to an interpretation that would support changes in national boundaries.

In the 1990s women's rights were proclaimed as human rights. The impetus for this development was the World Conference on Women held in Beijing in 1995. It became clear that states should be held accountable for failing to protect women from human rights violations committed in private realms such as the family, religious institutions, and corporations. The main treaty for women, the Convention on the Elimination of All Forms of Discrimination Against Women, was found lacking because it did not specifically address violence against women, including forms of violence occurring in the private sphere. Although CEDAW was widely ratified, many states undercut its efficacy by attaching reservations, understandings, and declarations (RUDs) specifying that they would enforce the treaty only so far as was consistent with Islamic law.

Children's rights also were recognized in the 1990s, although Poland first proposed the idea of international legal protection for children's rights within the UN system in 1962. Following the usual pattern of drafting a **nonbinding declaration** followed by a treaty, the UN completed the Convention on the Rights of the Child in 1989. It quickly became one of the most widely ratified instruments. Despite this success, governments could not agree on the interpretation of childhood, and the definition of a child was not entirely resolved. A child is a person under the age of eighteen, but international law does not specify the point at which children's rights begin. It remains unclear whether the unborn child, or fetus, has human rights.

transnational: extending beyond the jurisdiction of one single nation

marginalize: to move to the outer borders, or to move one to a lower position

hierarchy: a group of people ranked according to some quality, for example, social standing

enumerate: to expressly name, as in a list

self-determination: the ability of a people to determine their own destiny or political system

secede: to break away from, especially politically

nonbinding declaration: a statement of a government or government body that has no legal standing or force of law

In 2005 a human rights treaty for persons with disabilities was in the process of being drafted. The campaign to create the Convention to Promote and Protect the Rights of Persons with Disabilities occurred because of a paradigm shift from the medical model—which treated disability as a condition inhering in the individual—to the sociopolitical model, which focuses on the failure of the state to make environmental adaptations to ensure the full participation of persons with disabilities in all aspects of social life. Accordingly, instead of having the World Health Organization control disability policy (e.g., the International Classification of Impairments, Disabilities, and Handicaps), disability came to be understood as a matter of human rights, and thus human rights institutions came into play. The new disability **jurisprudence** is reflected in the new treaty.

Some minority groups have launched campaigns for greater international protection. Gays and lesbians have succeeded in some major decisions (e.g., the *Toonen* decision of the Human Rights Committee and the *Dudgeon* decision of the European Court of Human Rights). The reasoning in these cases turned on the right of privacy rather than on equal protection. The next issue on the agenda for sexual minorities—that is, same-sex marriage—has raised the

jurisprudence: the body of precedents already decided in a legal system

IN LONDON, AMNESTY INTERNATIONAL PROTESTS AGAINST FORMER CHILEAN DICTATOR AUGUSTO PINOCHET ON DECEMBER 9, 1998. Since its formation in 1961, London-based Amnesty International (AI) has served as a nonpartisan, international protector of human rights with about one million members in over 160 countries. AI rallied against Chile's former dictator Augusto Pinochet following his arrest in London via a Spanish warrant. (SOURCE: © TOUHIG SION/CORBIS SYGMA)

question of whether same-sex couples are entitled to equal protection of the laws, a question that remains largely unresolved in most countries except Belgium, the Netherlands, and a few provinces in Canada, where same-sex marriage is legal. The debate about gay rights shows how various general norms, such as privacy, equality, and nondiscrimination, can be inadequate to the task of protecting members of some minority groups.

In 2005 some marginalized groups lacked their own treaties (e.g., gays and lesbians, religious minorities, and **indigenous** peoples). The social movements for new instruments have occurred with little coordination or realization of the tensions between treaties—for example, women's rights versus cultural rights. Additional rights, such as environmental human rights, the right to health, and cultural rights, also are being put forward. New human rights are always emerging.

ENFORCEMENT MECHANISMS

In addition to some of the innovations in standard setting, there are new institutional mechanisms to enforce human rights throughout the world. Within the international community there are two major sets of institutions: charter-based bodies and treaty-based mechanisms. The UN Charter mandated the creation of the Human Rights Commission, which drafted the Universal Declaration of Human Rights. The Commission, the Subcommission on the Protection and Promotion of Human Rights, and the High Commissioner for Human Rights are referred to as the Charter-based institutions. As for the second type, each human rights treaty has its own committee of experts whose responsibility it is to enforce human rights in that convention.

The regional bodies include the Inter-American Commission and Court, the European Court of Human Rights and its **appellate** mechanism, the African Commission and Court on Human and Peoples Rights, and the revived Arab League for Human Rights; as of 2005 no Asian system existed. Although the regional bodies may have the advantage of rendering decisions in accordance with the values of the countries over which they have **jurisdiction**, the existence of multiple systems involves the disadvantage of increasing the likelihood that there will be competing interpretations of human rights.

Domestic courts increasingly have used international human rights law in their decision making. To the extent that governments of the world see fit to rely on international law either as the basis for their decisions or as an interpretive guide to clarify the scope of legal principles in their national constitutions, the standards will be enforceable. The willingness of national courts to reject the ancient doctrine of sovereign immunity so that it no longer will be a barrier to litigation bodes well for future attempts to hold leaders accountable. For example, when former Chilean dictator Augusto Pinochet (b. 1915) traveled to the United Kingdom in 1998 for medical treatment, he was arrested under a Spanish warrant to stand trial for human rights abuses.

The establishment of the International Criminal Court (ICC) is another significant development. The tribunal has the potential to enforce both human rights standards and humanitarian law. This institution provides a reason to be optimistic about the possibility not only of punishing officials who commit gross violations of human rights but also of deterring future misconduct. However, the reluctance of the U.S. government to join the ICC by ratifying the Rome Statute threatens to undermine the efficacy of this promising enforcement mechanism.

The trend toward using truth commissions to document state practice of human rights violations accompanied by **impunity** for leaders has raised

indigene: a person who has his origin in a specific region

appellate: a court having jurisdiction to review the findings of lower courts

jurisdiction: the territory or area within which authority may be exercised

impunity: an exemption from punishment

restitution: the transfer of an item back to an original owner, or, compensation for that item

questions about the possibility of holding leaders accountable. The phenomenon of state apologies for human rights violations, which usually substitute for **restitution**, is another development that some consider troubling. Although there is no reason why truth commissions and apologies should be used in lieu of punishment and restitution, this has been the practice in most countries. International scrutiny of governmental action may call into question the validity of both truth commissions and state apologies in their current forms.

The future of human rights depends not on legal instruments or institutional mechanisms but ultimately on the willingness of states to adhere to human rights standards themselves and to hold others accountable as well. Social movements play a crucial role in motivating governments to take human rights standards seriously by mobilizing shame and demonstrating widespread support for the values on which human rights are based.

See also: Children's Rights; Convention for the Elimination of All Forms of Discrimination Against Women; Economic, Social, and Cultural Rights; International Criminal Court; International Human Rights Law; International Humanitarian Law; Universal Declaration of Human Rights; Women's Rights.

BIBLIOGRAPHY

An-Na'im, Abdullahi A. "Toward a Cross-Cultural Approach to Defining International Standards of Human Rights: The Meaning of Cruel, Inhuman, or Degrading Treatment or Punishment." In *Human Rights in Cross-Cultural Perspectives: A Quest for Consensus*, ed. Abdullahi A. An-Na'im. Philadelphia: University of Pennsylvania Press, 1992.

Brooks, Roy L. *When Sorry Isn't Enough: The Controversy over Apologies and Reparations for Human Injustice*. New York: New York University Press, 1999.

Degener, Theresia. "Disabled Persons and Human Rights: The Legal Framework." In *Human Rights and Disabled Persons*, ed. Theresia Degener and Yolan Koster-Dreese. Dordrecht, The Netherlands: Martinus Nijhoff, 1995.

Donnelly, Jack. "Human Rights and Human Dignity: An Analytic Critique of Non-Western Conceptions of Human Rights." *American Political Science Review* 76 (1982):303–316.

Dudgeon v. United Kingdom. European Court of Human Rights, Series A, No. 45. September 23, 1981.

Hahn, Harlan. "The Political Implications of Disability Definitions and Data." In *The Psychological and Social Impact of Disability*, ed. Robert Marinelli and Arthur E. Dell Orto. New York: Springer, 1999.

Hersch, Jeanne. *The Birthrite of Man*. Paris: UNESCO, 1969.

Jayawickrama, Nihal. *The Judicial Application of Human Rights Law: National, Regional and International Jurisprudence*. Cambridge, UK: Cambridge University Press, 2002.

Keck, Margaret, and Kathryn Sikkink. *Activists Beyond Borders: Advocacy Networks in International Politics*. Ithaca, NY: Cornell University Press, 1998.

Laurent, Paul Gordon. *The Evolution of International Human Rights: Visions Seen*, 2nd ed. Philadelphia: University of Pennsylvania Press, 2003.

Lawrance, Benjamin N. "Refreshing Historical Accounts of Human Rights in Africa." *Oriental Anthropologist* 4 (2004):34–59.

Mutua, Makau. *Human Rights: A Political and Cultural Critique*. Philadelphia: University of Pennsylvania Press, 2002.

Panikkar, Raimundo. "Is the Notion of Human Rights a Western Concept?" *Diogenes* 120 (1982):75–102.

Rajagopal, Balakrishnan. *International Law from Below: Development, Social Movements, and Third World Resistance.* Cambridge, UK: Cambridge University Press, 2003.

Renteln, Alison Dundes. *International Human Rights: Universalism Versus Relativism.* Thousand Oaks, CA: Sage Publications, 1990.

Riles, Anneliese. *The Network Inside Out.* Ann Arbor: University of Michigan Press, 2000.

Toonen v. Australia. UN Human Rights Committee, Communication No. 488/1992 (adopted March 31, 1994).

Alison Dundes Renteln

Hungary

Hungary is a landlocked country located in East-Central Europe bordered by Austria on the west, Slovakia on the north, Ukraine on the northeast, Romania on the east, and Serbia and Montenegro, Croatia, and Slovenia on the south. Hungary's total land area is 57,809 square miles. The capital of Hungary is Budapest, which is the largest city in the country with a population of about 2 million people.

In 2003, the total population of Hungary was estimated at approximately 10.1 million. Hungary is predominantly **homogeneous**: Approximately 90 percent of the population are Hungarian. The remaining 10 percent are Romani (gypsies), German, Serb, Slovak, Romanian, Armenian, and other ethnicities. About 67.5 percent of Hungarians are Roman Catholic, 20 percent Calvinist, 5 percent Lutheran, and 7.5 percent other faiths.

homogeneous: simple; consisting of components that are identical or similar

BRIEF HISTORY

The Hungarian Kingdom was first established under Szent István (977–1038; Stephen I) in c.e. 1000. In 1541 Ottoman Turks occupied parts of the Hungarian Kingdom, but the Turks were expelled in 1686 and Hungary came under the domination of the Habsburg Empire. In 1867 a dual monarchy of Austria and Hungary was established, replacing the Habsburg Empire with the Austro-Hungarian Empire. From 1867 to 1920 Hungary remained part of that empire. In the wake of the Austro-Hungarian Empire's defeat in World War I, Hungary lost two-thirds of its population and territory. In the aftermath of World War II (post-1945), Hungary, along with other Central and Eastern European nations, came under the domination of a **communist** regime supported by the Soviet Union. The official name of the country became the Hungarian People's Republic. In 1955 Hungary joined the Warsaw Treaty Organization and became a member of the United Nations (UN).

communism: an economic and social system characterized by the absence of class structure and by common ownership of the means of production and subsistence

After the death of Soviet leader Joseph Stalin in 1953, the new leadership in Moscow undertook the so-called New Course—mandating a more flexible policy in Central and Eastern Europe. Perhaps in response to this policy, an anti-communist revolution arose in Budapest on October 23, 1956, and Hungarian Prime Minister Imre Nagy (1896–1958) officially withdrew Hungary from the Warsaw Treaty, abolished the one-party system, and formed a new **coalition** government, which lasted for two weeks only. János Kádár (1912–1989) immediately formed a counter-government and sought the USSR's military support.

coalition: an alliance, partnership, or union of disparate peoples or individuals

The revolution was viciously suppressed by Soviet forces. Kádár became the prime minister of Hungary in 1956 as well as the leader of the Hungarian Socialist Workers Party (HSWP). Hungary remained a one-party state, dominated by the Communist Party, until 1989, when the Party was dissolved and a multiparty political system with free elections was established as communist control over Central and Eastern Europe disintegrated.

MAJOR POLITICAL LEADERS SINCE 1945

Mátyás Rákosi (1892–1971) was Hungary's most powerful official from 1947 to 1956. Rákosi held the positions of the first secretary and premier, and reorganized the economy according to the Soviet model. As a Stalinist, Rákosi was removed from the post of premier in 1953, but until 1956 he retained the position of the first general-secretary—the most influential position under the communist regime. In 1956 Rákosi was forced to resign; he soon fled to the Soviet Union.

Imre Nagy became Rákosi's successor in 1953. He served as prime minister from 1953 to 1955, until the HSWP forced him to resign in 1955. Nagy was critical of the Soviet brand of communism. In the Hungarian revolution of October 1956 he once again assumed the position of prime minister, but only for a few days. He was subsequently executed in 1958 for his role in promoting the abortive uprising. In 1989, after the fall of the communist regime, Nagy's reputation was officially rehabilitated; he was reburied with full state honors.

In 1956 János Kádár, a cabinet member under Nagy, formed a countergovernment with Soviet support and, after crushing the Hungarian revolution, became prime minister. Kádár resigned as prime minister in 1958, but he reassumed the post from 1961 to 1965. He was a consistent supporter of Soviet foreign policy. However, Kádár's social and economic policies were relatively liberal. In 1968 Kádár implemented a reform program known as the New

(MAP BY MARYLAND CARTOGRAPHICS/THE GALE GROUP)

Economic Mechanism, which allowed for flexible management strategies and a policy of **decentralization**. He served as general-secretary until May 1988.

Miklós Németh (b.1948), a young economist, served as prime minister of Hungary from November 1988 to May 1990, when Hungarian political officials were evenly split: the communists on one hand and reformers on the other.

In 1990 the first free multiparty parliamentary elections in forty-three years were held. They resulted in the formation of a coalition government led by museum director József Antall (1932–1993), the president of the Hungarian Democratic Forum. Antall died in December 1993, and Peter Boross (b. 1928) headed the government until the next election in July 1994.

Gyula Horn (b. 1932), a socialist, held the position of prime minister from 1994 to 1998. Horn formed a coalition with the Alliance of Free Democrats in order to dispel foreign concerns about ex-communists returning to power.

In 1998 Victor Orbán (b. 1963) succeeded Horn. Orbán came to be known as an advocate of minority rights for ethnic Hungarians living abroad. In 2002 Peter Medgyessy (b. 1942) was elected prime minister; not a Communist Party member, he had been nominated as a candidate by the Hungarian Socialist Party. Medgyessy held different positions in the Ministry of Finance between 1966 and 1987. The tax system he initiated was essential in Hungary's move toward a **free market economy**.

SOCIOECONOMIC CONDITIONS

Hungary introduced some elements of market-based reforms before the collapse of the communist regime. Since communism's decline, Hungary has made a relatively smooth transition from a centrally planned to market economy, demonstrating strong economic growth. Inflation declined from 14 percent in 1998 to 4.7 percent in 2003. Hungary's **per capita** income in 2003 was estimated at $13,900. The private sector represents over 80 percent of the gross domestic product (GDP). In 2002 17 percent of the total population lived below the national poverty line, the unemployment rate was 5.8 percent, and infant mortality was eight per 1,000 live births.

NATURE OF GOVERNMENT

Hungary's government could be described as a parliamentary democracy. According to its constitution, the country is an independent, democratic state existing under the **rule of law**. The constitution declares that civil and human rights must be protected; a multiparty parliamentary system maintained; and executive, legislative, and judicial functions separated. Hungary became a full member of the North Atlantic Treaty Organization (NATO) in March 1999 and the European Union (EU) on May 1, 2004.

Hungary operates under a constitution that was adopted in 1949, but was dramatically amended in 1972, 1989, and 1997. The constitution underwent especially significant amendments in 1989, when the role of the Communist Party disintegrated. The 1989 amendments provided new legal rights for individuals and constitutional checks on the authority of the prime minister. The amendments also established the principle of parliamentary oversight. The 1997 amendments were intended to streamline the judicial system.

The transition to a capitalist economic system occurred via the groundwork that had been established in a series of steps toward **economic liberalization** in the years preceding 1989. The reform policies of Soviet leader Mikhail

decentralize: to move power from a central authority to multiple periphery government branches or agencies

free market economy: an economy with no or very little government regulation and ownership

per capita: for each person, especially for each person living in an area or country

rule of law: the principle that the law is a final grounds of decision-making and applies equally to all people; law and order

economic liberalization: the reduction or elimination of trade barriers and government regulations in an economy

■ ■ ■

THE HUNGARIAN CONSTITUTIONAL COURT

The Hungarian Constitutional Court, established in 1989, is a creation of the post-Communist phase of Hungary's transition to democracy. In the first nine years of the Court's existence it had the responsibility of creating a body of constitutional law within a very short time frame compared to other European countries. The Hungarian judges relied to some extent on the example of the German Constitutional Court but were careful to adapt its principles to their own country's situation.

The Hungarian Constitutional Court relies on a centralized model of judicial review. It has used the powers given to it to cooperate with the legislature and make some far-reaching decisions limiting the authority of the president of Hungary, maintaining judicial independence, and protecting freedom of speech and privacy. Other noteworthy rulings have concerned the death penalty, abortion, and economic reforms.

The Hungarian Constitutional Court sits in Budapest and is composed of eleven judges elected by Parliament for nine-year terms. The judges in turn elect a president and vice president to represent them for three-year terms. The judges may be re-elected to a second nine-year term but must retire at age seventy. The Court underwent a rapid and nearly complete turnover of judges in the three years between 1996 and 1999; its first female member was elected in June 1999.

---

unicameral: comprised of one chamber, usually a legislative body

---

Gorbachev (b. 1932)—*glasnost* (openness) and *perestroika* (restructuring)—became the trigger for the collapse of the communist regime in Soviet-bloc countries, including Hungary. Hungary took important steps toward creating a democracy in 1989. It initiated political and economic reforms, including the introduction of a capitalist market economy and the emergence of a multiparty system. In October 1989 the Hungarian People's Republic came to an official end, and under the new amendments to the constitution that same year, the country was renamed the Republic of Hungary.

Compared to what occurred in other post-communist countries, the transition from communist regime to democracy was relatively smooth and speedy in Hungary. Hungary is considered to have one of the most solid democratic systems among the rest of the post-communist states.

POLITICAL LIFE

The executive branch is composed of a president, prime minister, and cabinet. Before 1989 Hungary had a 21-member Presidential Council, instead of a president. The Presidential Council maintained combined legislative and executive powers, and the constitution described it as subordinate to the National Assembly and superordinate to the Council of Ministers. In 1989, however, the Presidential Council was replaced by an indirectly elected state president. The National Assembly elects this individual for a five-year term; he or she serves as commander in chief of the armed forces. The president's role as commander in chief is mainly ceremonial. Both the prime minister and cabinet members are approved by the National Assembly based on the president's recommendations. The prime minister usually is the leader of the most influential party of the winning coalition in parliament.

According to the Hungarian constitution, the president and Constitutional Court are intended to provide a system of checks and balances against the parliament and government. The work between the government and National Assembly can be described as open and transparent.

The post of prime minister in Hungary is quite powerful. The constitution extends considerable authority to the government and prime minister. The prime minister has the right to dismiss ministers at his or her own discretion. Only he or she has responsibility before parliament for the entire government. The prime minister can only be ousted through the electoral process. A no-confidence proceeding and vote may only be launched against the prime minister on the written proposal of at least one-fifth of the members of parliament. A no-confidence motion against the prime minister is regarded as a no-confidence action against the government.

Hungary's legislative branch consists of a **unicameral** National Assembly called the *Országgyülés*. The National Assembly has 386 members who are elected through two rounds of popular vote under the system of proportional and direct representation to serve four-year terms. Only four political parties have been represented in the recent National Assembly, as political parties must have 5 percent or more of the vote to win parliamentary representation.

The judicial system is composed of local courts, county courts, the Supreme Court, and the Constitutional Court. The Supreme Court has ultimate control over the operation of all other courts. The Constitutional Court was established in 1989; it has eleven members who are elected by the National Assembly for nine-year terms. The president appoints these justices for three-year terms. Judges may be reappointed for an indefinite period based on their performance. They cannot be affiliated with political parties, however, and are not permitted to engage in any type of political activity. The Constitutional Court in Hungary has wide powers including a power of checks and balances against the parliament and government.

CITIZEN PARTICIPATION, RIGHTS AND LIBERTIES

In Hungary approximately 200 officially registered political parties exist. However, only a limited number of political parties are viable. In the 1994 elections eight parties successfully won representation in the National Assembly, in 1998 six, and in 2002 four. The main political parties represented in the 2004 National Assembly were the Hungarian Socialist Party (with 46% of the vote), Hungarian Civic Union (42%), Hungarian Democratic Forum (6%), and Alliance of Free Democrats (5%). The last three political parties were founded from 1988 to 1990, whereas the Hungarian Socialist Party dates back to June 1948, when the Communist and Social Democratic Parties merged and came to be known as the Hungarian Workers Party. In 1956 this same party was reorganized as the Hungarian Socialist Workers Party (HSWP). In October 1989 the HSWP publicly renounced Marxism and adopted the name of the Hungarian Socialist Party. The Hungarian Socialist Party and Alliance of Free Democrats represent the left-wing coalition of the National Assembly, whereas the Hungarian Civic Union and Hungarian Democratic Forum represent the right-wing coalition.

Interest groups and non-governmental organizations (NGOs) came into existence in the mid-1980s. The total number of NGOs is well over 50,000, and upwards of 10 percent of the population are registered members of NGOs. Hungarian law permits interest groups to have any form of participation in politics. However, there are specific provisions that disqualify judges, members of the National Assembly, armed forces personnel, and civil servants from engaging in an interest group's activities. A large number of trade unions also exist. The most politically active trade unions are represented in the Interest Reconciliation Council (IRC), a formal forum where government officials discuss conflicts between employers and employees. Professional associations such as teachers' and doctors' groups are also active in lobbying for social and economic improvements.

Everyone over eighteen years of age has the right to vote. Since 1989 and the collapse of the communist regime, four rounds of national and local elections have taken place at four-year intervals. The first multiparty national legislative elections were held in March 1990, and in June 1990 the National Assembly elected Arpad Goncz (b. 1922) as president for a five-year term. Voter turnout in Hungary was particularly high in the 1990 legislative elections—over 75 percent of eligible voters cast ballots. However, voter turnout decreased to 69 percent in the 1994 legislative elections and 59 percent in the 1998 legislative elections. In 2002 voter turnout was again exceptionally high, reaching 73 percent.

The Hungarian constitution provides for the right to life and human dignity; the privacy and protection of personal data; liberty and personal security; freedom of thought, conscience, and religion; free expression of opinion; and peaceful assembly. The document further bans torture; inhuman, cruel, or humiliating treatment or punishment; and discrimination on the grounds of race, color, sex, language, religion, political orientation or another opinion. The Constitutional Court has also banned the death penalty.

In 2003 Freedom House rated Hungary as a free nation, giving it the best possible score of 1 on political rights and the next best score of 2 on civil rights and liberties. These assessments indicate that the promises of rights and liberties contained in Hungary's constitution are well-protected.

See also: European Union; Stalin, Joseph.

BIBLIOGRAPHY

Banks, Arthur S., ed. *Political Handbook of the World, 2000–2002.* Washington, DC: CQ Press, 2004.

Freedom House. "Hungary." *Freedom in the World 2003: The Annual Survey of Political Rights and Civil Liberties.* New York: Freedom House, 2004. <http://www.freedom-house.org/research/freeworld/2003/countryratings/hungary.htm>.

"Hungary." In *CIA World Factbook.* Washington, DC: Central Intelligence Agency, 2005. <http://www.cia.gov/cia/publications/factbook/geos/hu.html>.

Karatnycky, Adrian, et al., eds. *Nations in Transit 2003: Democratization in East Central Europe and Eurasia.* New York: Rowman & Littlefield, 2003.

Körössényi, Andrá. *Government and Politics in Hungary.* Budapest: Central European University Press, 1999.

Olson, David, and Philip Norton. *The New Parliaments of Central and Eastern Europe.* London: Frank Cass, 1996.

Lucy Dadayan

Iceland

Located in the middle of the northern Atlantic Ocean, Iceland is the second largest island in Europe. The shortest distance to Greenland is 278 kilometers (172.7 miles), to Scotland 708 kilometers (440 miles) and to Norway 970 kilometers (602.7 miles). Icelanders are descendents of the Norse and the Celts, and most Icelanders belong to the Evangelical Lutheran Church. Iceland's population in 2005 was nearly 300,000, a number that has more than tripled in the past century. The majority lives in the southwestern region, in and around the capital of Reykjavik.

Urbanization was very rapid in the twentieth century and was associated with a move from farming into industry, construction, commerce, and services. The transformation of Icelandic society almost perfectly traces the aftermath of the European industrial revolution, only at a higher speed. After centuries of almost total isolation, Iceland increasingly came into contact with both European and North American countries. The present process of **globalization** thus constitutes an even more radical departure for Iceland than for other Western countries. In the early twenty-first century Iceland ranked among those nations of the world that enjoy the highest standard of living, even though less than one-fifth of its land surface is arable. Equal access to education and health care services have for a long time been key elements in the social policy of Iceland. With nearly 100 percent literacy, the Icelandic people are highly educated. Iceland possesses a relatively equalitarian and cohesive social structure, partly because unlike most other European nations, Iceland has never had a national monarchy or **aristocracy**.

HISTORY

Iceland was founded in the ninth century by Nordic seafarers. In C.E. 930 a legal code for Iceland was accepted and the Icelandic parliamentary body, the *Althingi*, was established. The code of law and the procedure were derived from a body of Norwegian law adapted to meet Icelandic conditions. It was not put down in writing. The **rule of law** was of great significance from the earliest Icelandic history. From 930 to 1264 much of the law was recited during the

globalization: the process of expanding regional concerns to a worldwide viewpoint, especially politics, economics, or culture

aristocracy: a ruling financial, social, or political elite

rule of law: the principle that the law is a final grounds of decision-making and applies equally to all people; law and order

meeting of *Althingi* and some contend that it was not until later that written law took precedence over oral law.

In 1262 Icelanders established a union with Norway. In 1380, when the Danish and Norwegian monarchies united, Iceland followed suit and became part of the combined kingdom. The king obligated himself to preserve peace and to allow Iceland to have its own laws and maintain the *Althingi* until 1662, when Iceland gave formal approval for the **absolute** powers of the Danish king.

Icelanders were inspired by the ideas of **nationalism** and **liberalism** emerging from Europe during the nineteenth century. As a result, they formed a campaign to gain independence from Denmark. Proclamation of a constitution in 1874 marked an important step when the parliament regained legislative power. In 1904, home rule was developed in the form of an Icelandic minister of local affairs in Iceland who was answerable to the *Althingi*. In 1918 Iceland became an independent kingdom in loose union with Denmark, with the understanding that either party could leave after 25 years. From that point, Denmark abstained from further interference in Iceland's internal affairs. During World War II (1939–1945) the final step toward autonomy was reached when Iceland declared its full independence from Denmark with the establishment of the Icelandic Republic on June 17, 1944.

Iceland's independence was gained by completely peaceful, non-violent means. Moreover, Iceland has never had a standing army, and controls on handgun ownership have been extensive.

STRUCTURE OF GOVERNMENT

Iceland has a written constitution formally dated from the establishment of the republic in 1944. The opening article states that Iceland is a republic with a parliamentary government. The second article states that legislative authority

absolute: complete, pure, free from restriction or limitation

nationalism: the belief that one's nation or culture is superior to all others

liberalism: a political philosophy advocating individual rights, positive government action, and social justice, or, an economic philosophy advocating individual freedoms and free markets

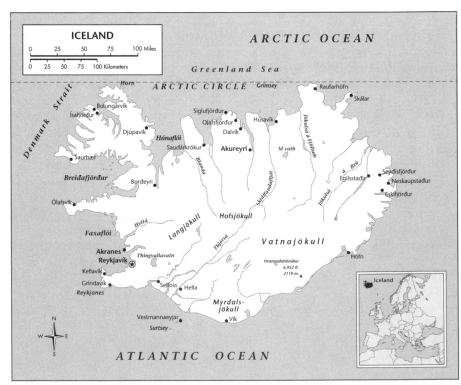

(MAP BY MARYLAND CARTOGRAPHICS/THE GALE GROUP)

is vested jointly in the *Althingi* and the president, executive authority in the president, and other governmental authorities in accordance with the constitution and other laws of the land, and judicial authority in the courts. The government consists of twelve cabinet ministers, among whom all significant matters are discussed. The cabinet at any time must be supported by the majority of the members of the *Althingi*, or, at a minimum, that a majority must be ready to tolerate the cabinet in power and defend it against a motion of no-confidence. All governments in Iceland have been **coalition** governments because none of the political parties has been able to gain a clear majority of the parliament. Two-party coalitions are usually the most stable type of government, whereas larger ones—usually three-party coalitions—have had a far shorter life expectancy.

The *Althingi* debates draft legislation and approves it when appropriate. The budget is also approved by the *Althingi*, resulting in a great impact on the executive sector. Among other tasks allotted to the *Althingi* are appointments by election to a considerable number of posts, usually to membership of boards and committees, and certain duties connected with the auditing of state finances. The *Althingi* does not need to produce legislation in order to declare its position on a certain issue. It can instead adopt a parliamentary resolution. At the request of the *Althingi* or by their own choice, the cabinet ministers are entitled to report on official issues.

coalition: an alliance, partnership, or union of disparate peoples or individuals

POLITICAL LIFE AND CITIZEN PARTICIPATION

The general public elects the *Althingi*, and parliament members face election every four years. The voter can only vote for a list of candidates offered by political parties. Elections take place on a Saturday by secret ballot. With many polling places in each constituency, is easy for the voters to get to the polls. Registration is automatic, and **suffrage** is universal for adults 18 years and older. Absentee ballots can be cast in the eight-week period preceding election day. Turnout in *Althingi* elections has been stable, around 90 percent in the late twentieth century.

suffrage: to vote, or, the right to vote

The Icelandic party system has mostly been characterized by a right wing party, (the Independence Party) a united center, (dominated by the provincial Progressive Party), and two left-wing parties, (the Social Democratic Alliance and the Left Green Party). A fifth political party (the Liberal Party) also had a seating in the *Althingi* in the early twenty-first century. The size of the Independence Party has made it strong in the coalition game and almost always the only political party capable of forming two-party coalitions. The Progressives, nonetheless, have made skillful use of their **ideological** center position and remain an effective competitor with the Independence Party for government leadership. The government in 2005 was made up of the Independence Party and the Progressive Party. Formed in 1995, this coalition, led by Prime Minister Halldor Asgrimsson (b. 1947) representing the Progressives, was in its third term in 2005.

ideology: a system of beliefs composed of ideas or values, from which political, social, or economic programs are often derived

Due to Iceland's small population, the inhabitants and the democratically elected members of parliament share a closer relationship than most other countries in Europe. Popular vote determines the elected president, who is then in office for a term of four years. New presidential candidates experience fierce competition, but a president seeking re-election, so far, has only been defeated twice.

The first president, Sveinn Björnsson (1881–1952), was elected by the *Althingi* in 1944. In 1945 and 1949, Björnsson was the only candidate for nationwide direct election, so no actual election was held. In 1952 *Althingi* member Asgeir Asgeirsson (1894–1972), was elected president. In 1968 the director of the National Museum, Kristjan Eldjarn (1916–1982), was elected, and in 1980 the director of the Reykjavik Theater, Vigdis Finnbogadottir (b. 1930), became the first popularly elected female

FAST FACTS

The Icelandic people are highly educated, with a nearly 100% literacy rate.

head of state in the world. President Olafur Ragnar Grimsson (b. 1943), an *Althingi* member and former university professor of political sciences, was first elected in 1996 and began his third term in 2004. If there are multiple candidates, the president only needs to receive the most votes, not a majority of the votes cast.

Because there is no vice president, a committee consisting of the prime minister, the speaker of the *Althingi*, and the president of the Supreme Court will take on presidential functions if necessary. The president must agree to all legislation passed by the *Althingi* before it becomes a law. Although the constitution prescribes supreme executive power to the president, it is the cabinet ministers who enact that power.

System of Local Government. Towns and rural districts constitute basic local administrative units in Iceland. The main principle of local government is autonomy. In each locality there is a town or district council, elected by general suffrage. The local council manages affairs of the locality according to what is further provided for by law. The main local government revenue sources are twofold: direct local personal income taxation, and grants from the central government.

ICELAND'S HOUSE OF PARLIAMENT BUILDING IN REYKJAVIK. Dating back to 930, Iceland's 63-member *Althingi* is the world's oldest parliament and has convened at the House of Parliament building in the capital of Reykjavik since its construction in 1881 by architect Ferdinand Meldahl (1827–1908). (SOURCE: © MACDUFF EVERTON/CORBIS)

The local council is elected, in a general secret ballot, for a term of four years. Locality councils make their decisions at meetings that are open to the public.

ROLE OF LEGISLATORS AND THE JUDICIARY SYSTEM

The 1944 constitution traces its roots to the Danish constitution of 1849 and clearly demonstrates that the Icelandic government is democratic. The government is based upon the principle of representative democracy, that power originates with the people, who delegate this power to their elected representatives.

Founded in 1919, the Supreme Court of Iceland held its first session in 1920. The court holds the highest judicial authority in Iceland with jurisdiction over the whole country. After being nominated by the minister of justice, the judges are appointed by the president of Iceland. They have to be Icelandic citizens of at least 35 years of age with no prior criminal record. Separated into two divisions, three or five Supreme Court judges reside over court to hear a case; there are nine justices total. The president of the court, appointed by the other justices for a two-year period, manages the affairs of the court, directs court sessions and divides tasks among the justices. For especially important cases, the president of the court may choose to have seven justices preside over a case.

Appointed for life, Supreme Court judges cannot be removed from office without court judgment, although it is possible to be released from office at the age of 65. Iceland's court procedures stem largely from Scandinavian and Germanic principles.

A provision calling for separation of three governmental powers: the legislative apparatus, the executive, and the judicial, is one of the basic principles of the constitution. However, this legal separation was not put into action outside the capital until 1991. In that year, the whole judiciary in Iceland underwent fundamental reforms, mainly aimed at a complete separation between executive and judicial powers. Under this legislation the regular courts consist of eight district courts formed based on the electoral areas. These courts have power over both civil and criminal matters. The nature of the prosecution itself changed. Under the new law local magistrates, in cases where penalties handed out do not exceed a fine, the confiscation of property, or short term confinement during an initial investigation, are able to hand down indictments. The decentralization of Iceland's government powers has been enacted.

GOVERNMENT AND FOREIGN RELATIONS

After Iceland became a republic in 1944, the main objectives of the foreign policy have been to safeguard independence and to reinforce Iceland's control over its natural resources, including marine resources. The exercise of national sovereignty was believed by many Icelanders to be identical to neutrality in foreign relations. After 1945 a neutral position was no longer believed feasible for major armed conflicts in Europe, and Icelandic leaders sought to foster close cooperation with other Western nations.

In 1946, Iceland joined the United Nations and, in 1951, the Council of Europe. Iceland strengthened its relationship with the European Union in 1994 through an agreement with the Western European Union in which its exports to European markets were granted virtually tariff-free access. This agreement also caused Iceland to use European Union trade and commercial legislation.

jurisdiction: the territory or area within which authority may be exercised

FAST FACTS

In Iceland, police officers and prison guards do not carry guns.

magistrate: an official with authority over a government, usually a judicial official with limited jurisdiction over criminal cases

decentralize: to move power from a central authority to multiple periphery government branches or agencies

sovereignty: autonomy; or, rule over a political entity

neutrality: the quality of not taking sides, as in a conflict

The decision by Iceland to join the North Atlantic Treaty Organization (NATO) as a founding member in 1949 provided further confirmation of Iceland's movement toward direct involvement in European security affairs. Iceland granted the United States permission to base a group of armed forces in its territory, allowing them to use Keflavik airport. The base was originally met with some resistance, as it was felt that the presence of foreign troops undermined Iceland's independence. With increasing globalization during the late twentieth century, objections to the NATO base diminished.

See also: Denmark; European Union; Norway; Parliamentary Systems.

BIBLIOGRAPHY

Althingi. The Icelandic Parliament. <http://www.althingi.is/vefur/upplens.html>.

Gunnlaugsson, Helgi, and John F. Galliher. *Wayward Icelanders: Punishment, Boundary Maintenance and the Creation of Crime*. Madison: The University of Wisconsin Press, 2000.

Gunnlaugsson, Helgi. "Iceland." In *Legal Systems of the World: A Political, Social, and Cultural Encyclopedia*, Herbert M. Kritzer, ed. Santa Barbara, CA: ABC-CLIO, 2002.

Hardarson, Ólafur Th. "Iceland." In *World Encyclopedia of Political Systems and Parties*, George E. Delury ed., third edition, Deborah A. Kaple, ed. New York: Facts On File, 1999.

Nordal, Johannes and Valdimar Kristinsson, eds. *Iceland: The Republic*. Reykjavik: The Central Bank of Iceland, 1996.

Helgi Gunnlaugsson

Immigration and Immigrants

emigration: the migration of individuals out of a geographic area or country

Immigrants are individuals who leave their country of origin to settle in another state. For the receiving state, this process is known as immigration, and for the sending state this phenomenon is **emigration**. For much of history, there were no restrictions on immigration. Thus, millions of Western European people migrated to the New World—now known as North and South America—as well as to areas of Africa and the South Pacific.

Unlike almost all other countries, the United States, Canada, and Australia continue to consider themselves to be "immigrant states," and to a large extent the data bear this out. From 1820 until the mid-1990s, over 60 million immigrants arrived on America's shores. In the decade of the 1990s, more than 10 million immigrants came to the United States. The immigration influence in Canada can be seen in the fact that immigrants presently make up more than 16 percent of the population. And, with the exception of Israel, Australia has the highest proportion of the population born in other nations.

Yet, there has been a dark, racist side to this immigration story. In the United States, ethnic restrictions were first directed against Chinese immigrants in the 1880s and Japanese immigrants after 1907. In the 1920s, the United States took aim at all of those who were not from Northwestern Europe by instituting the National Origins Quota System, which severely limited immigration from all other areas of the globe. It was not until the mid-1960s that the nativist and racist premise behind U.S. immigration policy was removed. This brought about an enormous change in U.S. immigration policy, and by the early 2000s Asians had become the largest segment of U.S. immigration (37.3%) whereas Northwestern Europeans constituted only 5.2 percent (and falling).

Australia followed a "white Australia" immigration policy until 1964. However, by the end of the twentieth century, a large and growing proportion of the immigrant population were coming from Asia as well as from non-English-speaking countries in Europe and the Middle East. Finally, although Canada's 1923 Immigration Act barred Chinese and most other Asians from immigrating (this was removed in 1962), Asians presently make up more than half (53%) of the immigrant population.

WHAT DO ALIENS LOOK LIKE TODAY?

Notwithstanding the language in Emma Lazarus's famous poem at the base of the Statue of Liberty—"Give me your tired, your poor, your huddled masses yearning to breathe free"—the vast majority of immigrants (at least legal immigrants) are not the "wretched refuse" referred to by Lazarus. Rather, immigrants often look much like the native population in terms of age, education, and professional status. This is true not only for those who are admitted on the basis of possessing certain kinds of job skills but also to a certain extent for those who are immigrating for family reunification purposes as well. For example, the median age of the foreign born population who entered the United States between 1980 and 1990 was 28.0 years, whereas the native-born population was 32.5 years. Although 37 percent of the immigrant population did not finish high school before coming to the United States, 26 percent of both native and immigrant populations held at least a bachelor's degree, although immigrants are twice as likely to hold a doctorate as native-born Americans.

> ". . . the vast majority of immigrants (at least legal immigrants) are not the 'wretched refuse' referred to by [Emma] Lazarus."

NATURALIZATION

One of the longstanding concerns of receiving states is that immigrants groups will not assimilate and will not become "members" of their new country. In upholding restrictions directed against Chinese nationals in the case of *Chae Chan Ping v. United States* (1889), the U.S. Supreme Court accused Chinese immigrants of remaining "strangers" in their new country, "residing apart by themselves, and adhering to the customs and usages of their own country. It seemed impossible for them to assimilate." Certainly, Chinese migration no longer looks anything like this—if, in fact, it ever did look like this. However, the rates in which immigrants **naturalize** (or become citizens in their new country) vary widely. In Australia only 50 percent of the immigrants from English-speaking countries take Australian citizenship compared with 80 to 90 percent for all other immigrant groups. In the United States, the highest rates of naturalization are from immigrants from Asia and Africa, and the lowest rates are from the neighboring nations of Canada and Mexico.

naturalize: to grant the privileges and rights of citizenship

ILLEGAL IMMIGRATION

Legal migration constitutes only one segment of the worldwide migration phenomenon. In addition to this, many developed countries have a sizeable (although that size is seldom known) population of undocumented aliens. In the United States in the mid-1980s the undocumented alien population was estimated somewhere between 5 and 16 million. This, in turn, prompted passage of the

sanction: economic, political, or military reprisals, or, to ratify

Immigration Reform Control Act of 1986 (IRCA), which granted legal status to millions of illegal aliens who had been living in the United States. Also as part of this act, the government instituted a program of employer **sanctions** that made it a federal crime to employ illegal aliens. Supporters of IRCA claimed that it would eliminate illegal migration to the United States. However, it has been ineffective, and there are presently millions of illegal aliens in the United States.

ASYLUM SEEKERS

As noted previously, most countries do not see themselves as immigrant states. Because of this, many foreign nationals seek entry as asylum seekers. In Western Europe these numbers have increased exponentially. Great Britain is typical of this phenomenon. In 1979 there were only 1,600 applicants for asylum.

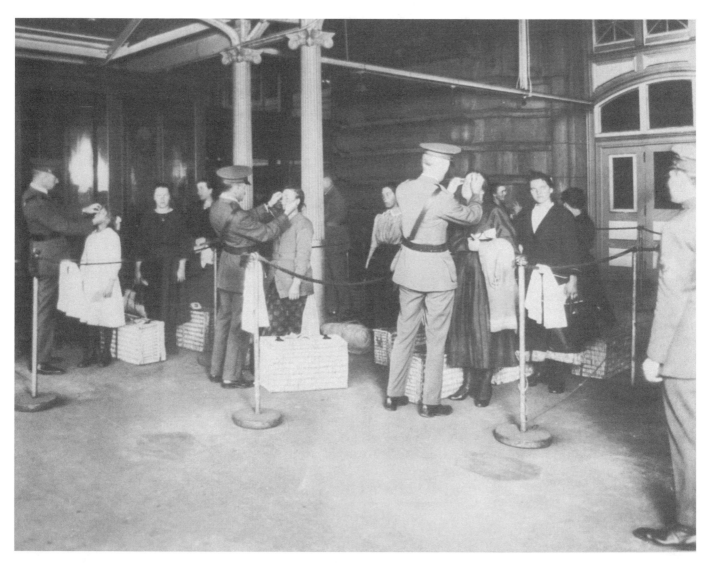

IMMIGRANTS ARRIVE AT ELLIS ISLAND IN NEW YORK AND ARE EXAMINED BY IMMIGRATION OFFICERS. In the shadow of the Statue of Liberty, historic Ellis Island in New York witnessed about 12 million immigrants enter the country between 1892 and 1954. During that time, two agencies were charged with processing—the U.S. Public Health Service and the U.S. Bureau of Immigration. (SOURCE: NATIONAL ARCHIVES AND RECORDS ADMINISTRATION)

This number increased to 30,000 in 1990 and then 44,000 in 1991. In 1999 there were 71,000 applications. In 1996, 40 percent of the asylum applications were from Africa, 35 percent from Asians, and 25 percent by Europeans (mainly those fleeing from the fighting in the former Yugoslavia), although it is noteworthy that more than half of the successful grants came from the latter group.

One of the great challenges now facing Western states is the large numbers of individuals from poor and violent states that continue to attempt to immigrate, much like Westerners did not so long ago.

See also: Citizenship; Naturalization.

BIBLIOGRAPHY

Adler, Leonore Loeb, and Uwe P. Gielen, eds. *Immigration: Immigration and Emigration in International Perspective*. Westport, CT: Praeger, 2003.

Alienikoff, T. Alexander, David Martin, and Hiroshi Motomura. *Immigration and Citizenship: Process and Policy*. 5th ed. St. Paul, MN: West Publishing, 2003.

Borjas, George J. *Friends or Strangers: The Impact of Immigrants on the U.S. Economy*. New York: Basic Books, 1990.

Castles, Stephen. *Ethnicity and Globalization: From Migrant Workers to Transnational Citizen*. London: Sage, 2000.

Chae Chan Ping v. United States, 130 U.S. 581 (1889).

Lynch, James P., and Rita Simon. *Immigration the World Over: Statutes, Policies, and Practices*. Lanham, MD: Rowman & Littlefield, 2003.

Pickus, Noah M., ed. *Immigration and Citizenship in the 21st Century*. Lanham, MD: Rowman & Littlefield, 1998.

Portes, Alejandro, and Ruben G. Rumbaut. *Immigrant America: A Portrait*. 2nd ed. Berkeley, CA: University of California Press, 1996.

Linda Cornett, Mark Gibney

India

One of the largest countries on the globe, India embodies an ancient and highly distinctive civilization. It is home to Hinduism, one of the major world religions. The military, political, and economic leader in its area, by 2004 India was rapidly becoming a twenty-first-century global economic powerhouse.

HISTORY

India, which includes most of the historical cultural area of pre-modern India, inherited a high civilization that developed more than 5,000 years ago in the Indus (now part of Pakistan) and, to a lesser certain extent, the Gangetic Valley. At about 1500 B.C.E. a series of invasions by Indo-Aryan peoples led to a synthesis with the native civilization. Minor Arab incursion began around C.E. 800, followed by larger Muslim invasions from the northwest starting in the twelfth century. Muslims soon became the dominant political group in northern India. European merchants and adventurers began arriving in the sixteenth century, and by the nineteenth century Britain had established its **hegemony**. Rising Indian resistance, the election of an anti-imperialist **socialist** government in London, and British political fatigue at the end of World War II (1939–1945)

hegemony: the complete dominance of one group or nation over another

socialism: any of various economic and political theories advocating collective or governmental ownership and administration of the means of production and distribution of goods

resulted in the establishment of Indian (and Pakistani) independence in 1947. In 1971 previously established Pakistan was divided into present-day Pakistan and Bangladesh.

Under the British, participatory government was well established at much of the local and provincial level. The leaders of the independence movement, principally under the domination of the broad-based Indian National Congress Party, were strongly committed to popular democracy. India's first prime minister, Jawaraharlal Nehru (1889–1964), was largely unchallenged; no leader since has been able to exercise the same sort of power. The other great leader of the movement, Mahatma Gandhi, was assassinated at the inception of the new independent government. Nehru's daughter, Indira Gandhi (1917–1984), was elected prime minister in 1966, but her attempt to subvert India's democratic system resulted in her dismissal in 1977. Reelected in 1980, Indira Gandhi's rule was cut short by her assassination in 1984. The subsequent decline of the Congress Party, the successor to the powerful pre-Independence Indian National Congress, and the rise of Hindu revivalist parties have since led to frequent changes in ruling **coalitions**.

India is a federal republic with twenty-six states and six union territories. Despite many challenges, India remains a democratic country with universal

coalition: an alliance, partnership, or union of disparate peoples or individuals

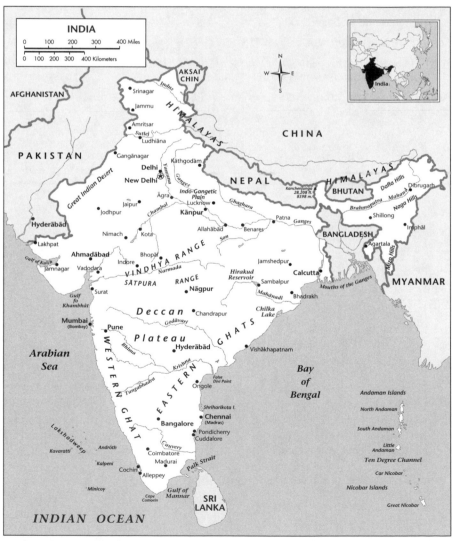

(MAP BY MARYLAND CARTOGRAPHICS/THE GALE GROUP)

suffrage at eighteen. As in many democracies, those with the greatest economic resources and the highest social status wield disproportionate influence. Nevertheless, freedoms of speech, assembly, and especially of the press are vigorously exercised. Although the local police often apply illegal forms of coercion in criminal cases, such tactics are rarely employed for political purposes. In its annual surveys, Freedom House, a prominent independent advocacy foundation, has recognized India's essentially free and democratic character, but given it less than the highest ratings on its protection of political rights (a rating of 2 out of 3 on civil rights and liberties) because of persistent **communal** violence that the government does not always effectively confront.

suffrage: to vote, or, the right to vote

communal: something owned or used by the entire community

POLITICAL GEOGRAPHY

At 3,287,590 square kilometers (2,054,700 square miles) India is approximately one-third the size of the United States. Excluding China whose Xizang Zizhiqu (Tibet) province it borders, India dwarfs the neighboring countries of Pakistan, Bangladesh, Sri Lanka, Nepal, and Bhutan. Only nearby Pakistan is of a closer, albeit limited, size.

Excepting its western border with Pakistan and its eastern with Bangladesh, India is bounded by the sea. Its borders with its neighbors, however, are ill defined. Nevertheless, India's sheer size and military strength provide it with a significant measure of security. In earlier centuries India was successfully invaded from the northwest by Muslims and from the sea by Europeans. More recently Japan launched an unsuccessful invasion in the northeast during World War II and China made a brief incursion in 1962. In the early twenty-first century some areas bordering China, Nepal, and Bangladesh are in dispute, and a military presence remains along the Chinese border. However, barring a substantial decline in either military power or national unity, India remains very unlikely to face a major external threat.

There are, however, potential internal threats. Politically, India may be divided into five major regions. Historically, the Gangetic plain, lying just south of the Himalayas, is India's religious, political, and economic heartland. Its citizens share a common ethnicity, religion, and family of languages. No political group can hope to rule India without a major power base in this region. The west consists of the economically dynamic and politically active coastal regions of the states of Maharashtra and Gujarat as well as the desert state of Rajasthan. The east is India's most diverse region. The state of West Bengal is a heavily populated, politically incendiary center of Indian political and cultural life. However, several sparsely populated, agriculturally rich areas further north and west are plagued by strong ethnic conflict. The center of India, largely occupied by the state of Madhya Pradesh, although rich in natural resources, remains economically poor and lightly populated.

Southern India is emerging as a rival to the heavily populated, politically dominant states of the Gangetic plain. It is the wealthiest and best educated part of India and may become a rallying point for the rest of the country. South Indians are racially different from their fellow citizens and share a family of languages unrelated to those of the north. India's high-tech "Silicon Valley" centers on Bangalore in the south Indian state of Karnataka.

POLITICS AND POPULATION

With approximately 1.1 billion people, India is second only to China in population. Roughly one out of every six people on earth is a citizen of India.

heterogeneous: complex; consisting of parts or components that are different from one another

Racially, religiously, and linguistically, India is more **heterogeneous** than Europe. India has two major racial groups, two major and several minor religions, and a wide variety of economic and cultural groupings.

The Indo-Aryans of the north, representing about 70 percent of the population, are the largest ethnic or racial group. With only minor exceptions, the Indo-Aryans speak languages from the Indo-European family. The most important, Hindi, is the national language and is spoken by approximately a third of all Indians, although there are fifteen nationally recognized official languages. The Dravidians of the south constitute another quarter of the population. Dravidian languages are also interrelated and are rarely spoken outside southern India. Other racial groups, including, for example, Mongoloid, account for approximately 5 percent of the population. Further divisions exist within all ethnic groups. For the most part, India's state borders follow linguistic boundaries.

English functions as the language of commerce and integration. It is the language of opportunity providing India's passport to world markets. Even in remote areas it is generally possible to find someone who can speak or at least read basic English.

Religion is a powerful and often violent political force in India. Over 80 percent of the population is Hindu. Perhaps the most ancient of all major religions, Hinduism has many branches. Some Hindus reject violence in any form. Many Hindus, however, are not opposed to violence and war.

Hindu society is divided into categories referred to as castes. Four traditional castes or *varna* exist: priest/scholar; warrior/ruler; merchant; and laborer. These terms and categories are imprecise and seldom used in daily life. Indians are generally referred to by subcaste or *jati*. There are approximately 3,000 *jatis,* which typically suggest the individual's linguistic group, traditional occupation, and ritual status. Hindus are keenly aware of their own and others' *jatis.* Outside the higher *jatis* is a broad and various but much devalued mixture of groups—variously called untouchables, harijans, scheduled castes, scheduled tribes, or *dalits* —that faces severe discrimination. Political and violent conflict often occurs both among the *jatis* and between harijans and non-harijans. Although illegal, the practice of untouchability is common. India has developed a controversial system of quotas to lessen caste discrimination.

sect: a group of people with a common distinctive view of religion or doctrine

Islam, representing about 12 percent of the population, is India's second major religion. Most Indian Muslims are Sunni, with the Shia being a small minority. The conflict between the two **sects**, so common elsewhere, is muted in India due to the discrimination that Muslims as a whole face. Violent conflict is common between Muslims and radical Hindu revivalists. Muslims, traditionally treated as untouchables, are also the beneficiaries of some government discrimination in their favor.

Largely concentrated in the northwest, Sikhs are a third important religious group, although they make up only 2 percent of the overall population. In the late twentieth and early twenty-first centuries, there has been intense pressure from militant, highly observant Sikhs to establish a separate Sikh state. By 2004, a compromise appeared to have been reached, but this often bitter conflict may not have been permanently settled.

The remaining 6 percent of the population is divided approximately equally between Christians and other religions, primarily Buddhists, Jains, and Parsis. For the most part, adherents to these religions work peacefully within the general political system and are accepted by the other groups.

ABOARD ELEPHANTS, ELECTION OFFICIALS TRANSPORT VOTING MACHINES TO LURI, INDIA, ON APRIL 19, 2004, FOR THE GENERAL ELECTION. In 2004, elections were held for 543 of the 545 People's Assembly's (*Lok Sabha*) lower house seats. The 2004 elections took place with more than 700,000 voting stations for about 670 million voters; electronic voting machines were used for the first time at some stations. (SOURCE: AP/WIDE WORLD PHOTOS)

■ ■ ■

ENVIRONMENTAL ISSUES

India's climate varies from tropical monsoon in the south to temperate in the north; natural hazards range from droughts to widespread and destructive flooding from monsoon rains. The country is also susceptible to severe thunderstorms and earthquakes. Chief problems that affect the Indian environment include deforestation, soil erosion, overgrazing, and desertification. Air pollution from industrial effluents and vehicle emissions is increasingly a problem, as is water pollution from raw sewage and runoff of agricultural pesticides. In some portions of the country, tap water is not potable.

India has the fourth-largest coal reserves in the world, but the growing population causes great strain on natural resources, including iron ore, manganese, mica, titanium ore, natural gas, diamonds, petroleum, and limestone.

In the early twenty-first century India faces, but is increasingly overcoming, a great division between its upwardly mobile modern (or at least semimodern) citizens and its more traditional population. Sixty percent of the population is employed in agriculture, producing 25 percent of the gross domestic product (GDP). This group, as well as half of the nonagricultural population, is largely traditional, meaning that approximately three-quarters of all Indians are not considered modern in outlook and style. Another way of dividing the population is by illiteracy rates: 40 percent of the population (52% of women and 30% of men) remain illiterate.

POLITICS AND THE ECONOMY

From 1947, when the country achieved independence, through the early 1990s, India pursued economic policies that discouraged foreign investment, severely restricted imports, and imposed stringent regulations on the internal economy. This course created near economic stagnation, leaving India far behind both the great Asian economic victors of the post-World War II period—Japan, South Korea, Taiwan, Singapore, Hong Kong, Malaysia, and Thailand—and China, its one-time competitor for Asian leadership.

To a great extent, although not completely, by the start of the twenty-first century India had opened its markets and welcomed foreign investment. Its strong educational system for the middle- and upper-middle-class segments of the population and the prevalence of the English language have transformed India into a major international competitor. From 1990 to 2004, India's average annual real growth rate was approximately 4 percent. In 2004, although 60 percent of the labor force remained in agriculture, industries such as textiles, chemicals, food processing, transportation equipment, mining, machinery, and software development were rising in importance.

Nevertheless, overpopulation and poverty remain significant problems, with approximately a quarter of the population living below the poverty line. Moreover, in 2004 India's public-sector deficit stood at a worrisome 10 percent of the GDP. Deep regional, ethnic, and linguistic conflicts are also likely to remain barriers to further economic progress.

NATURE AND STRUCTURE OF THE GOVERNMENT

India is a constitutional, parliamentary democracy. Unlike the situation in many other countries, these terms accurately describe Indian political reality. Its constitution is far more detailed and much easier to amend than that of the United States and other Western countries.

The titular head of state is the president who is only able to exercise significant influence in extraordinary circumstances. This office is filled every five years through an electoral process involving the two houses of parliament and the state legislatures. The prime minister is the dominant executive leader; he or she is elected by a majority vote of the lower house of parliament. With rare exceptions, the cabinet consists of members of the legislature chosen by the prime minister.

India has a **bicameral** parliament. The upper house is the Council of States (*Rajya Sabha*). Members are partially elected by the states and partially appointed by the president. The dominant lower house or House of the People (*Lok Sabha*) is chosen by popular election. Members of the upper house serve six-year terms. Representatives of the lower house serve a maximum of five years; most serve a shorter term.

■ ■ ■

bicameral: comprised of two chambers, usually a legislative body

Political Parties. India has a vigorous electorate with nearly fifty competitive political parties, many of which are strictly regional. The two leading national parties are the India National Congress (populist) and the Bharatiya Janata Party (Hindu populist). Together, these two parties typically command half of the votes cast. The third and fourth parties—the **Communist** Party of India-Marxist and the Harijan-oriented Bahuan Samaj Party—follow well behind, with each only accounting for 5 percent of the vote nationwide.

Interest Groups. Most interest groups found worldwide also exist in India. However, India is unusual in that groups which are extremely active elsewhere— for example, women's groups and trade associations—take a decidedly second place to its traditional religious, linguistic, and regional groupings.

The Judiciary. Especially at its upper levels, the Indian judiciary generally enjoys the respect of its citizens. Because of the specificity of the Indian constitution and the ease by which it is amended, as well as the strong tradition of judicial restraint inherited from British rule, the judiciary plays a considerably less important role in the political system than it does in many other countries, particularly the United States.

As many as twenty-five members may sit on the Supreme Court, all appointed by the president; they serve until the age of sixty-five. The independence of the court is defended by the fact that members can only be removed through a complex process involving action by the president and an overwhelming majority of both houses of parliament. The only causes warranting such removal are incapacity (e.g., severe illness) and misbehavior (e.g., corruption).

Unusual among federal systems, India's state courts do not function as separate units. The system is integrated. At lower levels, the judiciary is for the most part self-selecting, with senior justices naming their colleagues from within the justice system to positions.

THE BUREAUCRACY

India's 8-million-strong **bureaucracy** is rivaled in size only by that of China. Although often criticized for corruption and inefficiency, India's enormous civil service is largely responsible for this diverse nation's democratic and social successes.

On the national level alone, approximately thirty different groupings exist. The most prestigious are the Indian Administrative Service and the India Foreign Service, followed closely by the Indian Police Service. There are many others as well, such as the Postal and Railway Services. In addition, each state and union territory has its own civil service.

FOREIGN AFFAIRS

Although India lost the international influence it commanded in the late 1940s and 1950s, by 2004 it was recovering its global stature. India, a nuclear power, entered the twenty-first century as a strong second-tier international actor. For the most part, however, it chooses to keep a relatively low profile in international issues, despite being a member of the United Nations. Clearly, within its own geographical area India has no real competitor. Although the relationship between India and Pakistan remains tenuous and openly hostile at times, India's territorial integrity and its dominance in southern Asia would only be jeopardized if these tensions **proliferated** well beyond 2004 levels.

communism: an economic and social system characterized by the absence of class structure and by common ownership of the means of production and subsistence

bureaucracy: a system of administrating government involving professional labor; the mass of individuals administering government

proliferate: to grow in number; to multiply at a high rate

CONCLUSION

Despite its considerable problems, India may be viewed as a success: socially, politically, and, increasingly, economically. The challenges of the future will increasingly be those associated not with stagnation and decay, but with growth and prosperity.

See also: Gandhi, Mahatma.

BIBLIOGRAPHY

Cohen, Stephen P. *India.* Washington, DC: Brookings Institution Press, 2001.

Freedom House. "Hungary." *Freedom in the World 2003: The Annual Survey of Political Rights and Civil Liberties.* New York: Freedom House, 2004., <http://www. freedomhouse.org/research/freeworld/2003/countryratings/india.htm>.

Hardgrave, Robert, and Stanley Kochanek. *India.* Davis, CA: Wadsworth Press, 1999.

"India." In *CIA World Factbook.* Washington, DC: Central Intelligence Agency, 2005., <http://www.cia.gov/cia/publications/factbook/geos/in.html>.

Jodhka, Surindar S., ed. *Communities and Identities: Contemporary Discourses on Culture and Politics in India.* Beverly Hills, CA: Sage Publications, 2002.

Sivamakrishnan, K., and Arun Agrawal, eds. *The Cultural Politics of Development in India.* Stanford, CA: Stanford University Press, 2003.

Robert S. Robins

Indigenous Peoples' Rights

The Centre for World Indigenous Studies estimated that the number of indigenous peoples worldwide in 1999 was between 300 and 500 million. This figure includes more than 7,000 indigenous societies or cultures, living in more than seventy countries, constituting approximately 5 percent of the global population. In the absence of reliable statistics, however, these figures are only approximate.

WHO ARE INDIGENOUS PEOPLES?

Indigenous peoples are generally referred to in the plural, because they include many different communities. The use of the plural *peoples* indicates the diversity of people within the concept as a whole.

There is currently no agreed-upon definition of who is indigenous. Indigenous peoples themselves claim the right to define who they are. They argue that self-identification as indigenous is one of the basic rights. Nevertheless, the term indigenous peoples is generally used to describe a non-dominant group in a particular territory, with a more or less acknowledged claim to be aboriginal—or the "original" inhabitants.

Although the Aboriginal peoples of Australia, the Mäori of New Zealand, and the Maya of Guatemala were clearly there first, in some places the issue is more ambiguous. For example, in Africa many people consider all groups to be indigenous, and in Asia, where successive waves of people moved here and there, displacing other populations, similar problems with the term *first* also apply. It is safer to say, therefore, that indigenous peoples are those who arrived in a territory before single **nation-states** were formed.

nation-state: a relatively homogeneous state with only one or few nationalities within its political borders

Indigenous peoples have distinct social, political, and cultural identities, and languages, traditions, legal, and political institutions that are distinct from those of the national society. They have a special relationship with the land and natural resources, which is often fundamental to their cultural identity and therefore their survival as distinct peoples. Hundreds of thousands of indigenous peoples continue to be **pastoralists**, hunters and gatherers, and peasant farmers or shifting cultivators, whether full- or part-time. In most cases, the subsistence economy remains the bedrock of how indigenous peoples make their living.

pastoralist: supporter of a social organization whose main economic activity is raising livestock

OFFICIAL DEFINITIONS

There is no single official definition of indigenous peoples. However, there are three main working definitions within the United Nations (UN). The first definition of indigenous and tribal peoples was provided by the International Labor Organization's (ILO) Convention No. 169 Concerning Indigenous and Tribal Peoples in Independent Countries (1989), which came into force in 1991. In Article 1, the convention describes indigenous peoples as those who descended from the populations that inhabited the country at the time of colonization and who enjoy some or all of their own social, economic, cultural, or political institutions.

The other two widely used definitions were suggested by UN **Rapporteurs** Jose R. Martinez Cobo and Erica-Irene Daes. In his 1986 Report for the UN Sub-Commission on the Prevention of Discrimination and Protection of Minorities, Cobo stated that indigenous peoples are those who have a historical continuity with precolonial societies and who consider themselves distinct from the majority community. Daes, chairperson of the UN Working Group on Indigenous Populations, likewise has suggested that indigenous peoples are those who are descendants of groups that were in the country at the time of colonial invasion and who, have through their isolation from the majority community, preserved their ancestor's customs and traditions, and who are placed under a state structure that is fundamentally alien to theirs. Each of these definitions emphasizes self-identification as one of the main variables in any definition of indigenous peoples.

rapporteur: one that reports on a committee's work

VIOLATIONS OF INDIGENOUS PEOPLES' RIGHTS

Wherever they may live, in an industrialized or a lesser developed country, in a rural or urban area, indigenous peoples are often the most vulnerable sector of society; they tend to be **marginalized**—socially, economically, and politically—and suffer from oppression, discrimination, and poverty. When the Europeans first set foot in their prospective colonies they paid little notice of the local people and their rights. In many cases they pursued policies of exploitation (e.g., the Mäori in New Zealand), assimilation (e.g., the Aborigines and Torres Strait Islanders in Australia) or sometimes extermination (e.g., the Native American Indians in the United States). Native rights to land and resources were rarely recognized and huge swathes of land were settled by colonists in the mistaken belief that they were uninhabited.

marginalize: to move to the outer borders, or to move one to a lower position

In the early twenty-first century, indigenous peoples are facing a new form of putative exploitation in **globalization**, with its imposition of the culture and system of the global capitalist **market economy**. A key element in this ongoing colonization process is land.

globalization: the process of expanding regional concerns to a worldwide viewpoint, especially politics, economics, or culture

market economy: an economy with little government ownership and relatively free markets

Different mechanisms and tools have been devised to take the land away from indigenous peoples; all seem inherently discriminatory. They include projects such as the building of roads, construction of dams, laying of oil pipelines, mining and processing projects, deforestation and forestation programs, and the creation of natural parks in lands traditionally occupied by indigenous peoples; sometimes, these projects have required the actual eviction of indigenous groups from their traditional homelands.

In most countries where indigenous peoples are in the minority, they are among the poorest and most disadvantaged segment of the national population. As land is their main source of income and livelihood, this continuing erosion of their land rights is a major cause of the ongoing impoverishment of indigenous peoples.

Another area in which indigenous peoples often face discrimination is education. Indigenous peoples often face discrimination in access to educational facilities, resulting in poor educational achievement, and most national educational programs and curricula do not take into account the special characteristics and needs of indigenous peoples. The end result is that many indigenous children can feel marginalized.

Indigenous peoples who are still engaged in hunting and gathering are popularly viewed as backward and unprogressive and seen as impediments to economic development. This can result in official intimidation. Indigenous peoples are often arrested and jailed for continuing to hunt and gather on ancestral lands that have been made into reservations or declared protected areas. Indigenous peoples thus often face prejudice and discrimination when applying for jobs or trying to gain access to higher positions.

As a result of institutionalized state discrimination against indigenous peoples, they can also suffer from racial prejudice. In many parts of the world, indigenous peoples remain politically excluded, and their right to **self-determination** is routinely ignored or dismissed. Across the globe, indigenous peoples are significantly underrepresented in decision-making processes. Indigenous peoples are often the victims of official violence. They are routinely seen as scapegoats for crimes committed and are often overrepresented in criminal prosecutions.

The right to political, economic, social, and cultural self-determination and legal recognition of the rights to own, manage, and control their ancestral lands and resources are key demands of indigenous peoples and are at the heart of what it means to be indigenous in the twenty-first century.

INTERNATIONAL MECHANISMS TO PROTECT INDIGENOUS PEOPLES' RIGHTS

There have been significant advances in international thinking and action on indigenous issues and rights during the waning years of the twentieth and into the twenty-first century. The international community now recognizes that indigenous peoples have particular collective as well as individual rights that afford them a specified level and quality of protection under international human rights law.

ILO

The ILO Convention on Indigenous and Tribal Populations, (No. 107, 1957) was the first international document designed to protect indigenous peoples against discrimination and to ensure their continued existence. The convention

"Different mechanisms and tools have been devised to take the land away from indigenous peoples; all seem inherently discriminatory."

self-determination: the ability of a people to determine their own destiny or political system

is in force for twenty countries. In 1989, the ILO adopted the Convention on Indigenous and Tribal Peoples (No. 169), based on the premise that indigenous peoples have the right to survive as separate peoples with their own cultures and traditions. It also highlights the need for special measures to protect these peoples not only from discrimination but also cultural extinction. Fourteen countries have signed the convention, and **ratification** was under active consideration in a number of other countries in 2005. ILO Convention No. 107 and Convention No. 169 are the only binding instruments exclusively focused on indigenous peoples' rights as of early 2005.

ratify: to make official or to officially sanction

THE UN

A variety of UN committees and agencies have directed their attention to the condition of the world's indigenous peoples:

- The UN Sub-Commission on Prevention and Discrimination and Protection of Minorities study, completed in 1984, concluded that the continuous discrimination against indigenous peoples threatened their very existence.
- The Vienna Declaration and Program of Action adopted at the World Conference on Human Rights in 1993 recommended that states take positive steps to ensure respect for the human rights and fundamental freedoms of indigenous peoples.
- The Durban Declaration and Plan of Action, arising from the UN World Conference against Racism, Racial Discrimination, **Xenophobia** and Related Intolerance (2001), recognized that indigenous peoples have been victims of

xenophobia: a fear of foreigners, often leading to isolationism, reduction in immigration, and racism

TWO GUATEMALAN INDIGENOUS FARMERS PROTEST AGAINST THE GOVERNMENT'S LAND POLICIES IN GUATEMALA CITY ON MARCH 30, 2004. For indigenous and peasant farmers in Guatemala, the Agreement on Socio-Economic Issues and Agrarian Situation of 1996 would have atoned for decades of discrimination involving unfair land distribution. As of 2005, it had yet to be implemented. (SOURCE: © DANIEL LECLAIR/REUTERS/CORBIS)

discrimination for centuries and affirmed that they should not suffer any discrimination, particularly on the basis of their indigenous origin and identity.

- In 2001, the UN Commission on Human Rights appointed a Special Rapporteur on the situation of the human rights and fundamental freedoms of indigenous people to gather and receive information and communications from governments and indigenous peoples on violations of their human rights and fundamental freedoms.
- In 2002, at the UN World Summit on Sustainable Development, the international community affirmed that indigenous people play a vital role in sustainable development.

The UN, its partners, and indigenous peoples have developed a program that sets standards in regards to indigenous peoples and their rights and reviews developments regularly. The Working Group on Indigenous Populations, established in 1982, was the first arena in the UN system in which indigenous peoples could state their views. One of the principle outcomes in terms of standard setting is the draft declaration on the rights of indigenous peoples under discussion in the Working Group of the Commission on Human Rights. As of early 2005 this draft declaration was working its way up through the UN system to the General Assembly.

The UN observed the International Decade of the World's Indigenous Peoples from 1995 through 2004. The objective of the special observation was for governments to strengthen their efforts for international cooperation for the solution of problems faced by indigenous peoples in areas such as human rights, the environment, development, and health. The Decade helped to focus efforts in the UN system on two primary goals: the creation of a Permanent Forum on Indigenous Issues and the drafting of the declaration on the rights of indigenous peoples.

The Permanent Forum on Indigenous Issues—the first permanent mechanism within the UN system to address the problems facing indigenous peoples—was established in April 2000. Consisting of eight governmental experts and eight indigenous representatives, the Permanent Forum is the most significant and concrete step taken to date to address indigenous peoples' issues. Many indigenous peoples have high hopes that the forum will make a real difference to improving their lives.

The tenth session of the working group on the draft declaration occurred in September 2004. The challenge facing indigenous peoples and governments is to agree on a final text, enabling its adoption. However, there continue to be serious disagreements over the wording of the documents, especially over issues of internal self-determination and autonomy. For indigenous peoples the right to self-determination is the cornerstone of the draft declaration. Self-determination

■ ■ ■

A DEFINITION OF INDIGENOUS

In his 1986 Report for the UN Sub-Commission on the Prevention of Discrimination and Protection of Minorities, Martinez Cobo writes:

Indigenous communities, peoples and nations are those which, having a historical continuity with pre-invasion and pre-colonial societies that developed on their territories, consider themselves distinct from other sectors of the societies now prevailing in those territories or parts of them. They form at present non-dominant sectors of society and are determined to preserve, develop and transmit to future generations their ancestral territories, and their ethnic identity, as the basis of their continued existence as peoples, in accordance with their own cultural patterns, social institutions and legal systems. (Cobo 1986)

is a prerequisite for the exercise of their political, social, cultural, and spiritual rights, as well as their practical survival.

The draft declaration, if and when adopted, will not be legally binding on states. It will nevertheless have great moral force and will provide minimum standards to guide states in their dealings with indigenous peoples.

EUROPEAN UNION

The European Council passed a resolution in 1998 on indigenous peoples and has since mainstreamed indigenous peoples' issues in both its development and human rights strategies. The working document from the European Commission, prepared at the time of the council resolution, recognizes the economic, social, and political marginalization of indigenous peoples; their unique contribution to the sustainable use of resources; and the importance of their participation and inclusion in decision-making processes. It also acknowledges the importance of self-determination to indigenous peoples. The European Parliament has been getting increasingly involved in the issue of indigenous peoples, passing resolutions in 1994, calling for effective protection for indigenous peoples, and in 1995, calling for support for the Decade.

AFRICAN UNION

The 34th Ordinary Session of the African Commission on Human and People's Rights (2003) adopted the *Report of the African Commission's Working Group on Indigenous Populations/Communities*. The report contains an analysis of criteria for identifying indigenous peoples in Africa, an analysis of their human rights situation seen in the light of the provisions of the African Charter on Human and Peoples' Rights (1986) and an analysis of the African charter/jurisprudence and its potential for promoting and protecting their human rights. This was a major development as there remains considerable confusion in many African states in identifying and protecting indigenous peoples' rights.

THE CARIBBEAN COMMUNITY AND COMMON MARKET

In 1997, the Caribbean Community and Common Market (with fifteen member states from Latin America and the Caribbean) recognized in the Charter of Civil Society the contribution of indigenous peoples to the development process. It protects their historical rights and respects their culture (Article 11). The charter has the status of a regional, **intergovernmental** human rights declaration.

ORGANIZATION OF AMERICAN STATES

The Organization of American States (OAS; thirty-five independent countries of the Americas as of 2004) has turned its attention to the rights of its indigenous peoples. In 1997, the Inter-American Commission on Human Rights approved the OAS Proposed Declaration on the Rights of Indigenous Peoples in the Americas. As of 2004, the Declaration was under discussion by governments and indigenous representatives. The OAS proposed declaration is one of the most important exercises underway to address the human rights of indigenous peoples. In some countries of the Americas, the OAS is a substantial and far-reaching step forward relative to existing rights found in domestic law. However, there are fears that the OAS could do harm by undermining the high human rights standards that are being proposed for indigenous peoples at the UN.

THE CONCEPT OF INDIGENOUS

Erica-Irene Daes, Chairperson of the UN Working Group on Indigenous Populations (WGIP), while concluding in 1995 that "the concept of 'indigenous' is not capable of a precise definition that can be applied in the same manner to all regions of the world," has nevertheless suggested this variation, designating certain peoples as indigenous:

1. Because they are descendants of groups which were in the territory of the country at the time when other groups of different cultures or ethnic origins arrived there;
2. because of their isolation from other segments of the country's population they have preserved almost intact the customs and traditions of their ancestors which are similar to those characterised as indigenous; and
3. because they are, even if only formally, placed under a State structure which incorporates national, social and cultural characteristics alien to theirs. (Daes 1995)

intergovernmental: between or involving multiple governments, with each government retaining full decision-making power

INTERNATIONAL JURISPRUDENCE

Intergovernmental human rights bodies overseeing universal and regional human rights instruments, such as the UN Committee on the Elimination of Racial Discrimination, have frequently commented on government reports concerning the violation of the rights of indigenous peoples. In August 1997, the committee adopted General Recommendation XXIII, which states its concern at the continuing discrimination against indigenous peoples, calls for the **restitution** of their lands and territories, and, where this is not possible, for just, fair, and prompt compensation including comparable lands. Similarly, the Human Rights Committee, which is responsible for monitoring the implementation of the International Covenant of Civil and Political Rights (1966), is increasingly commenting on the inconsistency of state policy relating to indigenous peoples with international human rights law.

See also: International Covenant of Civil and Political Rights; United Nations Commission on Human Rights.

restitution: the transfer of an item back to an original owner, or, compensation for that item

BIBLIOGRAPHY

Anaya, S. James. *Indigenous Peoples in International Law*. New York: Oxford University Press, 2004.

Blaser, Mario. *In the Way of Development: Indigenous Peoples, Life Projects and Globalisation*. London: Zed Books, 2004.

Cobo, Jose R. Martinez. "Study of the Problem of Discrimination against Indigenous Populations." UN Sub-Commission on the Prevention of Discrimination and the Protection of Minorities. UN Doc. E/CN.4/Sub.2/1986/7 (1986).

Colchester, Marcus. *Conservation and Mobile Indigenous People: Displacement, Forced Settlement and Sustainable Development*. Oxford, UK: Berghahn Books, 2001.

Hughes, Lotte. *The No-Nonsense Guide to Indigenous Peoples*. London: Verso, 2003.

International Labour Organisation. *ILO Convention on Indigenous and Tribal Peoples, 1989 (No. 169): A Manual*. Geneva: International Labour Organisation, 2005. <http://www.ilo.org/ilolex/cgi-lex/convde.pl?C169>.

International Work Group on Indigenous Affairs. *The Indigenous World 2004*, ed. Diana Vinding. Copenhagen, Denmark: International Work Group on Indigenous Affairs, 2004.

Office of the United Nations High Commissioner for Human Rights. *Draft United Nations Declaration on the Rights of Indigenous Peoples*. Geneva: Office of the United Nations High Commissioner for Human Rights, 1994. <http://www.unhchr.ch/huridocda/huridoca.nsf/(Symbol)/E.CN.4.SUB.2.RES.1994.45.En?OpenDocument>.

Thornberry, Patrick. *Indigenous Peoples and Human Rights*. Manchester, UK: Manchester University Press, 2002.

Helena Whall

Indonesia

Located in Southeast Asia, Indonesia is the largest archipelagic nation (i.e., one consisting entirely of island groups), the fourth most-populous nation (211.7 million in 2002, according to the World Bank), the third largest electoral democracy, and the most populous predominantly Muslim nation (Muslims make up approximately 88% of the population) in the world. There are 400 volcanoes across the country, about 100 of which are deemed to be currently active.

The single fact linking the very diverse territories that make up Indonesia is that they were all part of the Netherlands' East Indies colony. Nationalism began to grow on an Indies-wide basis in the second quarter of the twentieth century, and out of these religiously, ethnically, and linguistically diverse areas, a single nation was born. Independence was proclaimed at the end of World War II, on August 17, 1945, by Sukarno (also Soekarno; 1901–1970)—who, like many Indonesians, used only one name—however, the Indonesians were forced to fight against and negotiate with the Dutch for four years before independence was finally secured in December 1949.

From 1945 to 1959, Indonesia was led by President Sukarno, in conjunction with various prime ministers arising out of Indonesia's parliament. The first nation-wide elections were held only in 1955, and a nominated parliament operated prior to the elections. Governments were unstable and ineffective, however. Declaring Indonesia's parliamentary regime modeled on the West incompatible with Indonesia's cultural traditions, the charismatic Sukarno overthrew parliamentary democracy and installed what he called "Guided Democracy." The parliament was reorganized to reflect parties and groups (representatives of the military, along with women, veterans, youth, and other organizations) willing to accommodate themselves to Sukarno's authoritarian regime.

The most significant political forces under Guided Democracy were Sukarno himself, the military, and the Indonesian Communist Party (*Partai Komunis Indonesia*; PKI), the largest communist party outside of the communist bloc at the time. The military and the communists were in rough balance, with Sukarno swinging one way or the other, attempting to keep the two forces in some kind of antagonistic balance.

Ultimately, Sukarno's regime could not maintain such a divided society. Polarization and suspicion between the non-communist forces, spearheaded by segments of the military and joined by a number of Muslim groups, and the

nationalism: the belief that one's nation or culture is superior to all others

regime: a type of government, or, the government in power in a region

authoritarianism: the domination of the state or its leader over individuals

bloc: a group of countries or individuals working towards a common goal, usually within a convention or other political body

polarize: to separate individuals into adversarial groups

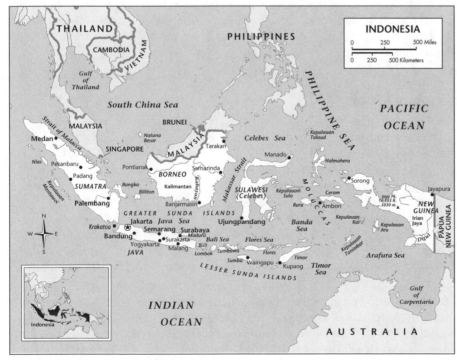

(MAP BY MARYLAND CARTOGRAPHICS/THE GALE GROUP)

communists, led by the PKI, propelled the country toward violence. The international environment was also unstable as Sukarno verbally attacked the West, launched a low-intensity war against neighboring Malaysia, and increasingly aligned the country with the communist People's Republic of China. In domestic affairs, Sukarno sought to keep a permanent revolution in motion. Bureaucrats were forced to demonstrate loyalty to Sukarno's political movements and parrot his slogans. The president paid little attention to management of the economy. Inflation exceeded 650 percent in 1965. Poverty and hunger grew widespread.

On the night of September 30, 1965, a mysterious **coup** occurred in which numerous top generals were targeted for assassination—by the communists, it was later asserted. The military, led by General Suharto (also Soeharto; b. 1921), then struck, sidelining Sukarno and gradually establishing a durable military-led government. Communists and their supposed sympathizers among the country's ethnic Chinese population were killed in the 1965 to 1966 period by members of the military and mass organizations, particularly Muslim groups, operating in tandem with the military. There is no consensus figure for the number of deaths in this period, although a number between 250,000 and 500,000 is not unreasonable. With this slaughter, communism was effectively eliminated in Indonesia.

Suharto's regime (1965–1998), called the New Order, removed the national focus from politics and turned it toward economic development. Suharto assumed the presidency in 1967 and gradually earned the sobriquet "the father of development." The Indonesian people were considered a "floating mass," which would have no involvement in politics, except for once every five years when they turned out to vote for the regime.

Political parties were **amalgamated** to just two that were allowed to compete in elections with the government-dominated Golkar, the **de facto** government party organized around functional groups in society. Through the six elections of the New Order period, Golkar achieved 62 to 75 percent of the national vote. Through a mix of coercion and violence imposed by the military working at all levels of government, legal constraints on popular participation in politics, control of the press, and some legitimacy earned through guaranteeing stability in the country and leading a successful program of economic expansion, Suharto was able to maintain control of Indonesia for almost thirty-three years.

THE ECONOMY

The base from which Suharto worked was a potentially rich one. The country had a wealth of oil, natural gas, timber, and minerals including gold, nickel, and bauxite to be exploited, in addition to a vast pool of cheap labor. Economic growth and poverty reduction policies helped to spread the benefits of economic growth around the nation. According to the World Bank, the poverty rate was reduced by 82 percent in the period from 1970 to 1995, and per capita incomes increased 4.8 percent annually during the same period. However, this is controversial for one of the most notable characteristics of Indonesia's economic growth was the emergence of an elite of superwealthy businesspersons within Suharto's own family and among those closely connected to the first family.

The economic growth delivered by the regime eventually carried the seeds of Suharto's downfall. Indonesians' rising levels of education and wealth led many to reject Suharto's top-down, military-dominated rule. The excessive wealth of Suharto's family was a prime focus of antigovernment student demonstrations that began in 1998, following the onset of the 1997 East Asian financial crisis. The crisis sent the country's currency plunging, pushed banks and

coup: a quick seizure of power or a sudden attack

FAST FACTS

Many Indonesians use only one name, referring to each other solely by their first names.

amalgamate: to merge together two or more things into one form; combine

de facto: (Latin) actual; in effect but not officially declared

businesses into bankruptcy, and saw prices soar. Students argued that the crisis was not simply an economic matter but that, rather, it was related to the failings of Suharto's crony-capitalist regime (i.e., a regime in which economic favors are doled out to politically favored individuals). In May 1998, deserted by long-time allies, the parliament occupied by exuberant students, and the city of Jakarta still smoldering in the wake of fires and riots that left hundreds dead, Suharto was forced to step down from the presidency.

TRANSITION TO DEMOCRACY

Suharto was succeeded by his vice president, B. J. Habibie (b. 1936), and a transition to democratic rule was initiated. Laws on association and organization were liberalized. Political parties were permitted to form freely. Transitional elections in 1999 delivered no definitive winner, leaving the parties in parliament to negotiate, which led to the selection of Abdurrahman Wahid (b. 1940), leader of Indonesia's largest Muslim organization, *Nahdlatul Ulama* (the Rise of the Islamic Scholars), as president. Abdurrahman's presidency was tumultuous, however, and he was **impeached** in 2001 and replaced by Megawati Sukarnoputri (b. 1947), the daughter of founding president Sukarno and leader of the Indonesian Democracy Party-Struggle. For the first time in 2004, Indonesians were allowed to elect their president directly. Susilo Bambang Yudhoyono (b. 1949) won in a second-round run-off, defeating **incumbent** president Megawati.

impeach: to accuse of a crime or misconduct, especially a high official; to remove from a position, especially as a result of criminal activity.

incumbent: one who currently holds a political office, or, holding a political office

The parties have been among the most conspicuous features of Indonesia's new democracy. Many of the top parties are personalistic, relying on the charisma of a single individual. Several Muslim-based political parties were among the top finishers in 1999 and 2004, including the National Awakening Party, the United Development Party, the Prosperous Justice Party, the National Mandate Party, and the Crescent Star Party. Of these parties, only two (the United Development Party and the Crescent Star Party, jointly earned 14.2 percent of the vote in 2004) have agitated for the rapid enforcement of Islamic law, or Shari'a. Broadly, among mainstream political actors, there is a recognition that the country, which is home to large populations of Christians, Hindus, and Buddhists, is too pluralistic to Islamize the state.

Elections in 1999 and 2004 were lively and largely peaceful. Transparency at the level of the individual polling station is high, and democratic norms are being slowly **inculcated** in the population through public education efforts.

inculcate: to teach through repetition

A vigorous civil society has arisen in the transition from authoritarian rule. Students served as the muscle that brought Suharto down, but in the day-to-day operation of Indonesia's democracy, more significant are reformist civil society groups that have established a strong voice in the contemporary political dialogue. Groups agitating against corruption and human rights violations and for women, the urban poor, and electoral reform contribute to a lively debate and act as a check on the newly empowered political parties.

THE GOVERNMENT

Indonesia's government is unitary in nature, unlike the federal system in the United States. However, a **devolution** of power to local districts, which took effect in 2001, has attempted to **decentralize** the government from the capital of Jakarta to the localities. In the early twenty-first century, the country was continuing an ongoing battle with large-scale (in the province of Aceh) and smaller-scale (in Papua) movements for independence. Executives and legislatures operate at the national, provincial, and district levels.

devolve: to move power or property from one individual or institution to another, especially from a central authority

decentralize: to move power from a central authority to multiple periphery government branches or agencies

The national government is a hybrid, or combination, presidential–parliamentary regime. Constitutional reforms have confined the president to two terms only and allowed bills to become law thirty days after parliament's approval, even without the president's signature.

Parliament is composed of three organs: the *Dewan Perwakilan Raykat* (DPR; People's Representative Assembly; 550 members), the *Dewan Perwakilan Daerah* (DPD; Regional Representative Assembly; 128 members), and finally, the DPR and DPD come together to form the third body, the *Majelis Permusyawaratan Rakyat* (MPR; People's Consultative Council). The MPR is the supreme repository of the nation's **sovereignty** to which the president is responsible. The DPR functions as the powerful lower house of parliament. The DPD, created in the wake of constitutional reforms, is designed to guarantee the regions a voice in central policy making.

A court system exists, crowned by a Supreme Court and a Constitutional Court, the latter of which is empowered to conduct **judicial review**, try the president, and **arbitrate** election disputes. The court system is weak after its long subservience to Suharto; it has an unusual Dutch legal heritage, low salaries for judges and prosecutors, and inadequately trained individuals.

sovereignty: autonomy; or, rule over a political entity

judicial review: the ability of the judicial branch to review and invalidate a law that contradicts the constitution

arbitration: a method of resolving disagreements whereby parties by agreement choose a person or group of people familiar with the issues in question to hear and settle their dispute

THE CONSTITUTION

Indonesia operates under its 1945 constitution, agreed in the year of the nation's proclamation of independence from Dutch rule. This constitution, written hurriedly by the republic's founders, was not intended to be permanent. However, attempts in the post-Suharto period (since 1998) to engage in a full-scale rewriting of the constitution, sought by students and other reformers, have been rebuffed. The constitution, whatever its flaws, is seen as a pillar of national identity and a guarantee of the country's territorial integrity. Although a total overhaul of the document has not been possible in the post-Suharto period, four major amendments to the constitution, providing important guarantees of rights and liberties and limits on executive power, were enacted from 1999 to 2002. The weakness of the court system is a significant barrier to the enjoyment of rights by many Indonesians.

■ ■ ■

STUDENT-LED PROTESTS OF 1998–1999

Student groups in Indonesia helped to bring an end to the Suharto (b.1921) regime in the spring of 1998. Beginning in late 1997, university students on several campuses demanded economic reforms. The 1998 Trisakti incident, however, was the immediate cause of widespread rioting that in turn led to Suharto's resignation. On May 12, 1998, while returning from a peaceful demonstration, four students at Trisakti University outside the capital of Jakarta were shot in the back by soldiers. The next day anti-Chinese rioters caused the deaths of fifteen hundred people in Jakarta and gang-raped Chinese women.

Human rights inquiries into the Trisakti incident as well as the two later episodes of violence against students known as Semanggi I and Semanggi II have not yielded significant results as of mid-2005. Semanggi I occurred in November 1998, when security troops fired on students protesting recent emergency legislation. Thirteen students died in the shooting. Semanggi II took place in September 1999, when Jakarta students demonstrated in opposition to President B. J. Habibie's (b. 1936) nomination for a second term. One student was killed.

The student movement fell short of transforming Indonesia's political system for two reasons: it split into factions after Suharto resigned, and it failed to broaden its appeal to the general population.

POLITICAL LIFE

Indonesia's emergent democracy has been severely challenged. Although the country was once considered an economic miracle similar to the success stories of Singapore and Taiwan, since 1998 the nation has struggled to get beyond what is referred to as its "multidimensional crisis." In politics, the initial transition to democracy was fraught with tension. Reformers wondered if the old status quo powers would allow themselves to be simply voted out of office, and students kept up the pressure in the streets to ensure that they did. Demonstrations became a daily fact of life in many of Indonesia's cities in the 1998 to 1999 period. This was a step forward for freedom of expression but a step backward for stability. During one tense stand-off between Habibie's transitional regime and the reform forces in November 1998, thirteen students were killed in what has come to be called the "Semanggi incident." The impeachment of the first democratic president Abdurrahman Wahid in 2001 was also preceded by months of political tension and escalating demonstrations. Terrorism has also taken a toll on the nation's stability, including church bombings in 2000; the Bali nightclub bombings in October 2002, in which 202 people died; the Jakarta J. W. Marriott Hotel bombing in August 2003, in which twelve died; and the Australian embassy bombing in Jakarta in September 2004, which killed nine.

In economics, the country has had difficulty finding its feet after stumbling during the East Asian financial crisis of the late 1990s. The economy declined 13 percent in 1998. Although far from being a miraculous recovery, annual economic growth at the rate of 3 to 4 percent did return to the country within a few years. Nonetheless, Indonesia struggles to convince investors, both domestic and foreign, that it is a safe place to do business. The country's economy has been hurt by perceptions of political instability, terrorism, difficult adjustments required to meet international lending demands, and renewed labor union activism.

This multidimensional crisis sets the stage in which politics happens on a daily basis for most Indonesians. Indonesians' day-to-day economic security has

■ ■ ■

THE EAST ASIAN FINANCIAL CRISIS

The 1997 financial crisis, also known as the Asian currency crisis, began in July 1997 with the collapse of Thailand's currency, the *baht*. This event caused Western investors to reassess the stability of financial systems throughout East and Southeast Asia. When these investors began to take their money out of other countries in the region, local currencies lost their value and their stock markets fell rapidly. Indonesia, South Korea, and Thailand were most heavily affected. In Indonesia the value of the *rupiah* began to fall in August 1997, declining dramatically in November in spite of help from the International Monetary Fund (IMF).

The 1997 crisis has been attributed to the role of psychological factors in financial markets and to poor risk management in Asian banking systems, and these undoubtedly exacerbated the situation. However, the primary causes were economic, including massive speculation, particularly in real estate, financed by borrowing; the rise in value of the American dollar, to which many Asian governments tied their currencies' value; and growing Chinese competition on world markets. In Indonesia, major corruption involving the ruling family, anti-Chinese policies (the ethnic Chinese minority makes up the bulk of the Indonesian merchant class), and the costly occupation of East Timor (eventually lost in 1999) explain why the crisis affected that country more severely than Singapore or Hong Kong. By the winter of 1997 Indonesia's long-term bonds were downgraded to junk status. The resulting inflation led to steep increases in the price of food and other necessities, which in turn sparked riots throughout Indonesia.

In response, President Suharto fired the governor of Bank Indonesia in February 1998, but this measure was inadequate. After massive protests as well as the loss of the army's support, Suharto resigned on May 20 after ruling for thirty-two years.

plethora: a large, sometimes overwhelming, amount

been challenged. The law and order situation has declined in many areas. The political situation, too, is in flux. Although elections have been held and a **plethora** of reforms enacted, many old powers continue to haunt the national corridors of power.

THE CONTINUING POWER OF OLD FORCES LIMITS DEMOCRACY

Golkar, the ruling party of the Suharto era, is the largest in Indonesia's parliament elected in 2004, holding 128 of 550 seats. Suharto himself continues to live comfortably in his Jakarta home, untried for human rights violations committed during his long, corrupt rule. He maintains his and his family's vast wealth, estimated by Transparency International to be between $15 and $35 billion dollars.

The military has been institutionally removed from several prominent areas of power, such as appointed positions in the legislatures, and its relationship to the police has been severed. However, the military remains powerful, and in some areas of the far-flung archipelago, it is still the most powerful institution. No high-ranking military officers have been held accountable for human rights violations committed during Suharto's rule, including the revenge slaughter of many East Timorese, following East Timor's vote for independence in 1999. Domestic and international human rights groups continue to point to military targeting of civilians in operations to quell the rebellious provinces of Aceh and Papua.

Additionally, prominent military leaders have now retired their uniforms and joined the country's political parties, seeking power through the new democratic processes. Susilo Bambang Yudhoyono (b. 1949), elected president in 2004, is a former general. Evidence suggests people chose him for his charisma, **populist** message, nonconfrontational style, and perceived ability to move the country forward. A competitor in the first round of the presidential election was Golkar candidate retired General Wiranto (b. 1947), who has been indicted for crimes against humanity by courts in East Timor, but was able to run for president and secure 22 percent of the vote in Indonesia.

populist: someone who advocates policies for the advancement of the common man

Like the military, the power of the **bureaucracy**, too, is a legacy from the Suharto period. Bureaucrats, enjoying a privileged position under authoritarian rule, have been slow to change to a new democratic way of doing business. Attempts to turn bureaucrats into "public servants" have been resisted, as have attempts to make the bureaucracy accountable to the public. There is no tradition of openness of information in Indonesia, so reformers' attempts to pry open the government for access to information continue to meet only halting successes.

bureaucracy: a system of administrating government involving professional labor; the mass of individuals administering government

Indonesia continually ranks as one of the most corrupt nations on earth, according to the Transparency International Corruption Perceptions Index. In 2003, the country ranked as one-hundred-twenty-second most corrupt out of 133 nations included in the survey.

The exercise of basic freedoms guaranteed by Indonesia's amended constitution continues to be problematic. As previously discussed, the weakness of the courts plays a role as there is little way for people to enforce their rights. Also, old laws that circumscribe freedom of the press, for example, have been recycled by the democratic governments to deter criticism. Journalists have also been subject to intimidation, violence, and even murder for daring to report on stories threatening to powerful interests.

See also: East Timor; Shari'a.

BIBLIOGRAPHY

Badan Pusat Statistik [Statistics Indonesia]. "Population of Indonesia by Province 1971, 1980, 1990, 1995 and 2000." <http://www.bps.go.id/sector/population/table1.shtml>.

Frederick, William H., and Robert L. Worden, eds. *Indonesia: A Country Study*. Washington, DC: Library of Congress, 1992. <http://lcweb2.loc.gov/frd/cs/idtoc.html>.

King, Dwight. *Half-Hearted Reform: Electoral Institutions and the Struggle for Democracy in Indonesia*. Westport, CT: Praeger, 2003.

Komisi Pemilihan Umum [Indonesian Elections Commission]. <http://www.kpu.go.id>.

Permanent Mission of Indonesia to the United Nations. "About Indonesia," 2004. <http://www.indonesiamission-ny.org/indonesia/indonesia/indonFrameSet2.html>.

Ricklefs, M. C. *A History of Modern Indonesia Since c. 1200*. Basingstoke, UK: Palgrave, 2001.

TempoInteractive. <http://www.tempointeractive.com/>.

"Tigers Adrift." *Economist.com*, March 5, 1998. <http://www.economist.com>.

Transparency International. *International Corruption Perceptions Index 2004*. <http://www.transparency.org/cpi/2004/dnld/media_pack_en.pdf>.

Transparency International. "Plundering Politicians and Bribing Multinationals Undermine Economic Development, says TI" March 25, 2004. <http://www.transparency.org/pressreleases_archive/2004/2004.03.25.gcr_relaunch.html>.

Van Dijk, Kees. *A Country in Despair: Indonesia Between 1997 and 2000*. Leiden, The Netherlands: KITLV Press, 2002.

The World Bank Indonesia. <http://www.worldbank.org/id>.

Paige Johnson Tan

Inter-American Commission and Court of Human Rights

The Organization of American States (OAS) created the Inter-American Commission on Human Rights in 1959 by resolution of the Fifth Meeting of Consultation of Ministers of Foreign Affairs. The commission's function originally was to promote respect for the human rights set forth in the American Declaration of the Rights and Duties of Man, approved by the OAS in 1948. Over time, the **mandate** of the commission expanded and its legal status was enhanced when it became a formal organ of the OAS in 1970.

mandate: to command, order, or require; or, a command, order, or requirement

Today, the Inter-American Commission on Human Rights is the principal OAS organ to promote the observance and protection of human rights and serve as a consultant to the OAS on human rights matters. The commission also has specific competence over matters relating to the fulfillment of obligations undertaken by states parties to all human rights conventions adopted in the regional framework (with the exception of the Convention on Persons with Disabilities, which creates a separate supervisory committee). Details of the functions and procedures of the commission are contained in its **statute** and regulations.

statute: a law created by a legislature that is inferior to constitutional law

The commission consists of seven independent experts elected to four-year terms by the OAS General Assembly. It is based in Washington, D.C., and is assisted by a secretariat headed by an executive secretary. Funding for the commission comes from the OAS budget. Commission sessions are normally held in Washington, D.C., but they also may be held in cities in other member states. During its sessions, the commission holds hearings during which, on request, it hears from individuals and representatives of human rights organizations and states.

Article 33 of the American Convention on Human Rights lists the Commission and the Inter-American Court of Human Right as the organs having "competence with respect to matters relating to the fulfillment of the commitments made by States Parties to [the] Convention." The court also has some functions extending to all OAS member states and to parties to the Convention on Violence against Women and the Disappearances. The court consists of seven judges, nominated and elected for six-year terms by the parties to the American Convention. Judges may be re-elected once. The court's functions and procedures are set forth in the American Convention and its Statute and Rules of Procedure. The court's permanent seat is in San Jose, Costa Rica.

The commission operates through thematic or country studies concerning human rights issues and by considering **petitions**. Provided that the formal and substantive requirements are met, individuals or groups may file a petition with the commission against any state that violates its human rights obligations. For states that are not party to the convention, the recognized rights are those contained in the American Declaration. For parties to the American Convention, the rights contained in the convention are protected in relation to all events that occur after the date of **ratification**, including continuing violations that may have begun prior to that date.

In processing petitions, the commission is directed to attempt a friendly settlement and may undertake a mission on site or hold hearings if it deems it necessary and appropriate. Commission practice commonly includes informal visits to a country by the commissioner who is the **rapporteur** for the country along with a staff attorney. The visits typically concern more than one case and are directed at fact finding, obtaining evidence or engaging the parties in friendly settlements. The petition process may result in a commission decision on the merits, together with specific recommendations to the state concerned. The commission may call for the state to pay appropriate compensation when it finds a violation has occurred, but it does not itself set the amount of compensation it views as appropriate.

In serious and urgent cases, the commission may, on its own initiative or as requested by a party, request that the state concerned adopt precautionary measures to prevent irreparable harm to persons. The commission may request information from the parties on any matter related to the adoption and observance of the precautionary measures. The commission may also request that the court order provisional measures in urgent cases that involve danger to persons. Precautionary measures have become very important in the commission's practice. Such measures have been sought to protect witnesses and petitioners from violence or to conserve evidence.

For the Inter-American Court to have **jurisdiction** over an individual case, the state concerned must be a party to the American Convention and have accepted the optional jurisdiction of the court; proceedings before the commission must be completed, and the case must be referred by the commission or the state concerned within three months after the commission has completed its work on the case. An individual petitioner cannot invoke the court's jurisdiction.

Under the rules of the commission, there is a presumption that all cases should go to the court if the commission has found one or more violations and

petition: a written appeal for a desired action, or, to request an action, especially of government

ratify: to make official or to officially sanction

rapporteur: one that reports on a committee's work

jurisdiction: the territory or area within which authority may be exercised

the responsible state has not complied with the commission's recommendations within the time period specified by the commission. A reasoned decision by an **absolute** majority of the commission is required to withhold such a case from the court. The position of the petitioner can be influential in this respect. Other factors that the commission may consider include the nature and seriousness of the violation, the need to develop or clarify case law, the future effect of the decision on member states, and the quality of the evidence. If the court finds a violation of the convention, it may order that the situation be remedied and may award compensation to the injured party. States are legally obliged to comply with a judgment of the court, and a **remedial** order may be enforced in the appropriate domestic courts.

As with other human rights institutions around the world, the Inter-American bodies exercise influence through the compelling moral claim of human rights, through careful fact finding of human rights violations, and through public pressure. Both the commission and the court have follow-up procedures to monitor compliance with their decisions and judgments. The binding nature of the court's judgments enhances compliance, which has generally

absolute: complete, pure, free from restriction or limitation

remedial: intended as a solution

OUTSIDE THE HONDURAS NATIONAL CONGRESS IN LATE 1995, MEMBERS OF THE COMMITTEE OF THE DETAINED-DISAPPEARED IN HONDURAS (COFADEH) PLACE PHOTOS OF MILITARY PERSONNEL BELIEVED RESPONSIBLE FOR THE DISAPPEARANCES. The Honduran COFADEH was founded by Zenaida Velasquez Rodriguez, whose brother, Manfredo Velasquez, was killed by Honduran security forces in 1981. COFADEH estimates that about 180 people were abducted between 1981 and 1989 by the Honduran government.
(SOURCE: ORLANDO SIERRA/AFP/GETTY IMAGES)

been good thus far. At the same time, the commission and court suffer from lack of human and financial resources coupled with a growing caseload. An absence of political will to confront human rights abuses, observed on the part of some OAS member states, also hampers the work of the commission and court to achieve more effective realization of internationally guaranteed human rights.

The first cases successfully brought to the Inter-American Court were originally filed at the Inter-American Commission by a Honduran non-governmental organization and concerned Honduran disappeared persons. Decisions on the Honduran cases were reached in 1988 and 1989. In 2003, the Inter-American Commission submitted fifteen cases to the Inter-American Court of Human Rights. This compares with only four cases submitted five years before in 1998. In an appraisal written in 1999 one scholar lauds the Court:

[I]ts orders have compensated victims and their families, secured lives and physical integrity, freed persons unjustly imprisoned, and led to reforms of national laws and judicial doctrine. Its opinions articulate a jurisprudence of fundamental rights that placed the inherent dignity of human persons . . . at the center of law. (Cassel 1999, p. 175)

See also: American Declaration of the Rights and Duties of Man and the American Convention on Human Rights.

jurisprudence: the body of precedents already decided in a legal system

BIBLIOGRAPHY

Buergenthal, Thomas, and Dinah Shelton. *Protecting Human Rights in the Americas: Cases and Materials.* 4th ed. Arlington, VA: N. P. Engel, 1995.

Buergenthal, Thomas, Dinah Shelton, and David Stewart. *International Human Rights in a Nutshell.* 3rd ed. Eagan, MN: West Publishing, 2002.

Cassel, Douglass. "Peru Withdraws from the Court: Will the Inter-American Rights System Meet the Challenge?" *Human Rights Law Journal* 20, nos. 4–6 (1999):167–175.

Medina-Quiroga, Cecilia. *The Battle of Human Rights: Gross, Systematic Violations and the Inter-American System.* Dordrecht, The Netherlands, Martinus Nijhoff, 1988.

Dinah Shelton

Interest Groups

Interest groups are an integral part of democratic systems: They allow individuals to become involved in the political process by advocating a cause or interest that is important to them. They are outlets for the people's expression of concern over certain issues. Interest groups in the United States have undergone many changes since the 1960s, but they still remain a strong and significant part the political process. Much can also be learned from studying interest groups through a comparative perspective.

An influential comparative analysis distinguishes two significant types of organized interest groups: institutional and associational groups. Institutional groups include large-scale organizations such as churches, militaries, and bureaucracies that serve important social or governmental functions that are not directly related to the interests of their members. Because of their size and importance, institutional interest groups are important participants in the political and policy making process in most countries, despite their nominal lack of focus on their members' political interests.

Associational interest groups are the types of groups that are most frequently referred to as interest groups in political analyses. They can be defined as groups of individuals or organizations that have come together in an organized way to promote an interest or set of interests. By organizing themselves into groups, individuals or organizations hope to influence the government to adopt policies that will further their cause. In addition to trying to influence policymakers, interest groups also provide valuable (if self-serving) information to the government on the costs, benefits, and consequences of proposed policies. Because forming and operating interest groups takes economic resources, time, and skill, they are much more frequent and important in the politics. Associational interest groups are often few in number and weak in power in the world's economically and politically less privileged nations.

Since the 1960s there has been an explosion of interest groups on the American political scene. There have also been changes in the types of activity of interest groups. In the past the predominant activity of an interest group was to attempt to influence the government to adopt policies that were favorable to its **platform**. In the twenty-first century, interest groups also provide the government with information and help to implement policies. This makes them an invaluable source to busy legislators who do not have time to become experts on all the policies that are put before them. However, interest groups are not without their problems. Just as a lack of wealth prevents the formation of associational interest groups in underprivileged nations, so it can lead to the inadequate representation of the interests of less powerful and underprivileged groups in the politics of wealth nations and a consequent policy bias against the interests of such groups.

Regardless of the resource bases, all interest groups must try to cope with the "free-rider" problem, which occurs when the fruits of an interest group's labor cannot be limited to members. If a group lobbies for a cleaner environment and achieves its goal; cleaner air is not enjoyed solely by the groups' members—everyone enjoys the cleaner air. Rational individuals see that there is no reason that they should expend their time and possibly their money to belong (or perhaps participate actively) to this group because they will enjoy the results no matter what. To combat this, groups offer a variety of benefits. Larger interest groups face this problem more frequently than smaller groups because smaller groups do not provide the anonymity that larger groups do with the result that face-to-face pressure can be applied to individuals to force them to actively participate.

Interest groups provide material, solidary, and purposive benefits for individuals as a way to entice them to join. Material benefits include discounted services or memberships to other organizations along with other economic benefits. A solidary benefit is the satisfaction that one derives from association and interaction with like-minded individuals. A purposive benefit is the satisfaction that one derives from contributing to an abstract cause. The benefits offered depend on the size of the interest group, with larger groups able to offer material benefits more easily than smaller groups. Benefits may be either tangible or symbolic, but interest groups are sure to offer some type of benefit to mobilize individuals to express their common concern and achieve their common goal.

Democratic governments are very conducive to the activities of interest groups. The structure of the U.S. government, for example, is **decentralized** and **pluralistic**, which means that there are points of access to the government at the local, state, and national level. Decentralization provides many opportunities for interest groups to **lobby** for their particular cause at the most appropriate level of government. Pluralism allows many groups to compete at once for the

platform: a statement of principles or legislative goals made by a political party

decentralize: to move power from a central authority to multiple periphery government branches or agencies

pluralism: a system of government in which all groups participate in the decision-making process

lobby: to advocate for a specific political decision by attempting to persuade decision makers

regime: a type of government, or, the government in power in a region

attention of the government. It helps to create a balance in the political order, and it also allows more individuals to become involved and more interests to be represented. Interest groups are thus a natural part of a democratic **regime**. Democratic government fosters interest groups and the activity of interest groups fosters democratic government because they allow many individuals to become involved in the political world.

Interest groups in Western European governments are also beneficial to their governments. In European countries economic groups are much stronger and more influential than in the United States. Economic interest groups in the United States are weak as a result of fragmentation. In European countries, there may be one or two main economic groups that dictate what the government policy should be. Noneconomic groups, on the other hand, have better participation levels in the United States than in Western European governments.

Interest groups have the important job of articulating the interests of the people. This is particularly important in democratic countries because the very form of the government relies on the activity and interest of the people. Participation through interest groups empowers individuals to become active in the political process. The politics of democratic countries are the politics of interests and interest groups help articulate and facilitate the implementation of the interests of the people.

See also: Democracy.

IN TALLAHASSEE IN 2004, LOBBYISTS MEET PRIOR TO THE START OF THE FLORIDA HOUSE OF REPRESENTATIVEÍS SESSION AT THE CAPITOL BUILDING. A function of local, state, and federal government, lobbying on behalf of an interest group is guaranteed by the First Amendment to the U.S. Constitution and spans many divergent types of industries and organizations. (SOURCE: AP/WIDE WORLD PHOTOS)

BIBLIOGRAPHY

Almond, Gabriel, and G. Bingham Powell. *Comparative Politics: System, Process, and Policy*. Boston: Little Brown and Company, 1969.

Hays, R. Allen. *Who Speaks for the Poor?* New York: Routledge, 2001.

Loomis, Burdett A., and Allan J. Cigler. "Introduction: The Changing Nature of Interest Group Politics." In *Interest Group Politics*, ed. Allan J. Cigler and Burdett A. Loomis. Washington DC: Congressional Quarterly Press, 1995.

Miller, Stephen. "The 1970s: The Rise of Public Interest Groups." In *Special Interest Groups in American Politics*. New Brunswick, NJ: Transaction Books, 1983.

Petracca, Mark P., ed. *The Politics of Interests: Interest Groups Transformed*. Boulder, CO: Westview Press, 1992.

Rossiter, Clinton, ed. *The Federalist Papers*. New York: Mentor, 1961.

Thomas, Clive S., ed. *Political Parties and Interest Groups*. Boulder, CO: Lynne Rienner Publishers, 2001.

Emily Corwin

International Convention on the Elimination of All Forms of Racial Discrimination

See International Human Rights Law.

International Court of Justice

The International Court of Justice (ICJ) is the principal judicial organ of the United Nations (UN). As such, its primary role is to assist the other organs of the UN achieve the objective of the United Nations Charter (UN Charter); namely, the peaceful resolution of disputes between states. The Court fulfills this responsibility by resolving legal questions so that either the parties or the UN can find a political solution. The Court sits in the famous Peace Palace in The Hague, the Netherlands.

HISTORY

The ICJ is the successor to the Permanent Court of International Justice (PCIJ), which was forced to relocate to Geneva during World War II (1939–1945). Although the PCIJ continued with administrative matters, its operations effectively ceased. No mention of a world court occurred in the initial planning for postwar reconstruction (the Atlantic Charter and the Four Nations Declaration on General Security in Moscow). Instead, separate committees in Latin America, the United States, and Great Britain began discussions on the subject, the key issue being whether to retain the PCIJ or create a new international court.

The Inter-American Juridical Committee formed in January 1942 emphasized the need to maintain continuity with the PCIJ. In late 1942 the U.S. Special Subcommittee on Legal Problems favored the creation of a new court based on a revised **statute** of the PCIJ. A report of the Informal Inter-Allied Committee of Experts in England concluded in May 1943 that the PCIJ Statute

statute: a law created by a legislature that is inferior to constitutional law

should form the basis for a world court; however, it viewed a decision on whether the PCIJ should be that court as beyond the committee's competence. Even the Dumbarton Oaks Proposals remained inconclusive, despite mentioning an international court of justice.

Some consensus emerged when the Committee of Jurists, comprising representatives from a total of forty-four nations, as well as the PCIJ, met in Washington, D.C., on April 9, 1945, and drafted a new statute for the forthcoming San Francisco Conference. At San Francisco it was decided that a new court would be created, but one having continuity with the PCIJ by referring to the PCIJ Statute in Article 92 of the new court's statute, itself an integral part of the UN Charter.

On April 18, 1946, the League of Nations voted itself and the PCIJ out of existence. The very same day the ICJ held its inaugural session at the Peace Palace and heard its first matter, the Corfu Channel case, on May 22, 1947.

BOSNIA BRINGS GENOCIDE CHARGES AGAINST SERBIA AT THE INTERNATIONAL COURT OF JUSTICE (ICJ) AT THE HAGUE'S PEACE PALACE IN 1996.
Hearing disputes between countries, the International Court of Justice (ICJ) resides in the Peace Palace at The Hague and replaced the Permanent Court of International Justice after a statute created the ICJ in 1946. (SOURCE: AP/WIDE WORLD PHOTOS)

STRUCTURE AND JURISDICTION

The ICJ is comprised of fifteen full-time judges, each a different nationality. In accordance with Article 9 of its Statute, the Court must represent the main forms of civilization and the world's principal legal systems. Thus, seats on the bench are allocated as follows: Western Europe and other states, five seats; Asia, three seats; Africa, three seats; Eastern Europe, two seats; and Latin America, two seats.

Members are elected independently by a majority in both the Security Council and the General Assembly and serve for nine years. Elections are staggered so that they are held every three years for five members, unless a member dies or resigns. The Court elects its president and vice president by **absolute** majority, and each holds office for three years. The president may cast a vote in split decisions.

In addition, **ad hoc** judges may be appointed to ensure that one member of the bench is the same nationality as each party in a dispute. This procedure has been criticized on the grounds that it destroys the international character of the Court and contravenes the legal principle that no man or woman should be a judge in his or her own cause.

To shorten resolution times, the ICJ Statute permits the creation of chambers: the Chamber of Summary Procedure, established annually and consisting of a president and vice president ex officio, and three other members; a special chamber, consisting of three or more members; and an ad hoc chamber that can be set up as required with as many judges as the Court determines and the parties approve.

Pursuant to its Statute, the Court can consider only questions of international law in both its advisory (Article 65) and contentious jurisdictions (Article 36). The Court exercises its advisory **jurisdiction** when a principal organ of the UN, such as the General Assembly, requests advice on a question of international law. Only states have standing to appear in the contentious jurisdiction, and a state must be a party to the ICJ Statute (all members of the UN are automatically a party). Further, this jurisdiction is consensual. Parties consent by a compromise, a special agreement between parties, or when a bilateral or multilateral treaty contains a clause referring disputes to the Court, and by a **unilateral** declaration made in advance accepting jurisdiction in a range of matters listed in Article 36(2) of the ICJ Statute (on **compulsory** jurisdiction). Such consent is usually subject to reservations excluding specific matters.

Article 37 of the ICJ Statute enables the ICJ to hear disputes that the PCIJ was entitled to hear by way of treaty. The Court resolves any questions regarding its jurisdiction.

STRENGTHS AND WEAKNESSES

Consensual jurisdiction is the Court's greatest weakness, since not all states have granted their consent. States can also withdraw their consent, and their reservations to Article 36(2) often render their consent meaningless. Second, when the Court seeks to invoke its compulsory jurisdiction, the risk of nonappearance by parties exists. There were many incidents of nonappearance during the 1970s and 1980s, the most famous being the U.S. absence in the Nicaragua case. The nonappearance of parties raises concerns that justice has not been

absolute: complete, pure, free from restriction or limitation

ad hoc: created for a specific purpose or to address a certain problem

jurisdiction: the territory or area within which authority may be exercised

unilateral: independent of any other person or entity

compulsory: mandatory, required, or unable to be avoided

■ ■ ■

NICARAGUA V. UNITED STATES

Nicaragua v. United States was a case heard by the International Court of Justice (ICJ) in 1986 concerning the United States' support of the Contra guerillas in Nicaragua's civil war and the mining of the country's harbors. The United States initially denied that the ICJ had jurisdiction in the matter. The ICJ disputed this claim, although the judges differed considerably among themselves regarding the extent of the court's powers.

The court issued its ruling in favor of Nicaragua on June 27, 1986. It found that the United States had broken its obligations under international law not to intervene in the affairs of another state; not to use force against another state; not to violate the sovereignty of another state; and not to interfere with peaceful commerce on the seas.

The United States' refused to accept the court's decision and withdrew of its previous acceptance of the court's jurisdiction. The United States also refused to pay the fine imposed by the Court. The case is often cited as an example of the ICJ's inability to enforce its rulings, often being disempowered by the same nations that created it.

done, arguably weakening the final decision. Alternatively, the legal process could be stymied.

States also have a history of noncompliance with the Court's rulings. Although the Court's judgments can be enforced through a Security Council resolution, no international police force exists to ensure compliance. Instead, enforcement is achieved by peer group pressure from other states.

Other criticisms include the following: the Court's reluctance to use provisional measures; its alleged lack of proactivity; its slow progress in hearing cases on the docket; and most controversial, the lack of standing for non-state entities.

The ICJ has one important advantage over the UN political organs: All parties are guaranteed a fair and impartial hearing. Despite concerns that its judges may be biased, studies have shown that in their decisions, they (even the ad hoc judges) willingly vote against their own national governments. One example involved Justice Stephen M. Schwebel (b. 1929) of the United States in the case concerning *Delimitation of the Maritime Boundary in the Gulf of Maine Area (Canada v. United States of America)*. In his dissenting opinion, Judge Schwebel voted against the United States' position and held it was correct to divide the Georges Bank between the United States and Canada. He disagreed with the Chamber's line of delimitation because it gave the United States a significantly greater proportion of the Gulf of Maine, and therefore was "inequitable." Moreover, no evidence exists of judges ever having been influenced by their national government. By restricting itself to the legal issues involved, the Court remains free from the political considerations and entanglements found elsewhere within the UN. This enables the Court to fully exploit its expertise and significantly aids its ability to sift through dubious statements made by national representatives in the guise of evidence, crucial when assisting parties or advising the political organs of the UN. The integrity of the Court is its greatest strength.

THE COURT'S SUCCESS

The ICJ, like any court, has been criticized for its individual decisions or advice given: for example, the controversial South West Africa cases, second phase (1966); the East Timor case (1995); or the nuclear weapons opinion (1986). However, the major criticism has been that the Court is ineffective. Given the consensual nature of the Court's jurisdiction and the highly political environment of international relations, this is no surprise. In the Nicaragua case (1986), for example, the United States withdrew from the case, revoked its Article 36(2) consent, and ignored the Court's determination of its liability.

Such criticisms ignore the results the Court can achieve [e.g., as a consequence of the Court's determination in the Libyan Arab Jamahiriya/Chad case (1994), a peace agreement was signed, and Libyan forces withdrew from disputed territory], and its often subtle successes. The Court's decision in the Nicaragua case played a crucial role in the U.S. government's decision to change its policy in Nicaragua and may have hastened the subsequent end to the conflict. Furthermore, many smaller states viewed the ICJ as standing firm against the world's most powerful state.

Although the potential for noncompliance exists, the fact remains that many states willingly comply with international law, as it is continually developed through both the Court's decisions and advisory opinions. In the Pakistani prisoners of war case, the mere threat of legal proceedings resulted in the 1974 Simla Agreement between India and Pakistan.

Since the Nicaragua case a marked **resurgence** of interest in the Court has occurred. In January 2004 two matters were heard: the controversial Legal Consequences of the Construction of a Wall in the Occupied Palestinian Territory (Request for Advisory Opinion) and Avena and Other Mexican Nationals (*Mexico v. United States of America*), with nine cases currently being heard and an additional twenty-one matters pending. They included border disputes, questions of **sovereignty**, the legality of the use of force, assets seized during World War II, allegations of genocide, and maritime law.

The increased use of the Court, rather than violence, as a means of resolving disputes is the Court's greatest achievement, and proof that it successfully meets its responsibilities under the UN Charter.

See also: United Nations.

resurgence: a return to action from a diminished state

sovereignty: autonomy; or, rule over a political entity

BIBLIOGRAPHY

Case Concerning East Timor. *Australia v. Portugal.* ICJ Report 89 (1995).

Coleman, Andrew. "The International Court of Justice and Highly Political Matters." *Melbourne Journal of International Law* 4, no. 1 (2003):29.

Corfu Channel Case (Merits). *UK v. Albania.* ICJ Report 4 (1949).

Gill, Terry. *Litigation Strategy at the International Court: A Case Study of the* Nicaragua v. United States *Dispute.* The Hague: Martinus Nijhoff, 1989.

Hensley, Thomas. "National Bias and the International Court of Justice." *Midwest Journal of Political Science* 12 (1968):568.

Highet, Keith. "The Peace Palace Heats Up: The World Court in Business Again?" *American Journal of International Law* 85 (1991):646.

Legality of the Threat or Use of Nuclear Weapons (Advisory Opinion). ICJ Report 22 (1996).

Military and Paramilitary Activities in and Against Nicaragua. *Nicaragua v. the United States of America.* ICJ Report 392 (1984).

Peck, Connie, and Roy Lee, eds. *Increasing the Effectiveness of the International Court of Justice: Proceedings of the ICJ/UNITAR Colloquium to Celebrate the 50th Anniversary of the Court.* The Hague: Martinus Nijhoff, 1997.

Rosenne, Shabtai. *The World Court, What It Is and How It Works,* 5th ed. The Hague: Martinus Nijhoff, 1996.

Szafraz, Renata. *The Compulsory Jurisdiction of the International Court of Justice.* The Hague: Martinus Nijhoff, 1993.

Stanimir, Alexandrov. *Reservations in Unilateral Declarations Accepting the Compulsory Jurisdiction of the International Court of Justice.* The Hague: Martinus Nijhoff, 1995.

Territorial Dispute (Libyan Arab Jamahiriya/Chad) (Judgment). ICJ Report 6 (1994).

Tiefenbrun, Susan. "The Role of the World Court in Settling International Disputes: A Recent Assessment." *Loyola of Los Angeles International and Comparative Law Journal* 20 (1997):1.

Weiss, E. B. "Judicial Independence and Impartiality." In *The International Court of Justice at a Crossroads,* ed. Lori Damrosch. Dobbs Ferry, New York: Transnational Publishers, 1987.

Andrew Coleman

International Covenant on Civil and Political Rights

■ ■ ■

FAST FACTS

Rights considered inalienable include the right to life; the freedom from torture and slavery; and the freedom of thought, conscience, and religion.

■ ■ ■

ratify: to make official or to officially sanction

self-determination: the ability of a people to determine their own destiny or political system

recourse: a resource for assistance

The International Covenant on Civil and Political Rights (CCPR) is part of the "international bill of rights" that also includes the Universal Declaration of Human Rights (1948) and the International Covenant on Economic, Social and Cultural Rights (CESCR) (1976). Drafts of the CESCR and CCPR were completed in 1953 and 1954. The United Nations (UN) General Assembly reviewed those drafts at its ninth session, in 1954, and voted to publish the drafts, circulate them widely, and solicit worldwide feedback. It also recommended that its Third Committee begin a detailed consideration of the drafts at its tenth session, in 1955. It was not until 1966, however, that a consensus was reached on both covenants. The Covenant on Civil and Political Rights (CCPR) was submitted for state approval on December 16, 1966; it entered into force on March 23, 1976, after thirty-five states had **ratified** it.

Among the rights of nation-states specified in the CCPR are the right of **self-determination**, the right of free trade, and the right to subsistence. The rights of individuals in the CCPR include the right to legal **recourse** when one's rights have been violated; the right to life, liberty, and freedom of movement; the right to equality before the law; due process rights in criminal proceedings; the right to privacy; and freedom of thought, conscience, religion, expression, assembly, and association.

The CCPR also prohibits torture, inhumane or degrading treatment, slavery or involuntary servitude, arbitrary arrest and detention, and the use of debtors' prisons. In addition, it guarantees the rights of children and prohibits discrimination based on race, sex, color, national origin, or language.

The CCPR allows states to suspend (or derogate) some of these rights in the event of a temporary civil emergency, but lists those rights that shall not be subject to derogation. Nonderogable rights include the right to life; the prohibition of torture and slavery; freedom of thought, conscience, and religion; and the prohibition of categorical discrimination. The abolition of the death penalty in the Second Optional Protocol is nonderogable for nation-states that have ratified this provision.

As of 2004, 151 state parties adhered to the Covenant. The CPPR was sent to the U.S. Senate for ratification in 1978, but the United States finally agreed to comply with it after years of delay on September 8, 1992. So far 151 states have adhered to the First Optional Protocol to the Covenant that allows individuals from adhering states to file complaints with the eighteen-member UN Human Rights Committee, which is the institution created by the Covenant for monitoring and implementing the CCPR. The Human Rights Committee hears complaints from individuals in closed meetings and the identity of all complainants is protected. All findings of the Committee are public and included in its annual report to the UN General Assembly. The Second Optional Protocol to the

CCPR focuses on the abolition of the death penalty, and it has been ratified by fifty state parties. The United States has not ratified either optional protocol.

See also: International Covenant on Economic, Social and Cultural Rights; Universal Declaration of Human Rights.

BIBLIOGRAPHY

Ian Brownlie, ed. *Basic Documents in International Law*, 5th ed. Oxford, UK: Clarendon Press, 2002.

Steiner, Henry J., and Philip Alston. *International Human Rights in Context: Law, Politics, Morals*. Oxford, UK: Clarendon Press, 2000.

United Nations High Commissioner on Human Rights. <http: unhchr.ch/html/menu3/ b/a_ccpr.htm>.

Donald W. Jackson

International Covenant on Economic, Social and Cultural Rights

The International Covenant of Economic, Social and Cultural Rights (CESCR), which after some twenty years of debates was adopted in the United Nation's (UN) General Assembly, opened for signature on December 16, 1966, and entered into force on January 3, 1976. The CESCR binds 148 state parties. The United States signed the CESCR on October 5, 1977, but it has not yet **ratified** the covenant and seems unlikely to do so for the foreseeable future. The U.S. government has consistently been more reluctant to recognize economic and social rights, such as the right to health, education, and minimal standards of food, clothing, and shelter, than it has the civil and political rights recognized in the UN's International Covenant of Civil and Political Rights, a distinction that was often pointed out by the Soviet Union before its collapse.

ratify: to make official or to officially sanction

The rights set out in the CESCR are monitored by the eighteen-member Committee on Economic, Social and Cultural Rights, which was established in its current form in 1985 by the UN Economic and Social Council and first convened in 1987. A draft optional protocol to CESCR, calling for the right of individual or group complaints concerning noncompliance with the Covenant, was adopted by the Committee on Economic, Social and Cultural Rights in 1996, but it has not yet been adopted by the UN Commission on Human Rights, a necessary precondition for submission for ratification.

The CESCR begins by acknowledging the rights of all peoples to **self-determination** through which they may "freely determine their political status and freely pursue their economic, social and cultural development" (Article 1). The positive rights recognized in the CESCR are the right to work (Article 6); the right to the "enjoyment of just and favorable conditions of work," including fair wages and equal remuneration for work of equal value (Article 7); the right to form trade unions and labor federations and the right to strike (Article 8); the right to social security, including social insurance (Article 9); the protection and assistance of families, mothers, and children (Article 10); the right to an adequate standard of living, including food (to be free from hunger), clothing, and shelter (Article 11); the right to the

self-determination: the ability of a people to determine their own destiny or political system

UNITED NATIONS EDUCATIONAL, SCIENTIFIC, AND CULTURAL ORGANIZATION (UNESCO) BUILDING IN PARIS, FRANCE. The United Nation's Committee on Economic, Social, and Cultural Rights, which supervises the execution of the CESCR, works closely with UNESCO on the subject of the right to education. (SOURC: LOOMIS DEAN/TIME LIFE PICTURES/GETTY IMAGES)

"enjoyment of the highest attainable standards of physical and mental health" (Article 12); the right to education (Article 13); and the right to take part in cultural life, to enjoy the benefits of science, and to reap the benefits of intellectual property (Article 15).

State parties that are bound by the CESCR have the duty of reviewing their implementation of these rights and reporting periodically to the Committee on Economic, Social and Cultural Rights. The eighteen members of the Committee are elected by the UN Economic and Social Council for four-year terms. The Committee seeks to determine whether the rights set out in the CESCR are being supported by states' parties and ways that the implementation of those rights might be improved.

At its fiftieth session in 1996, the Committee on Economic, Social and Cultural Rights developed a comprehensive program for more effective implementation of economic, social, and cultural rights and forwarded it to the UN High Commissioner on Human Rights for review by all the relevant UN institutions within the human rights domain. Still, for most of the states' parties, the rights contained in the CESCR remain fond aspirations rather than recognized realities.

See also: Convention on the Elimination of All Forms of Discrimination Against Women; International Covenant on Civil and Political Rights; Universal Declaration of Human Rights.

BIBLIOGRAPHY

Brownlie, Ian, ed. *Basic Documents in International Law*. 5th ed. Oxford, UK: Clarendon Press, 2002.

Office of the United Nations High Commissioner for Human Rights. *International Covenant on Economic, Social and Cultural Rights*. <http://www.unhchr.ch/html/menu3/b/a_cescr.htm>.

Steiner, Henry J. and Philip Alston. *International Human Rights in Context: Law, Politics, Morals*. Oxford, UK: Clarendon Press, 2000.

Donald W. Jackson

International Criminal Court

In the aftermath of the international war crimes trials before the Nuremberg and Tokyo Tribunals in 1946, the international community began to direct its energies toward the establishment of a permanent international criminal court (ICC). In 1948 the United Nations (UN) General Assembly requested the UN International Law Commission to study the feasibility of establishing a permanent war crimes tribunal. The International Law Commission submitted a draft **statute** for such a court in 1953, but the project was shelved during the Cold War because of U.S. and Soviet suspicions that the existence of such a court might imperil their national security policies.

With the creation of the **ad hoc** Former Yugoslavia and Rwanda Tribunals by the UN Security Council in the early 1990s, there was a growing consensus that similar international justice mechanisms should be employed on a case-by-case basis to prosecute crimes against humanity elsewhere in the world. Even the most ardent opponents of a permanent ICC had come to see the ad hoc tribunals as a useful foreign policy tool. The experience with the Former Yugoslavia and Rwanda tribunals proved that an international indictment and arrest warrant could serve to isolate offending leaders diplomatically, strengthen the hand of domestic rivals, and fortify international political will to impose economic **sanctions** and take more aggressive actions if necessary.

However, something known in government circles as "tribunal fatigue" eventually set in. The process of reaching agreement on the tribunal's statute; electing judges; selecting a prosecutor; hiring staff; negotiating headquarters agreements and judicial assistance pacts; erecting courtrooms, offices, and prisons; and appropriating funds turned out to be too time-consuming and exhausting for the members of the Security Council to undertake on a repeated basis. China and other permanent members of the Security Council let it be known that Rwanda would be the last of the ad hoc tribunals established by the Security Council.

Consequently, many UN members began to see the establishment of a permanent ICC as an improvement over the ad hoc approach. In 1994, the UN International Law Commission produced a new draft statute for an ICC that largely was based on the statutes and rules of the popular ad hoc tribunals. The International Law Commission's draft subsequently was refined through a series of preparatory conferences, culminating in a diplomatic conference held in Rome during the summer of 1998.

statute: a law created by a legislature that is inferior to constitutional law

ad hoc: created for a specific purpose or to address a certain problem

sanction: economic, political, or military reprisals, or, to ratify

jurisdiction: the territory or area within which authority may be exercised

THE POLITICS OF ROME

The statute that emerged from the Rome diplomatic conference envisioned a permanent ICC, based in The Hague (a city in the Netherlands), with **jurisdiction** over genocide, crimes against humanity, and war crimes. The most controversial issue at Rome was how the court would exercise its jurisdiction.

The Rome diplomatic conference represented a point of tension between the United States, which sought a Security Council-controlled court, and most of the world's other countries. The latter felt that no one accused of serious war crimes or genocide, regardless of country, should be exempt from the jurisdiction of a permanent ICC. Moreover, these countries were concerned about the possibility that the Security Council would once again slide into the state of paralysis that characterized the Cold War years, rendering a Security Council–controlled court ineffective. The justification for the American position was that, as the world's greatest military and economic power, more than any other country the United States is expected to intervene to halt humanitarian catastrophes around the world. The United States' unique position renders U.S. personnel uniquely vulnerable to the potential jurisdiction of an ICC. In sum, the U.S. administration feared that an independent ICC prosecutor would turn out to be a rogue official who would bedevil U.S. military personnel and officials and frustrate U.S. foreign policy.

Many of the countries at Rome were sympathetic to the United States' concerns. Thus, what emerged from Rome was a court with a two-track system of jurisdiction. The first track would apply to situations referred to the court by the Security Council. This track would create binding obligations on all states to comply with orders for evidence or the surrender of indicted persons under Chapter VII of the UN Charter. This track would be enforced by Security Council–imposed embargoes, the freezing of assets of leaders and their supporters, and/or by authorizing the use of force. The United States favored this track and would likely employ it in the event of a future Bosnia or Rwanda. The second track would apply to situations referred to the court by individual countries or the ICC prosecutor. This track would have no built-in process for enforcement, but instead would rely on the good-faith cooperation of the parties to the court's statute. Most of the delegates in Rome recognized that the real power was in the first track. However, the United States still demanded protection from the second track of the court's jurisdiction. In order to mollify U.S. concerns, the following protective mechanisms were incorporated into the court's statute at the urging of the United States:

First, the court's jurisdiction under the second track would be based on a concept known as "complementarity," which was defined as meaning the court would be a last resort that is activated only when domestic authorities are unable or unwilling to prosecute. At the insistence of the United States, the delegates at Rome strengthened the concept of complementarity by providing in Article 18 of the court's statute that the prosecutor must notify states with a prosecutive interest in a case of his or her intention to commence an investigation. If, within one month of notification, such a state informs the court that it is investigating the matter, the prosecutor must defer to the state's investigation, unless it can convince the pre-trial chamber that the investigation is a sham. The decision of the pre-trial chamber is subject to interlocutory appeal to the appeals chamber.

Second, the ICC would not have retroactive jurisdiction. Thus, it could not prosecute any crimes that were committed before the Rome statute took effect.

Third, the crime of aggression was omitted from the ICC's jurisdiction because the negotiators could not agree on a definition or triggering mechanism. Thus, actions similar to the U.S. bombing of Libya in 1986, the U.S. invasion of Panama in

1989, and the U.S. invasion of Iraq in 2003 would not be within the ICC's jurisdiction unless individual war crimes were committed during the conflicts.

Fourth, Article 8 of the court's statute specifies that the Court would have jurisdiction only over "serious" war crimes that represent a "policy or plan." Thus, random acts of U.S. personnel involved in a foreign peacekeeping operation would not be subject to the court's jurisdiction. Neither would incidents such as the July 3, 1988 accidental downing of an Iranian airbus by the USS *Vincennes*, or the August 20, 1998 U.S. attack on the suspected chemical weapons facility in Sudan that turned out to be a pharmaceutical plant.

Fifth, Article 15 of the court's statute guards against spurious complaints by the ICC prosecutor by requiring the approval of a three-judge pre-trial chamber before the prosecution can launch an investigation. Further, the decision of the chamber is subject to interlocutory appeal to the appeals chamber.

Finally, Article 16 of the statute allows the Security Council to affirmatively vote to postpone an investigation or case for up to twelve months on a renewable basis. While this does not amount to the individual veto the United States had sought, it does give the United States and other Security Council members a collective veto over the court.

The U.S. delegation obtained nearly everything it sought in Rome, substantially weakening the ICC in the process. These protections proved sufficient for other major powers including the United Kingdom, France, and Russia, which joined 117 other countries in voting in favor of the Rome treaty. However, without what would amount to an ironclad veto of jurisdiction over U.S. personnel and officials, the United States felt compelled to join China, Libya, Iraq, Israel, Qatar, and Yemen as the only seven countries voting in opposition to the Rome treaty.

AFTERMATH OF ROME

In the following months, the United States tried to secure international backing for a clause to be included in the agreement that was being prepared to govern the relations between the United Nations and the ICC. Without actually amending the ICC statute, the U.S. proposal would prevent the ICC from taking custody of official personnel of non-party states where the state has acknowledged responsibility for the act in question. Prior to the Rome Diplomatic Conference, many countries felt that the success of a permanent ICC would be in question without U.S. support. However, as it became increasingly obvious that the United States was not going to sign the Rome treaty, the willingness to compromise began to evaporate. This culminated in an overwhelming vote against the U.S. amendment requiring the consent of the state of nationality at the Rome Diplomatic Conference. The United States soon discovered that it would have no more luck with the issue through a series of bilateral negotiations than it did in the frenzied atmosphere that characterized the final days of the Rome conference.

By late 2000, the Clinton administration realized that the ICC ultimately would enter into force with or without U.S. support. A growing number of countries had **ratified** the Rome treaty by December, and more than 120 countries had signed it, indicating their intention to ratify. Sixty ratifications are necessary to bring it into force. The **signatories** included every other NATO state except for Turkey, three of the Security Council's permanent members (France, Russia, and the United Kingdom), and both of the United States' closest neighbors (Mexico and Canada). Even Israel, which had been the only Western country to join the United States in voting against the ICC Treaty in Rome in 1998, later changed its position and announced that it would sign the treaty. Israel's change of position was made possible when the ICC preparatory conference provided

ratify: to make official or to officially sanction

signatory: one who signs an agreement with other parties and is then bound to that agreement

definitions of the crimes over which the ICC has jurisdiction. This clarified that the provision in the ICC statute that made altering the demographics of an occupied territory a war crime would be interpreted no more expansively than the existing law contained in the Geneva Conventions.

In the waning days of his presidency, U.S. President William J. Clinton (b. 1946) authorized the signature of the Rome treaty, making the United States the 138th country to sign the treaty by the December 31st deadline. According to the ICC statute, after December 31, 2000, states must accede to the treaty, which requires full ratification—something that was not likely for the United States in the near term, given the current level of Senate opposition to the treaty. While signature is not the equivalent of ratification, it set the stage for U.S. support of Security Council referrals to the ICC, as well as other forms of U.S. cooperation with the court. In addition, it put the United States in a better position to continue to seek additional provisions to protect American personnel from the court's jurisdiction.

Clinton's last-minute action drew immediate ire from Senator Jesse Helms, then Chairman of the U.S. Senate Foreign Relations Committee, who had been one of the treaty's strongest opponents. Senator Helms responded by pushing for passage of the American Servicemembers' Protection Act of 2001, which

THE FIRST INTERNATIONAL CRIMINAL COURT (ICC) IN THE HAGUE IS BROUGHT TO SESSION BY UN SECRETARY-GENERAL KOFI ANNAN ON MARCH 11, 2003. Drawn from the Rome Statute of 1998, the International Criminal Court (ICC) handles cases primarily involving genocide, crimes against humanity, and war crimes, and is the first permanent international criminal court. (SOURCE: AP/WIDE WORLD PHOTOS)

would require the U.S. executive branch to take a number of steps to protect U.S. personnel from the jurisdiction of the ICC. Upon entering office a few weeks later, President George W. Bush signed the American Servicemembers' Protection Act into law, and he sent a representative to the United Nations to withdraw the U.S. signature from the Rome treaty. Pursuant to the act, under threat of veto, it forced the UN Security Council to insert a provision granting immunity from the ICC's jurisdiction to troops involved in UN–authorized actions, and under threat of terminating aid, it compelled fifty countries to enter into agreements with the United States, preventing them from surrendering U.S. personnel to the ICC.

U.S. opposition did not prevent the Rome statute from entering into force. The sixtieth ratification was received on April 11, 2002, and the ICC came into being on July 1, 2002. To date, ninety-four countries have ratified the Rome treaty, including every member of the European Union.

During its first two years, the annual budget for the ICC was 55 million euros. Funding comes from the states that have ratified the Rome treaty, rather than from the United Nations. On March 26, 2003, eighteen judges were elected from the following countries: Bolivia, Brazil, Canada, Costa Rica, Cyprus, Finland, France, Germany, Ghana, Ireland, Italy, Latvia, Mali, Samoa, South Korea, South Africa, Trinidad and Tobago, and the United Kingdom.

On June 16, 2003, Luis Moreno Ocampo of Argentina was selected by the Assembly of States' Parties to be the tribunal's chief prosecutor. At the time he was selected, Ocampo had been serving as a law professor at Harvard Law School. He had gained international recognition when he successfully led the prosecution of the military officers that participated in the 1990 rebellion against Argentine democracy. In the spring of 2004, the chief prosecutor announced that the ICC's first two investigations would involve crimes against humanity committed in the Congo and Uganda. In June of 2005, the chief prosecutor started a formal investigation in Sudan's Darfur region, where war crimes were suspected to have been committed by the Sudan government.

See also: Bosnia and Herzegovina; Crimes Against Humanity; Genocide; International Court of Justice; International Humanitarian Law; Israel; Rwanda; United Nations; United States; War Crimes.

BIBLIOGRAPHY

Bassiouni, M. Cherif. *The Legislative History of the International Criminal Court.* Ardsley, NY: Transnational Publishers Inc., 2005.

Cassese, Antonio, et al. *The Rome Statute of the International Criminal Court: A Commentary.* Oxford, UK: Oxford University Press, 2002.

Coalition for the International Criminal Court. <http://www.iccnow.org>.

The Frederick K. Cox International Law Center War Crimes Research Portal. Case Western Reserve University School of Law. <http://www.law.case.edu/war-crimes-research-portal>.

International Criminal Court. <http://www.icc-cpi.int>.

Lee, Roy S. *The International Criminal Court: The Making of the Rome Statute, Issues, Negotiations, Results.* The Hague: Kluwer Law International, 1999.

Sadat, Leila Nadya. *The International Criminal Court and the Transformation of International Law: Justice for the New Millennium (Innovation in International Law).* Ardsley, NY: Transnational Publishers Inc., 2002.

Schabas, William A. *An Introduction to the International Criminal Court*. Cambridge, UK: Cambridge University Press, 2001.

Scharf, Michael P. *Balkan Justice: The Story Behind the First International War Crimes Trial Since Nuremberg*. Durham, NC: Carolina Academic Press, 1997.

Sewall, Sarah B., and Carl Kaysen. *The United States and the International Criminal Court*. Lanham, MD: Rowman & Littlefield Publishers, 2000.

Michael P. Scharf

International Human Rights Law

Section 701 of the *Restatement of the Law, Third, The Foreign Relations Law of the United States,* defines human rights as "freedoms, immunities and benefits which, according to widely accepted contemporary values, every human being should enjoy in the society in which he or she lives." International human rights law binds states to recognize certain rights that all individuals should enjoy regardless of their nationality, ethnicity, religion, or place of residence. Although the specific content and enforcement of international human rights laws are often subject to debate, nearly everyone agrees that there should be universal standards to protect individuals. International human rights law is distinct from international humanitarian law. While the former is primarily concerned with state treatment of individuals in times of peace and the absence of extraordinary circumstances, the latter is primarily concerned with limiting the effects of war on nonparticipants and regulating the conduct of war itself.

Scholars and theorists disagree on the source and justification for human rights. Some argue that rights are justified by religion or natural law. Others argue that the battle for rights emerged in response to the growing problems faced by workers during the Industrial Revolution. Still others justify rights based on the standards needed for the realization of human dignity or the need to be free from fear. Whatever the theoretical source, human rights can all be categorized as rights granted to individuals, or in the case of collective rights, to groups of people at a level below the state. Before rights were regulated at the international level, rights were conferred and enforced by states. If a state did not grant or respect the rights of its citizens, the citizens had no one to whom they could appeal. By regulating rights at the international level, however, individuals have a legal basis above the state that legitimizes their rights claims and, in some cases, assists in the enforcement of rights.

The protection of individuals by human rights law challenges the traditional practice of international law, a **corpus** of law that evolved to regulate the behavior of states in their interactions with one another. Although international law established complex mechanisms to handle day-to-day interaction between states and to provide a foundation for the settlement of disputes, until the twentieth century it left the treatment of citizens almost entirely up to the state. To regulate human rights at the international level, however, requires the **codification** of rules on the treatment of individuals by states. By doing so, international human rights law transcends the regulation of state-to-state relations and provides legal guidelines for the treatment of citizens. International human rights law is a direct challenge to the **sovereignty** of states over their citizens, a fact that helps to explain why the enforcement of human rights law has not evolved as quickly as the law itself.

corpus: a body, as in a body of work

codification: the making of official law

sovereignty: autonomy; or, rule over a political entity

HISTORICAL FOUNDATION

The earliest efforts to regulate human rights through treaties can be traced to the Protestant Reformation in Europe. Religious leaders and heads of state were concerned about the **persecution** of those who shared their religious views but lived under a ruler of a different faith. Both the Peace of Augsburg (1555) and the Treaty of Westphalia (1648) included provisions regarding religious freedoms. These provisions were designed to prevent conflicts between rulers and states with different religious practices and could largely be considered as **reciprocal** agreements that created obligations to protect rights only as part of a larger treaty between states. Later efforts to regulate human rights at the international level included the effort to abolish the international slave trade and the protection of minority rights. The latter even received attention in the Treaty of Versailles (developed in 1919 after World War I [1949–1918]), parts of which called for the protection of certain minority groups within states. These provisions of the Treaty of Versailles were not meant to be generally applicable, however. They mentioned specific groups in specific countries whose rights should be protected in an effort to prevent conflicts between the states where the minorities lived and the states with which they had an ethnic bond. Nevertheless, the Treaty of Versailles did call for colonial powers to maintain certain standards of treatment for individuals in their colonies (Article 23).

At the outbreak of World War II (1939–1945), individual rights were still recognized and enforced primarily at the state level. Individuals only had legal rights to the extent that they were recognized by the state of which they were a citizen and in which they resided. The atrocities committed in World War II highlighted the problem of having a system of rights that depended upon states. Although international humanitarian law had evolved to provide some regulation of the conduct of war and the treatment of noncombatants, no real standard of international law existed to address the treatment of German citizens by the German government. Officially, the only laws that regulated Germany's treatment of its own citizens were German laws. In response to the charges regarding the Holocaust prosecuted at the International Military Tribunal at Nuremberg, many German officers claimed that they had not violated any law. To justify its prosecution of defendants for their role in the Holocaust, the Charter for the Nuremberg military tribunals applied the concept of crimes against humanity—crimes that were, by their very nature, reprehensible to the human conscience even if no custom or treaty had explicitly prohibited the practice. The decision to try German officials for crimes against humanity set an important legal **precedent** by holding individual representatives of a state legally accountable not only for their conduct in war, but also for the abuse of any civilian, including German nationals.

The other major development at the end of World War II was the signing and entry into force of the United Nations (UN) Charter (1945). The Charter was the first multilateral document that explicitly included the words "human rights." Article 68 of the Charter even included language requiring the Economic and Social Council (ECOSOC) to establish a Commission on Human Rights. One of the first tasks assigned to this commission was the drafting of an international bill of rights. Its work culminated in the Universal Declaration of Human Rights (UDHR), adopted by the UN General Assembly on December 10, 1948. Although not in the form of a legally binding treaty, this document was the first truly international **enumeration** of human rights. Almost immediately, the commission began working toward a legally binding instrument (or instruments) that would require states to abide by the standards set forth in the UDHR. Several factors delayed the implementation of these standards, however, including Cold War disputes between the United States and the former Soviet

persecute: to belittle, harass, injure, or otherwise intimidate, especially those of a different background or group

reciprocity: mutual action or help that benefits both parties

precedent: an established ruling, understanding, or practice of the law

enumerate: to expressly name, as in a list

Union and the rapid increase in UN membership as former colonies gained independence. The International Covenant on Civil and Political Rights (CCPR) and the International Covenant on Economic, Social, and Cultural Rights (CESCR) were not opened for signature until 1967 and did not enter into force

AT THE SUPREME COURT IN SANTIAGO, CHILE IN 2000, CITIZENS DEMAND THAT FORMER PRESIDENT AUGUSTO PINOCHET FACE CHARGES OF VIOLATING HUMAN RIGHTS. As a lifelong member of the Chilean Senate with immunity from prosecution, former president Augusto Pinochet eluded indictment on violation of human rights laws during his rule (1973–1990). Charges levied in the United Kingdom in 1998 were dropped because the British government claimed he was too ill to stand trial. As of 2005, Pinochet had yet to be convicted of any crime. (SOURCE: © REUTERS/CORBIS)

until 1976. Collectively, these three instruments—the two covenants plus the UDHR—are known as the International Bill of Rights.

While the covenants encompass a broad range of rights for all individuals, the UN has also worked to create legally binding instruments to secure specific types of rights and rights for particular populations. Among the many multilateral human rights conventions created under the UN system are the Convention on the Prevention and Punishment of the Crime of Genocide (CAG, 1948), International Convention on the Elimination of All Forms of Racial Discrimination (CERD, 1969), Convention on the Elimination of All Forms of Discrimination Against Women (CEDAW, 1981), Convention Against Torture and Other Cruel, Inhuman, or Degrading Treatment or Punishment (CAT, 1987), Convention on the Rights of the Child (CRC, 1990), and International Convention on the Protection of Rights of All Migrant Workers and Members of Their Families (CMW, 2003). These treaties have varying degrees of membership reflecting their level of global acceptance. As of 2004, for example, 192 member states had **ratified** the CRC. Of UN member states, only the United States and Somalia had failed to ratify the CRC; although neither country had ratified the treaty, both had signed it. At the other end of the spectrum, only twenty-six states had ratified the CMW.

ratify: to make official or to officially sanction

STATUS AS LAW

The two most common ways for human rights norms to become binding on a state are through the signing of treaties that contain human rights norms and through the evolution of customary international law concerning human rights. States agree to human rights provisions in treaty form by signing and ratifying a treaty containing human rights provisions. For example, as of 2004 the United States had signed and ratified the CCPR with certain reservations, but it had neither signed nor ratified the CMW. Because it has ratified the CCPR, the United States is legally obligated to follow its provisions. It has no such obligation under the CMW.

States may also be obligated to abide by certain human rights norms even if they have not signed a treaty containing those provisions. The primary way that a state may be bound to abide by standards of law not contained in a treaty is when a common state practice evolves to the point where it becomes customary international law. Traditionally, a norm becomes customary international law if a significant number of states around the world follow a certain practice to the extent that they begin to believe in a legal obligation to follow the practice. An example of such a norm outside the realm of human rights is the practice of diplomatic immunity. For centuries before the practice of giving foreign diplomats immunity from prosecution was codified in the Vienna Convention on Diplomatic Relations (1964), states recognized the practice as a legal obligation of states.

Human rights norms may take on the status of custom if a sufficient number of states abide by them on a consistent basis, even if they do not sign and ratify treaties obligating them to do so. In addition, a human rights norm may obtain customary legal status if it receives near-unanimous support in international forums such as the UN, even if all states do not ratify treaties containing those norms. Norms that are widely adopted in state constitutions and in regional documents in addition to international documents may also obtain customary status. Based on this standard, many scholars consider the principles contained in the UDHR to have evolved to customary status based on the universal acceptance of that document in the early twenty-first century. Many of the norms embodied in human rights treaties eventually take on customary legal status. Although most international treaties are designed to create obligations from one state to another, human rights treaties are written in such

jurisdiction: the territory or area within which authority may be exercised

derogate: to remove or deny, as a right; to disparage or belittle

a manner that their intention is to create norms of behavior for all states in regard to their citizens or to others in their jurisdiction.

Some human rights norms have achieved what is known as peremptory status. When a norm is peremptory, no state may **derogate** from it (not adhere to it) under any circumstance. This principle is also known as *jus cogens,* a Latin phrase meaning "compelling law." Among the norms that have reached the level of acceptance necessary to be considered peremptory are those banning genocide, slavery, extrajudicial killings, torture, arbitrary detention, systematic racial discrimination, and consistent violations of international recognized human rights. Most states would agree that committing any of these acts would qualify as a violation of international human rights law.

ENFORCEMENT

Traditionally, international law is enforced primarily by the states themselves. When one state violates its international obligations to another state, the victim state pursues any of a number of actions against the offending state. When international human rights law is violated, however, the primary victims are normally individuals residing in the offending states. While other states may make a claim against the offending state, they may not be as compelled to do so as they would be if they were the victim of a legal transgression. For this reason, international organizations such as the UN have primary responsibility for investigating violations of international human rights law. The United Nations Commission on Human Rights (CHR) actively investigates human rights abuses in particular countries or categories of abuse across a number of countries. Though it does not have the power to punish states guilty of human rights abuses, the UN and CHR do have the power to bring violations of human rights to the attention of the world.

sanction: economic, political, or military reprisals, or, to ratify

This unwanted scrutiny is often enough to trigger some changes in policy; moreover, international condemnation may result in economic **sanctions**, such as those imposed on South Africa in the 1980s. In certain cases, the UN Security Council has established special tribunals to try individuals accused of committing particularly widespread violations of human rights. The first two examples of this practice were the creation of the International Criminal Tribunal for the Former Yugoslavia (ICTY) and the International Criminal Tribunal for Rwanda (ICTR). Both these tribunals have tried individuals for violations of international humanitarian law and for certain human rights abuses.

In addition to initiating investigations by member states and by the CHR, individuals who are the victim of human rights abuses also have the ability to report their situation to the UN through special mechanisms in the CHR. In addition to this mechanism, six human rights treaties—the CCPR, CESCR, CERD, CEDAW, CAT, and CRC—have special treaty-monitoring bodies to evaluate the implementation of the rights contained in each document. Four of these committees can hear complaints about human rights abuses from individuals.

adjudicate: to settle a case by judicial procedure

In addition to efforts at the UN, some national and regional courts are able to **adjudicate** international human rights abuses. For example, a number of victims of human rights abuses have taken advantage of the United States' Alien Tort Claims Act to sue foreign governments in U.S. courts for violations of their rights. Other courts around the world have allowed for the arrest of prominent individuals implicated in widespread human rights abuses. One of the most famous examples of this was the 1998 arrest of former Chilean President Augusto Pinochet (b. 1915) in the United Kingdom based on a Spanish arrest warrant. Pinochet was accused of massive violations of rights while president of Chile, including the murder of Spanish citizens. The 1998 arrests did not directly lead to

Pinochet's facing trial (the United Kingdom returned him to Chile based on health concerns), but his arrest set an important precedent. In January 2005, the Chilean Supreme Court found that Pinochet's failing health was not a sufficient reason for him to avoid standing trial for crimes committed during his presidency. The European Court of Human Rights, one of the most powerful regional courts in the world, has the authority to overturn the laws of states under its jurisdiction that it determines to be in violation of certain human rights.

CONCLUSION

Despite some disagreement over certain human rights treaties and their implementation, international human rights law has made remarkable progress since World War II. Debate on human rights law is no longer focused on whether or not it exists, but rather on its specific content and the degree to which it should be enforced. Many of the debates at the UN concerning human rights involve the cultural interpretation of rights. Reflecting this diversity of opinion, human rights treaties are written only with input from all members of the UN. At the start of the twenty-first century the CHR, in charge of the codification and implementation of human rights standards, represented some fifty-three member states, elected according to regional distribution. The continued codification and implementation of international human rights law depend upon the input of, and agreement among, states around the world.

See also: Crimes Against Humanity; Human Rights; International Humanitarian Law; United Nations Commission on Human Rights; War Crimes.

BIBLIOGRAPHY

American Law Institute. *Restatement of the Law, Third: The Foreign Relations Law of the United States*. St. Paul, MN: American Law Institute, 1990.

Gearty, Conner, and Adam Tomkins. *Understanding Human Rights*. New York: Mansell, 1996.

Goldstein, Judith L., Miles Kahler, Robert O. Keohane, and Anne-Marie Slaughter. *Legalization and World Politics*. Cambridge, MA: MIT Press, 2001.

Meron, Theodor. *Human Rights in International Law: Legal and Policy Issues*. Oxford, UK: Clarendon Press, 1984.

Meron, Theodor. *Human Rights and Humanitarian Norms as Customary Law*. New York: Clarendon Press, 1989.

Steinger, Henry J., and Philip Alston. *International Human Rights in Context: Law, Politics, Morals*, 2d ed. New York: Oxford University Press, 2000.

Eric W. Cox

International Humanitarian Law

International humanitarian law (IHL) is the body of treaty and customary international law that regulates the behavior of states in armed conflict. IHL has two primary purposes. First, it protects those who do not participate or are no longer participating in armed conflict, including sick and wounded soldiers, prisoners of war, and civilians. Second, it regulates the means and methods that states may legally use to carry out armed conflict. The primary sources for modern IHL are the four Geneva Conventions of 1949 and the Additional Protocols of 1977.

Although much of IHL is concerned specifically with international armed conflict, each of the Geneva Conventions contains an identical article, known as Common Article Three, that concerns non-international conflicts. The Additional Protocol II of 1977 also regulates behavior in non-international conflicts. A number of other international agreements have sought to regulate the types of weapons that may be used in war. These conventions include the Biological Weapons Convention (1972), the Conventional Weapons Convention (1980), the Chemical Weapons Convention (1993), and the Landmines Convention (1997). These treaties have sought to ban certain types of conventional and unconventional weapons that cause excessive civilian casualties or are otherwise deemed to be inhumane.

corpus: a body, as in a body of work

The **corpus** of IHL consists of a wide range of laws intended to limit the effects of warfare. The major provisions of modern IHL include a responsibility to provide medical assistance to sick and wounded soldiers (even those of the enemy), to treat prisoners of war with dignity and respect, and to protect civilian populations. Prisoners of war cannot be put on trial or punished simply for fighting in a war, and they have a right to have contact with family and friends even while they are being detained. IHL also requires states to minimize the effects of armed conflict on civilian populations and to meet the needs of the population of any territory that they may occupy. Finally, IHL obligates states to allow international humanitarian organizations, such as the International Committee for the Red Cross (ICRC), to monitor their compliance with the provisions of IHL during armed conflict.

HISTORICAL DEVELOPMENT OF INTERNATIONAL HUMANITARIAN LAW

rule of law: the principle that the law is a final grounds of decision-making and applies equally to all people; law and order

Modern IHL dates to the mid-nineteenth century. As conflict became more destructive with the advent of modern industrial warfare, both private individuals and states began to recognize the need to regulate it. In 1863, the United States issued the Lieber Code to the Union Army. Among the provisions in the code were rules regarding the continuation of the **rule of law** in occupied areas; respect for foreign diplomats and consuls; protection of works of art from destruction, theft, or sale; and protection for prisoners of war.

■ ■ ■

WEAPONS CONVENTIONS

Weapons conventions are relatively recent in human history, although the use of biological and chemical weapons goes back to the Middle Ages. The earliest international effort to ban chemical weapons was the 1899 Hague Peace Conference, which failed to prevent the use of poison gas in World War I (1914–1918). The 1925 Geneva Protocol was the most significant attempt to control the production and deployment of biological as well as chemical agents between the two world wars.

The Biological Weapons Convention (BWC) of 1972 was the first disarmament treaty banning production of an entire category of weapons. Intended to supplement the Geneva Protocols, the BWC had been ratified by 150 nations by 2005.

The Chemical Weapons Convention (CWC) of 1993 had been ratified by 167 countries as of 2004. The CWC set up a timetable for the destruction of chemical weapons, from 1 percent in April 2000 to 45 percent by April 2004 and 100 percent by April 2007. By April 2004, however, only about 14 percent of stockpiled chemical weapons had been destroyed.

Since 2001 there has been increased concern regarding the possible use of biological and chemical weapons by terrorist groups. The Centers for Disease Control (CDC) lists no fewer than 47 viruses and bacteria that could be used for bioterrorism, and thirteen categories of chemicals (nerve gases, vomiting agents, biotoxins, and others) that could be used against civilians.

With regard to prisoners of war, the code is quite detailed as to what type of combatants may lawfully receive prisoner-of-war status and the protections and rights they possess. One interesting aspect of the code was its declaration that "the law of nations knows of no distinction of color" (Article 58). Even though the code was considered to be reflective of customary international law of the time, it was not an international treaty and was not binding on other states.

Around the same time, however, the movement that would become the ICRC began to press European governments to adopt a code of conduct for the treatment of sick and wounded soldiers. After an initial conference in Geneva in 1863 at which several states agreed to resolutions concerning the recognition of medical personnel during battle, the Swiss Federal Council sponsored a conference in 1864 for the purpose of adopting a convention concerning the treatment of the sick and wounded. This convention included provisions that required governments to treat any sick or wounded soldier regardless of nationality, recognized the **neutrality** of medical personnel, and established a red cross on a white background to be the official international symbol for medical personnel. States around the world would agree to the convention, including the United States in 1882.

neutrality: the quality of not taking sides, as in a conflict

The 1864 Geneva Convention was designed to protect the sick and the wounded. It did little to regulate the practice of warfare itself, however. Both governments and private individuals began to press for a formal **codification** of the laws of war, including the treatment of prisoners of war, the types of weapons that could be used in war, and the rights of belligerent and neutral parties. The culmination of this movement came at the International Peace Conference held in The Hague in 1899. At this conference, states adopted a number of conventions and declarations regarding the laws of war. Among the provisions adopted were protections for prisoners of war, including recognition that captured soldiers could not be forced to contribute to the capturing state's war effort, an expansion of the 1864 Geneva Convention's rules regarding the sick and wounded to **maritime** situations, and several limitations on the types of weapons that could be used in war. In particular, the conference placed a five-year ban on the use at any time of weapons dropped from the air, the use of poisonous gases, and the use of certain types of bullets that were considered to cause unnecessary and cruel injuries.

codification: the making of official law

maritime: relating to the sea or the coast

Both the 1864 Geneva Convention and the Hague Conventions were updated in the early twentieth century: the Geneva Convention in 1906 and the Hague Conventions in 1907. Those states that chose not to **ratify** the updated conventions were bound to respect the earlier conventions if they had ratified them.

ratify: to make official or to officially sanction

World War I (1914–1918) marked both an advance and a setback in the creation of IHL. Although the use of poisonous gas and other methods of warfare that states had attempted to ban represented a failure to regulate the methods of warfare, the war itself saw the ICRC take an active role in protecting sick and wounded soldiers and in extending protections to prisoners of war, even though it had no explicit authority to do so. During the war, the ICRC visited prisoner-of-war camps and reported violations of the principles of protection of prisoners of war to the governments involved in the war. After the war, several efforts were made to advance IHL, both in the regulation of weapons and in the protection of those not taking part in combat. In 1925, the Geneva Protocol prohibited the use of poisonous gases and biological weapons. In 1929, both the 1906 Geneva Convention and the 1907 Hague Convention were strengthened with respect to the treatment of prisoners of war, and the Red Crescent became officially recognized as a symbol equivalent to the Red Cross.

Despite the advances in formal IHL after World War I, the conduct of World War II (1939–1945) led to grave violations of both customary and treaty-based IHL.

Beyond the conduct of Nazi Germany toward Jews, Roma (gypsies), and other populations, the conduct of the war itself led to the targeting of civilian populations by all sides. Advancements in aerial bombing made it possible to target entire cities, including civilians. German developments in missile technology led to the use of the V1 and V2 rockets against the United Kingdom. Submarine warfare was used indiscriminately in multiple theaters of combat, often destroying vessels that were officially neutral or otherwise protected by IHL. The targeting of civilians was justified by the argument that civilian populations were an integral part of the war effort in modern battles. The fire bombings of Dresden and Tokyo and the use of atomic weapons against Hiroshima and Nagasaki were the logical extension of this argument, despite the existence of international law to the contrary.

If the war itself presented major challenges to IHL, the aftermath of the war did contribute to the development of the law through the Nuremberg and Tokyo War Crimes Tribunals. The charter of the International Military Tribunal, the governing document for the Nuremberg Tribunal, included reference to crimes against peace, war crimes, and crimes against humanity. Included in

RED CROSS WORKERS PASS BRITISH SOLDIERS EN ROUTE TO BASRA, IRAQ IN 2003. Founded by Jean Henri Dunant, the International Committee of the Red Cross (ICRC) traces its roots and emblem back to the 1864 Geneva Convention. There it was stipulated that wartime victims must be able to receive proper care by medical professionals identified by the ICRC's symbolic red cross printed on a white flag. (SOURCE: © REUTERS/CORBIS)

these crimes were the mistreatment of prisoners of war and civilian populations and the destruction and plunder of public and private property (Article 6). The trials themselves were groundbreaking in that they held individuals responsible for acts that were contrary to international law and were, at least in theory, legal according to the domestic laws of Germany. Sovereign immunity—that is, immunity from prosecution for heads of state or government representatives—was not recognized for those who were charged.

Although many of those responsible for violating IHL during World War II were brought to justice, one major criticism of the tribunals was that they represented victor's justice. Germany certainly did commit acts that violated international law and norms of behavior, especially in carrying out the mass murder of Jews and other populations. At the same time, however, some of the crimes for which the Germans were tried were committed by the Allied powers as well, especially the indiscriminate use of force against civilian populations.

World War II itself also pointed to weaknesses in IHL and led to further efforts to strengthen the formal treaty law that encompasses IHL. The 1948 Genocide Convention created a binding treaty that outlawed any attempt to eliminate a group based on its race, religion, or ethnicity. In 1949 the four Geneva Conventions, the cornerstone of modern humanitarian law, came into existence. Convention I concerns the treatment of sick and wounded soldiers on land; Convention II does the same for soldiers at sea; Convention III details laws related to the treatment of prisoners of war, and Convention IV describes the treatment of civilians in war, including the responsibilities of an occupying power. The major part of these treaties pertains to international armed conflict. Common Article Three of the treaties, however, is specific to non-international conflict—the wording of Article 3 in each treaty is identical. The treaties themselves refer to the role that international humanitarian bodies such as the ICRC should play in helping to ensure that states involved in armed conflict abide by the conventions. The vast majority of the world's states have accepted these treaties.

Since 1949, a number of other treaties have been created that contribute to IHL. Many of these treaties have concerned the types of weapons that may legally be used in war. The Biological Weapons Convention (1972), the Chemical Weapons Convention (1993), and the Landmines Convention (1997) all seek to ban entire classes of weapons. The Conventional Weapons Treaty (1980) seeks to ban weapons that are designed to cause excessive or cruel injuries. Of these treaties, the most successful is the Chemical Weapons Convention. Most of the world's largest powers have ratified that treaty and have worked to create an enforcement protocol and an agency to supervise its implementation. Little real progress has been made to achieve similar steps for the Biological Weapons Convention, however, and the Landmines Convention has met with opposition from many powerful states, including the United States.

The nature of armed conflict in the post–World War II era has also led to advancements in laws regulating the treatment of noncombatants. At the time that the Geneva Conventions of 1949 were written, the majority of armed conflicts occurred between states. As decolonization progressed in the wake of World War II, however, intrastate (as opposed to interstate) conflicts became more common. Although the Geneva Conventions did contain Common Article Three regarding non-international conflict, many viewed that provision as inadequate to address some of the abuses occurring in internal conflicts. In response to those concerns, two protocols to the Geneva Conventions were created in 1976, one of which dealt specifically with internal conflict.

INTERNATIONAL HUMANITARIAN LAW IN THE 1990S

During the Cold War and into the 1990s, many states and other actors violated the tenets of IHL. In many conflicts civilian populations were directly targeted, individuals were forced to serve in military forces against their will, and the treatment of prisoners of war often did not conform to international legal standards. Two conflicts in the early 1990s were particularly violent, however. In Rwanda and the former Yugoslavia, militias and government forces were involved in the indiscriminate targeting of civilian populations, including acts of genocide. In response to the actions in these two states, the United Nations Security Council created the International Criminal Tribunal for Rwanda (ICTR) and the International Criminal Tribunal for the Former Yugoslavia (ICTY). Both of these tribunals based their **jurisdiction**, in part, on the 1949 Geneva Conventions and the 1948 Genocide Convention. The ICTY dealt with both international and domestic conflict, whereas the ICTR's jurisdiction was primarily for an internal conflict. Common Article Three and the 1977 Additional Protocol II to the Geneva Conventions provided the legal justification for much of the ICTR's work. Although both of these tribunals have faced significant difficulties, they do represent an international effort to bring individuals to justice for committing violations of IHL. They also created important **precedents**. For example, cases under the tribunals reaffirmed that individuals could not argue that they were ordered to commit certain acts as a defense. In addition, the courts found that civilians participating in certain acts of genocide or violations of IHL could be also be held accountable, whereas IHL traditionally had applied to individuals acting in official capacities.

Despite their importance, however, the ICTY and ICTR also demonstrated a major weakness of IHL—the relative lack of enforcement. Despite the active role that the ICRC and other humanitarian aid agencies have played in international conflicts, major violations of IHL often go unpunished. In the 1990s, several states and organizations began to actively push for a permanent court to punish individuals for violations of IHL and other international criminal acts. The result of these efforts was the creation of the Rome Statute of the International Criminal Court (ICC), opened for signature in 1998. The ICC came into existence in July 2002, after enough state parties had ratified it.

The ICC has jurisdiction over a number of crimes including genocide, crimes against humanity, war crimes, and aggression. Article 8.2(a) of the statute includes "grave breaches of the Geneva Conventions of 12 August 1949" in the jurisdiction of the court. Despite the advance in the enforcement of IHL that the ICC represents, it is not a panacea. The ICC is dependent on states that have ratified the statute to aid in the capture of accused individuals. Many states object to the jurisdiction of the ICC, including the United States. The lack of consensus regarding the ICC makes its task difficult as it begins to address criminal breaches of international law.

CHALLENGES TO IHL IN THE TWENTY-FIRST CENTURY

The major new challenge presented to IHL in the twenty-first century is the changing nature of those involved in conflict. The terrorist attacks on the United States on September 11, 2001 pointed to the difficulties of modern conflict. Non-state actors that may contain members from a wide range of states can carry out incredibly sophisticated attacks. The conflict, or "War on Terror," that the United States began to wage after the September 11 attacks is not a war in the traditional sense, as the enemy does not possess a specific territory or a defined nationality. For IHL, one of the problems this presents is the lack of a clear status for prisoners captured in conflict.

jurisdiction: the territory or area within which authority may be exercised

precedent: an established ruling, understanding, or practice of the law

The Geneva Conventions and the two protocols contain rules for the treatment of prisoners of war and for those participating in armed combat outside the traditional rules of war, but the determination of who is a legal or illegal combatant has proved to be problematic. A related problem is the lack of a defined end to combat operations. In traditional war, prisoners are returned to their territory once combat has ceased. Armed conflicts involving non-state actors may not have clearly defined endpoints, making the decision on when to repatriate prisoners of war difficult.

Despite these challenges, IHL continues to affect the decisions states make in armed conflict. Despite its disagreement with some of the decisions of the ICRC, the United States still allows the ICRC to visit its detention facilities and to report on the United States's treatment of prisoners. Although many violations of IHL go unpunished, mechanisms such as the ICTY, ICTR, and ICC mean that some of those who violate IHL do so with impunity. Unlike many other areas of international law, IHL has gained widespread acceptance from states around the world in principle, if not always in practice.

See also: Crimes Against Humanity; Human Rights; International Criminal Court; International Human Rights Law; War Crimes.

repatriate: to return to the country of one's birth or citizenship

impunity: an exemption from punishment

BIBLIOGRAPHY

Chadwick, Elizabeth. "'Rights' and International Humanitarian Law." In *Understanding Human Rights*, ed. Conor Gearty and Adam Tomkins. New York: Mansell Publishing, 1996.

International Committee of the Red Cross. <http://www.icrc.org/eng>.

Steiner, Henry J., and Philip Alston. *International Human Rights in Context: Law, Politics, Morals.* 2d ed. Oxford, UK: Oxford University Press, 2000.

Eric W. Cox

Iran

Iran, formerly known as Persia, is located in the center of Middle East, bordering the Gulf of Oman, the Persian Gulf, and the Caspian Sea. It is slightly larger than Alaska, with an area of 1.648 million square kilometers (636,400 square miles). Iran's population was approximately 70 million in 2004. The population includes many ethnic groups. Persians (who speak Farsi or Persian) make up slightly more than half the population. About a quarter of the population is Azari (who speak a dialect of Turkish). Other major ethnic groups are Gilaki, Mazandarani, Kurd, Arab, Lur, Balooch, and Turkmen. Approximately 98 percent of the population is Muslim. Eighty-five percent of Iranian Muslims practice Shia Islam, which is a minority sect in the worldwide Islamic faith. The rest of the population is Zoroastrian, Jewish, or Christian. The literacy rate in Iran is relatively high for the Middle East, approximately 80 percent. According to the 2003 *CIA World Factbook,* the literacy rate was higher among men (85%) than women (73%).

sect: a group of people with a common distinctive view of religion or doctrine

BRIEF HISTORY

Persia was one of earliest sites of civilization and one of the greatest empires of the ancient world. It saw many wars and experienced foreign occupations by Greeks, Arabs, Mongols, and then by Allied forces during World War II

(MAP BY MARYLAND CARTOGRAPHICS/THE GALE GROUP)

(1939–1945). Iranians managed to gain their independence shortly after each invasion. Even after the Arab invasion and subsequent adoption of Islam, Iran maintained its distinct cultural identity within the Islamic world, first by retaining its own language and later by adhering to the Shia branch of Islam.

Iran continued to be a major power until the nineteenth century. After the founder of the Qajar dynasty (which ruled from 1794 to 1925) was assassinated, a long period of weak, self-indulgent monarchic rule coincided with increasing European involvement in the region. Iran began to lose its territories and independence. In the first quarter of nineteenth century Iran lost a large portion of its territories to Russia, including the entire Caucasian region (the area that contains the Caspian Sea). In 1856 it suffered the loss of the eastern part of contemporary Afghanistan to the British Empire. During the nineteenth century Russia and the British Empire competed to influence Iran's internal affairs. Iran's strategic location, historical significance, market for industrial goods, and natural resources made it a strategic target for the world's superpowers. The later discovery of huge reservoirs of oil and natural gas added to its global significance.

With many Iranians dissatisfied with the Qajar dynasty, the predominance of **despotic** (and often corrupt) local governors, and the lack of progress and order, Iran experienced its first revolution: the Constitutional Revolution of 1906. This uprising led the country to adopt its first constitution, which limited the power of the king and established a modern government with three separate branches of power.

After a short period of unstable governments and deteriorating security, Reza Khan Pahlavi (1878–1944), an army officer, staged a **coup** in 1921. He contained the rebels in different parts of country and established law, order, and security. The public, highly critical of the Qajar dynasty, did not stand in

despot: a ruler who does not govern in the interest of those governed

coup: a quick seizure of power or a sudden attack

his way when he seized the throne in 1925 and became the new king, or Reza Shah. Pahlavi initiated widespread reforms to modernize the country. He established a strong central government, built a modern army, and expanded the **bureaucracy**. He created an extensive system of **secular** primary and secondary schools and, in 1935, established the country's first European-style university. These schools and institutions of higher education became training grounds for the new bureaucracy and, along with economic expansion, helped to create a new middle class. The Shah also expanded the road network, completed the trans-Iranian railroad, and established a string of state-owned factories.

Many of the Shah's measures were consciously designed to break the power of the clerics. His educational reforms ended the clerics' near-monopoly on education. To further limit their power, he undertook a **codification** of the laws that created a body of secular law, applied and interpreted by a secular judiciary outside the control of the religious establishment. He excluded the clerics from judgeships, created a system of secular courts, and transferred many clerical duties to bureaucracies and state-licensed notaries. Perhaps the most controversial part of the Shah's reforms was his enforcement of European dress. These regulations included the forceful abolishment of the Islamic veil for women in 1936, which led to considerable dissatisfaction in some parts of the country.

Iran declared **neutrality** in World War II, refusing to expel German citizens or allow Allied forces to use Iranian soil. Consequently, joint Soviet, British, and American forces invaded Iran in 1941. Reza Shah went into exile and his son, Mohammad Reza Pahlavi (1919–1980), became the new Shah. In 1951 Mohammad Mosaddeq (1880–1967), a member of parliament and later the prime minister, led a movement that caused Iran to **nationalize** its oil industry and put an end to Great Britain's dominance in this part of the economy. In 1953 the United States and Britain staged a coup that overthrew Mosaddeq and renewed the power of the Shah. The coup effectively terminated the moderately conservative **nationalist** movement and helped to spread radical opposition, who sought to overthrow the monarchy.

REVOLUTION OF 1979

In the years following the 1953 coup, the Shah gradually established despotic rule. Iran became the most important military power in the region. The United States replaced Britain and Russia as the most influential foreign ally in the country's military, industrial, higher education, and administrative sectors. Iran thus entered into a strong alliance with the United States and became a major stabilizing force in the Middle East. During this period, oil income skyrocketed and was soon the major source of national income. As a result, Iran began to experience rapid population growth and a high rate of urbanization. Oil income enabled the government to drastically reduce the prices of energy, foreign currency, food, and other merchandise. The Shah, as had his father, advocated a speedy process of state-enforced Westernization. Many Iranians, however, saw the Shah's forced Westernizations as depriving them of cultural values, debasing their identity, and dividing the society. The Shah's brand of nationalism, which disproportionately emphasized the pre-Islamic cultural heritage of Iran, made it easy for his opponents to portray him as antireligious and corrupt, on top of being a dictator backed by the U.S. government.

In 1978 an extraordinary combination of factors, including the existence of a young, dissatisfied middle class and the unpopularity of the Shah following

bureaucracy: a system of administrating government involving professional labor; the mass of individuals administering government

secularism: a refutation of, apathy toward, or exclusion of all religion

codification: the making of official law

neutrality: the quality of not taking sides, as in a conflict

nationalization: the process of giving control or ownership of an entity to the government

nationalism: the belief that one's nation or culture is superior to all others

socialism: any of various economic and political theories advocating collective or governmental ownership and administration of the means of production and distribution of goods

fundamentalism: a philosophy marked by an extreme and literal interpretation of religious texts and an inability to compromise on doctrine or policy

ideology: a system of beliefs composed of ideas or values, from which political, social, or economic programs are often derived

years of despotic rule and oppression, gave birth to a public revolt. A wide range of **socialist** and leftist groups effectively organized riots and strikes. At the same time, a fall in oil revenues added to general public dissatisfaction. The growing power of a charismatic **fundamentalist** leader, Ayatollah Ruhollah Khomeini (1902–1989), and the Shah's reluctance to crush the riots only accelerated the revolution. Within a year the Shah lost power to revolutionary forces.

A period of chaos, disorder, and violence followed. Many prominent Iranians, including army officers, dependents of the former regime, politicians, and bureaucrats, were executed. Most industries were nationalized and many people lost their personal possessions and property. Bureaucrats were purged from government, leading to paralyzed bureaucracies. Eventually, Khomeini alienated secular revolutionaries and established the Islamic Republic of Iran (IRI). In this new regime the Ayatollah dominated. Other rebels and political activists were executed or forced to leave the country; in exile, they formed opposition groups. The revolution of 1979 and the new government radically transformed almost every aspect of Iranian society, including religious views, government administration, the economy, art, culture, and the legal system.

THE ISLAMIC REPUBLIC OF IRAN

The IRI is a theocratic republic. In this regime, a clergyman, chosen as the lifetime supreme leader, is the highest authority. The IRI is based on Khomeini's political **ideology**, which mixes politics with religion to the ultimate degree. He believed that the ultimate objective of Islam was to establish an Islamic state. Furthermore, he thought that the establishment and preservation of the Islamic state should take precedence over other religious duties. The Islamic state requires its citizens to enforce Islamic rules, including the protection of the state. Although the Islamic state gains its legitimacy from Allah, it must forge a covenant with its people, through the voting process and elected officials, to maintain power and acceptability. Therefore, Khomeini centered religion around politics and the state in an unprecedented manner, departing from the conventional conservative Islamic doctrine and teachings of the leading theologians.

The legal structure of the IRI consists of a highly complicated and controversial system of institutions. Figure 1 shows the relationships between

FIGURE 1

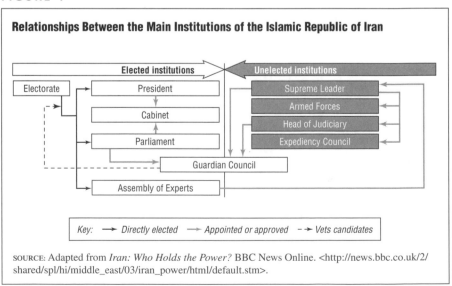

SOURCE: Adapted from *Iran: Who Holds the Power?* BBC News Online. <http://news.bbc.co.uk/2/shared/spl/hi/middle_east/03/iran_power/html/default.stm>.

the major institutions of the Islamic republic. The complexity of the constitution has led to a fragmented structure of government. Redundant, parallel institutions exist in all branches of government, even in the military and security forces.

Most Iranian revolutionary forces, both secular and religious, held largely socialist views about the economy and administration. This perspective, which was incorporated into the constitution and indoctrinates a huge administrative body, puts the government in control of most enterprises. In fact, the IRI has resembled doctrinaire socialist governments in many aspects during its lifetime. In addition to having a huge public sector, other similarities include pervasive state involvement in people's private lives, close engagement with leftist movements and socialist regimes, and reliance on propaganda and the enforcement of a revolutionary **hegemony**.

hegemony: the complete dominance of one group or nation over another

AN ERA OF CRISES

Iran experienced much turbulence in the early years of the IRI. The biggest challenge was the state of the economy. As a result of the socialization of the economy, a huge inflexible administration, chaos, and war, Iran's gross domestic product (GDP) dropped consistently for at least a decade after the IRI was established. The other source of crisis in Iran derived from domestic and **transnational** reactions to the country's revolutionary ideology. Attempting to purify society from any influences perceived as un-Islamic, the revolutionary forces imposed many social restrictions. They had little tolerance for social activities not approved by the government. They banned or restricted many social activities, including music, dance, and numerous traditional celebrations. They also propagated and enforced the revolutionary hegemony through mosques and schools. For the first time in Iranian history, most cultural entities, including

transnational: extending beyond the jurisdiction of one single nation

■ ■ ■
THE 1979 IRAN HOSTAGE CRISIS

The Shah of Iran had been reinstalled in power by a CIA-executed coup against a popular nationalist government in 1953. A corrupt, abusive and oppressive ruler, the Shah was supported strongly by the United States, which he supplied with cheap oil and a strategic base in the Persian Gulf region. In 1979 a revolution brought about by the combined social and religious opposition overthrew the Shah and he went into exile.

In late 1979 the Shah was allowed into the United States by President Jimmy Carter for medical treatment, provoking outrage in Iran. The new leader of Iran, Ayatollah Ruhollah Khomeini, encouraged Iranians to demonstrate their anger. In response, on November 4, 1979 a crowd of students seized the American embassy in Tehran and took 66 hostages (six other diplomats found refuge in the Swedish and Canadian embassies, and left Iran with fake Canadian passports on January 20, 1980). Thus began the Iran hostage crisis, which lasted for 444 days. Fourteen hostages, including one person with multiple sclerosis, were released between November 19, 1979 and July 11, 1980.

President Carter tried to resolve the hostage crisis with a series of economic and diplomatic measures. Two poorly planned air rescue attempts in April and October 1980 failed. Iran became more receptive to ending the crisis, however, when the Shah died in July 1980 and Iraq invaded Iran two months later. Carter's inability to end the crisis is considered a major reason for his loss to Ronald Reagan in the 1980 presidential election. Negotiations between the United States and Iran resumed immediately after the election. Iran released the remaining 52 hostages on January 20, 1981, just minutes after President Reagan had been sworn into office. Later, evidence emerged that the Reagan campaign, fearing an "October surprise" had secretly been in illegal contact with the Iranians during the campaign and made a deal with them to release the hostages only after Reagan had taken office. In return it promised to unfreeze Iranian assets and to supply much-needed armaments. Both of these actions were in fact carried out by the Reagan administration.

religious institutions, lost their independence from the government. Prominent religious scholars, who did not support the revolution and its associated radical ideology, were banned or isolated.

The IRI has also experienced major challenges in the area of foreign relations. For a few years after the revolution, it eagerly pursued a radical strategy of **proliferation** of ideological teachings to other Islamic countries and sought to destabilize regional governments. This strategy involved Iran in numerous regional and international conflicts and created many enemies.

In November 1979 the Iran hostage crisis began when a mob of angry Iranian students seized the U.S. embassy, took diplomats and employees hostage, and held them for 444 days. The seizure of the embassy and its aftermath further radicalized domestic politics and had a huge impact on the Iranian economy and the country's international relationships.

In 1980 Saddam Hussein (b. 1937), the former Iraqi dictator, launched a full-scale war against Iran in the hope of capturing its Arab-inhabited region. Iran's army had lost many of its military commanders in the revolution of 1979, and Hussein perceived the country to be in a severely weakened and disorganized condition. He also tried to take advantage of the international unpopularity of the Iranian revolutionary regime at that time. During this conflict, Iraq enjoyed the support of the Soviet Union, Western governments—including the United States—and most Arab countries. However, the war resulted in a stalemate, lasted for eight years, claimed more than a million lives on both sides, and cost hundreds of billions of dollars. Khomeini died in 1989, one year after the war's end.

ECONOMY AND POLITICS IN THE POST-KHOMEINI ERA

Ayatollah Khomeini's dominance in Iranian politics masked the differences among his followers. Following Khomeini's death his followers entered into a political struggle. Many Iranian political groups and parties became active inside and outside of the country. Most of these parties lacked a clear political theory and agenda. They were often vague about their positions on different issues and, not surprisingly, they often took dramatic turns in their views. In the late twentieth and early twenty-first century, political struggle in Iran was confined to ideological and propaganda wars, and had thus failed to bear practical fruit. No one political group can count on significant public support and the people are largely apathetic to the political process. According to official voting records, in the February 2004 election the winning **coalition** had the approval of less than 15 percent of eligible voters.

A tension between practicality and ideology has been the center of political conflict in the post-Khomeini era. The IRI has attempted to open its economy and also to separate itself, albeit hesitantly and slowly, from Khomeini's ideological foreign policy, adopting a stance of greater compromise with the international community.

Since none of Khomeini's disciples were prominent theologians, Ali Khamenei (b. 1939), who was the president at the time, was chosen as Khomeini's successor. Therefore, the religious qualifications for leadership were practically ignored in favor of revolutionary credentials. Shortly afterward, Hafsemi Rafsanjani (b. 1934) won the presidential election. In the subsequent years, the initial union and mutual support between Khamenei and Rafsanjani turned to a rivalry. Pragmatic forces quickly gathered around the president and more radical fundamentalists gathered around Khamenei. Khamenei gradually built up a separate governmental apparatus and strengthened his subordinate organizations, including the armed forces. The rivalry between this shadow government with radical cultural and military tendencies and the more pragmatic

proliferate: to grow in number; to multiply at a high rate

coalition: an alliance, partnership, or union of disparate peoples or individuals

executive branch became a main feature of the post-Khomeini politics. Khamenei also tried to gain theological credentials and promote himself to a Grand Ayatollah. Although he failed to get the religious recognition he sought, Khamenei did seize control of the mosques and most of the religious schools. Indeed, the invasion of mosques and religious schools by the government and suppression of independent voices of traditional Islam were completed during Khamenei's time. Khamanei also used his firm grip on public media and judiciary to propagate his revolutionary Islamic views. Khomeini's successors have lacked his charisma and religious authority; therefore, they have increasingly relied on military, **paramilitary**, and other security forces to maintain power.

In 1997, Mohammed Khatami (b. 1943) won the presidential election in a landslide victory against other candidates who were associated with Khamenei. Khatami was affiliated with the leftist groups loyal to Khomeini. Although Khatami and the rest of candidates all claimed to strictly adhere to principles of the 1979 revolution and Khomeini's doctrine of Islamic government, Khatami was generally perceived a more moderate candidate who was more independent. Khatami's victory was viewed as a sign of growing disillusionment with the leadership, a widespread desire for change, and a yearning for greater **pragmatism** and **liberalization**.

With the promise of reform, Khatami kept the popular support and remained president for two consecutive terms. In practice, however, Khatami's positions on economy and foreign relations, freedom, and the legal system were vague. Khatami's inconsistency and timidity combined with the aggressive campaign of radicals led to a blockage of any possible reform and added to public discontent and apathy.

In 2004 Iran still did not have formal diplomatic relations with the United States. The international community's biggest problem with Iran has been its nuclear weapons program. The country's foreign diplomacy has also been continuously undermined by the lasting side effects of its past policies, including its opposition to the Middle East peace process in Israel and interference in the affairs of neighboring countries.

After years of decline, the economy has experienced steady growth since the death of Khomeini. Unemployment and inflation rates remained high as of 2004, however. Some of the economic problems stem from the population boom that followed the 1979 revolution. In the early years after the revolution, and also during the Iran-Iraq War (1980–1988), the government largely ignored the need to institute population control programs. The resulting large generation of Iranians has put new added pressure on the economy and sought social changes. Moreover, the financial burden of public subsidies has intensified with population growth and rapid urbanization, and it has overwhelmed the government. The high rate of fuel consumption, the lack of an adequate infrastructure, and scant urban development have led to severe traffic and air pollution problems and one of the highest rates of fatal car accidents in the world.

Overall, demographic changes, restrictive social policies, and poor economic conditions have generated popular dissatisfaction with the government and created powerful pressure for reforms. As a result, Iran continues to experience a high rate of **emigration**.

THE LEGAL SYSTEM

After Khomeini's death the legal system was reorganized to resemble the courts of the early Islamic period. As a result, the modern structure of judicial power was completely deconstructed and many experienced lawyers and judges left the system. In 1999 the head of the judiciary was removed. Since

paramilitary: modeled after a military, especially as a possible supplement to the military

pragmatism: a belief that only that which can be practically accomplished should be advocated

liberalization: the process of lowering trade barriers and tariffs and reducing government economic regulations

emigration: the migration of individuals out of a geographic area or country

then some efforts have been made to return the legal system to normal status. However, administrative fragmentation, the shortage of qualified judges, and the judiciary's involvement in politics have slowed judicial reforms.

In the Iranian legal system, laws are supposed to derive from traditional Islamic **jurisprudence**; however, many laws have little to do with Islam. Economic laws are largely influenced by the constitution, which has a strong socialist tone. Family laws are most consistent with Islamic jurisprudence, yet they are not fundamentally different from pre-revolutionary laws. Although the constitution guarantees freedom of speech and political activity, in the early 2000s several laws have imposed major restrictions on the media and political activity. Political activists must remain loyal to the nation's supreme leader and the constitution. Criticism of the government, Khomeini, or the 1979 revolution is strictly prohibited, as is questioning the regime. The red light in the Islamic republic remains any activity that may be construed as a threat to the legitimacy of the supreme leader. Citizens do have some freedom and flexibility, however, in criticizing the executive and legislative branches, and to a lesser extent the judicial branch.

See also: Iraq; Shari'a.

BIBLIOGRAPHY

Daniel, Elton. *The History of Iran*. Westport, CT: Greenwood Press, 2001.

Hooglund, Eric, ed. *Twenty Years of Islamic Revolution, Political and Social Transition in Iran since 1979*. Syracuse, NY: Syracuse University Press, 2002.

"Iran." In *CIA World Factbook*. Washington, DC: Central Intelligence Agency, 2005. <http://www.cia.gov/cia/publications/factbook/geos/ir.html>.

"Iran: Who Holds the Power?" *BBC News Online.* <http://news.bbc.co.uk/2/shared/spl/hi/middle_east/03/iran_power/html/default.stm.>

Jahanbegloo, Ramin. *Iran: Between Tradition and Modernity*. Lanham, MD: Lexington Books, 2004.

Keddie, Nikki R. *Modern Iran: Roots and Results of Revolution.* New Haven, CT: Yale University Press, 2003.

Kurzman, Charles. *The Unthinkable Revolution in Iran.* Cambridge, MA: Harvard University Press, 2004.

Library of Congress, Federal Research Division. *Iran.* <http://countrystudies.us/iran/>.

Menashri, David. *Post-Revolutionary Politics in Iran: Religion, Society and Power*. Portland, OR: Frank Cass, 2001.

Mohammadi, Ali. *Iran Encountering Globalization: Problems and Prospects*. New York: Routledge Curzon, 2003.

Moslem, Mehdi. *Factional Politics in Post-Khomeini Iran*. Syracuse, NY: Syracuse University Press, 2002.

Statistical Center of Iran. <http://www.sci.or.ir>.

Hassan S Dibadj

Iraq

Few countries have received more of the world's attention during the late twentieth and early twenty-first century than Iraq. During those years, the country was involved in open warfare on three occasions. In the Iran-Iraq War

(MAP BY MARYLAND CARTOGRAPHICS/THE GALE GROUP)

(1980–1988), Iraq, led by its long-time dictator Saddam Hussein (b. 1937), clashed in an extended, brutal, and bitter war with its neighbor to the east, the Islamic Republic of Iran, that took many thousands of lives on both sides.

In the Persian Gulf War (1990–1991), Iraq was attacked and defeated by the United States and a sizable **coalition** of allies after Saddam Hussein had invaded Iraq's southern neighbor, Kuwait. Although his country lost the war and was subjected to significant international **sanctions**, Saddam Hussein retained dictatorial power and continued to be regarded by many of his neighbors and the United States as a danger to regional and world peace.

In the third conflict, the United States in 2003 again attacked Iraq in a war that was widely opposed throughout the world, even by many of the United States' staunchest allies from the earlier war and substantial segments of the American public. The controversial and bitterly debated justifications for this war put forward by U.S. President George W. Bush (b. 1946) and his administration were that Saddam Hussein's Iraq was implicated in supporting the terrorist organizations that attacked the United States on September 11, 2001, killing several thousand civilian Americans, and that Saddam Hussein possessed or was actively building weapons of mass destruction. Subsequent events demonstrated that neither of these justifications were based on fact, but, by the time this became known, the United States and its small coalition of allies had conquered

coalition: an alliance, partnership, or union of disparate peoples or individuals

sanction: economic, political, or military reprisals, or, to ratify

regime: a type of government, or, the government in power in a region

insurgency: a rebellion against an existing authority

Iraq, chased Saddam Hussein and his allies from power, and initiated a military occupation and an effort to build a new democratic **regime** in Iraq.

The U.S. military occupation of Iraq was unpopular with many Iraqis. The occupation regime and the transitional Iraqi regimes it supported were faced with apparently unanticipated serious opposition from a variety of **insurgent** groups. Nevertheless, the United States steadily transferred formal and, to a lesser degree, effective power to governments formed and led by Iraqis. Cooperating with United Nations (UN) officials, the United States sponsored democratic elections in January 2005 that were, in the eyes of many observers, remarkably high in voter participation and highly valued by a substantial majority of Iraqis.

The elected Iraqi leaders spent the first half of 2005 negotiating to construct a government that would represent all of Iraq's most important ethnic and religious groups and still have some chance of governing effectively. Their task continued to be greatly hampered by suicide bombings and other violent activities undertaken by insurgents, and as of mid-2005, the future of Iraq's first democratically elected government remained uncertain.

IRAQ AND ITS HISTORY

Iraq is located in the Middle East, bordering Iran, Jordan, Turkey, Saudi Arabia, Syria, and Kuwait. Iraq separates Arab countries from the non-Arab peoples that live in the Middle East, such as Iranians, Turks, and Kurds. Iraq also separates the mostly dry deserts of the Arabian countries from the mountainous lands to the east. The area of Iraq is 437,072 square kilometers (168,754 square miles), which is slightly more than twice the size of Idaho. Approximately 25 million people live in Iraq. The population is very young, with more than 40 percent of the population under the age of fourteen. The majority of people (97%) are Muslim, who are divided into two main groups. Most Muslims are Shia (60–65%), and the rest are Sunni (35–40%). Iraq consists of three distinct regions. Shias are concentrated in the south and center, Sunnis live mostly in the center and west, and Kurds live in the north. Most people speak Arabic, but Kurdish is the official language in the Kurdish regions.

Ancient History. Contemporary Iraq occupies the area of the former Mesopotamia, the area between the Tigris and Euphrates Rivers. This region was the site of the earliest civilizations of the ancient Near East, dating as far back as 6000 B.C.E. Many of the basic signs of civilization and early forms of science, such as astronomy and agricultural studies, first developed in this area. Some of the oldest stories found in the Hebrew Bible, such as those of the lives of Noah and Abraham, are set in ancient Mesopotamia. Consequently, the first known empire emerged from Mesopotamia in approximately 2400 B.C.E.

The Islamic Period. In C.E. 634, a small army of Arab tribesmen invaded and conquered Mesopotamia. They were followers of the prophet Muhammad (c. 570–672), who had introduced the monotheistic faith of Islam in C.E. 610 and established an Islamic state on the Arabian Peninsula. Within two years the Arabs had captured all of Mesopotamia and introduced Islam to the population. By C.E. 650 Islamic rule extended from Egypt to modern Afghanistan.

Four caliphs governed the Islamic state between 632 and 661. The events of the early Islamic period and the dispute over who was considered the legitimate successor of Muhammad divided the Muslims into the Shia and Sunni **sects**. Shia Muslims believed that Ali (656–661), the fourth caliph, was the real successor of Muhammad and should have been named the first caliph. The early years of the Islamic period, especially the reigns of the third caliph Othman (c. 588–656)

sect: a group of people with a common distinctive view of religion or doctrine

and that of Ali, were shaped by old rivalries between Arab tribes. These disputes led to the murder of several important Shia leaders (or imams) that further deepened the Shias' wounds. Because four Shia imams are buried in Iraq, it remains a significant place for Shia Muslims.

Iraq became the center of the Islamic world when the Abbasid dynasty (r. 750–1258) built Baghdad as its capital. Baghdad became the second largest city in the world and an important center of commerce, culture, science, and literature. After 806, the Iranians and other Muslim nations formed their own governments and separated from the Abbasid Empire.

Mongolian Attack, the Ottoman Empire, and British Rule. The Abbasid empire was conquered in 1258 by Mongolian tribes, who destroyed most of the cities, burned thousands of books, and massacred millions of people. The Mongolian invasion, scholars suggest, shifted the focus of Iraqi history from the urban-based Abbasid culture to pastoral nomadism and tribalism that lasted until the twentieth century.

After the Mongolian attack, Baghdad and other Iraqi cities lost their economic and cultural significance. After the establishment of the Safavid dynasty (r. 1502–1736) in neighboring Iran, Shia Islam was declared as the official religion in that country, and Iran's interest in Iraq increased. The establishment of the Safavids in Iran coincided with expansion of the Ottoman Empire (1299–1922), which was a Sunni government. From the sixteenth to the nineteenth centuries, the course of Iraqi history was determined by the continuing conflicts between the Safavid Empire in Iran and the Ottoman Turks. These continuing conflicts deepened the Shia–Sunni rift.

During the Ottoman period, the Sunni dominated government in Iraq and gained the administrative experience that would allow them to monopolize political power in the twentieth century. In the nineteenth and twentieth centuries, the Sunnis were able to take advantage of new economic and educational opportunities, while the Shias remained politically impotent and economically depressed. This growing gap further separated the two groups and made the Shia–Sunni rift an important element of Iraqi politics and social structure.

During World War I (1914–1918) Iraq became a battleground between British and Ottoman forces. After four years of war, the British took control of most parts of Iraq. Although Iraqis did not like the Turkish rule, they did not like the rule of non-Muslims either. A resistance movement started against British forces. The Great Iraqi Revolution (as the 1920 rebellion is called) united Sunni and Shia tribes and cities for the first time. The revolt, however, did not last long. Iraqi independence came in 1932.

INDEPENDENCE OF IRAQ

After World War I, when the British and the French started to grant independence to their occupied areas in the Middle East, they set the borders of these countries artificially without giving any consideration to their ethnic mix, commercial ties, or historical background. Many of these newly born countries had been parts of a larger Islamic empire for hundreds of years, and most of these societies still were largely composed of tribal communities. They were given little opportunity or input to define their own **nation-state**. The quest for a national identity gave rise to various political **ideologies** and groups which derived their legitimacy from sources such as language, religion, and national borders.

These forces shaped the contemporary politics of the Middle East. Iraq, in particular, was a region of ideological rivalry as well as tribal and ethnic conflicts.

nation-state: a relatively homogeneous state with only one or few nationalities within its political borders

ideology: a system of beliefs composed of ideas or values, from which political, social, or economic programs are often derived

coup: a quick seizure of power or a sudden attack

The clashes made the Iraqi government unstable. Since its independence, Iraq has experienced the greatest number of military **coups** and regime changes of any country in the Middle East.

Two major developments had a great impact on the Arab world and Iraq after World War II (1939–1945). The first was the establishment of state of Israel in 1948,

IRAQIS CELEBRATE AS A STATUE OF FORMER PRESIDENT SADDAM HUSSEIN TOPPLES IN BAGHDAD ON APRIL 9, 2003. The destruction of former Iraqi dictator Saddam Hussein's 40-foot statue in Firdos Square represented the end of Hussein's regime and the takeover of U.S. troops in Baghdad during the 2003 U.S.-led invasion of Iraq. (SOURCE: © REUTERS/CORBIS)

which initiated a long clash between Arab countries and Muslim populations in general against Israel and its Western allies. The main consequence of the establishment of Israel and the Arab–Israeli conflict was the growth of anti-Western sentiments and radical ideologies. These radical ideologies, which were also influenced by the **socialist** agenda, gave birth to military coups in Egypt, Iraq, and Syria.

As Arab countries looked for military support against Israel and Western countries, they solicited the former Soviet Union as their ally. Gradually, communist and socialist groups gained power in most of these countries. These socialist governments used pan-Arabism (and later Islamicist ideology) to create a dominant political group to support their anti-Western agenda and to soften the opposition to their governments.

The other development that greatly affected Iraq and other Persian Gulf countries was a great jump in oil incomes. The oil income boosted the population, accelerated the growth of the middle class, and helped **authoritarian** regimes to enforce and maintain their power.

The post–World War II Arab world witnessed both economic and political cooperation among Arab countries as well as rivalry for the role of leader. For the most part, Iraq and Egypt were considered the intellectual centers of the Arab world; consequently, they competed for the position of leadership. In Egypt, Gamal Abdel Nasser (1918–1970) used pan-Arabic propaganda against Iraq to support anti-regime activities and to destabilize the monarchy. Finally, in 1958 the Iraqi monarchy was overthrown by a military coup and was replaced by a republic led by army officers. From establishment of that republic until 1969, Iraq politics was riddled by military coups. As the oil economy grew and the role of government became more important, Iraq's class antagonisms intensified long-standing religious and sectarian hatreds. Each regime change revived suppressed sectarian, tribal, and ethnic conflicts. The strongest of these conflicts were those that occurred between Kurds and Arabs and between Sunnis and Shias.

In 1968, the Sunni Baath party seized power in a coup. Ahmed Hassan al-Bakr (1914–1982) became the president and Saddam Hussein, his vice president. Gradually, Hussein increased his power; by 1979, after Bakr's abdication, Hussein became the president of Iraq. Hussein soon gained a reputation as a brutally savage dictator. He appointed his relatives and people from his hometown Takrit to influential government posts and demanded strict obedience from them. He was very quick to punish anyone who was suspected of disloyalty, even his own family members.

The 1979 revolution in Iran had important implications for the region. After the seizure of the American embassy in Tehran by a mob of students, Iran's relation with the international community deteriorated. Hussein used this opportunity to wage a full-scale war against Iran in order to acquire its Arab-inhabited region. Although Iraq had the support of Western countries including the United States, other Arab countries, and the Soviet Union, the war lasted eight years and ended inconclusively in 1988. It claimed the lives of hundred of thousands of Iraqis and cost billions of dollars. The war also strained the domestic politics between Sunnis, Shias, and Kurds in Iraq. During the war, in violation of international conventions, Hussein used chemical weapons extensively against Iranian forces and later against the Kurdish population.

In 1990 Hussein attacked Kuwait and declared it to be part of Iraq. Armies composed of an international coalition led by the United States swiftly expelled the Iraqi army from Kuwait and forced the Iraqi dictator to accept weapon inspections. After the retreat of Iraqi army, President George H. W. Bush (b. 1924) encouraged the Iraqi people to overthrow Hussein's regime. Hussein,

socialism: any of various economic and political theories advocating collective or governmental ownership and administration of the means of production and distribution of goods

authoritarianism: the domination of the state or its leader over individuals

infrastructure: the base on which a system or organization is built

interim: for a limited time, during a period of transition

federalism: a system of political organization, in which separate states or groups are ruled by a dominant central authority on some matters, but are otherwise permitted to govern themselves independently

nationalism: the belief that one's nation or culture is superior to all others

subsidy: a government grant used to encourage some action

however, succeeded in crushing Shia and Kurdish uprisings and massacred thousands of rebels and their families. U.S. policy shifted to preserve Iraq's territorial integrity and implement economic sanctions imposed by the UN Security Council to contain Iraq's armament. The economic sanctions, however, increased the poverty rate, stifled the economy, and devastated public health and Iraqi **infrastructure**. Hussein's relations with the United States continued to be strained; a few years later, in 2003, his regime was defeated by a coalition composed mostly of U.S. and U.K. forces.

The U.S.-led takeover resulted in the shutdown of much of Iraq's central economic and administrative structure. Iraq's people had already been struggling under UN sanctions, and the Iraqi infrastructure, including roads and utilities, was severely damaged by the consecutive wars and the UN sanctions. Many Iraqis felt that the U.S. occupation failed to improve their lives. Widespread chaos and looting took place and many conflicts erupted.

In the wake of the war, the United States appointed an **interim** government with limited power to rebuild the Iraqi bureaucracies, the armed forces, and the police, as well as to prepare Iraq for its first free election. The Iraqi Governing Council, which was established under that interim government, unanimously approved an interim constitution to serve until a permanent constitution is adopted in late 2005. The interim constitution recognized Islam as a source of legislation and banned any laws that violate the tenets of the Muslim faith. The document entails a comprehensive bill of rights. Details of Kurdish autonomy were not determined, but the document established Iraq as a **federal** system. Furthermore, it specified as a goal that 25 percent of the national assembly seats were to be reserved for women. Although the charter was intended to be temporary, council members and U.S. executives expected it to serve as the basis for the permanent constitution.

For the first time in history after long periods of oppressive governments, Iraqis have been given a chance to establish a democracy. The elections of January 2005 and the resulting government were a major step toward that establishment. The political leaders chosen in that election were Jalal Talabani (b. 1933), a Kurd, who was chosen to be president of the new Iraq, and Ibrahim al-Jaafari (b. 1947), a Shia, who was elected prime minister.

However, Hussein's loyalists, criminal gangs, and international terrorists continue to try to destabilize the new government. With deep-rooted anti-Western sentiments that are propagated both by pan-Arab and **nationalist** media as well as radical Islamic and socialist groups, any group could face difficulties in cooperating with the occupying U.S. forces. Additionally, old ethnic and religious conflicts are intensified by a disagreement over the distribution of oil incomes. The Sunnis, who had ruled Iraq for centuries, must operate within a government whose majority comes from other groups. Moreover, some religious leaders wish to try to imitate Iran and establish a religious state in Iraq. The youthful population and widespread poverty can radicalize any political movement. As a result, security in Iraq had continually deteriorated after the fall of Hussein.

Any single Iraqi political group will likely have a hard time gaining enough legitimacy to defuse old conflicts and maintaining the ideological zeal necessary to construct a new order. Any future government also faces difficult economic challenges, as a major percentage of government money is spent on public **subsidies**. In a country stricken by wars and domestic conflicts, it will be hard to find enough popular support for necessary economic reforms.

See also: Iran; Shari'a.

BIBLIOGRAPHY

Helms, Christine Moss. *Iraq, Eastern Flank of the Arab World*. Washington, DC: Brookings Institution Press, 1984.

"Iraq." In *CIA World Factbook*. Washington, DC: Central Intelligence Agency, 2005. <http://www.cia.gov/cia/publications/factbook/geos/iz.html>.

Mackey, Sandra. *The Reckoning, Iraq and the Legacy of Saddam Hussein*. New York: W.W. Norton, 2002.

Metz, Helen Chapman. "Iraq." *Profile in Country Studies*. Washington, DC: Federal Research Division of the Library of Congress, 1988. <http://countrystudies.us/iraq/>.

U.S. Department of State, Bureau of Democracy, Human Rights, and Labor. "Iraq." *Country Reports on Human Rights*. Washington, DC: U.S. Department of State, Bureau of Democracy, Human Rights, and Labor, 2005. <http://www.state.gov/g/drl/rls/hrrpt/2004/41722.htm>.

Hassan S Dibadj

Ireland

Ireland, the second-largest island in Europe, lies in the Atlantic Ocean on the western periphery of the European continent, separated from Great Britain to the east by the Irish Sea. Although the island is 84,433 square kilometers (32,595 square miles) in size, the jurisdiction of the Republic of Ireland covers 70,280 square kilometers (27,135 square miles). With a population estimated at 3.97 million in 2004, Ireland remains relatively underpopulated with a population density of just fifty-six persons per square kilometer (22 persons per square mile), in contrast to the European Union (EU) average of 115 persons per square kilometer (44 persons per square mile).

Geographically, Ireland is a saucer-like territory, encircled by low mountains on the coast and relatively flat plains in the center. The country is divided into the four provinces—Connacht, Leinster, Munster, and Ulster—with these provinces further subdivided into thirty-two counties. Twenty-six of these counties constitute the Republic of Ireland; six of Ulster's nine counties form Northern Ireland, now a part of the United Kingdom. Dublin is the capital city of Ireland, with an estimated population in 2002 of 1.058 million. The two official state languages are Irish and English.

HISTORY

One of the more significant dates in Irish history is May 1, 1169, when the Normans invaded Ireland. Two years later, when the Norman/English King Henry II (1133–1189) was made Lord of Ireland in 1171, this marked the beginning of a period of English rule that was to last until 1922. Numerous insurrections occurred throughout the centuries against this domination, but because they were not popular widespread uprisings and because the Irish factions could not unite as they had done in 1014, when they defeated the Vikings at the Battle of Clontarf, their rebellions were all crushed. On Easter morning of 1916 insurgents took to the streets of Dublin in a failed attempt to begin the revolution. What became known as the Easter Rising resulted in the rise to prominence of *Sinn Féin* (meaning "we ourselves"), initially a minority movement which did not take part in the uprising but which grew rapidly as it was taken over by rebel nationalists in the aftermath of 1916. In 1919 the elected members of *Sinn Féin* formed

jurisdiction: the territory or area within which authority may be exercised

insurrection: an uprising; an act of rebellion against an existing authority

factionalism: a separation of people into competing, adversarial, and self-serving groups, usually in government

insurgency: a rebellion against an existing authority

IRELAND

| 0 | 25 | 50 | 75 | 100 Miles |
| 0 | 25 | 50 | 75 | 100 Kilometers |

SCOTLAND

NORTH
ATLANTIC
OCEAN

NORTHERN
IRELAND
(U.K.)

Letterkenny
Finn

Donegal

*Donegal
Bay*

Sligo

Monaghan

Carrick on
Shannon

Dundalk

*Lough
Conn*

Drogheda

Castlebar

Longford

Boyne

*Irish
Sea*

Achill I.

*Lough
Mask*

Roscommon

Mullingar

Swords

Lough Ree

*Lough
Corrib*

Athlone

Dublin

Galway

Tullamore

Dun
Laoghaire

Galway Bay

Naas

WICKLOW
MTS.

*Aran
Is.*

Cliffs of
Moher

*Lough
Derg*

Shannon

Wicklow

Ennis

Carlow

Arklow

Barrow

Limerick

Kilkenny

Suir

Tipperary

Clonmel

Wexford

Tralee

Waterford

Saint George's Channel

Killarney

Blackwater

*Blarney
Castle*

Dingle Bay

▲ Carrauntuohill
3,414 ft.
1041 m.

Lee

Cork

Bantry

*Bantry
Bay*

Celtic Sea

Ireland

N
W E
S

(MAP BY MARYLAND CARTOGRAPHICS/THE GALE GROUP)

agrarian: having to do with farming or farming communities and their interests; one involved in such a movement

socioeconomic: relating to the traits of income, class, and education

per capita: for each person, especially for each person living in an area or country

their own parliament, *Dáil Éireann*, where they produced a Proclamation of Independence modeled on the French and American versions.

Following a war of independence waged by *Sinn Féin*'s military wing, the Irish Republican Army (IRA), against British forces from 1919 to 1921, Ireland regained independence under the 1921 Anglo-Irish Treaty. This granted twenty-six of the thirty-two counties the same dominion status held by other members of the British Commonwealth such as South Africa and Canada. This partition was the main crux of the treaty, and it divided the country bitterly, resulting in a civil war from June 1922 to May 1923 that claimed 4,000 lives. The pro-treaty side, which formed the new government, won the civil war, but the anti-treatyites did not enter parliament until 1927. It was not until Eamon de Valera (1888–1975), founder of the anti-treaty party *Fianna Fáil*, was elected as president of the executive council (prime minister) in 1932 that democracy was consolidated in Ireland. In 1949 Ireland left the commonwealth and formally established a republic. After lengthy negotiations it joined the European Economic Community (now known as the EU) in 1973.

The issue of partition was never resolved, and the eruption of violence in the North between Nationalists/Republicans (predominantly Catholic) and Unionists/Loyalists (predominantly Protestant) in 1969 demanded the attention of the Republic's government. A peace process begun in the 1990s helped engineer a ceasefire and culminated in the 1998 Good Friday Agreement, which among other things, involved the Republic dropping its constitutional claim on Northern Ireland.

SOCIOECONOMIC STATUS

For a long time Ireland was an underdeveloped **agrarian** economy, lacking the major deposits of natural resources that elsewhere fueled the Industrial Revolution of the nineteenth century. However, the country has witnessed a dramatic change in its **socioeconomic** structure since the 1960s, with one of the major causes being the transformation of the economy from an agricultural to a post-industrial base. Agriculture had declined in importance to such a degree that, by 2002, it provided only 8 percent of employment and 5 percent of the gross domestic product (GDP), whereas the services sector employed 64 percent of the labor force and provided 49 percent of GDP. Ireland's rapid economic growth rate (the fastest in Europe) saw the country's **per capita** GDP increasing from 60 percent of the EU average in 1973 to 126 percent in 2002, earning the economy the title of the "Celtic Tiger," in recognition of its growth rate rivaling the dynamic "Asian Tiger" economies.

These changes have radically improved the quality of life, confirmed by the United Nations Human Development Index, which ranked Ireland tenth of 177 countries in 2004. However, a breakdown of this index reveals that although Ireland lies third in terms of GDP per capita, it lags behind its Western partners in terms of life expectancy (twenty-eighth), proportion living under the poverty line (twentieth), and its functional literacy rate (fourteenth).

SYSTEM OF GOVERNMENT

Ireland is a liberal democracy with a parliamentary system of government. It is also a republic, with a directly elected president as head of state.

Origins. This system of government is a legacy of Ireland's colonial rule under Britain. The vast majority of the new state's leaders were political novices, and, as their main aim was simply to consolidate the fledgling state, they adopted a system they knew best, the **Westminster** model of parliamentary democracy. This legacy—and the small size of the country—also explains the decision to create a **centralized**, unitary state.

Conversely, another by-product of British colonial rule was the decision to reject the constitutional monarchy model in favor of a republican form of government. Although Ireland did not formally become a republic until 1949, it was one in all but name from 1937 onward. Although Ireland veered from the Westminster model in having a president as head of state, the post is largely a ceremonial role with very few powers, such that the Irish presidency is recognized as the weakest in Europe. This mixture of parliamentarism and presidentialism has led some to classify the system as "semi-presidential," similar to France and Austria, although this is open to debate, with most observers preferring to categorize it as a parliamentary system with a directly elected president.

Constitutional Basis. Ireland deviated from the Westminster model and followed the American and French republican traditions by adopting a written constitution. The 1922 Constitution of the Irish Free State did not have an auspicious beginning: Because it was written under duress from the British government, it never carried the necessary air of authority. It was ultimately replaced in 1937 by *Bunreacht na hÉireann*, written free of any external influences and approved by the people in a **referendum**.

OPERATION OF GOVERNMENT

Ireland follows the classical model of liberal democratic theory, with the parliament representing the people as the supreme decision-making body. Parliament elects a prime minister (*Taoiseach*) and **ratifies** the prime minister's choice of government, or cabinet ministers. The *Taoiseach* and government are answerable and accountable to parliament, which is free to dismiss the government at any time they wish. Parliament also has the ultimate power to make laws, which the government is obliged to execute.

Division of Powers. The Irish political system is modeled on the writings of Montesquieu (1689–1755), with power **devolved** among the separate branches of the legislature, the executive, and the judiciary. A **bicameral** legislature, the houses of the *Oireachtas*, consists of a directly elected lower house, *Dáil Éireann* (House of Representatives), and an indirectly elected upper house, *Seanad Éireann* (Senate). The *Oireachtas* consists of the legislature and the president, and even though it has the sole and exclusive power for making legislation, almost all laws are government-sponsored. The *Dáil* can veto any bill, which the government has no power to override, but the disciplined nature of party governments ensures that this is a rare occurrence. The *Seanad* has few powers: It can veto any bill (except a money bill), but this veto automatically lapses after ninety days. The president can refer any bill (except a money bill or a proposal to amend the constitution) to the Supreme Court to check the constitutionality of the bill, but this power was only employed fifteen times up to March 2005, and it is generally expected that the president signs into law most bills passed by parliament.

Westminster: a democratic model of government comprising operational procedures for a legislative body, based on the system used in the United Kingdom

centralize: to move control or power to a single point of authority

referendum: a popular vote on legislation, brought before the people by their elected leaders or public initiative

ratify: to make official or to officially sanction

devolve: to move power or property from one individual or institution to another, especially from a central authority

bicameral: comprised of two chambers, usually a legislative body

TABLE 1

Irish Taoisigh (Prime Ministers) since 1945

Taoiseach	Years of office	Reason for leaving office
Éamon de Valera	1932–1948	Electoral defeat
John A. Costello	1948–1951	Electoral defeat
Éamon de Valera	1951–1954	Electoral defeat
John A. Costello	1954–1957	Electoral defeat
Éamon de Valera	1957–1959	Resigned
Seán Lemass	1959–1966	Resigned
Jack Lynch	1966–1973	Electoral defeat
Liam Cosgrave	1973–1977	Electoral defeat
Jack Lynch	1977–1979	Resigned
Charles J. Haughey	1979–1981	Electoral defeat
Garret FitzGerald	1981–1982	Electoral defeat
Charles J. Haughey	1982	Electoral defeat
Garret FitzGerald	1982–1987	Electoral defeat
Charles J. Haughey	1987–1992	Resigned
Albert Reynolds	1992–1994	Resigned
John Bruton	1994–1997	Electoral defeat
Bertie Ahern	1997–	

SOURCE: Courtesy of author.

de facto: (Latin) actual; in effect but not officially declared

de jure: (Latin) by right

judicial review: the ability of the judicial branch to review and invalidate a law that contradicts the constitution

bureaucracy: a system of administrating government involving professional labor; the mass of individuals administering government

technocracy: government by technicians using scientific expertise and analysis to optimize conditions for the public

nonpartisan: not relating to a political party or any division associated with the party system

Practice. Like most parliaments, the *Dáil*'s **de facto** powers deviate greatly from its **de jure** authority. The government is the real seat of authority, as it makes almost all laws, and the *Dáil* is little more than a glorified rubber stamp, used to confirm its decisions. This digression occurs because Ireland conforms to the Westminster model of democracy, with no effective separation of powers between government and parliament. They are not separate, distinct bodies, as the government is chosen from the parliament; all ministers must be members of either house of parliament, although because the provision that up to two senators can be appointed to government is rarely used, in effect virtually all ministers are also members of the *Dáil*, or *Teachta Dála* (TDs). In addition, the *Dáil* is not an atomized group of individuals, but rather a collection of a few tightly disciplined parties; because party TDs rarely rebel against their respective leaders, a majority government can act relatively independently of the *Dáil*, largely wielding unchecked power.

Judiciary. The final branch of government, the judiciary, deviates from the comparative European model in that the government is the sole appointee of judges. Nevertheless, the judiciary is recognized and acts as an independent body. Neither the legislative nor the executive branches have the authority to interfere with judicial decisions, and judges can only be dismissed by a majority of the *Dáil* and *Seanad* for obvious misbehavior or incapacity. The judiciary possesses the additional power of **judicial review**, which is the authority to interpret the constitutionality of legislation, any actions based on legislation, or the actions of any public body. This is a power they share with their common law U.S. counterparts, but which is different to the conventional European civil law model, in which designated constitutional courts alone have the power of judicial review.

Bureaucracy. The Irish **bureaucracy** conforms to the British generalist style of civil service, whereby officials are assessed according to their general administrative skills, in contrast to the **technocratic** ethos of most European bureaucracies. The distinguishing feature of the Irish civil service is the strictly **nonpartisan** nature of appointments, which is in contrast to the politicized nature of bureaucracy in the United States, where changes of civil servants occur in accordance with changes in the presidency. Until 1997, government ministers were responsible for everything done within, and by, their departments. This masked the role of departmental officials, some of whom exerted a considerable role on government policy. A change in legislation in 1997 went a little way to recognizing this de facto situation by acknowledging and allocating some responsibilities and powers to senior civil servants.

POLITICAL LIFE

The two dominant political parties of post-independence Ireland stem from the 1922–1923 civil war, with *Fianna Fáil* (meaning "Soldiers of Destiny") representing the anti-treaty tradition, and *Fine Gael* (meaning "Tribe of Gaels"), the pro-treaty tradition. Both are centrist parties, and they have led every single government, although they have never been in power together. *Fianna Fáil* has been the largest party at every election since 1932, spending fifty-five of seventy-three years in government from 1932 to 2005, and *Fine Gael*, which has been the second largest party at every election since 1932, has been in government for only eighteen years over the same time period. The third main party is the Labour Party, but their electoral performance has been the weakest of any European left-wing party, averaging only 11 percent of the vote from 1922 to 2004. Other minor parties include the Progressive Democrats, a liberal-style party; the Green Party, a quintessential ecology-based party; and *Sinn Féin*, an all-island **nationalist** party, which has close political links with the **paramilitary** IRA.

Interest Groups. Interest groups exert a considerable influence on government policy, with notable examples including the Irish Farmers' Association and the Irish Congress of Trade Unions. Elements of both the corporatist and pluralist models are evident in the role of interest groups in the policy-making process. The former takes the form of a tradition of three-way consultation between government, industry, and trade unions that expanded from the late 1980s onward to include a wide range of economic and social policies. The pluralist model is seen in the significant influence cause-centered groups can wield on public policy. This has especially been the case in the area of "moral politics," whereby groups such as the Society for the Protection of the Unborn Child and the Divorce Action Group dominated the campaigns of the various abortion and divorce referendums of the 1980s and 1990s.

Elections and Voting. Elections are free and fair, with Irish citizens having the right to vote at all elections and referendums. In addition, British citizens residing in Ireland can vote in *Dáil*, European, and local elections. Resident EU citizens can vote at European and local elections, and any resident can vote at local elections. The minimum voting age is eighteen. Unlike in some European countries (e.g., Belgium, the Netherlands, and Luxembourg), voting is not **compulsory** in Ireland, but electoral turnout remained relatively high, averaging over 75 percent until the 1980s, when it began to decline in line with a similar European pattern, falling to 62 percent in 2002.

The electoral system, proportional representations by means of the single transferable vote (PR-STV), is employed at all elections for the distributing and counting of votes. PR-STV is a system that elects members to multi-seat constituencies (three to five in Ireland). Voters rank the candidates in their order of preference (first, second, third, and so on), and a candidate needs to receive a specific quota of votes to be elected. Should a voter's first preference be neither sufficient nor necessary to get their desired candidate elected, their vote is transferred to their next preferred candidate, a process which continues until all

■ ■ ■
IRELAND

The term "Ireland" can be confusing. The entire island is known as Ireland, which was the name of the territory prior to 1922. However, under the Anglo-Irish Treaty of 1921, the southern state was known as the Irish Free State until 1937, and as *Éire*, Ireland, the Republic of Ireland, or simply the Republic since then; the northern jurisdiction is commonly referred to as Northern Ireland or the North. In this article, the Republic is simply referred to as Ireland.

nationalism: the belief that one's nation or culture is superior to all others

paramilitary: modeled after a military, especially as a possible supplement to the military

compulsory: mandatory, required, or unable to be avoided

seats have been filled by candidates who have received the required quota of votes, or when there are no more votes left to transfer. Because it is a relatively unique voting system (Malta is the only other country using PR-STV to elect its lower house of parliament), Ireland has attracted a disproportionate amount of attention from scholars of electoral systems. One other source of attention is the frequent use of the referendum (only Switzerland and Italy have held more in Europe), which occurs because any constitutional change requires a referendum. From 1937 to 2004, there were twenty-nine referendums, with sixteen since 1992. The two most common reasons for change have been related to moral issues and European integration.

PERSONAL FREEDOMS

Freedoms of assembly, association, expression, and religion are all constitutionally guaranteed. The Freedom House index ranks Ireland as "free," awarding it the maximum score of 1 (on a scale of 1 to 7) in terms of political rights and civil liberties. Irish residents have a relatively high level of personal security, with a crime rate of just 2,541 per 100,000 persons in 2003, the

PARLIAMENT BUILDING IN DUBLIN, IRELAND. Constructed in 1745, Leinster House in downtown Dublin, Ireland has housed the Irish parliament's legislature, or *Oireachtas*, since 1922. Parliament is comprised of a 60-member upper house (*Seanad Éireann*) and a 166-member lower house (*Dáil Éireann*). (SOURCE: © MICHAEL NICHOLSON/CORBIS. REPRODUCED BY PERMISSION.)

second lowest in the EU. However, the impact of the conflict in Northern Ireland has sometimes transgressed into the Republic, and there have been several high-profile incidents of terrorism, most notably simultaneous car bombings in Dublin and Monaghan in 1974 that killed thirty-three people. In addition, the prevalence of drug-running criminal gangs has increased since the 1990s. One high profile incident occurred in 1996 when one such gang murdered a prominent journalist, Veronica Guerin (1959–1996), who was investigating their activities.

Politics in Ireland have been greatly influenced by the country's relationship with Britain. As shown above, the form of government adopted is both a positive and negative reaction to the legacy of colonial rule.

The British influence also had an indirect effect as it sheltered Ireland from various social and political phenomena (e.g., centuries of warfare) that shaped European political systems. It is therefore distinct from the European paradigm for the general absence of social bases in guiding political choice, the weak role **ideology** has had to play in political competition, and the survival of parliamentary democracy in a small underdeveloped state.

ideology: a system of beliefs composed of ideas or values, from which political, social, or economic programs are often derived

However, it is in relation to Northern Ireland that the British influence is still most noticeably felt. It is this issue above all others that explains the disproportionate global coverage given to politics on the island, as violence and civil unrest have been a feature of political life since the twelfth century, although it is now by and large confined to the Northern jurisdiction.

See also: European Union; Northern Ireland; Parliamentary Systems; United Kingdom.

BIBLIOGRAPHY

Bunreacht na hÉireann (Constitution of Ireland). <http://www.irlgov.ie/publications.asp>.

Central Statistics Office. <http://www.cso.ie>.

Chubb, Basil. *The Government and Politics of Ireland.* 3rd ed. London: Longman, 1992.

Coakley, John, and Michael Gallagher, eds. *Politics in the Republic of Ireland.* 4th ed. London: Routledge, 2004.

Freedom House. "Ireland." *Freedom in the World 2004.* New York: Freedom House, 2004. <http://www.freedomhouse.org/research/freeworld/2004/countryratings/ireland.htm>.

Gallagher, Michael. "Republic of Ireland." In *Semi-Presidentialism in Europe,* ed. Robert Elgie. Oxford, UK: Oxford University Press, 1999.

Gallagher, Michael, Michael Marsh, and Paul Mitchell, eds. *How Ireland Voted 2002.* London: Palgrave, 2003.

Government of Ireland. <http://www.irlgov.ie>.

"Ireland." In *CIA World Factbook.* Washington, DC: Central Intelligence Agency, 2005. <http://www.cia.gov/cia/publications/factbook/geos/ei.html>.

Lalor, Brian, ed. *The Encyclopaedia of Ireland.* Dublin: Gill & Macmillan, 2003.

Lee, J. J. *Ireland 1912–1985: Politics and Society.* Cambridge, UK: Cambridge University Press, 1989.

Mitchell, Paul, and Rick Wilford, eds. *Politics in Northern Ireland.* Boulder, CO: Westview, 1999.

Official Report of the Parliamentary Debates of the Houses of the Oireachtas. <http://historical-debates.oireachtas.ie/>.

Sinnott, Richard. *Irish Voters Decide: Voting Behaviour in Elections and Referendums since 1918*. Manchester, UK: Manchester University Press, 1995.

United Nations Development Programme. "Ireland." *Human Development Report 2004.* New York: United Nations Development Programme, 2004. <http://hdr.undp.org/reports/global/2004/>.

Liam Weeks

Islamic Law

See: Shari'a.

Israel

The State of Israel is located at the eastern end of the Mediterranean Sea. Its borders—indeed its very existence—have been in dispute since it proclaimed its independence in May 1948. Those nations (and the United Nations) that recognize Israel as a legitimate **nation-state** generally are agreed on the following boundaries: the Mediterranean Sea forms Israel's western border; Lebanon and Syria are to the north; Egypt is to the south; and the territory commonly designated as the West Bank (including East Jerusalem) is to the east. The area within these boundaries comprises approximately 22,145 square kilometers (8,000 square miles)—about the size of the U.S. state of New Jersey.

In 2004, Israel had a population of 6.8 million. Ethnically, Israel's population was 80 percent Jewish; its 20 percent non-Jewish population was mostly Arab. In terms of religion, the population was 80 percent Jewish, 15 percent Muslim, 2 percent Christian, 1 percent Druze, and 2 percent other.

The semi-arid landscape provides limited opportunity for agriculture, so as Israel developed, it increasingly turned to industry and technology. In the twenty-first century, Israel had become a modern, Western-oriented nation, and Israelis had a standard of living (measured by gross domestic product **per capita**) comparable to European countries such as Spain.

GENERAL HISTORICAL BACKGROUND

It is a commentary on Jewish history that the **nationalist** movement—Zionism—that gave birth to the State of Israel had its organizational roots in Western Europe, its sociological roots in Eastern Europe, and its emotional roots in the Biblical homeland of the Jews, the territory usually called Palestine.

After their dispersion by the Roman Empire in the second century, the vast majority of the world's Jews lived outside Palestine. In 1881, the twenty-five thousand Jews who lived in what was then Ottoman Palestine were the remnant of a people who had inhabited the land since biblical times. Comprising roughly 6 percent of the region's population, they were desperately poor, totally apolitical, and completely involved in a way of life molded by their ancestral religion, which is now called Orthodox Judaism. This community did not appear to be fertile soil in which to plant a modern nationalist movement.

Yet, it was the tradition represented by that community that provided the affective ties of unity needed by the Zionist nation builders. Until the nineteenth

nation-state: a relatively homogeneous state with only one or few nationalities within its political borders

per capita: for each person, especially for each person living in an area or country

nationalism: the belief that one's nation or culture is superior to all others

century, all Jews, wherever they happened to reside, lived according to the norms of the Jewish religious tradition. Not only did those norms specify a Jew's relation to God, but in specifying the relation of person to person, especially within the Jewish community, those norms also defined the Jewish people. Traditional Judaism makes no distinction between religious belief and national identity; it entails both a religious and a national commitment. The religious tradition—its precepts and practices—also bound the Jewish people to Palestine. For Judaism connects God's covenant with the Jewish people to that land and to no other. So strong was this traditional attachment to the land that when Jewish nationalism did emerge, even the children of secularized European Jews could identify their nation only with the Zion of tradition—Palestine.

Western European Jewry had ceased to be a traditional religious community during the nineteenth century. In the aftermath of the French Revolution (1789–1799), Jews began assimilating into the societies of Western Europe. Their major concern was adapting themselves to the dominant cultures. Eventually, they modified or discarded some of their religious practices, and they began to make a distinction between their religion and their nationality. They were now French citizens who were Jewish, Germans who were Jewish, and so on. Because these Jews functioned as members of the modern Western societies in which they lived, they developed the skills and resources needed to create and sustain a nationalist movement.

The Jews' entry into Western societies was frequently met with resistance, which occasionally turned violent. This anti-Semitism led a secular Jew, Theodor Herzl (1860–1904), to form the World Zionist Organization in 1897. Its aim was to facilitate the return of the Jewish people to the land of Palestine and to establish an internationally recognized nation in which Jews could live free from persecution. The World Zionist Organization provided the ideological momentum and the institutional apparatus to wage the political fight for a Jewish state.

Most Western Jews, however, despite their anxieties about anti-Semitism, continued their struggle for full acceptance in their countries of birth. However, most Jews in Eastern Europe—in the Austro-Hungarian Empire and Czarist Russia—were regarded, and regarded themselves, as a distinct alien people merely cohabiting the same territory. When the economic structures that had sustained those communities collapsed at the end of the nineteenth century and incidents of violent anti-Semitism multiplied, however, the Jews of Eastern Europe sought to escape. Between 1882 and 1914, approximately 2.5 million Jews, almost one-third of the entire Jewish population, left the Eastern European empires. A minority went to Palestine and established the first Zionist settlements there. Despite the enmity of the Ottoman (Turkish) authorities and the hostility of the indigenous Arab population, those Zionist immigrants from Eastern Europe laid the foundations for a viable Jewish community in Palestine.

During World War I (1914–1918), the World Zionist Organization's leadership in Europe was able to negotiate a political arrangement for establishing an autonomous Jewish

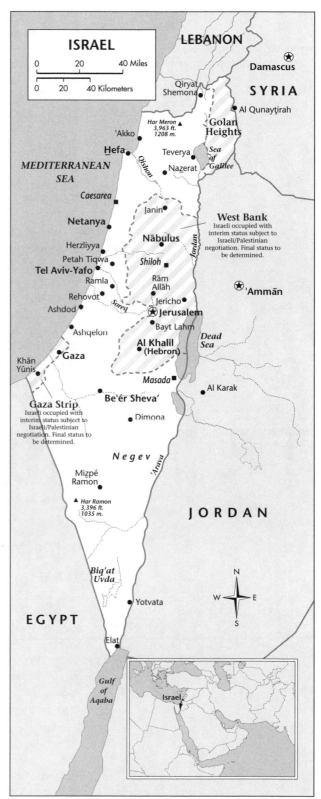

(MAP BY MARYLAND CARTOGRAPHICS/THE GALE GROUP)

imperialism: extension of the control of one nation over another, especially through territorial, economic, and political expansion

mandate: to command, order, or require; or, a command, order, or requirement

armistice: a cease fire or temporary end to hostilities

community in Israel. Led by Chaim Weizmann (1874–1952), they helped persuade the British War Cabinet that the Zionists' goals were not incompatible with its imperial interests. The result was the Balfour Declaration of November 1917. Although it did not grant the Zionists their ultimate objective (i.e., an independent Jewish state), it promised them the opportunity to establish a "national home" in Palestine. After the war, the San Remo Treaty (1920), which recognized Britain as the League of Nations' mandate authority governing Palestine, also incorporated the Balfour Declaration. From the Zionists' perspective, this provided international legitimacy for an autonomous Jewish community.

The majority Arab population of Mandate Palestine, however, never accepted the arrangement. They opposed the Zionist settlement from the outset because the continued arrival of Jewish immigrants would shift the balance of power within Palestine. Thus at the heart of the conflict were rival Jewish and Arab claims to the same territory. Both groups believed in their future right to rule the country after the mandate expired. The British were unable to resolve this conflict during their administration, as were the United Nations (UN) and the Allied nations after World War II (1939–1945). The dilemma continued into the twenty-first century.

Events in the post–World War I period, particularly the rise of Nazi Germany, soon exacerbated the situation in the region. Large numbers of European Jews sought refuge in Palestine, and the Palestinians revolted. Palestine was generally calm during World War II, but the destruction of six million Jews by the Nazis led many non-Jews to support the Zionist plan. In 1947, the UN sought to resolve the conflict by partitioning the territory into Jewish and Arab states. Although the Zionists reluctantly agreed (they had wanted their state to include all of Mandate Palestine), the Palestinians refused to surrender any part of the land they considered to be their own.

In May 1948, the Jews implemented the UN resolution by proclaiming an independent Jewish state named Israel. The Palestinians and seven surrounding Arab states militarily attempted to destroy Israel but were repulsed. In 1949, UN–sponsored armistice agreements established the boundaries previously noted and led to Israel's admission into the UN.

In the years since then, Israel fought wars with its Arab neighbors in 1956, 1967, 1973, and 1982. Israel signed peace treaties with Egypt (1979) and Jordan (1994) that settled the boundaries with those countries. But as of 2005 Israel had been unable to reach comparable agreements with Syria, Lebanon, and, most importantly, the Palestinians in the West Bank and Gaza Strip.

ISRAEL'S DEMOCRATIC POLITICAL SYSTEM

The 1947 UN Partition Resolution called for both of the proposed democratic states to function under written constitutions. However, the Constituent Assembly elected in March 1949, immediately after the War of Independence, was unable to complete the task in Israel. The enterprise foundered on disagreements between Orthodox Jews and the non-Orthodox majority about the role of Jewish religious law (*Halakhah*) in the Jewish state. Unable to resolve the issue without doing irreparable harm to the much-needed consensus of all elements within the community, the Constituent Assembly became the first Knesset (parliament).

As a compromise, in June 1950, the Knesset agreed that a constitution would be constructed, chapter by chapter, on the enactment of Basic Laws. By 1992, the Knesset had passed eleven Basic Laws, although a full bill of rights was not enacted. Nonetheless, in a 1995 decision, the Israeli Supreme Court declared that henceforth it would treat those Basic Laws as the constitution of Israel and as superior to ordinary legislation.

From the Basic Laws and the stable practices that have emerged over the subsequent decades, it is possible to describe the nation's actual institutional practices. Israel is a secular **republic**, with a theoretically supreme parliament (the Knesset), a powerful cabinet (the government), an independent judiciary, and a weak, ceremonial president. The protections accorded human rights are a result of its democratic political processes and of its civil law system.

Israel is a parliamentary democracy with a single-chamber elected assembly, the Knesset. National elections occur every four years, unless they are called earlier by a Knesset majority. All Israeli citizens over the age of eighteen have the right to vote, and voter turnout in elections during the late 1990s and early 2000s exceeded 75 percent of the eligible electorate. An Israeli votes for a list of candidates prepared by a political party (or group of parties), not an individual representative. The 120 members of Knesset are selected via a nationwide, **proportional system**. That is, the whole country is considered a single electoral district, and Knesset seats are allocated in proportion to the strength of a list at the polls. Any list that receives 2 percent of the vote is guaranteed some representation in the Knesset. This 2-percent requirement is the lowest threshold of any democracy utilizing a proportional election system.

Moreover, it easier to form a new political party and to submit an electoral list in Israel than in any other democratic nation. Only 100 citizens and a $10,000 deposit are needed to register a new party. The signatures of only 1,500 supporters are needed for a new party to submit a new list of candidates to compete in a Knesset election.

The combination of electoral rules that facilitate the creation of new parties (and electoral lists) with the law guaranteeing at least one Knesset seat to any list that receives only 2 percent of the national vote results in Israeli citizens having an extremely broad choice at the polls. In the 1996 elections, there were twenty lists on the ballot; in 1999, there were twenty-eight choices available to the Israeli elector.

The nationwide, proportional election system has meant that no single party (or party list) has ever achieved a Knesset majority. Because the government requires the support of at least sixty-one members of Knesset to be installed, all Israeli governments have been **coalitions**. Usually the government is cobbled together by the leader of the largest single Knesset party from among the eight to fifteen parties represented in that chamber. To form a coalition, the prime minister–designate must agree to support some of the programs favored by the smaller parties and to assign the administration of certain government ministries to the leaders of those parties.

The politics of coalition formation and maintenance supports Israeli democracy. As in all parliamentary systems, real effective power resides in the government (i.e., the prime minister and cabinet), not the Knesset. The government makes all significant policies because it has the support of a built-in parliamentary majority. The opposition (the parties comprising the minority) can only criticize the government in the hopes of gaining sufficient support to be part of a future ruling parliamentary coalition. In Israel, however, government policy is invariably based on bargaining and compromise rather than the dictates of a single individual or group, because the prime minister must worry about losing the support of coalition partners.

Nonetheless, the highly politicized and **centralized** structure of Israeli democracy creates a potential danger to human rights from arbitrary governmental operations. There are no institutional checks and balances once a Knesset majority agrees. The civil courts of Israel, particularly the Supreme Court, have responded

republic: a form of democratic government in which decisions are made by elected representatives of the people

proportional system: a political system in which legislative seats or offices are awarded based on the proportional number of votes received by a party in an election

coalition: an alliance, partnership, or union of disparate peoples or individuals

centralize: to move control or power to a single point of authority

rule of law: the principle that the law is a final grounds of decision-making and applies equally to all people; law and order

partisan: an ideologue, or a strong member of a cause, party, or movement

by actively protecting human rights. The Supreme Court is the final authoritative interpreter of the law and has utilized its authority to reinforce the **rule of law** as a hedge against potentially destructive governmental actions. The judges are selected by a nine-member nominating committee whose dominant members are the chief justice and two other Supreme Court justices. This procedure has successfully insulated the civil court judges from **partisan** politics and enabled them to protect individual rights even in the absence of a constitutional bill of rights.

HUMAN RIGHTS IN ISRAEL

According to Freedom House, all Israelis—Jew and non-Jew, secular and religious—enjoy nearly all of the basic human rights that are exercised by citizens in other Western democracies. They have freedoms of speech, of the press, and of association that are necessary to conduct competitive, democratic elections and to pursue their artistic, cultural, and intellectual interests. Israelis are guaranteed fair treatment in the criminal justice system. This record is a considerable achievement for a nation that has never been completely free from the threat of armed attack.

LOOKING AT A JEWISH SETTLEMENT, AN ISRAELI BOY STANDS IN A WATCHTOWER IN SOUTHERN GAZA STRIP ON APRIL 13, 2005. Upon seizing the Gaza Strip in 1967, Israel held power until a 1993 agreement between Israel and the Palestine Liberation Organization (PLO) that allowed for the creation of the interim Palestinian Authority (PA) to maintain control of the Gaza Strip, excluding Jewish settlements occupied by Israelis. In 2005, Israeli settlers withdrew from the Gaza Strip. (SOURCE: AP/WIDE WORLD PHOTOS)

As with other democracies, however, there are some problems. The non-Jewish Israeli citizens (roughly 20 percent of the population) are not functionally treated as equals. Although they have all the formal legal rights, they find it impossible to identify with the symbols and civic rituals of the Jewish state. The vast majority of non-Jewish Israelis are ethnically Palestinian, the same national group that has contested the very existence of the state of Israel since its establishment. Israeli-Palestinians generally turn out to vote in national elections in only slightly lower proportion than their Jewish fellow citizens and have formed their own political parties that receive their proportional share of Knesset seats. But Arab parties have never been included in government coalitions, which is the real source of power and influence. In sum, those citizens who are Palestinian in origin are isolated from the mainstream of Israeli life; their political effectiveness is limited by the Jewish nature of the state of Israel and by the state's omnipresent security concerns.

Another area of concern involves religious liberty and court proceedings for those who are not Jewish by religion. The Jewish state is not a **theocracy**. Judaism has not become the official religion of Israel, as Islam has become the state religion of other Middle Eastern countries. Nor does Israel enforce the norms of Judaism as part of its public and criminal law. Also, as a democracy, it seeks to guarantee freedom of religion and conscience to all its inhabitants. Unlike the United States, Israel's policy of religious liberty has not been implemented by a separation between religion and the state. Instead, Israel has continued the practice of the Ottoman Empire (1299–1922) and British Mandate, the *millet* system, under which the courts of the fourteen recognized religions have the sole authority to resolve such family matters as marriage, divorce, adoption, and so on. This prevents the religion of the majority (in Israel's case, Judaism) from interfering in the religious practices of minority groups.

theocracy: a state governed by its religious leaders

This arrangement also means, however, that a member of a particular religious group who deviates from the practices recognized by that group's religious authorities confronts major obstacles. For example, because there is no civil marriage, a divorced Roman Catholic cannot be married in Israel because it would violate the tenets of the Catholic religion. Again, because most religions frown on the practice, a couple from two different communities cannot marry each other in Israel. Similarly, an individual can only be divorced by the courts of his or her community. If the individual does not satisfy the clerical requirements, divorce is impossible. Numerous Israelis are legally "chained" to a partner from whom they have long parted. The examples can be multiplied, but they all point to the same problem: The medieval *millet* system is not functional in a contemporary liberal democracy.

Nonetheless, these blemishes should not dominate the assessment of the system. For more than fifty years, Israel has been—and continues to be—a vital democracy. There is no indication whatsoever, despite the absence of real peace in the region, that the Israeli leadership or the Israeli people will abandon their commitment to democracy and human rights.

See also: Gaza Strip; Halakhah; Palestine; West Bank.

BIBLIOGRAPHY

Arian, Asher. *Politics in Israel: The Second Republic*. Washington, DC: Congressional Quarterly Press, 2005.

Dowty, Alan. *The Jewish State: A Century Later*. Berkeley: University of California Press, 1998.

Edelman, Martin. *Courts, Politics, and Culture in Israel*. Charlottesville: University Press of Virginia, 1994.

Freedom House. *Freedom in the Middle East and North Africa*. Lanham, MD: Rowman & Littlefield, 2004.

Ghanem, As'ad. *The Palestinian–Arab Minority in Israel, 1948–2000*. Albany: State University Press of New York, 2001.

Mahler, Gregory. *Politics and Government in Israel: The Maturation of a Modern State*. Lanham, MD: Rowman & Littlefield, 2004.

Martin Edelman

Italy

Situated in southern Europe, Italy is a peninsula of 301,230 square kilometers (116,275 square miles) that includes two large islands: Sicily, which is separated by the Straits of Messina (only 3 kilometers, or less than 2 miles, wide), and Sardinia, which lies between Italy and Spain, separated by the Tyrrhenian Sea. On the north, the Alpine arc separates Italy from France, Switzerland, Austria, and Slovenia. Enclosed within the Italian territory are the Holy See (the Vatican City) and the Republic of San Marino (39 square kilometers; 15 square miles).

Italy had a population estimated in July 2003 at 57,998,353. The capital is Rome, with more than 2.5 million inhabitants. Important cities include Milan (3.5 million inhabitants), Turin (2 million inhabitants), Naples (3 million inhabitants), and Palermo (more than 1 million inhabitants). Other cities of significance include Bologna, Florence, and Bari.

The Italian currency was the lira, but like ten other European countries, on January 1, 2002, the euro became the only legal tender.

Italy has a strategic location, dominating the central Mediterranean region and representing the southern part of Europe facing the ethnic and cultural areas of North Africa and the Arabic-Islamic civilization.

Contemporary Italy has an increasingly diversified economy, but with a still strong internal division between a developed industrial North and an agricultural South, the latter of which depends heavily on government social assistance and is characterized by an average unemployment rate of 20 percent, which is quite high in comparison with the national average of about 9 to 10 percent.

THE HISTORY OF UNIFIED ITALY

The history of a unified Italy starts in the nineteenth century with the *Risorgimento*, a struggle for liberation from foreign rule and for the unification of the several Italian micro-states. The leaders of the *Risorgimento* were Giuseppe Mazzini (1805–1872), an **idealist** and republican, and Giuseppe Garibaldi (1807–1882), who represented the military myth of the *Risorgimento*. Unification of Italy was achieved when Rome was finally conquered and declared capital of Italy in July 1871.

The new state was established as a monarchy with a parliamentary government. Unified Italy embraced many liberal values, but was not democratic. The government was guided by **aristocratic** oligarchs and supported by a very narrow electoral base. Universal **suffrage** was not established in Italy until 1946.

idealism: the theory that ideas larger than reality guide human actions

aristocracy: a ruling financial, social, or political elite

suffrage: to vote, or, the right to vote

(MAP BY MARYLAND CARTOGRAPHICS/THE GALE GROUP)

Economic and social conditions were miserable, particularly in the southern part of the country, where only a few peasants owned land and labor contracts were oppressive. Most of the country's approximately 25 million people could not read or write, and the entire country suffered from a high mortality rate. The conditions of labor, extreme poverty, harsh taxation, and the birth of the **socialist** party provoked episodes of strongly repressed **insurrection** and the assassination of King Umberto I (1844–1900) in Monza on July 1, 1900.

FASCISM

World War I (1914–1918) revealed the weakness of the old aristocrat-liberal regime and its inability to face new challenges. The ruin and disillusionment following the war, the growth of the socialist party, anarchy, and the efforts for the **bourgeoisie** to maintain the political and economic control to reach higher levels of development prepared the ground for the success of fascism. Benito Mussolini (1883–1945), leader of the National Fascist Party, gained power in 1922 via revolution, with only thirty deputies of his party seated in the parliament. Fascist propaganda promised a new political system that would be neither capitalist nor communist and that would offer solutions to the working class and rationalize Italian capitalism. But fascism soon developed into an **authoritarian** regime. It failed only after the disaster of World War II (1939–1945).

socialism: any of various economic and political theories advocating collective or governmental ownership and administration of the means of production and distribution of goods

insurrection: an uprising; an act of rebellion against an existing authority

bourgeoisie: the economic middle class marked by wealth earned through business or trade

authoritarianism: the domination of the state or its leader over individuals

coup: a quick seizure of power or a sudden attack

The landing of Allied troops in Sicily on July 10, 1943, provoked a strong reaction against Mussolini. He was arrested after a palace **coup**, and a new government was formed. Mussolini was, however, rescued by a German commando raid and created a new rival government in the northern Italy under Nazi protection. This led to a civil war, which started spontaneously in September 1943 by the youth, who were disillusioned with fascism, and members of the Resistance Movement. These groups included people of different political ideas: communists, socialists, republicans and Christian Democrats. After the collapse of the last German defense lines in the North, Mussolini was caught and summarily shot.

THE FIRST ITALIAN REPUBLIC AND THE NEW POLITICAL SYSTEM

On June 2, 1946, the electorate voted by a majority of 54 percent to establish the Italian Republic, although the monarchy was still supported by a substantial margin in the South. The people also elected a constitutional assembly, in which all the parties that had supported the resistance movement were represented. A new constitution was approved on December 22, 1947, and went into effect on January 1, 1948.

The Republican constitution founded a new political and social order based on a pluralistic democracy. It recognized human labor as a fundamental right, provided recognition for the role of political parties and trade unions, institutional pluralism, political and administrative **decentralization**, and protection of ethnic, religious and linguistic minorities. It created twenty regions, including special status regions to protect linguistic and cultural minorities.

decentralize: to move power from a central authority to multiple periphery government branches or agencies

The political system was organized on the principle that the people are the true holders of **sovereign** power, which may be exercised both directly, through elections, and indirectly, through institutional representation. Through the ballot, which is universal, direct, and secret, the people choose their political representatives; through **referendums** they can decide directly to repeal a law or modify the constitution and also change regional and local laws.

sovereignty: autonomy; or, rule over a political entity

referendum: a popular vote on legislation, brought before the people by their elected leaders or public initiative

The political institutions of the Italian Republic include an executive branch, composed of two offices. The president of the republic is elected for a seven-year term by an electoral college, consisting of both houses of parliament and fifty-eight regional representatives. The executive also includes a chief of government or prime minister, who serves as the president of the Council of Ministers. The ministers are confirmed by the president of the Republic on the proposal of the prime minister. To be installed, a new government must appear before parliament, present its political program, and receive a vote of confidence.

bicameral: comprised of two chambers, usually a legislative body

The legislative branch is composed of a **bicameral** parliament, consisting of the Chamber of the Deputies (*Camera dei Deputati*) and Senate of the Republic (*Senato*). The 315 members of the *Senato* are elected by all citizens aged 25 and older for five-year terms. Three-quarters of the senators are elected through a majority system by region. A small number of senators, including all former presidents of the Republic, serve for life. The 630 members of the Chamber of Deputies are elected by all citizens aged 18 and older for five-year terms. Three-quarters of the deputies are elected with a majority system in single-member districts; the others are elected on a regional basis but only from among those parties that obtain at least 4 percent of the vote nationally.

The judicial branch consists of the Constitutional Court (*Corte Costituzionale*), composed of fifteen judges (one-third appointed by the president of the Republic, one-third elected by parliament, and one-third elected by the ordinary and administrative supreme court judges), and ordinary and administrative courts. The Constitutional Court is charged with controlling the correct application of the constitution and constitutional laws. A Superior Council of the Magistracy (*Consiglio Superiore della Magistratura*) monitors the selection and discipline of all judges.

The ordinary judiciary system includes 165 local trial courts, the same number of public prosecutors' offices (*Procure della Repubblica*), and 29 courts of appeals. Italian **magistrates** can be appointed to serve as either judges or prosecutors. Italian courts are organized by function into ordinary (civil and criminal) and administrative courts. At the top of the system there are two autonomous supreme courts: the first, the Court of Cassation (*Corte di Cassazione*), receives appeals from criminal and civil courts, and the second, the Council of State (*Consiglio di Stato*), receives appeals from the administrative courts. The most relevant problems of the system concern the careers of judges and the average length of trials, which may exceed several years.

magistrate: an official with authority over a government, usually a judicial official with limited jurisdiction over criminal cases

ITALIAN POLITICAL DEVELOPMENT

Historically, political institutions and civil society were linked by political parties and trade unions, organizations regulated also by the constitution. Since the early postwar years the two major trade unions, the *Confederazione Generale Italiana del Lavoro* (CGIL), which is close to the former Communist party, and the *Confederazione Italiana Sindacati Lavoratori* (CISL), which is close to the Christian Democratic party, played an important role not only in the economic life of the country but also in the political one. In the period from 1960 to 1990 the trade unions emerged as a strong political force and achieved some important social reforms. However, slowly the force of the trade unions declined, and the trade unions were increasingly threatened by single issue organizations or separate categories of workers' unions and by the local groups.

The Italian constitution regulates political pluralism by ensuring citizens the freedom to create political parties. The structure, function, and regulation of political parties remains a difficult issue for the entire Italian political system. The uncertainty and the comparative instability of democratic life in Italy result from a party-dominated system (*partitocrazia*). Political parties flourish and divide because of the difficulty of a stable representation system in a very fluid, fragmented, and individualistic civil society.

In the years following World War II (post-1945) formal democratic institutions often played a minor role in governance in comparison to the interests of individual parties and the pressure groups that influence the parties. This resulted in rapid changes in governments, with more than 50 prime ministers in the first 50 years of the Republic. These continuous changes in governments were caused more by internal conflict within the parties or among parties than by serious public policy differences.

The constitution does not regulate pressure groups and the activities of lobbies. In addition to the trade unions, important interest groups are the industrial and merchants' associations (*confindustria* and *confcommercio*), organized farm-groups (*confagricoltura*) and the Roman Catholic Church. Ownership and control of the mass media are also not regulated by the constitution and yet emerged as important instruments of social power and the target of a bitter struggle for their control.

polarize: to separate individuals into adversarial groups

coalition: an alliance, partnership, or union of disparate peoples or individuals

The life of the so-called First Republic (1946–1994) was determined by a **polarized** conflict between the Christian Democratic Party and the Communist Party. Important roles were also played by the Socialist Party and minor parties like Social Democrats, Liberals, and Republicans in creating governments **coalitions**.

The most popular party, the Christian Democratic, maintained the dominant political position during the First Republic and was central to all political coalitions. Its adherents were placed in key public institutions and in the most important social and economic structures and counted on the benevolent abstention of the left or of the Monarchists or neo-fascists on the right to maneuver through many delicate parliamentary situations. The Christian Democratic Party was reinforced by the trust of the Catholic Church, which saw in it an important defense again the strongest Communist Party in Europe.

After the period immediately following World War II, the Communists appealed to the left of the Christian Democrats to open new ways to reformism and publicly affirmed that the Marxist view of class struggle made no sense in modern developed countries. They respected parliamentary democracy and the multiparty system. In 1978 Aldo Moro (1916–1978), the leader of the Christian

THE PALAZZO DI MONTECITORIO IN ROME, ITALY. Italy's parliament has been located in Rome's Palazzo di Montecitorio since 1871. The legislature is composed of a 630-member lower house, Chamber of Deputies, and a 326-seat upper house, the Senate. (SOURCE: © DENNIS MARSICO/CORBIS)

Democrats, promoted the "historical compromise" to allow the Communist Party to join in governing coalitions.

Political life in Italy during the First Republic may have been complex, but the nation experienced rapid and unforeseen social and economic development. In 1945, Italy was one of the poorest countries in the West, but within a few years Italy generated one of the fastest growing economies in the world and became one of the most industrialized countries.

THE CRISIS OF THE SYSTEM

Economic success could not compensate after the 1970s for the slow collapse of the political system of the First Republic. The kidnapping and murder of Christian Democratic Party leader Moro by the Red Brigades in 1978 demonstrated that the political system was no longer able to react to terrorist groups and that the rigid political parties could not cope with the new social and political situation. Concentration of economic power and the strong ties of economic magnates with politics generated scandals and mistrust. Antiestablishment forces became more aggressive toward the system.

Public mistrust of politics and politicians led to the growth of parties outside of the institutions of government. The loss of **ideological** strength by the traditional parties oriented the electorate more and more toward **localism**. The traditional political parties could no longer exert political control in the country and that opened the way to growing activities by organized criminal groups. These criminal organizations represented a power in southern Italy that extended to the economic and social spheres and, indeed, to some politicians. In 1992, with the assassination of the two anti-Mafia judges Giovanni Falcone (1939–1992) and Paolo Borsellino (1940–1992), these criminal organizations became a threat to Italian institutions and forced a realization that there existed a real necessity for a radical change.

A decisive event contributed to political change in Italian politics. In 1992 Italian magistrates from the Milan Court, and especially Judge Antonio Di Pietro (b. 1950), accused leading politicians of large-scale corruption. The investigation discovered a scandal of political kickbacks and payoffs that touched many top politicians. The scandal and the ensuing moralizing process that began throughout the Italian economy created conditions that allowed the Italian business and industrial systems to develop in the context of European and global competition.

The social and political climate also changed. The ideological climate based on rigid distinctions among political parties was replaced by new political tendencies open to new political organizations. The electorate was no longer a party electorate: It became a public opinion electorate, which was more fluid, more present-oriented, and more guided by contemporary events and needs. A new **populist** mentality emerged on the political scene. This mentality was represented by Umberto Bossi (b. 1941) and his regionally oriented Northern League, by Silvio Berlusconi (b. 1936) and *Forza Italia* ("Go Italy!"), and by a form of media populism. In the general elections of 1994, the right wing alliance of *Forza Italia*, the Northern League, and the National Alliance (born from the old neo-fascist party *Movimento Sociale Italiano*) won a majority in the House of Deputies and a **plurality** in the Senate. The first party in the coalition was *Forza Italia*, which obtained 155 of the 366 seats in the lower house of Parliament, and Berlusconi was named prime minister. It was a very surprising success for the party that was founded only three months before the elections.

ideology: a system of beliefs composed of ideas or values, from which political, social, or economic programs are often derived

localism: a phrase or behavior specific to a certain area

populist: someone who advocates policies for the advancement of the common man

plurality: more votes than any other candidate, but less than half of the total number of votes

A NEW POLITICAL LANDSCAPE

The emergence of a new political climate was clear in the decline of strong political attachments, as well as in the difficulty of linking together new and different political forces and keeping the promises of a populist program. An internal dispute in the coalition the election in April 1996 of a new center-left coalition (The Olive Tree) and a new government led by Romano Prodi (b. 1939). The new coalition included the new Democratic Left Party, derived from the reform branch of the Communist Party. Disputes in the center-left coalition again led to new elections in May 2001, which gave a large majority to a center-right coalition (The House of Freedom) in which *Forza Italia*, National Alliance, and Northern League were joined by the Democratic-Christian Centre and United Christian Democrats, both linked to the tradition of the old Christian Democrats. The new government of Berlusconi was more stable and appeared better able to cope with an old political structure and a new kind of public opinion. In the early twenty-first century, very difficult internal problems, such as constitutional reforms, financial crises, new scandals, and new difficulties in controlling the public opinion again tested the viability of the government coalition. Populism, mass media, and the mass-regime seem to be very serious threats for Italian democracy.

CITIZENS' RIGHTS AND FREEDOMS

The Italian constitution defines rights and freedoms of the citizens. Equality before the law and equal rights for men and women are guaranteed as well as the right to strike and the right to an adequate health care. Among the freedoms, the constitution guarantees in particular the freedom of religious faiths, personal beliefs and ideologies, spoken and written expression, freedom of association, and the freedom of teaching and research. Some rights and freedoms are not derived directly from the constitutional text but rather indirectly from the decisions of the Constitutional Court, such as the guarantee of media pluralism.

bureaucracy: a system of administrating government involving professional labor; the mass of individuals administering government

juridical: relating to, created by, or pertaining to the judiciary

The real practice of such rights and freedoms is, to a point, actually limited by the pressure of **bureaucracy**, by the lack of an effective pluralism and of mechanisms of **juridical** defense, and by the relative incapacity of the people to elaborate creative and proactive organizations. Suspicion of power and passivity in the active exercise of rights and freedoms allow the powerful to increase their control of the masses through the monopolistic use of mass media and permit a peculiar kind of populism that may become a strong threat to freedom. The extension of rights and freedoms is very wide in the Italian law, but the opportunity, the ways, and the conditions to use them are actually restricted, thus diminishing the real sense of democracy.

See also: Dictatorship; European Microstates; European Union; Parliamentary Systems; Political Parties; Political Party Systems; Vatican.

BIBLIOGRAPHY

Istituto Geografico De Agostini. *Calendario Atlante De Agostini*. Novara, Italy: Istituto Geografico De Agostini, 2003.

Istituto Nazionale di Statistica. *Rapporto sull'Italia*. Bologna: Il Mulino, 2003.

Kogan, Norman. *A Political History of Postwar Italy*. New York: Praeger Publishers, 1981.

Mignone, Mario B. *Italy Today: At the Crossroads of the New Millennium*. New York: Peter Lang, 1998.

Mongardini, Carlo. *Ripensare la democrazia. La politica in un regime di massa*. Milan: Franco Angeli, 2002.

Montanelli, Indro, and Mario Cervi. *L'Italia di Berlusconi*. Milan: Rizzoli, 1994.

Montanelli, Indro, and Mario Cervi. *L'Italia dell'Ulivo*. Milan: Rizzoli, 1997.

Pasquino, Gianfranco. *Sistemi politici comparati*. Bologna: Bonomia University Press, 2003.

Poggi, Gianfranco. *Forms of Power*. Cambridge, UK: Polity Press, 2001.

Prospero, Michele. *La politica moderna. Teorie e profili istituzionali*. Rome: Carocci editore, 2002.

Putnam, Robert D., Robert Leonardi, and Raffaella Y. Manetti. *Making Democracy Work: Civic Traditions in Modern Italy*. Princeton, NJ.: Princeton University Press, 1993.

Carlo Mongardini

Ivory Coast

See: Côte d'Ivoire.

APPENDICES

Additional Protocol to the American Convention on Human Rights in the Area of Economic, Social and Cultural Rights

Introduction: The Additional Protocol, "Protocol of San Salvador," which entered into force in 1999, bolsters the American Convention on Human Rights. The Protocol obliges parties to it to take progressive action, according to their degree of development, to achieve observance of, among other rights, the right to work and to just, equitable, and satisfactory conditions of work; the right to organize trade unions and to strike; the right to a healthy environment; the right to education; and the right to the formation and protection of families.

PREAMBLE

The States Parties to the American Convention on Human Rights "Pact San José, Costa Rica,"

Reaffirming their intention to consolidate in this hemisphere, within the framework of democratic institutions, a system of personal liberty and social justice based on respect for the essential rights of man;

Recognizing that the essential rights of man are not derived from one's being a national of a certain State, but are based upon attributes of the human person, for which reason they merit international protection in the form of a convention reinforcing or complementing the protection provided by the domestic law of the American States;

Considering the close relationship that exists between economic, social and cultural rights, and civil and political rights, in that the different categories of rights constitute an indivisible whole based on the recognition of the dignity of the human person, for which reason both require permanent protection and promotion if they are to be fully realized, and the violation of some rights in favor of the realization of others can never be justified;

Recognizing the benefits that stem from the promotion and development of cooperation among States and international relations;

Recalling that, in accordance with the Universal Declaration of Human Rights and the American Convention on Human Rights, the ideal of free human beings enjoying freedom from fear and want can only be achieved if conditions are created whereby everyone may enjoy his economic, social and cultural rights as well as his civil and political rights;

Bearing in mind that, although fundamental economic, social and cultural rights have been recognized in earlier international instruments of both world and regional scope, it is essential that those rights be reaffirmed, developed, perfected and protected in order to consolidate in America, on the basis of full respect for the rights of the individual, the democratic representative form of government as well as the right of its peoples to development, self-determination, and the free disposal of their wealth and natural resources; and

Considering that the American Convention on Human Rights provides that draft additional protocols to that Convention may be submitted for consideration to the States Parties, meeting together on the occasion of the General Assembly of the Organization of American States, for the purpose of gradually incorporating other rights and freedoms into the protective system thereof, Have agreed upon the following Additional Protocol to the American Convention on Human Rights "Protocol of San Salvador:"

ARTICLE 1

Obligation to Adopt Measures The States Parties to this Additional Protocol to the American Convention on Human Rights undertake to adopt the necessary measures, both domestically and through international cooperation, especially economic and technical, to the extent allowed by their available resources, and taking into account their degree of development, for the purpose of achieving progressively and pursuant to their internal legislations, the full observance of the rights recognized in this Protocol.

ARTICLE 2

Obligation to Enact Domestic Legislation If the exercise of the rights set forth in this Protocol is not already guaranteed by legislative or other provisions, the States Parties undertake to adopt, in accordance with their constitutional processes and the provisions of this Protocol, such legislative or other measures as may be necessary for making those rights a reality.

ARTICLE 3

Obligation of Nondiscrimination The State Parties to this Protocol undertake to guarantee the exercise of the rights set forth herein without discrimination of any kind for reasons related to race, color, sex, language, religion, political or other opinions, national or social origin, economic status, birth or any other social condition.

ARTICLE 4

Inadmissibility of Restrictions A right which is recognized or in effect in a State by virtue of its internal legislation or international conventions may not be restricted or curtailed on the pretext that this Protocol does not recognize the right or recognizes it to a lesser degree.

ARTICLE 5

Scope of Restrictions and Limitations The State Parties may establish restrictions and limitations on the enjoyment and exercise of the rights established herein by means of laws promulgated for the purpose of preserving the general welfare in a democratic society only to the extent that they are not incompatible with the purpose and reason underlying those rights.

ARTICLE 6

Right to Work

1. Everyone has the right to work, which includes the opportunity to secure the means for living a dignified and decent existence by performing a freely elected or accepted lawful activity.

2. The State Parties undertake to adopt measures that will make the right to work fully effective, especially with regard to the achievement of full employment, vocational guidance, and the development of technical and vocational training projects, in particular those directed to the disabled. The States Parties also undertake to implement and strengthen programs that help to ensure suitable family care, so that women may enjoy a real opportunity to exercise the right to work.

ARTICLE 7

Just, Equitable, and Satisfactory Conditions of Work The States Parties to this Protocol recognize that the right to work to which the foregoing article refers presupposes that everyone shall enjoy that right under just, equitable, and satisfactory conditions, which the States Parties undertake to guarantee in their internal legislation, particularly with respect to:

a. Remuneration which guarantees, as a minimum, to all workers dignified and decent living conditions for them and their families and fair and equal wages for equal work, without distinction;

b. The right of every worker to follow his vocation and to devote himself to the activity that best fulfills his expectations and to change employment in accordance with the pertinent national regulations;

c. The right of every worker to promotion or upward mobility in his employment, for which purpose account shall be taken of his qualifications, competence, integrity and seniority;

d. Stability of employment, subject to the nature of each industry and occupation and the causes for just separation. In cases of unjustified dismissal, the worker shall have the right to indemnity or to reinstatement on the job or any other benefits provided by domestic legislation;

e. Safety and hygiene at work;

f. The prohibition of night work or unhealthy or dangerous working conditions and, in general, of all work which jeopardizes health, safety, or morals, for persons under 18 years of age. As regards minors under the age of 16, the work day shall be subordinated to the provisions regarding compulsory education and in no case shall work constitute an impediment to school attendance or a limitation on benefiting from education received;

g. A reasonable limitation of working hours, both daily and weekly. The days shall be shorter in the case of dangerous or unhealthy work or of night work;

h. Rest, leisure and paid vacations as well as remuneration for national holidays.

ARTICLE 8

Trade Union Rights

1. The States Parties shall ensure:

   a. The right of workers to organize trade unions and to join the union of their choice for the purpose of protecting and promoting their interests. As an extension of that right, the States Parties shall permit trade unions to establish national federations or confederations, or to affiliate with those that already exist, as well as to form international trade union organizations and to affiliate with that of their choice. The States Parties shall also permit trade unions, federations and confederations to function freely;

   b. The right to strike.

2. The exercise of the rights set forth above may be subject only to restrictions established by law, provided that such restrictions are characteristic of a democratic society and necessary for safeguarding public order or for protecting public health or morals or the rights and freedoms of others. Members of the armed forces and the police and of other essential public services shall be subject to limitations and restrictions established by law.

3. No one may be compelled to belong to a trade union.

ARTICLE 9

Right to Social Security

1. Everyone shall have the right to social security protecting him from the consequences of old age and of disability which prevents him, physically or mentally, from securing the means for a dignified and decent existence. In the event of the death of a beneficiary, social security benefits shall be applied to his dependents.

2. In the case of persons who are employed, the right to social security shall cover at least medical care and an allowance or retirement benefit in the case of work accidents or occupational disease and, in the case of women, paid maternity leave before and after childbirth.

ARTICLE 10

Right to Health

1. Everyone shall have the right to health, understood to mean the enjoyment of the highest level of physical, mental and social well-being.

2. In order to ensure the exercise of the right to health, the States Parties agree to recognize health as a public good and, particularly, to adopt the following measures to ensure that right:

   a. Primary health care, that is, essential health care made available to all individuals and families in the community;

   b. Extension of the benefits of health services to all individuals subject to the State's jurisdiction;

   c. Universal immunization against the principal infectious diseases;

   d. Prevention and treatment of endemic, occupational and other diseases;

   e. Education of the population on the prevention and treatment of health problems, and

   f. Satisfaction of the health needs of the highest risk groups and of those whose poverty makes them the most vulnerable.

ARTICLE 11

Right to a Healthy Environment

1. Everyone shall have the right to live in a healthy environment and to have access to basic public services.

2. The States Parties shall promote the protection, preservation, and improvement of the environment.

ARTICLE 12

Right to Food

1. Everyone has the right to adequate nutrition which guarantees the possibility of enjoying the highest level of physical, emotional and intellectual development.

2. In order to promote the exercise of this right and eradicate malnutrition, the States Parties undertake to improve methods of production, supply and distribution of food, and to this end, agree to promote greater international cooperation in support of the relevant national policies.

ARTICLE 13

Right to Education

1. Everyone has the right to education.

2. The States Parties to this Protocol agree that education should be directed towards the full development of the human personality and human dignity and should strengthen respect for human rights, ideological pluralism, fundamental freedoms, justice and peace. They further agree that education ought to enable everyone to participate effectively in a democratic and pluralistic society and achieve a decent existence and should foster understanding, tolerance and friendship among all nations and all racial, ethnic or religious groups and promote activities for the maintenance of peace.

3. The States Parties to this Protocol recognize that in order to achieve the full exercise of the right to education:

   a. Primary education should be compulsory and accessible to all without cost;
   b. Secondary education in its different forms, including technical and vocational secondary education, should be made generally available and accessible to all by every appropriate means, and in particular, by the progressive introduction of free education;
   c. Higher education should be made equally accessible to all, on the basis of individual capacity, by every appropriate means, and in particular, by the progressive introduction of free education;
   d. Basic education should be encouraged or intensified as far as possible for those persons who have not received or completed the whole cycle of primary instruction;
   e. Programs of special education should be established for the handicapped, so as to provide special instruction and training to persons with physical disabilities or mental deficiencies.

4. In conformity with the domestic legislation of the States Parties, parents should have the right to select the type of education to be given to their children, provided that it conforms to the principles set forth above.

5. Nothing in this Protocol shall be interpreted as a restriction of the freedom of individuals and entities to establish and direct educational institutions in accordance with the domestic legislation of the States Parties.

ARTICLE 14

Right to the Benefits of Culture

1. The States Parties to this Protocol recognize the right of everyone:

   a. To take part in the cultural and artistic life of the community;

   b. To enjoy the benefits of scientific and technological progress;

   c. To benefit from the protection of moral and material interests deriving from any scientific, literary or artistic production of which he is the author.

2. The steps to be taken by the States Parties to this Protocol to ensure the full exercise of this right shall include those necessary for the conservation, development and dissemination of science, culture and art.

3. The States Parties to this Protocol undertake to respect the freedom indispensable for scientific research and creative activity.

4. The States Parties to this Protocol recognize the benefits to be derived from the encouragement and development of international cooperation and relations in the fields of science, arts and culture, and accordingly agree to foster greater international cooperation in these fields.

ARTICLE 15

Right to the Formation and the Protection of Families

1. The family is the natural and fundamental element of society and ought to be protected by the State, which should see to the improvement of its spiritual and material conditions.

2. Everyone has the right to form a family, which shall be exercised in accordance with the provisions of the pertinent domestic legislation.

3. The States Parties hereby undertake to accord adequate protection to the family unit and in particular:

   a. To provide special care and assistance to mothers during a reasonable period before and after childbirth;

   b. To guarantee adequate nutrition for children at the nursing stage and during school attendance years;

   c. To adopt special measures for the protection of adolescents in order to ensure the full development of their physical, intellectual and moral capacities;

   d. To undertake special programs of family training so as to help create a stable and positive environment in which children will receive and develop the values of understanding, solidarity, respect and responsibility.

ARTICLE 16

Rights of Children Every child, whatever his parentage, has the right to the protection that his status as a minor requires from his family, society and the State. Every child has the right to grow under the protection and responsibility of his parents; save in exceptional, judicially-recognized circumstances, a child of young age ought not to be separated from his mother. Every child has the right to free and compulsory education, at least in the elementary phase, and to continue his training at higher levels of the educational system.

ARTICLE 17

Protection of the Elderly Everyone has the right to special protection in old age. With this in view the States Parties agree to take progressively the necessary steps to make this right a reality and, particularly, to:

a. Provide suitable facilities, as well as food and specialized medical care, for elderly individuals who lack them and are unable to provide them for themselves;

b. Undertake work programs specifically designed to give the elderly the opportunity to engage in a productive activity suited to their abilities and consistent with their vocations or desires;

c. Foster the establishment of social organizations aimed at improving the quality of life for the elderly.

ARTICLE 18

Protection of the Handicapped Everyone affected by a diminution of his physical or mental capacities is entitled to receive special attention designed to help him achieve the greatest possible development of his personality. The States Parties agree to adopt such measures as may be necessary for this purpose and, especially, to:

a. Undertake programs specifically aimed at providing the handicapped with the resources and environment needed for attaining this goal, including work programs consistent with their possibilities and freely accepted by them or their legal representatives, as the case may be;

b. Provide special training to the families of the handicapped in order to help them solve the problems of coexistence and convert them into active agents in the physical, mental and emotional development of the latter;

c. Include the consideration of solutions to specific requirements arising from needs of this group as a priority component of their urban development plans;

d. Encourage the establishment of social groups in which the handicapped can be helped to enjoy a fuller life.

ARTICLE 19

Means of Protection

1. Pursuant to the provisions of this article and the corresponding rules to be formulated for this purpose by the General Assembly of the Organization of American States, the States Parties to this Protocol undertake to submit periodic reports on the progressive measures they have taken to ensure due respect for the rights set forth in this Protocol.

2. All reports shall be submitted to the Secretary General of the OAS, who shall transmit them to the Inter-American Economic and Social Council and the Inter-American Council for Education, Science and Culture so that they may examine them in accordance with the provisions of this article. The Secretary General shall send a copy of such reports to the Inter-American Commission on Human Rights.

3. The Secretary General of the Organization of American States shall also transmit to the specialized organizations of the inter-American system of which the States Parties to the present Protocol are members, copies or pertinent portions of the reports submitted, insofar as they relate to matters within the purview of those organizations, as established by their constituent instruments.

4. The specialized organizations of the inter-American system may submit reports to the Inter-American Economic and Social Council and the Inter-American Council for Education, Science and Culture relative to compliance with the provisions of the present Protocol in their fields of activity.

5. The annual reports submitted to the General Assembly by the Inter-American Economic and Social Council and the Inter-American Council for Education, Science and Culture shall contain a summary of the information received from the States Parties to the present Protocol and the specialized organizations concerning the progressive measures adopted in order to ensure respect for the rights acknowledged in the Protocol itself and the general recommendations they consider to be appropriate in this respect.

6. Any instance in which the rights established in paragraph a) of Article 8 and in Article 13 are violated by action directly attributable to a State Party to this Protocol may give rise, through participation of the Inter-American Commission on Human Rights and, when applicable, of the Inter-American Court of Human Rights, to application of the system of individual petitions governed by Article 44 through 51 and 61 through 69 of the American Convention on Human Rights.

7. Without prejudice to the provisions of the preceding paragraph, the Inter-American Commission on Human Rights may formulate such observations and recommendations as it deems pertinent concerning the status of the economic, social and cultural rights established in the present Protocol in all or some of the States Parties, which it may include in its Annual Report to the General Assembly or in a special report, whichever it considers more appropriate.

8. The Councils and the Inter-American Commission on Human Rights, in discharging the functions conferred upon them in this article, shall take into account the progressive nature of the observance of the rights subject to protection by this Protocol.

ARTICLE 20

Reservations The States Parties may, at the time of approval, signature, ratification or accession, make reservations to one or more specific provisions of this Protocol, provided that such reservations are not incompatible with the object and purpose of the Protocol.

ARTICLE 21

Signature, Ratification or Accession Entry into Effect

1. This Protocol shall remain open to signature and ratification or accession by any State Party to the American Convention on Human Rights.

2. Ratification of or accession to this Protocol shall be effected by depositing an instrument of ratification or accession with the General Secretariat of the Organization of American States.

3. The Protocol shall enter into effect when eleven States have deposited their respective instruments of ratification or accession.

4. The Secretary General shall notify all the member states of the Organization of American States of the entry of the Protocol into effect.

ARTICLE 22

Inclusion of other Rights and Expansion of those Recognized

1. Any State Party and the Inter-American Commission on Human Rights may submit for the consideration of the States Parties meeting on the occasion of the General Assembly proposed amendments to include the recognition of other rights or freedoms or to extend or expand rights or freedoms recognized in this Protocol.

2. Such amendments shall enter into effect for the States that ratify them on the date of deposit of the instrument of ratification corresponding to the number representing two thirds of the States Parties to this Protocol. For all other States Parties they shall enter into effect on the date on which they deposit their respective instrument of ratification.

Human Rights Act of the United Kingdom

Introduction: Introduced in late 1998 in the United Kingdom, the Human Rights Act, partially reproduced here, incorporated into national law the European Convention on Human Rights. The Act gave the courts in England and Wales the right to enforce civil and political rights. Beyond the courts, the Act bound all public authorities to work in compliance with the Convention.

An Act to give further effect to rights and freedoms guaranteed under the European Convention on Human Rights; to make provision with respect to holders of certain judicial offices who become judges of the European Court of Human Rights; and for connected purposes. [9th November 1998]

BE IT ENACTED by the Queen's most Excellent Majesty, by and with the advice and consent of the Lords Spiritual and Temporal, and Commons, in this present Parliament assembled, and by the authority of the same, as follows:

PART I

RIGHTS AND FREEDOMS

Article 2: Right to Life

1. Everyone's right to life shall be protected by law. No one shall be deprived of his life intentionally save in the execution of a sentence of a court following his conviction of a crime for which this penalty is provided by law.

2. Deprivation of life shall not be regarded as inflicted in contravention of this Article when it results from the use of force which is no more than absolutely necessary:

    (a) in defence of any person from unlawful violence;
    (b) in order to effect a lawful arrest or to prevent the escape of a person lawfully detained;
    (c) in action lawfully taken for the purpose of quelling a riot or insurrection.

Article 3: Prohibition of Torture
No one shall be subjected to torture or to inhuman or degrading treatment or punishment.

Article 4: Prohibition of Slavery and Forced Labour

1. No one shall be held in slavery or servitude.

2. No one shall be required to perform forced or compulsory labour. . . .

Article 5: Right to Liberty and Security

1. Everyone has the right to liberty and security of person. No one shall be deprived of his liberty save in the following cases and in accordance with a procedure prescribed by law:

    (a) the lawful detention of a person after conviction by a competent court;

(b) the lawful arrest or detention of a person for non-compliance with the lawful order of a court or in order to secure the fulfilment of any obligation prescribed by law;

(c) the lawful arrest or detention of a person effected for the purpose of bringing him before the competent legal authority on reasonable suspicion of having committed an offence or when it is reasonably considered necessary to prevent his committing an offence or fleeing after having done so;

(d) the detention of a minor by lawful order for the purpose of educational supervision or his lawful detention for the purpose of bringing him before the competent legal authority;

(e) the lawful detention of persons for the prevention of the spreading of infectious diseases, of persons of unsound mind, alcoholics or drug addicts or vagrants;

(f) the lawful arrest or detention of a person to prevent his effecting an unauthorised entry into the country or of a person against whom action is being taken with a view to deportation or extradition.

2. Everyone who is arrested shall be informed promptly, in a language which he understands, of the reasons for his arrest and of any charge against him.

3. Everyone arrested or detained in accordance with the provisions of paragraph 1(c) of this Article shall be brought promptly before a judge or other officer authorised by law to exercise judicial power and shall be entitled to trial within a reasonable time or to release pending trial. Release may be conditioned by guarantees to appear for trial.

4. Everyone who is deprived of his liberty by arrest or detention shall be entitled to take proceedings by which the lawfulness of his detention shall be decided speedily by a court and his release ordered if the detention is not lawful.

5. Everyone who has been the victim of arrest or detention in contravention of the provisions of this Article shall have an enforceable right to compensation.

Article 6: Right to a Fair Trial

1. In the determination of his civil rights and obligations or of any criminal charge against him, everyone is entitled to a fair and public hearing within a reasonable time by an independent and impartial tribunal established by law. Judgment shall be pronounced publicly but the press and public may be excluded from all or part of the trial in the interest of morals, public order or national security in a democratic society, where the interests of juveniles or the protection of the private life of the parties so require, or to the extent strictly necessary in the opinion of the court in special circumstances where publicity would prejudice the interests of justice.

2. Everyone charged with a criminal offence shall be presumed innocent until proved guilty according to law.

3. Everyone charged with a criminal offence has the following minimum rights:

(a) to be informed promptly, in a language which he understands and in detail, of the nature and cause of the accusation against him;

(b) to have adequate time and facilities for the preparation of his defence;

(c) to defend himself in person or through legal assistance of his own choosing or, if he has not sufficient means to pay for legal assistance, to be given it free when the interests of justice so require;

(d) to examine or have examined witnesses against him and to obtain the attendance and examination of witnesses on his behalf under the same conditions as witnesses against him;

(e) to have the free assistance of an interpreter if he cannot understand or speak the language used in court.

Article 7: No Punishment without Law

1. No one shall be held guilty of any criminal offence on account of any act or omission which did not constitute a criminal offence under national or international law at the time when it was committed. Nor shall a heavier penalty be imposed than the one that was applicable at the time the criminal offence was committed.

2. This Article shall not prejudice the trial and punishment of any person for any act or omission which, at the time when it was committed, was criminal according to the general principles of law recognised by civilised nations.

Article 8: Right to Respect for Private and Family Life

1. Everyone has the right to respect for his private and family life, his home and his correspondence.

2. There shall be no interference by a public authority with the exercise of this right except such as is in accordance with the law and is necessary in a democratic society in the interests of national security, public safety or the economic well-being of the country, for the prevention of disorder or crime, for the protection of health or morals, or for the protection of the rights and freedoms of others.

Article 9: Freedom of Thought, Conscience and Religion

1. Everyone has the right to freedom of thought, conscience and religion; this right includes freedom to change his religion or belief and freedom, either alone or in community with others and in public or private, to manifest his religion or belief, in worship, teaching, practice and observance.

2. Freedom to manifest one's religion or beliefs shall be subject only to such limitations as are prescribed by law and are necessary in a democratic society in the interests of public safety, for the protection of public order, health or morals, or for the protection of the rights and freedoms of others.

Article 10: Freedom of Expression

1. Everyone has the right to freedom of expression. This right shall include freedom to hold opinions and to receive and impart information and ideas without interference by public authority and regardless of frontiers. This Article shall not prevent States from requiring the licensing of broadcasting, television or cinema enterprises.

2. The exercise of these freedoms, since it carries with it duties and responsibilities, may be subject to such formalities, conditions, restrictions or penalties as are prescribed by law and are necessary in a democratic society, in the interests of national security, territorial integrity or public safety, for the prevention of disorder or crime, for the protection of health or morals, for the protection of the reputation or rights of others, for preventing the disclosure of information received in confidence, or for maintaining the authority and impartiality of the judiciary.

Article 11: Freedom of Assembly and Association

1. Everyone has the right to freedom of peaceful assembly and to freedom of association with others, including the right to form and to join trade unions for the protection of his interests.

2. No restrictions shall be placed on the exercise of these rights other than such as are prescribed by law and are necessary in a democratic society in the interests of national security or public safety, for the prevention of disorder or crime, for the protection of health or morals or for the protection of the rights and freedoms of others. This Article shall not prevent the imposition of lawful restrictions on the exercise of these rights by members of the armed forces, of the police or of the administration of the State.

*Article 12: **Right to Marry*** Men and women of marriageable age have the right to marry and to found a family, according to the national laws governing the exercise of this right.

*Article 14: **Prohibition of Discrimination*** The enjoyment of the rights and freedoms set forth in this Convention shall be secured without discrimination on any ground such as sex, race, colour, language, religion, political or other opinion, national or social origin, association with a national minority, property, birth or other status. . . .

*Article 16: **Restrictions on Political Activity of Aliens*** Nothing in Articles 10, 11 and 14 shall be regarded as preventing the High Contracting Parties from imposing restrictions on the political activity of aliens.

*Article 17: **Prohibition of Abuse of Rights*** Nothing in this Convention may be interpreted as implying for any State, group or person any right to engage in any activity or perform any act aimed at the destruction of any of the rights and freedoms set forth herein or at their limitation to a greater extent than is provided for in the Convention.

*Article 18: **Limitation on use of Restrictions on Rights*** The restrictions permitted under this Convention to the said rights and freedoms shall not be applied for any purpose other than those for which they have been prescribed.

PART II
THE FIRST PROTOCOL

*Article 1: **Protection of Property*** Every natural or legal person is entitled to the peaceful enjoyment of his possessions. No one shall be deprived of his possessions except in the public interest and subject to the conditions provided for by law and by the general principles of international law.

The preceding provisions shall not, however, in any way impair the right of a State to enforce such laws as it deems necessary to control the use of property in accordance with the general interest or to secure the payment of taxes or other contributions or penalties.

*Article 2: **Right to Education*** No person shall be denied the right to education. In the exercise of any functions which it assumes in relation to education and to teaching, the State shall respect the right of parents to ensure such education and teaching in conformity with their own religious and philosophical convictions.

*Article 3: **Right to Free Elections*** The High Contracting Parties undertake to hold free elections at reasonable intervals by secret ballot, under conditions which will ensure the free expression of the opinion of the people in the choice of the legislature.

PART III

THE SIXTH PROTOCOL

Article 1: Abolition of the Death Penalty The death penalty shall be abolished. No one shall be condemned to such penalty or executed.

Article 2: Death Penalty in Time of War A State may make provision in its law for the death penalty in respect of acts committed in time of war or of imminent threat of war; such penalty shall be applied only in the instances laid down in the law and in accordance with its provisions. The State shall communicate to the Secretary General of the Council of Europe the relevant provisions of that law.

International Covenant on Civil and Political Rights

Source: United Nations Publications, March 23, 1966. The United Nations is the author of the original material. Available from <http://www.ohchr.org>. Reproduced by permission.

Introduction: One-third of the "international bill of rights," with the Universal Declaration of Human Rights and the International Covenant on Economic, Social and Cultural Rights, the CCPR acknowledges the rights to free trade, due process and equality before the law, among other enumerated rights, of the people of its member nations. Partially reproduced below, the Covenant also sets forth the right to political self-determination and non-derogable rights such as freedom of thought and religion.

Adopted and opened for signature, ratification and accession by General Assembly resolution 2200A (XXI) of 16 December 1966 entry into force 23 March 1976, in accordance with Article 49.

PART I

Article 1

1. All peoples have the right of self-determination. By virtue of that right they freely determine their political status and freely pursue their economic, social and cultural development.

2. All peoples may, for their own ends, freely dispose of their natural wealth and resources without prejudice to any obligations arising out of international economic co-operation, based upon the principle of mutual benefit, and international law. In no case may a people be deprived of its own means of subsistence.

3. The States Parties to the present Covenant, including those having responsibility for the administration of Non-Self-Governing and Trust Territories, shall promote the realization of the right of self-determination, and shall respect that right, in conformity with the provisions of the Charter of the United Nations.

PART II

Article 2

1. Each State Party to the present Covenant undertakes to respect and to ensure to all individuals within its territory and subject to its jurisdiction the rights recognized in the present Covenant, without distinction of any kind, such as

race, colour, sex, language, religion, political or other opinion, national or social origin, property, birth or other status.

2. Where not already provided for by existing legislative or other measures, each State Party to the present Covenant undertakes to take the necessary steps, in accordance with its constitutional processes and with the provisions of the present Covenant, to adopt such laws or other measures as may be necessary to give effect to the rights recognized in the present Covenant.

3. Each State Party to the present Covenant undertakes:

(a) To ensure that any person whose rights or freedoms as herein recognized are violated shall have an effective remedy, notwithstanding that the violation has been committed by persons acting in an official capacity;

(b) To ensure that any person claiming such a remedy shall have his right thereto determined by competent judicial, administrative or legislative authorities, or by any other competent authority provided for by the legal system of the State, and to develop the possibilities of judicial remedy;

(c) To ensure that the competent authorities shall enforce such remedies when granted.

Article 3 The States Parties to the present Covenant undertake to ensure the equal right of men and women to the enjoyment of all civil and political rights set forth in the present Covenant.

Article 4

1. In time of public emergency which threatens the life of the nation and the existence of which is officially proclaimed, the States Parties to the present Covenant may take measures derogating from their obligations under the present Covenant to the extent strictly required by the exigencies of the situation, provided that such measures are not inconsistent with their other obligations under international law and do not involve discrimination solely on the ground of race, colour, sex, language, religion or social origin.

2. No derogation from articles 6, 7, 8 (paragraphs I and 2), 11, 15, 16 and 18 may be made under this provision.

3. Any State Party to the present Covenant availing itself of the right of derogation shall immediately inform the other States Parties to the present Covenant, through the intermediary of the Secretary-General of the United Nations, of the provisions from which it has derogated and of the reasons by which it was actuated. A further communication shall be made, through the same intermediary, on the date on which it terminates such derogation.

Article 5

1. Nothing in the present Covenant may be interpreted as implying for any State, group or person any right to engage in any activity or perform any act aimed at the destruction of any of the rights and freedoms recognized herein or at their limitation to a greater extent than is provided for in the present Covenant.

2. There shall be no restriction upon or derogation from any of the fundamental human rights recognized or existing in any State Party to the present Covenant pursuant to law, conventions, regulations or custom on the pretext that the present Covenant does not recognize such rights or that it recognizes them to a lesser extent.

PART III

Article 6

1. Every human being has the inherent right to life. This right shall be protected by law. No one shall be arbitrarily deprived of his life.

2. In countries which have not abolished the death penalty, sentence of death may be imposed only for the most serious crimes in accordance with the law in force at the time of the commission of the crime and not contrary to the provisions of the present Covenant and to the Convention on the Prevention and Punishment of the Crime of Genocide. This penalty can only be carried out pursuant to a final judgement rendered by a competent court.

3. When deprivation of life constitutes the crime of genocide, it is understood that nothing in this article shall authorize any State Party to the present Covenant to derogate in any way from any obligation assumed under the provisions of the Convention on the Prevention and Punishment of the Crime of Genocide.

4. Anyone sentenced to death shall have the right to seek pardon or commutation of the sentence. Amnesty, pardon or commutation of the sentence of death may be granted in all cases.

5. Sentence of death shall not be imposed for crimes committed by persons below eighteen years of age and shall not be carried out on pregnant women.

6. Nothing in this article shall be invoked to delay or to prevent the abolition of capital punishment by any State Party to the present Covenant.

Article 7

No one shall be subjected to torture or to cruel, inhuman or degrading treatment or punishment. In particular, no one shall be subjected without his free consent to medical or scientific experimentation.

Article 8

1. No one shall be held in slavery; slavery and the slave-trade in all their forms shall be prohibited.

2. No one shall be held in servitude.

3. (a) No one shall be required to perform forced or compulsory labour;
   (b) Paragraph 3 (a) shall not be held to preclude, in countries where imprisonment with hard labour may be imposed as a punishment for a crime, the performance of hard labour in pursuance of a sentence to such punishment by a competent court;
   (c) For the purpose of this paragraph the term "forced or compulsory labour" shall not include: (i) Any work or service, not referred to in subparagraph (b), normally required of a person who is under detention in consequence of a lawful order of a court, or of a person during conditional release from such detention; (ii) Any service of a military character and, in countries where conscientious objection is recognized, any national service required by law of conscientious objectors; (iii) Any service exacted in cases of emergency or calamity threatening the life or well-being of the community; (iv) Any work or service which forms part of normal civil obligations.

Article 9

1. Everyone has the right to liberty and security of person. No one shall be subjected to arbitrary arrest or detention. No one shall be deprived of his liberty except on such grounds and in accordance with such procedure as are established by law.

2. Anyone who is arrested shall be informed, at the time of arrest, of the reasons for his arrest and shall be promptly informed of any charges against him.

3. Anyone arrested or detained on a criminal charge shall be brought promptly before a judge or other officer authorized by law to exercise judicial power and shall be entitled to trial within a reasonable time or to release. It shall not be the general rule that persons awaiting trial shall be detained in custody, but release may be subject to guarantees to appear for trial, at any other stage of the judicial proceedings, and, should occasion arise, for execution of the judgement.

4. Anyone who is deprived of his liberty by arrest or detention shall be entitled to take proceedings before a court, in order that court may decide without delay on the lawfulness of his detention and order his release if the detention is not lawful.

5. Anyone who has been the victim of unlawful arrest or detention shall have an enforceable right to compensation.

Article 10

1. All persons deprived of their liberty shall be treated with humanity and with respect for the inherent dignity of the human person.

2. (a) Accused persons shall, save in exceptional circumstances, be segregated from convicted persons and shall be subject to separate treatment appropriate to their status as unconvicted persons;

   (b) Accused juvenile persons shall be separated from adults and brought as speedily as possible for adjudication.

3. The penitentiary system shall comprise treatment of prisoners the essential aim of which shall be their reformation and social rehabilitation. Juvenile offenders shall be segregated from adults and be accorded treatment appropriate to their age and legal status.

Article 11

No one shall be imprisoned merely on the ground of inability to fulfil a contractual obligation.

Article 12

1. Everyone lawfully within the territory of a State shall, within that territory, have the right to liberty of movement and freedom to choose his residence.

2. Everyone shall be free to leave any country, including his own.

3. The above-mentioned rights shall not be subject to any restrictions except those which are provided by law, are necessary to protect national security, public order (*ordre public*), public health or morals or the rights and freedoms of others, and are consistent with the other rights recognized in the present Covenant.

4. No one shall be arbitrarily deprived of the right to enter his own country.

Article 13

An alien lawfully in the territory of a State Party to the present Covenant may be expelled therefrom only in pursuance of a decision reached in accordance with law and shall, except where compelling reasons of national security otherwise require, be allowed to submit the reasons against his expulsion and to have his case reviewed by, and be represented for the purpose before, the competent authority or a person or persons especially designated by the competent authority.

Article 14

1. All persons shall be equal before the courts and tribunals. In the determination of any criminal charge against him, or of his rights and obligations in a suit at law, everyone shall be entitled to a fair and public hearing by a competent, independent and impartial tribunal established by law. The press and the public may be excluded from all or part of a trial for reasons of morals, public order (*ordre public*) or national security in a democratic society, or when the interest of the private lives of the parties so requires, or to the extent strictly necessary in the opinion of the court in special circumstances where publicity would prejudice the interests of justice; but any judgement rendered in a criminal case or in a suit at law shall be made public except where the interest of juvenile persons otherwise requires or the proceedings concern matrimonial disputes or the guardianship of children.

2. Everyone charged with a criminal offence shall have the right to be presumed innocent until proved guilty according to law.

3. In the determination of any criminal charge against him, everyone shall be entitled to the following minimum guarantees, in full equality:

   (a) To be informed promptly and in detail in a language which he understands of the nature and cause of the charge against him;
   (b) To have adequate time and facilities for the preparation of his defence and to communicate with counsel of his own choosing;
   (c) To be tried without undue delay;
   (d) To be tried in his presence, and to defend himself in person or through legal assistance of his own choosing; to be informed, if he does not have legal assistance, of this right; and to have legal assistance assigned to him, in any case where the interests of justice so require, and without payment by him in any such case if he does not have sufficient means to pay for it;
   (e) To examine, or have examined, the witnesses against him and to obtain the attendance and examination of witnesses on his behalf under the same conditions as witnesses against him;
   (f) To have the free assistance of an interpreter if he cannot understand or speak the language used in court;
   (g) Not to be compelled to testify against himself or to confess guilt.

4. In the case of juvenile persons, the procedure shall be such as will take account of their age and the desirability of promoting their rehabilitation.

5. Everyone convicted of a crime shall have the right to his conviction and sentence being reviewed by a higher tribunal according to law.

6. When a person has by a final decision been convicted of a criminal offence and when subsequently his conviction has been reversed or he has been pardoned on the ground that a new or newly discovered fact shows conclusively that there has been a miscarriage of justice, the person who has suffered punishment as a result of such conviction shall be compensated according to law, unless it is proved that the non-disclosure of the unknown fact in time is wholly or partly attributable to him.

7. No one shall be liable to be tried or punished again for an offence for which he has already been finally convicted or acquitted in accordance with the law and penal procedure of each country.

Article 15

1 . No one shall be held guilty of any criminal offence on account of any act or omission which did not constitute a criminal offence, under national or international law, at the time when it was committed. Nor shall a heavier penalty be imposed than the one that was applicable at the time when the criminal offence was committed. If, subsequent to the commission of the offence, provision is made by law for the imposition of the lighter penalty, the offender shall benefit thereby.

2. Nothing in this article shall prejudice the trial and punishment of any person for any act or omission which, at the time when it was committed, was criminal according to the general principles of law recognized by the community of nations.

Article 16

Everyone shall have the right to recognition everywhere as a person before the law.

Article 17

1. No one shall be subjected to arbitrary or unlawful interference with his privacy, family, home or correspondence, nor to unlawful attacks on his honour and reputation.

2. Everyone has the right to the protection of the law against such interference or attacks.

Article 18

1. Everyone shall have the right to freedom of thought, conscience and religion. This right shall include freedom to have or to adopt a religion or belief of his choice, and freedom, either individually or in community with others and in public or private, to manifest his religion or belief in worship, observance, practice and teaching.

2. No one shall be subject to coercion which would impair his freedom to have or to adopt a religion or belief of his choice.

3. Freedom to manifest one's religion or beliefs may be subject only to such limitations as are prescribed by law and are necessary to protect public safety, order, health, or morals or the fundamental rights and freedoms of others.

4. The States Parties to the present Covenant undertake to have respect for the liberty of parents and, when applicable, legal guardians to ensure the religious and moral education of their children in conformity with their own convictions.

Article 19

1. Everyone shall have the right to hold opinions without interference.

2. Everyone shall have the right to freedom of expression; this right shall include freedom to seek, receive and impart information and ideas of all kinds, regardless of frontiers, either orally, in writing or in print, in the form of art, or through any other media of his choice.

3. The exercise of the rights provided for in paragraph 2 of this article carries with it special duties and responsibilities. It may therefore be subject to certain restrictions, but these shall only be such as are provided by law and are necessary:

(a) For respect of the rights or reputations of others;
(b) For the protection of national security or of public order (*ordre public*), or of public health or morals.

Article 20

1. Any propaganda for war shall be prohibited by law.

2. Any advocacy of national, racial or religious hatred that constitutes incitement to discrimination, hostility or violence shall be prohibited by law.

Article 21

The right of peaceful assembly shall be recognized. No restrictions may be placed on the exercise of this right other than those imposed in conformity with the law and which are necessary in a democratic society in the interests of national security or public safety, public order (*ordre public*), the protection of public health or morals or the protection of the rights and freedoms of others.

Article 22

1. Everyone shall have the right to freedom of association with others, including the right to form and join trade unions for the protection of his interests.

2. No restrictions may be placed on the exercise of this right other than those which are prescribed by law and which are necessary in a democratic society in the interests of national security or public safety, public order (*ordre public*), the protection of public health or morals or the protection of the rights and freedoms of others. This article shall not prevent the imposition of lawful restrictions on members of the armed forces and of the police in their exercise of this right.

3. Nothing in this article shall authorize States Parties to the International Labour Organisation Convention of 1948 concerning Freedom of Association and Protection of the Right to Organize to take legislative measures which would prejudice, or to apply the law in such a manner as to prejudice, the guarantees provided for in that Convention.

Article 23

1. The family is the natural and fundamental group unit of society and is entitled to protection by society and the State.

2. The right of men and women of marriageable age to marry and to found a family shall be recognized.

3. No marriage shall be entered into without the free and full consent of the intending spouses.

4. States Parties to the present Covenant shall take appropriate steps to ensure equality of rights and responsibilities of spouses as to marriage, during marriage and at its dissolution. In the case of dissolution, provision shall be made for the necessary protection of any children.

Article 24

1. Every child shall have, without any discrimination as to race, colour, sex, language, religion, national or social origin, property or birth, the right to such measures of protection as are required by his status as a minor, on the part of his family, society and the State.

2. Every child shall be registered immediately after birth and shall have a name.

3. Every child has the right to acquire a nationality.

Article 25

Every citizen shall have the right and the opportunity, without any of the distinctions mentioned in article 2 and without unreasonable restrictions:

(a) To take part in the conduct of public affairs, directly or through freely chosen representatives;

(b) To vote and to be elected at genuine periodic elections which shall be by universal and equal suffrage and shall be held by secret ballot, guaranteeing the free expression of the will of the electors;

(c) To have access, on general terms of equality, to public service in his country.

Article 26

All persons are equal before the law and are entitled without any discrimination to the equal protection of the law. In this respect, the law shall prohibit any discrimination and guarantee to all persons equal and effective protection against discrimination on any ground such as race, colour, sex, language, religion, political or other opinion, national or social origin, property, birth or other status.

Article 27

In those States in which ethnic, religious or linguistic minorities exist, persons belonging to such minorities shall not be denied the right, in community with the other members of their group, to enjoy their own culture, to profess and practise their own religion, or to use their own language.

International Covenant on Economic, Social and Cultural Rights

Source: United Nations Publications, December 16, 1966. The United Nations is the author of the original material. Available from <http:// www.ohchr.org>. Reproduced by permission.

Introduction: One-third of the "international bill of rights," with the Universal Declaration of Human Rights and the International Covenant on Civil and Political Rights, the CESCR acknowledges the rights to work, education, and an adequate standard of living, among other enumerated rights, of the people of its member nations. Partially reproduced below, the Covenant also sets forth the right to freedom from torture and slavery and the right to benefit from intellectual property.

PART I

Article 1

1. All peoples have the right of self-determination. By virtue of that right they freely determine their political status and freely pursue their economic, social and cultural development.

2. All peoples may, for their own ends, freely dispose of their natural wealth and resources without prejudice to any obligations arising out of international economic co-operation, based upon the principle of mutual benefit, and international law. In no case may a people be deprived of its own means of subsistence.

3. The States Parties to the present Covenant, including those having responsibility for the administration of Non-Self-Governing and Trust Territories, shall promote the realization of the right of self-determination, and shall respect that right, in conformity with the provisions of the Charter of the United Nations.

PART II
Article 2

1. Each State Party to the present Covenant undertakes to take steps, individually and through international assistance and co-operation, especially economic and technical, to the maximum of its available resources, with a view to achieving progressively the full realization of the rights recognized in the present Covenant by all appropriate means, including particularly the adoption of legislative measures.

2. The States Parties to the present Covenant undertake to guarantee that the rights enunciated in the present Covenant will be exercised without discrimination of any kind as to race, colour, sex, language, religion, political or other opinion, national or social origin, property, birth or other status.

3. Developing countries, with due regard to human rights and their national economy, may determine to what extent they would guarantee the economic rights recognized in the present Covenant to non-nationals.

Article 3 The States Parties to the present Covenant undertake to ensure the equal right of men and women to the enjoyment of all economic, social and cultural rights set forth in the present Covenant.

Article 4 The States Parties to the present Covenant recognize that, in the enjoyment of those rights provided by the State in conformity with the present Covenant, the State may subject such rights only to such limitations as are determined by law only in so far as this may be compatible with the nature of these rights and solely for the purpose of promoting the general welfare in a democratic society.

Article 5

1. Nothing in the present Covenant may be interpreted as implying for any State, group or person any right to engage in any activity or to perform any act aimed at the destruction of any of the rights or freedoms recognized herein, or at their limitation to a greater extent than is provided for in the present Covenant.

2. No restriction upon or derogation from any of the fundamental human rights recognized or existing in any country in virtue of law, conventions, regulations or custom shall be admitted on the pretext that the present Covenant does not recognize such rights or that it recognizes them to a lesser extent.

PART III
Article 6

1. The States Parties to the present Covenant recognize the right to work, which includes the right of everyone to the opportunity to gain his living by work which he freely chooses or accepts, and will take appropriate steps to safeguard this right.

2. The steps to be taken by a State Party to the present Covenant to achieve the full realization of this right shall include technical and vocational guidance and training programs, policies and techniques to achieve steady economic, social and cultural development and full and productive employment under conditions safeguarding fundamental political and economic freedoms to the individual.

Article 7 The States Parties to the present Covenant recognize the right of everyone to the enjoyment of just and favourable conditions of work which ensure, in particular:

(a) Remuneration which provides all workers, as a minimum, with: (i-Fair wages and equal remuneration for work of equal value without distinction of any kind, in particular women being guaranteed conditions of work not inferior to those enjoyed by men, with equal pay for equal work; (ii) A decent living for themselves and their families in accordance with the provisions of the present Covenant;

(b) Safe and healthy working conditions;

(c) Equal opportunity for everyone to be promoted in his employment to an appropriate higher level, subject to no considerations other than those of seniority and competence;

(d) Rest, leisure and reasonable limitation of working hours and periodic holidays with pay, as well as remuneration for public holidays.

Article 8

1. The States Parties to the present Covenant undertake to ensure:

(a) The right of everyone to form trade unions and join the trade union of his choice, subject only to the rules of the organization concerned, for the promotion and protection of his economic and social interests. No restrictions may be placed on the exercise of this right other than those prescribed by law and which are necessary in a democratic society in the interests of national security or public order or for the protection of the rights and freedoms of others;

(b) The right of trade unions to establish national federations or confederations and the right of the latter to form or join international trade-union organizations;

(c) The right of trade unions to function freely subject to no limitations other than those prescribed by law and which are necessary in a democratic society in the interests of national security or public order or for the protection of the rights and freedoms of others;

(d) The right to strike, provided that it is exercised in conformity with the laws of the particular country.

2. This article shall not prevent the imposition of lawful restrictions on the exercise of these rights by members of the armed forces or of the police or of the administration of the State.

3. Nothing in this article shall authorize States Parties to the International Labour Organisation Convention of 1948 concerning Freedom of Association and Protection of the Right to Organize to take legislative measures which would prejudice, or apply the law in such a manner as would prejudice, the guarantees provided for in that Convention.

Article 9 The States Parties to the present Covenant recognize the right of everyone to social security, including social insurance.

Article 10 The States Parties to the present Covenant recognize that:

1. The widest possible protection and assistance should be accorded to the family, which is the natural and fundamental group unit of society, particularly for its establishment and while it is responsible for the care and education of dependent children. Marriage must be entered into with the free consent of the intending spouses.

2. Special protection should be accorded to mothers during a reasonable period before and after childbirth. During such period working mothers should be accorded paid leave or leave with adequate social security benefits.

3. Special measures of protection and assistance should be taken on behalf of all children and young persons without any discrimination for reasons of parentage or other conditions. Children and young persons should be protected from economic and social exploitation. Their employment in work harmful to their morals or health or dangerous to life or likely to hamper their normal development should be punishable by law. States should also set age limits below which the paid employment of child labour should be prohibited and punishable by law.

Article 11

1. The States Parties to the present Covenant recognize the right of everyone to an adequate standard of living for himself and his family, including adequate food, clothing and housing, and to the continuous improvement of living conditions. The States Parties will take appropriate steps to ensure the realization of this right, recognizing to this effect the essential importance of international co-operation based on free consent.

2. The States Parties to the present Covenant, recognizing the fundamental right of everyone to be free from hunger, shall take, individually and through international co-operation, the measures, including specific programs, which are needed:

(a) To improve methods of production, conservation and distribution of food by making full use of technical and scientific knowledge, by disseminating knowledge of the principles of nutrition and by developing or reforming agrarian systems in such a way as to achieve the most efficient developement and utilization of natural resources;

(b) Taking into account the problems of both food-importing and food-exporting countries, to ensure an equitable distribution of world food supplies in relation to need.

Article 12

1. The States Parties to the present Covenant recognize the right of everyone to the enjoyment of the highest attainable standard of physical and mental health.

2. The steps to be taken by the States Parties to the present Covenant to achieve the full realization of this right shall include those necessary for:

(a) The provision for the reduction of the stillbirth-rate and of infant mortality and for the healthy development of the child;

(b) The improvement of all aspects of environmental and industrial hygiene;

(c) The prevention, treatment and control of epidemic, endemic, occupational and other diseases;

(d) The creation of conditions which would assure to all medical service and medical attention in the event of sickness.

Article 13

1. The States Parties to the present Covenant recognize the right of everyone to education. They agree that education shall be directed to the full development of the human personality and the sense of its dignity, and shall strengthen the respect for human rights and fundamental freedoms. They further agree that education shall enable all persons to participate effectively in a free society, promote understanding, tolerance and friendship among all nations and all racial, ethnic or religious groups, and further the activities of the United Nations for the maintenance of peace.

2. The States Parties to the present Covenant recognize that, with a view to achieving the full realization of this right:

(a) Primary education shall be compulsory and available free to all;

(b) Secondary education in its different forms, including technical and vocational secondary education, shall be made generally available and accessible to all by every appropriate means, and in particular by the progressive introduction of free education;

(c) Higher education shall be made equally accessible to all, on the basis of capacity, by every appropriate means, and in particular by the progressive introduction of free education;

(d) Fundamental education shall be encouraged or intensified as far as possible for those persons who have not received or completed the whole period of their primary education;

(e) The development of a system of schools at all levels shall be actively pursued, an adequate fellowship system shall be established, and the material conditions of teaching staff shall be continuously improved.

3. The States Parties to the present Covenant undertake to have respect for the liberty of parents and, when applicable, legal guardians to choose for their children schools, other than those established by the public authorities, which conform to such minimum educational standards as may be laid down or approved by the State and to ensure the religious and moral education of their children in conformity with their own convictions.

4. No part of this article shall be construed so as to interfere with the liberty of individuals and bodies to establish and direct educational institutions, subject always to the observance of the principles set forth in paragraph I of this article and to the requirement that the education given in such institutions shall conform to such minimum standards as may be laid down by the State.

Article 14

Each State Party to the present Covenant which, at the time of becoming a Party, has not been able to secure in its metropolitan territory or other territories under its jurisdiction compulsory primary education, free of charge, undertakes, within two years, to work out and adopt a detailed plan of action for the progressive implementation, within a reasonable number of years, to be fixed in the plan, of the principle of compulsory education free of charge for all.

Article 15

1. The States Parties to the present Covenant recognize the right of everyone:

(a) To take part in cultural life;

(b) To enjoy the benefits of scientific progress and its applications;

(c) To benefit from the protection of the moral and material interests resulting from any scientific, literary or artistic production of which he is the author.

2. The steps to be taken by the States Parties to the present Covenant to achieve the full realization of this right shall include those necessary for the conservation, the development and the diffusion of science and culture.

3. The States Parties to the present Covenant undertake to respect the freedom indispensable for scientific research and creative activity.

4. The States Parties to the present Covenant recognize the benefits to be derived from the encouragement and development of international contacts and co-operation in the scientific and cultural fields.

FILMOGRAPHY

Afghanistan

Afghan Stories (2002)
d. Taran Davies

Afghan-American filmmaker Davies and producer Walied Osman traveled to the Afghanistan front line during the U.S. invasion in order to chronicle the lives of ordinary Afghanis who have lived in a state of war for more than twenty years but who continue to have hope for the future.

Osama (2003)
d. Siddiq Barmak

Depicts the Taliban's oppression of women by showing a young girl who must pose as a boy to support her family and who is later forced into a local religious/military training camp where she struggles to hide her true identity. Dari with subtitles.

Albania

Albanian Journey: End of an Era (1991)
d. Paul Jay

Examines the rise and fall of socialism from Albania's 1944 establishment as a communist republic by Enver Hoxha to its emergence after Hoxha's death in 1985. Albanian with subtitles.

Algeria

The Battle of Algiers (1966)
d. Gillo Pontecorvo

Depicts the uprisings against French colonial rule in 1954 Algeria. English, French, and Arabic with subtitles.

1968 Academy Award: Best Director, Best Story and Screenplay

The Conspiracy (1973)
d. René Gainville

When Charles de Gaulle announces his intention to abandon Algeria, several French army officers stage a coup. French with subtitles.

Rachida (2002)
d. Yamina Bachir-Chouikh

A teacher at an elementary school becomes the target of terrorists when she refuses to help them during Algeria's civil conflict of the 1990s. Arabic and French with subtitles.

Apartheid

Bopha! (1993)
d. Morgan Freeman

A township police officer and his activist son clash as both township unrest and the freedom movement grow. Title is a Zulu word for arrest or detention.

Whether documentary, docudrama, or fictional narrative, film often exposes to the light what some would prefer remained hidden in darkness. The films selected for this filmography examine governments, political parties, historical tragedies, and the fight for freedom that is universal to the human spirit.

A Dry White Season (1989)
d. Eyzhan Palcy

A white Afrikaner must confront the apartheid system when his black gardener is persecuted and murdered.

Argentina

Evita (1996)
d. Alan Parker

Andrew Lloyd Webber/Tim Rice rock opera about the life and death of Eva Perón, who went from poverty to the wife of dictator Juan Perón and a would-be champion of the people.

Funny Dirty Little War (1983)
d. Hector Olivera

Rightist Peronists plot to oust the leftist mayor of their town, but he refuses to budge. Spanish with subtitles.

Spoils of War (2000)
d. David Blaustein

Blaustein spent three years interviewing the "Grandmothers of the Plaza de Mayo" who gathered to discover the fate of their missing family members during Argentina's dirty war of the late 1970s and early 1980s. Spanish with subtitles.

Armenia

Ararat (2002)
d. Atom Egoyan

Modern-day Armenian Canadians struggle to deal with the legacy of the 1915 genocide of Armenians by the Turks.

The Yearning (1990)
d. Frunze Dovaltyan

Arakel Aloyan, a survivor of the 1915 genocide, has built a new life with his family in Soviet Armenia, but he longs to visit his home village, now a part of Turkey. However, the Soviet government views his journey as treasonous. Armenian with subtitles.

Australia

Dead Heart (1996)
d. Nick Parsons

A 1930s culture clash occurs in the outback community of Wala-Wala between the aboriginals, who regard the area as sacred, and the white townspeople.

Gallipoli (1981)
d. Peter Weir

Follows the fortunes of two young Australian soldiers and their confrontation with the German-allied Turks in World War I.

Rabbit-Proof Fence (2002)
d. Philip Noyce

In 1930s Australia, racist government policies force three mixed-raced Aboriginal girls from their families and into an institution designed to train them as domestic workers. They escape and begin a 1,500 mile journey back to their home.

Austria

The Inheritors (1982)
d. Walter Bannert

A misfit teenager is drawn into a neo-Nazi youth group as Austria experiences a resurgence in fascist activity. German with subtitles.

Biko, Stephen

Cry Freedom (1987)
d. Richard Attenborough

South African journalist Donald Woods struggles to get to the truth behind the suspicious death of his friend, black activist Stephen Biko, who died while in police custody.

1987 Academy Award Nominee: Best Supporting Actor, Best Music, Best Song

Bosnia and Herzegovina

A Cry From the Grave (1999)
d. Leslie Woodhead

Depicts the 1995 massacre of more than 7,000 Muslim men and boys in Srebrenica, Bosnia, which was carried out by Serbian troops.

No Man's Land (2001)
d. Danis Tanovic

In 1993 Bosnia, a Croatian and a Serbian soldier wind up sharing the same trench behind enemy lines that is booby-trapped by a land mine. Bosnian with subtitles.

Welcome to Sarajevo (1997)
d. Michael Winterbottom

A group of journalists find themselves caught in the 1992 siege of the city and become disillusioned when the conflict is largely ignored by the rest of the world.

Brazil

The Burning Season (1994)
d. John Frankenheimer

Chico Mendes, a socialist union leader, fights to protect the homes and land of Brazilian peasants in the western Amazon rain forest.

Four Days in September (1997)
d. Bruno Barreto

In 1969 a group of young Brazilian idealists kidnap the American ambassador in order to draw attention to their country's military dictatorship.

1997 Academy Award Nominee: Best Foreign Language Film

The Mission (1986)
d. Roland Joffe

Eighteenth-century Jesuits in Brazil struggle against the slave trade legalized by the country's Portuguese rulers.

1987 Academy Award: Best Cinematography

Burkina Faso

Haramuya (1995)
d. Drissa Toure

A family is caught between modern life and their traditions while living in Ouagadougou. French with subtitles.

Cambodia

The Killing Fields (1984)
d. Roland Joffe

New York Times reporter Sydney Schanberg tries to rescue his Cambodian interpreter Dith Pran when Pol Pot and the Khmer Rouge begin their cleansing campaign.

1985 Academy Award: Best Supporting Actor, Best Cinematography, Best Film Editing

S21: The Khmer Rouge Killing Machine (2003)
d. Rithy Panh

Looks at the period between 1975 and 1979 when almost two million Cambodians lost their lives to murder and famine at the hands of the Khmer Rouge; focuses primarily on the S21 detention center. Khmer with subtitles.

Canada

Black Robe (1991)
d. Bruce Beresford

In 1634 a French Jesuit priest is sent across the Canadian wilderness to bring the word of God to the Hurons, but instead he is seduced by their native culture.

Censorship

Control Room (2004)
d. Jehane Noujaim

Examines the inner workings of Al Jazeera, the Arab television network, as the network reports on the 2003 U.S. war with Iraq.

Chad

Daresalam (2000)
d. Issa Serge Coelo

Dijmi and Kkoni find their friendship strained when political turmoil causes them to join rival factions of a revolutionary movement. Arabic and French with subtitles.

Chile

Missing (1982)
d. Constantin Costa-Gavras

After a young American writer disappears in Chile during the Pinochet coup,

his father tries to discover what has happened.

1983 Academy Award: Best Adapted Screenplay

The Pinochet Case (2001)
d. Patricio Guzmán

Investigates the legal origins of the case against Chilean dictator Gen. Augusto Pinochet, who was arrested in 1998 for crimes against humanity while on a trip to London.

China (PRC)

The Blue Kite (1993)
d. Tian Zhuangzhuang

During the cultural revolution, Teitou and his friends and family experience political and social upheavals. Mandarin with subtitles.

Tibet: Cry of the Snow Lion (2003)
d. Tom Piozet

Examines the struggle between Buddhist Tibet and Communist China and the contrast between the monasteries and ancient ceremonies and the graphic accounts of Chinese repression. Alternate title: *Tibet: Cry of the Snow Leopard*.

To Live (1994)
d. Yimou Zhang

Follows the life of one Chinese family from the 1940s through the cultural revolution of the 1960s. Mandarin with subtitles.

Civil Rights Movement in the United States

Boycott (2001)
d. Clark Johnson

Recreates the Montgomery, Alabama, bus boycott by the city's black population during 1955 and 1956.

Malcolm X (1992)
d. Spike Lee

Biography of the black activist who became a leader in the Nation of Islam and who was assassinated in 1964.

Rosewood (1997)
d. John Singleton

Based on the true story of a prosperous African-American town in Florida that was destroyed by a white mob in 1923.

Colombia

Welcome to Colombia (2003)
d. Catalina Villar

The filmmaker travels across the country during Colombia's 2002 presidential election to examine the consequences of the decades-long civil war.

Colonies and Colonialism

Indochine (1992)
d. Regis Wargnier

Follows twenty-five years in the life of a French colonist, born and raised in Indochina, from 1930 to the communist revolution. French with subtitles.

1992 Academy Award: Best Foreign Language Film

Zulu Dawn (1979)
d. Douglas Hickox

Increasing tension between the British colonial government and the Zulus lead to an epic battle at Ulandi in 1878. (The battle itself is depicted in the 1964 film *Zulu*).

Congo, Democratic Republic of (Zaire)

Lumumba (2000)
d. Raoul Peck

Biography of Patrice Lumumba, the first elected prime minister of the Congo, who was assassinated only months after the country gained its independence from Belgium.

Mobutu: King of Zaire (1999)
d. Thierry Michel

Rise and fall of Joseph Mobutu, ruler of Zaire for over thirty years until his overthrow in 1997.

Constitutional Monarchy

The Windsors: A Royal Family (2002)
d. Annie Fienburgh

Traces the British royal family from 1917—when King George V renamed his family the "House of Windsor" during World War I to distance himself from his German ancestors—to the death of Princess Diana in 1997.

Croatia

Vukovar (1994)
d. Boro Draskovic

Vukovar is a Croat town just across the Danube from Serbia, where ethnic groups coexist peacefully until nationalist demonstrations begin and the town comes under siege. Serbo-Croatian with subtitles.

Cuba

Balseros (2003)
d. Carlos Bosch and Joseph M. Domenech

Follows the plight of seven Cuban refugees who risk their lives to flee by raft to America, their detention at the Guantanamo naval base, and their first years in America.

2003 Academy Award Nominee: Best Feature Documentary

Before Night Falls (2000)
d. Julian Schnabel

Writer Reinaldo Arenas is imprisoned and tortured by the Cuban government but is eventually allowed to become a part of the 1980 Mariel boatlift to the United States.

Fidel: The Untold Story (2002)
d. Estela Bravo

Footage from Cuban State archives and interviews with historians, public figures, friends, and Castro himself provide insight into Castro's public and private lives.

Czech Republic

Divided We Fall (2000)
d. Jan Hrebejk

In German-occupied Czechoslovakia, a young couple goes to extreme measures to provide shelter to a Jewish neighbor. Czech with subtitles.

Dalai Lama

Ethics and the World Crisis: A Dialogue with the Dalai Lama (2003)
d. Steven Lawrence

The Dalai Lama attends a Town Hall meeting in New York City and discusses ethical dilemmas with various journalists, politicians, economists, and environmentalists.

Kundun (1997)
d. Martin Scorsese

Portrait of the Fourteenth Dalai Lama from 1937 through 1959, when he was forced to flee Chinese-occupied Tibet for exile in India.

El Salvador

Romero (1989)
d. John Duigan

Biography of Oscar Romero, the archbishop of San Salvador, who was assassinated in 1980 for his outspoken opposition to the Salvadoran death squads.

Roses in December (1982)
d. Ana Carrigan and Bernard Stone

Examines the life and death of lay missionary Jean Donovan, who worked with the Maryknolls in El Salvador. In 1980 Donovan and three American nuns were murdered by El Salvador's national security forces.

Elections

Secret Ballot (2001)
d. Babak Payami

A female polling official travels through remote Iranian villages collecting votes on election day, accompanied by a surly military border guard. Farsi with subtitles.

A Very British Coup (1988)
d. Mick Jackson

A former steelworker and left-wing radical is elected as Britain's prime minister, but his policies threaten the status quo.

The War Room (1993)
d. Chris Hegedus and D. A. Pennebaker

Behind-the-scenes look at Bill Clinton's presidential campaign from June 1992 to election night.

Ethiopia

Harvest: 3,000 Years (1976)
d. Haile Gerima

A peasant family struggles to survive under the demands of an uncaring landowner—the legacy of a colonialist past. Amharic with subtitles.

Imperfect Journey (1994)
d. Haile Gerima

The filmmaker journeys from his hometown to the capital city of Addis Ababa after the country's Soviet-backed junta has fallen.

France

Heart of a Nation (1943)
d. Julien Duvier

Saga of a Montmarte family through three wars—from the Franco-Prussian War through the Nazi occupation. French with subtitles.

Is Paris Burning? (1966)
d. René Clément

An account of the liberation of Paris from Nazi occupation. French with subtitles.

The Sorrow and the Pity (1969)
d. Marcel Ophuls

Ophuls mixes archival footage with interviews depicting France's Vichy government collaboration with Nazi Germany from 1940 to 1944. English, French, and German with subtitles.

Gandhi, Mahatma

Gandhi (1982)
d. Richard Attenborough

Biography of Gandhi, from the prejudice he encountered as a young attorney in South Africa to his role as a spiritual leader and his use of passive resistance against British colonial rule in India.

1982 Academy Award: Best Picture, Best Director, Best Actor, Best Original Screenplay, Best Cinematography, Best Film Editing, Best Art/Set Decoration, Best Costume Design, Best Sound

Gaza Strip

Gaza Strip (2002)
d. James Longley

A look at the realities of Palestinian life following the election of Israeli prime minister Ariel Sharon. Arabic with subtitles.

Genocide

Genocide (1981)
d. Arnold Schwartzman

Features period film and photographs concerning Adolf Hitler's "final solution."

1982 Academy Award: Best Feature Documentary

The Genocide Factor (2000)
Robert J. Emery

Historical coverage of genocide beginning with the Bible and continuing through the twentieth century in Cambodia and East Timor.

Germany

Good Bye, Lenin! (2003)
d. Wolfgang Becker

Set during the political turmoil of 1989; a young man keeps the fact that the Berlin Wall has fallen from his socialist East German mother who is recovering from a heart attack and a coma.

Heimat (1984)
d. Edgar Reitz

A sixteen-hour made-for-television drama following the fortunes of one German family from 1919 to 1982 as a microcosm of twentieth-century history. German with subtitles.

The Nasty Girl (1990)
d. Michael Verhoeven

A young German girl plans to enter an essay contest by writing about her hometown's history during the Third Reich and finds herself harassed by members of her community who do not want the truth revealed. German with subtitles.

Greece

Z (1969)
d. Constantin Costa-Gavras

In this political thriller a magistrate investigates the assassination of a Greek nationalist and ties it to a secret organization supported by the government and the police. French with subtitles.

1969 Academy Award: Best Foreign Language Film, Best Film Editing

Guatemala

The Devil's Dream (1991)
d. Mary-Ellen Davis

Shows the socio-political realities when the majority of the population are illiterate agricultural workers exploited by landowners and repressed by the military. Spanish with subtitles.

El Norte (1983)
d. Gregory Nava

Persecuted in their homeland, a Guatemalan brother and sister struggle to journey north to America and safety. English and Spanish with subtitles.

The Silence of Neto (1994)
d. Luis Argueta

A young boy comes of age in 1950s Guatemala—a period of political upheaval and Cold War paranoia. Spanish with subtitles.

Hitler, Adolf

The Architecture of Doom (1991)
d. Peter Cohen

Captures the inner workings of the Third Reich from Nazi Party rallies to the last days inside Hitler's bunker.

Downfall (2004)
d. Oliver Hirschbiegel

Dramatization of Hitler's final days in his Berlin bunker. German with subtitles.

2004 Academy Award Nominee: Best Foreign Language Film

The Life of Adolf Hitler (1961)
d. Paul Rotha

Archival footage depicts the rise of the Nazi Party to Hitler's Berlin retreat.

Hungary

Angi Vera (1978)
d. Pal Gabor

A teenager living in 1948 Hungary is sent to a socialist reeducation school. Hungarian with subtitles.

Sunshine (1999)
d. Istvan Szabo

Four generations of a Hungarian-Jewish family struggle to prosper while seeking to avoid the anti-Semitism pervading their society, but they can neither avoid the Nazis nor the Hungary Revolution of 1956.

Immigration and Immigrants

Dirty Pretty Things (2002)
d. Stephen Frears

Depicts the plight of illegal immigrants to Great Britain and the exploitation they face because of their status.

In America (2002)
d. Jim Sheridan

An Irish family sneaks into America from Canada and tries to make a better life for themselves despite poverty and their illegal status.

Journey of Hope (1990)
d. Xavier Koller

A Kurdish family tries to immigrate legally to Switzerland but instead is forced to try to cross the Alps on foot. Turkish with subtitles.

1990 Academy Award: Best Foreign Language Film

India

Bandit Queen (1994)
d. Shekhar Kapur

Lower-caste Phoolan Devi is sold into marriage and brutalized by her husband. She eventually escapes and joins with a group of hill bandits, helping them to rob and kidnap the rich and higher castes. Hindi with subtitles.

The Jewel in the Crown (1984)
d. Christopher Morahan and Jim O'Brien

Epic made-for-television saga of the last years of British colonial rule in India from 1942 to 1947.

Indonesia

The Year of Living Dangerously (1982)
d. Peter Weir

In 1965 a naïve Australian journalist is assigned to cover the political situation in Indonesia amidst rioting in Jakarta following a coup against President Sukarno.

Iran

Blackboards (2000)
d. Samira Makhmalbaf

A group of nomadic teachers travels the mountainous Kurdistan region of Iran, searching for students while trying to avoid land mines and Iraqi soldiers. Kurdish with subtitles.

Iraq

Dreams of Sparrows (2005)
d. Hayder Mousa Daffar

Daffer leads a team of six filmmakers through pre-reconstruction Baghdad and examines both the gratitude expressed for the overthrow of Saddam Hussein and the despair over the post-war situation. English and Arabic with subtitles.

Gunner Palace (2005)
d. Michael Tucker

Soldiers in a U.S. artillery company, stationed in one of Saddam Hussein's personal palaces, speak about their experiences in Iraq.

Ireland

Michael Collins (1996)
d. Neil Jordan

A revolutionary leader with the Irish Volunteers (a precursor to the Irish Republican Army), Collins is dedicated to freeing Ireland from British rule, though his part in negotiating the Anglo-Irish Treaty will divide the country in two.

Israel

Cup Final (1991)
d. Eran Riklis

An Israeli soldier being held by Palestine Liberation Organization guerrillas forms a relationship with the group's leader based on their mutual obsession with the Italian national soccer team. Hebrew with subtitles.

On the Objection Front (2004)
d. Shiri Tsur

In 2002 a group of reserve officers and soldiers in the Israel Defense Forces issues a public statement that they refuse to fight beyond the country's 1967 borders and will not help perpetuate Israel's control over the Palestinians regardless of the consequences. Hebrew with subtitles.

Italy

Amarcord (1974)
d. Federico Fellini

Fascism, family life, and religion in 1930s Italy all come together in the town of Rimini (director Fellini's birthplace). Italian with subtitles.

1974 Academy Award: Best Foreign Language Film

The Garden of the Finzi-Continis (1970)
d. Vittorio De Sica

An aristocratic Jewish family lives under increasing Fascist oppression on the eve of World War II but tries to ignore the uncertainty of their situation. Italian with subtitles.

1971 Academy Award: Best Foreign Language Film

Open City (1945)
d. Roberto Rossellini

A leader in the Italian underground resists the Nazi control of Rome. Italian with subtitles.

Japan

Hiroshima (1995)
d. Roger Spottiswoode and Koreyoshi Kurahara

Recreates the circumstances surrounding the dropping of the first atomic bomb in 1945; includes newsreel footage and contemporary interviews. English and Japanese with subtitles.

Juries

Twelve Angry Men (1957)
d. Sidney Lumet

One man sounds the voice of reason as a jury inclines toward a quick-and-dirty verdict against a boy on trial.

Kenya

Black Man's Land Trilogy (1986)
d. David Koff and Anthony Kowarth

Vol. 1: White Man's Country; Vol. 2: Mau Mau; Vol. 3: Kenyatta. The films cover colonialism, nationalism, and revolution from Kenya's transformation from British East Africa and colonial rule through a guerrilla war for independence and a biography of Jomo Kenyatta, the country's first prime minister.

King Jr., Martin Luther

Citizen King (2004)
d: Orlando Bagwell

Traces the steps of the civil rights leader from his 1963 "I have a dream" speech at the Lincoln Memorial to his 1968 assassination in Memphis.

"King" (1978)
d. Abby Mann

Explores the life of Martin Luther King Jr. from 1954 through 1968.

Korea, South

Tae Guk Gi: The Brotherhood of War (2004)
d. Je-Kyu Kang

Two brothers are drafted to fight in the Korean War and follow divergent paths while serving on the front lines. Korean with subtitles.

Kosovo

Warriors (2002)
d. Daniel Calparsoro

A group of Spanish soldiers stationed as peacekeepers in Kosovo in 1999 is caught in the middle of a guerrilla war between Serbs and Albanians. Spanish with subtitles.

Lebanon

Hostages (1993)
d. David Wheatley

Docudrama about the Beirut hostage crisis of the late 1980s in which five Westerners were held by Islamic militants.

West Beirut (1998)
d. Ziad Doueiri

Three friends try to have a normal adolescence as civil war tears their city apart. Arabic and French with subtitles.

Macedonia

Before the Rain (1994)
d. Milcho Manchevski

Follows the stories of three people whose lives are affected by ethnic strife and pervasive violence in war-torn Macedonia. English, Macedonian, and Albanian with subtitles.

Malaysia

The Killing Beach (1992)
d. Stephen Wallace

An Australian photojournalist travels to Malaysia in the late 1970s to report on the plight of the Vietnamese boat people seeking refuge, and the resentment of the Malays.

Mali

Life on Earth (1998)
d. Abderrahmane Sissako

The France-based director returns to his poor village in Mali to visit his father and realizes how little has changed despite the coming of the twenty-first century. French and Bambara with subtitles.

Mandela, Nelson

Mandela (1987)
d. Philip Saville

Traces the trials of Nelson and Winnie Mandela from the couple's early opposition to apartheid to Nelson's sentence to life imprisonment in 1964.

Mandela and de Klerk (1997)
d. Joseph Sargent

Story of white Afrikaner president F. W. de Klerk, who declared an end to apartheid in 1992, and black activist Nelson Mandela, who succeeded him to the presidency in 1994.

Mexico

Mojados: Through the Night (2004)
d. Tommy Davis

Follows four men across a 120-mile journey from Mexico to the United States and the lives of illegal immigrants. Spanish with subtitles.

Viva Zapata! (1952)
d. Elia Kazan

Chronicles the life of Mexican revolutionary Emiliano Zapata, who led a peasant revolution from 1910 to 1919.

Myanmar (Burma)

Beyond Ragoon (1995)
d. John Boorman

An American is stranded in Burma amidst political unrest when she loses her passport and tries to flee from the repressive regime with the aid of a dissident.

Netherlands, The

Soldier of Orange (1977)
d. Jan De Bont

The lives of six Dutch students are changed forever by the Nazi invasion of Holland during World War II. Based on the exploits of resistance leader Erik Hazelhoff. Dutch with subtitles.

Nicaragua

Carla's Song (1996)
d. Ken Loach

A Nicaraguan refugee raising money for the Sandinista cause in Great Britain returns home to confront her past.

Under Fire (1983)
d. Roger Spottiswoode

Three foreign correspondents witness the 1979 revolution while on assignment in Managua.

The World Stopped Watching (2003)
d. Peter Raymont

This sequel to The World Is Watching (1988) follows journalists who covered the U.S.-financed Contra war against the Sandinista revolutionary government when they return to the country fourteen years later.

Northern Ireland

Bloody Sunday (2002)
d. Paul Greengrass

Depicts the civil-rights march through Derry [Londonderry], Northern Ireland, on January 30, 1972, to protest the policy of British internment without trial.

The Informant (1997)
d. Jim McBride

An ex–Irish Republican Army soldier is pressured into assassinating a Belfast judge but instead is captured and interrogated by a British Army officer and a local police inspector.

War and Peace in Ireland (1998)
d. Arthur Mac Caig

A look at the conflict in Northern Ireland from 1968 to the peace process that began in the early 1990s.

Palestine

Occupied Palestine (1987)
d. David Koff

Examines the realities of what it means to live under occupation, reflecting the Palestinian experience of Zionism and Palestinian resistance to it.

Panama

Noriega: God's Favorite (2000)
d. Roger Spottiswoode

Docudrama about Panamanian strongman Gen. Manuel Noriega, who was deposed after the U.S. invasion in 1989.

The Panama Deception (1992)
d. Barbara Trent

Details the 1989 U.S. invasion of Panama amidst allegations of illegal conduct.

Peru

Fire in the Andes (1985)
d. Ilan Ziv

Investigates the disappearance of thousands of Peruvians targeted as members of the insurgent group Shining Path by the Peruvian military.

Philippines

Fires on the Plain (1959)
d. Kon Ichikawa

An unhinged Japanese soldier in the Philippines during World War II roams the war-torn countryside encountering horror and devastation. Japanese with subtitles.

Poland

A Generation (1955)
d. Andrzej Wajda

A young man escapes the Warsaw Ghetto during World War II and joins the Polish resistance. Part 1 of Wajda's war trilogy, followed by _Kanal_ (1956) and _Ashes and Diamonds_ (1958). Polish with subtitles.

Man of Marble (1976)
d. Andrzej Wajda

A bricklayer is persecuted by the government for being a champion for workers' rights. Followed by _Man of Iron_ (1981), dealing with the 1980s Gdansk shipyard strike. Polish with subtitles.

Political Protest

Fahrenheit 9/11 (2004)
d. Michael Moore

News clippings, interviews, and political satire encompass the director's scathing critique of George W. Bush's presidency.

Refugees

In This World (2002)
d. Michael Winterbottom

Two Afghan boys endure a harrowing journey from Pakistan to London in search of refuge. English, Pashtu, and Persian with subtitles.

Letters to Ali (2004)
d. Clara Law

Focuses on the plight of Middle Eastern refugees living in Australian detention centers and one Australian family's determination to free an orphaned Afghan boy.

Romania

Children Underground (2001)
d. Edet Belzberg

Examines the social and political conditions that led to the problems of homeless children in Bucharest, Romania. Romanian with English subtitles.

Roosevelt, Eleanor

Eleanor: First Lady of the World (1982)
d. John Erman

Depicts the former first lady's life after the president's death as she goes to work for the United Nations.

The Eleanor Roosevelt Story (1965)
d. Richard Kaplan

Biography of Eleanor Roosevelt from her unhappy childhood to her work as a humanitarian and as the chairwoman of the United Nations Commission on Human Rights.

Russia

The Battleship Potemkin (1925)
d. Sergei Eisenstein

A 1905 mutiny aboard the Potemkin leads to an uprising against the Czar in Odessa. Silent.

Prisoner of the Mountains (1996)
d. Sergei Bodrov

Two Russian soldiers are taken hostage in a remote Muslim village high in the Caucasus mountains because the village leader wishes to trade them for his own captive son. Russian with subtitles.

1996 Academy Award Nominee: Best Foreign Language Film

October (Ten Days That Shook the World) (1927)
d. Sergei Eisenstein

Chronicles the Bolshevik Revolution of 1917. Silent.

Rwanda

Hotel Rwanda (2004)
d. Terry George

In 1994, Kigali hotel manager Paul Rusesabagina, a Hutu, and his Tutsi wife, Tatiana, shelter more than 1,000 Hutu refugees from the genocidal chaos that surrounds them. English and French with subtitles.

2004 Academy Award Nominee: Best Actor, Best Supporting Actress, Original Screenplay

Sometimes in April (2005)
d. Raoul Peck

Augustin Mugaza is a middle-class Hutu, married to a Tutsi, who struggles to survive the Rwandan genocide of 1994.

Senegal

Moolaadé (2004)
d. Ousmane Sembene

In a small Sengalese village, four young girls escape to the home of the wife of a village elder to avoid the purification practice of female circumcision and to pit the rights of women against tradition. Sengalese with subtitles.

Serbia and Montenegro

Pretty Village, Pretty Flame (1996)
d. Srdjan Dragojevic

In 1992 members of a Serbian patrol are trapped by Muslim militiamen in a tunnel connecting Zagreb and Belgrade with no hope for escape. Serbo-Croatian with subtitles.

South Africa

Amandla! A Revolution in Four-Part Harmony (2002)
d. Lee Hirsch

A history of black South African music and its role in the fight against apartheid.

South Africa: Beyond a Miracle (2002)
d. John Michalczyk

Chronicles the evolution of South Africa from the apartheid years to the release of Nelson Mandela, the country's first free elections in 1994, and subsequent efforts to build a strong democracy.

Spain

Land and Freedom (1995)
d. Ken Loach

A British communist heads to Spain in 1937 to fight fascism and discovers infighting and betrayal within the Republican forces.

The War Is Over (1966)
d. Alain Resnais

Diego, a Spanish revolutionary now exiled in France, wonders if his twenty-five years of struggle against Franco have achieved anything. French with subtitles.

Sudan

Lost Boys of Sudan (2003)
d. Megan Mylan and Jon Shenk

Two teenage Sudanese refugees, members of the Dinka tribe, try to adjust to life in a U.S. resettlement program.

Turkey

Journey to the Sun (1999)
d. Yesim Ustaoglu

Berzan is a Kurdish rebel who befriends Mehmet while living in Istanbul. When Mehmet is mistaken for a Kurd and arrested, he begins to understand Berzan's tenuous situation. Turkish and Kurdish with subtitles.

Uganda

General Idi Amin Dada (1974)
d. Barbet Schroeder

Schroeder documents the madness of the Ugandan dictator in his own words and actions.

Ukraine

Eternal Memory: Voices from the Great Terror (1997)
d. David Pultz

Focuses on the Ukraine where Stalinist purges in the 1930s and 1940s cost the lives of millions.

United Kingdom

The Murder of Stephen Lawrence (1999)
d. Paul Greengrass

Institutional racism is explored when a Jamaican-British family seeks justice for the murder of their teenage son by neo-Nazis and encounters only police indifference.

My Son the Fanatic (1997)
d. Udayan Prasad

A Pakistani living in England for twenty-five years discovers his British-born son has turned to Islamic fundamentalism.

Vietnam

A Bright Shining Lie (1998)
d. Terry George

Chronicles the Vietnam War as seen through the eyes of Lt. Col. John Paul Vann, a U.S. advisor to the Vietnamese Army who eventually exposed falsified battle reports to newspeople.

The Quiet American (2002)
d. Philip Noyce

A British journalist working in Saigon is suspicious of a brash American who may be working for the Central Intelligence Agency. Set amidst the communist insurgence of Ho Chi Minh into French-held Indochina.

West Bank

Promises (2001)
d. Justine Shapiro, B. Z. Goldberg, and Carlos Bolado

Explores the lives of Palestinian and Israeli children living in settlements and refugee camps in the West Bank. Arabic, Hebrew, and English with subtitles.

A

abdicate: to renounce or give up power, usually referring to royalty

abrogate: to abolish or undo, usually a law

absolute: complete, pure, free from restriction or limitation

absolutism: a way of governing, usually monarchic, that reflects complete control and an unwillingness to compromise or deviate from dogma or principles

ad hoc: created for a specific purpose or to address a certain problem

adjudge: to settle a case by judicial procedure

adjudicate: to settle a case by judicial procedure

adversarial system: a legal system in which two opposing sides present arguments and a third party renders a verdict

adversary: an enemy, rival, or opponent

agrarian: having to do with farming or farming communities and their interests; one involved in such a movement

amalgamate: to merge together two or more things into one form; combine

amparo: a legal action or law that offers protection of rights

annex: to incorporate; to take control of politically and/or physically

apartheid: an official policy of racial segregation in the Republic of South Africa with a goal of promoting and maintaining white domination

appellate: a court having jurisdiction to review the findings of lower courts

arable land: land suitable for the growing of crops

arbitrary: capricious, random, or changing without notice

arbitration: a method of resolving disagreements whereby parties by agreement choose a person or group of people familiar with the issues in question to hear and settle their dispute

archipelago: a chain of islands in close proximity to one another

aristocracy: a ruling financial, social, or political elite

armistice: a cease fire or temporary end to hostilities

atheism: the belief that God does not exist

atoll: an island, usually formed from a coral reef, that has a ring shape

austere: extremely stern; simple and undecorated

autarkic: self-sufficient and independent, as in a national economy free of imports

authoritarianism: the domination of the state or its leader over individuals

autocracy: a political system in which one individual has absolute power

B

beleaguer: to bully, harass, or attack another

bicameral: comprised of two chambers, usually a legislative body

bicephalic: possessing two heads, as in government with two heads of state

bloc: a group of countries or individuals working toward a common goal, usually within a convention or other political body

bourgeoisie: the economic middle class marked by wealth earned through business or trade

bureaucracy: a system of administrating government involving professional labor; the mass of individuals administering government

C

cadre: a close group of skilled individuals

canon: a law governing the administration of the church

canton: a political subdivision, especially in Switzerland

caste and class system: a stratified social system marked by an uneven distribution of political or economic power between classes regardless of population

caucus: a group of individuals with common traits or goals, or a meeting of such a group

caudillistic: dictatorial; from *caudillo*, Spanish for dictator

cede: to relinquish political control of lands to another country; surrender

centralize: to move control or power to a single point of authority

chancery: a court of equity, especially in the United States, England, or Wales

Charter law: a law that allows a government to contract out its functions to private companies or entities

city-state: a system of government common in ancient Greece, marked by a city with authority over surrounding territory

clientelism: a system of personal relations in which clients exchange services, money, or votes for protection or favors

coalition: an alliance, partnership, or union of disparate peoples or individuals

codification: the making of official law

collectivity: the state of being whole or complete, as a group

commodity: an article of trade or commerce that can be transported, especially an agricultural or mining product

commonwealth: a government created to advance the common good of its citizens

communal: something owned or used by the entire community

communism: an economic and social system characterized by the absence of class structure and by common ownership of the means of production and subsistence

comparative-historical perspective: a way of studying events or situations by comparing them to similar events or situations throughout history

compulsory: mandatory, required, or unable to be avoided

conquistador: one of the leaders of the Spanish conquest of Central and South America in the sixteenth century; derived from the Spanish for "conqueror"

conscript: to draft an individual into the armed services against his will

consociational: belonging to an association, especially a church or a religious association

constituency: the people who either elect or are represented by an elected official

constitutional republic: a system of government marked by both a supreme written constitution and elected officials who administer the powers of government

conventional weapon: a weapon that uses traditional explosives, not one which is biological, chemical, or nuclear in nature

corpus: a body, as in a body of work

cosmopolitanism: a philosophy advocating a worldwide focus as opposed to a focus on the concerns of a specific country or region

countersignature: a second signature on a document confirming its validity

coup: a quick seizure of power or a sudden attack

court of first instance: the first or lowest court in which a case or suit can be decided

coverture: a state of protection under the law given to a married woman

cronyism: favoritism for one's friends or supporters in the appointment to positions or granting of other benefits

cultural autonomy: the state in which a group's beliefs and behavior patterns do not incorporate influences from other groups

cultural revolution: a radical change in a culture usually caused by new ideas, events, or technology

customary law: a law created by the traditions of a community but never officially declared in force

D

de facto: (Latin) actual; in effect but not officially declared

de jure: (Latin) by right

decentralize: to move power from a central authority to multiple periphery government branches or agencies

delegate: to assign power to another, or, one who represents another

deliberate: to present contradicting arguments and choose a common course of action based upon them, or, characterized by such careful discussion

delineate: to depict, portray, or outline with detail

democratization: a process by which the powers of government are moved to the people of a region or to their elected representatives

deputy: one who has been given authority by another to act in that person's absence

derogate: to remove or deny, as a right; to disparage or belittle

despot: a ruler who does not govern in the interest of those governed

devolve: to move power or property from one individual or institution to another, especially from a central authority

dissident: one who disagrees with the actions or political philosophy of his or her government or religion

docket: a list or schedule of cases to be heard by a court

duopoly: a political system dominated by two political parties, or a market dominated by two firms

E

echelon: from the French for "rung," one level of a hierarchical society or other institution

economic liberalization: the reduction or elimination of trade barriers and government regulations in an economy

electoral college: the system for selection of the president in the United States, in which states or localities elect individuals pledged to support a specific candidate who then officially elect the president

emigration: the migration of individuals out of a geographic area or country

emir: a ruler in a country with a government based on Islamic religious beliefs

endemic corruption: longstanding and pervasive lawlessness of government officials

entente cordiale: an agreement resulting in the peaceful co-existence between parties, for example, nations

enumerate: to expressly name, as in a list

envisage: to hold a picture of something in one's mind

eradicate: to destroy or eliminate a population of items, people, or other living things

ethnic cleansing: the systematic murder of an entire ethnic group

ethnocracy: a state ruled by people of one particular common background, thought to be the superior ethnicity

ethnography: the study of the origin, characteristics, or interaction of cultures or racial groups

export economy: an economy dominated by selling products internationally as opposed to domestically

expropriate: to take property from its owner and give it to another, especially oneself; usually accomplished through government decree or legal procedures

extrajudicial: outside the legal system; lacking the legitimating authority of the government

F

Fabian socialist: one committed to a gradual rather than an immediate adoption of socialist principles

factionalism: a separation of people into competing, adversarial, and self-serving groups, usually in government

federalism: a system of political organization, in which separate states or groups are ruled by a dominant central authority on some matters, but are otherwise permitted to govern themselves independently

Fertile Crescent: the land between the Tigris and Euphrates Rivers in Iraq, where the earliest human civilizations formed

fiat: an authoritative, sometimes arbitrary, order, usually by a government

figurehead: an individual with a title of leadership, but no real authority or power

first-past-the-post system: an electoral system consisting of single-member, winner-take-all districts common in countries with a British political history

franchise: a right provided by statutory or constitutional law; to give such a right

free market economy: an economy with no or very little government regulation and ownership

free trade: exchange of goods without tariffs charged on importing or exporting

fundamentalism: a philosophy marked by an extreme and literal interpretation of religious texts and an inability to compromise on doctrine or policy

G

gendarme: a soldier used in civilian police operations, especially in France

gerrymandering: the artful drawing of legislative districts in order to give advantage to one political party, race, or other group

globalization: the process of expanding regional concerns to a worldwide viewpoint, especially politics, economics, or culture

governorate: a political subdivision, often associated with Middle Eastern states

governor-general: a governor who rules over a large territory and employs deputy governors to oversee subdivided regions

grand duchy: a territory ruled by a grand duke or duchess

grassroots: at the lowest level, often referring to support from members of the public rather than from political elites

guerrilla: a soldier engaged in nontraditional methods of warfare, often separate from any structured military group

H

habeas corpus: a written order to determine whether one's detention or imprisonment is lawful; Latin for "you shall have the body"

hard money: money raised by a political candidate that can be spent directly on campaign activities but is subject to fund-raising limits

Hays Code: a law governing the regulation of moral content in motion picture production; it was put into force from 1930 through 1967

hegemony: the complete dominance of one group or nation over another

heresy: an opinion about religion that contradicts that of an organized church

heterogeneous: complex; consisting of parts or components that are different from one another

hierarchy: a group of people ranked according to some quality, for example, social standing

homogeneous: simple; consisting of components that are identical or similar

humanist: one who places a great deal of importance on humankind and its experiences

humanitarian assistance: aid to individuals or countries used for the basic needs of people, including food and shelter

I

idealism: the theory that ideas larger than reality guide human actions

ideology: a system of beliefs composed of ideas or values, from which political, social, or economic programs are often derived

impeach: to accuse of a crime or misconduct, especially a high official; to remove from a position, especially as a result of criminal activity

imperialism: extension of the control of one nation over another, especially through territorial, economic, and political expansion

impunity: an exemption from punishment

in extremis: at the point of death; pushed to the furthest limitations possible

inalienable right: a right that cannot be taken away

inculcate: to teach through repetition

incumbent: one who currently holds a political office, or, holding a political office

indigene: a native

infrastructure: the base on which a system or organization is built

infringe: to exceed the limits of; to violate

institutionalism: a focus on the importance and role of the organization, especially a religious organization, in public and private matters

insurgency: a rebellion against an existing authority

insurrection: an uprising; an act of rebellion against an existing authority

intercommunal: between or involving multiple communities

interdiction: a prohibitory decree, especially to halt trade between two nations

intergovernmental: between or involving multiple governments, with each government retaining full decision-making power

interim: for a limited time, during a period of transition

international socialism: a movement to expand socialism worldwide, advocating greater economic cooperation between countries for the benefit of all people

interparty: between or involving more than one party

interpellation: a formal questioning regarding public conduct or an official action of government

interregnum: the period of time between the reigns of two successive monarchs

interventionism: the policy of involving oneself in another's affairs, especially one nation to another

intransigent: an inability to compromise or to deviate from principle

J

Jacksonian: characteristic of a strong presidency; refers to the period of the U.S. presidency of Andrew Jackson in the late 1820s and 1830s

judicial review: the ability of the judicial branch to review and invalidate a law that contradicts the constitution

junta: a group of individuals holding power, especially after seizing control as a result of a coup

juridical: relating to, created by, or pertaining to the judiciary

jurisdiction: the territory or area within which authority may be exercised

jurisprudence: the body of precedents already decided in a legal system

jurist: a person learned in legal matters; most often, a judge

K

kleptocracy: a government controlled by those seeking personal gain

Kremlin: in Moscow, the seat of government in the former USSR as well as in the Russian Federation

L

landlocked: sharing no border with a body of water

legal positivism: a philosophy that laws have no moral standing, being merely man-made

legalism: strict adherence to laws

liberalism: a political philosophy advocating individual rights, positive government action, and social justice, or, an economic philosophy advocating individual freedoms and free markets

liberalization: the process of lowering trade barriers and tariffs and reducing government economic regulations

liberation theology: a hybrid of Marxism and Catholic doctrine, advocating social justice through salvation; especially posited by some Latin American clergy

lingua franca: a universal or very common language

litigate: to bring a disagreement or violation of the law before a judge for a legal decision

litmus test: a simple test in which a single quality determines the outcome

lobby: to advocate for a specific political decision by attempting to persuade decision makers

localism: a phrase or behavior specific to a certain area

logographic writing system: a system of written language in which each word is represented not by a series of letters, but by a picture

lumpenproletariat: the lowest stratum of the working classes, consisting of those who are poor and under-educated

M

macroeconomics: a study of economics in terms of whole systems, especially with reference to general levels of output and income and to the interrelations among sectors of the economy

magistrate: an official with authority over a government, usually a judicial official with limited jurisdiction over criminal cases

majoritarianism: the practice of rule by a majority vote

malapportionment: the use of legislative boundaries to create districts that do not have approximately equal populations

Mandarin: an individual in the Chinese government, or, the official language of the Chinese government

mandate: to command, order, or require; or, a command, order, or requirement

marginalize: to move to the outer borders, or to move one to a lower position

maritime: relating to the sea or the coast

market economy: an economy with little government ownership and relatively free markets

marriage of convenience: a marriage performed solely for economic or social benefits

martial law: rule by military forces in an occupied territory or rule by military officials declared during a national emergency

Marxist-socialism: an economic system in which government owns industry or heavily regulates the economy

Mau Mau Revolt: a failed rebellion in Kenya against British rule in the 1950s; it preceded independence by twelve years

merit plan: a method for the selection of judges, based on performance or quality of work rather than political views or affiliation

meritocracy: a system of society or government in which individuals are rewarded based on individual achievement

micro-nationalism: nationalism not for a county but for a community resembling a state on paper or in cyberspace

migrant labor: workers who relocate seasonally, following job opportunities

militarism: pertaining to the military or the culture of the military, or aggressive military preparation

militia: a group of citizens prepared for military service in emergency situations

mixed-member proportional voting: an electoral system in which some representatives are elected from first-past-the-post districts and some are appointed through proportional representation

modernism: a philosophy advocating ideas and elements specific to modern times, or the integration of those ideas into preexisting cultures or beliefs

modernization: the act of incorporating new ideas or technology

monarchical: of or relating to a monarchy

money laundering: to cause illegally obtained money to appear legitimate by moving or converting it

monopoly: the domination of a market by one firm or company

Monroe Doctrine: the statement by U.S. President James Monroe in 1823 declaring that Europe should stay out of American and Latin American affairs

monsoon: heavy rainfall usually associated with India and Southeast Asia

mores: the moral values, customs, or traditions in a specific region

mosaic: politically, the alliance of diverse people or groups

motherland: one's country or region of origin

multilateral lending: the lending of money to countries by institutions that pool funds from multiple sources, such as the International Monetary Fund and the World Bank

multipartyism: the state of having multiple parties in a party system

municipality: local governmental units, usually cities or towns

N

Napoleonic Code: French law first established in 1804; it is the first known legal code within a civil legal system

nascent: new or recently created or brought into existence

nationalism: the belief that one's nation or culture is superior to all others

nationalization: the process of giving control or ownership of an entity to the government

nation-state: a relatively homogeneous state with only one or few nationalities within its political borders

natural right: a basic privilege intrinsic to all people that cannot be denied by the government

naturalize: to grant the privileges and rights of citizenship

neo-imperialism: the belief in the building of political or cultural empires in the contemporary world

neo-liberalism: a belief in economic liberalism with a willingness to compromise on some ideological points in order to advance liberal goals

neo-patrimonialism: a system of government that outwardly delineates between the personal and the public realm, but in which political patronage by the ruler is the reality, with personal relationships defining one's wealth or power

nepotism: favoritism for one's own family in the appointment to positions or granting of other benefits

neutrality: the quality of not taking sides, as in a conflict

no confidence (vote of): a vote in a parliament on a government's policies that, if lost, will result in dissolution of the parliament and new elections

Nonaligned Movement: an organization of countries, formed in 1961, that did not consider themselves allied with either the western or the eastern blocs

nonbinding declaration: a statement of a government or government body that has no legal standing or force of law

nonpartisan: not relating to a political party or any division associated with the party system

North Atlantic Treaty Organization: a military alliance chiefly involving the United States and Western Europe that stated that, in the event of an attack, the member countries would have a mutual defense

O

offshore banking: banking that takes place in a foreign country, usually to escape domestic taxation

oligarchy: government by a few or an elite ruling class, whose policies are often not in the public interest

ombudsman: a government official that researches the validity of complaints and reports his findings to an authority

ordinary court: a court that hears civil cases, especially in the United Kingdom

Ottoman Empire: (1299–1922) an empire centered in Turkey (and defeated in World War I) that once spanned Northern Africa, the Middle East, and parts of Southeast Europe and contemporary Russia

P

pacifism: the belief that war and violence are inferior methods of conflict resolution, to be avoided

pan-Africanist: an advocate for the unity of all African nations

pan-Arabist: an advocate for the unity of the Arab world

pandemic: affecting a large segment of the population or a large geographic area

paramilitary: modeled after a military, especially as a possible supplement to the military

parity: a state of equality, or being identical

parliamentary override: the ability of a parliament to override decisions of other government bodies

partisan: an ideologue, or a strong member of a cause, party, or movement

party apparatus: the process used by a political party to make decisions, nominate candidates, choose leaders, or win elections; the manpower, expertise, or money needed to accomplish those goals

pastoralist: supporter of a social organization whose main economic activity is raising livestock

patrimonialism: a system of government in which the ruler personally controls all aspects of life, including politics and the economy, and personal wealth or power is a function of an individual's personal relationship to the ruler

per capita: for each person, especially for each person living in an area or country

peripheral: marginal; on the outer limits

perpetrate: to commit a crime or injustice

persecute: to belittle, harass, injure, or otherwise intimidate, especially those of a different background or group

petition: a written appeal for a desired action, or, to request an action, especially of government

pillage: to plunder; to loot or steal during an emergency or war

plantation system: a system of farming in which landowners use slaves or poorly paid workers to farm large tracts of land

platform: a statement of principles or legislative goals made by a political party

plebiscite: a vote by which the people of a country make known their opinions on a proposal or regime

plenary: complete or absolute; attended by all members or delegates to a convention

plethora: a large, sometimes overwhelming, amount

pluralism: a system of government in which all groups participate in the decision-making process

plurality: more votes than any other candidate, but less than half of the total number of votes

pogrom: a planned annihilation of a specific people, especially the Jews

polarize: to separate individuals into adversarial groups

policy advocate: a lobbyist

political autonomy: the state of a country or region within a country that holds sovereignty over its own affairs

political nomadism: the movement of an official elected as a member of a specific political party away

from that party, usually to another party

polity: a form of government held by a specific country or group

polygamy: the practice of having more then one mate or spouse at one time

popular mandate: authorization granted by the electorate, derived from the support of at least the majority

populist: someone who advocates policies for the advancement of the common man

pragmatism: a belief that only that which can be practically accomplished should be advocated

precedent: an established ruling, understanding, or practice of the law

primordialism: a way of studying nationalism that advocates looking at familial and ethnic connections and their relation to underlying conflicts

probity: honesty

procedural right: a right to due process of the law when defending other liberties

proletariat: the lower class of workers and laborers in a society

proliferate: to grow in number; to multiply at a high rate

promulgation: an official declaration, especially that a law can start being enforced

proportional system: a political system in which legislative seats or offices are awarded based on the proportional number of votes received by a party in an election

protectorate: a territory or country under the protection of another sovereign country's military

proto state: an entity that adopts most of the characteristics of a state but does not have complete sovereignty, such as an interim government or the European Union

proxy: an authorized substitute, or, the ability to act in another's place

prurient: lewd, immature, or childlike

purchasing power parity: a way of measuring the buying power of countries' currencies based on the cost of identical goods

Q

quasi-presidential: similar to a president or presidential system, or, having the identical effect of a presidential system

R

rapporteur: one that reports on a committee's work

ratify: to make official or to officially sanction

Realpolitik: policies or actions rooted in the practical rather than the abstract

recession: a period of negative economic growth associated with high unemployment

reciprocity: mutual action or help that benefits both parties

recourse: a resource for assistance

redress: to make right, or, compensation

referendum: a popular vote on legislation, brought before the people by their elected leaders or public initiative

regime: a type of government, or, the government in power in a region

regional integration: the movement of economic or political power to a central authority from regional centers of power

relativism: a belief that ethical values are dependent on individuals or groups and are not common to all humanity

remedial: intended as a solution

remittance: a shifting of funds from one entity to another

reparation: funds or other compensation offered as a remedy for damages

repatriate: to return to the country of one's birth or citizenship

reprisal: retaliation for a negative action

republic: a form of democratic government in which decisions are made by elected representatives of the people

restitution: the transfer of an item back to an original owner, or, compensation for that item

resurgence: a return to action from a diminished state

retrocession: the act of returning, as in territory

rule of law: the principle that the law is a final grounds of decision making and applies equally to all people; law and order

S

sage: a wise person

sanction: economic, political, or military reprisals, or, to ratify

schism: a separation between two factions or entities, especially relating to religious bodies

secede: to break away from, especially politically

sect: a group of people with a common distinctive view of religion or doctrine

sectoral specialization: the ability of a country to organize its economy in such a way that it dominates or performs better in a specific sector

secularism: a refutation of, apathy toward, or exclusion of all religion

self-determination: the ability of a people to determine their own destiny or political system

seminal: original; at the basis of

separatism: a belief that two regions should be separated politically

serf: a peasant, or laborer under the feudal system, who worked the land of the feudal lord

shah: the ruler of Iran

sheikhdom: a geographic region ruled by a Arab chief known as a sheikh

signatory: one who signs an agreement with other parties and is then bound to that agreement

social cleavage: a division of membership in or voting for a political party, based on social class

socialism: any of various economic and political theories advocating collective or governmental ownership and administration of the means of production and distribution of goods

socioeconomic: relating to the traits of income, class, and education

soft money: money that can be spent on a political campaign, independent of a candidate, in order to avoid fund-raising limits

sovereignty: autonomy; or, rule over a political entity

statist economy: an economy highly regulated by a state's central authority

statute: a law created by a legislature that is inferior to constitutional law

statutory codification: the act of making common law or tradition into official law passed by a legislature

subjugate: to force into submission

subsidiary: a small component of a larger entity

subsidy: a government grant used to encourage some action

subsistence farming: farming which does not turn a profit, providing only enough food for the farmers themselves

suffrage: to vote, or, the right to vote

sultanate: a country governed by the sovereign of an Islamic state, called a sultan

super-majority: a legislative majority so large that the party can pass whatever legislation it wishes

supernational: composed of multiple nations and having control over those nations, which themselves are independent states

super-presidential: referring to a republic with a very strong presidency, especially Russia

supranational: between or involving multiple governments, with all governments sharing control, usually through independent representatives and majority rule

suzerain: a state that dominates the foreign affairs of a subordinate state, while allowing it autonomy in domestic affairs

syncretism: an attempt to meld disparate or opposing schools of thought

T

technocracy: government by technicians using scientific expertise and analysis to optimize conditions for the public

tenure: the right to hold land, position, or status over the long term, or the act of doing so

theocracy: a state governed by its religious leaders

tort: a civil crime for which the law provides a remedy

totalitarianism: a form of absolute government that demands complete subjugation by its citizens

transnational: extending beyond the jurisdiction of one single nation

treatise: a type of scholarly essay that outlines principles and draws conclusions from the factual discussion included

tribunal: a type of court of law, usually military in nature

tripartite: involving three parties, especially in negotiations

U

ultranationalism: an extreme belief, stemming from a fear of foreigners, that one's home country is superior to all others

umbrella organization: a corporation that controls many smaller subsidiaries

unconventional warfare: a war in which open confrontation between opposing forces is limited; tactics might include terrorism or the use of biological, chemical, or nuclear weapons

unicameral: comprised of one chamber, usually a legislative body

unilateral: independent of any other person or entity

unitary: centralized

untouchability, practice of: segregation of the bottom caste in India, who are believed to be "untouchable"

V

vagary: a sudden, unexpected change

vendetta: a protracted, often violent dispute, especially in the name of revenge

venerate: to hold something or someone in extremely high regard

vestige: a remnant of a lost or vanished entity, as in a nation or an institution

viceroy: one who governs a territory as the representative of the monarch

W

warlord: a leader, usually over a small region, who governs by military force

welfare state: a political state that assumes liability for the wellbeing of its people through government-run social programs

Westminster: a democratic model of government comprising operational procedures for a legislative body, based on the system used in the United Kingdom

X

xenophobia: a fear of foreigners, often leading to isolationism, reduction in immigration, and racism

Page numbers in **boldface** type indicate article titles; those in *italic type* indicate illustrations. An italic *t* after a page number indicates a table. The number preceding the colon indicates the volume number; the number after a colon indicates the page number.

China (PRC),   **1:183–189**
  background,   **1:**183, **1:**318
  Chinese Communist Party (CCP),
    1:184–188
  constitution,   **1:**185–186, **1:**257
  dictatorship,   **1:**186, **1:**318
  government, structure of,   **1:**186,
    1:187–188, **1:**257
  history,   **1:**183–184
  Hong Kong,   **2:**209, **2:**210, **2:**211–212
  hostility to religion,   **2:**127–128,
    2:130, *2:130*, **2:**132
  human rights,   **1:**188–189
  map,   *1:184*
  palatial complex of the Forbidden City,
    1:187
  political life,   **1:**186–187
  reproductive rights,   **4:**39
  socioeconomic conditions,   **1:**184
  Tiananmen Square, protests in,
    2:211, **3:**304, *3:305*, **3:**306
  Tibet,   **1:**188
Chirac, Jacques,   **2:**96, *4:9*
Chissano, Joaquim,   **3:**155
CHR. *See* United Nations Commission on
    Human Rights
Chun Doo Hwan,   **3:**61, **3:**63
Cicero,   **1:**168, **4:**43
Citizenship,   **1:189–195**
  American concept of,   **1:**190–191,
    *1:*193, **1:**194–195
  in ancient Greece,   **1:**190
  Citizenship Day on Ellis Island,   *3:172*
  ethnic membership conception,
    1:192, **1:**193–194
  franchise and voting rights,   **1:**191
  geographical dimension,   **1:**190
  German concept of,   **1:**192, **1:**194
  historical background,   **1:**189–191
  Israeli concept of,   **1:**192, **1:**194
  legal element,   **1:**189–190
  perpetual allegiance of subjects,
    1:191–192
  political theory,   **1:**189, **1:**190, **1:**194
  Roman law,   **1:**190
  territorial conception,   **1:**191–192,
    1:193
  Voting Rights Act of 1965,   **1:**191,
    1:208, **4:**138, **4:**282
  See also individual countries
City-state, defined,   **1:**189
Civil law,   **1:195–199**
  case law, lack of binding effect,   **1:**197
  codification,   **1:**195–196
  contrasts with common law,   **1:**198,
    1:223–225
  convergence with common law,
    1:198–199, **1:**221, **1:**225–226
  history,   **1:**222–223

Justinian's compilation *(Corpus Juris
    Civilis),*   **1:**197, **1:**223
Napoleonic Code (French Code
    Civil),   **1:**195–196, **1:**197–198,
    1:223
  political and historical context,   **1:**198
  Roman law heritage,   **1:**197, **1:**222–223
  supra-national law in European Union,
    1:198
  Twelve Tables,   **1:**222–223
Civil liberties in emergencies,   **1:199–205**
  affirmative action,   **1:**209
  busing of school students,   **1:**209
  Civil Rights Act of 1991,   **1:**209
  domestic terrorism,   **1:**201–202
  line between crimes and acts of war,
    1:203–204
  line between crimes and minor public
    order disturbances,   **1:**203,
    1:204–205
  list of liberties affected by emergencies,
    1:201
  quasidictatorial powers in times of
    emergency,   **1:**318
  September 11, effect on civil liberties,
    1:166, **1:**202–203
  social contract theory,   **1:**199–200,
    1:202
  terrorism and right to privacy,   **4:**49,
    4:51
  terrorism as emergency,   **1:**200–201
  transnational terrorism,   **1:**202–205
  USA Patriot Act,   **1:**203, **2:**106,
    2:119–120, *4:48*, **4:**52
  war on terrorism,   **1:**203
  See also Terrorism
Civil rights movement in the United
    States,   **1:206–210**
  affirmative action,   **2:**36, **2:**38, **2:**39
  background,   **1:**206
  Brown v. Board of Education, **1:**206,
    1:208, **2:**35–36, *2:37*, **2:**39, **2:**87
  Civil Rights Act of 1957,   **1:**206
  Civil Rights Act of 1964,   **1:**208, **2:**39
  early civil rights acts,   **1:**206–208
  Grutter v. Bollinger,   **1:**209
  "Jim Crow" segregation,   **1:**206
  Little Rock, Arkansas, school desegre-
    gation,   **1:**206–207, **1:**208
  marches and demonstrations,
    1:207–208
  Montgomery, Alabama, bus boycott,
    1:206
  nonviolent civil disobedience,
    1:206–207, *1:207*
  Plessy v. Ferguson "separate but equal"
    decision,   **1:**206, **2:**35, **2:**37
  *Regents of the University of California v.
    Bakke,*   **1:**209

"sit-in" demonstrations,   **1:**207
Three-Fifths Compromise in U.S.
    Constitution,   **1:**206
universities, desegregation of,
    1:207–208
Voting Rights Act of 1965,   **1:**191,
    1:208, **4:**138, **4:**282
See also Equal protection of the law
Clientelism, defined,   **1:**154
Clinton, William J.,   **3:**242, 272
Coalition, defined,   **1:**4
Coard, Bernard,   **2:**181
Codification, defined,   **1:**224
CoE. *See* Council of Europe
Coke, Edward,   **1:**222, **2:**7
Collectivity,   **2:**152
Collor de Mello, Fernando,   **1:**114–115
Colombia,   **1:210–217**
  April 19th Movement (*Movimiento 19
    de Abril,* or M–19),   **1:**213
  background,   **1:**210
  Cali Cartel,   **1:**213
  civil conflict, effects of,   **1:**213–214,
    1:215
  Conservative Party,   **1:**212–214
  contemporary politics,   **1:**213–214,
    1:216
  government, structure of,   **1:**214–216
  illicit drug trade,   **1:**211–212,
    1:213–214
  La Violencia,   **1:**212–213
  leftist guerrilla movements,   **1:**210,
    1:211, **1:**212–214
  Liberal Party,   **1:**212–214
  map,   *1:211*
  Medellín Cartel,   **1:**213
  National Front,   **1:**212–213
  National Liberation Army (*Ejército de
    Liberación Nacional,* or ELN),
    1:213–214
  1991 Constitution,   **1:**213–216
  Patriotic Union (*Union Patriótica,* or
    UP),   **1:**213
  People's Liberation Army (*Ejército
    Popular de Liberación,* or EPL),
    1:213
  political history,   **1:**212–213
  Revolutionary Armed Forces of
    Colombia (*Fuerzas Armadas
    Revolucionarias de Colombia,* or
    FARC),   **1:**213–214
  right-wing paramilitary forces,   **1:**210,
    1:211, **1:**213–214
  separation of Venezuela, Ecuador, and
    Panama,   **1:**212
  socioeconomic conditions,   **1:**210–212
Colonies and colonialism,   **1:217–221**
  colonialism, definition,   **1:**218
  colony, defined,   **1:**217

M